Edward Taylor's

Gods Determinations

and

Preparatory Meditations

Rosemary Fithian
Guruswamy

Oh Pardon hold, Lord give, forgive me, I pray.
Fixing my Heart: it being in Snow.
I strive myselfe, being myselfe again
In heart & heate to thee. I frozen grow.
Stir my dull Spirits: make them sharp & bright.
Then fetch forthyselfe, & thy delight.

My stains are dark, & sin too deep, if all
The Excellency in Created Shells
Too low, & little is to make it fall
Out of my tender throate wherein it dwells.
This Excellence is but a shade to that
Which is enough to make my stains go back.

The glory of this world Slickton in types,
In all Choise things thosen to typifie,
His glory upon whom the world doth light,
Within's a Shaddow, or a Butterfly.
How glorious then, my Lord, art thou to mee
Being to cleanse me, & worke alone for thee.

The glory of all Types doth meet in thee.
Thy glory doth their glory quite excell:
More than the Sun excells in its bright glee
A nat, an Earewig, Weevill, Snaile, or Shell.
Wonders in Crowds stand here; & your eyes may see
Viewing his Excellence, & blessing see.

Oh that I had but halfe an eye to view
This Excellence of thine, undazled so
Therewith to give my heart a death anew
Untill I quickened am & made to glow.
All is too little for thee: but alas
Most of my little all hath other pass.

Then Pardon, Lord, my fault, & let thy beams
Of Holiness pierce thro this Heart of mine.
Ope to thy Blood la passage thro my veins.
Let thy pure Blood my impure Blood refine
Then with new Blood & Spirit I will deck
My turns upon thy Excellency good.

Edward Taylor's
Gods Determinations
and
Preparatory Meditations

A CRITICAL EDITION

Edited and with an introduction by Daniel Patterson

Frontispiece: Meditation 2.1. Beinecke Rare Book and Manuscript Library, Yale University.

© 2003 by The Kent State University Press, Kent, Ohio 44242
All rights reserved.
Library of Congress Catalog Card Number 2002006024
ISBN 0-87338-749-x
Manufactured in the United States of America

07 06 05 04 03   5 4 3 2 1

Taylor, Edward, 1642–1729.
Edward Taylor's Gods determinations and Preparatory meditations : a critical edition / edited and with an introduction by Daniel Patterson.
p. cm.
ISBN 0-87338-749-x (pbk. : alk. paper)
1. Christian poetry, American. I. Taylor, Edward, 1642–1729. Gods determinations. II. Taylor, Edward, 1642–1729. Preparatory meditations. III. Patterson, Daniel, 1953– IV. Title.
PS850.T2 G638 2002
811'.1—dc21
2002006024

British Library Cataloging-in-Publication data are available.

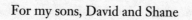 For my sons, David and Shane

Oh! Bright! Bright thing! I fain would something say:
Lest Silence should indict me.

Contents

Preface and Acknowledgments

The work of discovering and clarifying Edward Taylor's significance began with Thomas H. Johnson's request to see Taylor's "Poetical Works" manuscript at Yale University's library in 1936. Throughout the 1950s and 1960s, Donald E. Stanford contributed his great work, and in the 1960s, 1970s, and 1980s subsequent editors labored—Norman Grabo, Charles Mignon, the Davises. This new edition of Taylor's major works, *Gods Determinations* and his *Preparatory Meditations*, makes possible now an even fuller view of the poet's achievement.

This first critical edition of Edward Taylor's *Gods Determinations* and *Preparatory Meditations* also offers the first complete text of all the Meditations that Taylor transcribed into his "Poetical Works" manuscript. The reliability and accuracy of this edition are, in part, based on the work of past editors; and so collectively we have restored Taylor's poetry to what he probably intended. This Puritan poet's art can now be seen to lack a significant portion of the flaws and glitches that previous editions reported, and we can be more confident that we are reading what Taylor wrote.

I gratefully acknowledge permission from Yale University's Beinecke Rare Book and Manuscript Library to publish material from Edward Taylor's "Poetical Works" manuscript. The many days I have spent there, scuffing up balls of carpet fiber around my feet, have been intense and arduous, and conditions for my work there could not have been better.

Preparatory Meditation 2.162[A] and some of the material on *Gods Determinations* in the introduction first appeared in *Early American Literature*. I thank the journal's editor for permission to use that material in this volume.

I am deeply and somewhat luxuriously in debt to a scattered coterie of Taylor scholars for much of what I know and believe about this poet. In the Introduction I have tried to represent accurately their findings, and in my notes I have acknowledged their work. I am grateful to them all.

I am especially happy to acknowledge, in gratitude, the shaping influence of Thomas M. Davis. When I went to him with a dissertation idea, he said, "Fine," and then left the country for two years. I have never forgotten that. By the time he returned from Greece, I had a much deeper appreciation for the work on the Taylor manuscripts that he and Virginia L. Davis were doing. Their seven volumes of Taylor's writings are impressive, a truly daunting achievement, and Tom's *A Reading of Edward Taylor* stands among the most informed and perceptive analyses of Taylor's poetry. *A Reading* demonstrates the value of learning everything Taylor knew before writing about the man's art.

I wish also to acknowledge the work of Donald E. Stanford. He established Taylor's place in the history of literature by being the first to make available the breadth of Taylor's poetic achievement. As a textual editor, I am grateful for and humbled by Professor Stanford's work.

Joanna Hildebrand Craig, editor-in-chief of The Kent State University Press, has worked creatively and assiduously to make this volume a much better book than it otherwise would have been. She has also made the multistage process of publication a very pleasant experience. I am grateful. I suspect that Christine Brooks, the Press's production manager, has acquired a new understanding of the "pain" in "painstaking," having arranged Taylor's poem headings and titles on the many pages of this volume so that readers can for the first time see Taylor's use of the brace to set off the dates of his Meditations. I am grateful to her as well.

Central Michigan University has provided institutional support. For much-needed assistance in the final stages of proofing galleys, I thank H. Nellie Corder. I also thank colleagues Greg Spinner and Bill Reader for pointing out a theological stone unturned.

This project has occupied and preoccupied me for several years. It has thus loomed as a sometimes puzzling presence in the minds of my two sons, David and Shane, through most of their young years. Throughout they have been vital companions in my mind, on my shoulders, and by my side on the trail. If I live to 2053, I will not meet better people. These two young men make my life good. I dedicate this volume to them.

Editorial Principles and Procedures

The text of this edition of Edward Taylor's *Gods Determinations* and *Preparatory Meditations* is based on the unique copy of the poems transcribed by Taylor into his "Poetical Works" manuscript, which is housed in the Beinecke Rare Book and Manuscript Library at Yale University.

I follow Taylor's script exactly, with the following exceptions:

- Spell out "and" for Taylor's ampersand (he typically spelled out the word only at the beginning of a line) and capitalize it when the ampersand follows end punctuation.
- Spell out Taylor's abbreviations. The following is a complete listing:

Chch (Church)	y^e (the)
Ld (Lord)	y^{ir} (their)
o^r (our)	y^{is} (this)
sd (said)	y^m (them)
S^r (Sir)	y^n (then)
S^t (Saint)	y^r (your)
w^{ch} (which)	y^t (that)
w^n (when)	y^{ts} (that's)
w^{th} (with)	y^y (they or thy).

- Modernize medial *u* (*aboue* becomes *above*), initial *v* (*vpon* becomes *upon*), the long *s*, and *ff* for *F*.
- Double the consonant where Taylor used the tilde to indicate the double consonant (*Com̃it* becomes *Commit*).
- Spell out *though, through,* and *although.* Before July 1701, Taylor typically abbreviated these words by using the circumflex (*thô, thrô, althô*). Beginning in July 1701, Taylor switched to the apostrophe to contract these words (*tho'*); he did not return to the circumflex.

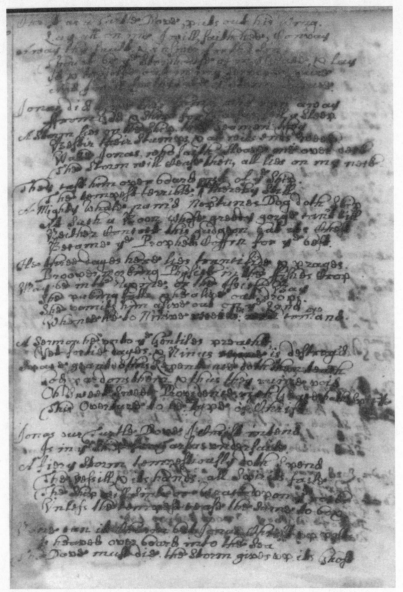

Meditation 2.30, ll. 13–51. *Beinecke Rare Book and Manuscript Library, Yale University.*

- Modernize Taylor's hyphen, which in most cases is a double horizontal stroke (=).
- Regularize the punctuation of poem titles, Bible references, and the names of speakers in dialogues and spell out these names where Taylor abbreviated them.

- Omit the ruled left margin and the catchword that Taylor supplied for each page but retain the line he drew across the page at the end of each poem. In the few places where he omitted this line, I silently add it.
- On the few occasions when Taylor reached the right edge of a page before completing the line's final word or two and then simply wrote the remaining letters below the line in the margin, I silently emend it.
- Regularize Taylor's indentation pattern that becomes irregular and constantly varying beginning with *PM* 2.157[A].

All other changes are specified in the emendations list; other textual matters are discussed in the textual notes.

Taylor numbered the pages of *Gods Determinations*, and I indicate these in square brackets in the text. He numbered no other pages in the "Poetical Works" manuscript; in recent years, however, the pages of the entire manuscript have been numbered in pencil continuously from 1 to 400. For the *Preparatory Meditations*, I indicate this pagination in square brackets placed to the right of the last line that appears on the indicated page.

Taylor's capital *S* is inconsistent. I follow the Davises' practice of considering "as a capital only those *S*'s in which the lower downward stroke terminates on the line *and* closes with the initial upward stroke, unless the size and shape of the character itself suggest that he intended it for a capital" (*MP* xxiii). Similarly, Taylor was occasionally inconsistent with a capital *V, W,* or *Y.* Whenever one of these letters has only one tall vertical stroke (a clear capital *V, W,* or *Y* has two), I report that letter as lower-case unless its size or shape suggest that Taylor intended it as upper-case.

Although Taylor generally prepared his manuscripts with care, his punctuation is not always consistent and becomes increasingly inconsistent in his last two decades. While a central principle of this edition is to avoid emendation, I do make changes for clarity. For example, I supply the apostrophe for a contraction where Taylor has omitted one because his usual practice was to use such apostrophes. I do not, however, supply the apostrophe to possessive endings because Taylor rarely did so himself. I emend a period that is followed by a word beginning with a lower-case letter if the emendation is needed for clarity and does not violate Taylor's usual practice. Wherever I add or alter punctuation, I note the change in the emendations list.

Taylor made several errors in numbering the Meditations in the Second Series. His numbering runs thus: 1–54, 56, 58–59, 60, 60–68, 67, 68–123, 123, 125–39, 129–31, 134–44, one unnumbered poem, 146–48, 148–53, 152–56. He skips 55, 57, 88, 124; and he duplicates 60, 67, 68, 123. When he reached 139 (and the end of his manuscript), he took up a new gathering of pages and began with 129; thereafter he skipped 132 and 133, omitted the number for 145, and duplicated 148, 152, and 153. I follow Stanford's practice of distinguishing duplicated numbers up to the first 139 by [A] and [B]. After the first 139, I change Taylor's numbering, renumbering the second 129 (which follows the first 139) as 140, and so forth. Thereafter, wherever Taylor duplicated a number, I again distinguish the poems with [A] and [B], but the numbers are my emended numbers. Again, all changes are noted in the emendations list.

I avoid o±ering conjectural readings; in rare cases, however, I do supply in square brackets a reading or partial reading that seems highly probable ("marv[els]" at *PM* 2.24.18). Most of these occur where a Bible verse or chapter number is too faded or where a biblical quotation is partially blotted. In a number of cases a word or phrase is partially legible; I place the illegible portion inside square brackets and indicate the approximate number of illegible letters with unspaced asterisks.

Six spaced asterisks in the text indicate an entire line missing. Three spaced asterisks indicate that some part of a line is either missing or illegible. In all cases I explain the textual problem in the textual notes.

At the end of each poem, I report all recoverable evidence of Taylor's revisions. Because of the great number of illegible cancellations, I include these in the textual notes and only when they seem of unusual importance. I indicate interlinear insertions with *ins.* and legible original readings with *orig.* Taylor's earlier drafts of Meditations 1.1–8, the three titled Meditations, and Meditation 1.9.1–12 exist in a manuscript (described in Stanford, *Poems* 506). I do not report the variants between these drafts and the final versions in the "Poetical Works" manuscript because the variants are so extensive that the only useful representation of those drafts would be an edition of the complete texts.

It is clear that the graphic arrangement of poem titles was important to Taylor. Therefore, the placement and spacing of the titles in this edition imitate their appearance in PW; this includes the use of braces to frame the dates of the Meditations. Note also that Taylor uses the Old Style dating, the system in which March is the first month of the year and February the last.

. . .

I prepared the first transcription of Taylor's manuscript by typing into a computer while reading from a microfilm copy of the manuscript. I then took the typescript to the Beinecke Library, where I checked the typescript against the manuscript itself. For passages that were difficult to read, I was able to use—in various combinations—magnifying lenses, a light table, a manuscript microscope, and an ultraviolet light. A corrected and completed transcription of Taylor's manuscript grew out of this stage of the work. As a means of checking the accuracy of this document, I collated it against the Stanford edition of *Gods Determinations* and *Preparatory Meditations*. At every point where my document and the Stanford edition varied, I checked Taylor's manuscript again in order to resolve the question. I then made the emendations, all of which are noted at the back of this volume, as are the variants between this edition and Stanford's.

Abbreviations

C   *Edward Taylor's Christographia*. Ed. Norman S. Grabo. New Haven: Yale University Press, 1962.

CR   *Edward Taylor's "Church Records" and Related Sermons*. Ed. Thomas M. and Virginia L. Davis. Boston: Twayne, 1981. [Note: The Davises indicate with brackets and italics readings they adopt from two earlier transcriptions (449, n. 1); quotations herein from *CR* reproduce these indicators.]

ETvsSS   *Edward Taylor vs. Solomon Stoddard: The Nature of the Lord's Supper*. Ed. Thomas M. and Virginia L. Davis. Boston: Twayne, 1981.

GD   *Gods Determinations*. Line numbers are cited in parentheses.

HG   *Edward Taylor's Harmony of the Gospels*. Ed. Thomas M. and Virginia L. Davis, with Betty L. Parks. 4 vols. Delmar, NY: Scholar's Facsimiles and Reprints, 1983.

MHC   *A Transcript of Edward Taylor's Metrical History of Christianity*. Ed. Donald E. Stanford. Cleveland: Micro Photo, Inc., 1962.

MP   *Edward Taylor's Minor Poetry*. Ed. Thomas M. and Virginia L. Davis. Boston: Twayne, 1981.

PM   *Preparatory Meditations*. A specific poem is cited by its series number (either 1 or 2), poem number, and line number (separated by periods).

PW   Taylor's "Poetical Works" manuscript.

TCLS   *Edward Taylor's Treatise Concerning the Lord's Supper*. Ed. Norman S. Grabo. East Lansing: Michigan State University Press, 1966.

UTOT   *Upon the Types of the Old Testament*. Ed. Charles W. Mignon. 2 vols. Lincoln: University of Nebraska Press, 1989.

INTRODUCTION

An Overview of Edward Taylor's Life and Work

When Edward Taylor reluctantly made the treacherous journey to the frontier settlement of Westfield, Massachusetts, in November 1671, he was about twenty-eight years old, highly educated, and the author of a few poems. Fifty-eight years later, when the minister-poet died in Westfield, he had delivered several thousand sermons, written more than 2,000 manuscript pages of original prose, and composed some 40,000 lines of poetry—practically all of which remained only in manuscript form for more than two hundred years, and very little of which was read by anyone other than a few family members and friends.

Edward Taylor was born in Sketchley, Leicestershire, in 1642, 1643, or 1644. No more specific information of the year of his birth exists than two conflicting reports of his age upon his death in 1729: his obituary in the *Boston News Letter* cites his age as eighty-five, while his tombstone reads eighty-seven.[1]

Born into England's turbulent 1640s, the young Edward Taylor apparently matured through the 1650s and 1660s into a nonconformist. After mentioning that Taylor was educated by a nonconformist schoolmaster and that he then kept a school himself for a brief time, his obituary speculates that "this Part of the World" would never have known

---

1. Donald E. Stanford's dissertation, "An Edition of the Complete Poetical Works of Edward Taylor," contains or refers to practically all sources of information about Taylor's life known at that time. Constance J. Gefvert, *Edward Taylor: An Annotated Bibliography, 1668–1970*, includes convenient listings of sources known through 1970. Since then, important manuscript material has contributed to a more coherent reconstruction of his life: see especially Walter L. Powell, "Edward Taylor's Westfield: An Edition of the Westfield 'Town Records'"; *CR, MP, ETvsSS, HG,* and *UTOT;* see also Thomas M. Davis, "Edward Taylor's Elegy on Deacon David Dewey."

Taylor if he had agreed to take the oaths then required of ministers and schoolmasters. With the death of his yeoman father, William, in 1658 (his mother was dead by then); the Restoration of 1660 and the Act of Uniformity of 1662; and his reaching the age of twenty-one, the age at which he would receive forty pounds from his father's estate,[2] Taylor was free and inclined to consider migrating to Puritan New England. Of the five poems that survive from this period before Taylor's migration (*MP* 3–18), two express his pious love for a school friend and his brother and sister-in-law, and the other three take a position against external and internal challenges to Puritanism in his native land. With limited opportunities in England for a nonconformist Bible scholar, Taylor chose New England.

In his brief diary are accounts of the passage from England, his time at Harvard College, and his move to Westfield. Taylor boarded a ship at Execution Dock in Wapping on April 26, 1668, and came ashore at Boston ten weeks later, on July 5. The voyage was frequently unpleasant; Taylor noted many days of seasickness and occasional disturbing dreams involving his brothers. The end of his entry for June 19 is especially telling: "After dinner, I reading the 4[th chapter of] John in greek, was so sleepy that when I had done, I lay down, and dropping into a sleep, and dreaming of my brethern, was so oppressed with sorrow that I had much to do to forbea[r] weeping out, but being over-pressed with this passion, I awaked and was almost down-right sick" (*Diary* 33).

For his second and third nights on shore, Taylor lodged at the home of Increase Mather. For the following two weeks he was the guest of John Hull; while there he arranged to begin his studies at Harvard College, where he was admitted and given the position of college butler, making him responsible for the buttery and dining area as well as the college's "Vessells, and Utensells" (Stanford, "An Edition" ix). That he was given this position reflects his greater age and maturity than most of the other students, a distinction reflected also in an incident Taylor mentions in his diary. A group of scholars who objected to the "too much austerity" of tutor Thomas Graves discovered that they could trap him in the lecture hall by driving "a nail above the Hall Doore Catch" while Taylor and others were reciting to Graves within (37). In order to learn who the culprits were, the tutor pressured Taylor to spy

2. Donald E. Stanford discovered the will of Taylor's father; see "The Parentage of Edward Taylor."

on his fellows to "watch who did it." Taylor bungled the mission but demonstrated his alliance with authority, even if too austere.

By the end of his third year at Harvard, and although "the Lord gave me the affections of all, both in the Colledge and in the town, whose love was worth having," Taylor was afflicted by the gossip of some who envied the "Charitable and well grounded Esteem" he received from a married woman who had approached him for spiritual counseling (38). He was so troubled by this gossip that he considered leaving Cambridge, even offering to forego his place at commencement. However, Harvard's president, Charles Chauncy, who had high regard and affection for Taylor, convinced him to stay.

At Harvard Taylor was known as a poet who on public occasions could produce fitting and competent verse. The five poems that survive from Taylor's three years at the college are all of a public nature (*MP* 19–35), four being elegies commemorating the lives of prominent New England Puritans. At his commencement on May 5, 1671, Taylor read his only Harvard poem that is not an elegy, "My last Declamation in the Colledge Hall," a vigorous and complex defense of the English language as well as an early and modest critique of his poetic abilities.

Taylor's stay at Harvard ended abruptly. Six months after his commencement—a period not accounted for in the diary—on November 16, 1671, he settled in as "scholar of the house." The next day, Thomas Dewey arrived, a man Taylor characterized as "a Messenger sent from Westfield on Connecticut River, to the Bay for to get a Minister for that People" (38). On the advice of elders he had met in Boston, and carrying a letter from Increase Mather, Dewey approached Taylor about taking the call. Taylor did not know what to do. He consulted with friends and advisers, including President Chauncy, who wanted Taylor to stay, and Increase Mather, who advised him to go. On November 26 Dewey pressed Taylor to go with him to Westfield. Taylor's narration of this decision in his diary makes his extreme uncertainty and ambivalence clear: "I not knowing how to cast down Goodman Dewy's expectation[s] after I had raised them, set forward" (38–39). He does not explain his reasoning any further than this, except to say that when he spoke with President Chauncy on the night of the 26th, Chauncy could, if sadly, support the move since Taylor's "proceedings were by Prayer and cou[n]sell" (39).

Taylor expresses quite clearly, however, his anxiety about the travel conditions he faced, as "a great snow" had begun falling on November 23:

... the snow being about Mid-leg deepe, the way unbeaten, or the track filled up againe, and over rocks and mountains, and the journey being about an 100 miles; and Mr. Cooke of Cambridge told us it was the desperatest journey that ever Connecticut men undertooke. ... [O]n the next [i.e. third] day we ventured to lead our Horses, in great danger over Connecticut River, though altogether against my will, upon the ice, which was about 2 dayes in freezing; but mercy going along with, though the ice cracked every step, yet we came over safely, and well, to the wonder almost of all that knew it. (39)

Although his references to the number of days and the dates of this journey are rather confused (he writes that they arrived in Westfield after traveling for two full days and part of a third but gives November 27 as the day they began and December 2 as the day of arrival), Taylor gives December 3, 1671, as the date of his first sermon in the Westfield meetinghouse. For his text he turns significantly to the beginning of the Gospel account of John the Baptist's wilderness ministry, specifically Matthew 3:2. Taylor's decision to conjure the Bible's preeminent wilderness preacher in his first sermon on the western frontier of British North America following "the desperatest journey that ever Connecticut men undertooke" is rich with suggestions about how he saw his role in Westfield.

While some twenty-five years later, he was able to joke with Samuel Sewall about his distance from Boston and Harvard College—"I am far off from the Muses Copses: and the Foggy damps assaulting my Lodgen in these remotest Swamps from the Heliconian quarters, where little Save Clonian Rusticity is Al-A-Mode, will plead my apology" ([Letter] 125)—in his first two days in Westfield, Taylor was no doubt in a serious frame of mind, considering whether or not he could spend the rest of his life there and praying for guidance. The example of John the Baptist would have more than thematic relevance. Although we do not have this first sermon, we do have the interpretation of John's ministry Taylor developed in his *Harmony of the Gospels* some years later (II:106–39). There, with his Westfield auditory in mind, he sheds the light of Scripture on his Westfield experience. Though far from the intellectual and spiritual community of Boston, Taylor saw in John's experience "That God doth sometime make the most wilderness & unlikely places partakers of the pouring out of his Spirit when the most gent, & Courtly Citie go without" and that "you may finde the Church in the Wilderness." With this in mind, Taylor could consider his Westfield ministry and reason that "we are not to look on things according to the outward Looks" (II:106). Similarly, he could find encouragement also in knowing "That John the Baptist fell upon his publick ministry in the Wilderness" (II:115).

Taylor also used John's ministry to teach his parishioners something about his and their own responsibilities: "those that are imployed aright in the ministry of the word, are sent of God. . . . So that they have good warrant to be faithfull & the refusall to receive their Message is a rejecting of God"; and since God's messengers "are of Angellical imployment & honour," "it will be bad to slight their message." John's call to "prepare . . . the way of the Lord" for Taylor was a call to prepare "the heart, & [af]fections & practice" of those who heard his voice "crying in the wilderness." Taylor felt the heavy weight of this responsibility, since "man naturally is very much unprepared for Christ" yet "must be prepared" (II:121). And while John's ministry can be tremendously encouraging to a minister's confidence that "the voice of one Crying, a powerful voice oftimes is the instrument of a powerful dispensation" (II:122), Taylor cautions that even though a "Copious Auditory" can be attracted to so inspired a ministry, "its no new thing to have a multitude of vile persons flock after the sealing ordinances." These "vipers," he warns, ought to be met "with sore rebuke," since they "have no right to Gospell Seals." He refers here to the Lord's Supper, which he would maintain throughout his fifty-eight years in Westfield was a "Gospell Seal" that only God's Elect should be allowed to enjoy in any church on Earth. With his emphasis on the need to prepare, Taylor suggests the means by which he and his hearers would examine their souls' worthiness to be admitted to the Lord's Supper. We cannot know whether Taylor, fresh from Harvard, developed every one of these points when he delivered the first Westfield sermon, but he clearly was convinced of parallels between his wilderness experience and that of John: a lone messenger of God crying in the wilderness about the needs to repent and to prepare for Christ.

At the time Taylor arrived in Westfield, it was the youngest and westernmost township in Massachusetts. Its first home lots had been established only four years earlier, in the spring of 1667, and it had become independent of Springfield in May 1669, at the same time that its name was officially recorded as Westfield instead of Woronoco, its original Algonquin name meaning "the winding land" (Lockwood 58–62, 72). Since a priority of every new town in the Colony was a full religious life, including baptism and the administration of the Lord's Supper, the first citizens of Westfield had tried to find and keep a suitable minister. Their first, John Holyoke, apparently served only a few months, desisting, as Taylor puts it, after "finding the Mini[sterial] work too heavie for him." About a year passed before their second pastor, Moses Fisk, was brought up from the Bay, but (again according to Taylor's record) "[he be]ing here in their beginnings met with many temptations" (which remain unspecified), and he left after serving "the Lord amongst them about 3 years" (*CR* 3–4). Taylor, too, seemed to have settled in reluctantly at first, but he remained in Westfield until his death fifty-eight years later.

More than seven years passed before Taylor officially "gathered" the church in Westfield. In those seven years, the maturing minister reconceived his life and work: he became the leader of a congregation, a husband, and a father; he endured the anxiety of war; and he more deeply incorporated his art into his life. The causes of his reluctance to gather the church and thereby satisfy the wishes of the families of Westfield are unclear but likely have something to do with not wanting to live so far away from an engaged intellectual community and with not wanting to be distracted by a rustic life: the production of food, the control of predators, the fear of attacks by indigenous peoples. He may have argued during his second year that Westfield lacked a sufficient number of Christians convinced of their regenerate state to sustain a church. Three men from Westfield wrote letters to church members in Northampton, where Solomon Stoddard was pastor, asking them to help encourage Taylor in his ministry, possibly even by asking one of their own members to move to Westfield. But Stoddard and his members were of the opinion that their brethren in Westfield were "already furnisht with a Compitancy of men for the Comfortable beginning of Ecclesiasticall work" and offered Taylor no encouragement (*CR* 450). Writing in 1679, Taylor characterized this early period: "I being now brought amongst them, did not determine any Settlement [*at once*] but when I had served some two years here, we set up Conference me[eting in] which I went over all the Heads of Divinity unto the means of the Application [of Re]demption, in order to prepare them for a Church State before we did [*enter.*] Tho' we began this Course, yet I was not determined within myselfe [*what to do*]" (*CR* 4).

Shortly after his move to frontier Westfield, Taylor constructed the first of his two most elaborate acrostic poems (*CR* 32–35). It is an elegy that consists of a ten-line double acrostic set atop a quadruple acrostic of twenty-eight iambic pentameter lines arranged in two columns of fourteen lines each. This literal monument honors the deceased president of Harvard College whom Taylor relied upon as counselor and friend, Charles Chauncy. So complex and public a work reflects more than Taylor's profound affection for Chauncy; it shows also that Taylor still identified with the Bay and that in his mind the audience he wrote for was still the college and communities he left behind.

The audience for the second of these complex displays of acrostic wit was Elizabeth Fitch, the daughter of the Reverend James Fitch of Norwich, Connecticut. By 1674, the year of an extant letter and two poems to Elizabeth (*MP* 37–43)—who wrote her name as "Elisa" in several apparently available spaces in Taylor's manuscripts—Westfield's third minister in five years was deciding to stay: "But at length my thoughts being more settled, I determined within [*myself that*] in case things could go comfortably on, to Settle with them: & in [*order thereto*] Changed my Condition, & entred into a married State; hop[*ing that the following*] Summer would open a doore to l[et] us into a Church State" (*CR* 4).

During his first three years, Taylor's conception of his role in Westfield evolved; and, as the second of the poems to Elizabeth shows, the role that Taylor's art would play in his life was deepening, taking on new significance. In "My Last Declamation" Taylor reveals that he saw poetry in 1671 as ornamentation, and certainly both the Chauncy elegy and the first love poem to Elizabeth, "This Dove & Olive Branch to you," are evidence of this idea's continuing sway in Taylor's mind. But in "Were but my Muse an Huswife Good" a new notion arises in Taylor's work, which he perhaps inadvertently acknowledges to his future wife by writing that his muse had never before "Spun" "Such Silken Huswifery" or verse. In this poem, dated October 27, 1674, Taylor develops a fairly common weaving conceit so that it implicates his love for Elisa Fitch, their marriage, and the elect condition of his soul. Ornamentation is subordinated to the expression of his thoughts about the sacrificial nature of their marriage, and from this date onward, Taylor's poetry shows that he fully unifies the ministerial and artistic realms of his mind. He seems never again satisfied with the aesthetic that imbues "My Last Declamation" or his first love poem to Elizabeth.[3]

Further evidence of Taylor's artistic development at this time is his decision to begin his own metrical paraphrase of the Hebrew Psalms (see *MP* 44–101). While he was deciding to marry and stay in Westfield

---

3. Dean G. Hall, "Edward Taylor: The Evolution of a Poet," develops this and other points (99–120). Hall's study remains the most thorough investigation of Taylor's early development, approximately through the beginnings of *PM*.

as a counselor of souls on the frontier, he also began to study very closely the work of the chief poet of the Bible. With this move he performed some linguistic apprentice work, surely, but he also made a turn inward to the discovery of his own meditative voice. One result was a shift in the concerns of his poetry ever farther from the more secular aesthetic of the earlier verse. His art could take even deeper root in his Westfield ministry, and the minister-poet's service to his God could acquire an even richer texture. Because the poetry seems from this point on to be conceived more as process than as product, Taylor seems to have found in David's 150 Psalms a compelling and satisfying model of poetry as life-long process (a point developed below in the discussion of the *Preparations Meditations*). His *Preparatory Meditations* would reflect this, but his duty to assist his parishioners in their spiritual growth prompted him to compose *Gods Determinations* first.

Edward Taylor and Elizabeth Fitch married on November 5, 1674.[4] Taylor had hoped that by the following summer he could formally gather the church, "[*But the summer coming*], opened a doore [to] that De[solating] war began by Philip Sac[*hem of the Pakanoket*] Indians, by which [*this handful was sorely pressed yet sovereignly preserved*]" (*CR* 4). The anxiety and danger that King Philip's War brought to Westfield no doubt delayed the formation of the church for a few months, but what further reasons for delay there may have been until 1679 are not clear. In the following passage from the "Church Records," Taylor records that Westfield came close to dissolution during this time and then alludes, but only cryptically, to an even more serious cause of delay in gathering the church:

> Thus tho' we lay in the very rode of the Enemy were we preserved; onely the war had so impoverisht us that many times were we ready to leave the place, & many did, yea many of those that were in full Communion in other places, for their number in all being but nine, four of them removed. & worse than this, a sore [tem]ptation was

4. In her fifteen years of marriage, Elizabeth bore eight children: Samuel (b. Aug. 27, 1675); Elizabeth (b. Dec. 27, 1676, d. Dec. 25, 1677); James (b. Oct. 12, 1678, d. Jan. 30, 1701); Abigail (b. Aug. 6, 1681, d. Aug. 22, 1682); Bathshuah (b. Jan. 17, 1684); Elizabeth (b. Feb. 5, 1685, d. July 26, 1685); Mary (b. July 3, 1686, d. May 15, 1687); Hezekiah (b. Feb. 10 or 18, 1688, d. Mar. 3, 1688). This information (and that supplied in note 21 below) is compiled from Stanford, "An Edition," xxii, xxv; and from Taylor's baptismal records (*CR* 243–49). I use Taylor's spellings.

thrust in amo[n]gst us by the Adversary that seem'd to threaten the overthrow of all proceedings unto a Church state, by those on whom that intrest was before, most apparently devolved. (*CR* 5)

What this sore temptation was we do not know.

Late in the summer of 1679 when Taylor and the array of visiting ministers and elders gathered the church in Westfield, the extension of baptism to the children of "halfway members" (those professing members who had not publicly related their conversion experience and thereby gained full membership) of New England's congregations had practically lost its controversial edge. The debate over the Halfway Covenant had quieted, and a dialogue of hope was emerging from the rhetoric of the Jeremiad. Although ministers throughout New England were responding to changing conditions by emphasizing the Gospel promises over Old Testament wrath, a few were considering opening the church doors wider or more readily than the earlier generations had. The Reforming Synod would convene in the same year and, through its condemnation of sinful behaviors and its guidelines for reformation, bear indirect witness to the diversification of New England's population as well as to the pressure this placed on Puritan ecclesiology. But "hypocrites" still had to be kept from the central sacrament of New England Congregationalism, as the "Result" of the Halfway Synod of 1662 reiterated: "It is requisite that persons be not admitted unto Communion in the Lords Supper without making a personal and publick profession of their Faith and Repentance, either orally, or in some other way, so as shall be to the just satisfaction of the Church; and that therefore both Elders and Churches be duely watchfull and circumspect in this matter" (Walker 433).

During this time of uneasy but needed adaptation in New England's Congregational polity, Edward Taylor worked diligently and consistently amid "Clonian rusticity" to maintain the original vision of the Bay Colony's first Puritan ministers, who had required the public relation of saving faith for full membership in a congregation and for admission to the Lord's Supper. Throughout his ministry of nearly sixty years that began in 1671, Taylor found ways to maintain this requirement within the framework of the 1648 "Cambridge Platform," and his controversy with Northampton's Solomon Stoddard arose because of differences with his liberal (and, to Taylor, even apostate) neighbor on this point of doctrine. Because the Lord's Supper offered the Elect the highest of spiritual experiences and because it occupied a central place in Taylor's conception of religious experience, Taylor gave decades of intellectual energy to this theological controversy.[5]

Solomon Stoddard was present to help gather the church at Westfield and ordain its minister in August 1679, and he extended Taylor on that day the right hand of fellowship. On the same day, in Taylor's founding sermon, Stoddard heard a thorough defense of Congregational orthodoxy as it had evolved through the synods of 1648 and 1662. God's minister in Westfield, Taylor clearly announced, would work to keep God's "Habitation" as free of hypocrites as possible in this world by requiring a public relation of saving faith of all who would approach the Lord's Supper. The children of halfway members would be baptized and enjoy church discipline, but only those who met the standards set by New England's first generation of Puritan ministers would find admission to Communion in Westfield. Stoddard, of course, did not engage Taylor in a theological debate on this long-delayed foundation day; but a few weeks later, at the first meeting of the Reforming Synod of 1679, he began openly to advocate two changes in church polity: admit halfway members to the Lord's Supper and no longer require the public relation of saving faith.[6]

In Taylor's view, the sacrament of the Lord's Supper was appointed by God as the highest of all mortal experiences; in his treatise on the subject, he characterizes it as "the highest communication of grace and favor" (TCLS 51). More specific to religious life in New England was Taylor's view that the Bay Colony was settled as a place where hypocrites could be prevented from approaching the Table: "to avoid such mixt administrating of the Lord's Supper, and to enjoy an holy administrating of it to the visibly worthy was that that brought this people from all things near and dear to them in their native country to encounter with the sorrows and difficulties of the wilderness" (TCLS 126). Because the sanctity of the Lord's Supper was thus fundamental to Taylor's conception of the meaning of human life, and because Stoddard's ideas posed a radical threat to that conception, Taylor devoted much of his

5. *ETvsSS* includes all the manuscript evidence of Taylor's debate with Stoddard; Thomas M. Davis's introduction to that volume provides a complete, insightful account of the entire history.

6. In Taylor's account, Stoddard's formal welcome of Westfield's new church ("I do in the Name of the Churches give you the Right hand of Fellowship") was less than satisfactory because it was not "done in the Name of Christ" (*CR* 159).

intellectual and artistic energy from this time forward to defending the
public relation. Beginning in the first year of the new decade, then, much
of Taylor's prose and poetry can be seen as a reaction against Stoddardean
thinking, which, if adopted, would loosen the admission standards of
Congregational churches and subordinate the spiritual experience of
the Lord's Supper to the conversion experience. In Stoddard's view, requiring the public relation effectively denied many good people a spiritual experience that could help them along the way to their conversions.
But in the view of Taylor and of almost every other New England minister in 1679, opening the Lord's Supper to all nonscandalous, professing Christians would mean "the begining of New Englands Apostasy"
(*ETvsSS* 65).

So from the gathering of the Westfield church in 1679 until the ordination of Nehemiah Bull on October 26, 1726, as the town's new minister, Taylor saw one of his central roles as God's instrument as defending the sanctity of the Lord's Supper by continuing to require a public
relation of one's conversion experience. In 1728 the members of the
Westfield church voted it "a matter of indifferency" whether a person
seeking membership give a public relation or not (Lockwood 333).

Edward Taylor believed that the highest work any mortal could perform was the conversion of souls to Christ, and in this context his art
found motive and growth. His two major poetic accomplishments, *Gods
Determinations* and the *Preparatory Meditations*, comprise his public and
private artistic responses to this central challenge of his life's work: building and maintaining a worthy and pure "habitation" for the Puritans'
God in New England.

Gods Determinations

Before the founding of the Westfield church, New England's ministers
had been adapting to changing conditions in order to survive a perceived
membership crisis. Reconsidering their 1648 refusal to baptize children
whose parents were not full members of a congregation, they compro-
mised in 1662 because of the ever-increasing number of parishioners
left thus in Puritan limbo. Some six months before Taylor left Harvard
for Westfield, the last opponent to this compromise, Increase Mather,
reluctantly approved extended baptism. As did practically every other
Massachusetts church founded after 1675, Taylor's Westfield church

adopted the Halfway Covenant from its inception. Taylor's "Foundation Day Sermon" makes this clear. Even with this "halfway" measure in place, however, in the 1670s and 1680s commonly 50, 60, and even 70 percent of a given congregation's halfway members never achieved full membership (Pope 233–36). These are the conditions that called forth Solomon Stoddard's radical proposal to open Communion (and thus grant full membership) to all nonscandalous, professing Christians.

Among the early deeds Taylor performed for his Westfield ministry at about the time of his ordination was the composition of *Gods Determinations touching his Elect: &c The Elects Combat in their Conversion, and Coming up to God in Christ: together with the Comfortable Effects thereof,* a 2,102-line primer of spiritual growth and full membership. In this strikingly original poem, Taylor embodies his fully developed plan to preserve the sanctity of the Lord's Supper by coaching New Englanders at every stage of spiritual growth toward the collective goal of full Communion in a congregation. Everyone has a role to play in Taylor's response to this crucial moment in New England Congregationalism.

As Taylor indicates in the title of the poem, the main concern of *Gods Determinations* is with the "Elect."[7] This includes residents of Westfield and, by extension, all members of New England's Puritan communities who might be among God's Elect: a saint of the church, his pious and dutiful children, his less pious (or more scrupulous) children, the children or even the grandchildren of those who had owned the Covenant but never attained full membership. Even a town resident who had no ancestral claim to the Covenant[8] could not be excluded from those who might be among the Chosen. Since God's determinations touching his damned would be a relatively simple matter, Taylor focuses in the allegorical action of the poem on the needs and spiritual experience of the Elect. The "Royall Coach," which God sends to carry some of fallen humankind to the "mighty Sumptuous feast," has the effect of splitting

7. Michael J. Colacurcio, *"Gods Determinations Touching Half-Way Membership:* Occasion and Audience in Edward Taylor," discusses *GD* in the context of the Halfway Crisis, arguing that halfway members are the specific audience of the entire poem. In *"Gods Determinations:* The Occasion, the Audience and Taylor's Hope for New England," I argue for a more diverse audience and thereby highlight the deeper design features of the poem. Where Colacurcio sees "emphatic repetition" (303), I see distinct divisions that Taylor designs for the varied spiritual needs of his parishioners.

8. In Congregationalism, to "own the Covenant" was to profess publicly one's acceptance of church doctrine and discipline and to commit oneself and children to strive for full membership in that congregation.

"All mankinde . . . in a Dicotomy." All those fortunate enough to find God's favor ride in this coach; "The rest do slite the Call and Stay behinde" (371–84). Taylor then effectively removes from the poem those not in the coach by having them "Scull unto eternal woe" (403) and clearly announces that the exclusive concern of the remainder of the poem is with those in the coach, God's Chosen Few: "These therefore and their journey now do come / For to be treated on, and Coacht along" (417–18).

Having established the Elect as the exclusive concern of the poem, Taylor then begins to represent the diversity of this group. He first identifies various degrees of resistance to "the Work of Conversion" by dividing the Elect into four groups. The first group answers the call of Grace immediately: "Grace therefore calls them all, and Sweetly wooes. / Some won come in, the rest as yet refuse, / And run away . . ." (435–37). Those who run away are pursued by Mercy, and some of them surrender after only a short attempt to flee (437–40). This group becomes the poem's First Rank. Taylor further divides those who continue to resist into two groups, which later become the poem's Second and Third Ranks. Justice captures the Second Rank when they run into "Strong Barracadoes" (446); then Justice pursues the Third Rank until they surrender when they see "Mercy stand with Justice" (457). The clearest distinction Taylor makes in this four-fold division of the Elect is between the first two groups, who surrender easily to Mercy, and the other two, who offer much more resistance and must be captured by Justice, with, in the last case, Mercy's assistance.

The spiritual diversity of Taylor's audience moved him to divide the Elect into these categories. He deliberately distinguishes the spiritual experiences of the First Rank from those of the Second and Third Ranks in order to demonstrate to every member of the Puritan community who might possibly be one of the Elect two contrasting approaches to full membership. In the first, the elect soul comes relatively easily to an awareness and acceptance of its fortunate condition. The First Rank representative, Soul, effectively withstands Satan's various assaults (605–774) and then turns away from Satan to seek "Succour" directly from Christ (775–98). Christ replies favorably, explaining that Satan's assaults function simply "to make thee Cling / Close underneath thy Saviours Wing" and that the First Rank's sins are "Dead'ned" and "shall not rise again" (814–34). Soul is able to accept this good news from Christ and is moved by joy to attempt a song of praise (925–1016). The souls of the First Rank, then, come to a recognition of their elect state without allowing their natural fears and doubts (i.e., Satan's assault) to seriously hinder their progress. Their conversion is complete.

When Taylor presents the second of his two possible approaches to full Communion, however, he distinguishes it from the first in two important ways: he shows the progress of the Second and Third Ranks to be considerably slower and more difficult; and he has the troubled Second and Third Ranks find help in Saint, the full member of the Puritan church, and not, as the First Rank does, immediately in Christ. As does the First Rank's, the ordeal of the Second and Third Ranks begins with an attack by Satan that effectively convinces them of their sinfulness (1017–66). They are unable, however, to offer effective resistance to Satan's attacks, as the First Rank does, and fall into a debate over which is the more sinful rank of souls, each arguing that it has reason to envy the more hopeful condition of the other (1167–238).

As the First Rank does following Satan's assault, so now do the Second and Third Ranks plead for mercy from Christ: "Then pardon, Lord, and put away our guilt. / So we be thine, deale with us as thou wilt" (1289–90). But here Taylor makes an important variation in the pattern established by the First Rank's experience: no "Christs Reply" follows the remaining ranks' humble plea for mercy. Taylor does not have Christ step in and gently remove their agony, as he does for the First Rank; instead, the now-unified voice of the Second and Third Ranks reverts to a lament over the utterly sinful condition of both its body and soul (1291–318). The grip of despair slackens, however, and the Second and Third Ranks resolve to search for some hope of their salvation (since their plea directly to Christ apparently goes unanswered) under the guidance of "the Pious Wise" (1340). Taylor introduces in the work's second "Preface," Saint, the full church member, who for approximately the next 500 lines (1347–842) helps Soul find reason to believe that it is among God's Elect. The role Christ performs in the conversion experience of the First Rank, Saint performs for the Second and Third Ranks, who face much greater difficulties than does the First Rank in their progress toward an awareness of their elect condition.

By thus distinguishing the experience of the First Rank from that of the Second and Third Ranks, Taylor effectively represents the two main types of conversion experience members of the Puritan community underwent in their progress toward full membership in a church. The first requires a relatively shorter period of time and, after a time of initial doubt, leads the individual directly to Christ. The second takes a considerably longer time, and the individual, after apparently receiving no succor from Christ directly, must find help instead in those who already are full members in the congregation. The experience of Taylor's First Rank represents what the founding generation of Puritans had hoped would be the common experience of all the children of the Covenant: following baptism as a child, the individual experiences in due course an action of God's grace on his or her soul; examines that soul for a time in order to accept this action, with some confidence, as a sign of his or her own elect state; and convincingly relates this experience to the church elders, who then grant full membership. This person does not become stalled and suspended in a state of halfway membership.

The majority of the later generations, however, did not come so quickly to a belief that they were among the Elect; they were generally more hesitant than the founders. Taylor's Second and Third Ranks represent those elect souls who in New England in the latter part of the seventeenth century were beset with persistent doubts and fears concerning their election.[9] These halfway members had at least one professing ancestor and had renewed their Covenant with a particular congregation, but they continually surrendered to doubts and fears and were unable to give a public relation of an action of grace on their souls. There were also some who, although having no professing ancestor, had owned the Covenant after attending the converting ordinance, the preaching of the Word, but who failed to become full members. Even residents of a town who had neither professing ancestors nor halfway membership could be among the Elect; they were, after all, required to attend public sermons[10] and became thereby potential converts. Taylor's Second and Third Ranks, then, represent all of God's Elect whom Taylor perceived as being in need of greater assistance than those represented by the First Rank, who had moved more easily from self-examination to full Communion.

9. For the general background of piety and spirituality in New England at this time, see Edmund S. Morgan, *Visible Saints: The History of a Puritan Idea;* Norman Petit, *The Heart Prepared: Grace and Conversion in Puritan Spiritual Life;* Robert G. Pope, *The Half-Way Covenant: Church Membership in Puritan New England;* and E. Brooks Holifield, *The Covenant Sealed: The Development of Puritan Sacramental Theology in Old and New England, 1570–1720.* Specifically on spiritual doubts and "scrupulous melancholy," see John Gatta Jr., *Gracious Laughter: The Meditative Wit of Edward Taylor,* 33–49.

10. The 1648 "Platform of Church Discipline" points out that the "ignorant or Scandalous" were "required by wholsome lawes to attend" public sermons (Williston Walker, *The Creeds and Platforms of Congregationalism,* 200).

Taylor's Saint in *Gods Determinations* manifests this greater concern with encouraging those who were not in full Communion that emerged in New England following the general adoption of extended baptism and halfway membership.[11] Hence, when Taylor introduces Saint, he is not only showing the humble, more hesitating souls where to find greatly needed guidance, but he is also including the full members of New England's Puritan congregations in the intended audience of his poem. By illustrating the role Saint plays in the conversion experience of the Second and Third Ranks, Taylor, in effect, admonishes New England's communicants to perform their duty, as defined in the synod reports of 1648 and 1662, of assisting the spiritual growth of the entire congregation.

In his foundation sermon, and probably shortly before he began working on *Gods Determinations*, Taylor addresses his congregation in two groups: those "Without" and those "Within a Church State" (*CR* 145). Taylor exhorts both groups to "Enter your names among the living in Jerusalem" (150); for the replenishment of the congregation, it was essential that they become full members. Taylor then charges specifically those "Within a Church State," the saints, to "Be knit together in Love" and to perform the duties of "Gods Habitation" (154); one of their duties is to "be a means and instrument of handing down this glorious intrest of Gods house unto those that shall succeed in a glorious way" (156–57). Thus, during the period he was working on *Gods Determinations*, Taylor publicly announced the important role the full members, the saints, would play in the spiritual growth of those members of the congregation who were experiencing some difficulties in their progress toward full Communion.

Taylor's vision in *Gods Determinations* is of a community of God's Elect who have either obtained or are striving for full membership in the church, for which probable assurance of salvation is necessary. "It is a duty in all," Taylor writes in his *Treatise Concerning the Lord's Supper,*

---

11. The emergence of this concern is also apparent in differences between the documents drawn up by the Synods of 1648 and 1662. The 1648 document emphasizes maintaining the purity of the church and the undesirable consequences of not doing so. The 1662 document, however, the "Propositions Concerning the Subject of Baptism and Consociation of Churches," while in essential agreement with the 1648 "Platform," places a much stronger emphasis on the extension of the Covenant promises to the offspring of the faithful and on the great need to train and educate these young people within the church environment. Walker, *Creeds and Platforms*, contains both documents; Pope, *The Half-Way Covenant*, tells the full story.

"to make after assurance" (156). In Taylor's religious community, it was an additional duty of the saints to assist the rest of the congregation (whether halfway or non-members) in the difficult task of discovering this probable assurance. In *Gods Determinations* he addresses this entire community of God's Elect: the full members, the halfway members, and the non-members. He addresses all those in attendance at his sermons, anyone in the Puritan community who might be one of the Elect.

The options available to Taylor for directing the future of Congregationalism in New England were, of course, limited. Had it been possible, he would no doubt have rekindled in his contemporaries the militant zeal and faith of those who had experienced the European persecutions and had later come to New England on a divine mission. However, admitting to Communion practically anyone willing to come who was not scandalous, as reports suggested Solomon Stoddard considered doing, might possibly have increased membership; but a church so formed would have been too far removed from Taylor's vision of a Congregational church as "Christ's Curious Garden fenced in / With Solid Walls of Discipline," where church elders examined those requesting membership and opened "onely to the right" (1940–41, 1953). Taylor's strategy, rather, was to stress the more liberal Puritan interpretation of what one might accept as sufficient evidence of election. He would continue to preach the basic Calvinistic doctrines of predestination and total depravity; but rather than dwell on the sins of the congregation and the dreadful possibility that they were damned, he chose to focus on the promises of grace and on convincing the unconverted that they very likely were among the Elect. He chose to put within the reach of all in his congregation a well-grounded hope of election and then to make clear to them that they needed only that.

The scriptural basis for this strategy is the Pauline doctrine that even the weakest faith is adequate to salvation: "Him that is weak in the faith receive ye . . ." (Romans 14:1). St. Paul's authority, of course, is Christ, who taught that "If ye have faith as a grain of mustard seed . . . nothing shall be impossible unto you" (Matthew 17:20). The prominent Puritan theologian William Perkins developed some of the implications this teaching could have for those seeking full membership. In his commentary on the first five chapters of Galatians, Perkins elaborates on the degree of faith one might judge sufficient. The "common faith of true beleevers," he writes, is apprehended sometimes only very slightly, but "it sufficeth": "For in this world wee rather live by hungring and thirsting, then by ful apprehending of Christ. . . ." In fact, he continues, the "highest degree of faith" (that is, "a full perswasion of Gods Mercie") is attainable only by "the Prophets, Apostles, martyrs; and such as have beene long exercised in the schoole of Christ" (209). The logical extreme of Perkins's discussion of faith is that God will accept even "the will to beleeve for faith it selfe, & the wil to repent for repentance" (208). Even in the Cambridge "Platform" of 1648, where the emphasis is primarily on maintaining the purity of New England's congregations rather than on liberalizing admission standards, this New Testament doctrine occurs: "The weakest measure of faith is to be accepted in those that desire to be admitted into the church: becaus weak christians if sincere, have the substance of that faith, repentance & holiness which is required in church members. . . ." Full members are admonished to use "Such charity & tenderness" that "the weakest christian if sincere, may not be excluded, nor discouraged"; the implication is that the weakest Christians have sometimes been excluded: "Severity of examination is to be avoyded" (Walker 222). The promises of covenant theology, which received greater emphasis in the 1662 Synod report, provided the rationale for the charitable view of weak faith: "Children of the Covenant . . . have frequently the beginning of grace wrought in them in younger years. . . . they have Faith and Repentance indefinitely given to them in the Promise . . . which continues valid . . . while they do not reject it" (330).

The solution to the membership crisis Taylor presents in *Gods Determinations*, then, is not original; it does not involve any radical theological innovation. His view does, however, require a shift of emphasis. In the first decades of New England Congregationalism, the churches were often overly strict, even harsh, in their judgment of public confessions because a militant zeal led them to emphasize the need to maintain the purity of their congregations.[12] Taylor, however, more readily acknowledges the inherent fallibility of human judgment in eternal matters and emphasizes the need for "Christian Charity." At the formal gathering of the Westfield church, Taylor warned that judgments "concerning the worke of Grace" were "fallable" because they were "made from the Appearance of things"; therefore, he advised his congregation, "appearing holiness with men, nothing appearing to the Contrary but Such humane infirmities, as are to be found in the best of Gods people doth sway our judgment to hope & therefore to pass the Sentence of Christian Charity

---

12. See, for example, Morgan, *Visible Saints*, 106–8.

Concerning the reallity of Such a Persons Holiness, & so to recieve such for Saints, & fitt Matter" (*CR* 126). For Taylor, the concept of hope was crucial, as the reasoning expressed in the phrase "to hope & therefore" implies. Hope of salvation was the essential requirement for full membership at Westfield. In his *Treatise Concerning the Lord's Supper,* Taylor makes very clear the role of hope in his view of salvation: "That knowledge is a good and warrantable ground for thy approach to the wedden feast that is a good ground for thy hope in Christ to stand upon. For a grounded hope is sufficient in this case. For it lays hold upon the promises of God. Christ dwells in the soul by hope. It is the instrument of communicating much of the love of God to the soul. Hence it makes not ashamed. Nay, by hope are we saved" (158). The "will to beleeve," for Taylor, was apparently acceptable "for faith it selfe."

Taylor dramatizes at length the theoretical effectiveness of his interpretation of what should be accepted as signs of election. He makes clear in the poem that the chief difficulty most elect souls faced was avoiding being caught in a dilemma between hope and fear. It was equally sinful to presume one's election or to despair over one's expected damnation. As Taylor's Satan says, "You'l then have sharper Service than the Whale, / Between the Sword fish, and the Threshers taile" (505–6). The main goal of the long middle sections of the poem is to direct the various ranks of elect souls to a successful resolution of this dilemma through the doctrines of hope and Christian charity. Taylor hoped that this strategy would obviate the need for Solomon Stoddard's "apostacy."

Further strategies appear in the formal aspects of the poem. Of primary importance are its homiletic structure and rhetoric.[13] The Protestant sermon's long-established pattern was designed to reflect "the order

13. Because *GD* is so original and complex, a rich history of diverse interpretations precedes the homiletic reading presented here: Nathalia Wright, "The Morality Tradition in the Poetry of Edward Taylor," describes the work's structure as dramatic and as influenced (if only indirectly) by the medieval morality plays. Jean L. Thomas, "Drama and Doctrine in *Gods Determinations,*" diverges from Wright by positing the sixteenth- and seventeenth-century "literature of religious instruction" and the medieval homiletic tradition behind this body of writing as the source of Taylor's allegorical devices. In *Edward Taylor,* Norman S. Grabo has suggested that *Gods Determinations* "is primarily lyric in structure rather than narrative or dramatic" and has also pointed out similarities to "five-act drama" and to "formal Ignatian meditation" (165–67). In the revised edition of *Edward Taylor,* Grabo adds the possibility of musical influence on the poem; that is, the rhapsody, the cantata, or the chamber opera could be musical analogs for the "purposeful disunity" and "virtuosity" he sees in the poem (100–107). Robert D. Arner, "Notes on the Structure of Edward Taylor's *Gods Determinations,*" locates Taylor's plan, rather, in what he sees as the four thematic

of Nature" (Chappell l); that is, it was designed to move the truth of Scripture from the head to the heart, from the memory and understanding to the will and affections. The Puritan view of human psychology included an epistemology that accounted for humankind's fallen condition.[14] Since any mortal's perception and understanding were confined to a state of corrupt nature, and since God wished neither to abandon nor confound humans, he adapted the manner in which he revealed his truth and will to the capacity of his creatures. The outward and natural senses—usually sight and hearing—must first be acted upon. The senses conveyed information to the mind where the power of memory was engaged. The understanding, the rational faculty, then analyzed the information and made it ready for the heart, the seat of the will and the affections. Any person's acquisition of knowledge conformed to this hierarchy of the powers of the soul (see Miller 239–79). Likewise, however, Puritans believed that God's grace acted on humankind in accordance with the same "order of Nature" and affected first the head and then the heart. For this reason, the Puritan sermon was designed to address, in order, the memory, understanding, and finally the will and affections. The auditor's memory was engaged by the first part of the sermon, the reading of the biblical text. Next, the understanding or judgment was addressed by the explication, or opening, of the text and by the demonstration and proof of the doctrine derived from the text. Finally, the will and affections were stirred by the "uses" or "applications" of the doctrine, usually the longest section of the sermon.

William Perkins provides a convenient outline for the "sacred and onely methode of Preaching" in *The Arte of Prophecying*, a sermon manual known well among Puritans in the seventeenth century:

---

divisions indicated in the poem's full title. Gatta demonstrates Taylor's use of "comic" strategies to aid the spiritual growth of the poem's audience ("The Comic Design of *Gods Determinations touching his Elect*"; *Gracious Laughter*, 101–40). William J. Scheick, "The Jawbones Schema of Edward Taylor's *Gods Determinations*," analyzes the poem's thematic concern with the hope/fear dilemma as an "underlying schema" that provides "an autonomous inner dynamic." David L. Parker, "Edward Taylor's Preparationism: A New Perspective on the Taylor-Stoddard Controversy," and George Sebouhian, "Conversion Morphology and the Structure of *Gods Determinations*," have discussed the degree to which the form of *GD* is dependent on Taylor's understanding of spiritual growth. Jeffrey A. Hammond's *Edward Taylor: Fifty Years of Scholarship and Criticism*, provides a thorough, facilitating (and occasionally witty) guide to all studies of Taylor.

14. William J. Scheick, *The Will and the Word: The Poetry of Edward Taylor*, discusses the role of faculty psychology in Taylor's work.

1. To reade the Text distinctly out of the Canonicall Scriptures.
2. To give the sense and understanding of it being read, by the scripture it selfe.
3. To collect a few and profitable points of doctrine out of the naturall sense.
4. To apply (if he have the gift) the doctrines rightly collected, to the life and manners of men, in a simple and plaine speech. (672)

Richard Bernard, author of another popular manual, *The Faithfull Shepherd*, clarifies the epistemological design of the sermon structure: "When the judgment is informed by Doctrine, the use must bee made to gaine the affection. These two cannot in nature bee severed, yet are they in themselves distinct. That precedes, this ever followes; the one is for the understanding, the other is for the will, both for the bettering of the soule, and to build us up in the way of life" (272).

This same epistemological pattern was apparent to Puritans even in the arrangement of the books of the Bible. As William Perkins demonstrates in *The Arte of Prophecying*, for example, the Old Testament opens with "Historicall" books (Genesis through Job), providing "stories of things done." Next are the "Dogmaticall" books (Psalms through Song of Solomon), "which teach and prescribe the Doctrine of Divinitie." The last section of the Old Testament comprises the "Propheticall" books (Isaiah through Malachi), "Predictions, either of the judgements of God for the sinnes of the people, or of the deliverance of the Church, which is to bee perfitted at the comming of Christ." It is also significant that "with these predictions . . . they doe mingle the doctrine of repentance, and doe almost alwaies use consolation in Christ to them that doe repent." The New Testament also followed this pattern, moving from histories through the Epistles and finally to Revelations, "a propheticall history" (647–48). Thus, God had adapted to humankind's pattern of perception the manner in which he revealed his Word and thereby had provided the instruments of his Word, the gospel ministers, with a structural model.

Edward Taylor relied on this structural model, using it to shape his sermons through nearly six decades of preaching and using it as an organizational device as well in his *Treatise Concerning the Lord's Supper*, the *Christographia*, and the *Harmony of the Gospels*. His use of this homiletic structure reflects an important premise in Taylor's aesthetic: that is, the *causal* relationship that exists between the public purpose of *Gods Determinations* and the poem's homiletic structure and rhetoric. Whenever

Taylor wants to move knowledge or an awareness of grace from the rational to the affective faculty, he addresses the powers of the soul in their "natural" sequence. Since his purpose in *Gods Determinations* is public, he uses a public, homiletic structure and rhetoric.

In its overall structure, *Gods Determinations* parallels the general plan of the standard Puritan sermon. Within this general structural plan, the poem has five main divisions, corresponding to a doctrine section followed by four "uses," or one "use" and three "applications":

Division One (ll. 1–418): Doctrine of Election.

Division Two (ll. 419–604): Use by way of information for all of the Elect.

Division Three (ll. 605–1016): Application of Election to those who come up to mercy with relative ease.

Division Four (ll. 1017–914): Application of Election to those who come up with greater difficulty.

Division Five (ll. 1915–2102): Application of Election to all of the Elect by way of consolation.

The first division begins with the opening "Preface" and ends with "Gods Selecting Love in the Decree" (1–418). Taylor's primary concern in this section is to establish the basic doctrinal truths on which the remainder of the poem rests: that God created the world from nothing and gave it to humankind so that "Through nothing man all might him Glorify" (38); that mortals by their own actions sinned; that they became thereby utterly undeserving and helpless; that God, while remaining both just and merciful, of his own sovereign will and love to humankind, extended grace to some of the fallen creatures; and that many elect souls will face difficulty in their efforts to believe in their election since they will be caught between "Proud Humility, and Humble Pride" (238). This division's chief concern is with describing, proving, and giving reasons for God's election of some for salvation.

The second division of the poem—beginning with "The Frowardness of the elect in the Work of Conversion" and ending with "The Effect of this Reply with a fresh Assault from Satan" (419–604)—represents the most general application of the doctrine to all of the Elect. In this section, the Elect are drawn from Satan to Christ by Mercy and Justice. Then Christ, without assuring any particular group of grace, makes a general statement of the condition of grace: "To him that smiteth hip, and thigh, / My foes as his: Walks warily, / I'le give him Grace: he'st give me praise" (565–67). The division then concludes with an encouraged First Rank and no suggestion that those souls will face serious difficulties in what follows but, rather, with "Still Drooping" Second and Third Ranks and a strong intimation that Satan will effectively challenge them (571–92). Then, as if heeding William Perkins's instruction that a doctrine should be applied "according to the divers conditions of men and people" (*Arte* 665), in the third and fourth divisions Taylor addresses the Elect according to his two main groups and more specifically applies the doctrine of election to the particular case of each, treating first those captured by Mercy, or the First Rank (605–1016), and then those captured by Justice, or the Second and Third Ranks (1017–914). Finally, in a carefully detailed rhapsody of consolation, the poem's fifth division applies election again to all of the Elect now in their ultimate mortal condition as "the Lambs espoused Wife" (1915–2102).

Within these divisions, Taylor applies the doctrine of election first to the rational faculty and then to the will and affections. He treats first, by way of instruction, the effect of election on all of the Elect; then in a more specific treatment he demonstrates the effect of election on the diverse conditions of his audience; and finally he addresses the affections directly in an attempt to present the consoling and "Comfortable Effects" of election. And as the application of doctrine in any sermon was designed primarily to stir the will and affections, throughout the last four divisions of *Gods Determinations* there runs an implicit exhortation to the poem's audience to find hope of their own election in the examples presented.

One of the rhetorical conventions Puritan ministers used to assist in their proof of a sermon's doctrine, or to obviate objections to an application of that doctrine, was a series of questions (or objections) and answers, often also presented as problems and solutions. This technique is an appeal to reason amid a general effort to move the will and affections. Bernard, for example, lists as the first use to be made of a doctrine that "of Confutation," "because if the truth delivered have any adversaries, they must be confuted first: for, where the doctrine is gaine-said, there no other uses can be made; till it bee approved, and the errours or heresies be overthrown" (274).

Taylor's training and demonstrable skill in the use of this homiletic rhetorical device manifest themselves in *Gods Determinations* in the abundant use of dialogue, where Taylor's keen perception of the hopes and fears of those in his congregation emerges—a perception that grew out of his experience as a pastor counseling "froward" souls. Throughout the portions of the poem that apply the doctrine of election rationally to his audience (divisions two, three, and four), Taylor relies on this method of objections and answers. In "A Dialogue between Justice and Mercy," for example, where Taylor revels in the Christian paradox that God remains just even when merciful, Taylor's pastoral interest in anticipating the various ways in which individuals might resist his exhortations is apparent in the companion stanzas of Mercy and Justice, both of whom "foresee" that "Proud man will me abuse" and that "the Humble Soul" will likewise resist the offer of grace (209–44). In the First Rank's direct confrontation with Satan ("First Satans Assault against those that first Came up to Mercy's terms"), Satan voices some of the persistent fears and doubts of Puritans. He begins by questioning the First Rank's very calling: "Why to an Empty Whistle did you goe?" (606). The First Rank then makes an immediate answer as well as a nicely logical turn on Satan's own words: "It's not an Empty Whistle: yet withall, / And if it be a Whistle, then a Call" (609–10). First Rank Soul consistently counters each of Satan's challenges with an effective answer. And, finally, throughout the lengthy dialogues between Saint and Soul (1347–842), Taylor's skill with this standard homiletic strategy of presenting real and often entangling objections to a proposition (in order the more dramatically to demonstrate the clear and satisfying solutions to them) is apparent in Saint's steady supply of answers to Soul's doubts. If Soul's sins "Swim in Mercies boundless Ocean," then, says Saint, "they'l . . . swim quite away / On Mercies main, if you Repenting Stay" (1367, 1371–72). When Soul claims that "my Hopes do witherd ly, / Before their buds breake out, their blossoms dy," Saint counters that "The Apple plainly prooves the blossom were. / Thy withred Hopes hold out Desires as Cleare" (1481–82, 1485–86). And so on. Taylor, of course, developed this ability in his training and experience as a spiritual counselor and composer of sermons.

Beyond the use of dialogue, the diction, the use of proverbs, the allegorical devices, and the imagery also contribute to the general homiletic design by conforming to the theory that words, images, and tropes must be intelligible to the understanding of the "plain man" before they can have the ultimate desired effect on his or her will and affections. The significance of the diction and use of proverbs in *Gods Determinations* is best seen by contrast with the greater number of difficult words and the relative lack of proverbial expressions in the *Preparatory Medita-*

tions.[15] In *Gods Determinations*, however, Taylor's homiletic purpose and accompanying awareness of his audience lead him to choose words his audience is more likely to be familiar with. All dialect words in the poem, for example, are in general usage in the seventeenth century, with the sole exception of "Squitchen" (30), Taylor's diminutive form of "squitch." Only two borrowings from Hebrew occur, and both would have been familiar from their use in the King James translation: "Shekel" (216) and "Epha" (1246). Only five specialized words from law and theology occur, and they represent simple, basic concepts: "Quittance" (203), surety" (241), "Acquittance" (314), "Amercement" (635), and "distraint" (638). Taylor's use of proverbs in *Gods Determinations* indicates a similar contrast with his private Meditations, which contain almost no proverbs. Taylor goes beyond simply adopting known proverbs: by occasionally using the form of the proverb for nonproverbial material, he further acknowledges the usefulness of the form. Mercy, for example, in her dialogue with Justice, laments: "Some will have Farms to farm, Some wives to wed: / Some beasts to buy; and I must waite their Will" (222–23). These lines, based on a passage from Christ's parable of the "great supper" (Luke 14:18–20), demonstrate Taylor's artistry with the proverb, for they have the sound and imagery of an authentic folk proverb (with especially fine half-line alliteration). Later in the poem, Saint sums up a long speech to Soul with a proverb that does not appear in any of the standard collections of proverbs: "Give but a Child a Knife to Still his Din: / He'l Cut his Fingers with it ere he blin" (1555–56). Taylor makes abundant use of proverbial expressions in *Gods Determinations;* and this fact taken together with the near absence of proverbs in the *Preparatory Meditations* indicates that in *Gods Determinations* Taylor consciously keeps his rhetoric within the reach of even the least educated.

Further evidence of the poem's homiletic design is apparent in the relative simplicity of its conceits. Most of the poetry Taylor wrote before *Gods Determinations* shows a clear, even central, interest and delight in complex poetic elements, such as the pun, the acrostic, and the extended conceit.[16] Likewise, in the *Preparatory Meditations*, the involved, intricate conceit is a characteristic feature.[17] In *Gods Determinations*, however, Taylor

15. On diction, see Charles W. Mignon, "Diction in Edward Taylor's 'Preparatory Meditations'"; on proverbs, see Robert D. Arner, "Proverbs in Edward Taylor's *Gods Determinations.*"

16. See Hall's chapters on Taylor's early verse, "Edward Taylor," 1–134.

17. As Karl Keller, for example, explains in *The Example of Edward Taylor:* "the *conceit,*

very noticeably and significantly alters his usual handling of conceits. Relative to the rest of his poetry, the conceits in this poem are remarkably simple and thereby a further indication that Taylor here designs his imagery for the understanding of even the least sophisticated in his audience. For example, nowhere in the poem does a conceit become more complex than in the "mudwalld Lodge" passage in Taylor's debate between body and soul, where the soul accuses the body of staining both the body and the pure soul within it by soaking in the puddles of worldly sin. His conclusion to this conceit is an excellent proverbial verse that contains appropriately liquid imagery and effectively summarizes in a single image what the preceding nine lines establish: "A Musty Cask doth marre rich Malmsy Wine" (1309–18). Thus, the relative simplicity of the conceits reflects the poem's homiletic structure and purpose. In curbing his usual poetic tendency to enhance and explore the implications of a conceit by elaborating it, Taylor draws on the homiletic tradition for this public poem.

The design of *Gods Determinations* is pervasively homiletic and reflects the artist's deliberate and adept pairing of form and meaning. Because the poem's basic concern is the Elect's "Coming up to God in Christ," Taylor derived the structure from the standard sermon form, the divinely appointed means for communicating that meaning. Accordingly, the poem's rhetoric follows the same "order of Nature" that controls the sermon structure. By viewing its structure as significantly influenced by Puritan sermon structure, we can see the epistemological basis for the arrangement and design of the poem. And we ultimately see that the poet of *Gods Determinations* was in complete control of a complex and coherent work.

As an occasional poem, *Gods Determinations* responded to its own generation as Wigglesworth's *Day of Doom* responded to its earlier, more conservative generation, one closer to the European persecutions and the felt emergencies that drove them and their parents to a distant and unknown wilderness. Wigglesworth used fear to keep the faith; Taylor used hope to obviate innovations Solomon Stoddard soon would advocate. Westfield's new minister praised his wife, Elizabeth, for having been so faithful a member of her generation that she knew by heart the homiletic poem that expressed their moment in the history of redemp-

---

whether humorously brief or hyperbolically extended as a structure for a poem, is Taylor's way of reaching out again for God through 'the faculty of enjoyment' throughout his sacramental poems. His yearning for salvation was so intense that it needed the most strained form of language he knew how to use" (185–86).

tion, *The Day of Doom*.[18] That was his generation and his poem, too. Now to control the change that was underway and to shape his culture, his theocracy, he composed the next voice in what he believed to be the historical evolution of Christ's work on Earth, *Gods Determinations*.

Finally, the aesthetic relationship between sermon and poem in *Gods Determinations* has deep meaning in its culture. As Harry S. Stout points out, by redistributing "power among many hands in local contexts," Congregationalism in New England marks an adaptation to the new environment, to the "open spaces of the New World"—an environment in which the sermon became more authoritative and influential than it was in England because of the near identity of civil and ecclesiastical authority in New England: "Sermons were authority incarnate" (20–26). Seen in this context, Taylor's most thoroughly homiletic poem becomes a significant cultural artifact since the aesthetic impulse, or the cultural need for its homiletic design, was caused by the new environment. Taylor spent several years learning how to adapt to the strange, new conditions of frontier Westfield. By the time he decided to stay and gathered his church there in 1679, he was ready to compose a public poem that was—by design—indigenous to his new world's culture.

Preparatory Meditations

With Westfield's church gathered and functioning, and with *Gods Determinations* complete and in a finished manuscript, Taylor approached his fortieth year as the leader of his town, his congregation, and his family. And in the relative solitude of his study, after having experimented with the many stanza forms and the variety of voices in *Gods Determinations*, the more confident—or at least more experienced and accomplished—poet was in transition. Edward Taylor's distinctive voice was about to emerge.[19]

Integral to this transition are the metrical paraphrases of the Psalms

18. At the end of his elegy for Elizabeth, Taylor writes: "The Doomsday Verses much perfum'de her Breath, / Much in her thoughts, & yet she fear'd not Death" (*MP* 114).

19. The following discussion of Taylor's evolving view of his art and of the relationship between Taylor's poetry and his other writings and his life in Westfield, except where noted, is based on Thomas M. Davis, *A Reading of Edward Taylor*, esp. 106–98. Davis's study provides the most comprehensive account of the stages and development of Taylor's poetic voice and career.

that he had begun as early as 1674 and further developed through the early 1680s (*MP* 44–101). This work not only deepened his knowledge of biblical poetics and helped him maintain his facility with biblical Hebrew, but it also seems to have shown him a dimension of the poetic life that he had not explored before in his own work: the dimension within which poetry takes on the sustained momentum of a lifelong process rather than being conceived within the focused activity that produces an individual poem.[20] The eight numbered, occasional poems that he wrote in the early 1680s (*MP* 102–14) show a brief and apparently experimental interest in limited works that interpreted natural phenomena (consistent with the sort of observations that Increase Mather regularly gathered at this time[21]), but the Bible's chief poet, David, offered Edward Taylor a more biblical use for his talents as well as a model of personal meditation. Meditation for the purpose of examining one's spiritual condition was always necessary for Puritans; but for Taylor, meditation would be useful as a means of assuring himself that he was worthy of administering the emblems of Communion to his parishioners. His studied paraphrasing of the Hebrew Psalms coincided with this emerging need for a new kind of meditative practice, and he had recently discovered in *Gods Determinations* a broad range of usefulness for a six-line stanza of iambic pentameter rhyming ababcc. These are crucial factors in the origins of the decades-long process of writing his *Preparatory Meditations*.

Although the *Preparatory Meditations* as a kind of spiritual autobiography often strike readers as remarkably regular and disappointingly unresponsive to events in Taylor's family and town, the reader sees throughout both Series the evolution of the poet's spiritual history as well as Taylor's responses to worldly events. In the First Series, for example, the first nine poems (1–6 and the three unnumbered, titled poems) seem to be occasional Meditations written before Taylor had decided definitely to write a continuous series of poems. Meditations 8–13 are unified by a concern with the Lord's Supper. Taylor next developed a group (poems 14–18) on Christ as priest, prophet, and king. In poems 19–22 Taylor

20. Keller develops the concern with process as opposed to product in Taylor's conception of his art (*The Example* 88–93). Davis discusses the role of the paraphrases in Taylor's development (*MP* xiii–xiv; *A Reading* 23–24).

21. In a letter to Increase Mather dated March 22, 1682 or 1683, Taylor describes several observations for Mather's use in his *Illustrious Providences* (1684). Taylor also refers in this letter to "my diary" (not the one edited by Francis Murphy), suggesting the possibility that yet more Taylor manuscripts may be found.

meditates on the purpose of his poetry. And in 23–30, which lack a unify-
ing idea or text, we see emerging the link Taylor develops between the
quality of his poetry and his spiritual condition: "Shoddy poetry now
begins to be seen in the context of sin" (Davis, *A Reading* 97).

This concern with the quality of his verse, however, disappears from
the First Series after the death of Elizabeth on July 7, 1689, which is also
the date Taylor gave Meditation 33. All the evidence suggests that Westfield's minister had a deep emotional attachment to his wife (Davis, *A Reading* 110–19), and in this poem, which does not refer to her directly, the
surviving husband meditates on the theological problem his deep love presents. Twenty weeks pass before the date of the next poem, during which
time he seems to have reevaluated the meaning of his poetry. Whereas
earlier he had asked that Christ's "Image" be "foild" in his words of praise
(*PM* 1.7.13–18), he now, more humbly, wants Christ to find the attempted
praise in his childish "Lisping." The nearly arrogant posture he strikes in
the last stanza of Meditation 19 ("And setting Foot upon its neck I sing")
has been replaced by the quieter, subdued "Make me thy bell / To ring thy
Praise." Taylor's impulse to poetry survived the deaths of Elizabeth and
five of their children, but the meaning of his art was changing.

Other events affected his work as well. In the fall of 1689, smallpox
was spreading in Boston; by early November 1690, ten of Taylor's parishioners had died of the disease. On October 5, 1690, Stoddard preached
a sermon in which he urged his congregation to view the Lord's Supper
as "appointed by Jesus Christ, for the begetting of Grace" (*ETvsSS* 129–
47); this came at a time when the Supper was moving ever more clearly
to the center of Taylor's thought. Amid this period of extreme affliction,
Taylor's heightened awareness of his own sinfulness moves him to open
Meditation 39 in November 1690 with a rending amalgam of David's
nearly despondent cry of lament ("My God, my God, why hast thou
forsaken me?" [Psalm 22]) and a description of what he has seen while
serving as both physician and minister to the victims of smallpox:

> My Sin! my Sin, My God, these Cursed Dregs,
>   Green, Yellow, Blew streakt Poyson hellish, ranck,
> Bubs hatcht in natures nest on Serpents Eggs,
>   Yelp, Cherp and Cry; they set my Soule a Cramp.

Two months later, his condition has not improved; he still represents his
heart as sinful in the extreme: "A Dunghill Pit, a Puddle of mere slime"

and "A Bag of Poyson." By contrast, all previous representations of Taylor's sin seem innocuous; yet both Meditations 39 and 40 turn ultimately to gratitude and praise without any intervening consideration of a possible link between the quality of his art and grace. Christ's sacrifice is the focus of these lamentations. The overt concern with the quality of his poetry that emerged between Meditations 19–22 and Elizabeth's death has now been completely subsumed by his focus on Christ and the Lord's Supper. Through the experiences of several years, Taylor's view of his poetry evolved from the ambitious "dedication to art" group (19–22) to the more balanced and restrained role for his poetry expressed in Meditation 43: "Till then I cannot sing, my tongue is tide. / Accept this Lisp till I am glorifide."

Sometime between February and May 1691, Taylor copied final versions of Meditations 1–40 and the three titled Meditations into a manuscript. On June 2, 1692, Taylor married Ruth Wyllys of Hartford after three years of being a single parent to his three children.[22] In the following spring, he transcribed the final versions of the last nine poems of the First Series and without any manuscript explanation began numbering his poems from "one" again.

With the greater stability brought by his marriage to Ruth, Taylor began a series of Meditations on the Old Testament types—poems Thomas M. Davis sees as reflecting this new view of his art's meaning. In the types poems, the poet subordinates the making of poetry to his apprehension of God's revealed Word in the types. The variety and inventiveness of the earlier poems are largely replaced by a devotional focus on doctrine. At the same time, Taylor was also burying his talent in the Job paraphrases and beginning his versified history of Christianity (*MHC*), which seems a kind of monument to the insignificance of art. This time of greater stability also allowed Taylor to focus on Stoddard's troubling actions, and he thus began his most productive period of prose. In 1693 he added lengthy anti-Stoddard arguments to his "Foundation Day Sermon"[23] and began both *Upon the Types of the Old Testament* and *Treatise Concerning the Lord's Supper*. In addition, he continued work on his largest project, the *Harmony of the Gospels*, which he had begun in the mid-1680s.

---

22. Ruth bore five daughters and a son, all of whom lived to adulthood: Ruth (b. April 16, 1693); Naomi (b. March 1695); Anna (b. July 7, 1696); Mehetable (b. August 13, 1699); Kezia (b. late March or early April 1702); Eldad (b. April 1708). Ruth died in January 1730.

23. See Dean Hall and Thomas M. Davis, "The Two Versions of Edward Taylor's Foundation Day Sermon," for the two versions of this sermon.

As Taylor approached the end of the century, and the end of his third decade in Westfield, difficulties between the minister and the town were becoming more common. Among other sources of tension were a salary dispute (see *CR* 463–65 n.66), meetinghouse and road repairs, and disciplinary cases.[24] A serious personal tragedy was the death of Taylor's son James early in 1701; he died of a fever in the Barbados after venturing out as a young merchant. With James's death, only two of Elizabeth's children survived. Nevertheless, Taylor began another large project that summer, his *Christographia*, a series of sermons devoted to the apprehension of Christ in his incarnation. For just over two years, into October 1703, he sustained this theme in the sermons and a parallel series of Meditations (2.43–56). In 1711, soldiers based in Westfield because of Queen Anne's War brought influenza, and ten town residents died that November, including both of Taylor's deacons. Yet, through all this difficult time, only the one personal reference to James appears in the Meditations (2.40; in fact, "James" is the only family name to appear in all of Taylor's Meditations).

Davis suggests that this distinct absence of allusions to his life in Westfield shows that Taylor was associating his poetry less and less with the concerns of this world. After the sustained series of types Meditations, and as he advanced into and beyond his sixties, Taylor also moved his poetry conceptually ever closer to the liberating poetic inspiration of the Canticles. Among the other changes of a more secular and diverse population in New England, ministerial authority was eroding. In his late sixties, Taylor stopped work on his *Harmony of the Gospels*, even though it was only about one-third complete; around the same time, he lost interest in his "Metrical History of Christianity" and left it not quite finished. Between June 1711 and October 1712, he developed a unit of Meditations (2.102–10) that methodically refute Stoddard's beliefs about the Lord's Supper. This is the last grouping of Meditations before he turned to Canticles for the rest of his life. By September 1713, when he began the Canticles-inspired Meditations, his poetry had become a meditative refuge from the mundane. These poems reveal a minister who does not seriously doubt that he is one of the Elect and a poet who has ceased to apologize for the limitations of his poetry.[25]

24. See Powell, "Edward Taylor's Westfield," for the full history of Taylor's relationship to the town of Westfield.

25. It is important to note here a number of works not otherwise referred to in this Introduction. Following a serious illness in December 1720, Taylor wrote "A Valediction

Beyond Taylor's life in Westfield, however, several theological and biblical contexts are crucial for an understanding of his art. One such informing context for the *Preparatory Meditations* is the Protestant cosmology and the resultant theory of metaphor. Often the distance between the vehicle and tenor of Taylor's metaphors (that is, between Taylor's "signe" and "signatum" [*PM* 2.106.48]) strikes readers as so great that the metaphor distracts from the point the poet intends to make and becomes thus a poetic weakness.[26] Taylor's specifically Protestant poetic, however, supplies a needed context for an informed reading of his *Preparatory Meditations.*

In Protestant theology, original sin caused a gulf between the divine realm and the created world that can be crossed only by means of Christ. An emphasis on original sin in Puritan thought becomes an emphasis on the perilous abyss between the fallen realm of human striving and the eternal realm of salvation. You can't get there from here—except by means of the appointed medium, the incarnate Christ. The Catholic doctrine of transubstantiation, from the Puritan point of view, directly opposed their pious emphasis on the gulf dividing the two realms and led Taylor to conclude that "The Pope's a whore" (*PM* 2.108.16) for maintaining that the earthly bread and wine of the Lord's Supper actually become the body and blood of Christ. For Taylor the bread and wine remain what they are, serving as "signs" (*TCLS* 13) to assist the mortal contemplation of Christ's sacrifice. Similarly, Taylor's metaphors, which he draws attention to in the *Preparatory Meditations,* are earthly and remain such—that is, inherently inferior to the divine praise he aspires to and mere "signs" of their meanings. His theory of metaphor thus parallels his view of the emblems of Communion; by consciously emphasizing the earthly inferiority of the bread and wine and of his metaphors, Taylor amplifies the disparity between the two realms and stresses the glory of his God. His metaphors are legitimate for the same

---

to all the World preparatory for Death 3[d] of the 11[m] 1720"; he left three manuscript versions of this poem (*MP* 219–41). After another illness in the following December, he left two versions of "A Fig for thee Oh! Death" (*MP* 261–64). After Increase Mather died in August 1723, Taylor worked through four versions of an elegy (*MP* 241–48). In these final years, he was also trying to develop his "Pope Joan" project, leaving some six versions and fragments (*MP* 248–61).

26. See Herbert Blau, "Heaven's Sugar Cake: Theology and Imagery in the Poetry of Edward Taylor," for a discussion of this argument. The discussion here of Taylor's Protestant poetic and of his theory of metaphor is indebted to Kathleen Blake, "Edward Taylor's Protestant Poetic: Nontransubstantiating Metaphor"; see also Barbara Kiefer Lewalski's chapter on Taylor (*Protestant Poetics and the Seventeenth-Century Religious Lyric,* 388–426).

reasons that the bread and wine are, as he explains in his *Treatise Concerning the Lord's Supper:*

> Natural things are not unsuitable to illustrate supernaturals by. For Christ in his parables doth illustrate supernatural things by natural, and if it were not thus, we could arrive at no knowledge of supernatural things, for we are not able to see above naturals.
>
> God hath a sweet harmony of reason running the same throughout the whole creation, even through every distinct sort of creatures; hence Christ on this very account makes use of natural things to illustrate supernaturals by, and the Apostle argues invisible things from the visible. (43)

What might seem to us, then, as Taylor's inept, deliberately shocking, or even sacrilegious metaphors are rather the metaphors of a Puritan poet deliberately and self-consciously drawing attention to the great distance between his earthly vehicles and their holy tenors.[27] When Taylor signifies Christ's blood with "beere" (*PM* 2.60[B].21), he violates no standard of decorum because he points to no comparison; rather, he flaunts the disparity with pious impunity.

The full title that Taylor gave the manuscript in which he transcribed these poems is "Preparatory Meditations before my Approach to the Lords Supper. Chiefly upon the Doctrin preached upon the Day of administration." The tradition of formal, devotional meditation most influential among Puritans in Taylor's day had been adapted from Catholic practices for Protestant use as a means of helping the truth of Scripture have a life-altering effect in the will of the reader or auditor. The three steps of meditation on a scriptural text or doctrine progressed through the three faculties of the human soul: the memory, the understanding or the rational faculty, and the will or affections. Richard Baxter's *The Saints Everlasting Rest* (London, 1650) contains one of the most influential Puritan discussions of meditation. In it Baxter refers to the meditative work of the rational faculty as "Consideration," which he says can be called "a Preaching to ones self" in order to "quicken" the heart; "Enter into a serious debate

27. Gatta discusses this quality in Taylor's writing in the context of the comic, the ludic, and wit. Incongruity between a metaphor's vehicle and tenor can often be understood as Taylor's "reverent parody" of scriptural language, images, or larger patterns: by "drawing on a sense of polar continuity between *ridiculum* and *admiratio* . . . reverent parody aims . . . to magnify the Lord" (*Gracious Laughter,* esp. 14–15).

with it: Plead with it in the most moving and affecting language: Urge it with the most weighty and powerful *Arguments*." Legitimate aids in meditation were prayer, which "keeps the Soul in mind of the *Divine Presence*," and a reliance on sensory detail; that is, in order to make divine truth more vivid in the fallen human mind, Baxter argued, the faithful could make use of concrete images and objects as aids to this end.[28] Taylor's meditative use of vivid imagery certainly reflects a similar epistemology, and his understanding of the structure and usefulness of meditation is generally informed by this tradition in Protestant thought.

The fact that the *Preparatory Meditations* do not regularly follow this structure shows that Taylor's specific meditative practice was free of anxiety about strictly following a prescribed three-stage structure.[29] He maintained, however, that meditation was nonetheless helpful in preparing one's soul for approaching the Lord's Supper. He coached the eligible residents of Westfield to prepare themselves by meditating: "Meditate upon the feast: its causes, its nature, its guests, its dainties, its reason and ends, and its benefits, etc. For it carries in its nature and circumstances an umbrage, or epitomized draught of the whole grace of the gospel. For here our Savior is set out in lively colors" (*TCLS* 203). As a means of achieving the larger goal of an altered will, meditation for Taylor seems to have been a rational contemplation of God's Word that accompanied faith. In the only Meditation wherein the word "meditation" occurs (2.138), Taylor interprets the top and bottom teeth of the Canticles Bride (which the Bridegroom in Canticles 6:6 compares to sheep) to mean faith and meditation:

> This Faith, and Meditation a pair appeare
>   As two like to the two brave rows of Teeth
> The Upper and the neather, well set cleare
>   Exactly meet to chew the food, beliefe
>   Doth eate by biting; meditation
>   By Chewing spiritually the Cud thereon. (ll. 53–58)

28. See Louis Martz, *The Poetry of Meditation*, for a full study of this tradition, and Martz's "Foreword" for his discussion of Taylor's place in it. I am indebted to Martz for his discussion of Richard Baxter, including the quoted material.

29. Rosemary Fithian Guruswamy discusses the disparities between meditative structure and Taylor's *PM* ("The Influence of the Psalm Tradition on the Meditative Poetry of Edward Taylor," 127; "'Words of My Mouth, Meditations of My Heart': Edward Taylor's *Preparatory Meditations* and the Book of Psalms," 113, nn.23 and 27).

For Taylor, preparation for the Lord's Supper began with "Examination" of the soul (*TCLS* 200–201) and then turned to a "Contemplation" of the Sacrament achieved by means of "Meditation." And meditation, as the rational faculty's "Chewing," transformed what the presumably elect soul accepted on faith (the initial "biting") into knowledge that could be digested and thereby made efficacious in the will and affections. The effectiveness of meditation did not depend entirely on the rigorous following of a prescribed structure; it depended, rather, on the spiritual condition of the soul, for Taylor modeled by David, the biblical soul in meditation: "Let the words of my mouth, and the meditation of my heart, be acceptable in thy sight, O Lord . . ." (Psalm 19:14).[30]

Just as Taylor's *Preparatory Meditations* are informed by a particularly Protestant tradition of meditation, so too are they informed by a Protestant aesthetic based on the Bible. The Logos-centered thought of the Reformation gave new life to several centuries of loosely focused interest in the poetic aspects of God's Word. As far as Protestants were concerned, the Bible should provide the basis not only for human society but also for each person's apprehension of deity. The philological and literary implications of this Protestant aesthetic caused many in England in the sixteenth and seventeenth centuries to reconceive poetry. Beyond simply heightening their awareness of the beauty of hexameter in the book of Job or of the lyric achievement of the range of metrical forms in the Psalms, this Protestant focus on biblical poetics offered poets freshly authorized models for their work—especially models that, like David's Psalms, corroborated the Protestant theory of spiritual growth. The Bible's shaping influence reached the rhetoric, modes of symbolic representation, and genres of poetry. The result in England was "the remarkable flowering of the religious lyric in the seventeenth century" (Lewalski 5).[31] At least one result in New England was the biblical poetic of Edward Taylor.

An important premise for Taylor's art appears in a notebook draft of the "Heads of Divinity" that he drew up shortly after moving to Westfield. Here Taylor rather elliptically notes that the ultimate purpose of

---

30. See Grabo for a discussion of Taylor's understanding of meditation (*Edward Taylor* 59–66; rev. ed. 34–39).

31. For a fuller discussion of this rise of Protestant biblical poetics, see Lewalski, *Protestant Poetics*, 3–13. For a discussion of the biblically sanctioned "intertextual patterning" that informs Taylor's Meditations, see Raymond A. Craig, "The 'Peculiar Elegance' of Edward Taylor's Poetics."

humankind is to glorify God—"Mans End ultimate Gods Glory"—and, furthermore, that the Bible is the only guide available to show God's creatures how to achieve this purpose: "Mans Rule to this End: The Word of God, Isa. 8.20" (*CR* xvi). Taylor's *Preparatory Meditations* are the sustained series of meditative poems that Taylor created and nurtured as a private means for glorifying his God. As he writes in the "Prologue," even though he is a "Crumb of Dust," he is "design'd / To make my Pen unto thy Praise alone." And since Scripture guides mortals in their attempts at praise, it provides also the crucial informing context within which to read the *Preparatory Meditations.*

Taylor knew the ways of formal meditation, and he knew the literary models of the Bible in their original Hebrew. When he turned his art inward and began his poetry of praise. This new, complex work came to have more in common with the Psalms than with Protestant formal meditative practices, which were also influenced by the Psalms, a meditative book long admired as an anatomy of the soul.[32] Taylor's *Preparatory Meditations* reflect a pervasive affinity with the Hebrew Psalms that helped him find his way to his own private poetry of spiritual examination and praise.[33]

The influence of the Psalms is so pervasive that Guruswamy concludes that in the *Preparatory Meditations*, "Taylor wrote his own Book of Psalms" ("'Words'" 110). This influence appears in three major aspects of poetic technique Taylor employs in his meditations: voice, structure, and imagery. Just as the voice of the Psalmist manifests the many moods of the soul seeking evidence of God's favor, Taylor's meditative voice ranges from that of the troubled, contrite soul to that of the joyous elect soul. Furthermore, in the expression of this voice, Taylor relies on five techniques regularly used by David: directing questions at his God (see, for example, *PM* 1.1, 1.20, 2.12, 2.91); shifting the audience within a poem from the poet's soul to Christ (as in *PM* 1.12, 1.23, 2.14, 2.68[B]); amplifying both the expression of praise and the poet's unworthiness (as in *PM* 1.11, 1.29, 1.39, 2.18); emphasizing through

32. See Lewalski, *Protestant Poetics*, esp. 39–53.

33. The discussion here of the affinities the *Preparatory Meditations* have with the Psalms is indebted to the extensive demonstrations worked out in Guruswamy's "Influence" and "'Words.'" Consult Guruswamy also for convenient and thorough references to the specific Psalms that manifest the various elements of voice, structure, and imagery she explores in her studies. The evidence she presents is extensive and detailed and can only be sampled here.

antithesis the distance between the glory of God and the depravity of humankind (as in *PM* 1.9, 1.21, 2.49, 2.109); and the occasional weaving of a public voice into the private voice (as in *PM* 1.27, 1.34, 2.44, 2.105). The three poetic structures relied on in the Psalms—those of the lament, the supplication, and the hymn of praise or thanksgiving—aided the Psalmist in manifesting his dynamic voice; and the Puritan poet apparently found in these structures a biblical model for his own psalms. The lament has a three-part structure: an opening invocation that often includes a petition for spiritual help, an affirmation of faith in God's ability to supply this help, and a concluding vow to praise God or words of praise (as in *PM* 1.16, 1.31, 2.17, 2.26, 2.69). The supplication has a similar three-part structure but is free of the self-deprecation of the lament; it is essentially a rather confident petition that moves from the opening invocation through an account of the poet's struggle to please God and the poet's petition to the concluding expression of some degree of belief that God will grant the petition, this last often ending in a vow to praise (as in *PM* 1.21, 1.42, 2.1, 2.53, 2.70). The Psalm of praise or thanksgiving opens with a call to praise, proceeds through an account of what the poet has to be thankful for, and concludes in expressions of gratitude and praise. This model appears in Taylor's *Preparatory Meditations* that focus on Christ's goodness rather than on the poet's plight (as in *PM* 1.9, 1.19, 2.2, 2.41, 2.98).

Taylor's use of David's imagery nearly permeates his meditative poems and extends to varying degrees of paraphrase. Perhaps most tangible are the transliterated Hebrew musical terms that Taylor borrows to associate his poems directly with those of David (for example, "Muth Labben" [*PM* 2.28.36] and "Michtam" [*PM* 1.18.48 and elsewhere]). Direct paraphrases occasionally contribute to the private nature of Taylor's *Preparatory Meditations* by introducing obscure references; for example, Taylor paraphrases Psalm 110:7 ("He shall drink of the brook in the way: therefore shall he lift up the head") as "This Lamb in laying of these Lyons dead; / Drank of the brooke: and so lift up his Head" (*PM* 1.19.17–18). Taylor's borrowings are often broader, extending to longer passages that encompass entire ideas; for example, Psalm 8:3–5 reads: "When I consider thy heavens, the work of thy fingers, the moon and the stars, which thou hast ordained; / What is man, that thou art mindful of him? and the son of man, that thou visitest him? / For thou hast made him a little lower than the angels, and have crowned him with glory and honour." Taylor's

rendering serves his more Christological purpose while relying on the
idea in David's Psalm, the structure of that idea, and the chief imagery:

> That thou, my Lord, that hast the Heavens bright
>   Pav'd with the Sun, and Moon, with Stars o're pinckt,
> Thy Tabernacle, yet shouldst take delight
>   To make my flesh thy Tent, and tent within't.
> Wonders themselves do Seem to faint away
> To finde the Heavens Filler housd in Clay. (*PM* 2.24.7–12)

In other ways as well, the pervasiveness of the psalmic influence on
Taylor's conception of his *Preparatory Meditations* makes this a crucial
context for an informed reading of this body of poetry.

Taylor's reliance on typology in the *Preparatory Meditations* is as pervasive as his reliance on the Psalms and further reflects his biblical poetic. For Taylor, and for Protestants generally, Adam, Moses, Jonah,
and other Old Testament figures were foreshadowings, or "types," of
Christ, just as circumcision and Passover were "types" of baptism and
the Lord's Supper, respectively. With the Reformation's emphasis on
the letter of the Word came a method of reading Old Testament persons, ceremonies, and events as "shadows" or "types" of their divine
fulfillment in the person of Christ and in New Testament ceremonies
and events relevant to spiritual salvation. As the revealed Word of God,
the Bible essentially relates the history of the Elect and exists in the
mind of God outside of time. This belief allowed Protestants to maintain that Old Testament types had historical reality but no soteriological
meaning except by their fulfillment in Christ. Their scriptural basis for
typology came from the Pauline books. Thus, when Taylor sees Christ
"in the shine / Out Spouted so from Adams typick Streame" (*PM* 2.3.8–
9), he is not guilty of the condemned Patristic allegorical readings; rather,
he is a Puritan biblicist relying on Paul's teaching that Adam "is the
figure of him that was to come" (Romans 5:14). Similarly following Paul,
where he speaks of baptism as "the circumcision made without hands"
(Colossians 2:11), Taylor refers to baptism as "a better marke" and as
"Circumcisions Rightfull Heir" (*PM* 2.70.34–35). Taylor's circumcised
nostrils (*PM* 1.3) become less alarming in this context.[34]

---

34. Like any other code, typology has it keys, and Taylor's main references were those
by Thomas Taylor and Samuel Mather. Michael Schuldiner, "Edward Taylor's 'Problematic' Imagery," explains the nostril reference in *PM* 1.3.

While Taylor drew on the usefulness of the Old Testament types in his poetry and prose throughout his ministry, typology became one of the chief hermeneutic tools of his trade between May 1693 and November 1706 while he developed the series of sermons he titled "Upon the Types of the Old Testament" and a series of corresponding poems (*PM* 2.1–30, 2.58–61, 2.70–71).[35] Though these poems generally strike readers as less inventive than Taylor's other work, because of his reliance on the established code of correspondences between the types and their antitypes (see, for example, *A Reading* 138–41), while working with types Taylor did develop one of the original elements of his art, what Karen Rowe has called the "typological conceit."[36] Whereas the metaphysical conceit yokes unlikes together to demonstrate surprising similarities, the goal of Taylor's typological conceit is to move beyond the given correspondences between worldly type and spiritual antitype and then undermine those surficial similarities in order to emphasize the more significant disparities, which indicate humankind's unworthiness and Christ's glory. In his most successful typological poems, Taylor uses this conceit to enact the resolution of the hope-fear dilemma. In *PM* 2.27, for example, Taylor represents his own sinful condition in the typological terms of leprosy and then writes of his spiritual recovery in terms of the ritual cleansing of lepers conducted by the Hebrew priests of Leviticus 14. Thus far in the poem (ll. 1–36), Taylor affirms that the leprosy and the cleansing of Leviticus shadow forth sin and Christ's forgiveness of sin, but then he pushes beyond the simple correspondences to a personal and metaphoric synthesis of type and antitype, asking Christ to "Wash me also in / The Poole of Shiloam" and to "put thy Blood upon my Right Eare fair." This synthesis—the typological conceit—becomes the poet's means to the hopefulness expressed at the end of the poem, and what could have remained a rational affirmation of typology becomes the art of a Puritan poet.

Throughout his fifties and on into his early sixties, Taylor focused on the types; the next and last major focus of his work began as he entered his seventies and turned to the Song of Solomon, or Canticles, for the

35. Taylor interrupted work on *UTOT* to develop first *TCLS* and then *C*. See Charles W. Mignon's "Introduction" for a detailed chronology of Taylor's work on all three treatises (l–lvii).

36. Karen E. Rowe, *Saint and Singer: Edward Taylor's Typology and the Poetics of Meditation*, provides a comprehensive study of typology in the work of Edward Taylor; Mignon's "Introduction" is also essential. The discussion here of the typological conceit and of *PM* 2.27 is based on Rowe, *Saint and Singer*, 138–42.

final twelve years of his *Preparatory Meditations*. With only four exceptions, Taylor chose texts from Canticles for the last fifty-four of these poems (*PM* 2.115–65). Canticles had new meaning for the aging theologian and spiritual counselor because it was understood to celebrate the promised wedding between Christ and the church on Earth or between Christ and the elect soul. To meditate on and identify with the Bride of the Canticles' Bridegroom was to contemplate the promised joys of spiritual salvation in an allegory of the individual soul's search for assurance of Christ's love. In this one book of the Bible, Protestants justified deemphasizing the literal meaning of the Word, arguing that in this case God relied on allegory.[37] Since Protestants read Canticles as essentially eschatological, Taylor, in contemplating the Bridegroom, moved beyond the leaden mediation of the types (the Bridegroom was not considered historical) to the affective symbolism of the divinely inspired Song of espousal. The Christ Taylor constructs in these poems helps him anticipate an eternal afterlife of consummated union. This is not the historical Christ of the miracles and the Passion. Since the erotic language and imagery of the Song are subordinated by Taylor (and Protestants generally) to the allegorical meaning, Taylor's renderings of these passages in his own poems always turn to his spiritual goals. Thus, when Taylor develops a description of the Bride's breasts (*PM* 150) as "like two little Roes that browse / Among the lillies in their shining dress" and "which are trust up fine," his meditative intent remains eschatological; he presents himself as Christ's "spirituall Babe" and promises to "sing forth thy praise." As he prepares for the end of his life through his Canticles Meditations, Taylor does not focus on his unworthiness as he did earlier; he dwells instead on his espousal to the spiritual Bridegroom.

After Taylor recorded his final Meditation, dated October 1725, he bound together all 219 "Preparatory Meditations," an act that suggests a project completed.

Because Edward Taylor knew so much, and because he drew on the full breadth of this knowledge for his poetry, his work, especially his private

---

37. Lewalski provides a convenient survey of Canticles exegesis (*Protestant Poetics*, 59–69); for the exhaustive survey of primary and secondary material on this subject, see Jeffrey A. Hammond, "Songs from the Garden: Edward Taylor and the Canticles," 19–101. Hammond's "A Puritan *Ars Moriendi:* Edward Taylor's Late Meditations on the Song of Songs" provides the basis for the discussion here of Canticles in Taylor's work. See also, however, Hammond, *Sinful Self, Saintly Self: The Puritan Experience of Poetry,* esp. 225–35.

meditations, can be quite challenging to readers three centuries removed from his day. Nonetheless, Taylor's art, while owing and owning certain allegiances to various literary traditions, is unique in the world and richly repays its close reading. Collectively his work is so nearly comprehensive of a mental and spiritual life expressed in its time and place that it offers a view, rare in its fullness, of a long moment when European traditions were brooding in the North American wilderness. It is as Robert Hass, one of our day's most accomplished poets, looking back on Taylor's verse, recently wrote: "now, some sixty years after the recovery of his verse, it still seems newly decanted, as if . . . it had been salvaged from the sea and the bottles opened and the odor were as sharp and unfamiliar as the day it was bottled" (264).

Taylor's More Polished Altar

Almost everyone who has tried to evaluate Taylor's poetic achievement has felt the need to apologize for or explain away "rough" and "crabbed" qualities (Johnson, "Edward Taylor" 319–20) or "surface crudities" (Martz xviii) of his verse. And certainly any poet who would try to make verse of "the Chariots of Aminadib" would at least occasionally challenge the generosity of even the most sympathetic readers. There is, then, some truth to the charge—but not nearly as much as has been thought. This new edition, by more accurately reporting Taylor's transcription of his *Gods Determinations* and *Preparatory Meditations*, sharpens our focus on the manuscript and reveals a body of poetry that is much more smoothly polished than previous editions have suggested. The following passages are examples of that sharper focus. On the left is a stanza (*PM* 2.35.13–18) as it appears in Donald Stanford's 1960 edition; to the right is the same stanza as presented herein.

Thy Ware to me's so rich, should my Returns	Thy Ware to me's so rich, should my Returns,
Be packt in sparkling Metaphors, out stilld	Be packt in sparkling Metaphors, out still'd
From Zion's garden flowers, by fire that burns	From Zion's garden flowers, by fire that burns
Aright, of Saphire Battlements up filld	Aright, of Saphire fuell and up filld

| And sent in Jasper Vialls it would bee | And [**]nt in Jasper Vialls, all would bee |
| A pack of guilded Non-Sense unto thee. | As packs of guilded Non-sense unto thee. |

In line 16, Taylor wrote "fuell"; this word, however, is somewhat obscured by a stain. Stanford enters his "Battlements" as a conjectural reading, as he does also for "sent" in the next line. Taylor's "fuell," however, is legible in the stain and is part of a consistently developed metaphor in the stanza. If "Battlements" and "sent" were the manuscript readings, Taylor's persona would be sending battlements in vials. Because I could not read all of the second word in line 17, I report the legible "nt" and show the approximate number of illegible letters by asterisks. A likely word in this place is "burnt" and would be consistent with Taylor's image here of fuel in a vial.

As a second sample of this sharper focus, I cite *PM* 2.164, where Taylor characterizes his poetry as a "mantle" not good enough for his "Dear Lord." Taylor expresses the fear that this mantle would

| . . . have a smoaky Smell, and Choaky lodge | . . . have a smoaky smell, and Choaky, lodge |
| Within its Clasp. And so it proove a blodge. | Within its Nap. And so it proove a bodge. |

In the Stanford edition, a "Clasp" is not a place where a smell can lodge, but Taylor's "Nap" is. Stanford's "blodge" causes him to speculate in his Glossary that Taylor might mean "blotch," or a "discolored patch"; Taylor's "bodge," however, meaning a botched piece of work, is legible in the manuscript and is consistent with the poet's humble view of his art. Taylor's comma following "Choaky" makes the lines less of a bodge than they would be without it.

Taylor's spiritual vision was clear, and his poetic skills were refined and stayed with him even into his last years. This edition should help us see his achievement much more clearly and completely.

Works Cited

Arner, Robert D. "Notes on the Structure of Edward Taylor's *Gods Determinations.*" *Studies in the Humanities* 3.2 (1973): 27–29.

———. "Proverbs in Edward Taylor's *Gods Determinations.*" *Southern Folklore Quarterly* 37.1 (1973): 1–13.

Bernard, Richard. *The Faithfull Shepherd.* Rev. ed. London, 1621.

Blake, Kathleen. "Edward Taylor's Protestant Poetic: Nontransubstantiating Metaphor." *American Literature* 43.1 (1971): 1–24.

Blau, Herbert. "Heaven's Sugar Cake: Theology and Imagery in the Poetry of Edward Taylor." *New England Quarterly* 26 (1953): 337–60.

Chappell, William. *The Preacher, Or the Art and Method of Preaching.* London, 1656.

Colacurcio, Michael J. "*Gods Determinations Touching Half-Way Membership*: Occasion and Audience in Edward Taylor." *American Literature* 39 (1967): 298–314.

Craig, Raymond A. "The 'Peculiar Elegance' of Edward Taylor's Poetics." In *The Tayloring Shop: Essays on the Poetry of Edward Taylor in Honor of Thomas M. and Virginia L. Davis.* Ed. Michael Schuldiner. Newark: University of Delaware Press, 1997. 68–101.

Davis, Thomas M. "Edward Taylor's Elegy on Deacon David Dewey." *Proceedings of the American Antiquarian Society* 96 (April 1986): 75–84.

———. *A Reading of Edward Taylor.* Newark: University of Delaware Press, 1992.

Gatta, John, Jr. "The Comic Design of *Gods Determinations touching his Elect.*" *Early American Literature* 10.2 (1975): 121–43.

———. *Gracious Laughter: The Meditative Wit of Edward Taylor.* Columbia: University of Missouri Press, 1989.

Gefvert, Constance J. *Edward Taylor: An Annotated Bibliography, 1668–1970.* Kent, Ohio: Kent State University Press, 1971.

Grabo, Norman S. *Edward Taylor.* New York: Twayne, 1961.

———. *Edward Taylor: Revised Edition.* Boston: Twayne, 1988.

[Guruswamy], Rosemary Fithian. "The Influence of the Psalm Tradition on the Meditative Poetry of Edward Taylor." Ph.D. diss. Kent State University, 1979.

———. "'Words of My Mouth, Meditations of My Heart': Edward Taylor's *Preparatory Meditations* and the Book of Psalms." *Early American Literature* 20 (1985): 89–119.

Hall, Dean G. "Edward Taylor: The Evolution of a Poet." Ph.D. diss. Kent State University, 1977.

Hall, Dean, and Thomas M. Davis. "The Two Versions of Edward Taylor's Foundation Day Sermon." *Resources for American Literary Study* 5 (Autumn 1975): 199–216.

Hammond, Jeffrey A. *Edward Taylor: Fifty Years of Scholarship and Criticism.* Columbia, S.C.: Camden House, 1993.

——. "A Puritan *Ars Moriendi:* Edward Taylor's Late Meditations on the Song of Songs." *Early American Literature* 17.3 (1982/83): 191–214.

——. *Sinful Self, Saintly Self: The Puritan Experience of Poetry.* Athens: University of Georgia Press, 1993.

——. "Songs from the Garden: Edward Taylor and the Canticles." Ph.D. diss. Kent State University, 1979.

Hass, Robert. "Edward Taylor: What Was He Up To?" *Green Thoughts, Green Shades: Essays by Contemporary Poets on the Early Modern Lyric.* Ed. Jonathan F. S. Post. Berkeley: University of California Press, 2002. 257–88.

Holifield, E. Brooks. *The Covenant Sealed: The Development of Puritan Sacramental Theology in Old and New England, 1570–1720.* New Haven: Yale University Press, 1974.

Johnson, Thomas H. "Edward Taylor: A Puritan 'Sacred Poet.'" *New England Quarterly* 10 (1937): 290–322.

——, ed. *The Poetical Works of Edward Taylor.* New York: Rockland Editions, 1939.

Keller, Karl. *The Example of Edward Taylor.* Amherst: University of Massachusetts Press, 1975.

Lewalski, Barbara Kiefer. *Protestant Poetics and the Seventeenth-Century Religious Lyric.* Princeton: Princeton University Press, 1979.

Lockwood, John H. *Westfield and Its Historic Influences, 1669–1919.* 2 vols. Springfield, Mass.: Press of Springfield Printing and Binding Co., 1922.

Martz, Louis. "Foreword." *The Poems of Edward Taylor.* Ed. Donald E. Stanford. New Haven: Yale University Press, 1960. xiii–xxxvii.

——. *The Poetry of Meditation.* New Haven: Yale University Press, 1954.

Mather, Samuel. *The Figures or Types of the Old Testament.* Dublin, 1683.

Mignon, Charles W. "Diction in Edward Taylor's 'Preparatory Meditations.'" *American Speech* 41(1966): 243–53.

——. "Introduction." *Upon the Types of the Old Testament.* Ed. Charles W. Mignon. 2 vols. Lincoln: University of Nebraska Press, 1989. 1:xix–lxxvii.

Miller, Perry. *The New England Mind: The Seventeenth Century.* Cambridge: Harvard University Press, 1939.

Morgan, Edmund S. *Visible Saints: The History of a Puritan Idea.* New York: New York University Press, 1963.

Nicolaisen, Peter. *Die Bildlichkeit in der Dichtung Edward Taylors.* Neumünster: Karl Wachholtz, 1966.

Parker, David L. "Edward Taylor's Preparationism: A New Perspective on the Taylor-Stoddard Controversy." *Early American Literature* 11.3 (1976/77): 259–78.

Patterson, J. Daniel. "*Gods Determinatons:* The Occasion, the Audience, and Taylor's Hope for New England." *Early American Literature* 22.1 (1987): 63–81.

Perkins, William. *The Arte of Prophecying.* In *The Workes of that Famous and Worthy Minister of Christ, in the Universitie of Cambridge.* 3 vols. London, 1613. 2:643–73.

———. *A Commentarie or Exposition Upon the Five First Chapters of the Epistle to the Galatians.* In *Workes* 2:153–432.

Petit, Norman. *The Heart Prepared: Grace and Conversion in Puritan Spiritual Life.* New Haven: Yale University Press, 1966.

Pope, Robert G. *The Half-Way Covenant: Church Membership in Puritan New England.* Princeton: Princeton University Press, 1969.

Powell, Walter L. "Edward Taylor's Westfield: An Edition of the Westfield 'Town Records.'" Ph. D. diss. Kent State University, 1982.

Rowe, Karen E. *Saint and Singer: Edward Taylor's Typology and the Poetics of Meditation.* Cambridge: Cambridge University Press, 1986.

Scheick, William J. "The Jawbones Schema of Edward Taylor's *Gods Determinations.*" In *Puritan Influences in American Literature.* Ed. Emory Elliott. Urbana: University of Illinois Press, 1979. 38–54.

———. *The Will and the Word: The Poetry of Edward Taylor.* Athens: University of Georgia Press, 1974.

Schuldiner, Michael. "Edward Taylor's 'Problematic' Imagery." *Early American Literature* 13.1 (1978): 92–101.

Sebouhian, George. "Conversion Morphology and the Structure of *Gods Determinations.*" *Early American Literature* 16.3 (1981/82): 226–40.

Stanford, Donald E. "An Edition of the Complete Poetical Works of Edward Taylor." Ph.D. diss. Stanford University, 1953.

———. "The Parentage of Edward Taylor." *American Literature* 33 (1961): 215–21.

———. *The Poems of Edward Taylor.* New Haven: Yale University Press, 1960.

Stout, Harry S. *The New England Soul: Preaching and Religious Culture in Colonial New England.* New York: Oxford University Press, 1986.

Taylor, Edward. *The Diary of Edward Taylor.* Ed. Francis Murphy. Springfield, Mass.: Connecticut Valley Historical Museum, 1964.

———. *Edward Taylor vs. Solomon Stoddard: The Nature of the Lord's Supper.* Ed. Thomas M. Davis and Virginia L. Davis. Boston: Twayne, 1981.

———. *Edward Taylor's Christographia.* Ed. Norman S. Grabo. New Haven: Yale University Press, 1962.

―――. *Edward Taylor's "Church Records" and Related Sermons.* Ed. Thomas
M. Davis and Virginia L. Davis. Boston: Twayne, 1981.

―――. *Edward Taylor's Harmony of the Gospels.* Ed. Thomas M. Davis and
Virginia L. Davis, with Betty L. Parks. 4 vols. Delmar, N.Y.: Scholar's
Facsimiles and Reprints, 1983.

―――. *Edward Taylor's Minor Poetry.* Ed. Thomas M. Davis and Virginia L.
Davis. Boston: Twayne, 1981.

―――. *Edward Taylor's Treatise Concerning the Lord's Supper.* Ed. Norman S.
Grabo. East Lansing: Michigan State University Press, 1966.

―――. [Letter to Increase Mather.] *Massachusetts Historical Society Collections,* Fourth Series, 8 (1868): 629–31.

―――. [Letter to Samuel Sewell.] In "The Pouring of the Sixth Vial: A Letter in a Taylor-Sewall Debate." Ed. Mukhtar Ali Isani. *Proceedings of the
Massachusetts Historical Society* 83 (1971): 123–29.

―――. *A Transcript of Edward Taylor's Metrical History of Christianity.* Ed.
Donald E. Stanford. Cleveland: Micro Photo, Inc., 1962.

―――. *Upon the Types of the Old Testament.* Ed. Charles W. Mignon. 2 vols.
Lincoln: University of Nebraska Press, 1989.

Taylor, Thomas. *Christ Revealed: Or The Old Testament Explained.* London,
1635.

Thomas, Jean L. "Drama and Doctrine in *Gods Determinations*." *American
Literature* 36 (1965): 452–62.

Walker, Williston. *The Creeds and Platforms of Congregationalism.* Boston:
Pilgrim Press, 1960.

Wright, Nathalia. "The Morality Tradition in the Poetry of Edward Taylor." *American Literature* 18 (1946): 1–17.

GODS DETERMINATIONS

Gods Determinations touching his Elect: &c
The Elects Combat in their
Conversion, and
Coming up to God in Christ:
together with the
Comfortable Effects thereof.

THE PREFACE.

    Infinity, when all things it beheld
In Nothing, and of Nothing all did build,
Upon what Base was fixt the Lath, wherein
He turn'd this Globe, and riggalld it so trim?
Who blew the Bellows of his Furnace Vast?   5
Or held the Mould wherein the world was Cast?
Who laid its Corner Stone? Or whose Command?
Where Stand the Pillars upon which it Stands?
Who Lac'de and Fillitted the earth so fine,
With Rivers like green Ribbons Smaragdine?   10
Who made the Sea's its Selvedge, and it locks
Like a Quilt Ball within a Silver Box?
Who Spread its Canopy? Or Curtains Spun?
Who in this Bowling Alley bowld the Sun?
Who made it alway when it rises Set   15
To go at once both down and up to get?
Who th'Curtain rods made for this Tapistry?
Who hung the twinckling Lanthorns in the Sky?
Who? who did this? or who is he? Why, know
It's Onely Might Almighty this did doe.   20
His hand hath made this noble worke which Stands
His Glorious Handy work not made by hands.
Who Spake all things from nothing; and with ease
Can Speake all things to nothing, if he please.
Whose Little finger at his pleasure Can   25
Out mete ten thousand worlds with halfe a Span:
Whose Might Almighty can by half a looks
Root up the rocks and rock the hills by th'roots.
Can take this mighty World up in his hande,
And Shake it like a Squitchen or a Wand.   30
Whose Single Frown will make the Heavens Shake
Like as an aspen leafe the Winde makes quake.
Oh! what a might is this Whose Single frown
Doth Shake the world as it would Shake it down?

{ 49 }

Which All from Nothing fet, from Nothing, All: 35
Hath All on Nothing Set, lets Nothing fall.
Gave All to nothing Man, indeed whereby
Through nothing man all might him Glorify. [1]
In Nothing man imbosst the brightest Gem
More pretious than all pretiousness in them. 40
But Nothing man did throw down all by Sin:
And darkened that lightsom Gem in him.
  That now his Brightest Diamond is grown
  Darker by far than any Coalpit Stone.

---

9 Fillitted *orig.* Fillatted
16 go at once both down and up *orig.* be at once down going and up
21 hand *orig.* had
32 quake *orig.* shake
33 this *orig.* this?
35 Which *orig.* He

THE EFFECTS OF MANS APOSTACY.

  While man unmarr'd abode his Spirits all 45
In vivid hue were active in their hall,
This Spotless Body, here and there mentain
Their traffick for the Universall gain.
Till Sin Beat up for Volunteers. Whence came
A thousand Griefs attending on the Same. 50
Which march in ranck, and file, proceed to make
A Battery, and the fort of Life to take.
Which when the Centinalls did Spy, the Heart
Did beate alarum up in every part.
The Vitall Spirits apprehend thereby 55
Exposde to danger great the Suburbs ly,
The which they do desert, and Speedily
The Fort of Life, the Heart, they Fortify.
The Heart beats up still by her Pulse to Call
Out of the outworks her train Souldiers all 60
Which quickly come hence; now the Looks grow pale

Limbs feeble too: the Enemies prevaile.
Do Scale the Outworks where there's Scarce a Scoute
That can be Spi'de sent from the Castle out.
  Man at a muze, and in a maze doth Stand,   65
While Feare the Generall of all the Band
Makes inroads on him: then he Searches why,
And quickly Findes, God stand as Enemy.
Whom he would fain Subdue, yet Fears affright
In Varnishing their Weapons in his Sight.   70
Troops after troops, Bands after Bands do high,
Armies of armed terrours drawing nigh:
He lookes within, and sad amazement's there,
Without, and all things fly about his Eares.
Above, and sees Heaven falling on his pate,   75
Below and Spies th'Infernall burning lake,
Before and Sees God storming in his Face,
Behinde, and Spies Vengeance persues his trace: [2]
To Stay he dares not, go he knows not where.
From God he can't, to God he dreads for Feare.   80
To Dy he Dreads; For Vengeance's due to him;
To Live he must not, Death persues his Sin:
He Knows not what to have, nor what to loose
Nor what to do, nor what to take or Choose:
Thus over Stretcht upon the Wrack of Woe,   85
Bereav'd of Reason, he proceeds now So,
Betakes himselfe unto his Heels in hast,
Runs like a Mad man till his Spirits wast,
Then like a Child that fears the Poker Clapp
Him on his face doth on his Mothers lap;   90
Doth hold his breath, lies still for fear least hee
Should by his breathing lowd discover'd bee.
Thus on his face doth see no outward thing
But Still his heart for Feare doth pant within.
Doth make its Drummer beate So loud it makes   95
The Very Bulworks of the City Quake:
Yet gets no aide: Wherefore the Spirits they
Are ready all to leave, and run away.
For Nature in this Pannick feare scarce gives
Him life enough, to let him feel he lives.   100

Yet this he easily feels, he liveth in
A Dying Life, and Living Death by Sin.
Yet in this Lifeless life wherein he lies,
Some Figments of Excuses doth devise
That he may Something say, when 'rain'd, although   105
His Say seems nothing, and for nought will go.
  But while he Sculking on his face close lies
  Espying nought the Eye Divine him Spies.
Justice and Mercy then fall to debate
Concerning this poore fallen mans estate,   110
Before the Bench of the Almighties Breast.
Th'ensuing Dialogues hint their Contest.

---

83 loose *orig.* Choose
89 like a *orig.* like the *orig.* like like

A DIALOGUE BETWEEN { JUSTICE AND
                        MERCY

Offended Justice comes in fiery Rage,
Like to a Rampant Lyon new assaild,
Array'de in Flaming fire now to engage,   115
With red hot burning wrath poore man unbaild.
  In whose Dread Vissage Sinfull man may Spy
  Confounding, Rending, Flaming Majesty.   [3]

Out Rebell, out (saith Justice) to the Wrack,
Which every joynt unjoynts, doth Streatch, and Strain,   120
Where Sinews tortur'de are untill they Crack
And Flesh is torn asunder grain by grain.
  What Spit thy Venom in my Face. Come out
  To handy gripes Seing thou art so Stoute.

Mercy takes up the Challenge, Comes as meeke   125
  As any Lamb, on mans behalfe, She Speakes
Like new blown pincks, breaths out perfumed reech
  And doth revive the heart before it breaks.

Justice (saith Mercy) if thou Storm so fast,
Man is but dust that flies before thy blast. 130

Justice.
My Essence is ingag'de, I cannot bate,
Justice not done no Justice is; and hence
I cannot hold off of the Rebells pate
The Vengeance he halls down with Violence.
If Justice wronged be She must revenge: 135
Unless a way be found to make all friends.

Mercy.
My Essence is engag'de pitty to show.
Mercy not done no Mercy is. And hence
I'le put my shoulders to the burden so
Halld on his head with hands of Violence. 140
As Justice justice evermore must doe:
So Mercy Mercy evermore must Show.

Justice.
I'le take thy Bond: But know thou this must doe.
Thou from thy Fathers bosom must depart:
And be incarnate like a Slave below, 145
Must pay mans Debts unto the utmost marke.
Thou must sustain that burden, that will make
The Angells Sink into th'Infernall lake.

Nay on thy shoulders bare must beare the smart
Which makes the Stoutest Angell buckling, cry, 150
Nay makes thy Soule to Cry through griefe of heart,
ELI, ELI, LAMA SABACHTANI.
If this thou wilt, come then, and do not spare,
Beare up the Burden on thy Shoulders bare.

Mercy.
All this I'le do, and do it o're, and o're, 155
Before my Clients Case shall ever faile.
I'le pay his Debt, and wipe out all his Score
And till the pay day Come I'le be his baile.

I Heaven, and Earth do on my Shoulders beare
Yet down I'le throw them all rather than Spare.   [4]160

Justice.
Yet notwithstanding still this is too Small,
    Although there was a thousand times more done
If Sinless man did, Sinfull man will fall;
    If out of debt, will on a new Score run.
    Then Stand away, and let me Strike at first: 165
    For better now, than when he's at the Worst.

Mercy.
If more a thousand times too little bee
    Ten thousand times yet more than this I'le do:
I'le free him from his Sin, and Set him free
    From all those faults the which he's Subject to.   170
    Then Stand away, and strike not at the first.
    He'l better grow when he is at the worst.

Justice.
Nay, this ten thousand times as much can still
    Confer no hony to the Sinners hive.
For man though Shrived throughly from all ill   175
    His Righteousness is merely negative.
    Though none be damnd but such as Sin imbrace:
    Yet none are Sav'd without Inherent Grace.

Mercy.
What though ten thousand times, too little bee?
    I will ten thousand thousand times more do.   180
I will not onely from his Sin him free,
    But fill him with Inherent grace also.
    Though none are Sav'd that wickedness imbrace.
    Yet none are Damn'd that have Inherent Grace.

Justice.
Yet this ten thousand thousand times more shall   185
    Though Doubled o're, and o're for little Stands.
The Righteousness of God should be his all

The which he cannot have for want of hands.
Then though he's Spar'de at first, at last he'l fall
For want of hands to hold himselfe withall. 190

Mercy.
Though this ten thousand thousand times much more
  Though doubled o're and o're for little go,
I'le double Still its double o're and ore
  And trible that untill I make it do.
  I'le make him hands of Faith to hold full fast. 195
  Spare him at first, then he'l not fall at last.

For by these hands he'l lay his Sins upon
  The Scape Goats head, o're whom he shall Confess
And with these hands he rightly shall put on
  My milkwhite Robe of Lovely Righteousness. 200
  Now Justice on, thy Will fulfilled bee.
  Thou dost no wrong: the Sinner's just like thee.

Justice.
If so, it's so: then I'l his Quittance seale:
  Or shall accuse myselfe as well as him:
If so, I Justice shall of Justice faile 205
  Which if I do, Justice herselfe should Sin.
  Justice unspotted is; and therefore must
  * * * * * * [5]

Mercy.
I do foresee Proud man will me abuse,
  He'th broke his Legs, yet's Legs his Stilts must bee: 210
And I may Stand untill the Chilly Dews
  Do pearle my Locks before he'l Stand on mee.
  For Set a Beggar upon horseback, See
  He'll ride as if no man so good as hee.

Justice.
And I foresee Proude man will me abuse. 215
  Judging his Shekel is the Sanctuaries:
He on his durty Stilts to walk will Choose:

Yea is as Clean as I, and nothing varies
Although his Shekel is not Silver good
And's tilting Stilts do stick within the mudd.   220

Mercy.
But most he'l me abuse, I feare, for Still
  Some will have Farms to farm, Some wives to wed:
Some beasts to buy; and I must waite their Will.
  Though while they Scrape their naile, or Scratch their head,
  Nay though with Cap in hand I Wooe them long   225
  They'l whistle out their Whistle e're they'l come.

Justice.
I See I'st be abusde by greate, and Small:
  And most will count me blinde, or will not see:
Me leaden heel'd, with iron hands they'l Call:
  Or am unjust, or they more just than mee.   230
  And while they while away their Mercy so,
  They set their bristles up at Justice do.

Mercy.
I feare the Humble Soul will be too Shie;
  Judging my Mercy lesser than his Sin.
Inlarging this, but lessoning that thereby.   ·   235
  'S if Mercy would not Mercy be to him.
  Alas! poore Heart! how art thou damnifide,
  By Proud Humility, and Humble Pride?

Justice.
The Humble Soul deales worse with me, doth Cry
  If I be just, I'le on him Vengeance take   240
As if I su'de Debtor, and surety
  And double Debt and intrest too would rake.
  If Justice Sue the Bonds that Cancelld ar'
  Sue Justice then before a juster bar.

Mercy.
But in this Case alas, what must be done   245
  That haughty Souls may humble be, and low?

That Humble Souls may suck the Hony Comb?
  And thou for Justice, I for Mercy go?   [6]
  This Query weighty is, Let's therefore Shew
  What must be done herein by me, and you.   250

Justice.
Lest that the Soule in Sin Securely ly,
  And do neglect Free Grace, I'le steping in
Convince him by the Morall Law, whereby
  He'st se in what a pickle he is in.
  For all he hath, for nothing stand it shall   255
  If of the Law one hair breadth short it fall.

Mercy.
And lest the Soule should quite discourag'de Stand
  I will Step in, and Smile him in the face,
Nay I to him will hold out in my hand
  The golden Scepter of my Rich-Rich Grace.   260
  Intreating him with Smiling lips most cleare
  At Court of Justice in my robes t'appeare.

Justice.
If any after Satans Pipes do Caper
  Red burning Coales from hell in Wrath I gripe,
And make them in his face with Vengeance vaper,   265
  Untill he dance after the Gospell Pipe.
  Whose Sun is Sin, when Sin in Sorrows shrow'd,
  Their Sun of Joy Set in a grievous Cloud.

Mercy.
When any Such are Startled from ill,
  And Cry, help, help, with tears, I will advance   270
The Musick of the Gospell Minsterill,
  Whose Strokes they Strike, and tunes exactly dance.
  Who mourn when Justice frowns, when Mercie playes
  Will to her Sounding Viall Chant out Praise.

Justice.
The Works of Merit-Mongers I will weigh   275

Within the Ballance of the Sanctuary:
Their Matter, and their Manner I will lay
    Unto the Standard-Rule t'see how they vary.
    Whos'ever trust doth to his golden deed
    Doth rob a barren Garden for a Weed.   280

Mercy.
Yet if they'l onely on my Merits trust
    They'st in Gods Paradise themselves solace,
Their beauteous garden knot I'le also thrust
    With Royall Slips, Sweet Flowers, and Herbs of Grace.
    Their Knots I'le weed, to give a Spangling Show   285
    In Order: and perfumes shall from them flow.

Justice.
Those that are ignorant, and do not know
    What meaneth Sin, nor what means Sanctity,
I will Convince that all Save Saints must go
    Into hot fire, and brinston there to fry.   290
    Whose Pains hot Scalding boyling Lead transcends,
    But evermore adds more and never Ends.   [7]

Mercy.
Though Simple, learn of mee, I will you teach,
    True Wisdom for your Souls Felicity,
Wisdom Extending to the Endless reach   295
    And blissful end of all Eternity.
    Wisdom that doth all else transcend as far
    As Sol's bright Glory doth a painted Star.

Justice.
You that Extenuate your Sins, come see
    Them in Gods multiplying Glass: for here   300
Your little Sins will just like mountains bee,
    And as they are just So they will appeare.
    Who doth a little Sin Extenuate
    Extends the Same, and two thereof doth make.

Mercy.
A little Sin is Sin: and is Sin Small?   305
  Excuse it not, but aggrivate it more.
Lest that your little Sin asunder fall
  And two become, each bigger than before.
  Who Scants his Sin will Scarce get grace to save.
  For little Sins, but little pardons have.   310

Justice.
Unto the Humble Humble Soule, I say,
  Cheer up, poor Heart, for Satisfi'de am I.
For Justice nothing to thy Charge can lay,
  Thou hast Acquittance in thy surety.
  The Court of Justice thee acquits: therefore   315
  Thou to the Court of Mercy are bound o're.

Mercy.
My Dove, come hither linger not, nor Stay.
  Though thou among the pots hast lai'n, behold
Thy Wings with Silver Colours I'le o're lay:
  And lay thy feathers o're with yellow gold.   320
  Justice in Justice must adjudge thee just:
  If thou in Mercies Mercy put thy trust.

---

110 fallen mans *orig.* mans fallen
120 unjoynts *orig.* doth
213 See *orig.* hee
214 He'll *orig.* Will
220 Stilts *orig.* Sticks
224 Scrape *orig.* Scratch
242 rake. *orig.* scrape
245 Case *ins.*
246 haughty *orig.* hauty
254 He'st *orig.* Ile
268 set *orig.* will set
289 Convince *orig.* Convence

Mans Perplexity when calld to an account.

Justice, and Mercy ending their Contest,
In Such a Sort, now thrust away the Desk.
And other titles come in Majesty,   325
All to attend Almighty royally.
Which Sparkle out, call man to come, and tell
How he his Cloath defild and how he fell?
   He on his Skirts with Guilt, and Filth out peeps
With Pallid Pannick Fear upon his Cheeks,   330
With Trembling joynts, and Quiverring Lips, doth quake
As if each Word he was about to make,
Should hackt asunder be, and Chopt as Small
As Pot herbs for the pot before they Call
Upon the Understanding to draw neer,   335
By tabbering on the Drum within the eare.
His Spirits are So low they'l Scarce afford
Him winde enough to waft a Single word   [8]
Over the Tongue unto one's eare: yet loe,
This tale at last with Sobs, and Sighs lets goe.   340
Saying, my Mate procurde me all this hurt,
Who threw me in my best Cloaths in the Dirt.
   Thus man hath lost his Freehold by his ill:
Now to his Land Lord tenent is at Will.
And must the Tenement keep in repare   345
What e're the ruins, and the Charges are.
Nay, and must mannage war against his Foes.
Although ten thousand Strong, he must oppose.
Some Seeming Friends prove Secret foes, which will
Thrust Fire i'th'thatch, nay Stob, Cut throate and kill.   350
Some undermine the Walls: Some knock them down,
And make them tumble on the Tenents Crown.
  He's then turnd out of Doors, and so must Stay,
  Till's house be raisd against the Reckoning day.

GODS SELECTING LOVE IN THE DECREE.

Man in this Lapst Estate at very best,   355
A Cripple is and footsore, sore opprest.
Can't track Gods Trace but Pains, and pritches prick
Like poyson'd Splinters Sticking in the Quick.
Yet jims in th'Downy path with pleasures Spread
As't was below him on the Earth to tread.   360
Can prance, and trip within the way of Sin,
Yet in Gods path moves not a little wing.
  Almighty this foreseing, and withall
That all this Stately worke of his would fall
Tumble, and Dash to pieces Did in lay   365
Before it was too late for it a Stay.
Doth with his hands hold, and uphold the Same.
Hence his Eternall Purpose doth proclaim.
Whereby transcendently he makes to Shine
Transplendent Glory in his Grace Divine.   370
Almighty makes a mighty Sumptuous feast:
Doth make the Sinfull Sons of men his guessts.
But yet in Speciall Grace he hath to Some,
(Because they Cripples are, and Cannot come)
He sends a Royall Coach forth for the same,   375
To fetch them in, and names them name by name.
A Royall Coach whose Scarlet Canopy
O're Silver Pillars, doth expanded ly:
All bottomed with purest gold refin'de,
And inside o're with lovely Love all linde.   380
Which Coach indeed you may exactly spy
All mankinde Splits in a Dicotomy.
  For all ride to the feast that favour finde.
  The rest do slite the Call and Stay behinde.   [9]

O! Honour! Honour! Honours! Oh! the Gain!   385
And all Such Honours all the Saints obtain.
It is the Chariot of the King of Kings:
That all who Glory gain, to glory brings.
Whose Glory makes the rest, (when Spi'de) beg in.
Some gaze and Stare. Some stranging at the thing.   390

Some peep therein; Some rage thereat, but all,
Like market people seing on a Stall,
Some rare Commodity Clap hands thereon
And Cheapen't hastily, but soon are gone.
For hearing of the price, and wanting pay   395
Do pish thereat, and Coily pass away.
So hearing of the terms, whist, they'le abide
At home before they'l pay so much to ride.
But they to whom it's sent had rather all,
Dy in this Coach, than let their journey fall.   400
They up therefore do get, and in it ride
Unto Eternall bliss, while down the tide
The other Scull unto eternall woe;
By letting Slip their former journey so.
For when they finde the Silver Pillars fair   405
The Golden bottom pav'de with Love as rare,
To be the Spirits Sumptuous building cleare,
When in the Soul his Temple he doth reare.
And Purple Canopy to bee (they spy)
All Graces Needlework and Huswifry;   410
Their Stomachs rise: these graces will not down.
They think them Slobber Sawces: therefore frown.
They loath the Same, wamble, keck, heave they do:
Their Spleen thereat, out at their mouths they throw.
Which while they do, the Coach away doth high   415
Wheeling the Saints in't to eternall joy.
   These therefore and their journey now do come
   For to be treated on, and Coacht along.

---

356 Cripple *orig.* Cripl
385 Honour! Honour! *orig.* Honour, Honour
411 Their *orig.* These

— They resist grace

THE FROWARDNESS OF THE ELECT IN THE WORK OF CONVERSION.

add Justice to Mercy

   Those upon whom Almighty doth intend
His all Eternall Glory to expend,   420
Lulld in the lap of Sinfull Nature Snugg,
Like Pearls in Puddles cover'd ore with mudd:
Whom, if you search, perhaps some few you'l finde,
That to notorious Sins were ne're inclinde.
Some Shunning Some, some most, some greate, some Small,   425
Some this, that or the other, Some none at all.
But all, or almost all you'st easly finde,
To all or almost all Defects inclinde: [10]
To Revell with the Rabble rout who say
Let's hiss this Piety out of our Day.   430
And those whose frame is made of finer twine   ?
Stand further off from Grace than Wash from Wine.
Those who suck Grace from th'breast, are nigh as rare
As Black Swans that in milkwhite Rivers are.
Grace therefore calls them all, and Sweetly wooes.   435
Some won come in, the rest as yet refuse,
And run away: Mercy persues apace,
Then Some Cast down their arms, Cry Quarter, Grace.   *— war imagery*
Some Chased out of breath drop down with feare
Perceiving the persuer drawing neer.   440
The rest persude, divide into two rancks,
And this way one, and that the other prancks.
   Then in comes Justice with her forces by her,
And doth persue as hot as Sparkling fire.
The right wing then begins to fly away.   445
But in the Streights Strong Baracadoes lay.
They're therefore forc'd to face about, and have
Their Spirits Queld, and therefore Quarter Crave.
These Captivde thus: justice persues the Game
With all her troops to take the other train.   450
Which being Chast in a Peninsula
And followd close, they finde no other way
To make escape, but t'rally round about:
Which if it faile them that they get not out,
They're forct into the Infernall Gulfe alive   455

Or hackt in pieces are or took Captive.
But Spying Mercy stand with Justice, they
Cast down their Weapons, and for Quarter pray.
Their lives are therefore Spar'de, yet they are ta'ne
As th'other band: and prisoners must remain.   460
And so they must now Justice's Captives bee
On Merices Quarrell: Mercy sets not free.
   Their former Captain is their Deadly foe.
   And now, poor Souls, they know not what to do.

---

449 persues *ins.*
455 They're forct *orig.* They forct are
463 Their *orig.* Ther

SATANS RAGE AT THEM IN THEIR CONVERSION.

   Grace by the Aide of Justice wins the day.   465
And Satans Captives Captives leads away.
Who finding of their former Captains Cheates,
To be Rebellion, him a Rebell Greate,
Against his Rightfull Sovereign, by whom
He shortly shall to Execution Come,   470
They Shew for Pardon do at Mercies Doore
Bewailing of that war they wag'd before.   [11]
   Then Satan in a red-hot-firy rage
Comes belling, roaring ready to ingage,
To rend, and tare in pieces Small all those,   475
Whom in the former Quarrell he did lose.
But's boyling Poyson'd madness, being by
A Shield Divine repelld, he thus lets fly.
You Rebells all, I Will you gripe, and fist,
I'le make my Jaws a Mill to grin'de Such Grists.   480
Look not for Mercy, Mercy well doth see
You'l be more false to her than Unto mee.
You're the first Van that fell; you're Traitors, Foes,
And unto Such Grace will no trust repose.
You Second Ranck are Cowards, if Christ Come   485

With you to fight his field, you'l from him run.
You third are feeble hearted; if Christs Crown
Must Stand or fall by you, you'l fling it down.
You last did last the longest: but being ta'ne
Are Prisoners made, and Jayle Birds must remain. 490
It had been better on the Turff to dy
Then in Such Deadly Slavery to ly.
Nay, at the best you all are Captive Foes.
Will Wisdom have no better aide than those?
Trust to a forced Faith? To hearts well known 495
To be (like yours) to all black Treason Prone?
For when I shall let fly at you, you'l fall:
And so fall foule upon your Generall.
Hee'l Hang you up alive then; by and by.
And I'le you wrack too for your treachery. 500
He will become your foe. You then shall bee
Flanckt of by him before, behinde by mee.
You'st stand between us two our Spears to dunce.
Can you Offend and Fence both wayes at once?
You'l then have sharper Service than the Whale, 505
Between the Sword fish, and the Threshers taile.
You'l then be mawld worse than the hand that's right
Between the heads of Wheelhorn'd Rams that fight.
    What will you do when you shall Squezed bee
    Between Such Monstrous Gyants Jaws as Wee? 510

---

479 all, I *orig.* all all, I I
484 Grace *orig.* Grace Grace
497 I *orig.* I'

THE SOULS ADDRESS TO CHRIST AGAINST THESE ASSAULTS.

Thou Gracious Lord, Our Honour'd Generall
  May't Suite thy Pleasure never to impute,
It our Presumption when presume we shall
  To line thy Noble Ears with our Greate suite?   [12]
  With ropes about our necks we come, and lie,   515
  Before thy pleasure's Will, and Clemency.

When we unto the height of Sin were grown,
  We Sought thy Throne to overthrow; but were
In this our Seeking Quickly overthrown:
  A Mass of Mercy in thy face shone cleare.   520
  We quarter had: though if we'de had our Share
  We had been quarter'd up as Rebells are.

Didst thou thy Grace on Treators arch expend?
  And force thy Favour on thy Stubborn Foe?
And hast no Favour for a failing Friend,
  That in thy Quarrell trippeth with his toe?   525
  If thus it be, thy Foes Speed better far,
  Than do thy Friends, that go to fight thy War.

But is it as the Adversary Said?
  Dost thou not hear his murdering Canons roare?   530
What Vollies fly? What Ambushments are laid?
  And still his Strategems grow more, and more.
  Lord, fright this frightfull Enemy away.
  A Trip makes not a Traitor: Spare we pray.

And if thou still Suspect us come, and search: 535
  Pluck out our hearts and Search them narrowly.
If Sin allow'd in any Corner learch,
  We beg a Pardon, and a Remedy.
  Lord Gybbit up Such Rebells Arch Who do
  Set ope the back doore to thy Cursed foe.   540

CHRISTS REPLY.

I am a Captain to your Will.
You found me Gracious, So shall Still.
Whilst that my Will is your Design.
    If that you stick unto my Cause
    Opposing whom oppose my Laws   545
I am your own, and you are mine.

The weary Soule I will refresh
And Ease him of his heaviness.
Who'le Slay a Friend? and Save a Foe?
    Who in my War do take delight,   550
    Fight not for prey, but Pray, and Fight,
Although they Slip, I'le mercy Show.   [13]

Then Credit not your Enemy
Whose Chiefest daintie is a lie.
I will you comfort Sweet extend.   555
    Behold I am a Sun and Shield
    And a Sharp Sword to win the field.
I'l surely Crown you in the End.

His murdering Canons which do roare
And Engins though as many more   560
Shoot onely aire: no Bullets fly.
    Unless you dare him with your Crest,
    And ope to him the naked breast,
Small Execution's done thereby.

To him that smiteth hip, and thigh,   565
My foes as his: Walks warily,   .
I'le give him Grace: he'st give me praise.
    Let him whose foot doth hit a stone
    Through weakness, not rebellion
Not faint, but think on former dayes.   570

---

544 If that you stick *orig.* If you stick stick Close
564 thereby *orig.* therefor
570 faint *orig.* faint faint

The Effect of this Reply with a fresh Assault from Satan.

Like as the Shining Sun, we do behold,
Is hot, and Light, when th'Weather waxeth Cold:
Like as brave Valour in a Captain Steels
His Armies Courage, when their Spirit reels.
As Aqua Vitæ when the Vitalls faile: 575
So doth this Speech the Drooping Soul availe.
How doth this Answer Mercies Captives Cheer?
Yet those whom Justice took Still Drooping were.
And in this nick of time the Foe through Spite
Doth like a glorious Angell seem of Light.   580
Yet though he painteth o're his Velvet smut,
He Cannot yet Conceal his Cloven foot.
Hence in their joy he Straweth poyson on,
Those Objects that their senses feed upon.
By Some odde straggling thought up poyson flies   585
Into the heart: and through the Eares, and Eyes.
Which Sick, lies gasping: Other thoughts then high
To hold its head; and venom'd are thereby.
Hence they are influenc't to Selfe Ends: these darts
Strike Secret Swelling Pride up in their hearts.   590
   The which he fosters till the bladder flies
   In pieces; then joy lies agast and dies.
Now Satan counts the Cast his own thus thrown:
Off goes the Angels Coate, on goes his own.   [14]
With Griping Paws, and Goggling Eyes, draws nigher,   595
Like some fierce Shagg'd Red Lion, belching fire:
Doth stoutly Charge them home that they did fall
And breake the Laws of their Choice Admirall.
And his attend: and so were his. For they
Must needs be his whom ever they obey.   600
Thus he in frightfull wise assaults them all,
Then one by one doth Singly on them fall.
   Doth winnow them with all his wiles, he can,
   As Wheate is winnow'd with the Sieve, and Fan.

First Satans Assault against those that first Came up to
Mercys terms.

Satan.
Soon ripe, Soon rot. Young Saint, Old Divell. Loe   605
Why to an Empty Whistle did you goe?
What Come Uncalld? and Run unsent for? Stay.
It's Childrens Bread: Hands off: out, Dogs, away.

Soul.
It's not an Empty Whistle: yet withall,
And if it be a Whistle, then a Call: 610
A Call to Childrens Bread, which take we may.
Thou onely art the Dog whipt hence away.

Satan.
If I then you: for by Apostasy
You are the Imps of Death as much as I.
And Death doth reign o're you through sin: you See,   615
As well as Sin doth reign to Death in mee.

Soul.
It is deni'd: Gods Mercy taking place,
Prepared Grace for us, and us for Grace.
And Graces Coach in Grace hath fetcht us in,
Unto her Feast. We shall not dy in Sin.   620

Satan.
If it be so, your Sins are Crucifide:
Which if they be; they Struggl'd when they di'de.
It is not so with you: you judge before
You felt them gird, you'de got them out of Doore.

Soul.
Mercy the Quartermaster Speedily,   625
Did stifle Sin, and still its hidious Cry.
Whose Knife at first Stuck in its heart to th'head:
That Sin, before it hard did Sprunt, fell dead.

Satan.
A mere Delusion! Nature shows that Life
Will strugle most upon the bloody Knife.   630
And so will Sin. Nay Christ doth onely Call,
And offer ease to Such as are in thrall.

Soul.
He offer'd unto mee, and I receiv'd
Of what hee wrought, I am not yet bereav'd.   ⟩ *a penalty*
Though Justice set Amercement on mee   635
Mercy hath took it off, and set me free.   [15]

Satan.
Is Mercy impudent? or Justice blinde?
I am to make distraint on thee Designd.
The North must wake before the South proves Kind.
The Law must breake before the Gospell binde.   640

Soul.
But Giliads Balm, like Balsom heald my wound
Makes not the Patient sore, yet leaves him Sound.
The Gospell did the Law prevent: my heart
Is therefore dresst from Sin: and did not smart.

Satan.
A likely thing! Oh Shame! presume on Grace!   645
Here's Sin in Grain: it hath a Double Face.
Come, Come with mee. I'le Shew your Outs, and Inns,
Your Inside, and your out: your Holy things.
    For these I will anatomize; then see,
    Believe your very Eyes, believe not mee.   650

---

615 you See *orig.* and See
634 hee *orig.* I

THE ACCUSATION OF THE INWARD MAN.

Satan speaks

You want Cleare Spectacles: your eyes are dim:
Turn inside out: and turn your Eyes within.
Your Sins like motes in th'Sun do swim: nay see
Your Mites are Mole hills, Mole hills Mountains bee.
Your Mountain Sins do magnitude transcend: 655
Whose number's numberless, and do want end.
The Understanding's dark, and therefore Will
Account of Ill for Good, and Good for ill.
As to a Purblinde man men oft appeare
Like Walking Trees within the Hemisphere.   660
So in the judgment Carnall things Excell:
Pleasures and Profits beare away the Bell.
The Will is hereupon perverted so,
It laquyes after ill, doth good foregoe.
The Reasonable Soule doth much delight   665
A Pick-pack t'ride o' th'Sensuall Appitite.
And hence the heart is hardened and toyes,
With Love, Delight, and Joy, yea Vanities.
   Make but a thorow Search, and you may spy
Your Soul atrudging hard, though Secretly   670
Upon the feet of your Affections mute,
And hankering after all forbidden fruite.
Ask but yourself in Secret laying neer
Thy head thereto: 't will Whisper in thine eare
That it is tickled much, though Secretly.   675
And greatly itches after Vilany.
'T will fleere thee in thy face, and though it say,
It must not tell, it Scorns to tell thee nay.
But slack the rains, and Come a Loophole lower:
You'l finde it was but Pen-coop't up before.   680
Nay, muster up your thoughts, and take the Pole
Of what walk in the Entry of your Soule   [16]
Which if you do, you certainly will finde
With Robbers, Cut-throats, Theives it's mostly linde.
And hundred Roagues you'l finde ly gaming there,   685
For one true man, that in that path appears.
Your True man too's oft foot sore, sildom is,

Sound Winde, and Limb: and still to adde to this,
He's but a Traviller within that Way:
Whereas the rest there pitch their Tents, and Stay.   690
Nay, nay, what thoughts Unclean? Lacivious?
Blasphemous? Murderous? and Malicious?
Tyranick? Wrathfull? Atheistick rise
Of Evills New, and Old, of e'ry Sise?
These bed, and board here, make the heart a sty   695
Of all Abominable Brothlery.
   Then is it pure? is this the fruite of Grace?
   If So, how do yee: You and I Embrace.

---

655 do *orig.* doth
656 do *orig.* doth
663 perverted *orig.* perveted
664 doth *orig.* and

THE OUTWARD MAN ACCUSED.

Turn o're thy Outward man, and judge aright;
Doth not a Pagans Life out Shine thy Light?   700
Thy fleering Looks, thy Wanton Eyes, each part
Are Painted Sign-Post of a Wanton heart.
If thou art weigh'd in Golden Scales; Dost do
To others as thou wouldst be done unto?
Weigh, weigh thy Words: thy Untruths, all which came   705
Out of thy mouth, and thou Confest the same.
Why did thy Tongue detract from any one,
Whisper Such tales thou wouldst not have be known?
When thou was got in Such a merry veane
How far didst thou exceed the golden mean?   710
When that thou wast at such a Boon, or Feast
Why didst thou rather ly, than lose thy jeast?
How wast thou tickled when thy droughty Eares
Allay'de their Thirst with filthy Squibs, and jears?
Why didst thou glaver men of Place? And why,   715
Scowle, Glout, and Frown, on honest Poverty?

Why did'st thou Spend thy State in foolish prancks?
And Peacock up thyselfe above thy rancks?
Why thoughtst thyselfe out of the World as shut,
When not with others in the Cony Cut?   720
Hold up thy head, is't thus or no? if yea,
How then is all thy folly purg'd away?
    If no, thy tongue belies itselfe, for loe
    Thou saidst thy heart was dresst from Sin also.

---

715 thou *orig.* thy

THE SOUL ACCUSED IN ITS SERVING GOD.

When thou dost go to Serve thy God, behold   725
What greate Distractions do thy Soule infold?
How thy Religious Worship's much abusde?
And with Confusion greate thy Soul's amuzde?   [17]
What thoughts to God on Errand dost thou send
That have not Sin therein, or in the End?   730
In Holy-Waters I delight to fish
For then I mudd them, or attain a Dish,
Of Holy things. I oft have Chiefest part,
And Cutting: nay do Carve the fat, and heart.
For in Gods worship still thy heart doth cling   735
Unto and follows toyish Earthly things.
And what thou offer'st God his Holy Eye
Sees, is an Offering of Hypocrisy.
And if thou saw'st no hell, nor heaven; I see,
My Soule for thine, thy Soule and mine agree.   740
What then's thy Love to God, and Piety?
Is it not Selfish? And Comes in by th'by?
For Selfe is all thine aim; not God thine end:
And what Delight hath he in Such a friend?
Lip Love is little else, but Such a ly,   745
As makes the matter but Hypocrisy.
    What's thy Repentance? Can'st thou come and Show
    By those Salt Rivers which do Ebb, and Flow

By th'motion of that Ocean Vast within,
Of pickled Sorrow rising for thy Sin?   750
For Sin prooves very Costly unto all.
It Cost Saint Peter bitter tears, and Paul.
Thy joy is groundless, Faith is false, thy Hope
Presumption, and Desire is almost broke.
Zeale Wild fire is, thy Pray'res are Sapless most,   755
Or like the Whistling of Some Dead mans Ghost:
Thy Holy Conference is onely like
An Empty Voice that tooteth through a pipe.
Thy Soule doth peep out at thine Eares, and Eyes
To bless those bawbles that are earthly toyes.   760
But when Gods Words in at those Windows peepe
To kiss thy Soul, thy Soul lies dead asleep.
Examine but thy Conscience. Her reply,
Will Suite hereto: For Conscience dare not ly.
When did thine Eyes run down for Sin as Sin,   765
That thus thy heart runs up with joy to Sing?
    Thy Sins do Sculk under a flowrisht paint.
    Hence thou a Sinner art, or I a Saint.

    Soul.
Well Satan, well: with thee I'le parle no more.
But do adjure thee hence: begone therefore.   770
If I as yet was thine, I thus do say
I from thy flag would quickly flag away.
    Begone therefore; to him I'le Send a groane
    Against thee drawn, who makes my heart his Throne.   [18]

---

737 his *orig.* thy
748 Flow *orig.* Flow?

The Souls Groan to Christ for Succour.

Good Lord, behold this Dreadfull Enemy 775
    Who makes me tremble with his fierce assaults,
I dare not trust, yet feare to give the ly,
    For in my Soul, my Soul finds many faults.
    And though I justify myselfe to's face:
    I do Condemn myselfe before thy Grace. 780

He Strives to mount my Sins, and them advance
    Above thy Merits, Pardons or Good Will
Thy Grace to lessen, and thy Wrath t'inhance
    As if thou couldst not pay the Sinners bill.
    He Chiefly injures thy rich Grace, I finde 785
    Though I confess my heart to Sin inclin'de.

Those Graces which thy Grace enwrought in mee;
    He makes, as nothing but a pack of Sins.
He maketh Grace no grace, but Crueltie,
    Is Graces Honey Comb, a Comb of Stings? 790
    This makes me ready leave thy Grace and run.
    Which if I do, I finde I am undone.

I know he is thy Cur, therefore I bee
    Perplexed lest I from thy Pasture Stray
He bayghs, and barks so veh'mently at mee. 795
    Come rate this Cur, Lord, breake his teeth I pray.
    Remember me I humbly pray thee first,
    Then halter up this Cur that is so Curst.

Christs Reply.

Peace, Peace, my Hony, do not Cry,
My Little Darling, wipe thine eye, 800
    Oh Cheer, Cheer up, come See.
Is any thing too deare, my Dove,

Is any thing too good, my Love
   To get or give for thee?

If in the severall thou art   805
This Yelper fierce will at thee bark:
   That thou art mine this shows.
As Spot barks back the Sheep again
Before they to the Pound are ta'ne,
   So he and hence 'way goes.   810

But yet this Cur that bayghs so sore
Is broken tootht, and muzzled sure,
   Fear not, my Pritty Heart.
His barking is to make thee Cling
Close underneath thy Saviours Wing.   815
   Why did my Sweeten start?   [19]

And if he run an inch too fur,
I'le Check his Chain, and rate the Cur.
   My Chick, keep clost to mee.
The Poles shall sooner kiss, and greet   820
And Paralells shall Sooner meet
   Than thou shalt harmed bee.

He Seeks to aggrivate thy Sin
And Screw them to the highest pin,
   To make thy faith to quaile.   825
Yet mountain Sins like mites should show
And then these mites for naught should goe
   Could he but once prevaile.

I Smote thy Sins upon the Head,
They Dead'ned are, though not quite dead: 830
   And shall not rise again.
I'l put away the Guilt thereof,
And purge its Filthiness cleare off:
   My Blood doth out the Stain.

And though thy judgment was remiss   835
Thy Headstrong Will too Wilfull is,
   I will Renew the Same.
And though thou do too frequently
Offend as heretofore hereby
   I'le not Severely blaim.   840

And though thy senses do inveagle
Thy Noble soul to tend the Beagle,
   That t'hunt her games forth go.
I'le Lure her back to me, and Change
Those fond Affections that do range   845
   As yelping beagles doe.

Although thy Sins increase their race,
And though when thou hast Sought for Grace,
   Thou fallst more than before
If thou by true Repentance Rise,   850
And Faith makes me thy Sacrifice,
   I'l pardon all, though more.

Though Satan Strive to block thy way
By all his Stratagems he may;
   Come, come though through the fire.   855
For Hell that Gulph of fire for Sins,
Is not So hot as t'burn thy Shins.
   Then Credit not the Lyar.

Those Cursed vermin Sins that Crawle
All ore thy Soul both Greate, and small   860
   Are onely Satans own: [20]
Which he in his Malignity
Unto thy Souls true Sanctity
   In at the doors hath thrown.

And though they be Rebellion high,   865
Ath'ism or Apostacy:
   Though blasphemy it bee:
Unto what Quality, or Sise

Excepting one, so e're it rise.
    Repent, I'le pardon thee.   870

Although thy Soule was once a Stall
Rich hung with Satans nick nacks all;
    If thou Repent thy Sin,
A Tabernacle in't I'le place
Fild with God's Spirit, and his Grace.   875
    Oh Comfortable thing!

I dare the World therefore to Show
A God like me, to anger Slow:
    Whose wrath is full of Grace.
Doth hate all Sins both Greate, and Small: 880
Yet when Repented, pardons all.
    Frowns with a Smiling Face.

As for thy outward Postures each,
Thy Gestures, Actions, and thy Speech,
    I Eye and Eying Spare.   885
If thou repent. My Grace is more
Ten thousand times still tribled ore
    Than thou canst want, or ware.

As for the Wicked Charge he makes,
That he of Every Dish first takes   890
    Of all thy holy things.
It's false, deny the Same, and Say,
That which he had he stool away
    Out of thy Offerings.

Though to thy Griefe, poor Heart, thou finde   895
In Pray're too oft a wandring minde,
    In Sermons Spirits dull.
Though Faith in firy furnace flags,
And Zeale in Chilly Seasons lags.
    Temptations powerfull.   900

These faults are his, and none of thine
So fur as thou dost them decline.
   Come then receive my Grace.
And when he buffits thee therefore
If thou my aid, and Grace implore   905
   I'le shew a pleasant face.   [21]

But Still look for Temptations Deep,
Whilst that thy Noble Sparke doth keep
   Within a Mudwald Cote.
These White Frosts and the Showers that fall   910
Are but to whiten thee withall.
   Not rot the Web they smote.

If in the fire where Gold is tride
Thy Soule is put, and purifide
   Wilt thou lament thy loss?   915
If Silver-like this fire refine
Thy Soul and make it brighter Shine:
   Wilt thou bewaile the Dross?

Oh! fight my Field: no Colours fear:
I'l be thy Front, I'l be thy reare.   920
   Fail not: my Battells fight.
Defy the Tempter, and his Mock:
Anchor thy heart on mee thy Rock.
   I do in thee Delight.

---

803 Is any *orig.* Can I thinke any
811 yet *orig.* th
843 t'hunt *orig.* hunts
911 thee *orig.* you
916 fire *orig.* refine

AN EXTASY OF JOY LET IN BY THIS REPLY RETURND IN
ADMIRATION.

My Sweet Deare Lord, for thee I'le Live, Dy, Fight.   925
    Gracious indeed! My Front! my Rear!?
    Almighty magnify a Mite!
       O! What a wonder's here?

Had I ten thousand times ten thousand hearts:
    And Every Heart ten thousand Tongues;   930
    To praise, I should but Stut odd parts
       Of what to thee belongs.

If all the World did in Alimbeck ly,
    Bleeding its Spirits out in Sweat;
    It could not halfe enlife a Fly,   935
       To Hum thy Praises greate.

If all can't halfe enlife a Fly to hum,
    (Which Scarce an Animall we call)
    Thy Praises then which from me come,
       Come next to none at all.   940

For I have made myselfe ten thousand times
    More naught then nought itselfe, by Sin.
    Yet thou extendst thy Gracious Shines
       For me to bath therein.

Oh! Stand amaizd yee Angells Bright, come run   945
    Yee Glorious Heavens and Saints, to Sing:
    Place yee your praises in the Sun,
       Ore all the world to ring.   [22]

Nay stand agast, ye sparkling Spirits bright!
    Shall little Clods of Dust you peere?   950
    Shall they toote Praises on your pipe?
       Oh! that we had it here.
What can a Crumb of Dust sally such praise
    Which do from Earth all heaven o're ring?

Who swaddle up the Suns bright rayes   955
   Can in a Flesh Flie's Wing?

Can any Ant Stand on the Earth and spit
   An other out to peer with this?
   Or Drink the Ocean up, and yet
     Its belly empty is?   960
Thou may'st this World as easily up hide
   Under the Blackness of thy naile:
   As scape Sins Gulph, without a Guide:
     Or Hell without a bale.

If all the Earthy Mass were rambd in Sacks   965
   And Saddled on an Emmet Small,
   Its Load were light unto those packs
     Which Sins do bring on all.
But Sure this burden'd Emmet moves no wing.
   Nay, nay, Compar'd with thee it flies.   970
   Yet man is easd his weight of Sin.
     From hell to Heav'n doth rise.

When that the World was new, its Chiefe Delight,
   One Paradise alone Contain'de:
   The Bridle of Mans Appetite   975
     The Appletree refrain'de.
The which he robbing, eat the fruit as good,
   Whose Coare hath Chokd him and his race.
   And juyce hath poyson'd all their blood,
     He's in a Dismall Case.   980

None can this Coare remove, Poyson expell:
   He, if his Blood ben't Clarifi'de
   Within Christs veans, must fry in Hell,
     Till God be Satisfi'de.
Christ to his Father saith, Incarnate make   985
   Mee, Mee thy Son; and I will doe't:
   I'le purify his Blood, and take
     The Coare out of his Throate.

All this he did, and did for us, vile Clay:
　　Oh! let our Praise his Grace assai'le.　　　　　　990
　　To free us from Sins Gulph each way,
　　　　He's both our Bridge, and Raile.
Although we fall and Fall, and Fall and Fall:
　　And Satan fall on us as fast.
　　He purgeth us and doth us call　　　　　　　　995
　　　　Our trust on him to Cast.　　　　　　　　[23]

My Lumpish Soule, why art thou hamper'd thus,
　　Within a Crumb of Dust?　Arise,
　　Trumpet out Praises.　Christ for us
　　　　Hath slain our Enemies.　　　　　　　　1000
Screw up, Deare Lord, upon the highest pin:
　　My Soul thy ample Praise to Sound.
　　O tune it right, that every String
　　　　May make thy praise rebound.

But oh! how Slack, Slow, dull? with what delay,　　1005
　　Do I this Musick to, repare;
　　While tabernacled in Clay
　　　　My Organs Cottag'de are?
Yet Lord accept this Pittance of thy praise
　　Which as a Traveller I bring,　　　　　　　　1010
　　While travelling along thy wayes
　　　　In broken notes I Sing.

And at my journies end in endless joyes
　　I'l make amends where Angells meet
　　And Sing their flaming Melodies　　　　　　　1015
　　　　In Ravishing tunes most Sweet.

---

966 Emmet *orig.* Emmets bac
1006 repare, *orig.* repare?

THE SECOND RANKE ACCUSED.

You that are branded for Rebellion
What whimsy Crotchets do you feed upon?
Under my Flag you fighting did Defie
And Vend much Venom Spit at God most high: 1020
You dar'de him as a Coward, out, and went
Flinging your Poyson'd darts against his tent.
When Grace did Sound her parle, you Stopt the Eare:
You backward drew as she to you drew neere.
But what's this Grace, which you, forsooth, so prize,   1025
For which you stand your own Sworn Enemies?
Who ever saw, Smelt, tasted, felt the Same?
It's but an airy notion, or a name.
Fine food for fools, or Shallow brains, who know
No better fair and therefore let all go.   1030
Did mercy better Cain, or make him thrive
When he pronounc'd himselfe a Figitive?
What Benefit had Esau who did weep
And in Repenting teares did scald his Cheek?
Or what King Ahab, that he softly went?   1035
Or what poore Judas that he did repent?
Grace doom'd them down to hellish flames, although
To Court the Same they Steep't their Souls in woe.
To whom she yields a Smile, She doth expect
That With a Smile, her Smile they Soon accept   1040
But you have hitherto like Stirdy Clowns
Affronted Grace, and paid her Smiles with Frowns.   [24]
Nay Mercy lookes before she Gives, to See
That those to whom she gives true Christians bee.
That all the Graces of the Spirit do   1045
Like Clouds of Sweet perfume from Such forth flow.
And that their Souls be to the Spirits feet
An Aromatick Spicery most Sweet.
Is't so with you? You from her Scepter fly,
As judging it a grace graceless to dy.   1050
Your Faith's a Phancy: Fear a Slavery.
Your Hope is Vain, Patience Stupidity.
Your Love is Carnall, Selfish, Set on toyes:

Your Pray'res are Prattle, or Tautologies.
Your Hearts are full of Sins both Small, and Greate.   1055
They are as full as is an Egge of meate.
Your Holy Conference and talkings do
But for a Broken Piece of Non-Sense go.
If So, you are accurst; God doth impart,
His Blessings onely on the broken heart.   1060
But Search your peace turnd o're, and view each Side.
Graces Magnetick touch will it abide?
Doth Mercys Sun through Peaces lattice clear
Shine in thy Soule? Then what's that Uproare there?
Look well about you, try before you trust.   1065
Though Grace is Gracious; Justice Still is just.
  If so it be with you, say what you can
  You are not Saints, or I no Sinner am.

1010 Traveller *orig.* Traviller
1022 Flinging *orig.* Fling
1040 That With *orig.* With
1056 They are *orig.* It is as

THE THIRD RANK ACCUSED.

  What thou art too for Christ, it seems? Yet fain
Thou wouldst the World with all her Pomps mentain.   1070
But Such as share of Christ, fall Short of these.
And have but faint affections to such fees.
Go Coach thy Eyes about the world, and eye
Those Rich inchanting Braveries there Cry
Give us your heart? Wherefore thy heart doth ake   1075
That it such Amorous Objects must forsake.
The Love whereto so Stuffs thy heart: no place
Is left therein for any Saving Grace.
It's folly then to think that Grace was Shown,
When in persute thy heart was overthrown.   1080
It was not Grace in Grace that made thee fall:
For unto Grace thou hast no heart at all.
Thou thoughtst these Objects of thy Love would faile.

The thoughts of which do make thy Spirits faile.
And this is easely prov'd: for thou didst goe 1085
Into the field with God, as with a foe. [25]
And bravely didst out brave the Notion Grace.
And Chose to flee rather than it imbrace.
And well thou mightst, A Bird in hand doth far
Transcend the Quires that in the Hedges are. 1090
And so it's still: turn o're thy heart, thou'lt finde
As formerly so still thou art inclinde.
In Sin thou hadst delight, didst grace defy:
And dost so still: For still thou dost reply.
Who ever went to Hell, and Came again 1095
To shew to any one, what is that pain?
Did ever any slip to Heaven to see
Whether there's there a God? and who is hee?
What is that fancide God rowld o're the tongue?
Oh! Brainsick Notion, or an Oldwifes Song! 1100
That he should wholy be in e'ry place
At once all here, and there, yet in no Space.
That all should be in any part though Small:
That any part of him should be him all.
And that he hath no parts though Head, and Heart. 1105
Hands, Ears, and Eyes he hath, he hath no part.
That he is all in all, yea all in thee,
That he is also all that time in mee.
That he should be all in each Atom small:
And yet the whole cannot contain him all. 1110
That he doth all things in a moment See,
At once, of things to Come, Past, and now bee.
That He no Elder, he no Younger is,
Than when the World began: (What wonder's this?)
That time that flies from all with him remains, 1115
These are Chamaera's Coin'd in Wanton brains.
Among which Fopperies mans Soul may go,
Concerning which thou mak'st so much ado.
Nay; what? or where is Hell Can any Show?
This Bug bare in the Darke 's a mere Scar-Crow. 1120
But say it's true: there is an Hell: a God.
A Soul Immortall in a mortall Clod:

Did God such principles infuse as egge
The Soul from him into Eternall plague?
Thou dost Confess that God doth not Demand   1125
Such things of us as had are of no hand.
Which Sure he doth, if he deny to Save
Whom live by Natures Law: which Law he Gave.
Yet grant this tenet which thy heart denies,
Christ saveth none but whom he Sanctifies.   1130
Thou art not Sanctifide in any part;
For sins keepe Centinall within thy heart
And there they train, therein they Rentdevouz.
Her troops therein do quarter: and do house.   [26]
   And hence as from a fountain Head there Streams   1135
Through ev'ry part Pollution in the Veans.
Hence sprouts Presumption making much too bold
To catch such Shaddows which no hand can hold.
Hence Harebrain'd Rashness rushes in the Brain:
Hence Madbrain'd Anger which no man can tame.   1140
Hence Crackbrain'd folly, or a shatter'd Wit
That none Can Plaster: none can med'cine it.
Hence a Stiff, Stubborn, and Rebellious Will
That sooner breakes than buckles to fulfill
Gods Laws: and so for other Sins thou'lt find   1145
A Forward Will joyn'd with a froward minde.
Thy Heart doth lip such Languague, though thy Lip
Is loath to let such Languague open Slip.
I see thy Secret thoughts: and such they bee,
That Wish there was no God, or I was Hee.   1150
Or that there was no Holiness, unless
Those Sins thou'rt given to, were Holiness.
Or that there was no Hell, except for those
Who stand for Holiness, and Sin oppose.
Or that there was no heaven t'enter in,   1155
Except for those Who pass their Lives in Sin.
Though thou the Languague of thy heart out face
Dost, yet thou huggest Sin, dost hiss out Grace.
Set Heaven, and Hell aside it's clearly shown,
Thou lov'st mee more than God thou seem'st to own.   1160
Hence was it not for these, it plainly 'pears

Thy God for Servants might go Shake his ears.
For thou to keep within my booke dost Still
Ungod thy God not walking by his Will.
   This Languague of thy heart doth this impart: 1165
   I am a Saint, if thou no Sinner art.

1073 Eyes *orig.* World
1074 Cry *orig.* ly
1089 A *orig.* for a
1105 Heart *orig.* Hands
1109 each *orig.* every
1118 mak'st *orig.* makest
1125 Demand *orig.* Cõmand
1129 Yet *orig.* H
1147 Languague *orig.* Language; thy *orig.* lip
1149 Secret *orig.* Secret Secret
1155 t'enter *orig.* to enter
1157 the *orig.* d
1158 dost *orig.* and
1165 impart *orig.* declare

A THRENODIALL DIALOGUE BETWEEN THE SECOND AND THIRD
RANKS.

   Second.
Oh you! How do you? Alas! how do things go
With you, and with your Souls? For once we know
You did as we, Welt, Wallow, Soake in Sin;
For which Gods ire infires our hearts within.   1170

   Third.
Ne're Worse, though when Secure in Sin much worse.
Though curst by Sin, we did not feele the Curse.
Now Seing we no help can See, we rue,
Would God it was with us as't is with you.

   Second.
With us! alas! a Flent would melt to See   1175

A Deadly foe, in Such a Case as wee.
God Seems our Foe, repent we Can't: but finde
To ill Goodwill, to Good a wayward minde.   [27]

   Third.
This is in you your Grace, we easely Spie
The Love of God within your looks to ly.   1180
But oh! our Souls Set in Sins Cramp stand bent
To Badness, and no Grace we have t'Repent.

   Second.
This is your Charity. But if you Saw
Those ugly Crawling Sins that do us knaw
You'd Change your minde. You mourn, and pray we See: 1185
We would not for a World, you were as wee.

   Third.
Repent! and Pray! Aye, so the Traytor Cast,
Cries, *Good my Lord!* yea, when his Doom is past.
You erre through your Abundant Charity.
We dare not wish, as we, our Enemy.   1190

   Second.
Your Low esteemings of yourselves enlarge
Ours of you much. But oh that Dismall Charge!
We don't Repent, Believe, we nothing do:
No Grace we have though something Gracelike show.

   Third.
Is't so with you who do so much out do   1195
Poor nothings us? Oh! whither Shall we go?
Our Grace a Mockgrace is: Of Ulcerous Boiles.
We are as full, as Satan is of Wiles.

   Second.
There's not a Sin that is not in our Heart.
And if Occasion were, it would out Start.   1200
There's not a Precept that we have not broke.
Hence not a Promise unto us is Spoke.

Third.
It's worse with us: The Preacher Speaks no word.
The Word of God no sentence doth afford;
But fall like burning Coals of Hell new blown   1205
Upon our Souls: and on our Heads are thrown.

Second.
It's worse with us. Behold Gods threatonings all;
Nay Law, and Gospell, on our Heads do fall.
Both Hell, and Heaven, God and Divell do
With Wracking Terrours Consummate our Woe.   1210

Third.
We'le ne're believe that you are worse than wee,
For Worse than us wee judge no Soul can bee.
We know not where to run, nor what to doe.
Would God it was no worse with us than you.

Second.
Than us, alas! what would you fain aspire   1215
Out of the Frying Pan into the Fire?
Change States with you with all our hearts we would,
Nay, and give boot therewith, if that we could.

Third.
Say what you can, we can't but thinke this true
That Grace's Ambush hath Surprized you.   1220
But Judgment layes an Ambush Strong to take
* * * * * *   [28]

Second.
What Charity have you for us? When thus
You judge amiss both of yourselves, and us?
What pitty is't? Yet God will you repay.   1225
Although we perish, and be cast away.

Third.
The Lord forbid the last, and grant we may
Deceived be wherein we be, you say.

We Cannot wish a Toade as wee, but Crave,
Your prayers for us, that we may pardon have.   1230

   Second.
Our Pray'res, are pray'reless: Oh! to what we bee
An ugly Toad's an Angell bright we See.
Oh pray, pray you, oh pray, for us that So
The Lord of Mercy Mercy on's may Show.

   Third.
O would we could! but oh Hells Gripes do grinde   1235
Yea writh our Souls with Cramps of e'ry kinde.
If Grace begrace us not we go to Hell.
The Good Lord help us both, thus fare you Well.

Title Second *orig.* Fir
1168 we *orig.* I
1182 no *orig.* we've not
1204 sentence *orig.* Comfort
1206 on *orig.* at
1209 God *orig.* both God
1219 but *orig.* believe
1220 Ambush *orig.* tender Ambush
1231 are *orig.* Case

THEIR CALL IN THIS SAD STATE FOR MERCY.

We humbly beg, oh Lord, to know our Crime.
That we thus tortur'de are before our time.   1240
Before our Time? Lord give's this Word again.
For we have long ago deserv'de Hells flame.
If Mercy wrought not Miracles none could
Us monuments of mercy now behold.
But oh! while mercy waits we Slaves to Sin,   1245
Heap up Sins Epha far above the brim.
What Shall we do when to account we're Calld?
How will abused Mercy burn, and Scald?
We know not How, nor Where to stay or goe.

We know not whom, nor What to trust or doe. 1250
Should we run hence from Mercy, Justice will
Run hotly after us our blood to Spill.
But should we run to Mercy, Justice may
Hold Mercies hands while Vengeance doth us slay.
And if we trust to Grace, necessity 1255
Binds us by force at Grace's Grace to ly.
But if we run from Grace, we headlong cast
Ourselves upon the Spiles of Ruine Vast.
And if we claim her ours, she'l Surely smite
Us, for presuming on an others right. 1260
  Who'le with a Leaking, old Crackt Hulk assay,
To brave the raging Waves of Adria?
Or who can Cross the Main Pacifick o're?
Without a Vessell wade from Shore to Shore?
What wade the mighty main from brim to brim, 1265
As if it would not reach above the Chin? [29]
But, oh! poor wee, must wade from brinck to brinck.
With Such a weight as would bright Angells Sink.
Or venture angry Adria, or drown
When Vengeance's Sea doth break her flood gates down. 1270
If Stay, or Go to Sea we drown. Then See
In what a wofull Pickle, Lord, we bee.
Rather than tarry, or the rough Sea trust,
On the Pacificke Ocean forth we thrust.
Necessity lies on's: we dare not Stay: 1275
If drown we must, we'l drown in Mercy's Sea.
Impute it not presumption if we high
To Cast ourselves on Mercies Clemency.
Is't not as great Presumption, Lord, to Stand
And gaze on ruine, but refuse the hand 1280
Which offers help? Or on Such Courses fall
Which fall to ruin, ruinating all?
Lord, pitty, pitty us, Lord pitty send:
A thousand pitties 'tis we Should offend.
But oh! we did, and are thereto propence: 1285
And what we count off, oft thou Countst offence.
We've none to trust: but on thy Grace we ly,
If dy we must, in mercy's arms wee'l dy.

Then pardon, Lord, and put away our guilt.
So we be thine, deale with us as thou wilt.   1290

1268 weight *orig.* with

The Soule Bemoning Sorrow rowling upon a resolution to seek Advice of Gods people.

Alas! my Soule, product of Breath Divine,
For to illuminate a Lump of Slime.
Sad Providence! Must thou below thus tent,
In such a Cote as strangles with ill sent?
Or in such Sensuall Organs make thy Stay   1295
Which from thy noble end do make thee Stray?
My nobler part, why dost thou laquy to
The Carnall Whynings of my Senses so?
What? thou become a Page, a Peasant, nay,
A Slave unto a Durty Clod of Clay!   1300
Why should the Kirnell bring Such Cankers forth
To please the Shell, as will devour them both?
Why didst thou thus thy Milkwhite Robes defile
With Crimson Spots of Scarlet Sins most vile?
  My Muddy Tent, Why hast thou done so ill   1305
To Court, and kiss my Soule, yet kissing kill?
Why didst thou Whyning, egg her thus away
Thy Sensuall Appetite to Satisfy?
Art thou So safe, and firm a Cabinet
As though thou soaking lie in nasty wet,   1310
And in all filthy Puddles: yet the thin
Can ne're drench through to Stain the Pearle within?   [30]
It's no Such thing: Thou'rt but a Cawle wrought Case.
And when thou fallst, thou foulst its Shining face.
Or but her mudwalld Lodge, which wet by Sin   1315
Diffuseth all in her that it rowles in.
One Stain Stains both, when both in one Combine.
A Musty Cask doth marre rich Malmsy Wine.
  Woe's mee! my mouldring Heart! What must I do?

When is my moulting time to shed my woe? 1320
Oh! Woefull fall! what fall from Heavenly bliss
To th'bottom of the bottomless Abyss?
Above an Angry God! Below, black-blew
Brimstony flames of hell where Sinners rue!
Behinde, a Traile of Sins! Before appeare 1325
An Host of Mercies that abused were!
Without a Raging Divell! And within
A Wracking Conscience Galling home for Sin!
What Canst not finde one Remedy, my Soule,
On Mercies File for mee? Oh! Search the Rowle. 1330
What freeze to death under Such melting means,
Of Grace's Golden, Life Enliv'ning Beams?
What? not one Hope? Alas! I hope there's Some.
Although I know not in what way it come.
Although there is no hope within my minde 1335
I'le force Hope's Faculty, till Hope I finde.
Some glimmerings of Hope, I hope to Spy
In Mercies Golden Stacks, or Remedy.
I therefore am Resolv'd a Search to make,
And of the Pious Wise some Counsill take. 1340
I'le then in Pensiveness myselfe apply
To them in hope, but yet halfe hopelessly.
Perhaps these thoughts are blessed motions, though
From whence they are, as yet I do not know.
 And if from Christ. Oh! then thrice Happy mee. 1345
 If not, I'st not be worser than I bee.

THE PREFACE.

 Soul.
Long lookt for Sir! Happy, right Happy Saint.
I long to lay before you my Complaint:
And gain your Counsill: but you're Strange. And I
Through backwardness lost opportunity. 1350

Saint.
How is't good Sir: methinks I finde there dart
Some pleasant Hopes of you within my heart.
What is your Rantery declinde, foregone?
Your looks are like the Earth you Tread upon.

Soul.
It's true: I do, and well may look so, too   1355
For worse than mee the world did never show.
My Sins are dide in grain: all Grace I lack.
This doth my Soul on tenterhooks enwrack.   [31]
Wherefore I Counsill Crave touching my Sin
My Want of Grace: Temptations too within.   1360

1355 look *orig.* do so too

THE SOULS DOUBTS TOUCHING ITS SINS ANSWERD.

Saint.
Is this thy Case, Poor Soul, Come then begin:
Make known thy griefe: anatomize thy Sin.
Although thy Sins as Mountains vast do show,
Yet Grace's fountain doth these mountains flow.

Soul.
True, true indeed, where Mountains Sinke but where   1365
They Swim, their Heads above these mountains peare.
Mine Swim in Merices boundless Ocean do:
Therefore their Heads above these waters goe.

Saint.
I thought as you, but loe the Lyon hee
Is not so fierce as he is feign'd to bee.   1370
But grant they Swim, they'l then swim quite away
On Mercies main, if you Repenting Stay.

Soul.
I Swim in Mercy: but my Sins are Sayles
That waft my barke to Hell by Graces Gales.
Is't possible for Such as Grace outbrave   1375
(Which is my Case) true Saving Grace to have?

Saint.
That's not thy Sin: thou didst not thus transgress,
Thy Grace-outbraveing Sin is bashfulness.
Thou art too backward. Satan strives to hold
Thee fast hereby, and saith, thou art too bold.   1380

Soul.
Alas! How are you out in mee, behold;
My best is poison in a Box of Gold.
If with mine Eyes you saw my hearts black Stain,
You'de judge my Sins were double dide in grain.

Saint.
Deluded Soul, Satan beguiles thee so   1385
Thou judgst the bend the back side of the bow,
Dost press thyselfe too hard: Straite wands appeare
Crookt in, and out, in running rivlets Clear.

Soul.
You raise the fabrick of your pious hope
Upon Such water Bells, as rots denote.   1390
For my Profession doth but cloake my Sin.
A guilded Maukin's Stufft with Chaff within.

Saint.
I love not thus to row in Such a Stream:
And if I did, I should so touch my Theme.
But muster up your Sins though more or few: 1395
Grace hath an Edge to Cut their bonds atwo.

Soul.
This is my Sin, My Sin I love, but hate

God and his Grace. And who's in such a state?
My Love, and Hatred do according rise
Unto Sins height, and unto Grace's Sise.   [32]1400

   Saint.
I thought as you when first to make me See
God powred out his Spirit Sweet on mee.
But oh Strange Fetch! What Love, yet hate to have?
And hate in heart what heartily you Crave?

   Soul.
Sometimes meethinks I wish, Oh! that there were   1405
No Heaven nor Hell. For then I need not feare.
I'm pestred with black thoughts of Blasphemy,
And after thoughts do with these thoughts Comply.

   Saint.
See Satans Wiles: while thou in Sin didst dwell
Thou Calledst not in Question Heaven, or Hell.   1410
But now thou'rt out with Sin he makes thee Call
In Question both, that thou in Hell mightst fall.

   Soul.
But, oh! methinks, I finde I Sometimes wish
There was no God, or that there was not this.
Or that his wayes were other than they bee.   1415
Oh! Horrid, horrid, Hellish thoughts in mee!

   Saint.
'T was thus, or worse with me. I often thought,
Oh! that there was no God: or God was Naught.
Or that his Wayes were other Wayes. Yet hee
In mighty mercy hath bemerci'de mee.   1420

   Soul.
My Heart is full of thoughts, and ev'ry thought
Full of Sad, Hellish, Drugstery enwrought.
Methinks it Strange to Faith that God should bee
Thus All in All, yet all in Each part. See.

Saint.
'T was so with me. Then let your Faith abound   1425
For Faith will Stand where Reason hath no ground.
This proves that God is Onely God: for hee
Surpasseth the Superlative degree.

Soul.
Methinks I am a Frigot fully fraught
And Stoughed full with each Ath'istick thought.   1430
Methinkes I hate to think on God: anone
Methinks there is no God to thinke upon.

Saint.
I thought as much at first: my thoughts, so vain,
Were thus that God was but Stampt i'th'brain.
But God disperst these wicked thoughts. Behold   1435
The various methods of the Serpent old!

Soul.
All arguments against mee argue Still:
I see not one bespeaks me ought, but ill.
What s'e're I use I do abuse: Oh! Shew,
Whether the Case was ever thus with you.   1440

Saint.
It was: But see how Satan acts, for his
He troubles not with Such a thought as this.
But Wicked thoughts he in the Saints doth fling,
And saith they're theirs, accusing them of Sin.

Soul.
Methinks my heart is harder than a flint;   1445
My Will is Wilfull, frowardness is [in]'t   [33]
And mine Affections do my Soule betray,
Sedaning of it from the blessed way.

Saint.
Loe, Satan hath thy thoughts inchanted quite.
And Carries them a pick pack from the right.   1450

Thou art too Credulous: For Satan lies.
It is not as you deeem: deem otherwise.

Soul.
But I allow of Sin: I like it well.
And Chiefly grieve, because it goes to hell.
And were it ever so with you, I see   1455
Grace hath prevented you which doth not mee.

Saint.
I thought as you: but now I clearly Spy,
These Satans brats will like their Curst Sire ly.
He Squibd these thoughts in you, you know not how.
And tempts you then to deem you them allow.   1460

Soul.
And so I do: would I could Sins disown:
But if I do, they'l own me for their own.
I have no Grace to do't: this prooves me in
A Lamentable State, a State of Sin.

Saint.
What ambling work within a Ring is here?   1465
What Circular Disputes of Satans Geer?
To proove thee Graceless he thy Sins persues:
To proove thee Sinfull, doth thy Grace accuse.
  Why dost thou then believe the Tempter so?
  He Seeks by helping thee thy Overthrow.   1470

1384 You'de judge *orig.* You'de my
1386 judgst *orig.* judge
1446 Wilfull, *orig.* Wilfulfull
1455 And *orig.* And if
1458 ly *orig.* dy
1465 within *orig.* is here within

DOUBTS FROM THE WANT OF GRACE ANSWERD.

Soul.
Such as are Gracious grow in Grace therefore
Such as have Grace, are Gracious evermore.
Who Sin Commit are Sinfull: and thereby
They grow Ungodly. So I feare do I.

Saint.
Such as are Gracious, Graces have therefore   1475
They ever more desire to have more.
But Such as never knew this dainty fare
Do never wish them 'cause they dainties are.

Soul.
Alas! alas! this Still doth me benight.
I've no desire, or no Desire aright: 1480
And this is Clear: my Hopes do witherd ly,
Before their buds breake out, their blossoms dy.

Saint.
When fruits do thrive, the blossom falls off quite.
No need of blossoms when the Seed is ripe.
The Apple plainly prooves the blossom were.   1485
Thy withred Hopes hold out Desires as Cleare.

Soul.
Alas! my Hopes Seem but like blasted fruit.
Dead on the Stoole before it leaves its root:
For if it lively were a growth it hath,
And would be grown e're this to Saving Faith.   1490

Saint.
* * * I'le make most plain
* * * * * *   [34]
Which lively is, layes hold on Christ too, though
Thou deem'st it doth like blasted blossoms show.

Soul.

If it was so, then Certainly I should,   1495
With Faith Repentance have. But, oh! behold,
This Grace leaves not in mee a Single print.
Mine Eyes are Adamant, my Heart is Flint.

Saint.

Repentance is not argued so from Tears.
As from the Change that in the Soul appears,   1500
And Faith Ruld by the Word. Hence ever Spare
To mete Repentance out by Satans Square.

Soul.

I fear Repentance is not Genuine.
It's Feare that makes me from my Sins decline.
And if it was, I should delight much more,   1505
To bathe in all Gods Ordinances pure.

Saint.

And dost thou not? Poore Soule thou dost I know.
Why else dost thou Relent, and Sorrow So?
But Satan doth molest thee much to fling
Thee from thy Dutie into e'ry Sin.   1510

Soul.

If these were my Delight, I should Embrace
The royall Retinue of Saving Grace,
Peace, Patience, Pray're, Meekness, Humility.
Love, Temp'rance, Feare, Syncerety, and Joy.

Saint.

You do: though not alike at all times sure.   1515
And you do much desire to have more.
I wonder that you judge them worth the having,
Or Crave them, if they are not got by Craving.

Soul.

My measure is so small, I doubt, alas!
It's next to none, and will for nothing pass.   1520

But if I had but this or that Degree,
Of all these Graces, then thrice Happy mee!

   Saint.
You have not what you Would, and therefore will
Not own you have at all. What Sullen Still?
If God Should fill you, and not work your bane,   1525
You would not be Content, but would Complain.

   Soul.
What must my vessell voide of Grace be thrust
By you in Glory thus among the just
As Gracious though the Dose of Grace I finde
Is scarce a Grain? Can this Content your minde?   1530

   Saint.
God, and his All, 's the Object of the Will:
All God alone can onely it up fill.
He'de kill the Willer, if his Will he Should
Fill to the brim, while Cabbined in mould.
What Mortall can contain immortall bliss;   1535
If it be poured on him as it is?   [35]
A Single Beam thus touching him would make
The Stoutest mortall man to ashes Shake.
Will nothing give Content unless you have
While here a mortall, all your Will can Crave?   1540
If so, the Promise which is made to those
That hunger after Righteousness you'l lose.
For being full, you could not hunger still
Nor Wish for more, you having once your Will.
You can't contain Halfe, what in truth you would   1545
Or do not Wish for Halfe of what you should.
Can't all the Sea o're fill an Acorn bole?
Can't God ore fill a little Whimpring Soul?
What Can a Nut shell all the World Enfold?
Or Can thy Heart all Heavens Glory Hold?   1550
And never break? What Canst thou here below
Weld Heavens bliss while mortall thus? Oh! No.
God Loves you better, than to grant your Cry,

the mortal condition [handwritten annotation]

When you do Cry for that which will destroy.
Give but a Child a Knife to Still his Din: 1555
He'l Cut his Fingers with it ere he blin.

  Soul.
Had I but any sparke of Grace, I might
Have much more than I have with much delight.
How can I trust to you? You do not know
Whether I have a Grain of Grace, or no.   1560

  Saint.
You think you might have more: you shall have So,
But if you'd all at once, you could not grow.
And if you could not grow, you'd grieving fall,
All would not then Content you had you all.
Should Graces Floodgate thus at once breake down   1565
You most would lose, or else it would you drown.
He'l fill you but by drops that so he may
Not drown you in't, nor Cast a Drop away.

1477 this *orig.* these
1528 just *orig.* just?

Doubts from Satans Temptations Answered.

  Soul.
But oh the Tempter harries me so fast
And on me falls to make me fall at last.   1570
Had I but Grace surely I might repell
His firy Darts that dart in fire from hell.

  Saint.
If you had none, he never would bestow
Such darts upon you Grace to overthrow.
Though Bullets shot are blinde, the fowlers eye   1575
Aims at the marke before he lets them fly.

Soul.

But he bewilders me: I scarce can finde
But lose, myselfe again within my minde.
My thoughts are Laberryntht, I can't enjoyn
Any thereof the rest to discipline.   [36]1580

Saint.

I once was thus. The Crooked Serpent old
Doth Strive to hinder what he can't withold.
And where he cannot keep from Grace, he's loath,
To keep from keeping Saving Grace from Growth.

Soul.

But if a Pious thought appeare, I finde   1585
It's brambled in the briers of my minde.
Or in those brambles lost, or Slinks away:
But Vip'rous thoughts do in these thickets Stay.
With these I pest'red am in Duty So,
I doubt I undo all thereby I do.   1590

Saint.

First Satan envies each Choice thought: then hee
To murder it, or make't Short winded bee
Doth raise a Fog, or fude of thoughts most vile
Within the Soul; and darkens all that ile.
And when he cannot hinder pray're he'le Strive   1595
To spoile the Same, but Still hold on, and thrive.

Soul.

But yet I feare there oft lurks Secretly
Under each Duty done Hypocrisy.
I finde no heart unto the Wayes of Grace.
It's but their End my heart would fain imbrace.   1600

Saint.

Why give you Credit to your deadly foe?
He turns ore ery stone Grace t'overthrow.
He'l fight on both sides Grace, Grace to destroy.

To ruinate your Souls Eternally.
He makes some thus red mad on mischiefe grow   1605
And not to matter what they say, or do.
He makes Civility to pass for Grace,
With Such as hunt riches hot Senting trace.
To such as God doth Call, he doth reply
That all their Grace is but Hypocrisy.   1610
   Contrarily, a Refuge Strong to make
For e'ry Sin, he doth this method take.
He tells the Doubting Soul, this is no Sin,
Untill he Diveth over head therein.
But then to breake his Heart he doth reply: 1615
That done is Sin, He Sinned willingly.
He to the Sinner saith, Great Sins are Small,
Small Sins he telleth him, are none at all.
And so to Such there is no Sin: for why
Great Sins are Small, Small None. But oh but eye   1620
If God awakes a Soul, he doth begin
To make him count indifferent things as Sin.
Nay Lawfull things wanting a Circumstance
Or having one too much, although by Chance.
And thus he doth involve the doubting Soule   1625
In dismall doubts and makes it fear to rowle
Himselfe on Christ for fear it should presume.
But if he doth he quickly turns his tune
And doth accuse, because he did not take
As soon as mercy did an offer make.   [37]1630
Oh! See the Craft the Serpent old doth use
To hopple Souls in Sin, and Sin to Choose.
One while he terms true Grace a morall thing.
One while morality a Splended Sin.

   Soul.
You shew the matter as the matter is   1635
But shew me how in Such a Case as this,
T'repell the Tempter, and the field t'obtain.
To Chaff away the Chaff and Choose the grain.

Saint.
Perform the Duty, leave th'event unto
His Grace that doth both in, and out side know.   1640
Beg pardon for your Sins: bad thoughts defy,
That are Cast in you by the Enemy.
Approove yourselfe to God, and unto his
And beg a pardon where you do amiss.
If wronged go to God for right, and pray   1645
Hard-thoughted saints black-thoughted thoughts away.
Renew your acts of Faith: believe in him,
Who died on the Cross to Cross out Sin.
Allow not any Sin: and if you sin
Through frailty, Faith will a new pardon bring.   1650
Do all Good Works, work all good things you know
As if you should be Sav'd for doing so.
Then undo all you've done, and it deny
And on a naked Christ alone rely.
Believe not Satan, Unbelieve his tales   1655
Lest you should misbelieve the Gospell bales.
    Do what is right, and for the right Contend.
    Make Grace your way, and Glory'l be your End.

Yet as a further Caution Still I'le shew
You other Wiles of Satan to eschue.   1660
And that a Saint may of a Saint account
Not as a Saint though once with God in th'mount.

1602 ore ery *orig.* each
1458 ly *orig.* dy*1618* Sins *orig.* thing

SOME OF SATANS SOPHESTRY.

The Tempter greatly Seeks, though secretly,
  With an Ath'istick Hoodwinke man to blinde,
That So the Footsteps of the Deity   1665
  Might Stand no longer stampt upon his minde.
  Which when he can't blot out, by blinding, quite,
  He strives to turn him from the Purer Light.

With Wiles enough, he on his thoughts intrudes,
  That God's a Heape of Contradictions high,   1670
But when these thoughts man from his thoughts excludes,
  Thou knowst not then (saith he) this Mystery.
  And when the first String breaks, he strives to bring
  Into Sins brambles by the other String.   [38]

When God Calls out a Soule, he Subtilly   1675
  Saith God is kinde: you need not yet forsake
Your Sins: but if he doth, he doth reply,
  Thou'st out Stood Grace. Justice will vengeance take.
  He'l tell you you Presume on Grace, to fright
  You to despare, beholding Justice bright.   1680

Though just before mans mountain Sins were mites,
  His mites were nothing. Now the Scales are turn'd.
His mites are mountains now, of mighty height
  And must with Vengeance-Lightening be burn'd.
  Great Sins are Small, till men repent of Sin: 1685
  Then Small are far too big to be forg'in.

While man thinks slightly, that he will repent,
  There's time enough (saith he), it's easly done.
But when repent he doth, the time is Spent,
  Saith he, it is too late to be begun,   1690
  To keep man from't, it's easly done saith he,
  To dant him in't, he saith, it Cannot bee.

So Faith is easy till the Soule resolves
  To Live to Christ, and upon Christ rely.

Then Saving Faith he bold presumption Calls,   1695
  Hast thou (saith he) in Christ propriety?
The Faithfulls Faith, he Stiles Presumption great,
But the Presumptuous, theirs is Faith Compleat.

Nay though the Faith be true he acts so Sly,
  As to raise doubts. And then it must not do: 1700
Unless Assurance do it Certify:
  Which if it do, it douts of it also.
Faith is without Assurance Shuffled out,
And if Assurance be, that's Still a Doubt.

But should the Soule assured once, once Doubt,   1705
  Then his Assurance no Assurance is:
Assurance doth assure the Soul right out
  Leave not a Single Doubt to do amiss.
But Satan Still will Seeke to Pick an hole
In thy Assurance to unsure thy Soul.   1710

Should any Soule once an Assurance get,
  Into his hands, Soon Satans Pick-Lock key
With Sinfull Wards Unlocks his Cabinet
  To Steal the Jewell in it thence away.
The Soul thus pillag'de, droops unto the grave.   1715
It's greater grief to lose than not to have.

He doth molest the Soule, it cannot See
  Without Assurance Extraordinary
Which Should it have, it would soon take to bee
  A Mere Delusion of the Adversary.   1720
Assurance would not Serve should God Convay
It in an Usuall or Unusuall way.   [39]

Thus I might search, Poor Soul, the Magazeen
  Of Gospell Graces over: I might paint
Out Satan Sculking each Side each unseen   1725
  To Hoodwinck Sinners, and to hopple Saints.
For he to dim their Grace, and Slick up Sin
Calls Brass bright Gold, bright Golde but brass or tin.

He tempts to bring the Soul too low or high,
  To have it e're in this or that extream: 1730
To See no want or want alone to eye:
  To keep on either side the golden mean.
  If it was in't to get it out he'l 'ledge,
  Thou on the wrong Side art the Pale or Hedge.

When God awakes a Soule he'l Seeke to thrust   1735
  It on Despare for want of Grace or get
And pufft with Pride, or in Securety hush't
  Or Couzen it with Graces Counterfet.
  Which if he can't he'l Carp at Grace, and raile
  And Say, this is not Grace, it thus doth faile.   1740

And thus he Strives with Spite, Spleen, bitter Gall
  That Sinners might Dishonour God Most high:
That Saints might never honour God at all.
  That those in Sin, These not in Grace might dy.
  And that the Righteous, Gracious, Pious, Grave,   1745
  Might have no Comfort of the Grace they have.

Lest you be foild herewith, watch well unto
  Your Soul, that thrice Ennobled noble Gem:
For Sins are flaws therein, and double woe
  Belongs thereto if it be found in them.   1750
  Are Flaws in Venice Glasses bad? What in
  Bright Diamonds? What then in man is Sin?

1719 would *orig.* quickly up would
1751 Venice *orig.* Venus

DIFFICULTIES ARISING FROM UNCHARITABLE CARIAGES
OF CHRISTIANS.

When these assaults proove vain, the Enemy
   One Saint upon an other oft doth Set,
To make each fret like to Gum'd Taffity   1755
   And fire out Grace thus by a Chafe or Fret.
   Uncharitable Christians inj'rous are.
   Two Freestons rubd together each do ware.

When Satan jogs the Elbow of the one
   To Spleenish Passions which too oft doth rise   1760
For want of Charity, or hereupon
   From some Uncharitable harsh Surmise,
   Then the Poore Doubting Soul is oft oppresst,
   By hard Reflections from an harder breast.

Th'Uncharitable Soul oft thus reflects,   1765
   After each Birth a Second birth doth Come.
Your Second Birth no Second Birth ejects,
   The Babe of Grace then's Strangld in the Womb.
   There's no New Birth born in thy Soul thou'lt finde   [40]
   If that the after Birth abide behinde.   1770

The Babe of Grace, thinks he, 's not born it's sure.
   Sins Secundine is not as yet out Cast.
The Soul no Bracelet of Graces pure
   Doth ware, while wrapt in nature's slough so fast.
   And thus he doth for want of Charity,   1775
   The wounded wound Uncharitably.

And thus some Child of God, when led awry
   By Satan, doth with Satan take a part,
Against Some Child of God, whom frowardly
   He by Reflections harsh wounds thus in heart.   1780
   Pough! Here's Religion! Strange indeed! Quoth hee.
   Grace makes a Conscience of things here that bee.

Grace Conscious makes one how to Spend ones time,
  How to perform the Duties of one's place
Not onely in the things which are Divine;   1785
  But in the things which ware a Sublune Face.
  Do you do so? and order good persue?
  Don't Earth and Heaven interfer in you?

Will God accept the Service if the time
  Is Stolen from our Calling him to pay?   1790
What will he yield that Sacrifice his Shine,
  That from anothers Altar's stole away?
  God and our Callings Call: and th'Sacrifice
  Stole from our Callings Altar he defies.

Yet if it falls on worldly things intense   1795
  It's Soon Scourgd then with whips of Worldliness;
It gives to many, nay to all, offence
  And gathers to itselfe great penciveness.
  Intense on God, or on the world, all's one,
  The Harmless Soule is hardly thought upon.   1800

Such Traps, and Wilds as these are, Satan Sets,
  For to intrap the Innocent therein:
These are his Wyers, Snares, and tangling Nets,
  To hanck, and hopple harmless Souls in Sin.
  If in Such briars thou enbrambled light   1805
  Call on the Mighty God with all thy might.

On God in Christ Call hard: For in him hee
  Hath Bowells melting, and Expanded arms:
Hath Sweet imbraces, Tender mercy free
  Hath Might Almighty too to save from harms.   1810
  Into his Dove streakt Downy bosom fly.
  In Spite of Spite, or Spiters Enmity.

These are Gods Way-Marks thus inscrib'd; this hand
  Points you the way unto the Land Divine,
The Land of Promise, Good Immanuels Land.   1815
  To New Jerusalem above the line.

Ten thousand times thrice tribled blesst he is,
That walketh in the Suburbs here of bliss.   [41]

His Wildred state will wane away, and hence
    These Crooked Passages will Soon appeare   1820
The Curious needlework of Providence
    Embrodered with golden Spangles Cleare.
    Judge not this Web while in the Loom, but stay
    From judging it untill the judgment day.

For while it's firled up the best Can See   1825
    But little of it, and that little too
Shews weather beaten but when it shall bee
    Hung open all at once, Oh beautious Shew!
    Though thrids run in, and out, Cross Snarle and twinde
    The Web will even be enwrought you'l finde.   1830

If in the golden Mashes of this Net
    (The Checkerwork of Providence) you're Caught
And Carride hence to Heaven, never fret:
    Your Barke Shall to an Happy Bay be brought.
    You'l Se both Good and Bad drawn up hereby,   1835
    These to Hells Horrour, those to Heavens Joy.

Fear not Presumption then, when God Invites:
    Invite not Fear, when that he doth thee Call:
Call not in Question whether he delights
    In thee, but make him thy Delight, and all.   1840
    Presumption lies in Backward Bashfulness,
    When one is backward though a bidden Guest.

1756 fire *orig.* ou
1765 oft *orig.* doth oft
1776 wounded wound *orig.* wound Uncharitably
1835 Good *orig.* God

THE EFFECT OF THIS DISCOURSE UPON THE SECOND,
AND THIRD RANCKS.

Rank Two.
Whence Come these Spicy Gales? Shall we abuse
    Such Sweet Perfumes with putrid noses?
Who did in this Diffusive Aire Diffuse   1845
    Such Aromatick fumes or Posies?
These Spirits are with Graces sweetly splic'te;
What Good Comes in them? Oh! they Come from Christ!

Rank Three.
Whence Come these Cloudy Pillars of Perfume?
    Sure Christ doth on his Garden blow   1850
Or open Graces Spice Box, I presume,
    From whence these Reechs do flow:
For oh! heart Ravishing Steams do scale my Soule,
And do in Heavenly Raptures it enrowle.

Rank Two.
Sure Grace a progress in her Coach doth ride,   1855
    Lapt up in all Perfumes, whose Sent,
Hath Suffocated Sin, and nullifi'de
    Sad Griefe, as in our Souls it went.
Sin Sincks the Soul to Hell: but here is Love
Sincks Sin to Hell; and Soars the Soul above.   1860

Rank Three.
I strove to Soar on high. But, oh! methought
    Like to a Lump of Lead my Sin
Prest down my Soul; But now it's off, she's Caught   [42]
    In holy Raptures up to him.
Oh! let us then Sing Praise: methinks I Soar   1865
Above the Stars, and Stand at Heavens Doore.

1846 Posies *orig.* Poses
1859 Sincks *orig.* Sinks
1860 Sincks *orig.* Sink ; to *orig.* to h

Our Insufficiency to Praise God Suitably,
for his Mercy.

Should all the World so wide to atoms fall,
　　Should th'Aire be Shred to motes. Should we
　　Se all the Earth hackt here So Small
　　　　That none Could Smaller bee?　　　　　　　　1870
Should Heaven, and Earth be Atomizd, we guess
The Number of these Motes were numberless.

But should we then a World each Atom deem,
　　Where dwell as many pious men
　　As all these Motes the world Could teem　　　　1875
　　　　Were it shred into them?
Each Atom would the World Surmount wee guess
Whose men in number would be numberless.

But had each pious man, as many Tongues
　　At Singing all together then　　　　　　　　　　1880
　　The Praise that to the Lord belongs
　　　　As all these Atoms men?
Each man would Sing a World of Praise, we guess,
Whose Tongues in number would be numberless.

And had each Tongue, as many Songs of Praise　　　1885
　　To Sing to the Almighty ALL.
　　As all these men have Tongues to raise
　　　　To him their Holy Call?
Each Tongue would tune a World of Praise, we guess
Whose Songs in number would be numberless.　　　　1890

Nay, had each Song as many Tunes most Sweet
　　Or one intwisting in't as many,
　　As all these Tongues have Songs most meet
　　　　Unparallelld by any?
Each Song a world of Musick makes we guess　　　　1895
Whose Tunes in number would be numberless.

Now Should all these Conspire in us that we

Could breath Such Praise to thee, Most High?
Should we thy Sounding Organs be
   To ring Such Melody?   1900
Our Musick would the World of Worlds out ring
Yet be unfit within thine Eares to ting.

Thou didst us mould, and us new mould when wee
   Were worse than mould we tread upon.
   Nay Nettles made by Sin wee bee.   1905
      Yet hadst Compassion.
Thou hast pluckt out our Stings; and by degrees
Hast of us, lately Wasps, made Lady-Bees.   [43]

Though e're our Tongues thy Praises due can fan
   A Weevle with the World may fly,   1910
   Yea fly away: and with a Span
      We may out mete the Sky.
Though what we can is but a Lisp, We pray
Accept thereof; We have no better pay.

1870 none *orig.* not

THE SOULE SEEKING CHURCH-FELLOWSHIP.

The Soul refresht with gracious Steams, behold,   1915
   Christs royall Spirit richly tended
With all the guard of Graces manifold
   Throngs in to Solace it amended
   And by the Trinity befriended.

Befriended thus! It lives a Life indeed   1920
   A Life! as if it Liv'd for Life.
For Life Eternall: wherefore with all heed
   It trims the Same with Graces rife
   To be the Lambs espoused Wife.

Yea like a Bride all Gloriously arraide   1925
　　It is arrai'de Whose dayly ware
Is an Imbrodery with Grace inlai'de,
　　Of Sanctuary White most Faire,
　　It's drest in Heavens fashion rare.

Each Ordinance, and Instrument of Grace   1930
　　Grace doth instruct are Usefull here.
They're Golden Pipes where Holy Waters trace
　　Into the Spirits Spicebed Deare,
　　To vivify what withering were.

Hence do their Hearts like Civit-Boxes Sweet   1935
　　Evaporate their Love full pure,
Which through the Chincks of their Affections reechs
　　To God, Christ, Christians all, though more,
　　To Such whose Counsills made their Cure.

Hence now Christ's Curious Garden fenced in   1940
　　With Solid Walls of Discipline
Well wed, and watered, and made full trim:
　　The Allies all Laid out by line:
　　Walks for the Spirit all Divine.

Whereby Corruptions are kept out, whereby   1945
　　Corrupters also get not in,
Unless the Lyons Carkass Secretly
　　Lies lapt up in a Lamblike Skin
　　Which Holy seems yet's full of Sin.

For on the Towers of these Walls there Stand   1950
　　Just Watchmen Watching day, and night,
And Porters at each Gate, who have Command
　　To open onely to the right.
　　And all within may have a Sight.   [44]

Whose Zeale, should it along a Channell Slide   1955
　　Not banckt with Knowledg right and Good,

Nor Bottomed with Love: nor wiers ti'de
　To hinder prejudiciall Blood
　The Currant will be full of mud.

But yet this Curious Garden richly set,　　　　　　　　　　　　1960
　The Soul accounts Christs Paradise
Set with Choice Slips, and flowers: and longs to get
　Itself Set here: and by advice
　To grow herein and so rejoyce.

1928 Faire *orig.* rare
1937 their *orig.* there
1963 Itselfe by advice *orig.* Heavenly wise
1964 and so rejoyce *orig.* it Seeks and joyes

THE SOUL ADMIRING THE GRACE OF THE CHURCH ENTERS INTO
CHURCH FELLOWSHIP.

How is this City, Lord, of thine bespangled　　　　　　　　　1965
　　With Graces Shine?
With Ordinances alli'de, and inam'led,
　　Which are Divine?
Walld in with Discipline her Gates obtaine
Just Centinalls with Love Imbellisht plain.　　　　　　　　　1970

Hence glorious, and terrible She Stands;
　　That Converts new
Seing her Centinalls of all demand
　　The Word to Shew;
Stand gazing much between two Passions Crusht　　　　　　1975
Desire, and Feare at once which both wayes thrust.

Thus are they wrackt. Desire doth forward Screw
　　To get them in,
But Feare doth backward thrust, that lies purdue.
　　And Slicks that Pin.　　　　　　　　　　　　　　　　1980

You cannot give the word, Quoth she, which though
You Stumble on't it's more than yet you know.

But yet Desires Screw Pin doth not Slack:
    It still holds fast.
But Fears Screw Pin turns back or Screw doth Crack   1985
    And breaks at last.
Hence on they go, and in they enter: where
Desire Converts to joy: joy Conquours Fear.

They now enCovenant with God: and His:
    They thus indent.   1990
The Charters Seal's belonging unto this
    The Sacrament
So God is theirs avoucht, they his in Christ.
In whom all things they have, with Grace are splic'te.

Thus in the usuall Coach of Gods Decree   1995
    They bowle and Swim
To Glory bright, if no Hypocrisie
    Handed them in.
For Such must Shake their handmaid off lest they
Be Shakt out of this Coach, or dy in th'way.   [45]2000

1969 obtaine *orig.* containe
1985 Yet turns back *orig.* Slips
1993 is *orig.* in

THE GLORY OF; AND GRACE IN THE CHURCH SET OUT.

    Come now behold
  Within this Knot What Flowers do grow:
    Spanglde like gold:
  Whence Wreaths of all Perfumes do flow.
Most Curious Colours of all Sorts you shall   2005
With all Sweet Spirits Sent. Yet that's not all.

    Oh! Look, and finde
These Choicest Flowers most richly Sweet
    Are Disciplinde
With Artificiall Angels meet.   2010
An heap of Pearls is precious: but they shall
When set by Art Excell: Yet that's not all.

    Christ's spirit Showers
Down in his Word, and Sacraments
    Upon these Flowers   2015
The Clouds of Grace Divine Contents.
Such things of Wealthy Blessings on them fall
As make them Sweetly thrive: Yet that's not all.

    Yet Still behold!
All flourish not at once. We See   2020
    While Some Unfold
Their blushing Leaves, Some buds there bee.
Here's Faith, Hope, Charity in flower, which call
On yonders in the Bud. Yet that's not all.

    But as they stand   2025
Like Beauties reeching in perfume
    A Divine Hand
Doth hand them up to Glories room:
Where Each in Sweet'ned Songs all Praises Shall
Sing all ore Heaven for aye. And that's but all.   2030

THE SOULS ADMIRATION HEREUPON.

What I such Praises Sing! How can it bee?
    Shall I in Heaven Sing?
    What I, that scarce durst hope to see
    Lord, Such a thing?
Though nothing is too hard for thee: 2035
One Hope hereof Seems hard to mee.

What, Can I ever tune those Melodies
    Who have no tune at all?   [46]
Not knowing where to stop nor Rise,
    Nor when to Fall.   2040
To Sing thy Praise I am unfit.
I have not learn'd my Gam-Ut yet.

But should these Praises on String'd Instruments
    Be Sweetly tun'de? I finde
I nonplust am: for no Consents   2045
    I ever minde.
My Tongue is neither Quill, nor Bow:
Nor Can my Fingers Quavers Show.

But was it otherwise, I have no Kit:
    Which though I had, I could   2050
Not tune the Strings, which soon would Slip
    Though others Should.
But should they not, I cannot play:
But for an F should Strike an A.

And should thy Praise upon Winde-Instruments   2055
    Sound all o're Heaven Shrill?
My Breath will hardly through Such Vents
    A Whistle fill,
Which though it should, it's past my Spell
By Stops, and Falls to Sound it Well.   2060

How should I then, joyn in Such Exercise?
    One Sight of thee'l intice
Mine Eyes to theft: whose Extasies
    Will Stob my Voice.
Hereby mine Eyes will bind my Tongue.   2065
Unless thou, Lord, do Cut the thong.

What Use of Uselesse mee, then there, poore Snake?
    There Saints, and Angells Sing,
Thy Praise in full Cariere, which make
    The Heavens to ring.   2070

Yet if thou wilt thou Can'st me raise
With Angels bright to sing thy Praise.

2061 joyn *orig*. Lord, joyn
2063 theft *orig*. Robbery
2064 Voice. *orig*. Vice

THE JOY OF CHURCH FELLOWSHIP RIGHTLY ATTENDED.

In Heaven Soaring up, I dropt an Eare
 On Earth: and oh! Sweet Melody:
And listening, found it was the Saints who were   2075
 Encoacht for Heaven that Sang for Joy.
 For in Christs Coach they Sweetly Sing;
 As they to Glory ride therein.   [47]

Oh! joyous hearts! Enfirde with holy Flame!
 Is Speech thus tassled with praise?   2080
Will not your inward fire of Joy contain;
 That it in open flames doth blaze?
 For in Christ's Coach Saints Sweetly Sing,
 As they to Glory ride therein.

And if a String do slip, by Chance, they soon,   2085
 Do screw it up again: whereby
They Set it in a more melodious Tune
 And a Diviner Harmony.
 For in Christs Coach they Sweetly Sing
 As they to Glory ride therein.   2090

In all their Acts, publick, and private, nay
 And Secret too, they praise impart.
But in their Acts Divine and Worship, they
 With Hymns do offer up their Heart.
 Thus in Christs Coach they Sweetly Sing   2095
 As they to Glory ride therein.

Some few not in; and some whose Time, and Place
   Block up this Coaches way do goe
As Travellers afoot, and so do trace
   The Road that gives them right thereto   2100
   While in this Coach these Sweetly Sing
   As they to Glory ride therein.

PROLOGUE.

Lord, Can a Crumb of Dust the Earth outweigh
  Outmatch all mountains, nay the Chrystall sky?
Imbosom in't designs that shall Display
  And trace into the Boundless Deity?
   Yea hand a Pen whose moysture doth guild ore   5
   Eternall Glory with a glorious glore.

If it its Pen had of an Angels Quill,
  And sharpend on a Pretious stone ground tite,
And dipt in Liquid Gold, and mov'de by skill
  In Christall leaves should golden Letters write   10
   It would but blot and blur: yea jag, and jar
   Unless thou makst the Pen, and scribener.

I am this Crumb of Dust which is design'd
  To make my Pen unto thy Praise alone,
And my dull Phancy I would gladly grinde   15
  Unto an Edge on Zions Pretious stone.
   And Write in Liquid Gold upon thy Name
   My Letters till thy glory forth doth flame.

Let not th'attempts breake down my Dust I pray
  Nor laugh thou them to Scorn but pardon give.   20
Inspire this Crumb of Dust till it display
  Thy Glory through't: and then thy dust shall live.
   Its failings then thou'lt overlook I trust,
   They being slips slipt from thy Crumb of Dust.

Thy Crumb of Dust breaths two words from its breast,   25
  That thou wilt guide its pen to write aright
To Prove thou art, and that thou art the best
  And shew thy Properties to shine most bright.
   And then thy Works will shine as flowers on stems
   Or as in Jewellary shops, do jems.   [129]30

5 doth *ins.*
9 *orig.* And golden Letters in
11 yea *orig.* yet
13 Dust *orig.* Dust and
18 My *orig.* my
24 slipt *orig.* washt
29 thy *orig.* thy Glorious ; will shine *ins.*

PREPARATORY MEDITATIONS,

FIRST SERIES

Preparatory Meditations
before my Approach to the Lords Supper.
Chiefly upon the Doctrin preached
upon the Day of administration.

WESTFIELD
23.5M   1. MEDITATION.
1682

What Love is this of thine, that Cannot bee
  In thine Infinity, O Lord, Confinde,
Unless it in thy very Person See,
  Infinity, and Finity Conjoyn'd?
  What hath thy Godhead, as not Satisfide   5
  Marri'de our Manhood, making it its Bride?

Oh. Matchless Love! filling Heaven to the brim!
  O're running it: all running o're beside
This World! Nay Overflowing Hell; wherein
  For thine Elect, there rose a mighty Tide!   10
  That there our Veans might through thy Person bleed,
  To quench those flames, that else would on us feed.

Oh! that thy Love might overflow my Heart!
  To fire the Same with Love: for Love I would.
But oh! my streight'ned Breast! my Lifeless Sparke!   15
  My Fireless Flame! What Chilly Love, and Cold?
  In measure Small! in Manner Chilly! See.
  Lord blow the Coal: Thy Love Enflame in mee.

12.9M   2. MEDITATION ON CAN. 1.3. THY NAME IS
1682   AN OINTMENT POURED OUT.

My Dear, Deare, Lord I do thee Saviour Call.
  Thou in my very Soul art as I Deem,
Soe High, not High enough, Soe Great, too Small:
  Soe Deare, not Dear enough in my esteem.

Soe Noble, yet so Base: too Low, too Tall: 5
Thou full, and Empty art: Nothing, yet ALL.

A Precious Pearle, above all price dost 'bide.
    Rubies no Rubies are at all to thee.
Blushes of burnisht Glory sparkling slide
    From every Square in various Colour'd glee   10
    Nay Life itselfe in Sparkling Spangles Choice.
    A Precious Pearle thou art above all price.

Oh! that my Soul, Heavens Workmanship (within
    My Wicker'd Cage,) that Bird of Paradise
Inlin'de with Glorious Grace up to the brim   15
    Might be thy Cabbinet, oh Pearle of Price.
    Oh! let thy Pearle, Lord Cabbinet in mee.
    I'st then be rich! nay rich enough for thee.   [165]

My Heart, oh Lord, for thy Pomander gain.
    Be thou thyselfe my Sweet Perfume therein.   20
Make it thy Box, and let thy Pretious Name
    My Pretious Ointment be emboxt herein.
    If I thy Box and thou my Ointment bee
    I shall be Sweet, nay, Sweet enough for thee.

Enough! Enough! oh! let me eat my Word.   25
    For if Accounts be ballanc'd any way,
Can my poore Eggeshell ever be an Hoard,
    Of Excellence enough for thee? Nay: nay.
    Yet may I Purse, and thou my Mony bee
    I have enough. Enough in having thee.   30

---

2 art as I Deem *orig.* indeed art Deemd
3 Soe High *orig.* Too High Soe Great *orig.* too Great
4 Soe *orig.* Too ; in *orig.* to ; esteem *orig.* esteem'd
5 Soe *orig.* Too
7 Pearle *orig.* Peale
22 herein *orig.* therein
23 thy *orig.* the

11.12M 1682 } 3. Meditation. Can. 1.3. Thy Good Ointment.

How Sweet a Lord is mine? If any should
  Guarded, Engarden'd, nay, Imbosomd bee
In reechs of Odours, Gales of Spices, Folds
  Of Aromaticks, Oh! how Sweet was hee?
  He would be Sweet, and yet his sweetest Wave   5
  Compar'de to thee my Lord, no Sweet would have.

A Box of Ointments, broke; Sweetness most sweet
  A surge of Spices: Odours Common Wealth,
A Pillar of Perfume: a Steaming Reech
  Of Aromatick Clouds: All Saving Health   10
  Sweetness itselfe thou art: And I presume
  In Calling of thee Sweet, who art Perfume.

But Woe is mee! who have so quick a Sent
  To Catch perfumes pufft out from Pincks, and Roses
And other Muscadalls, as they get Vent,   15
  Out of their Mothers Wombs to bob our noses.
  And yet thy sweet perfume doth seldom latch
  My Lord, within my Mammulary Catch.

Am I denos'de? or doth the Worlds ill Sents
  Engarison my nosthrills narrow bore?   20
Or is my Smell lost in these Damps it Vents?
  And shall I never finde it any more?
  Or is it like the Hawks, or Hownds whose breed
  Take Stincking Carrion for Perfume indeed?

This is my Case. All things smell sweet to mee: 25
  Except thy sweetness, Lord. Expell these damps.
Breake up this Garison: and let me see
  Thy Aromaticks pitching in these Camps.
  Oh! let the Clouds of thy sweet Vapours rise,
  And both my Mammularies Circumcise.   [166]30

Shall spirits thus my Mammularies Suck?
  (As Witches Elves their teats,) and draw from thee
My Dear, Dear Spirit after fumes of muck?
  Be Dunghill Damps more sweet than Graces bee?
  Lord, clear these Caves; these Passes take, and keep.   35
  And in these Quarters lodge thy Odours sweet.

Lord, breake thy Box of Ointment on my Head;
  Let thy sweet Powder powder all my hair:
My Spirits let with thy perfumes be fed.
  And make thy Odours, Lord, my nosthrills fare.   40
  My Soule shall in thy Sweets then Soar to thee:
  I'le be thy Love, thou my Sweet Lord shalt bee.

Title Good *orig.* Sweet
4 Aromaticks *orig.* Aramaticks
6 Sweetness *orig.* Sweeness
14 Catch *orig.* Cath
20 narrow *orig.* wide
24 indeed? *orig.* indeed.
32 (As] *orig.* As ; teats,) *orig.* teats, ; draw *orig.* drain

THE EXPERIENCE.

Oh! that I always breath'd in Such an aire,
  As I Suckt in, feeding on Sweet Content!
Disht up unto my soul ev'n in that pray're
  Pour'de out to God over last Sacrament.
  What Beam of Light wrapt up my sight to finde   5
  Me neerer God than ere Came in my minde?

Most Strange it was! But yet more strange that shine
  Which filld my soul then to the brim to spy
My Nature with thy Nature all Divine
  Together joynd in Him thats Thou, and I.   10
  Flesh of my Flesh, Bone of my Bone. there's run
  Thy Godhead, and my Manhood in thy Son.

Oh! that that Flame which thou didst on mee Cast
   Might me enflame, and Lighten ery where.
Then Heaven to me would be less at last   15
   So much of heaven I should have while here.
   Oh! sweet though Short! I'le not forget the Same.
   My neerness, Lord, to thee did me Enflame.

I'le Claim my Right: Give place, ye Angells Bright.
   Ye farther from the Godhead stande than I.   20
My Nature is your Lord; and doth Unite
   Better than Yours unto the Deity.
   Gods Throne is first, and mine is next: to you
   Onely the place of Waiting-men is due.

Oh! that my Heart, thy Golden Harp might bee   25
   Well tun'd by Glorious Grace, that e'ry string
Screw'd to the highest pitch, might unto thee
   All Praises wrapt in Sweetest Musick bring.
   I praise thee, Lord, and better praise thee would
   If what I had, my heart might ever hold.   30

---

6 neerer *orig.* nerer
8 spy *orig.* see,
14 enflame *orig.* inflame
18 Enflame *orig.* inflame
28 Praises wrapt *orig.* Praise wrapt up

THE RETURN.

Inamoring Rayes, thy Sparkles, Pearle of Price
   Impearld with Choisest Gems, their beams Display
Impoysoning Sin, Guilding my Soule with Choice
   Rich Grace, thy Image bright, making me pray,
   Oh! that thou Wast on Earth below with me   5
   Or that I was in Heaven above with thee.   [169]

Thy Human Frame with Beauty Dapled, and
  In Beds of Graces pald with golden layes,
Lockt to thy Holy Essence by thy hand,
  Yields Glances that enflame my Soul, that sayes   10
  Oh! that thou wast on Earth below with mee!
  Or that I was in Heaven above with thee.

All Love in God, and's Properties Divine
  Enam'led are in thee: thy Beauties Blaze
Attracts my Souls Choice golden Wyer to twine   15
  About thy Rose-Sweet Selfe. And therefore prayes
  Oh! that thou wast on Earth below with mee!
  Or, that I was in Heaven above with thee.

A Magazeen of Love: Bright Glories blaze:
  Thy Shine fills Heaven with Glory; smile Convayes   20
Heavens Glory in my soule, which it doth glaze
  All ore with amoring Glory; that she sayes,
  Oh! that thou wast on Earth below with mee!
  Or, that I was in Heaven above with thee!

Heavens Golden Spout thou art where Grace most Choice   25
  Comes spouting down from God to man of Clay
A Golden Stepping Stone to Paradise
  A Golden Ladder into Heaven! I'l pray
  Oh! that thou wast on Earth below with mee
  Or that I was in Heaven above with thee.   30

Thy Service is my Freedom Pleasure, Joy,
  Delight, Bliss, Glory, Heaven on Earth, my Stay,
In Gleams of Glory thee to glorify,
  But oh! my Dross and Lets. Wherefore I say
  Oh! that thou wast on Earth below with mee: 35
  Or that I was in Heaven above with thee.

If off as Offall I be put, if I
  Out of thy Vineyard Work be put away:
Life would be Death: my soule would Coffin'd ly,

Within my Body; and no longer pray   40
Oh! that thou wast on Earth below with mee:
But that I was in Heaven above with thee.

But I've thy Pleasant Pleasant Presence had
In Word, Pray're, Ordinances, Duties; nay,
And in thy Graces, making me full Glad,   45
In Faith, Hope, Charity. that I do say,
That thou hast been on Earth below with mee.
And I shall be in Heaven above with thee.

Be thou Musician, Lord, Let me be made
The well tun'de Instrument thou dost assume: 50
And let thy Glory be my Musick plaide.
Then let thy Spirit keepe my Strings in tune,   [170]
Whilst thou art here on Earth below with mee
Till I sing Praise in Heaven above with thee.

---

2 Impearld *orig.* Impald
11 wast *orig.* was
12, 18, 24, 30, 36, 42 was *orig.* wast *orig.* was
25 thou art *ins.*

22.2M } 4. MEDITATION. CANT. 2.1. I AM THE ROSE OF SHARON.
1683 }

My Silver Chest a Sparke of Love up locks:
And out will let it when I can't well Use.
The gawdy World me Courts t'unlock the Box
A motion makes, where Love may pick, and choose.
Her Downy Bosom opes, that pedlars stall   5
Of Wealth, Sports, Honours, Beauty, slickt up all.

Love pausing on't, these Clayey Faces she
Disdains to Court; but Pilgrims life designs,
And Walkes in Gilliads Land, and there doth see

The Rose of Sharon which with Beauty shines;   10
Her Chest unlocks; the sparke of Love out breaths
To Court this Rose: and lodgeth in its leaves.

No Flower in Garzia Horti shines like this:
    No Beauty sweet in all the World so Choice;
It is the Rose of Sharon sweet, that is   15
    The Fairest Rose that Grows in Paradise.
    Blushes of Beauty bright, Pure White, and Red
    In Sweats of Glory on Each Leafe doth bed.

Lord lead me into this sweet Rosy Bower:
    Oh! Lodge my Soul in this sweet Rosy bed: 20
Array my soul with this sweet Sharon flower:
    Perfume me with the Odours it doth Shed.
    Wealth, Pleasure, Beauty spirituall will line,
    My pretious Soul, if Sharons Rose be mine.

The Blood Red Pretious Syrup of this Rose   25
    Doth all Catholicons excell what ere.
Ill Humours all that do the Soule inclose
    When rightly usd, it purgeth out most clear.
    Lord purge my Soul with this Choice Syrup, and
    Chase all thine Enemies out of my land.   30

The Rosy Oyle, from Sharons Rose extract
    Better than Palma Christi far is found.
Its Gilliads Balm for Conscience when shes wrackt,
    Unguent Apostolorum for each Wound.
    Let me thy Patient, thou my Surgeon bee.   35
    Lord, with thy Oyle of Roses Supple mee.

No Flower there is in Paradise that grows
    Whose Vertues Can Consumptive souls restore
But shugar of Roses made of Sharons Rose
    When Dayly usd, doth never fail to Cure.   40
    Lord let my Dwindling Soul be dayly fed
    With Sugar of Sharons Rose. its dayly Bread.   [171]

God Chymist is, doth Sharons Rose distill.
  Oh! Choice Rose Water! Swim my soul herein.
Let Conscience bibble in it with her Bill.   45
  Its Cordiall, ease doth Heartburns Causd by Sin.
  Oyle, Syrup, Sugar, and Rose Water such.
  Lord, give, give, give; I cannot have too much.

But, oh! alas! that such should be my need,
  That this Brave Flower must Pluckt, Stampt, Squeezed bee,   50
And boyld up in its Blood, it Spirits Sheed,
  To make a Physick sweet, sure, safe for mee.
  But yet this mangled Rose rose up again
  And in its pristine glory, doth remain.

All sweets, and Beauties of all Flowers appeare   55
  In Sharons Rose, whose Glorious Leaves out vie
In Vertue, Beauty, sweetness, Glory Cleare.
  The Spangled Leaves of Heavens cleare Chrystall sky.
  Thou Rose of Heaven, Glory's Blossom Cleare
  Open thy Rosie Leaves, and lodge mee there.   60

My Dear-Sweet Lord, shall I thy Glory meet
  Lodg'd in a Rose, that out a sweet Breath breaths.
What is my way to Glory made thus sweet,
  Strewd all along with Sharons Rosy Leaves.
  I'le walk this Rosy Path: World fawn, or frown   65
  And Sharons Rose shall be my Rose, and Crown.

---

18 on *orig.* of
13 Garzia *orig.* Gartia
23 line *orig.* shine
34 each *orig.* all
53 Rose *orig.* flower
54 And *orig.* In

THE REFLEXION.

Lord, art thou at the Table Head above
  Meat, Med'cine, Sweetness, sparkling Beautys to
Enamour Souls with Flaming Flakes of Love,
  And not my Trencher, nor my Cup o'reflow?
  Be n't I a bidden Guest? Oh! Sweat mine Eye.   5
  Oreflow with Teares: Oh! draw thy fountains dry.

Shall I not Smell thy Sweet, oh! Sharons Rose?
  Shall not mine Eye Salute thy Beauty? Why?
Shall thy sweet leaves their Beautious sweets upclose?
  As halfe ashamde my sight should on them ly?   10
  Woe's me! for this my sighs shall be in grain
  Offer'd on Sorrows Altar for the same.

Had not my soule's thy Conduit, Pipes stopt bin
  With mud, what Ravishment would'st thou Convay?
Let Graces Golden Spade dig till the Spring   15
  Of tears arise, and cleare this filth away.
  Lord, let thy Spirit raise my sighings till
  These Pipes my Soule do with thy sweetness fill.

Earth once was Paradise of Heaven below
  Till inkefac'd Sin had it with poyson stockt   20
And Chast this Paradise away into
  Heav'ns upmost Loft, and it in Glory Lockt.   [172]
  But thou, Sweet Lord, hast with thy golden Key
  Unlockt the Doore, and made, a golden day.

Once at thy Feast, I saw thee Pearle-like stand   25
  'Tween Heaven, and Earth where Heavens Bright glory all
In Streams fell on thee, as a floodgate and,
  Like Sun Beams through thee on the World to Fall.
  Oh! Sugar Sweet then! my Deare sweet Lord, I see
  Saints Heavens-lost Happiness restor'd by thee.   30

Shall Heaven, and Earth's bright Glory all up lie
  Like Sun Beams bundled in the sun, in thee?

Dost thou sit Rose at Table Head, where I
  Do sit, and Carv'st no morsell Sweet for mee?
  So much before, So little now! Sprindge, Lord,   35
  Thy Rosie Leaves, and me their Glee afford.

Shall not thy Rose my Garden fresh perfume?
  Shall not thy Beauty my dull Heart assaile?
Shall not thy golden gleams run through this gloom?
  Shall my black Velvet Mask thy fair Face Vaile?   40
  Pass o're my Faults: Shine forth, bright Sun: arise
  Enthrone thy Rosy-Selfe within mine Eyes.

---

2 Beautys *orig.* Beautys shew
12 offer'd *orig.* Offed
18 sweetness *orig.* sweeness
37 Rose *orig.* Rose thy
40 Vaile *orig.* Vale

2:7M
1683   }   5. Meditation. Cant. 2.1. The Lilly of the Vallies.

My Blessed Lord, art thou a Lilly Flower?
  Oh! that my Soul thy Garden were, that So
Thy bowing Head root in my Heart, and poure
  Might of its seeds, that they therein might grow.
  Be thou my Lilly, make thou me thy knot: 5
  Be thou my Flowers, I'le be thy Flower Pot.

My barren heart thy Fruitfull Vally make:
  Be thou my Lilly flouerishing in mee:
Oh Lilly of the Vallies. For thy Sake,
  Let me thy Vally, thou my Lilly bee.   10
  Then nothing shall me of thy selfe bereave.
  Thou must not me, or must thy Vally leave.

How shall my Vallie's Spangling Glory spred,
  Thou Lilly of the Vallies Spangling

There Springing up? Upon thy bowing Head   15
All Heavens bright Glory hangeth dangling.
My Vally then with Blissfull Beams shall Shine,
Thou Lilly of the Vallys, being mine.

---

6 thou *orig.* thy
14 Spangling *orig.* Spangling?

ANOTHER MEDITATION AT THE SAME TIME.

Am I thy Gold? Or Purse, Lord, for thy Wealth;
  Whether in mine, or mint refinde for thee?
I'me counted So, but count me o're thyselfe,
  Lest gold washt face, and brass in Heart I bee.
  I Feare my Touchstone touches when I try   5
  Mee, and my Counted Gold too overly.   [173]

Am I new minted by thy stamp indeed?
  Mine Eyes are dim, I cannot clearly see.
Be thou my Spectacles that I may read
  Thine Image, and Inscription Stampt on mee.   10
  If thy bright Image do upon me Stand
  I am a Golden Angell in thy hand.

Lord, make my Soule thy Plate: thine Image bright
  Within the Circle of the Same enfoile.
And on its brims in golden Letters write   15
  Thy Superscription in an Holy style.
  Then I shall be thy Money, thou my Hord:
  Let me thy Angell bee, bee thou my Lord.

10:12M ⎤   7. MEDITATION. PS. 45.2. GRACE IN THY LIPS IS
1683   ⎦   POURED OUT.

Thy Humane Frame, my Glorious Lord, I spy,
  A Golden Still with Heavenly Choice drugs filld,
Thy Holy Love, the Glowing heate whereby,
  The spirit of Grace is graciously distilld.
  Thy Mouth the Neck through which these Spirits Still   5
  My soul thy Violl make, and therewith fill.

Thy Speech the Liquour in thy Vessell Stands,
  Well ting'd with Grace a blessed Tincture, Loe,
Thy Words distilld, Grace in thy Lips pourd, and,
  Give Graces Tinctur in them where they go.   10
  Thy words in graces tincture stilld, Lord, may
  The Tincture of thy Grace in me Convay.

That Golden Mint of Words thy Mouth Divine
  Doth tip these Words, which by my Fall were spoild;
And Dub with Gold dug out of Graces mine   15
  That they thine Image might have in them foild.
  Grace in thy Lips poured out's as Liquid Gold.
  Thy Bottle make my Soule, Lord, it to hold.

8:4M ⎤   8. MEDITATION. JOH. 6.51. I AM THE LIVING BREAD.
1684 ⎦

I kening through Astronomy Divine
  The Worlds bright Battlement, wherein I spy
A Golden Path my Pensill cannot line,
  From that bright Throne unto my Threshold ly.
  And while my puzzled thoughts about it pore   5
  I finde the Bread of Life in't at my doore.

When that this Bird of Paradise put in
  This Wicker Cage (my Corps) to tweedle praise

Had peckt the Fruite forbad: and so did fling
  Away its Food; and lost its golden dayes;   10
  It fell into Celestiall Famine sore:
  And never could attain a morsell more.   [174]

Alas! alas! Poore Bird, what wilt thou doe?
  The Creatures field no food for Souls e're gave.
And if thou knock at Angells dores, they show   15
  An Empty Barrell: they no Soul bread have.
  Alas! Poore Bird, the Worlds White Loafe is done.
  And cannot yield thee here the smallest Crumb.

In this sad state, Gods Tender Bowells run,
  Out streams of Grace: And he to end all strife   20
The Purest Wheate in Heaven, his deare-dear Son
  Grinds, and kneads up into this Bread of Life.
  Which Bread of Life from Heaven down came and stands
  Disht on thy Table up by Angells Hands.

Did God mould up this Bread in Heaven, and bake,   25
  Which from his Table came, and to thine goeth?
Doth he bespeake thee thus, This Soule Bread take;
  Come Eate thy fill of this thy Gods White Loafe?
  It's Food too fine for Angells, yet come, take
  And Eate thy fill. It's Heavens Sugar Cake.   30

What Grace is this knead in this Loafe? This thing
  Souls are but petty things it to admire.
Yee Angells, help: This fill would to the brim
  Heav'ns whelm'd-down Chrystall meele Bowle, yea and higher.
  This Bread of Life dropt in thy mouth, doth Cry.   35
  Eate, Eate me, Soul, and thou shalt never dy.

7:7M
1684 } 9. MEDITATION. JOH. 6.51. I AM THE LIVING BREAD.

Did Ever Lord Such noble house mentain,
  As my Lord doth? Or Such a noble Table?
'T would breake the back of kings, nay, Monarchs brain
  To do it. Pish, the Worlds Estate's not able.
  I'le bet a boast with any that this Bread   5
  I eate excells what ever Cæsar had.

Take earth's Brightst Darlings, in whose mouths all flakes
  Of Lushous Sweets she hath do croude their Head,
Their Spiced Cups, Sweet Meats, and Sugar Cakes
  Are but dry Sawdust to this Living Bread.   10
  I'le pawn my part in Christ, this Dainti'st Meate,
  Is Gall, and Wormwood unto what I eate.

The Boasting Spagyrist (Insipid Phlegm,
  Whose Words out Strut the Sky) vaunts he hath rife
The Water, Tincture, Lozenge, Gold, and Gem,   15
  Of Life itselfe. But here's the Bread of Life.
  I'le lay my Life, his Aurum Vitæ Red
  Is to my Bread of Life, worse than DEAD HEAD.   [175]

The Dainti'st Dish of Earthly Cookery
  Is but to fat the body up in print.   20
This Bread of Life doth feed the Soule, whereby
  It's made the Temple of Jehovah in't.
  I'le Venture Heav'n upon't that Low or High
  That eate this Living Bread shall never dy.

This Bread of Life, So excellent, I see   25
  The Holy Angells doubtless would, if they
Were prone unto base Envie, Envie't mee.
  But oh! come, tast how sweet it is. I say,
  I'le Wage my Soule and all therein uplaid,
  This is the Sweetest Bread that e're God made.   30

What wonder's here, that Bread of Life should come
  To feed Dead Dust? Dry Dust eate Living Bread?
Yet Wonder more by far may all, and Some
  That my Dull Heart's so dumpish when thus fed.
  Lord Pardon this, and feed mee all my dayes,   35
  With Living Bread to thy Eternall Prayse.

26.8M
        } 10. MEDITATION. JOH. 6.55. MY BLOOD IS DRINKE INDEED.
1684

Stupendious Love! All Saints Astonishment!
  Bright Angells are black Motes in this Suns Light.
Heav'ns Canopy the Paintice to Gods tent
  Can't Cover't neither with its breadth, nor height.
  Its Glory doth all Glory else out run,   5
  Beams of bright Glory to't are motes i'th'Sun.

My Soule had Caught an Ague, and like Hell
  Her thirst did burn: She to each spring did fly,
But this bright blazing Love did Spring a Well
  Of Aqua-Vitæ in the Deity.   10
  Which on the top of Heav'ns high Hill out burst
  And down came running thence t'allay my thirst.

But how it came, amazeth all Communion.
  Gods onely Son doth hug Humanity,
Into his very person. By which Union   15
  His Humane Veans its golden gutters ly.
  And rather than my Soule should dy by thirst,
  These Golden Pipes, to give me drink, did burst.

This Liquour brew'd, thy Sparkling Art Divine
  Lord, in thy Chrystall Vessells did up tun,   20
(Thine Ordinances,) which all Earth o're shine
  Set in thy rich Wine Cellars out to run.

Lord, make thy Butlar draw, and fill with speed
My Beaker full: for this is drink indeed.

Whole Buts of this blesst Nectar Shining stand   25
  Lockt up with Saph'rine Taps, whose splendid Flame
Too bright do shine for brightest Angells hands
  To touch, my Lord, Do thou untap the Same.   [176]
  Oh! make thy Chrystall Buts of Red Wine bleed
  Into my Chrystall Glass this Drink-Indeed.   30

How shall I praise thee then? My blottings jar
  And wrack my Rhymes to pieces in thy praise.
Thou breath'st thy Vean still in my Pottinger
  To lay my thirst, and fainting spirits raise.
  Thou makest Glory's Chiefest Grape to bleed   35
  Into my Cup: And this is Drink-Indeed.

Nay, though I make no pay for this Red Wine,
  And Scarce do say I thanke-ye-for't; Strange thing!
Yet were thy silver skies my Beer bowle fine
  I finde my Lord, would fill it to the brim.   40
  Then make my life, Lord, to thy praise proceed
  For thy rich blood, which is my Drink-Indeed.

31.3M ⎤
1685 ⎦   11. MEDITATION. ISAI. 25.6. A FEAST OF FAT THINGS.

A Deity of Love Incorporate
  My Lord, lies in thy Flesh, in Dishes Stable
Ten thousand times more rich than golden Plate
  In golden Services upon thy Table,
  To feast thy People with. What Feast is this!   5
  Where richest Love lies Cookt in e'ry Dish?

A Feast, a Feast, a Feast of spiced Wine
  Of Wines upon the Lees, refined well

Of Fat things full of Marrow, things Divine
   Of Heavens blesst Cookery which doth excell.   10
   The Smell of Lebanon, and Carmell Sweet
   Are Earthly damps unto this Heavenly reech.

This Shew-Bread Table all of Gold with white
   Fine Table Linen of Pure Love, 's ore spred
And Courses in Smaragdine Chargers bright   15
   Of Choicest Dainties Paradise e're bred.
   Wherein each Grace like Dainty Sippits lie
   Oh! brave Embroderies of sweetest joy.

Oh! what a Feast is here? This Table might
   Make brightest Angells blush to sit before.   20
Then pain my Soule! why wantst thou appitite?
   Oh! blush to thinke thou hunger dost no more.
   There never was a feast more rich than this:
   The Guests that Come hereto shall swim in bliss.

Hunger, and Thirst my Soule, goe Fast, and Pray,   25
   Untill thou hast an Appitite afresh:
And then come here; here is a feast will pay
   Thee for the same with all Deliciousness.
   Untap Loves Golden Cask, Love run apace:
   And o're this Feast Continually say Grace.   30

19:5M
        }   12. MEDITATION. ISAI. 63.1. GLORIOUS IN HIS APPARELL.
1685

This Quest rapt at my Eares broad golden Doores:
   Who's this that comes from Edom in this Shine   [177]
In Died Robes from Bozrah? this more ore
   All Glorious in's Apparrell; all Divine?
   Then through that Wicket rusht this buss there gave,   5
   It's I that right do speake mighty to Save.

I threw through Zions Lattice then an Eye
  Which Spide one like a lump of Glory pure.
Nay, Cloaths of gold button'd with pearls do ly
  Like Rags, or Shooclouts unto his he wore.   10
    Heavens Curtains blancht with Sun, and starrs of Light
    Are black as sackcloath to his Garments bright.

One shining Sun guilding the Skies with Light
  Benights all Candles with their flaming Blaze.
So doth the Glory of this Robe benight   15
  Ten thousand Suns at once ten thousand wayes.
    For e'ry thrid therein's dy'de with the shine
    Of All, and Each the Attributes Divine.

The Sweetest breath, the sweetest Violet
  Rose, or Carnation ever did gust out   20
Is but a Foist to that Perfume beset
  In thy Apparell Steaming round about.
    But is this so? My Peuling Soul then pine
    In Love untill this Lovely one be thine.

Pluck back the Curtains; back the Window shutts: 25
  Through Zions Agate Window take a view;
How Christ in Pinckted Robes from Bozrah puts
  Comes Glorious in's Apparell forth to Wooe.
    Oh! if his Glory ever kiss thine Eye,
    Thy Love will soon Enchanted bee thereby.   30

Then Grieve, my Soul, thy vessell is so small
  And holds no more for such a Lovely Hee.
That strength's so little, Love scarce acts at all.
  That sight's so dim, doth scarce him lovely See.
    Grieve, grieve, my Soul, thou shouldst so pimping bee,   35
    Now Such a Price is here presented thee.

All sight's too little sight enough to make.
  All Strength's too little Love enough to reare.
All Vessells are too Small to hold or take

Enough Love up for Such a Lovely Deare.   40
How little to this Little's then thy ALL.
For Him whose Beauty saith all Love's too small?

My Lovely One, I fain would love thee much
    But all my Love is none at all I see,
Oh! let thy Beauty give a glorious tuch   45
    Upon my Heart, and melt to Love all mee.
    Lord melt me all up into Love for thee
    Whose Loveliness excells what love can bee.

---

27 Pinckted *orig.* Pinckt
28 Wooe *orig.* Woe
30 Enchanted *orig.* inchanted
33 so *ins.*
34 doth *orig.* is
38 to *ins.*

27.7M   13. MEDITATION. COL. 2.3. ALL THE TREASURES
1685   OF WISDOM.

Thou Glory Darkning Glory, with thy Flame
    Should all Quaint Metaphors teem ev'ry Bud
Of Sparkling Eloquence upon the Same
    It would appeare as dawbing pearls with mud.   [178]
    Nay Angells Wits are Childish tricks, and like   5
    The Darksom night unto thy Lightsom Light.

Oh! Choicest Cabbinet, more Choice than gold
    Or Wealthi'st Pearles wherein all Pearls of Price
All Treasures of Choice Wisdom manifold
    Inthroned reign. Thou Cabinet most Choice   10
    Not Scant to hold, not Staind with cloudy geere
    The Shining Sun of Wisdom bowling there.

Thou shining Golden Lanthorn with pain'd Lights
    Of Chrystall cleare, thy golden Candles flame,

Makes such a shine, as doth the Sun benights. 15
  It's but a smoaky vapor to the Same.
All Wisdom knead into a Chrystall Ball,
  Shines like the Sun in thee, its azure Hall.

Thou rowling Eye of Light, to thee are sent
  All Dazzling Beams of Shine, the Heavens distille. 20
All Wisdoms Troops do quarter in thy Tents
  And all her Treasures Cabin in thy tills.
  Be thou, Lord, mine: then I shall Wealthy bee,
  Enricht with Wisdoms Treasures, stought in thee.

That little Grain within my golden Bowle, 25
  Should it attempt to poise thy Talent cleare,
It would inoculate into my Soule.
  As illookt Impudence as ever were.
  But, loe, it stands amaizd, and doth adore,
  Thy Magazeen of Wisdom, and thy Store. 30

---

15 doth *orig.* doth so
20 distille *orig.* distills
24 stought *orig.* stoughd

14:9M   }   14.
10:11M   }   15. MEDITATIONS. HEB. 4.14. A GREAT
1685   }   HIGH PRIEST.

Raptures of Love, Surprizing Loveliness,
  That burst through Heavens all, in Rapid Flashes,
Glances guilt o're with Smiling Comliness!
  (Wonders do palefac'd Stand smit by such dashes).
  Glory itselfe Heartsick of Love doth ly 5
  Bleeding out Love o're Loveless mee, and dy.

Might I a glance of this bright brightness shew;
  Se it in him who gloriously is dresst:
A Gold Silk Stomacher of Purple, blew

Blancht o're with Orient Pearles being on his Breast: 10
And all his Robes being answerable, but
This Glory Seen, to that unseen's a Smut.

Yea, Beauteous Hee, in all his Glory stands,
Tendring himselfe to God, and Man: where hee
Doth Justice thus bespeake, Hold out thy hands: 15
Come, take thy Penworths now for mine of mee.
I'le pay the fine that thou seest meet to set
Upon their Heads: I'le dy to cleare their debts.

Out Rampant Justice steps in Sparkling White,
Him rends in twain, who on her Altar lies   20
A Lump of Glory flaming in her bright
Devouring Flames, to be my sacrifice.
Untill her Fire goes out well Satisfide.
And then he rose in Glory to abide.   [179]

To Heav'n went he, and in his bright Throne Sits   25
At Gods right hand pleading poor Sinners Cases.
With Golden Wedges he of Promise, splits
The Heav'ns ope, to shew what Glory 'braces.
And in its thickness thus with Arms extended,
Calls, come, come here, and ever be befriended.   30

Frost bitten Love, Frozen Affections! Blush;
What icy Chrystall mountain lodge you in?
What Wingless Wishes, Hopes pinfeatherd tush!
Sore Hooft Desires, hereof do in you spring?
Oh hard black Kirnell at the Coare! not pant?   35
Encastled in an heart of Adamant!

What strange Congealed Heart have I when I
Under such Beauty shining like the sun
Able to make Frozen Affection fly,
And Icikles of Frostbitt Love to run.   40
Yea, and Desires lockt in an heart of steel
Or Adamant, breake prison, nothing feel.

Lord may thy Priestly Golden Oares but make
  A rowing in my Lumpish Heart, thou'lt See
My Chilly, Numbd Affections Charm and break   45
  Out in a rapid Flame of Love to thee.
  Yea, they unto thyselfe will fly in flocks
  When thy Warm Sun my frozen Lake unlocks.

Be thou my High Priest, Lord; and let my name
  Ly in some Grave dug in those Pearly rocks   50
Upon thy Ephods shoulder piece, like flame
  Or graved in thy Breast Plate-Gem: brave Knops.
  Thou'lt then me beare before thy Fathers Throne
  Rowld up in Folds of Glory of thine own.

One of these Gems I beg, Lord, that so well   55
  Begrace thy Breast Plate, and thy Ephod cleaver.
To Stud my Crown therewith: or let me dwell
  Among their Sparkling, glancing shades for ever.
  I'st then be deckt in glory bright to Sing
  With Angells, Hallelujahs to my King.   60

---

37 when *orig.* under
40 Icikles *orig.* Ickles ; frostbitt *orig.* frostbitten
50 Pearly *orig.* p

6.1M   ⎱   16. MEDITATION. Lu. 7.16. A GREATE PROPHET
1685/6   ⎰   IS RISEN UP.

Leafe Gold, Lord of thy Golden Wedge o'relaid
  My Soul at first, thy Grace in e'ry part
Whose peart, fierce Eye thou such a Sight hadst made
  Whose brightsom beams could break into thy heart
  Till thy Curst Foe had with my Fist mine Eye   5
  Dasht out, and did my Soule Unglorify.

I cannot See, nor Will thy Will aright.
  Nor See to waile my Woe, my loss and hew

Nor all the shine in all the Sun can light
  My Candle, nor its Heate my Heart renew.   10
  See, waile, and Will thy Will, I must, or must
  From Heavens Sweet shine to Hells hot flame be thrust.

Grace then Conseald in God himselfe, did rowle
  Even Snow Ball like into a Sun ball shine
And nestles all its Beams buncht in thy Soule   15
  My Lord, that sparkle in Prophetick Lines.
  Oh! Wonder more than Wonderfull! this Will
  Lighten the Eye which Sight Divine did Spill.   [180]

What art thou, Lord, this Ball of Glory bright?
  A Bundle of Celestiall Beams up bound   20
In Graces band fixt in Heavens topmost height
  Pouring thy golden Beams thence, Circling round.
  Which shew thy Glory, and thy glories Way.
  And ery Where will make Celestiall Day.

Lord let thy Golden Beams pierce through mine Eye   25
  And leave therein an Heavenly Light to glaze
My Soule with glorious Grace all o're, whereby
  I may have Sight, and Grace in mee may blaze.
  Lord ting my Candle at thy Burning Rayes,
  To give a gracious Glory to thy Prayse.   30

Thou Lightning Eye, let Some bright Beames of thine
  Stick in my soul, to light and liven it:
Light, Life, and Glory, things that are Divine;
  I shall be grac'd withall for glory fit.
  My Heart then stufft with Grace, Light, Life, and Glee   35
  I'le Sacrifice in Flames of Love to thee.

---

21 in *orig.* up in

13.4M ⎫
1686   ⎭ 17. Meditations. Rev. 19.16. King of Kings.

A King, a King, a King indeed, a King
  Writh up in Glory! Glorie's glorious Throne
Is glorifide by him, presented him.
  And all the Crowns of Glory are his own.
  A King, Wise, Just, Gracious, Magnificent.   5
  Kings unto him are Whiffles, Indigent.

What is his Throne all Glory? Crown all Gay?
  Crown all of Brightest shine of Glory's Wealth?
This is a Lisp of Non-Sense. I should say,
  He is the Throne, and Crown of Glory 'tselfe.   10
  Should sun beams come to gilde his glory they
  Would be as 'twere to gild the Sun with Clay.

My Phancys in a Maze, my thoughts agast,
  Words in an Extasy; my Telltale Tongue
Is tonguetide, and my Lips are padlockt fast   15
  To see thy Kingly Glory in to throng.
  I can, yet cannot tell this Glory just,
  In Silence bury 't, must not, yet I must.

This King of Kings's Brave Kingdom doth Consist
  Of Glorious Angells, and Blesst Saint alone   20
Or Chiefly. Where all Beams of Glory twist
  Together, beaming from, lead to his throne
  Which Beams his Grace Coiles in a Wreath to Crown
  His, in the End in Endless Bright Renown.

His Two-Edg'd Sword, not murdering steel So base,   25
  Is made of Righteousness, unspotted, bright
Imbellisht o're with overflowing Grace
  Doth killing, Cure the sinner, kills Sin right.
  Makes milkwhite Righteousness, and Grace to reign,
  And Satan and his Cubs wish Sin ly slain.   30

Were all Kings deckt with sparkling Crowns, and arm'd
  With flaming Swords, and firy Courage traind   [181]
And led under their King Abaddon, Charmd
  In battell out against their foes disdaind.
  One Smiling look of this bright shine would fell   35
  Them and their Crowns of Glory all to Hell.

Thou art my king: let me not be thy shame.
  Thy Law my Rule: my Life thy Life in mee.
Thy Grace my Badge: my Glory bright thy Name.
  I am resolv'd to live, and dy with thee.   40
  Keep mee, thou King of Glory on Record.
  Thou art my King of Kings, and Lord of Lords.

---

11 gilde *orig.* guilde
12 gild *orig.* guild
27 Imbellisht *orig.* Imbellesht

29:6M ⎤ 18. MEDITATION. ISAI. 52.14. HIS VISSAGE
1686 ⎦ WAS MARR'D MORE THAN ANY MAN.

Astonisht Stand, my soule; why dost not start
  At this surprizing sight shewn here below?
Oh! let the twitch made by my bouncing Heart
  Gust from my breast this Enterjection, Oh!
  A Sight so Horrid, sure it's Mercies Wonder   5
  Rocks rend not at't, nor Heavens split asunder.

Souls Charg'd with Sin, Discharge at God, beside
  Firld up in Guilt, Wrapt in Sins Slough, and Slime.
Wills wed to Wickedness, Hearts stonifide
  Flinty Affections, Conscience Chalybdine   10
  Flooding the World with Horrid Crimes, arise
  Daring Almighty God Contemptuouswise.

Hence Vengeance rose with her fierce Troops in Buff,
  Soul-piercing Plagues, Heart-Aching Griefs, and Groans,

Woes Pickled in Revenges Powdering Trough: 15
  Pain fetching forth their Proofs out of the boanes.
  Doth all in Flames of Fire Surround them So
  Which they can ne're o'recome, nor undergo.

In this Sad Plight the richest Beauty Cleare,
  That th'bravest Flower, that bud was big with, wore,   20
Did glorify those Cheeks, whose Vissage were
  Marr'd more than any mans, and Form spoild more.
  Oh! Beauty beautifull, not toucht with vice!
  The fairest Flower in all Gods Paradise!

Stept in, and in its Glory 'Counters all.   25
  And in the Belly of this Dismall Cloud,
Of Woes in Pickle is gulpht up, whose Gall
  He dranke up quite. Whose Claws his Face up plow'd.
  Yet in these Furrows Sprang the brightest Shine
  That Glory's Sun could make, or Love Enshrine.   30

Then Vengeance's Troops are routed, Pickled Woe
  Heart-aching Griefes, Pains plowing to the boanes,
Soul piercing Plagues, all Venom do foregoe.
  The Curse now Cures; though th'Griefe procureth groans.
  As th'Angry Bee doth often lose her Sting,   35
  The Law was Cursless made in Cursing him.

And now his shining Love beams out its rayes
  My Soul, upon thy Heart to thaw the same:
To animate th'Affections till they blaze;
  To free from Guilt, and from Sins Slough, and shame.   [182]40
  Open thy Casement wide, let Glory in,
  To Guild thy Heart to be an Hall for him.

My Breast, be thou the ringing Virginalls:
  Ye mine Affections, their sweet Golden strings,
My Panting Heart, be thou for Stops, and Falls: 45
  Lord, let thy quick'ning Beams dance o're the Pins.
  Then let thy spirit this Sweet note resume,
  ALTASCHATH MICHTAM, in Seraphick Tune.

---

16 boanes *orig.* bones

14:9M ⎫   19. Meditation. Phil: 2.9. God hath highly
1686 ⎭   exalted him.

Looke till thy Looks look Wan, my Soule; here's ground.
   The Worlds bright Eye's dasht out: Day-Light so brave
Bemidnighted; the sparkling Sun, palde round
   With flouring Rayes lies buride in its grave
   The Candle of the World blown out, down fell.   5
   Life knockt a head by Death: Heaven by Hell.

Alas! this World all filld up to the brim
   With Sins, Deaths, Divills, Crowding men to Hell.
For whose reliefe Gods milke-white Lamb stept in
   Whom those Curst Imps did worry, flesh, and fell.   10
   Tread under foot, did Clap their Wings and so
   Like Dunghill Cocks over their Conquourd, Crow.

Brave Pious Fraud; as if the setting Sun
   Dropt like a Ball of Fire into the seas,
And so went out. But to the East come, run: 15
   You'l meet the morn shrinde with its flouring Rayes.
   This Lamb in laying of these Lyons dead;
   Drank of the brooke: and so lift up his Head.

Oh! Sweet, Sweet joy! These Rampant Fiends befoold:
   They made their Gall his Winding Sheete; although   20
They of the Heart-ach dy must, or be Coold
   With Inflamation of the Lungs, they know.
   He's Cancelling the Bond, and making Pay:
   And Ballancing Accounts: it's Reckoning day.

See, how he from the Counthouse shining went,   25
   In Flashing Folds of Burnisht Glory, and
Dasht out all Curses from the Covenant
   Hath Justices Acquittance in his hand
   Pluckt out Deaths sting, the Serpents Head did mall.
   The Bars and Gates of Hell he brake down all.   30

The Curse thus Lodgd within his Flesh, and Cloy'de,
  Can't run from him to his, so much he gave.
And like a Gyant he awoke beside:
  The Sun of Righteousness rose out of's Grave.
    And setting Foot upon its neck I sing   35
    Grave, where's thy Victory? Death, Where's thy Sting?

---

14 seas *orig.* sea

9:11M   ⎫   20. MEDITATION. PHIL. 2.9. GOD HATH HIGHLY
1686   ⎭   EXALTED HIM.

View all ye Eyes above, this Sight which flings
  Seraphick Phancies in Chill Raptures high,
A Turffe of Clay, and yet bright Glories King
  From dust to Glory Angell like to fly.   [183]
    A Mortall Clod immortalizde, behold,   5
    Flyes through the skies Swifter than Angells could.

Upon the Wings he of the Winde rode in
  His Bright Sedan, through all the silver Skies
And made the Azure Cloud his Charriot bring
  Him to the Mountain of Celestiall joyes.   10
    The Prince o'th'Aire durst not an Arrow spend
    While through his Realm his Charriot did ascend.

He did not in a Fiery Charriot's shine,
  And Whirlewinde, like Elias upward goe.
But th'golden Ladders Jasper rounds did climbe   15
  Unto the Heavens high from Earth below.
    Each Step trod on a Golden Stepping Stone
    Of Deity unto his very Throne.

Methinks I see Heavens Sparkling Courtiers fly,
  In flakes of Glory down him to attend: 20

And heare Heart Cramping notes of Melody,
   Surround his Charriot as it did ascend
   Mixing their Musick making e'ry String
   More to inravish as they this tune Sing.

God is Gone up with a triumphant shout   25
   The Lord with Sounding Trumpets melodies.
Sing Praise, Sing Praise, Sing Praise, Sing Praises out,
   Unto our King Sing praise Seraphickwise.
   Lift up your Heads ye lasting Doore they sing
   And let the King of Glory Enter in.   30

Art thou ascended up on high, my Lord,
   And must I be without thee here below?
Art thou the sweetest Joy the Heavens afford?
   Oh! that I with thee was! what shall I do?
   Should I pluck Feathers from an Angells Wing,   35
   They could not waft me up to thee my King.

Lend mee thy Wings, my Lord, I'st fly apace.
   My Soules Arms stud with thy strong Quills, true Faith,
My Quills then Feather with thy saving Grace,
   My Wings will take the Winde thy Word displai'th.   40
   Then I shall fly up to thy glorious Throne
   With my strong Wings whose Feathers are thine own.

---

41 up to *orig.* unto

13.1M   }   21. MEDITATION. PHIL. 2.9. GOD HATH HIGHLY
1686/7   }   EXALTED HIM.

What Glory's this, my Lord? Should one small Point
   Of one small Ray of't touch my Heart't would spring
Such joy as would an Adamant unjoynt
   If in't, and tare it, to get out and Sing.

T'run on Heroick golden Feet, and raise   5
Heart Ravishing Tunes, Curld with Celestiall praise.

Oh! Bright! Bright thing! I fain would something say:
  Lest Silence should indict me. Yet I feare
To say a Syllable lest at thy day
  I be presented for my Tattling here.   [184] 10
  Course Phancy, Ragged Faculties, alas!
  And Blunted Tongue don't Suit: Sighs Soile the Glass.

Yet Shall my mouth stand ope, and Lips let run
  Out gliding Eloquence on each light thing?
And shall I gag my mouth, and ty my Tongue,   15
  When Such bright Glory glorifies within?
  That makes my Heart leape, dancing to thy Lute?
  And shall my telltale tongue become a Mute?

Lord Spare I pray, though my attempts let fall
  A Slippery Verse upon thy Royall Glory.   20
I'le bring unto thine Altar th'best of all
  My Flock affords. I have no better story.
  I'le at thy Glory my dark Candle light.
  Not to descry the sun, but use by night.

A Golden Throne whose Banisters are Pearles,   25
  And Pomills Choicest Gems: Carbuncle-Stayes
Studded with Pretious Stones, Carv'd with rich Curles
  Of Polisht Art, Sending out flashing Rayes,
  Would him Surround with Glory, thron'de therein.
  Yet this is to thy Throne a dirty thing.   30

Oh! Glorious sight! Loe, How Bright Angells stand
  Waiting with Hat in hand on Him alone
That is Enthron'de, indeed at Gods right hand:
  Gods Heart itselfe being his Happy Throne.
  The Glory that doth from this Person fall,   35
  Fills Heaven with Glory, else there's none at all.

12:4M ⎫   22. MEDITATION. PHIL. 2.9. GOD HATH HIGHLY
1687 ⎭   EXALTED HIM.

When thy Bright Beams, my Lord, do strike mine Eye,
  Methinkes I then could truely Chide out right,
My Hide bound Soule that stands so niggardly
  That scarce a thought gets glorified by't.
  My Quaintest Metaphors are ragged Stuff,   5
  Making the Sun Seem like a Mullipuff.

Its my desire, thou shouldst be glorifi'de:
  But when thy Glory shines before mine eye,
I pardon Crave, lest my desire be Pride.
  Or bed thy Glory in a Cloudy sky.   10
  The Sun grows wan; and Angells palefac'd shrinke,
  Before thy shine, which I besmeere with Inke.

But shall the Bird sing forth thy Praise, and shall
  The little Bee present her thankfull Hum?
But I who see thy shining Glory fall   15
  Before mine Eyes, stand Blockish, Dull, and Dumb?
  Whether I speake, or speechless stand, I spy,
  I faile thy Glory: therefore pardon Cry.   [185]

But this I finde; My Rhymes do better suite
  Mine own Dispraise than tune forth praise to thee.   20
Yet being Chid, whether Consonant, or Mute,
  I force my Tongue to tattle, as you see.
  That I thy glorious Praise may Trumpet right,
  Be thou my Song, and make Lord, mee thy Pipe.

This Shining sky will fly away apace,   25
  When thy bright Glory splits the same to make
Thy Majesty a Pass, whose Fairest Face
  Too foule a Path is for thy Feet to take.
  What Glory then, shall tend thee through the sky
  Draining the Heaven much of Angells dry?   30

What Light then flame will in thy Judgment seate,
   'Fore which all men, and angells shall appeare?
How shall thy Glorious Righteousness them treate,
   Rend'ring to each after his Works done here?
   Then Saints With Angells thou wilt glorify: 35
   And burn Lewd Men, and Divells Gloriously.

One glimps, my Lord, of thy bright Judgment day,
   And Glory piercing through, like fiery Darts,
All Divells, doth me make for Grace to pray,
   For filling Grace had I ten thousand Hearts.   40
   I'de through ten Hells to see thy Judgment Day
   Wouldst thou but guild my Soule with thy bright Ray.

---

24 make *orig.* maketh
39 doth me *orig.* doth

21.6M ⎫
      ⎬ 23. MEDITATION. CANT. 4.8. MY SPOUSE.
1687 ⎭

Would God I in that Golden City were,
   With Jaspers Walld, all garnisht, and made Swash,
With Pretious Stones, whose Gates are Pearles most cleare
   And street Pure Gold, like to transparent Glass.
   That my dull Soule, might be inflamde to See   5
   How Saints and Angells ravisht are in Glee.

Were I but there, and could but tell my story,
   'T would rub those Walls of Pretious stones more bright:
And glaze those Gates of Pearle, with brighter Glory;
   And pave the golden Street with greater light.   10
   'T would in fresh Raptures saints, and Angells fling.
   But I poore Snake Crawl here, Scarce mudwalld in.

May my Rough Voice, and my blunt Tongue but Spell
   My Tale (for tune they can't) perhaps there may

Some Angell catch an end of't up, and tell   15
    In Heaven, when he doth return that way,
He'l make thy Palace, Lord, all over ring,
    With it in Songs, thy Saint, and Angells Sing.

I know not how to speak't, it is so good:
    Shall Mortall, and Immortall marry? nay,   20
Man marry God? God be a Match for Mud?
    The King of Glory Wed a Worm? mere Clay?
    This is the Case. The Wonder too in Bliss.
    Thy Maker is thy Husband. Hearst thou this?   [186]

My Maker, he my Husband? Oh! Strange joy!   25
    If Kings wed Worms, and Monarchs Mites wed should,
Glory spouse shame, a Prince a Snake or Fly
    An Angell Court an Ant, all Wonder would.
    Let Such wed Worms, Snakes, Serpents, Divells, Flyes.
    Less Wonder than the Wedden in our Eyes.   30

I am to Christ more base, than to a King
    A Mite, Fly, Worm, Ant, Serpent, Divell is;
Or Can be, being tumbled all in sin,
    And shall I be his Spouse? How good is this?
    It is too good to be declar'de to thee.   35
    But not too good to be believ'de by mee.

Yet to this Wonder, this is found in mee,
    I am not onely base but backward Coy,
When Christ doth Wooe: and till his spirit bee
    His Spokesman to Compell me I deny.   40
    I am so base and Froward to him, Hee
    Appears as Wonders Wonder, wedding mee.

Seing, Dear Lord, it's thus, thy spirit take
    And send thy Spokesman, to my Soul, I pray.
Thy saving Grace my Wedden Garment make: 45
    Thy spouses Frame into my soul Convay.

I then shall be thy Bride Espousd by thee
And thou my Bridesgroom Deare Espousde shalt bee.

---

3 Pearles *orig.* Peales
15 of't *orig.* oft
20 Immortall *orig.* immortall
48 shalt bee *orig.* by mee

6:9M   24. MEDITATION. EPH. 2.18. THROUGH HIM WE HAVE—
1687   —AN ACCESS—UNTO THE FATHER.

Was there a Palace of Pure Gold, all Ston'de
  And pav'de with Pearles, whose Gates Rich Jaspers were,
And Throne a Carbuncle, whose King Enthronde
  Sat on a Cushion all of Sunshine Cleare;
  Whose Crown a Bunch of Sun Beams was: I should   5
  Prize Such as in his favour shrine me would.

Thy Milke white Hand, my Glorious Lord, doth this:
  It opes this Gate, and me Conducts into
This Golden Palace whose rich Pavement is
  Of Pretious Pearles: and to this King also.   10
  Thus Thron'de, and Crown'd: whose Words are 'bellisht all
  With brighter Beams, than e're the Sun let fall.

But oh! Poore mee, thy sluggish servant, I
  More blockish than a block, as blockhead, stand.
Though mine Affections Quick as Lightning fly   15
  On toys, they snaile like move to kiss thy hand.
  My Coal-black doth thy Milke white hand avoide,
  That would above the Milky Way me guide.

What aim'st at, Lord? that I should be so Cross.
  My minde is Leaden in thy Golden Shine.   20
Though all o're Spirit, when this dirty Dross
  Doth touch it with its smutting leaden lines.

What Shall an Eagle t'catch a Fly thus run?
Or Angell Dive after a Mote i'th' Sun?   [187]

What Folly's this? I fain would take, I thinke,   25
   Vengeance upon myselfe: But I Confess,
I can't. Mine Eyes, Lord, Shed no Tears but inke.
   My handy Works, are Words, and Wordiness.
   Earth's Toyes ware Knots of my Affections, nay,
   Though from thy Glorious Selfe they're Stoole away.   30

Oh! that my heart was made thy Golden Box
   Full of Affections, and of Love Divine,
Knit all in Tassles, and in True-Love Knots,
   To garnish o're this Worthy Worke of thine.
   This Box and all therein more rich than Gold,   35
   In sacred Flames, I to thee offer would.

With thy rich Tissue my poore Soule array:
   And lead me to thy Fathers House above.
Thy Graces storehouse make my soule I pray.
   Thy Praise shall then ware Tassles of my Love.   40
   If thou Conduct mee in thy Fathers Wayes,
   I'le be the Golden Trumpet of thy Praise.

---

35 Box *orig.* Box all

22:11M ⎫
          ⎬   25. MEDITATION. EPH. 5.27. A GLORIOUS CHURCH.
1687 ⎭

Why Should my Bells, which Chime thy Praise, when thou
   My Shew-Bread, on thy Table wast, my King,
Their Clappers, or their Bell ropes want even now?
   Or those that can thy Changes sweetly ring?
   What is a Scar-Fire broken out? No, no.   5
   The Bells would backward ring if it was So.

Its true: and I do all things backward run,
  Poor Pillard I have a Sad tale to tell:
My Soule Starke nakt, rowld all in mire, undone.
  Thy Bell may tole my passing Peale to Hell.   10
  None in their Winding sheet more naked stay
  Nor Dead than I. Hence oh! the Judgment Day.

When I behold Some Curious Piece of Art,
  Or Pritty Bird, Flower, Star, or Shining Sun,
Poure out o'reflowing Glory: oh! my Heart   15
  Achs Seing how my thoughts in Snick-snarls run.
  But all this Glory to my Lord's a spot
  While I in Stead of any, am all blot.

But, my sweet Lord, what glorious robes are those
  That thou hast brought out of thy Grave for thine?   20
They do out shine the Sun-Shine, Grace the Rose.
  I leape for joy to thinke, shall these be mine?
  Such are, as waite upon thee in thy Wars,
  Cloathd with the Sun, and Crowned with twelve Stars.

Dost thou adorn some thus, and why not mee?   25
  Ile not believe it, Lord, thou art my Chiefe.
Thou me Commandest to believe in thee.
  I'l not affront thee thus with Unbeliefe.
  Lord, make my Soule Obedient: and when so,
  Thou saist Believe, make it reply, I do.   [188]30

I fain the Choicest Love my Soule Can get,
  Would to thy Gracious Selfe a Gift present.
But cannot now unscrew Loves Cabbinet.
  Say not this is a Niggards Complement:
  For Seing it is thus I choose now rather   35
  To send thee th'Cabbinet; and Pearle together.

15:1M ⎫ 26. MEDITATION. ACT. 5.31. To GIVE —
1688 ⎭   FORGIVENESS OF SINS.

My Noble Lord, thy Nothing Servant I
  Am for thy sake out with my heart, that holds,
So little Love for Such a Lord: I Cry
  * * * * * *
    How should I be but angry thus to see   5
    My Heart so hidebound in her Acts to thee?

Thou art a Golden Theame: but I am lean,
  A Leaden Oritor upon the Same.
Thy Golden Web excells my Dozie Beam:
  Whose Linsy-Wolsy Loom deserves thy blame.   10
  It's all defild, unbiasst too by sin:
  An hearty Wish for thee's scarce shot therein.

It pitties mee who pitty Cannot show,
  That such a Worthy Theame abusd should bee.
I am undone, unless thy Pardons doe   15
  Undoe my sin I did, undoing mee.
  My sins are greate, and grieveous ones, therefore
  Carbuncle Mountains can't wipe out their Score.

But thou, my Lord, dost a Free Pardon bring.
  Thou giv'st Forgiveness: yet my heart through sin,   20
Hath naught but naught to file thy Gift up in,
  An hurden Haump doth Chafe a Silken Skin.
  Although I pardons beg, I scarce can See,
  When thou giv'st pardons, I give praise to thee.

O bad at best! what am I then at worst?   25
  I want a Pardon: and when pardon'd, want
A Thankfull Heart: Both which thou dost disburst.
  Giv'st both, or neither: for which Lord I pant.
  Two Such good things at once! methinks I could
  Avenge my heart, lest it should neither hold.   30

Lord tap mine Eyes, seing such Grace in thee,

So little doth affect my Graceless Soule.
And take my teares in lue of thanks of mee,
   New make my heart: then take it for thy tole.
   Thy Pardons then will make my heart to sing   35
   Its Michtam-David: With Sweet joy Within.

---

10 Whose *orig.* That all defild

1:5M ⎫   27. Meditation. Col. 1.19. In Him should all
1688 ⎭   Fulness Dwell.

Oh! Wealthy Theam! Oh! Feeble Phancy: I
   Must needs admire, when I recall to minde,
That's Fulness, This it's Emptiness, though spy
   I have no Flowring Brain thereto inclinde.
   My Damps do out my fire. I cannot though   5
   I would Admire, finde heate enough thereto.   [189]

What shall I say? Such rich rich Fullness would
   Make Stammering Tongues speake smoothly, and Enshrine
The Dumb mans mouth with silver streams like gold
   Of Eloquence making the Aire to Chime.   10
   Yet I am Tonguetide stupid, sensless stand,
   And Drier drain'd than is my pen I hand.

Oh! Wealthy Box: more Golden far than Gold
   A Case more Worth than Wealth: a richer Delph,
Than Rubies; Cabbinet, than Pearles here told.   15
   A Purse more glittering than Glory 'tselfe
   A Golden Store House of all Fulness: shelfe,
   Of Heavenly Plate. All Fulness in thyselfe.

Oh! Godhead Fulness! There doth in thee flow
   All Wisdoms Fulness: Fulness of all strength: 20
Of Justice, Truth, Love, Holiness also
   And Graces Fulness to its upmost length

Do dwell in thee. Yea and thy Fathers Pleasure.
Thou art their Cabbinet, and they thy Treasure.

All Office Fulness with all Office Gifts   25
    Imbossed are in thee, Whereby thy Grace,
Doth treat both God, and Man, bringst up by hifts
    Black sinner and White Justice to imbrace.
    Making the Glory of Gods Justice shine:
    And making Sinners to Gods glory Climbe.   30

All Graces Fulness dwells in thee, from Whom
    The Golden Pipes of all Convayance ly,
Through which Grace to our Clayie Panchins Come.
    Fullness of Beauty, and Humanity.
    Oh! Glorious Flow're; Glory, and sweetness splice,   35
    In thee to Grace, and Sweeten Paradise!

But, oh! the Fathers Love! herein most vast!
    Angells, engrave't in brightest Marble, t'see
This Flower that in his Bosom sticks so fast,
    Stuck in the Bosom of Such stuffe as wee   40
    That both his Purse, and all his Treasure thus,
    Should be so full, and freely sent to us.

Were't not more than my heart can hold, or hord,
    Or than my Tongue can tell; I thus would pray,
Let him in Whom all Fulness Dwells, dwell, Lord   45
    Within my Heart: this Treasure therein lay.
    I then shall Sweetly tune thy Praise, When hee
    In Whom all Fulness dwells, doth dwell in mee.

---

3 it's *orig.* is
11 Tonguetide *orig.* Tongtid
14 Wealth *orig.* Welth
15 Pearles *orig.* Peales
22 to *orig.* unto
26 thy *ins.*
35 and *ins.*

2:7M   28. MEDITATION. JOH: 1:16. OF HIS FULNESS WEE
1688   ALL RECEIVE: AND GRACE —

When I Lord, send some Bits of Glory home,
  (For Lumps I lack) my Messenger, I finde,
Bewildred, lose his Way being alone
    In my befogg'd Dark Phancy, Clouded minde.   [190]
    Thy Bits of Glory pack't in shreds of Praise   5
    My Messenger doth lose, losing his Wayes.

Lord Cleare the Coast: and let thy sweet sun shine.
  That I may better Speed a Second time:
Oh! fill my Pipkin with thy Blood red Wine:
    I'l drinke thy Health: To pledge thee is no Crime.   10
    Although I but an Earthen Vessell bee
    Convay some of thy Fulness into mee.

Thou, thou my Lord, art full, top full of Grace,
  The Golden Sea of Grace: Whose springs thence come,
And Pretious Drills, boiling in ery place.   15
    Untap thy Cask, and let my Cup Catch some.
    Although it's in an Earthen Vessells Case.
    Let it no Empty Vessell be of Grace.

Let thy Choice Caske, shed, Lord, into my Cue
  A Drop of Juyce presst from thy Noble Vine.   20
My Bowl is but an Acorn Cup, I sue
    But for a Drop: this will not empty thine.
    Although I'me in an Earthen Vessells place,
    My Vessell make a Vessell, Lord, of Grace.

My Earthen Vessell make thy Font also: 25
  And let thy Sea my spring of Grace in't raise.
Spring up oh Well; my Cup with Grace make flow.
    Thy Drops will on my Vessell ting thy Praise.
    I'le Sing this Song, when I these Drops Embrace.
    My Vessell now's a Vessell of thy Grace.   30

3 Bewildred, *orig.* Bewildred, and
4 Phancy *orig.* Pancy *orig.* f
26 thy *ins.*
28 Drops *orig.* Dops

11.9M ⎱ 29. MEDITATION. JOH. 20.17. MY FATHER, AND YOUR
1688 ⎰   FATHER, TO MY GOD, AND YOUR GOD.

My shattred Phancy stole away from mee,
  (Wits run a Wooling over Edens Parke)
And in Gods Garden Saw a golden Tree,
    Whose Heart was All Divine, and gold its barke.
    Whose glorious limbs, and fruitfull branches strong   5
    With Saints, and Angells bright are richly hung.

Thou! thou! my Deare-Deare Lord, art this rich Tree.
  The Tree of Life Within Gods Paradise.
I am a Withred Twig, dri'de fit to bee
    A Chat Cast in thy fire, writh off by Vice.   10
    Yet if thy Milke white-Gracious Hand will take mee
    And grafft mee in this golden Stock thou'lt make * * *

Thou'lt make me then its Fruite, and Branch to Spring.
  And though a nipping Eastwinde blow, and all.
Hells Nymps with Spite their Dog's sticks thereat ding   15
  To Dash the Grafft off, and its fruits to fall.
    Yet I shall stand thy Grafft and Fruits that are
    Fruits of the Tree of Life thy Grafft shall beare.   [191]

I being grafft in thee there up do stand
  In us Relations all that mutuall are.   20
I am thy Patient, Pupill, Servant, and
    Thy Sister, Mother, Doove, Spouse, Son, and Heire
    Thou art my Priest, Physician, Prophet, King,
    Lord, Brother, Bridegroom, Father, Ev'ry thing.

I being grafft in thee am graffted here   25
　　Into thy Family, and kindred Claim
To all in Heaven, God, Saints, and Angells there.
　　I thy Relations my Relations name.
　　Thy Fathers mine, thy God my God, and I
　　With Saints, and Angells draw Affinity.   30

My Lord, what is it that thou dost bestow?
　　The Praise on this account fills up, and throngs
Eternity brimfull, doth overflow
　　The Heavens vast with rich Angelick songs.
　　How Should I blush? how Tremble at this thing.   35
　　Not having yet my Gam-Ut, learnd to Sing.

But, Lord, as burnisht Sun Beams forth out fly
　　Let Angell-Shine forth in my Life out flame,
That I may grace thy gracefull Family
　　And not to thy Relations be a shame.   40
　　Make mee thy Grafft, be thou my Golden Stock.
　　Thy Glory then I'le make my fruits and Crop.

---

31 is it that *orig.* ist
41 my *ins.*

6:11M ⎫
　　　　⎬　30. MEDITATION. 2.COR. 5.17.—HE IS A NEW CREATURE.
1688   ⎭

The Daintiest Draught thy Pensill ever Drew:
　　The finest vessell, Lord, thy fingers fram'de:
The stateli'st Palace Angells e're did view,
　　Under thy Hatch betwixt Decks here Contain'd
　　Broke, marred, spoild, undone, Defild doth ly   5
　　In Rubbish ruinde by thine Enemy.

What Pittie's this? Oh Sunshine Art! What Fall?
　　Thou that more Glorious wast than glories Wealth!

More Golden far than Gold! Lord, on whose Wall
  Thy scutchons hung, the Image of thyselfe!   10
It's ruinde, and must rue, though Angells should
  To hold it up heave while their Heart strings hold.

But yet thou Stem of Davids stock when dry
  And shrivled held, although most green was lopt   [192]
Whose sap a Sovereign sodder is, whereby   15
  The breach repared is in which its dropt.
  Oh Gracious Twig! thou Cut off? bleed rich juyce
  T'Cement the Breach, and Glories shine reduce?

Oh Lovely One! how doth thy Loveliness
  Beam through the Chrystall Casements of the Eyes   20
Of Saints, and Angells sparkling Flakes of Fresh
  Heart Ravishing Beauty, filling up their joyes?
  And th'Divells too; if Envies Pupills stood
  Not peeping there these Sparkling Rayes t'exclude?

Thou Rod of Davids Root, Branch of his Bough   25
  My Lord, repare thy Palace. Deck thy Place.
I'm but a Flesh, and Blood bag: Oh! do thou
  Sill, Plate, Ridge, Rib, and Rafter me with Grace.
  Renew my Soule, and guild it all within:
  And hang thy saving Grace on ery Pin.   30

My Soule, Lord, make thy shining Temple, pave
  Its Floore all o're with Orient Grace: thus gild
It o're with Heavens gold: Its Cabbins have
  Thy Treasuries with Choicest thoughts up filld.
  Pourtray thy Glorious Image round about   35
  Upon thy Temple Walls within, and Out.

Garnish thy Hall with Gifts, Lord, from above
  With that Rich Coate of Male thy Righteousness,
Truths Belt, the spirits Sword, the Buckler Love
  Hopes Helmet, and the shield of Faith kept fresh.   40
  The Scutchons of thy Honour make my sign.
  As Garland Tuns are badges made of Wine.

New mould, new make me thus, me new Create
   Renew in me a Spirit right, pure, true.
Lord make me thy New Creature, then new make   45
   All things to thy New Creature here anew.
New Heart, New thoughts, New Words, New wayes likewise.
New Glory then shall to thyselfe arise.

---

2 vessell *orig.* vessill
6 thine *orig.* the
32 gild *orig.* guild
38 Male *orig.* Meale
39 Belt *orig.* Breast Plate

17.12M   ⎱   31. MEDITATION. 1.COR. 3.21.22. ALL THINGS
1688   ⎰   ARE YOURS.

Begrac'de with Glory, gloried with Grace,
   In Paradise I was, when all Sweet shines
Hung dangling on this Rosy World to face
   Mine Eyes, and Nose, and Charm mine Eares with Chimes.
   All these were golden Tills the which did hold   5
   My Evidences wrapt in glorious folds.

But as a Chrystall Glass, I broke, and lost
   That Grace, and Glory I was fashion'd in   [193]
And cast this Rosy World with all its Cost
   Into the Dunghill Pit, and Puddle Sin.   10
   All right I lost in all Good things, each thing
   I had did hand a Vean of Venom in.

Oh! Sad-Sad thing! Satan is now turnd Cook:
   Sin is the Sauce he gets for ev'ry Dish.
I cannot bite a bit of Bread or Roote   15
   But what is Sopt therein, and Venomish.
   Right's lost in what's my Right. Hence I do take
   Onely what's poison'd by th'infernall Snake.

But this is not the Worst: there's worse than this.
  My Tast is lost; no bit tasts sweet to mee,   20
But what is Dipt all over in this Dish.
  Of Ranck ranck Poyson: this my sauce must bee.
  Hell Heaven is, Heaven hell, yea Bitter Sweet:
  Poison's my Food: Food poison in't doth keep.

What e're we want, we cannot Cry for, nay,   25
  If that we could, we could not have it thus.
The Angell's can't devise, nor yet Convay
  Help in their Golden Pipes from God to us.
  But thou my Lord, (Heart leape for joy and Sing)
  Hast done the Deed: and't makes the Heavens ring.   30

By mee all lost, by thee all are regain'd.
  All things are thus fall'n now into thy hande.
And thou Steep'st in thy Blood what sin had Stain'd
  That th'Stains and Poisons may not therein Stand.
  And having stuck thy Grace all o're the Same   35
  Thou giv'st it as a Glorious Gift again.

Cleare up my Right, my Lord, in thee, and make
  Thy Name Stand Dorst upon my soule in print.
In Grace I mean, that So I may partake
  Of what I lost, in thee, and of thee in't.   40
  I'l take it then, Lord, at thy hand, and sing
  Out Hallelujah for thy Grace therein.

28.2M   ⎫   32. MEDITATION. 1.COR. 3.22. WHETHER PAUL
1689   ⎬   OR APOLLOS, OR CEPHAS.

Thy Grace, Deare Lord, 's my golden Wrack, I finde
  Screwing my Phancy into ragged Rhimes,
Tuning thy Praises in my feeble minde
  Untill I come to strike them on my Chimes.

Were I an Angell bright, and borrow could   5
King Davids Harp I would them play on gold.

But plung'd I am, my minde is puzzled,
  When I would Spin my Phancy thus unspun,
In finest Twine of Praise I'm muzzled
  My tazzled Thoughts twirld into snick-snarls run.   [194]10
  Thy Grace, my Lord, is such a glorious thing,
  It doth Confound me when I would it Sing.

Eternall Love an Object mean did smite
  Which by the Prince of Darkness was beguilde.
That from this Love it ran and Sweld with spite   15
  And in the way with filth was all defilde
  Yet must be reconcild, cleansd, and begrac'te
  Or from the fruits of Gods first Love displac'te.

Then Grace, my Lord, wrought in thy Heart a vent,
  Thy soft soft hand to this hard worke did goe,   20
And to the Milke White Throne of Justice went
  And entred bond that Grace might overflow.
  Hence did thy Person to my Nature ty
  And bleed through humane Veans to Satisfy.

Oh! Grace, Grace, Grace! this Wealthy Grace doth lay   25
  Her Golden Channells from thy Fathers throne,
Into our Earthen Pitchers to Convay
  Heavens Aqua Vitæ to us for our own,
  O! let thy Golden Gutters run into
  My Cup this Liquour till it overflow.   30

Thine Ordinances, Graces Wine-fats where
  Thy Spirits Walkes, and Graces runs doe ly
And Angells waiting stand with holy Cheere
  From Graces Conduite Head, with all Supply.
  These Vessells full of Grace are, and the Bowls   35
  In which their Taps do run, are pretious Souls.

Thou to the Cup dost say (that Catch this Wine,)
  This Liquour, Golden Pipes, and Wine fats plain,
Whether Paul, Apollos, Cephas, all are thine.
  Oh Golden Word! Lord Speake it ore again.   40
  Lord Speake it home to me, say these are mine,
  My Bells shall then thy Praises bravely chime.

---

13 Love *orig.* Love did
24 bleed *orig.* bled
37 Cup *orig.* Cups ; Catch *orig.* Catching

7:5M
1689 } 33. MEDITATION. 1 COR. 3.22 LIFE IS YOURES.

My Lord my Life, can Envy ever bee
  A Golden Vertue? Then would God I were
Top full thereof untill it colours mee
  With yellow streaks for thy Deare sake most Deare,
  Till I be Envious made by't at myselfe.   5
  As scarcely loving thee my Life, my Health.

Oh! what strange Charm encrampt my Heart with spite
  Making my Love gleame out upon a Toy?
Lay out Cart-Loads of Love upon a mite?
  Scarce lay a mite of Love on thee, my Joy?   10
  Oh, Lovely thou! shalt not thou loved bee?
  Shall I ashame thee thus? Oh! Shame for mee!   [195]

Nature's amazde, Oh monstrous thing Quoth shee,
  Not Love my life? What Violence doth split
True Love, and Life, that they should sunder'd bee?   15
  She doth not lay such Eggs, nor on them sit.
  How do I sever then my Heart with all
  Its Powers whose Love scarce to my Life doth crawle.

Glory lin'de out a Paradise in Power
  Where e'ry seed a Royall Coach became   20

For Life to ride in, to each shining Flower.
  And made mans Flower with glory all ore flame.
  Hells Inkfac'de Elfe black Venom Spat upon
  The Same, and killd it. So that Life is gone.

Life thus abusde fled to the golden Arke,   25
  Lay lockt up there in Mercie's Seate inclosde:
Which did incorporate it whence its Sparke
  Enlivens all things in this Arke inclosde.
  Oh, glorious Arke! Life's Store-House full of Glee!
  Shall not my Love safe lockt up ly in thee?   30

Lord arke my Soule safe in thyselfe, whereby
  I and my Life again may joyned bee.
That I may finde what once I did destroy
  Again Conferde upon my soul in thee.
  Thou art this Golden Ark, this Living Tree   35
  Where life lies treasurde up for all in thee.

Oh! Graft me in this Tree of Life within
  The Paradise of God, that I may live.
Thy Life make live in mee; I'le then begin
  To bear thy Liveing Fruits, and them forth give.   40
  Give mee my Life this way; and I'le bestow
  My Love on thee my Life, and it shall grow.

25.9m ⎫
        ⎬ 34. MEDITATION. 1 COR. 3.22. DEATH IS YOURS.
1689   ⎭

My Lord I fain would Praise thee Well but finde
  Impossibilities blocke up my pass.
My tongue Wants Words to tell my thoughts, my Minde
  Wants thoughts to Comprehend thy Worth. alas!
  Thy Glory far Surmounts my thoughts, my thoughts   5
  Surmount my Words: Hence little Praise is brought.

But seing Non-Sense very Pleasant is
　To Parents, flowing from the Lisping Child,
I Conjue to thee, hoping thou in this
　Wilt finde some hearty Praise of mine Enfoild,   10
　But though my Pen dropd golden Words, yet would
　Thy Glory far out shine my Praise in Gold.   [196]

Poor wretched man Death's Captive stood full Chuffe
　But thou my Gracious Lord didst finde reliefe.
Thou King of Glory didst to handy cuff   15
　With King of Terrours, and dasht out his Teeth.
　Pluckt'st out his sting, his Poyson quelst, his head
　To pieces brakest: hence Cruell Death lies Dead.

And still thou by thy gracious Chymistry,
　Dost of his Carkass Cordialls make rich, High,   20
To free from Death makst Death a remedy:
　A Curb to sin, a spur to Piety.
　Heavens brightsom Light shines out in Death's Dark Cave.
　The Golden Dore of Glory is the Grave.

The Painter lies who pensills death's Face grim   25
　With White bare butter Teeth bare Staring bones,
With Empty Eyeholes, Ghostly Lookes which fling
　Such Dread to see as raiseth Deadly groans,
　For thou hast farely Washt Deaths grim grim face
　And made his Chilly finger-Ends drop grace.   30

Death Tamde, subdude, Washt fair by thee! Oh Grace!
　Made Usefull thus! thou unto thine dost say
Now Death is yours, and all it doth in't brace
　The Grave's a Down bed now made for your clay.
　Oh! Happiness! How should our Bells hereby   35
　Ring Changes, Lord, and praises trust with joy.

Say I am thine, My Lord: Make me thy bell
　To ring thy Praise. Then Death is mine indeed.
A Hift to Grace, a spur to Duty; Spell
　To Fear; a Frost to nip each [***]hty Weede.   40

A Golden doore to Glory. Oh! I'le sing
This Triumph! o're the Grave! Death where's thy sting?

---

10 Wilt *orig.* Will
11 Pen dropd *orig.* Pell drilld
13 stood full *ins.*
14 Gracious *orig.* Graceous
15 Glory *orig.* Terr
27 Ghostly *orig.* Gostly
32 thus! *orig.* thus,
34 bed *orig.* now ; now *ins.*
39 a *ins.*
40 [***]hty *ins.*

19:11M ⎫
         ⎬   35. MEDITATION. 1 COR. 3.22. THINGS PRESENT.
1689   ⎭

Oh! that I ever felt what I profess.
　'T would make me then the happi'st man alive.
Ten thousand Worlds of Saints can't make this less
　　By living on't, but it would make them thrive.
　　Those Loaves and Fishes are not lessened   5
　　Nor Pasture overstockt, by being fed.

Lord am I thine? art thou, Lord, mine? So rich!
　How doth thy Wealthy bliss branch out thy sweets
Through all things Present? These the Vent-holes which
　　Let out those Ravishing Joys our souls to greet?   10
　　Impower my Powers, Sweet Lord, till up they raise
　　My 'ffections that thy glory on them blaze.   [197]

How many things are there now, who display'th?
　How many Acts each thing doth here dispense?
How many Influences each thing hath?   15
　　How many Contraries each Influence?
　　How many Contraries from Things do flow?
　　From Acts? from Influences? Who can show?

How Glorious then is he that doth all raise
　Rule and Dispose and make them all Conspire　　　　　　20
In all their Jars, and Junctures, Good-bad wayes
　To meliorate the selfe same Object higher?
　Earth, Water, Fire, Winds, Herbs, Trees, Beasts and Men,
　Angells, and Divells, Bliss, Blasts, advance one stem?

Hell, Earth, and Heaven with their Whole Troops, come　　25
　Contrary Windes, Grace, and Disgrace, Soure, Sweet,
Wealth, Want, Health, Sickness, to Conclude in Sum
　All Providences Works in this good meet?
　Who, who can do't, but thou, my Lord? and thou
　Dost do this thing; yea thou performst it now.　　　　　30

Oh, that the Sweets of all these Windings, Spoute
　Might, and these Influences streight, and Cross,
Upon my Soule, to make thy shine breake out
　That Grace might in get and get out my dross!
　My Soule up lockt then in this Clod of Dust　　　　　　35
　Would lock up in't all Heavenly Joyes most just.

But oh! thy Wisdom, Lord! thy Grace! thy Praise!
　Open mine Eyes to see the Same aright.
Take off their film, my sins, and let the Rayes
　Of thy bright Glory on my peepholes light.　　　　　　40
　I fain would love and better love thee Should,
　If 'fore me thou thy Loveliness unfold.

Lord, Cleare my sight: thy Glory then out dart:
　And let thy Rayes beame Glory in mine eye
And Stick thy Loveliness upon my heart,　　　　　　　　45
　Make me the Couch on which thy Love doth ly.
　Lord make my heart thy bed, thy heart make mine.
　Thy Love bed in my heart, bed mine in thine.

---

3 Ten orig. Th
5 Loaves orig. Loves
8 bliss orig. bless
10 our orig. out

16:1M ⎫
1689 ⎭   36. MEDITATION. 1 COR. 3.32. THINGS TO COME YOURS.

What rocky heart is mine? My pincky Eyes
   Thy Grace spy blancht, Lord, in immensitie.
But finde the Sight me not to meliorize,
   O Stupid Heart! What strang-strange thing am I?   [198]
   I many months do drown in Sorrows spring   5
   But hardly raise a sigh to blow down sin.

To find thee Lord, thus overflowing kinde,
   And t'finde mee thine, thus overflowing vile,
A Riddle seems unrivetted I finde.
   This reason saith, is hard to reconcile,   10
   Dost Vileness choose? Or can't thy kindness shown
   Me meliorate? Or am I not thine own?

The first two run thy glory would to Shame.
   The last plea doth my Soule to hell Confine.
My Faith therefore doth all these Pleas disdain.   15
   Thou kindness art, it saith, and I am thine.
   Upon this banck it doth on tiptoes stand
   To ken o're Reasons head at Graces hand.

But Did I say, I wonder, Lord, to spie
   Thyselfe so kind; and I so vile yet thine?   20
I eate my Word: and wonder more that I
   No viler am, though all ore vile do shine.
   As full of sin I am, as Egge of meate.
   Yet finde thy golden Rod my sin to treate.

Nay did I say, I wonder t'see thy store   25
   Of kindnesses, yet me thus vile with all?
I now unsay my say; I wonder more
   Thou dash me not to pieces with thy maule,
   But in the bed, Lord, of thy goodness lies
   The Reason of't, which makes my Wonders rise.   30

For now I wonder t'feele how I thus feele.
  My Love leapes into Creatures bosoms; and
Cold sorrows fall into my Soule as Steel,
  When faile they, yet [***]is[*] thy Love's White hand.
  I scarce know what t'make of myselfe. Wherefore   35
  I crave a Pardon, Lord, for thou hast store.

How wondrous rich art thou? Thy storehouse vast
  Holdes more ten thousandfold told ore and ore
Than this Wide World Can hold. The doore unhasp.
  And bring me thence a Pardon out therefore.   40
  Thou stoughst the World so tite with present things
  That things to Come, though crowd full hard, can't in.

These things to Come, tread on the heels of those.
  The presents breadth doth with the broad world run.
The Depth and breadth of things to come out goes   45
  Unto Times End which bloweth out the Sun.
  Their breadth and length meate out Eternity.
  These are the things that in thy storehouse ly.   [199]

A Cockle shell contains this World as well
  As can this World thy Liberallness contain.   50
And by thy Will these present things all fall
  Unto thy Children for their present gain.
  And things to Come too, to Eternity.
  Thou Willedst them: they're theirs by Legacy.

But am I thine? Oh! what strange thing's in mee?   55
  Enricht thus by thy Legacy? yet finde
When one small Twig's broke off, the breach should bee
  Such an Enfeebling thing upon my minde.
  Then take a pardon from thy Store, and twist
  It in my soule for help. 'Twill not be mist.   60

I am asham'd to say I love thee do.
  But dare not for my Life, and soule deny't.
Yet wonder much Love's springs should lie so low
  Thy Lovliness its Object shines so bright.

Shall all the Beams of Love upon me shine? 65
And shall my Love Love's Object still make pine?

I'me surely made a Gazing stock to all:
The Holy Angells Wonder: and the Mock
Of Divells (pining that they misse it all)
To see these beams gild me a stupid stock. 70
Thy Argument is good, Lord point it, come
Let't lance my heart, till True Loves Veane doth run.

But that there is a Crevice for one hope
To creep in, and this Message to Convay
That I am thine, makes me refresh. Lord ope 75
The Doore So wide that Love may scip, and play.
My spirits then shall dance thy Praise. I'me thine.
And Present things with things to come are mine.

---

1 pincky *orig.* pinky
5 spring *orig.* springs
6 sin *orig.* sins
15 these *orig.* Pleas
35 scarce *orig.* scare
44 doth *orig.* do
46 Unto *orig.* [*******] the End of
47 Their *orig.* These
66 Love's *orig.* Love object
70 gild *orig.* guild

4:3M
1690 } 37. MEDITATION. 1 COR. 3.23. YOU ARE CHRIST'S.

My Soule, Lord, quailes to thinke that I should bee
So high related, have such Colours faire
Stick in my Hat, from Heaven: yet should see
My soule thus blotcht: Hells Liveries to beare.
What Thine? New-naturizd? Yet this Relation 5
Thus barren, though't's a Priviledg-Foundation?

Shall I thy Vine branch be, yet grapes none beare?
  Grafft in thy Olive stand: and fatness lack?
A shackeroon, a Ragnell yet an Heire?
  Thy Spouse, yet; oh! my Wedden Ring thus slack?   10
  Should Angel-Feathers plume my Cap I should
  Be swash? but oh! my Heart hereat grows Cold.   [200]

What is my Title but an empty Claim?
  Am I a fading Flower within thy Knot?
A Rattle, or a gilded Box, a Flame   15
  Of Painted Fire, a glorious Weedy spot?
  The Channell ope of Union, the ground
  Of Wealth, Relation: yet I'me barren found?

What am I thine, and thou not mine? or dost
  Not thou thy spouse joyn in thy Glory Cleare?   20
Is my Relation to thee but a boast?
  Or but a blustring say-so, or spruice jeere?
  Should Roses blow more late, sure I might get,
  If thine, some Prim-Rose, or Sweet Violet?

Make me thy Branch to bare thy Grapes, Lord, feed   25
  Mee with thy bunch of Raisins of the Sun.
Me stay with apples: let me eate indeed
  Fruites of the tree of Life: it's richly hung.
  Am I thy Child, Son, Heir, thy spouse, yet gain
  Not of the Rights that these Relations claim?   30

Am I hop't on thy knees, yet not at ease?
  Sunke in thy bosom, yet thy Heart not meet?
Lodgd in thine Arms? yet all things little please?
  Sung Sweetly, yet finde not this Singing Sweet?
  Set at thy Table, yet scarce tast a Dish   35
  Delicious? Hugd, yet seldom gain a Kiss?

Why? Lord, why thus? Shall I in Question Call
  All my Relation to thyselfe? I know
It is no Gay to please a Child withall

But is the Ground whence Priviledges flow.   40
Then ope the sluce: let something spoute on me.
Then I shall in a better temper bee.

---

10 Ring *orig.* ring
12 hereat *ins.*
15 gilded *orig.* guilded
28 of *ins.*

6:5M   38. MEDITATION. 1 JOH. 2.1. AN ADVOCATE
1690   WITH THE FATHER.

Oh! What a thing is Man? Lord, Who am I?
   That thou shouldst give him Law (Oh! golden Line)
To regulate his Thoughts, Words, Life thereby.
   And judge him Wilt thereby too in thy time.
   A Court of Justice thou in heaven holdst   5
   To try his Case while he's here housd on mould.

How do thy Angells lay before thine eye.
   My Deeds both White, and Black I dayly doe?
How doth thy Court thou Pannellst there them try?
   But flesh complains. What right for this? let's know   10
   For right, or wrong I can't appeare unto't.
   And shall a Sentence Pass on such a Suite?   [201]

Soft; blemish not this golden Bench, or place.
   Here is no Bribe, nor Colourings to hide
Nor Pettifogger to befog the Case   15
   But Justice hath her Glory here well tri'de.
   Her Spotless Law all spotted Cases tends
   Without Respect or Disrespect them ends.

God's Judge himselfe: and Christ Atturny is,
   The Holy Ghost Regesterer is founde.   20
Angells the Sergeants are, all Creatures kiss

The booke, and doe as Evidences abounde.
All Cases pass according to pure Law
And in the sentence is no Fret, nor flaw.

What saist, my soule? Here all thy Deeds are tri'de.   25
Is Christ thy Advocate to pleade thy Cause?
Art thou his Client? Such shall never slide.
    He never lost his Case; he pleads such Laws
    As Carry do the same, nor doth refuse
    The Vilest sinners Case that doth him Choose.   30

This is his Honour, not Dishonour: nay.
No Habeas-Corpus gainst his Clients came.
For all their Fines his Purse doth make down pay.
    He Non-suites Satan's suite or Casts the Same.
    He'l plead thy Case, and not accept a Fee.   35
    He'l plead Sub Forma Pauperis for thee.

My Case is bad. Lord be my Advocate.
    My Sin is red: I'me under Gods Arrest.
Thou hast the Hit of Pleading; plead my state.
    Although it's bad thy Plea will make it best.   40
    If thou wilt plead my Case before the King:
    I'le Waggon Loads of Love, and Glory bring.

---

3 Words *orig.* his Words and
8 I dayly doe? *orig.* before thine eye
15 Pettifogger *orig.* Petty
22 doe *ins.*

9:9M ⎱   39. MEDITATION. FROM 1. JOH. 2.1. IF ANY
1690 ⎰   MAN SIN, WE HAVE AN ADVOCATE.

My Sin! my Sin, My God, these Cursed Dregs,
  Green, Yellow, Blew streakt Poyson hellish, ranck,
Bubs hatcht in natures nest on Serpents Eggs,
    Yelp, Cherp and Cry; they set my Soule a Cramp.
    I frown, Chide, strik and fight them, mourn and Cry   5
    To Conquour them, but cannot them destroy.

I cannot kill nor Coop them up: my Curb
  'S less than a Snaffle in their mouth: my Rains
They as a twine thrid, snap: by hell they're spurd:
    And load my Soule with swagging loads of pains.   [202]10
    Black Imps, young Divells, snap, bite, drag to bring
    And pick mee headlong hells dread Whirle Poole in.

Lord, hold thy hand: for handle mee thou may'st
  In Wrath but, oh! a twinckling Ray of hope
Methinks I spie thou graciously display'st.   15
    There is an Advocate: a doore is ope.
    Sin's poyson Swell my heart would till it burst,
    Did not a hope hence creep in't thus, and nurse't.

Joy, joy, Gods Son's the sinners Advocate.
    Doth plead the sinner guiltless, and a Saint.   20
But yet Atturnies pleas Spring from the State
    The Case is in: if bad it's bad in plaint.
    My Papers do contain no pleas that do
    Secure mee from, but knock me down to, woe.

I have no plea mine Advocate to give.   25
  What now? He'l anvill Arguments [g]reate store
Out of his Flesh and Blood to make thee live.
    O Deare bought Arguments: Good pleas therefore.
    Nails made of heavenly steel, more Choice than gold
    Drove home, Well Clencht, eternally will hold.   30

Oh! Dear bought Plea, Deare Lord, what buy't so deare?
  What with thy blood purchase thy plea for me?
Take Argument out of thy Grave t'appeare
  And plead my Case with, me from Guilt to free.
  These maule both Sins, and Divells, and amaze   35
  Both Saints, and Angells; Wreath their mouths with praise.

What shall I doe, my Lord? what do, that I
  May have thee plead my Case? I fee thee will
With Faith, Repentance, and obediently
  Thy service 'gainst satanick sins fulfill.   40
  I'l fight thy fields, while Live I do, although
  I should be hackt in pieces by thy foe.

Make me thy Friend, Lord, be my surety: I
  Will be thy Client, be my Advocate:
My Sins make thine, thy Pleas make mine; hereby   45
  Thou wilt mee Save, I will thee Celebrate.
  Thou'lt kill my Sins that cut my heart within:
  And my rough Feet shall thy smooth praises Sing.   [203]

---

12 Whirle *orig.* Whorle
27 his *ins.*

1:12   ⎫   40. MEDITATION. 1 JOH. 2.2. HE IS A
1690/1   ⎭   PROPITIATION FOR OUR SIN.

Still I complain; I am complaining Still.
  Oh! woe is me! Was ever Heart like mine?
A Sty of Filth, a Trough of Washing-Swill
  A Dunghill Pit, a Puddle of mere slime,
  A Nest of Vipers, Hive of Hornets; stings.   5
  A Bag of Poyson, Civit-Box of sins.

Was ever Heart like mine? So bad? black? Vile?
  Is any Divell blacker? Or can Hell

Produce its match? It is the very soile
   Where Satan reads his Charms, and sets his spell.   10
   His Bowling Ally, where he sheeres his fleece
   At Nine Pins, Nine Holes, Morrice, Fox and Geese.

His Palace Garden where his Courtiers walke,
   His Jewells Cabbinet. Here his Caball
Do sham it, and truss up their Privie talk.   15
   In Fardells of Consults and bundles all.
   His shambles, and his Butchers stall's herein.
   It is the Fuddling Schoole of every sin.

Was ever Heart like mine? Pride, Passion, fell.
   Ath'ism, Blasphemy, pot, pipe it, dance   20
Play Barlybreaks, and at last Couple in Hell.
   At Cudgells, Kit-Cat, Carts and Dice here prance.
   At Noddy, Ruff-and-trumpt, Jing, Post-and-Pare,
   Put, One-and-thirty, and such other ware.

Grace shuffled is away: Patience oft sticks   25
   Too soon, or draws itselfe out, and's out Put.
Faith's over trumpt, and oft doth lose her tricks.
   Repentance's Chalkt up Noddy, and out shut.
   They Post, and Pare off Grace thus, and its shine.
   Alas! alas! was ever Heart like mine?   30

[S]ometimes methinks the Serpents head I mall:
   Now all is Still: my spirits do recreute.
But ere my Harpe can tune sweet praise, they fall
   On me afresh, and tare me at my Root.
   They bite like Badgers now, nay worse, although   35
   I tooke them toothless sculls, not long agoe.   [204]

My Reason now's more than my sense, I feele
   I have more sight than sense. Which seems to bee
A Rod of sun beams t'whip mee for my steele.
   My spirit's spiritless, and dull in mee   40
   For my dead prayerless Prayers: the Spirits winde
   Scarce blows my mill about. I little grinde.

Was Ever Heart like mine? My Lord, declare.
  I know not what to do: What shall I doe?
I wonder, split I don't upon Despare.   45
  It's grace's wonder that I wrack not so.
  I faintly shun't: although I see this Case
  Would say, my sin is greater than thy Grace.

Hope's Day-peep dawns hence through this chinck. Christs name
  Propiciation is for Sins. Lord, take   50
It so for mine. Thus quench thy burning flame
  In that clear stream that from his side forth brake.
  I can no Comfort take while thus I see
  Hells Cursed Imps thus jetting strut in mee.

Lord take thy sword: these Anakims destroy: 55
  Then soake my Soule in Zions Bucking tub:
With Holy Soap, and Nitre, and rich Lye
  From all Defilement mee cleanse, wash and rub.
  Then wrince, and wring mee out till th'water fall
  As pure as in the Well: not foule at all.   60

And let thy sun shine on my Head out cleare.
  And bathe my Heart within its radient beams:
Thy Christ make my Propitiation Deare.
  Thy Praise shall from my Heart breake forth in streams.
  This reeching Vertue of Christs blood will quench   65
  Thy Wrath, slay Sin and in thy Love mee bench.

---

11 sheeres *orig.* shieres
16 and *orig.* b
17 stall's *orig.* state's
18 the *orig.* his
22 Cudgells *orig.* Cutgells and
26 Put *orig.* shut *orig.* Put
40 and dull *orig.* abide
49 Hope's *orig.* Hence
50 Propiciation is *orig.* Propiciation's ; Sins *orig.* our Sins ; take *orig.* take it
57, 58 *orig.* Oh! wash mee well and all my sin out rub, / Then rince, and wring
mee cleare out: till th'water fa[ll]
62 its *orig.* these

24.3M   41. MEDITATION. JOH. 14.2. I GO TO PREPARE A
1691   PLACE FOR YOU.

A Clew of Wonders! Clusterd Miracles!
   Angells, come whet your Sight hereon. Here's ground.
Sharpen your Phansies here, ye Saint in Spiracles.
   Here is enough in Wonderment to drownd's.
   Make here the shining [m]ark or White on which   5
   Let all your Wondring Contemplations pitch.   [205]

The Magnet of all Admiration's here.
   Your tumbling thoughts turn here. Here is Gods Son,
Wove in a Web of Flesh, and Bloode rich geere.
   Eternall Wisdoms Huswifry well spun.   10
   Which through the Laws pure Fulling mills did pass.
   And so went home the Wealthy'st Web that was.

And why thus shew? Hark, harke, my Soule. He came
   To pay thy Debt, and being come most Just.
The Creditor did sue him for the Same.   15
   Did winn the Case, and in the grave him thrust.
   Who having in this Prison paid the Debt.
   And took a 'Quittance, made Death's Velvet fret.

He broke her Cramping tallons, did unlute
   The Sealed Grave, and gloriously up rose   20
Ascendeth up to glory on this Sute.
   Prepares a place for thee where glorie glowes.
   Yea yea for thee, although thy griefe out gush
   At such black Sins at which the Sun may blush.

What Wonder's here? Big belli'd Wonders in't   25
   Remain, though wrought for saints as white as milk.
But done for me whose blot's as black as inke.
   A Clew of Wonders finer far than Silke.
   Thy hand alone that wound this Clew I finde
   Can to display these Wonders it unwinde.   30

Why didst thou thus? Reason stands gasterd here.
  She's overflown: this soares above her sight
Gods onely son for sinners thus appeare;
  Prepare for Durt a throne in glory bright!
  Stand in the Doore of Glory to imbrace   35
  Such dirty bits of Dirt, with such a grace!

Reason, lie prison'd in this golden Chain.
  Chain up thy tongue, and silent stand awhile.
Let this rich Love thy Love and heart obtain
  To tend thy Lord in all admiring style.   40
  Lord screw my faculties up to the skill
  And height of praise as answers thy good Will.

Then while I eye the Place thou hast prepar'de
  For Such as I, I'le Sing thy glory out
Untill thou welcome me, as 'tis declar'de   45
  In this sweet glory runing rounde about.   [206]
  I would do more but can't, Lord help me do
  That I may pay in glory what I owe.

---

1 Wonders! *orig.* Wonders,
16 win *orig.* wine
18 'Quittance *orig.* 'Quttance
19 did *orig.* and
30 these *orig.* this
41 the *ins.*
42 praise *orig.* praises ; thy *orig.* this
45 me, *orig.* me there,
46 runing *orig.* ruing

2:6M ⎤   42. MEDITATION REV. 3.22. I WILL GIVE HIM TO SIT
1691 ⎦   WITH ME IN MY THRONE.

Apples, of gold, in silver pictures shrin'de
  Enchant the appitite, make mouths to water.
And Loveliness in Lumps, tunn'd, and enrin'de
  In Jasper Cask, when tapt, doth briskly vaper:
  Brings forth a birth of Keyes t'unlock Loves Chest,   5
  That Love, Like Birds, may fly to 't from its nest.

Such is my Lord, and more. But what strang thing
  Am I become? Sin rusts my Lock all o're.
Though he ten thousand Keyes all on a string
  Takes out, scarce one, is found, unlocks the Doore.   10
  Which ope, my Love crincht in a Corner lies
  Like some shrunck Crickling: and scarce can rise.

Lord ope the Doore: rub off my Rust, Remove
  My sin, And Oyle my Lock. (Dust there doth shelfe)
My Wards will trig before thy Key: my Love   15
  Then, as enlivend, leape will on thyselve.
  It needs must be, that giving handes receive
  Again Receivers Hearts furld in Love Wreath.

Unkey my Heart; unlock thy Wardrobe: bring
  Out royall Robes: adorne my soule, Lord: so,   20
My Love in rich attire shall on my King
  Attend, and honour on him well bestow.
  In Glory he prepares for his a place
  Whom he doth all beglory here with grace.

He takes them to the shining threashould cleare   25
  Of his bright Palace, cloath'd in Grace's flame.
Then takes them in thereto, not onely there
  To have a Prospect, but possess the same.
  The Crown of Life, the Throne of Glorys Place,
  The Fathers House blancht o're with orient Grace.   [207]30

Can'an in golden print enwalld with jems:
  A Kingdome rim'd with Glory round: in fine.
A glorious Crown pal'de thick with all the stems
  Of Grace, and of all Properties Divine.
  How happy wilt thou make mee when these shall   35
  As a blesst Heritage unto mee fall?

Adorn me, Lord, with Holy Huswifry.
  All blanch my Robes with Clusters of thy Graces:
Thus lead me to thy threashold: give mine Eye
  A Peephole there to see bright glories Chases.   40
  Then take mee in: I'le pay, when I possess,
  Thy Throne, and thee the Rent in Happiness.

---

3 tunn'd *orig.* tun'd
23 In *orig.* He
28 a *ins.*
37 with *orig.* in
42 Throne *orig.* Glory

8.9M
1691 } 43. MEDITATION. REV. 2.10. A CROWN OF LIFE.

Fain I would sing thy Praise, but feare I feign.
  My sin doth keepe out of my heart thy Feare.
Damps Love: defiles my soule. Old Blots new stain.
  Hopes hoppled lie, and rusty Chains worn cleare.
  My Sins that make me stand in need of thee;   5
  Do keep me back to hugge all Sin I see.

Nature's Corrupt, a nest of Passion, Pride,
  Lust, Worldliness, and such like bubs: I pray,
But struggling finde, these bow my Heart aside.
  A Knot of Imps at barly breaks in't play.   10
  They do inchant me from my Lord, I finde,
  The thoughts whereof proove Daggers in my mind.

Pardon, and Poyson them, Lord, with thy Blood.
  Cast their Curst Karkasses out of my Heart.
My Heart fill with thy Love; let Grace it dub.   15
  Make this my Silver Studs by thy rich art.
  My Soule shall then be thy sweet Paradise.
  Thou'st be its Rose, and it thy Bed of Spice.

Why mayn't my Faith now drinke thy Health, Lord, ore,
  The Head of all my sins? and Cast her Eye,   20
In glorifying glances on the Doore
  Of thy Free Grace, where Crowns of Life do lie: [208]
  Thou'lt give a Crown of Life to such as bee
  Faithfull to Death. And shall Faith faile in mee?

A Crown of Life, of Glory, Righteousness,   25
  Thou wilt adorn them with, that will not fade.
Shall Faith in mee Shrinke up for Feebleness?
  Nor take my Sins by th'Crown, till Crownless made?
  Breath, Lord, thy Spirit on my Faith, that I
  May have thy Crown of Life; and sin may dy.   30

How spirituall? Holy shall I shine, when I
  Thy Crown of Righteousness ware on my Head?
How Glorious when thou dost me glorify
  To ware thy Crown of Glory pollished?
  How shall I when thy Crown of Life I ware   35
  In lively Colours flowrish, fresh, and fair?

When thou shalt Crown me with these Crowns I'l bend
  My shallow Crown to crown with Songs thy Name.
Angels shall set the tune, I'le it attend:
  Thy Glory'st be the burden of the same.   40
  Till then I cannot sing, my tongue is tide.
  Accept this Lisp till I am glorifide.

---

2 doth *ins.*
7 Corrupt *orig.* Corrupt's
15 Love. *orig.* Love of

17:11M }   44. Meditation. 2. Tim. 4.8. A Crown of
1691   }   Righteousness.

A Crown, Lord, yea, a Crown of Righteousness.
    Oh! what a Gift is this? Give Lord I pray
An Holy Head, and Heart it to possess
    And I shall give thee glory for the pay.
    A Crown is brave, and Righteousness much more   5
    The glory of them both will pay the score.

A Crown indeed consisting of fine gold
    Adherent, and Inherent Righteousness,
Stuck with their Ripe Ripe Fruits in every fold
    Like studded Carbuncles they do it dress.   10
    A Righteous Life doth ever ware renown
    And thrusts the Head at last up in this Crown.   [209]

A Milk whit hand sets't on a Righteous Head.
    An hand Unrighteous can't dispose it nay.
It's not in such an hande, such hands would bed   15
    Black smuts on't should they fingers on it lay.
    Who can the Crown of Righteousness suppose
    In an Unrighteous hand for to dispose.

When once upon the head it's ever green
    And altogether Usde in Righteousness,   20
Where blessed bliss, and blissfull Peace is Seen,
    And where no jar, nor brawler hath access,
    Oh! blessed Crown what hold the breadth of all
    The state of Happiness in Heavens Hall.

A Crown of Righteousness, a Righteous Head,   25
    Oh naughty man! my brain pan turrit is
Where swallows build and hatch: sins black, and red
    My head and heart do ach, and frob at this.
    Lord were my Turret cleansd, and made by thee,
    Thy Graces Dovehouse turret much might bee.   30

Oh! make it so: then Righteousness, pure, true
　Shall Roost upon my boughs, and in my heart
And all its fruits that in Obedience grew
　To stud this Crown like jems in evry part.
　I'st then be garnisht for this Crown, and thou   35
　Shalt have my songs to diadem thy brow.

Oh! Happy me, if thou wilt Crown me thus.
　Oh! naughty heart! What Swell with sin? fy fy.
Oh! Gracious Lord, me pardon: do not Crush
　Me all to mammocks: Crown and not destroy.   40
　I'le tune thy Prayses while this Crown doth come.
　Thy Glory bring I tuckt up in my Songe.

---

13 on *orig.* upon ; a *ins.*
15 It's not in *orig.* It is in no
19 upon *orig.* on
32 in *ins.*
34 To *orig.* That ; thy *orig.* this

24.2M ⎫　　45. Meditation. 1 Pet. 5.4. Ye shall receive a
1692 ⎭　　　　Crown of Glory.

A Crown of Glory! Oh! I'm base, it's true
　My Heart's a Swomp Brake, Thicket vile of Sin,
My Head's a Bog of Filth; Blood bain'd doth spew
　Its venom streaks of Poyson o're my skin.   [210]
　My Members Dung-Carts that bedung at pleasure   5
　My Life, the Pasture where Hells Hurdloms leasure.

Becrown'd with Filth! Oh! what vile thing am I?
　What Cast, and Charge to make mee Meddow ground?
To drain my Bogs? to lay my Frog-pits dry?
　To stub up all my brush that doth abound?   10
　That I may be thy Pasture fat and frim,
　Where thy choice Flowers, and Hearbs of Grace shine trim?

Vast charge thus to Subdue me: Wonders play
  Hereat like Gamesters; 'bellisht Thoughts dresst fine,
In brave attire, cannot a finger lay   15
  Upon it that doth not besmut the shine.
  Yet all this cost and more thou'rt at with me.
  And still I'm Sad, a Seing Eye may See.

Yet more than this: my Hands that Crown'd thy Head
  With sharpest thorns, thou washest in thy Grace.   20
My Feet that did upon thy Choice Blood tread
  Thou makest beautifull thy Way to trace.
  My Head that knockt against thy head, thou hugg'[st]
  Within thy bosom: boxest not, nor lugg'st.

Nay more as yet, thou borrow'st of each Grace   25
  That Stud the Hearts of Saints, and Angells bright
Its brightest beams, the beams too of the place
  Where Glory dwells: and all the Beames of Light
  Thy, and thy Fathers Glorious Face out spread,
  To make this Crown of Glory for my head.   30

If it was possible the thoughts that are
  Imbellisht with the riches of this tender
Could torment such as do this bright Crown ware
  Their Love to thee, Lord, 's lac'de so streight, and slende[r]
  These beams would draw up Griefe to cloude this Glo[r]y   35
  But not so then; though now Grace acts this story.   [211]

My Pen enravisht with these Rayes out Strains
  A Sorry Verse. And when my gold dwells in
A Purse guilt with the glory bright that flames
  Out from this Crown, I'le tune an higher pin.   40
  Then make me Lord heir of this Crown, Ile sing
  And make thy Praise in my Heroicks ring.

---

5 that *orig.* that with filth do
9 Bog *orig.* Bogs
12 thy choice *orig.* all the
14 'bellisht *ins.*

17 and more *ins.*
26 Stud *orig.* Studs
33 do *orig.* in bright *orig.* C

17:5M ⎤   46. MEDITATION. REV. 3.5. THE SAME SHALL BE
1692 ⎦   CLOATHED IN WHITE RAIMENT.

Nay, may I, Lord, believe it? Shall my skeg
  Be 'ray'd in thy White Robes. My thatcht old Cribb
(Immortall Purss hung on a mortall Peg)
  Wilt thou with fair'st array in heaven rig?
  I'm but a jumble of gross Elements.   5
  A snaile Horn where an Evill spirit tents.

A Dirt ball dresst in milk white Lawn, and deckt
  In Tissue tagd with gold, or Ermins flush,
That mocks the Starrs, and sets them in a fret
  To se themselves out shone thus; Oh they blush.   10
  Wonders stand gastard here. But yet my Lord,
  This is but faint to what thou dost afford.

I'm but a Ball of dirt. Wilt thou adorn
  Mee with thy Web wove in thy Loom Divine
The Whitest Web in Glory, that the morn,   15
  Nay that all Angell glory, doth ore shine?
  They ware no such: This whitest Lawn most fine
  Is onely worn, my Lord, by thee and thine.

This saye's no flurr of Wit, no new Coin'd shape
  Of frollick Fancie in a Rampant Brain.   20
It's juyce Divine bled from the Choicest Grape
  That ever Zions Vinyarde did mentain.
  Such Mortall bits immortalliz'de shall ware
  More glorious robes, than glorious Angells bare.   [212]

Their Web is wealthy, wove of Wealthy Silke   25
  Well wrought indeed, it's all brancht Taffity.

But this thy Web more white by far than milke
  Spun on thy Wheele twine of thy Deity
  Wove in thy Web, Fulld in thy mill by hand
  Makes them in all their bravery seem tand.   30

This Web is wrought by best, and noblest Art
  That heaven doth afford of twine most choice
All brancht, and richly flowerd in every part
  With all the Sparkling flowers of Paradise
  To be thy Ware alone, who hast no peere   35
  And Robes for g[***]ious Saints to thee most deare.

Wilt thou, my Lord, dress my poore wither'd stump
  In this rich web whose whiteness doth excell;
The Snow, though 'tis most black? And shall my Lump
  Of Clay ware more than e're on Angells fell?   40
  What shall my bit of Dirt bedeckt so fine
  That shall Angelick glory all out shine?

Shall things run thus? Then Lord, my tumberill
  Unload of all its Dung, and make it cleane.
And load it with thy wealthi'st Grace untill   45
  Its Wheeles do crack, or Axletree complain.
  I fain would have it cart thy harvest in,
  Before it's loosed from its Axlepin.

Then screw my strings up to thy tune that I
  May load thy Glory with my songs of praise.   50
Make me thy shalm, thy praise my songs, whereby
  My mean shoshannim may thy Michtams raise.
  And when my Clay ball's in thy White robes dress[t]
  My tune perfume thy praise shall with the best.   [213]

---

8 gold, or *orig.* golden
10 shone *ins.*
23 Such *orig.* Our
24 Angells *orig.* bare
29 Fulld *orig.* and Fulld
33 flowerd *ins.*

36 g[***]ious *ins.* ; deare *orig.* deere
41 shall ins.

9:8M   ⎫   47. MEDITATION ON MATT: 25.21. ENTER THOU
1692   ⎭   INTO THE JOY OF THY LORD.

Strang, strang indeed. It rowell doth my heart
  With pegs of Greefe and tents of greatest joy.
When I wore Angells Glory in each part
  And all my shirts wore flashes of rich die.
    Of Heavenly Colours, hedg'd in with rosie Reechs,   5
    A spider spit its Vomit on my Cheeks.

This ranckling juyce bindg'd in its cursed stain
  Doth permeat both Soul and Bodys Soile
And drench each Fibre, and infect each grain.
  Its ugliness Swells over all the ile.   10
    Whose Stain'd mishapen bulk's too high, and broad
    For th'Entry of the narrow gate to God.

Ready to burst, thus, and to burn in hell,
  Now in my path I finde a Waybred spring
Whose leafe drops balm that doth this Venom quell   15
  And juyce's a Bath, that doth all stains out bring.
    And sparkling beauty in the room convay.
    Lord feed me with this Waybred Leafe, I pray.

My stain will out: and swelling swage apace.
  And holy Lusters on my shape appeare   20
All Rosie Buds: and Lilly flowers of grace
  Will grace my turfe with sweet sweet glory here.
    Under whose shades Angells will bathing play
    Who'l guard my Pearle to glory, housd in clay.

Those Gates of Pearle, porter'd with Seraphims.   25
  On their Carbuncle joynts will open wide.
And entrance give me where all glory swims

Into the Masters Joy, e're to abide.
O sweet sweet thought. Lord take this praise though thin.
And when I'm in't I'le tune an higher pin.   [214]30

---

7 bindg'd *orig.* bing'd
22 with sweet *orig.* with sweetest

[**]10M   ⎱   48. MEDITATION ON MATT. 25.21. ENTER INTO THE
[1]692   ⎰   JOY OF THY LORD.

[W]hen I, Lord, eye thy Joy, and my Love, Small,
   My heart gives in: what now? strange! sure I love thee!
And finding brambles 'bout my heart to craul
   My heart misgives mee. Prize I ought above thee?
   Such great Love hugging them, such small Love, thee!   5
   Whether thou hast my Love, I scarce can See.

My reason rises up, and chides my Cup
   Bright Loveliness itselfe. What not love thee!
Tumbling thy Joy, Lord, ore; it rounds me up.
   Shall loves nest be a thorn bush: not thee bee?   10
   Set Hovells up of thorn kids in my heart!
   Avant adultrous Love; from me depart.

The Influences my vile heart sucks in
   Of Puddle Water boyld by Sunn beams till
Its spiritless, and dead, nothing more thin   15
   Tasts wealthier than those thou dost distill.
   This seems to numb my heart to think that I
   [S]hould null all good to optimate a toy.

Yet when the beamings, Lord, of thy rich Joys,
   Do guild my Soule, meethinks I'm sure I love thee.   20
They Calcine all these brambly trumperys
   And now I'm sure that I prize naught above thee.

Thy beams making a bonefire of my stack
Of Faggots, bring my Love to thee in 'ts pack.

For when the Objects of thy Joy impress   25
  Their shining influences on my heart
My Soule seems an Alembick doth possess
  Love Stilld into rich spirits by thy Art.
  And all my pipes, were they ten thousand would
  Drop spirits of Love on thee, more rich than gold.   30

Now when the world with all her dimples in't
  Smiles on me, I do love thee more than all:
And when her glory freshens, all in print,
  I prize thee still above it all, and shall.
  Nay all her best to thee, do what she can,   35
  Drops but like drops dropt in a Closestoole pan.   [215]

The waftings of thy Joy, my Lord therefore
  Let in the Cabbin of my Joy rise high,
And let thy Joy enter in mee before
  I enter do into my masters joy.   40
  Thy joyes in mee, will make my Pipes to play
  For joy thy Praise while teather'd to my clay.

---

3 craul *orig.* cral
7 my Cup *orig.* me
10 a *ins.*
22 prize *orig.* lov
23 my *ins.*
27 Alembick *orig.* Alimbeck
28 Love *orig.* Loves
36 Drops *orig.* Dops

26:12M
1692   }   49. MEDITATION. MATT. 25.21. THE JOY OF THY LORD.

Lord, do away my Motes: and Mountains great.
    My nut is vitiate, Its kirnell rots:
Come, kill the Worm, that doth its kirnell eate.
    And strike thy sparkes within my tinder box.
    Drill through my metall-heart an hole wherein   5
    With graces Cotters to thyselfe it pin.

A Lock of Steel upon my Soule, whose key
    The Serpent keeps, I fear, doth lock my doore.
O pick't: and through the key-hole make thy way
    And enter in: and let thy joyes run o're.   10
    My Wards are rusty. Oyle them till they trig
    Before thy golden key: thy Oyle makes glib.

Take out the splinters of the World that stick
    Do in my heart. Friends, Honours, Riches, and
The shivers in't of Hell whose venoms quick   15
    And firy make it swoln and ranckling stand.
    These wound and kill: those shackle strongly to
    Poore knobs of Clay, my heart, hence sorrows grow.

Cleanse, and enlarge my kask: It is too small:
    And's tartarizd with worldly dregs dri'de in't.   20
It's bad mouth'd too: and though thy joyes do Call
    That boundless are, it ever doth them stint.
    Make me thy Chrystall Caske: those wines in't tun
    That in the Rivers of thy joyes do run.

Lord make me, though suckt through a straw or Quill,   25
    Tast of the Rivers of thy joyes, some drop.
'T will sweeten me: and all my Love distill
    Into thy glass, and me for joy make hop.
    'T will turn my water into wine: and fill
    My Harp with Songs my Masters joyes distill.   [216]30

11 My *orig.* My Oyl
20 And's *orig.* Its
22 doth *orig.* set
23 me *orig.* my
27 'T *orig.* It
28 me *orig.* make

PREPARATORY MEDITATIONS,

SECOND SERIES

Oh Leaden heeld. Lord, give, forgive I pray.
  Infire my Heart: it bedded is in Snow.
I Chide myselfe seing myselfe decay
  In heate and Zeale to thee. I frozen grow.
  File my dull spirits: make them sharp and bright: 5
  Them firbush for thyselfe, and thy delight.

My Stains are such, and sinke so deep, that all
  Th'Excellency in Created shells
Too low, and little is to make it fall
  Out of my leather Coate wherein it dwells.   10
  This Excellence is but a Shade to that
  Which is enough to make my Stains go back.

The glory of the world slickt up in types
  In all Choice things chosen to typify,
His glory upon whom the worke doth light,   15
  To thine's a Shaddow, or a butterfly.
  How glorious then, my Lord, art thou to mee
  Seing to cleanse me, 's worke alone for thee.

The glory of all Types doth meet in thee.
  Thy glory doth their glory quite excell: 20
More than the Sun excells in its bright glee
  A nat, an Earewig, Weevill, snaile, or shell.
  Wonders in Crowds start up; Your eyes may strut
  Viewing his Excellence, and's bleeding cut.

Oh! that I had but halfe an eye to view   25
  This excellence of thine, undazled: so
Therewith to give my heart a touch anew
  Untill I quickned am, and made to glow.

All is too little for thee: but alass
Most of my little all hath other pass.   30

Then Pardon, Lord, my fault. And let thy beams
  Of Holiness pierce through this Heart of mine.
Ope to thy Blood a passage through my veans.
  Let thy pure blood my impure blood refine
  Then with new blood and spirits I will dub   35
  My tunes upon thy Excellency good.   [167]

---

1 forgive *orig.* forgive my
9 is *orig.* are
12 make *orig.* give
16 To thine's *orig.* Is but

[*****] ⎫   2. MEDITATION. COLL: 1.15. THE FIRST BORN OF
[*****] ⎭   EVERY CREATURE.

Oh! Golden Rose! Oh. Glittering Lilly White
  Spic'd o're with heavens File divine, till Rayes
Fly forth whose shine doth wrack the strongest Sight
  That Wonders Eye is tent of, while't doth gaze
  On thee. Whose Swaddle Bonde's Eternity.   5
  And sparkling Cradle is Rich Deity.

First Born of e'ry Being: hence a Son
  Begot o'th'First: Gods onely son begot.
Hence Deity all ore. Gods nature run
  Into a Filiall Mould: Eternall knot.   10
  A Father then, and Son: persons distinct.
  Though them Sabellians contrar'ly inckt.

This mall of Steell falls hard upon these foes
  Of truth, who melt the Holy Trinity
Into One Person: Arrians too and those   15
  Socinians calld, who do Christs Deity

Bark out against. But Will they, nill they, they
Shall finde this Mall to split their brains away.

Come shine, Deare Lord, out in my heart indeed
   First Born; in truth before thee there was none   20
First Born, as man, born of a Virgin's Seed:
   Before or after thee such up ne'er sprung.
   Hence Heir of all things lockt in natures Chest:
   And in thy Fathers too: extreamly best.

Thou Object of Gods boundless brightest Love,   25
   Invested with all Sparkling rayes of Light
Distill thou down, what hony falls above.
   Bedew the Angells Copses; fill our sight
   And hearts therewith within thy Father's joy.
   These are but Shreads under thy bench that ly.   30

Oh! that my Soul was all enamored
   With this First Born enough: a Lump of Love
Son of Eternall Father, Chambered
   Once in a Virgins Womb; dropt from above.
   All Humane royalty hereby Divin'de.   35
   The First Born's Antitype: in whom they're shrin'de.   [168]

Make mee thy Babe, and him my Elder Brother.
   A Right, Lord grant me in his Birth Right high.
His Grace, my Treasure make above all other.
   His Life my sampler: My Life his joy.
   I'le hang my Love then on his heart, and sing
   New Psalms on Davids Harpe to thee and him.

---

14 melt *orig.* th[*] d[**]ill
25 boundless *orig.* bounless

15.8M   }   3. Meditation. Rom. 5.14. Who is the Figure of
1693   }   Him that was to come.

Like to the Marigold, I blushing close
  My golden blossoms when thy sun goes down:
Moist'ning my leaves with Dewy sighs, halfe frose
  By the nocturnall Cold, that hoares my Crown.
  Mine Apples ashes are in apple shells   5
  And dirty too: strange and bewitching spells!

When, Lord, mine Eye doth Spie thy Grace to beame
  Thy Mediatoriall glory in the shine
Out Spouted so from Adams typick Streame
  And Emblemizd in Noahs pollisht shrine,   10
  Thine theirs out shines so far it makes their glory
  In brightest Colours, seem a Smoaky story.

But when mine Eye full of these beams doth cast
  Its rayes upon my dusty essence thin
Impregnate with a Sparke Divine, defacde,   15
  All Candid o're with Leprosie of Sin.
  Such Influences on my spirits light,
  Which them as bitter gall, or Cold ice smite.

My brissled sins hence do so horrid 'peare,
  None but thyselfe, (and thou deckt up must bee   20
In thy Transcendent glory sparkling cleare)
  A Mediator unto God for mee.
  So high they rise, Faith scarce can toss a Sight
  Over their head upon thyselfe to light.

Is't possible such glory, Lord, ere should   25
  Center its Love on me Sins Dunghill elfe?
My Case up take? make it its own? Who would
  Wash with his blood my blots out? Crown his shelfe
  Or Dress his golden Cupboard with such ware?
  This makes my pale facde Hope almost despare.   [217]30

Yet let my Titimouses Quill suck in
  Thy Graces milk Pails some small drop: or Cart
A Bit, or splinter of some Ray, the wing
  Of Grace's Sun sprindgd out, into my heart:
    To build there Wonders Chappell where thy Praise   35
    Shall be the Psalms sung forth in gracious layes.

---

2 sun *orig.* son
4 hoares *orig.* whores
6 and *ins.*
7 thy *ins.*
9 Out Spouted *orig.* Spouted out ; Streame] *orig.* Shrine
10 Emblemizd *orig.* Emblemisd
17 light *orig.* lite

24.10M   ⎱   4. MEDITATION. GAL. 4.24. WHICH THINGS ARE
1693   ⎰   AN ALLEGORIE.

My Gracious Lord, I would thee glory doe;
  But finde my Garden over grown with weeds:
My Soile is Sandy; brambles ore it grow;
  My stock is stunted; branch no good Fruits breeds.
    My Garden weed: Fatten my soile, and prune   5
    My stock, and make it with thy glory bloome.

O Glorious One, the gloriou'st thought I thincke
  Of thee falls black as Inck upon thy Glory.
The brightest Saints that rose, do Star like, pinck;
  Nay Abrams Shine to thee's an Allegory.   10
    Or fleeting sparke in th' smoke, to typify
    Thee, and thy Glorious selfe in mystery.

Should all the sparks in heaven, the Stars there dance
  A Galliard, Round about the sun and stay
His Servants (while on Easter morn his prance   15

Is o're, which old wives prate of) O brave Play.
Thy glorious Saints thus boss thee round, which stand
  Holding thy glorious Types out in their hand.

But can I thinck this Glory greate, its head
  Thrust in a pitchy cloude should strangled ly   20
Or tucking up its beams should go to bed
  Within the Grave, darke me to glorify?
  This Mighty thought my hearts too streight for, 'though
  I hold it by the hand, and let not goe.

Then, my Blesst Lord, let not the Bondmaids type   25
  Take place in mee. But thy blesst Promisd Seed.
Distill thy Spirit through thy royall Pipe
  Into my Soule; and so my Spirits feed,
  Then them, and me still into praises right
  Into thy Cup where I to swim delight.   30

Though I desire so much, I can't o're doe.
  All that my Can contains, to nothing comes   [218]
When summed up, it onely Cyphers grow
  Unless thou set thy Figure to my sums.
  Lord Set thy Figure 'fore them greate, or small.   35
  So make them some thing, and I'l give thee all.

---

9 an *ins.*
10 thee's an *orig.* thee's
18 Types out *orig.* out

4.1M   } 5. MEDITATION ON GAL. 3.16. AND TO THY SEED
1693/4   }   WHICH IS CHRIST.

Art thou, Lord, Abraham's Seed, and Isaac too?
  His Promis'd seed? That One, and Only Seed?
How can this bee? Paul certainly saith true.
  But one seed promisd. Sir this Riddle read.

Christ is the Metall: Isaack is the Oar.   5
Christ is the Pearle, in Abraham's tre[*]d therefore.

Christ's Antitype. Isaac his Type up spires.
  In many things, but Chiefly this because
This Isaac, and the Ram cought in the briars
  One sacrifice, foreshew by typick laws   10
  Christs Person, all Divine, joynd whereto's made
  Unperson'd Manhood, on the Altar's laid.

The full grown Ram, provided none knows how,
  Typing Christ's Manhood, made by God alone;
Cought in the brambles by the horns, must bow,   15
  Under the Knife. The manhoods Death, and Groan.
  Yet Isaac's leaping from the Altar's bed,
  Foretold its glorious rising from the Dead.

But why did things run thus? For sin indeed,
  No lesser price than this could satisfy.   .   20
Oh. costly Sin! this makes mine intraills bleed.
  What fills my shell, did make my Saviour die.
  What Grace then's this, of God, and Christ that stills
  Out of this Offering into our tills?

Lord with thine Altars Fire, mine Inward man   25
  Refine from dross: burn out my sinfull guise
And make my Soul thine Altars Drippen pan
  To Catch the Drippen of thy Sacrifice.
  This is the Unction thine receive; the which
  Doth teach them all things of an happy pitch.   30

Thy Altars Fire burns not to ashes down
  This Offering. But it doth roast it here.
This is thy Roastmeate cooked up sweet; brown,
  Upon thy table set for Souls good cheer.
  The Drippen, and the meate are royall fair   35
  That fatten Souls, that with it welcomd are.   [219]

My Trencher, Lord, with thy Roast Mutten dress:
  And my dry Bisket in thy Dripping Sap.
And feed my Soul with thy Choice Angell Mess:
  My heart thy Praise, Will, tweedling Larklike tap.   40
  My florid notes, like Tenderills of Vines
  Twine round thy Praise, plants sprung in true Love's Mines.

---

11 Divine, *orig.* Divine, unto its ty
12 on the Altar 's laid *orig.* and on th Altar ly
21 intraills *orig.* intralls
22 my *ins.*
25 burn *orig.* and burn
28 thy *orig.* this

27.3M   } 6. MEDITATION. ON ISAI. 49.3. THOU ART MY
1694   }   SERVANT, OH, ISRAEL.

I fain would praise thee, Lord, but finde black sin,
  To stain my Tunes my Virginalls to spoile.
Fetch out the same with thy red blood: and bring
  My Heart in kilter, and my spirits oyle.
  My Theme is rich: my skill is poore, untill   5
  Thy Spirit makes my hand its holy quill.

I spy thyselfe, as Golden Bosses fixt
  On Bible Covers, shine in Types out bright,
Of Abraham, Isaac, Jacob, where's immixt
  Their streaming Beames of Christ displaying Light.   10
{ Jacobs now jog my pen, whose golden rayes
{ Do of thyselfe advance an holy blaze.

His Name as Jacob, saith, there's stow'd in thee
  All Wisdom to mentain all Pious skill
And that the Divells Heels should tript up bee   15
  By thee alone; thou dost his brains out spill.
  The Name of Israel in Scutcheons shows
  Thou art Gods Prince to batter down his Foes.

His Fathers blessing him, shews, thou camest down
  Full of thy Fathers blessing: and his Griefe   20
That thou shouldst be a man of Grief; a Crown
  Of Thorns thou wor'st to purchase us reliefe.
  Isr'el by Joseph's had to Egypt, and
  Joseph thee thither, and from thence did hand.

Jacob doth from his Father go and seek   25
  A Spouse and purchasd by his Service two.
Thou from thy Father came'st, thy spouse most meek
  Of Jews, and Gentiles down to purchase, wooe
  And gain. And as Twelve stems did from him bud
  Thou twelve Apostles sentst, the Church to stud.   30

In all those Typick Lumps of Glory I
  Spy thee the Gem made up of all their shine
Which from them all in thickest glory fly
  And twist themselves into this Gem of thine.
  And as the shine thereof doth touch my heart,   35
  Joy sincks my Soule seeing how rich thou art.   [220]

How rich art thou? How poore am I of Love,
  To thee, when all this Glory at my Doore
Stands knocking for admission: and doth shove
  To ope't, and Cabbinet with all her store?   40
  Make Love inflamed rise, and all entwine
  About Thyselfe her Object all in shine.

Lord pardon mee, my sin, and all my trash.
  And bring my soule in surges of rich flame
Of Love to thee. I truely Envie dash   45
  Upon my selfe, my hidebound selfe for shame,
  I fain would prize, and praise thee: but do finde
  My Flame upsmootherd by a Carnall minde.

Oh! blow my Coale with thy blesst Bellows till
  It Glow, and [s]end Loves hottest steams on thee.   50
I shall be warm; and thou mine arms shall fill
  And mine Embraces shall thy Worship bee.

I'le sacrifice to thee my Heart in praise.
When thy Rich Grace shall be my hearty Phrase.

---

7 thy *orig.* thy thy
15 Heels *orig.* Heeld
26 two *orig.* too
28 down *orig.* camest
39 Stands *orig.* Stads
40 with *orig.* in
44 soule ins.

5.6M   }   7. MEDITATION Ps: 105.17. HE SENT A MAN
1694   }   BEFORE THEM, EVEN JOSEPH, WHO WAS SOLD ETC.

All Dull, my Lord, my spirits flat, and dead
  All water sockt and sapless to the skin.
Oh! Screw mee up, and make my spirits bed
  Thy quickening vertue. For my inke is dim
  My pensill blunt. Doth Joseph type out thee?   5
  Haraulds of Angells Sing out, Bow the Knee.

Is Josephs Glorious shine a Type of thee?
  How bright art thou? He Envi'de was as well.
And so was thou. He's stript, and pickt, poore hee,
  Into the pit. And so was thou; they shell   10
  Thee of thy Kirnell. He by Judah's Sold
  For twenty Bits; thirty for thee he'd told.

Joseph was tempted by his Mistress vile.
  Thou by the Divell, but both shame the foe.
Joseph was cast into the jayle a while.   15
tomb   And so was thou. Sweet apples mellow so.
  Joseph did from his jayle to glory run.
  Thou from Deaths pallot rose like morning sun.   [221]

Joseph layes in against the Famine, and
  Thou dost prepare the Bread of Life for thine.   20

He bought with Corn for Pharaoh th'men, and Land.
  Thou with thy Bread mak'st such themselves Consign
Over to thee, that eate it. Joseph makes
  His brethren bow before him. Thine too quake.

Joseph constrains his Brethren till their sins   25
  Do gall their Souls. Repentance bubbles fresh.
Thou treatest sinners till Repentance springs
  Then with him sendst a Benjamin like messe.
Joseph doth Cheare his humble brethren. Thou
  Dost stud with joy the mourning saints that bow.   30

Josephs bright shine th'Eleven Tribes must preach.
  And thine Apostles now Eleven, thine
They beare his presents to his Friends: thine reach
  Thine unto thine, thus now behold a shine.
  How hast thou pensild out, my Lord, most bright   35
  Thy glorious Image here, on Josephs Light.

This I bewaile, in me under this shine
  To see so dull a Colour in my skin.
Lord, lay thy brightsome Colours on me thine.
  Scoure thou my pipes then play thy tunes therein.   40
  I will not hang my Harp on Willows by,
  While thy Sweet praise, my Tunes doth glorify.

---

4 dim *orig.* thin
5 Doth *orig.* J
10 shell *orig.* shell thee
11 Kirnell *orig.* Kernell
18 Deaths *ins.*
21 th' *orig.* the
33 his *orig.* this
40 then play *ins.* ; tunes *orig.* tunes then blow

14:8M
1694
} 8. MEDITATION. ROM. 5.8. GOD COMMENDS HIS
LOVE UNTO US, IN THAT WHILE WE WERE YET
SINNER[S], CHRIST DIED FOR US.

Thou pry'st thou screw'st my sincking soul up to,
  Lord th'Highest Vane, amazements summit Bears
Seeing thy Love ten thousand wonders do.
  Breaking sins Back that blockt it up; us snares.
  The very stars, and sun themselves did scoule,   5
  Yea Angells too, till it shone out, did howle.

Poore sinfull man lay grovling on the ground.
  Thy wrath, and Curse to dust lay grinding him.
And sin, that banisht Love out of these bounds
  Hath stufft the world with curses to the brim.   10
  Gods Love thus Caskt in Heaven, none can tap
  Or breake its truss hoops, or attain a Scrap.   [222]

Like as a flock of Doves with feathers washt,
  All o're with yellow gold, fly all away
At one Guncrack, so Lord thy Love sin quasht   15
  And Chased hence to heaven (Darksom day.)
  It nestles there: and Graces Bird did hatch.
  Which in dim types we first Pen feather'd catch.

God takes his son, stows in him all his Love,
  (Oh Lovely One) him Lovely thus down sends   20
His rich Love Letter to us from above
  And chiefly in his Death his Love Commends.
  Writ all in Love from top to toe, and told
  Out Love more rich and shining far than gold.

For e'ry Grain stands bellisht ore with Love.   25
  Each Letter, syllable, Word, Action sounde
Gods Commendations to us from above
  But yet Loves Emphasis most cleare is found
  Engrav'd upon his Grave stone in his blood
  He shed for sinners, Lord what Love? How good?   30

It rent the Heavens ope that seald up were
  Against poore Sinners: rend the very Skie
And rout the Curse, Sin, Divell, Hell (Oh Deare)
  And brake Deaths jaw bones, and its sting destroy.
  Will search it[s] Coffers: fetch from thence the Dust   35
  Of saints, and it attend to glory just.

My God! this thy Love Letter to mee Send.
  Thy Love to mee spell out therein I will.
And What choice Love thou dost mee there commend,
  I'le lay up safely in my Souls best till.   40
  I'le read, and read it; and With Angells soon
  My Mictams shall thy Hallelujahs tune.

---

2 Bears *orig.* wears
13 Dove with *orig.* Doves whose

<table>
<tr><td>16:10M
1694</td><td>}</td><td>9. MEDITATION. DEUT. 18.[15.] THE LORD THY GOD
WILL RAISE UP UNTO THEE A PROPHET—
—LIKE UNTO MEE.</td></tr>
</table>

Lord, let thy Dazzling shine refracted fan'de
  In this bright Looking Glass, its favour lay
Upon mine Eyes that oculated stand
  And peep thereat, in button moulds of clay
  Whose glory otherwise that Courts mine eye   5
  Will all its sparkling family destroy.   [223]

Yea let thy Beams, better ten thousand times
  Than brightest Eyebright, cherishing revive
The Houshold that possesseth all the shrines
  In Visions Palace, that it well may thrive.   10
  Moses is made the Looking glass: in which
  Mine Eyes to spie thee in this Type I pitch.

Poore Parents bring him in, when bondage state
  On Israel lay: and So it was with thee.

He's persecuted; all male babes alate   15
  Are to be slain. Thy case was such we see.
  He's sav'de by miracle: and raisd up by
  A sire reputed. So thy matters ly.

Was he most Meeke, Courageous, Faithfull, Wise?
  Those all shine bright in thee: out shine the sun.   20
Did he his Father then in law suffice
  With faithfull Service? So thou well hast done.
  Did he a gentile Wed? Thy spouse so shines.
  Was he a Mediator? This thee twines.

Did he Gods Israel from Egypt through   25
  The Red Sea lead, into the Wilderness?
Thou bring'st Gods Israel from bondage too
  Of Sin into the World here through no less
  Than thy red blood: and in this Chace t'assoile
  The firy Serpents, whose black venoms boile.   30

He Fasted fourty days, and nights, did give
  Them Gods own Law. Thou didst the very same.
The Morall Law whereto we ought to live.
  The Gospell Law to laver out our shame.
  Then Israel's Church-hood, Worship, Ministry   35
  He founded: which thou didst too gospelly.

He did confirm his Office Worke with Wonders,
  And to the Covenant annexed seals.
Thou thine in miracles, and more in numbers.
  And Gospell Seals unto thy Church out dealst.   40
  He intercession made, and pardon gain'd
  Unto his people. Thou didst so, it's fam'de.

He led them to the border of Gods Land
  Sang like a swan his dying song (well known)
Laid down his hilts: and so discharg'd his hand   45
  Dy'de, Buri'de, Rose, and went to glories throne.   [224]
  All which shine gloriously in thee that wee
  Do Moses finde a Well drawn Map of thee.

Good God! what grace is this takes place in thee?
　How dost thou make thy Son to shine, and prize　　　　50
His glory thus? Thy Looking-glass give mee.
　　And let thy spirit wipe my Watry eyes.
　　That I may see his flashing glory-darte
　　Like Lightening quick till it infire my heart.

I long to see thy sun upon mee shine,　　　　55
　But feare I'st finde my selfe thereby shown worse
Yet let his burning beams melt, and refine
　　Me from my dross, yet not to singe my purse.
　　Then of my metall make thy Warbling harp:
　　That shall thy Praise deck't in Sweet tunes outwarp.　　　　60

---

1 shine *ins.*
10 well *ins.*
24 This *orig.* This 'bout
31 did give *orig.* then gave
34 our *orig.* their
55 sun *orig.* son
57 beams *orig.* beams are

10:12M
1694
} 10. MEDITATION, WHICH OUR FATHERS THAT
FOLLOW'D AFTER, BROUGHT IN WITH JESUS, INTO
THE POSSESSION OF THE GENTILES ACT. 7.45.

Moses fare well. I with a mournfull teare
　Will wash thy Marble Vault, and leave thy shine
To follow Josuah to Jordan where
　　He weares a Type, of Jesus Christ, divine.
　　Did by the Priests bearing the Arke off Cut　　　　5
　　Her stream, that Isr'el through it drieshod foot.

Doth twelve men call who in the Channell raise
　Twelve stones, and also other twelve up take
And Gilgal Stud therewith, like pearles that blaze
　　In Rings of Gold, this passage to relate.　　　　10

All speaking Types of Christ whose Ministry
Doth Jordans streams cut off, that 'fore them fly.

And brings the Church into the Promis'd Coast
And singles out his twelve Apostles who
Twelve flaming Carbuncles before his host   15
Out of the Channell take, and them bestow
As Monuments upon its banck most fair.
Twelve Articles th'Apostles Creed doth bare.

Now Farewell Wilderness, with all thy Fare.
The Water of the Rock, and Mannah too.   20
My Old-New Cloaths my Wildernesses Ware.
The Cloud and Pillar bright, adjue adjue.   [225]
You onely in the Wilderness did flower
As flowring Types. With Angells now I bower.

Let Gilgal speake for mee, where Egypts stain   25
Lapt in my Foreskin up clipt off offshook.
I feed on Can'ans Wheat, Mannah's plump grain
All Evangelicall our Bakers Cooke.
I drink the Drink of Life and weare Christs Web
And by the Sun of Righteousness am led.   30

Our Joshua doth draw his Troops out to
The Lunar coast, this Jericho the World
And rounds it while the Gospell Levites blow
Their Gospell Rams Horn Trumpits till down hirld
Its walls lie flat, and it his Sacrifice   35
Doth burn in Zeale, whose Flame doth Sindge the skies.

As Joshuah doth fight Haile stones smite down
The Can'anites: so Christ with Haile stones shall
Destroy his Enemies, and breake their Crown
The Sun and Moon shall stand to see them fall.   40
The Heavens Chrystall Candlestick-like stand
Holding for him their Candles in their hand.

Yet such as Rahab like come o're to him
  His Grace implanteth in his Golden Stock.
As Joshuah did each Tribe his lot out fling.   45
  So Christ doth his in Glory portions lot.
  As Joshua fixt Gods Worship, and envest
  Them with the Promise. Christ thus his hath blest.

That blazing Star in Joshua's but a Beam,
  Of thy bright Sun, my Lord, fix such in mee   50
My Dishclout Soul Rence, Wring, and make it cleane.
  Then die it in that blood that fell from thee.
  And make the Waiting men within my heart
  Attend thy Sweetest praise, in evry part.

---

1 with *orig.* will
8 also *ins.* ; that *orig.* whose
10 Rings *orig.* Rigs
16 take *orig.* wake
17 banck *orig.* bank
21 Cloaths *orig.* Claths
26 offshook *orig.* offtook
34 till *orig.* all
36 Flame *orig.* d
37 Joshuah *orig.* Josuah
45 Tribe his lot out *orig.* Tribes lot well
46 So *orig.* To
49 Beam *orig.* Ray
51 cleane *orig.* clem

19.3M } 11. MEDITATION. JUD: 13.3. THE ANGELL OF THE
1695   }   LORD APPEARED TO THE WOMAN. &c.

Eternall Love burnisht in Glory thick,
  Doth butt, and Center in thee, Lord, my joy.
Thou portrai'd art in Colours bright, that stick
  Their Glory on the Choicest Saints, Whereby
  They are thy Pictures made. Samson Exceld   5
  Herein thy Type, as he thy foes once queld.   [226]

An Angell tells his mother of his birth.
  An Angell telleth thine of thine. Ye two
Both Males that ope the Womb in Wedlock Kerfe
  Both Nazarited from the Womb up grew.   10
  He after pitchy night a sunshine grows
  And thou the Sun of Righteousness up rose.

His Love did Court a Gentile spouse; and thine
  Espousd a Gentile to bebride thyselfe.
His Gentile Bride apostatizd betime.   15
  Apostasy in thine grew full of Wealth.
  He Sindgd the Authours of't with Foxes tails.
  And foxy men by thee on thine prevaile.

The Fret now rose. Thousands upon him
  An asses Jaw his javling is, whereby   20
He slew a Thousand, heap by heap that hour.
  Thou by weake means mak'st many thousands fly.
  Thou ribbon like wast platted in his Locks
  And hence he thus his Enemies did box.

He's by his Friend betray'd, for money sold,   25
  Took, bound, blindfolded, made a May game Flout
Dies freely with great sinners, when they hold
  A Sacred Feast. With arms stretcht greatly out
  Slew more by death, than in his Life he slew.
  And all such things, my Lord, in thee are true.   30

Samson at Gaza went to bed to sleep.
  The Gazites watch him and the soldiers thee.
He Champion stout at midnight rose full deep.
  Took Gaza's Gate on's back away went hee.
  Thou rose didst from thy Grave and also tookst   35
  Deaths Doore away throwing it off o'th'hooks.

Thus all the Shine that Samson wore is thine,
  Thine in the Type. Oh, Glorious One. Rich glee
Gods Love hath made thee thus. Hence thy bright shine
  Commands our Love to bow thereto the Knee.   40

Thy Glory chargeth us in Sacrifice
To make our Hearts and Love to thee to rise.

But woe is me! my heart doth run out to
  Poor bits of Clay: or dirty Gayes embrace.
Doth leave thy Lovely selfe for loveless shows   45
  For lumps of Lust, nay sorrow and disgrace.   [227]
  Alas, poore Soule! a Pardon, Lord, I crave.
  I have dishonourd thee and all I have.

Be thou my Samson, Lord, a Rising Sun,
  Of Righteousness unto my soule, I pray.   50
Conquour my Foes, Let Graces Spouts all run
  Upon my Soule O're which thy sunshine lay.
  And set me in thy sunshine; make each flower
  Of Grace in me thy Praise perfum'd out poure.

---

4 on *orig.* in
11 grows *orig.* rose
18 on ins.
23 Thou *orig.* Thou'st
24 he ins.
27 hold *orig.* did hold
28 With *orig.* His ; greatly out *orig.* out amain
34 went hee *orig.* we see
42 thee *orig.* life
52 O're *orig.* ore
53 make *orig.* that

7.5M   }   12. MEDITATION. EZEK. 37.24. DAVID MY SERVANT
1695   }   SHALL BE THEIR KING.

Dull, Dull indeed! What shall it e're be thus?
  And why? Are not thy Promises, my Lord,
Rich, Quick'ning things? How should my full Cheeks blush
  To finde mee thus? and those a lifeless Word?
  My Heart is heedless: unconcernd hereat: 5
  I finde my Spirits spiritless, and flat.

Thou Courtst mine Eyes in Sparkling Colours bright,
    Most bright indeed, and soul enamoring,
With the most shining Sun, whose beames did smite
    Me with delightfull smiles to make mee spring.   10
    Embellisht knots of Love assault my minde
    Which still is Dull, as if this sun ne're shin'de.

David in all his gallantry now comes,
    Bringing to tende thy shrine, his Royall Glory,
Rich Prowess, Prudence, Victories, sweet songs,   15
    And Piety to Pensill out thy story;
    To draw my heart to thee, in this brave shine
    Of typick Beams most warm. But still I pine.

Shall not this Lovely Beauty, Lord, set out
    In Dazzling shining Flashes 'fore mine Eye,   20
Enchant my heart, Loves golden mine, till 't spout
    Out streames of Love refin'd that on thee lie.
    Thy Glory's great: Thou Davids Kingdom shalt
    Enjoy for aye. I want and that's my fault.   [228]

Spare me, my Lord, spare me, I greatly pray,   25
    Let me thy Gold pass through thy Fire untill
Thy Fire refine, and take my filth away.
    That I may shine like Gold, and have my fill
    Of Love for thee, untill my Virginall
    Chimes out in Changes sweet thy Praises shall.   30

Wipe off my Rust, Lord, with thy wisp me scoure,
    And make thy Beams pearch on my strings their blaze.
My tunes Cloath with thy shine, and Quavers poure
    My Cursing Strings on, loaded with thy Praise.
    My Fervent Love with Musick in her hand,   35
    Shall then attend thyselfe, and thy Command.

---

9 Sun *ins.*
11 knots *orig.* knot ; assault *orig.* assaults
13 now *orig.* doth
23 great *orig.* th'king
34 My *orig.* Upon My

1:7M ⎫   13. Meditation. Ps. 72. the title. A Psalm for
1695 ⎭   Solomon.

I fain would praise thee, Lord, but when I would,
  I finde my Sin my Praise dispraises bring.
I fain would lift my hands up as I should;
  But when I do, I finde them fould by Sin.
  I strive to heave my heart to thee, but finde   5
  When striving, in my heart an heartless minde.

Oh! that my Love, and mine Affections rich
  Did spend themselves on thee and thou hadst them.
I strive to have thy Glory on them pitch
  And fetch thee them. Hence Solomon thy jem,   10
  And glorious Type thy sparkling Beams out flings
  But in the same my Love but little springs.

Was He a bud of Davids stok? So thou.
  Was he a King? Thou art a King of Kings.
Was He a Make-peace King? Thy royall brow   15
  Doth weare a Crown which peace Eternall brings.
  Did He Excell in Wisdome? Thine doth flame.
  And thou art Wisdom's Storehouse whence his came.

I may aver him of all fallen men
  The perfect'st piece that Nature ever bred.   20
Thy Human nature is the perfect'st jem
  That Adams offspring ever brudled.
  No Spot nor Wrinckle did it ever smite.
  Adams in Paradise was ne're so bright.   [229]

Did He Gods Temple Build, in glory shown?   25
  Thou buildst Gods House, more gloriously bright.
Did he sit on a golden ivery Throne
  With Lions fenc'd? Thy Throne is far more White
  And glorious: garded with Angells strong.
  A streame of fire doth with the Verdict come.   30

Did he his Spouse, a glorious Palace build?
 The Heavens are the Palace for thy Spouse.
Gods house was by his pray're with Glory filld.
 God will for thine his Church in Glory house.
 Did Sheba's Queen faint viewing of his glory?   35
 Bright Angells stand amaz'd at thy story.

But hence griefe springs, finding these rayes of Light
 Scarce reach my heart, it is so ditcht with Sin.
I scarce can See I see it, or it smite
 Upon my Love that it doth run to him.   40
 Why so? my Lord! Why so? Shall Love up shrink?
 Or mine Affection to thee be a Shrimp?

Oh! feed mee at thy Table: make Grace grow
 Knead in thy Bread, I eate, thy Love to mee,
And Spice thy Cup, I take, with rich grace so,   45
 That at thy Table I may honour thee
 And if thy Banquet fill mee with thy Wealth.
 My growing Grace will glorify thyselfe.

---

13 bud *orig.* but
16 which *orig.* where
19 him *orig.* hee
20 piece *ins.* ; ever bred *orig.* bred ever
24 was *orig.* was not
25 glory *orig.* glory bright
36 amaz'd *orig.* amazed stand

3D.9M } 14. MEDITATION. COL. 2.3. IN WHOM ARE HID ALL THE
1695 } TREASURES OF WISDOM, AND KNOWLEDGE.

Halfe Dead: and rotten at the Coare: my Lord!
 I am Consumptive: and my Wasted lungs
Scarce draw a Breath of aire: my silver Coard
 Is loose. My buckles almost have no tongues.

My Heart is Fistulate: I am a Shell.   5
In Guilt and Filth I wallow, Sent and smell.

Shall not that Wisdom horded up in thee
   (One key whereof is Sacerdotall Types)
Provide a Cure for all this griefe in mee
      And in the Court of Justice save from stripes.   10
      And purge away all Filth and Guilt, and bring
      A Cure to my Consumption as a King?

Shall not that Wisdom horded in thee (which
   Prophetick Types enucleate) forth shine   [230]
With Light enough a saving Light to fix   15
      On my Poore Taper? and a Flame Divine?
      Making my Soule thy Candle and its Flame
      Thy Light to guide mee, till I Glory gain?

Shall not that Wisdom horded in thee up
   (Which Kingly Types do shine upon in thee)   20
Mee with its Chrystall Cupping Glasses cup
      And draine ill Humours wholy out of mee?
      Ore come my Sin? and mee adorn with Grace
      And fit me for thy Service, and thy Face?

How do these Pointers type thee out most right   25
   As Graces Officine of Wisdom pure
The fingers salves and Medicines so right
      That never faile, when usd, to worke a Cure?
      Oh! that it would my Wasted lungs recrute.
      And make my feeble Spirits upward shute.   30

How Glorious art thou, Lord? Cloathd with the Glory
   Of Prophets, Priests, and Kings? Nay all Types come
To lay their Glory on thee. (Brightsome Story)
      Their Rayes attend thee, as Sun Beams the sun.
      And shall my Ulcer'd Soule have such reliefe?   35
      Such glorious Cure? Lord strengthen my beliefe.

Why dost not love, my Soule? or Love grow Strong?
    These glorious Beams of Wisdom on thee shine.
Will not this sunshine make thy branch green long,
    And flowrish as it doth to heaven climbe?   40
    Oh! chide thyselfe out of thy Lethargie.
    And unto Christ on Angells wings up fly.

Draw out thy Wisdom, Lord, and make mee just.
    Draw out thy Wisdom. Wisdoms Crown give mee.
With shining Holiness Candy my Crust: 45
    And make mee to thy Scepter bow the knee.
    Let thy rich Grace mee save from Sin, and Death:
    And I will tune thy Praise with holy Breath.

---

25 most right *orig.* upright
27 The fingers *orig.* So fingering
39 make *ins.* ; thy branch green *orig.* Green and Long

WESTFIELD ⎫
12.10M   ⎬   15. MEDITATION. MAT. 2.23. HE SHALL BEE
1695/6   ⎭   CALLED A NAZARITE.   [231]

A Nazarite indeed. Not such another.
    More rich than Jasper, finer far than silke.
More cleane than Heavens froth the skies out pother:
    Purer than snow: and Whiter far than Milke.
    In Bodie ruddier than Rubies, nay   5
    Whose pollishing of Sapphires brave, and gay.

Devoted by thy Father and thyselfe.
    To all Examplary Holy Life.
Grace's Chiefe Flower pot on highest shelfe
    In all Gods Hall Here Holiness is rife.   10
    And higher Herbs of Grace can never grow
    In Bulk, or Brightness, than before us flow.

Thy Typick Holiness, more sweet than Muske,
    Ore tops the paltry Dainties of strong Drinke:

Or Vines whose Fruite is Casked in an huske,   15
   And Kirnelld with hard stones: though from their Chink
Bleeds royall Wine: and grapes sweet Raisens make
The Wine will Soure; types may not of it take.

The letter of the Law of Nazarites
   Concerns thee not; the spirit oft is meet   20
For thee alone. Thou art the Vine t'invite's.
   The Grape without Husk, stone, The Raisen sweet.
   Yea, thou thyselfe, the Wine, and strong Drink art
   E're sweet, nere Vinegar, or soureing sharp.

Thy Head that wares a Nazaritick Crown.   25
   Of Holiness Deckt with its purple Hair
Dide in the Blood thy Grape shed when presst down
   Derides the Rasor. Saints there nestled are.
   And when thy Vow is o're under the wing
   Of their Peace offering thy praise they'le sing.   30

Thou never wast defiled by the Dead.
   No Dead thing ever, yet disstained thee.
Life from thy Fingers ends runs, and ore spred
   Itselfe through all thy Works what e're they bee.
   Thy Thoughts, Words, Works are lively, frim, do still   35
   Out spirituall Life. Thy Spirit doth them fill.

Pare off, my Lord, from mee I pray my pelfe.
   Make mee thy Nazarite by imitation   [232]
Not of the Ceremony, but thyselfe.
   In Holiness of Heart, and Conversation.   40
   Then I shall weare thy Nazarite like Crown
   In Glory bright with songs of thy Renown.

---

13 Thy *orig.* The
18 may not of it *orig.* may nt it
24 soureing *orig.* sourer
25 that wares *orig.* doth ware
26 Holiness Deckt *orig.* Holiness set
31 defiled *orig.* defilled

WESTFIELD   } 16. MEDITATION. LU. 1.33 HE SHALL REIGN
9.1M 1695/6   }   OVER THE HOUSE OF JACOB FOREVER.

Thou art, my Lord, the King of Glory bright.
  A glory't is unto the Angells flame
To be thy Harauld publishing thy Light
  Unto the Sons of Men: and thy rich Name.
  They are thy Subjects. Yet thy realm is faire.   5
  Ore Jacobs House thou reignest: they declare.

Their brightest glory lies in thee their king.
  My Glory is that thou my king maist bee.
That I may be thy Subject thee to sing
  And thou may'st have thy kingdoms reign in mee.   10
  But when my Lips I make thy scepter Kiss
  Unheartiness hatcht in my heart doth hiss.

Rich Reason, and Religion Good thus cry,
  Be Subject, Soule: of Jacobs house be one.
Here is a king for thee. Whom Angells fly   15
  To greet and honour Sitting in his throne.
  Sins mutiny, and marr his intrest brave.
  My Pray'res grow Dead. Dead Corps laid in the grave.

The lowly Vine beares fruitfull clusters, Rich.
  The Humble Olive fat with oyle abounds.   20
But I like to the fiery Bramble, Which
  Jumps at a Crown, am but an empty sound.
  A guilded Cask of tauny Pride, and Gall,
  With Veans of Venom o're my spirits sprawle.

Like to the Daugh all glorious made when dresst   25
  In feathers borrowed of other birds
Must need be King of birds: but is distresst,
  When ery bird its feather hath, and Curbd
  Doth glout, and slouch her Wings. Pride acts this part.
  And base Hypocrisy. Oh! rotten heart!   30

Blesst Lord, my King, where is thy golden Sword?
    Oh! sheath it in the bowells of my Sin.
Slay my Rebellion, make thy Law my Word.
    Against thine Enemies Without within.   [233]
    Implant mee as a branch in Gods true vine   35
    And then my grape will yield thy Cup rich wine.

Shall I, now grafted in thy Olive tree
    The house of Jacob, bramble berries beare?
This burdens me to thinke of, much more thee
    Breake off my black brire Claws: mee Scrape, and pare.   40
    Lord make my Bramble bush thy rosie tree.
    And it will beare sweet Roses then for thee.

Kill my Hypocrisie, Pride, Poison, Gall.
    And make my Daugh thy Turtle Dove ore laid.
With golden feathers: and my fruites then shall   45
    Flock Dovelike to thy Lockers, oh! Choice trade.
    My Cooing then shall be thy Musick in,
    The House of Jacob, tun'de to thee my King.

---

5 Yet *orig.* yea
19 beares *orig.* grows
28 hath *ins.*
44 Daugh *orig.* Dawgh
46 Flock *orig.* flock

WESTFIELD } 17. MEDITATION. EPH. 5.2. AND GAVE HIMSELFE
16:6. 1696 }   FOR US AN OFFERING, AND A SACRIFICE TO GOD.

Thou Greate Supream, thou Infinite first One.
    Thy Being Being gave to all that be
Yea to the best of Beings thee alone
    To serve with service best for best of fee.
    But man the best servd thee the Worst of all   5
    And so the Worst of incomes on him falls.

Hence I who'me Capable to serve thee best
  Of all the ranks of Beings here below
And best of Wages win, have been a pest
  And done the Worst, earn'd thus the Worst of Woe.   10
  Sin that imploys mee findes mee worke indeed
  Me qualifies, ill qualities doth breed.

This is an hell indeed thus to be held
  From that which nature holdst her chiefe delights
To that that is her horrour and refelld   15
  Ev'n by the Law God in her Essence writes
  But for reliefe Grace in her tender mould
  Massiah cast all sacrifices told.

I sin'd. Christ bailes, Grace takes him surety,
  Translates my sin upon his sinless shine.   20
He's guilty thus, and Justice thus doth eye
  And Sues the band and brings on him the fine.
  All Sacrifices burn but yet their blood
  Can't quench the fire, When laid upon the Wood.   [234]

They type; thy Veane phlebotomizd must bee   25
  To quench thus Fire; no other blood nor thing
Can do't. Hence thou alone art made for mee
  Burnt, Meat, Peace, Sin, and Trespass Offering.
  Thy blood must fall: thy life must go or I
  Under the Wrath of God must ever fry.   30

This fire upon thee burnt, and is allay'd
  For all of thine. Oh make mee thine, I pray.
So shall this Wrath from me be retrograde.
  No fire shall Sindge my rags nor on them Stay.
  New qualify mee, I shall then on go   35
  Anew about thy service, and it do.

What Grace in God? What Love in Christ thus spring
  Up unto men, and to my poore poore heart?
That so thy burning fire no sparke can fling

Or sparkle on such Tinder. This impart   40
Unto thy servant. This will be my Health:
And for a gift to thee I send myselfe.

Oh! that my Love, was rowld all ore and ore
   In thine, and Candi'd in't: and so refin'd
More bright than gold, and grown in bulke far more   45
   Than tongue can tell of each best sort, and kind.
   All Should be thine, and I thine own will be.
   Accept my gift; no better is with mee.

Then own thine own. Be thou my sacrifice.
   Thy Father too, that he may father mee.   50
And I may be his Child, and thy blood prize.
   That thy attonement may my clearing bee.
   In hope of Which I in thy service sing
   Unto thy Praise upon my Harp within.

---

4 of *ins.*
18 Massiah cast *orig.* Did Cast Massiah
22 And *orig.* And sh[*]es
24 quench *orig.* wench
25 phlebotomizd *orig.* phlegmbotomizd
34 Sindge *orig.* Singe
37 spring *orig.* springs
47 and *orig.* and all

Westfield ⎫
            ⎬   18. Meditation. Heb. 13.10. Wee have an Altar.
18.8m 1696 ⎭

A Bran, a Chaff, a very Barly yawn,
   An Husk, a Shell, a Nothing, nay yet Worse.
A Thistle, Bryer prickle, pricking Thorn
   A Lump of Lewdeness, Pouch of Sin, a purse
   Of Naughtiness, I am, yea what not Lord?   5
   And wilt thou be mine Altar? and my bord?   [235]

Mine Heart's a Park or Chase of Sins: Mine Head
　'S a Bowling Alley; Sins play Ninehole here.
Phansy's a Green: Sin Barly breaks in't led.
　Judgment's a pingle: Blindeman's Buff's plaid there.　　10
　Sin playes at Coursy Parke within my Minde.
　My Will's a Walke in which it aires what's blinde.

Sure then I lack Attonement. Lord me help.
　Thy Shittim Wood ore laid With Wealthy brass
Was an Atoning altar, and Sweet Smelt:　　15
　But if ore laid with pure pure gold it was
　It was an Incense Altar, all perfum'd.
　With Odours, wherein Lord thou thus was bloom'd.

Did this ere during Wood when thus orespread
　With these erelasting Metalls altarwise　　20
Type thy Eternall Plank of Godhead Wed
　Unto our Mortall Chip, its Sacrifice?
　Thy Deity mine Altar. Manhood thine,
　Mine Offring on't for all mens Sins, and mine?

This Golden Altar puts such weight into　　25
　The Sacrifices offer'd on't, that it
Ore weighs the Weight of all the sins that flow
　In thine Elect. This Wedge, and beetle Split
　The Knotty Logs of Vengeance too to shivers:
　And from their Guilt and * * * them cleare delivers.　　30

This Holy Altar by its Heavenly fire
　Refines our Offerings: casts out their dross
And Sanctifies their Gold by its rich 'tire.
　And all their Steams with Holy Odours boss.
　Pillars of Frankincense and rich Perfume　　35
　They 'tone Gods nosthrills with, off from this Loom.

Good News, Good Sirs, more good than comes within
　The Canopy of Angells. Heavens Hall
Allows no better: this atones for Sin,
　My Glorious God, Whose Grace here thickest falls.　　40

May I my Barly yawn, Bran, Bryer Claw
Lay on't a Sacrifice? or Chaff or Straw?

Shall I my Sin Pouch lay, on thy Gold Bench
  My Offering, Lord, to thee? I've such alone
But have no better. For my Sins do drench   45
  My very best unto their very bone.
  And shall mine Offering by thine Altars fire
  Refin'd, and sanctifi'd to God aspire?

Amen, ev'n so be it. I now will climb,
  The stares up to thine Altar, and on't lay   50
Myselfe, and services, even for its shrine.
  My Sacrifice brought thee accept I pray.
  My Morn, and Evning Offerings I'le bring
  And on this Golden Altar Incense fling.

Lord let thy Deity mine Altar bee   55
  And make thy Manhood, on't my sacrifice.
For mine Atonement: make them both for mee
  My Altar t'sanctify my gifts likewise
  That so myselfe and Service on't may bring
  Its worth along with them to thee my king.   60

The thoughts whereof, do make my tunes as fume,
  From off this Altar rise to thee Most High.
And all their steams Stufft with thy Altars blooms,
  My Sacrifice of Praise in Melody.
  Let thy bright Angells catch my tune, and sing't.   65
  That Equalls Davids Michtam which is in't.

---

9 in't *orig.* it
10 a *ins.*
11 Coursy *orig.* Course
12 it aires *orig.* they aire
14 Thy *orig.* The
15 an *orig.* as
17 Incense *orig.* Insen
24 for all mens sins *orig.* for Sins of all
26 offer'd *orig.* offer'd up

28 Wedge *orig.* Widge
30 and *orig.* whereof
35 Perfume *orig.* Perfumes
42 on't *orig.* on't as
58 my *ins.*
61 tunes *orig.* tunes to
62 rise *orig.* run
65 Let thy *orig.* A tune ; my tune *orig.* the tunes
66 That *orig.* It ; which *orig.* that

Westfield   } 19. MEDITATION. CAN. 1.12. WHILE THE
7.10M 1696   }   KING SITS AT HIS TABLE, MY SPICKNARD
                    SENDS FORTH THE SMELL THEREOF.

Lord dub my tongue with a new tier of Words
  More comprehensive far than my dull speech
That I may dress thy Excellency, Lord
  In Languague welted with Emphatick [*]ich.
  Thou art my King: my Heart thy Table make   5
  And sit thereat untill my spicknard wake.

My Garden Knot drawn out most curiously
  By thy brave hand set with the bravest slips
Of spicknard: Lavender that thence may fly
  Their Wealthy spirits from their trunks and tips.   10
  That spicknard Oyle, and Oyle of spike most sweet
  May muskify thy Palace with their Reecke.   [237]

Then sit at thy round Table with delight,
  And feast in mee, untill my spicknard bloome,
And Crown thy head with Odour-Oyle rich bright,   15
  And croud thy Chamber with her Sweet perfume.
  The Spicknard in my knot then flourish will:
  And frindge thy Locks with odour it doth still.

And when thou at thy Circuite-Table sitst
  Thine Ordinances, Lord, to greet poor hearts   20
Such Influences from thyselfe thou slipst
  An[d] make their Spicknard its sweet Smell impart.

So make my Lavender to Spring, and Sent.
In Such attire her Spirits ever tent.

And as thou at thy Table Sitst to feast   25
Thy Guests thereat, Thy Supper, Lord, well drest.
Let my sweet spicknard breath most sweet, at least
Those Odours that advance thy Glory best.
And make my heart thine Alabaster Box
Of my Rich Spicknard to perfume thy locks.   30

If this thou grant, (and grant thou this I pray)
And sit my King at thy rich table thus,
Then my Choice spicknard shall its smell display,
That sweetens mee and on thee sweet doth rush.
My songs of Praise too sweeten'd with this fume   35
Shall scale thine Eares in Spicknardisick Tune.

---

6 my *ins.*
7 most *orig.* more
11 That *orig.* For
12 May *orig.* To ; Reeke *orig.* Reke
20 Thine *orig.* Even thine
22 An[d] *orig.* Ma
36 scale *orig.* skeall

7: 12M ⎫   20. MEDITATION. HEB. 9.11. BY A GREATER, AND
1696   ⎬   MORE PERFECT TABERNACLE.
       ⎭

Didst thou, Lord, Cast mee in a Worship-mould
That I might Worship thee immediatly?
Hath sin blurd all thy Print, that so I should
Be made in vain unto this End? and Why?
Lord print me ore again. Begon, begon,   5
Yee Fly blows all of hell. I'le harbour none.

That I might not receive this mould in vain
Thy Son, my Lord, my Tabernacle he

Shall be: me run into thy mould again.
  Then in this Temple I will Worship thee.   [238]10
  If he the Medium of my Worship stand
  Mee, and my Worship he will to thee hand.

I can't thee Worship now without an House.
  An house of Worship here will do no good,
Unless it type my Woe, in which I douse,   15
  And Remedy in deifyed Blood.
  Thy Tabernacle, and thy Temple they
  Such Types arose. Christ is their Sun, and Ray.

Thou wast their Authour: Art Christs too and his.
  They were of Choicest Matters. His's th'best blood.   20
Thy spirits over shaddowing form'd them, This
  Did overshaddow Mary. Christ did bud.
  The Laver, Altar, Shew Bread, Table Gold
  And Golden Light and Oyle, do Christs shine hold.

The Efficacy that's lodgd in them all   25
  Came from thyselfe in influences; nay
Their Glory's but a painted Sun on th'wall
  Compar'd to thine and that thou dost display.
  How glorious then art thou, when all their glory
  Is but a Paintery to thy bright story.   30

Thou art the Laver to wash off my Sin:
  The Altars for atonement out of hand:
The sweet sweet Incense cast the fire within:
  The Golden Table, where the Shew bread stand.
  The Golden Candlestick with holy Light   35
  Mentain'd by holy Oyle in Graces Pipe.

The flames whereof, enmixt with Grace assaile
  With Grace the heart in th'Light that takes the Eye
To light us in the way within the Vaile
  Unto the Arke in which the Angells prie   40
  Having the Law Stowd in't, up Coverd under
  The Mercy Seate, that Throne of Graces Wonder.

Thou art my Tabernacle, Temple right,
  My Cleansing, Holiness, Atonement, Food.
My Righteousness, My Guide of Temple Light   45
  Into the Holy Holies. (as is shewd)
  My Oracle, Arke, Mercy seat: the place
  Of Cherubims amazde at Such rich grace.   [239]

Thou art my Medium to God, thou art
  My Medium of Worship done to thee.   50
And of Divine Communion, sweet heart!
  Oh Heavenly intercourse! Yee Angells See!
  Art thou my Temple, Lord? Then thou Most Choice
  Art Angells Play-House, and Saints Paradise.

Thy Temples Influences stick on mee.   55
  That I in Holy Love may stow my heart
Upon thyselfe, and on my God in thee.
  And with its Holiness guild Every part
  Of me: and I will as I walke herein
  Thy Glory thee in Temple Musick bring.   60

25 that's *orig.* that
34 where the *orig.* and his
37 enmixt *orig.* inmixt ; assaile *orig.* out throws
38 With Grace *orig.* Grace on
44 Atonement *orig.* my Atonement
53 Most *orig.* bl
58 its Holiness *orig.* Holiness *orig.* Holy

16.3M
}
1697
21. MEDITATION. COL. 2.16.17.—IN RESPECT OF
AN HOLY DAY, OF A NEW MOON, OR A SABBATH.
WHICH ARE FIGURES.

Rich Temple Fair! Rich Festivalls my Lord,
  Thou makst to entertain thy Guests most dresst
In dishes up by SEVENS which afford
  Rich Mystery under their brims expresst.
  Which to discover clearly make the brain   5

Of most men wring, their kirnells to obtain.

Each Seventh Day a Sabbath Gracious Ware.
  A Seventh Week a yearly Festivall.
The Seventh Month a Feast nigh, all, rich fare.
  The Seventh Yeare a Feast Sabbaticall.   10
  And when Seven years are Seven times turnd about
  A Jubilee. Now turn their inside out.

What secret sweet Mysterie under the Wing
  Of this So much Elected number lies?
What Vean can e're Divine? or Poet sing?   15
  Doubtless most Rich. For such shew God most Wise
  I will adore the Same although my quill
  Can't hit the string that's tun'd by such right skill.

Sharpen my Sight my Lord that I may spie
  A lively Quickness in it jump for joy   20
And by the breaking of the shell let fly
  Such pleasant species as will folly 'Stroy.   [240]
  Out of these Feasts, although the Number Seven
  I leave untill my Soul is housd in Heaven.

And here I beg thy aide. Mine eyes refine.   25
  Untill my sight is strong enough to spy
Thyselfe my Lord deckt all in Sun-Like shine.
  And see myselfe cloathd in thy Beams that fly,
  My sight is dim: With Spectacles mee suite
  Made of a pair of Stars it to recrute.   30

Make mee thy Lunar Body to be filld
  In full Conjunction, with thy Shining Selfe
The Sun of Righteousness: whose beams let guild
  My Face turnd up to heaven, on which high shelfe
  I shall thy Glorys in my face that shine,   35
  Set in Reflected Rayes. Hence thou hast thine.

Moon-like I have no light here of mine own.
  My Shining beams are borrowd of this Sun.

With which when 'ray'd its Rayes on mee are shown
   Unto this World as I it over run.   40
   My black side's Earthward, Yet thy beams that flew
   Upon mee from thy face, are in its view.

Hence Angells will in heaven blow up aloud
   For joy thy Trumpet on my new Moon day.
And in its Prime, the Golden Rayes that shroud   45
   Within thy Face will guild my Edges gay.
   Oh! Happy Change. the Sun of Righteousness
   With's healing Wings my moon doth richly dress.

And though this world doth eye thy brightness most
   When most in distance from thyselfe I'm backt,   50
Yet then I most am apt even from this Coast
   To be Ecclipsd, or by its fogs be blackt.
   My back at best, and dark side Godward bee,
   And pitchy clouds do hide thy face from mee.

Oh! let not Earth, nor its thick fogs I pray   55
   E're Slip between me and thy lightsome Rayes
But let my Cloathing be thy Sunshine Ray.
   My New-Moon Trumpet then shall sound thy prai[se.]   [241]
   I then in Sweet Conjunction shall with thee
   The Sun of Righteousness abiding bee.   60

---

2 makst *orig.* make
6 wring *orig.* ring
10 Feast *orig.* Feast offer
12 Jubilee *orig.* Jubilee steps in
13 sweet Mysterie *orig.* Myteries
17 the *ins.* ; by *ins.*
18 the *ins.* ; by *ins.*
23 These Feasts all *canc.*
28 cloathd *orig.* cloathe ; thy *orig.* the
34 high *ins.*
35 Glorys *orig.* Glory ; shine *orig.* shines
42 mee *orig.* my
43 aloud *orig.* loud
44 my *ins.*

46 Edges *orig.* Edge all
49 brightness *orig.* bright
54 clouds do *orig.* cloud to
57 my *ins.*

22. MEDITATION. 1 COR. 5.7. CHRIST OUR
    PASSOVER IS SACRIFICED FOR US.

I from the New Moon of the first month high
  Unto its fourteenth day When she is Full
Of Light the Which the shining Sun let fly
  And when the Sun's all black to see Sins pull
  The sun of Righteousness from Heaven down   5
  Into the Grave, and weare a Pascall Crown.   [242]

A Bond slave in Egyptick Slavery
  This Noble Stem, Angellick Bud, this Seed
Of Heavenly Birth, my Soul, doth groaning ly.
  When shall its Pass o're come? when shall't be Free'd?   10
  The Lamb is slain upon the fourteenth day
  Of Month the first, my Doore posts do display.

Send out thy Slaughter Angell, Lord, and Slay
  All my Enslaving 'Gypsies Sins, while I
Eate this rost Mutten, Paschall Lamb, Display   15
  Thy Grace herein, while I from Egypt high.
  I'le feed upon thy Roast meat here updresst.
  With Bitter hearbs, unleaven'd bread the best.

I'le banish Leaven from my very Soule
  And from its Leanetoe tent: and search out all   20
With Candles lest a Crum thereof Should rowle
  Into its Corners or in mouseholes fall.
  Which when I finde I'le burn up, and will Sweep
  From every Corner all and all cleane keep.

My Bunch of Hyssop, Faith, dipt in thy blood   25
  My Paschall Lamb, held in thy Bason bright

Baptize my Doore Posts shall, make Crimson good
  Let nothing off this Varnish from them wipe.
  And while they weare thy Crimson painted dy,
    No Slaughter Angell Shall mine house annoy.   30

Lord, purge my Leaven out: my Tast make quick:
  My Souls Strong Posts baptize with this rich blood
By bunch of Hyssop, then I'le also lick
  Thy Dripping Pan: and eat thy Roast Lamb good.
  With Staff in hand. Loins Girt, and Feet well Shod   35
  With Gospell ware as walking to my God.

I'le Goshen's Ramesis now leave apace.
  Thy Flag I'le follow to thy Succoth tent
Thy sprinkled blood being my lintells grace
  Thy Flesh my Food, with bitter herbs attent   40
  To minde me of my bitter bondage State
  And my Deliverance from all Such fate.   [243]

I'le at this Feast my First sheafe bring, and Wave
  Before thee, Lord, my Crop to Sanctify
That in my first Fruits I my harvest have   45
  May blest unto my Cyckle Constantly.
  So at this Feast my harp shall Tunes advance
  Upon thy Lamb, and my Deliverance.

But now I from the Passover do pass.
  Easter farewell; rich jewells thou did shew,   50
And come to Whitsuntide, and turn the Glass
  To Search her sands for pearles therein anew
  For Isra'l a fifti'th day from Egypt broke,
  Gave Sinai's Law, and Crown'd the mount with Smoke.

And Christ our Passover had not passt o're   55
  Full fifty dayes before in fiery guise
He gave Mount Zions Law from graces store
  The Gospell Law of Spirit and Life out highs
  In fiery Tongue, that did confound all those
  At Pentecost that Zions King oppose.   60

The Harvest of the year through Grace now inn'd
  Enjoyd and Consecrated with Right praise,
All typifying that the right we Sind
  Away's restor'd by Christ: and all things raisd
  Fit for our use, and that we thankfully   65
  Unto the use thereof ourselves should ply.

Lord make me to this Pentecost repare,
  Make mee thy Guest too at this Feast: and live
Up to thy Gospell Law: and let my fare
  Be of the two white Loaves this feast doth give.   70
  If Prophets Seeding yield me harvest, I
  Will as I reap sing thee my harvest joy.

---

1 first *orig.* first pass
4 And when the Sun's *orig.* And the Sun
22 will *orig.* well
27 Crimson *orig.* Cris
39 being *orig.* being being
46 my *ins.*
57 Zions *orig.* Sions
64 things *orig.* things made

17.7M ⎫ 23. MEDITATION. 1. JOH. 2.2. HE IS THE
1697 ⎭ PROPITIATION FOR OUR SINS.

Greate Lord yea Greatest Lord of Lords thou art,
  And King of Kings, may my poor Creaking Pipe
Salute thine Eare. This thought doth Sink my heart
  Ore burdened with over sweet Delight.   [244]
  An Ant bears more proportion to the World   5
  Than doth my piping to thine eare thus hurld.

It is a Sight amazing strange to see
  An Emperour picking an Emmets Egge.
More strange it's that Almighty should to mee

E're lend his Eare. And yet this thing I beg.   10
I'm Small and Naught, thou mayst much less me Spare
Than I the Nit that hangeth on my hair.

But oh thy Grace! What glory on it hings,
In that thou makst thy Son to bare away
The marrow of the matter choice that Clings   15
Unto the service of Atonment's day?
This was his Type, He is its Treasure rich
That Reconciles for sin that doth us ditch.

Sins thick and threefold at my threshold lay
At Graces threshold I all gore in Sin.   20
Christ backt the Curtain. Grace made bright the day,
As he did our Atonement full step in.
So Glorious he. His Type is all unmeet
To typify him till aton'd and sweet.

A'ron as he atonement made, did ware   25
His milke white linen Robes, to typify
Christ cloath'd in human flesh pure White, all fair,
And undefild, atoneing God most High.
Two Goates he took, and lots to know Gods will
Which he should send away: and Which, should kill.   30

Dear Christ, thy Natures two are typ't thereby
Making one sacrifice, Humane, Divine.
The Manhood is Gods Lot, and this must dy.
The Godhead as the Scape Goate death declines.
One Goat atones, one beares all Sin away.   35
Thy natures do this work, each as they lay.

Aaron the blood must catch in's Vessell t' hold.
Lord let my Soule the Vessell be of thine.
Aaron must in a Censar all of Gold
Sweet incense burn with Altars fire Divine   [245]40
To Typify the incense of thy Prayer.
Perfuming of thy Service thou didst beare.

Aaron goes in unto the Holy place
  With blood of Sprinkling and sprinkles there
Atones the Tabernacle, Altars face   45
  And Congregation, for defild all were.
  Christ with his proper blood did enter in
  The Heavens bright, propitiates for Sin.

Aaron then burns the Goat without the Camp
  And Bullock too whose blood went in the Vaile.   50
Christ sufferd so without the Gate Deaths Cramp.
  And Cramped Hell thereby; the Divells quaile.
  Thus done with God Aaron aside did lay
  His Linen Robes, and put on's Golden 'Ray.

And in this Rich attire he doth apply   55
  Himselfe before the peoples very eyes,
Unto the other Service richly high
  To typify the gracious properties
  Wherewith Christs human nature was bedight
  In which he mediates within Gods Sight.   60

What wonder's here? Shall Such a Sorry thing
  As I have such rich Cost laid down for mee
Whose best at best as mine's not worth a Wing
  Of one poore Fly, that I should have from thee
  Such Influences of thy goodness smite mee   65
  And make me mute as by delight envite mee?

Lord let thy Gracious hand me chafe, and rub
  Till my numbd joynts be quickn'd and compleat,
With Heate and Spirits all divine, and good.
  To make them nimble in thy Service Greate.   70
  Oh! take my ALL thyself, allthough I bee
  All bad, I have no better gift for thee.

Although my gift is but a Wooden toole
  If thou receive it, thou wilt it enrich
With Grace, that's better than Apollo's Stoole.   75
  Thy Oracles't will utter out the which

Will make my Spirits thy bright golden Wyers
ALTASCHAT Michtam tune in Angells Quires.

---

6 piping *orig.* pipe
11 much *ins.*
17 his *orig.* thy ; Type, *orig.* Type, Th
19 lay *orig.* ly
24 aton'd *orig.* atone
34 death declines *orig.* deat doth fly
50 Vaile *orig.* Vale

25:10M ⎫ MEDITATION 24. JOH. 1.14. ἐσκήνωσε[ν] ἐν ἡμῖν
1697   ⎭ TABERNACLED AMONGST US.

My Soul would gazing all amazed Stand,
   To See the burning Sun, with'ts golden locks
(An hundred Sixty Six times more than th'land)
   Ly buttond up in a Tobacco box.
   But this bright Wonder, Lord, that fore us playes   5
   May make bright Angells gasterd, at it gaze.

That thou, my Lord, that hast the Heavens bright
   Pav'd with the Sun, and Moon, with Stars o're pinckt,
Thy Tabernacle, yet shouldst take delight
   To make my flesh thy Tent, and tent within't.   10
   Wonders themselves do Seem to faint away
   To finde the Heavens Filler housd in Clay.

Thy Godhead Cabbin'd in a Myrtle bowre,
   A Palm branch tent, an Olive Tabernacle,
A Pine bough Booth, An Osier House or tower   15
   A mortall bitt of Manhood, where the Staple
   Doth fixt, uniting of thy natures, hold,
   And hold out marv[els] more than can be tol[d.]

Thy Tabernacles floore Celestiall
   Doth Canopie the Whole World. Lord; and wilt   20

Thou tabernacle in a tent so small?
  Have Tent, and Tent cloath of a Humane Quilt
  Thy Person make a bit of flesh of mee,
  Thy Tabernacle, and its Canopee?

Wonders! my Lord, Thy Nature all With Mine   25
  Doth by the Feast of Booths Conjoynd appeare
Together in thy Person all Divine
  Stand House, and Householder. What Wonder's here?
  Thy Person infinite, without compare
  Cloaths made of a Carnation leafe doth war[e.]   30

What Glory to my nature doth thy Grace
  Confer, that it is made a Booth for thine
To tabernacle in? Wonders take place.
  Thou low dost step aloft to lift up mine.   [247]
  Septembers fifteenth day did type the Birth   35
  Of this thy tabernacle here on earth.

And through this leafy Tent the glory cleare
  Of thy Rich Godhead Shineth very much:
The Crowds of Sacrifices which Swarm here
  Shew forth thy Efficacy now is Such   40
  Flowing in from thy natures thus united
  As Clears off Sin, and Victims all benighted.

But yet the Wonder grows: and groweth much,
  For thou wilt Tabernacles change with mee.
Not onely Nature, but my person tuch.   45
  Thou wilst mee thy, and thee, my tent to bee.
  Thou wilt, if I my heart will to thee rent,
  My Tabernacle make thy Tenement.

Thou'lt tent in mee, I dwell in thee shall here.
  For housing thou wilt pay mee rent in bliss: 50
And I shall pay thee rent of Reverent fear
  For Quarters in thy house. Rent mutuall is.
  Thy Tenent and thy Teniment I bee.
  Thou Landlord art and Tenent too to mee.

Lord lease thyselfe to mee out: make mee give   55
  A Lease unto thy Lordship of myselfe.
Thy Tenent, and thy Teniment I'le live:
  And give and take Rent of Celestiall Wealth.
I'le be thy Tabernacle: thou shalt bee
  My Tabernacle. Lord thus mutuall wee.   60

The Feast of Tabernacles makes me Sing
  Out thy Theanthropy, my Lord, I'le spare
No Musick here. Sweet Songs of praises in
  The Tabernacles of the Righteous are.
  My Palmifer'd Hosannah Songs I'le raise   65
  On my Shoshannims blossoming thy praise.

---

1 Soul *orig.* Soul dot
3 more *orig.* bigger
17 Doth *orig.* Is
29 infinite *orig.* enfinite
37 the *orig.* thy
39 The *orig.* C
51 pay *orig.* b ; of Reverent *orig.* in S[**]ei[**]
53 and *ins.* ; Teniment *orig.* Pal[*****]
57 Teniment *orig.* Tenement
60 wee *orig.* bee

6:1M   }   MEDITATION 25. NUMB. 28.4.9 ONE LAMB SHALT
               THOU OFFER IN THE MORNING, AND THE OTHER AT
1698   }   EVEN. AND ON THE SABBATH DAY TWO LAMBS &C.

Guilty, my Lord, What can I more declare?
  Thou knowst the Case, and Cases of my Soule.
A Box of tinder: Sparks that falling are
  Set all on fire, and worke me all in shoals.
  A Pouch of Passion is my Pericarde.   5
  Sparks fly when ere my Flint and Steele strike hard.

I am a Dish of Dumps: yea ponderous dross,
  Black blood all clotted, burdening my heart.

That Anger's anvill and my bark bears moss
  My Spirits Soakt are drunke with blackish Art.   10
  If any Vertue Stir, it is but feeble.
  Th'Earth Magnet is, my heart's the trembling needle.

My Mannah breedeth Worms: Thoughts fly blow'd are.
  My heart's the Temple of the God of Flies.
My Tongue's an Altar of forbidden Wear,   15
  Fansy a foolish fire enflam'd by toys
  Perfum'de with reeching Offerings of Sins
  Whose steaming reechs delight hobgoblings.

My Lord, is there no help for this with thee?
  Must I abuse, and be abused thus?   20
There Morn, and Even Sacrifices bee:
  To cleans the Sins of Day, and Night from us,
  Christ is the Lamb: my Pray're each morn and night
  As Incense offer I up in thy Sight.

My morn, and evening Sacrifice I bring   25
  With Incense sweet upon mine Altar Christ.
With Oyle and wine two quarters of an Hin
  With flower for a Meat Offering all well Spic'dt,
  On bended knees, with hands that tempt the skies.
  This is each day's atoning sacrifice.   30

And thou the Sabbath settledst at the first.
  And wilt continue it till last. Wherefore   [249]
Who strike down Gospell Sabbaths are accurst.
  Two Lambs, a Meat, and Drinke offering God more
  Conferd on it than any other Day   35
  As types the Gospell Sabbaths to display.

Here is Atonement made: and Sprituall Wine
  Pourd out to God: and Sanctified Bread
From Heaven's givn us: What Shall we decline
  With God Communion, thus to be fed?   40
  This Heavenly fare will make true Grace to thrive.
  Such as deny this thing are not alive.

I'le tend thy Sabbaths: at thine Altar feed.
  And never make thy type a nullitie.
The Ceremonies cease, but yet the Creede   45
  Containd therein, continues gospelly.
  That makes my Feeble spirits will grow frim.
  Hence I in Sabbath Service love to swim.

My Vespers, and my Mattins I'le attend:
  My Sabbath Service carry on I will.   50
Atoning Efficacy God doth send
  To Sinners in this path. and grace here stills.
  Still this on me untill I glory Gain.
  And then I'le Sing thy praise in better strain.

Date orig. 1697
Title 9 orig. 10
12 the *ins.*
14 the Temple *orig.* a Temple
15 Wear *orig.* Wears
17 with *orig.* with with
18 steaming *orig.* steaing
29 with *orig.* and with
32 till last *orig.* untill the last
36 As Types *orig.* To typify
41 Heavenly *orig.* Heaven
47 make *orig.* makes
52 grace *orig.* d

26:4M   MEDITATION. 26. HEB. 9.13.14. HOW MUCH MORE SHALL
1698   THE BLOOD OF CHRIST, &c.

Unclean, Unclean: My Lord, Undone, all vile,
  Yea all Defil'd: What shall thy servant doe?
Unfit for thee: not fit for holy soile,
  Nor for Communion of Saints below.
  A bag of botches, Lump of Loathsomeness: 5
  Defild by Touch, by Issue: Leproast flesh.

Thou wilt have all that enter do thy fold
  Pure, Cleane, and bright, Whiter than whitest Snow
Better refin'd than most refined Gold:
  I am not so: but fowle: What shall I doe?   10
  Shall thy Church Doors be shut, and shut out mee?
  Shall not Church-fellowship my portion bee?   [250]

How can it be? Thy Churches do require
  Pure Holiness. I am all filth, alas!
Shall I defile them, tumbled thus in mire?   15
  Or they mee cleanse before I current pass?
  If thus they do, Where is the Niter bright
  And sope they offer mee to wash me White?

The Brisk Red heifers Ashes, when calcin'd,
  Mixt all in running Water is too Weake   20
To wash away my Filth: The Dooves assign'd.
  Burnt, and sin Offerings neer do the feate,
  But as they Emblemize the Fountain spring
  Thy Blood, my Lord, set ope to wash off Sin.

Oh! richest Grace! Are thy Rich Veans then tapt   25
  To ope this Holy Fountain (boundless Sea)
For Sinners here to lavor off (all Sapt
  With Sin) their Sins and Sinfulness away?
  In this bright Chrystall Crimson Fountain flows
  What washeth whiter than, the Swan or Rose.   30

Oh! wash mee, Lord, in this Choice Fountain, White
  That I may enter, and not sully here
Thy Church, whose floore is pav'de with Graces bright
  And hold Church fellowship with Saints most clear.
  My Voice all Sweet, with their melodious layes   35
  Shall make Sweet Musick blossom'd with thy prais[e.]

---

4 Nor *orig.* Or
13 require: *orig.* requre
15 them *orig.* them entering
24 off *orig.* away

4:7M   ⎫   MEDITATION 27. UPON HEB.9.13.14. HOW MUCH MORE
1698   ⎬   SHALL THE BLOOD OF CHRIST &c.

My mentall Eye, spying thy Sparkling Fold
  Bedeckt, my Lord, with Glories shine alone:
That doth out do all Broideries of Gold;
  And Pavements of Rich Pearles, and Precious Stone
  Did double back its Beams to light my sphere   5
  Making an inward search, for what springs there.

And in my Search I finde myselfe defild:
  Issues and Leprosies all ore mee streame.
Such have not Enterance. I am beguild:
  My Seate, Bed, Saddle, Spittle too's uncleane.   10
  My Issue Runs: my Leprosy doth Spread:
  My upper Lip is Coverd: not my Head.   [251]

Hence all ore ugly, Nature Poysond stands,
  Lungs all Corrupted, skin all botchd and scabd
A Feeble Voice, a stinking Breath out fand   15
  And with a Scurfy skale I'me all ore clagd
  Robes rent: Head bare, Lips Coverd too I cry.
  Uncleane, Uncleane, and from thy Camp do fly.

Woe's mee! Undone! Undone! my Leprosy!
  Without a Miracle there is no Cure.   20
Worse than the Elephantick Mange I spie
  My Sickness is. And must I it endure?
  Dy of my Leprosy? Lord, say to't nay:
  I'le Cure thee in my wonder working way.

I see thy Gracious hand indeed hath cought   25
  Two Curious pritty pure Birds, types most sure
Of thy two Natures. And the one is brought.
  To shed its blood in running waters pure
  Held in an Earthen Panchin which displays
  Thy Blood and Water preacht in Gospell dayes.   30

The slain Dove's buri'de: In whose Blood in water
  The Living Turtle, Ceder, Scarlet twine
And Hysop diptd are (as an allator)
  Sprinkling the Leper with it seven times.
  That typify Christs Blood by Grace appli'de   35
  To Sinners vile, and then they're purifi'de.

Sprindge Lord mee With it. Wash me also in
  The Poole of Shiloam, and shave mee bare
With Gospell Razer. Though the Roots of Sin
  Bud up again, again shave off its hair.   40
  Thy Eighth dayes Bath, and Razer make more gay,
  Than th'Virgin Maries Purifying day.

My Tresspass, Sin, and my Burnt Sacrifice
  My Flowre and Oyle, for my meate Offering
My Lord, thou art. Whether Lambs or Doves up rise   45
  And with thy Holy Blood atonement bring.
  And put thy Blood upon my Right Eare fair
  Whose tip shall it, its Onely jewell, Ware.

[A]nd put it Gold-Ring-like on my Right Thumbe
  And on my Right Greate toe as a Rich Gem.   50
[T]his Blood will not Head, Hand nor Foot benum.
  But satisfy and cleans all fault from them.   [252]
  Then put thy Holy Oyle upon the place
  Of th'Blood of my Right Eare, Thumb, Toe. Here's Grace.

Then Holiness shall Consecrate mine Eare.   55
  And sanctifie my Fingers Ends, and Toes.
And in my hearing, Working, Walking here
  The Breath of Sanctifying Grace out goes.
  Perfuming all these Actions, and my life.
  Oh! sweetest sweet. Hence Holiness is rife.   60

Lord, Cleanse mee thus with thy Rich Bloods sweet shower
  My Issue stop: destroy my Leprosy.
Thy Holy Oyle upon my Head out poure

And cloathe my heart and Life with sanctity.
My Head, my Hand and Foot shall strike thy praise.   65
If thus besprinkled, and Encamp thy Wayes.

---

2 shine *orig.* glittering shine
14 scabd *orig.* stabd
27 And *ins.*
33 Hysop diptd are *orig.* Hysop are diped
34 Sprinkling *orig.* And Sprinkl **e
45 art *orig.* art alone
50 a *ins.*
54 th' *ins.*
64 cloathe *orig.* clathe

11:10M   MEDITATION 28. ISAI 32.2. A MAN SHALL BE FOR
1698   A HIDING PLACE FROM THE WINDE.

That Bowre, my Lord, which thou at first didst build.
   Was pollished most gay, and ev'ry ranck
Of Creatures in't shone bright, each of them filld
   With dimpling Glory, Cield with golden planck
   Of Smiling Beauty. Man then bore the Bell;   5
   Shone like a Carbuncle in Glories Shell.

How brave, and bright was I then, Lord, myselfe?
   But woe is mee! I have transgresst thy Law.
Undone, defild, Disgrac'd, destroy'd my Wealth.
   Persu'de by flaming Vengeance, as fire dry straw.   10
   All Ranks I broake, their Glory I benighted,
   Their Beauty blasted, and their Bliss befrighted.

Hence Black-Blew, Purple spots of Horrid guilt,
   Rise in my Soule. Mee Vengeance hath in Chrase
To spill my blood, 'cause I her Glory Spilt.   15
   And did the Creatures Glory all disgrace.
   Shall I fall by the Venger's hand, before
   I get within the Refuge-Citie's doore?

Oh! give me Angells Wings to fly to thee.
    My Lord, all Stumbling Stones pick out of th'way: 20
Thou art my Refuge City: and Shalt bee.
    Receive me in, let not th'Avenger slay.
    I do attempt to over run my Sin:
    And fly to thee, my Refuge. Let mee in.

I've by my sin a man, the Son of man   25
    Slain, and myselfe, Selfe-Murderer, I slew.   [253]
Yet on the Golden Wings of Faith which fan
    The Gospell Aire the Altars Horns I wooe.
    Renouncing all my Sins, and Vanity
    And am resolv'd before the same to dy.   30

Accept me Lord, and give my Sailes thine Aire.
    That I may swiftly sayle unto thyselfe.
Be thou my Refuge, and thy Blood my faire.
    Disgrace my Guilt: and grace me with thy Wealth.
    Be thou my Refuge City; take me in.   35
    And I thy Praise will on Muth Labben sing.

---

2 pollished *orig.* pollished with
10 fire dry *orig.* fire doth
21 City *ins.*

5.12M }   MEDITATION. 29. 1.PET. 3.20. WHILE THE ARK
1698   }   WAS BUILDING.

What shall I say, my Lord? with what begin?
    Immence Profaneness wormholes ery part.
The World is Saddlebackt with Loads of Sin.
    Sin Craks the Axle tree of this greate Cart.
    Floodgates of Firy Vengeance open fly   5
    And Smoakie Clouds of Wrath darken the skie.

The Fountains of the Deep up broken are.
    The Cataracts of heaven do boile ore

With Wallowing Seas. Thunder, and Lightenings tare.
  Spouts out of Heaven, Floods out from hell do roare.   10
To overflow, and drownd the World all drownd
And overflown with Sin, that doth abound.

Oh! for an Ark, an Ark of Gopher Wood.
  This Flood's too stately to be rode upon
By other boats, which are base swilling tubs.   15
  It gulps them up as gudgeons. And they're gone.
But thou my Lord, dost Antitype this Arke.
And rod'st upon these Waves, that toss! and barke.

Thy Humane Nature, (oh Choice Timber Rich)
  Bituminated ore within, and out   20
With Dressing of the Holy Spirits pitch
  Propitiatory. Grace parg'd round about.
This Ark will ride upon the Flood, and live
Nor passage to a drop through Chink holes give.

This Ark will Swim upon the fiery flood;   25
  All showrs of fire the heavens rain on't will   [254]
Slide off: through Hells and Heavens spouts, out stood
  And meet upon't to crush't to shivers, still
  It neither sinks, breaks, Fires, nor Leaky prooves
But lives upon them all and upward mooves.   30

All that would not be drownded must be in't
  Be Arkd in Christ, or else the Cursed rout
Of Crimson sins their Cargoe will them Sinke
  And suffocate in Hell [b]ecause without.
  Then Ark me, Lord, thus in thyselfe, that I   35
  May dance upon these drownding Waves with joye.

Sweet Ark, with Concord Sweetend, in thee feed
  The Calfe, and Bare, Lamb, Lion at one Crib.
Here Rattlesnake and Squerrell jar not, breed.
  The Hawk and Dove, the Leopard, and the Kid   40
  Do live in Peace, the Child, and Cockatrice.
  As if Red Sin tantarrow'd in no vice.

Take me, my Lord, into thy golden Ark.
  Then when thy flood of fire shall come, I shall
Though Hell Spews streams of Flames, and th'Heavens spark   45
  Out storms of burning Coals, Swim safe ore all.
  I'le make thy Curled flames my Citterns Wire
  To toss my Songs of Praise rung on them, higher.

---

16 they're gone *orig.* good as none
21 Holy Spirits *orig.* Holy Ghost's Choice
26 showrs *orig.* showres
38 Lamb *orig.* Lam

9.2M
1699
} MEDITATION. 30. MATTH. 12.40. As JONAH WAS
THREE DAYES, AND THREE NIGHTS IN THE WHALES
BELLY. SO MUST &c.

Prest down with sorrow, Lord, not for my Sin!
  But with Saint 'Tony Cross I crossed groane.
Th[**] my leane Muses garden thwarts the Spring
  In Stead of Anthems, breatheth her ahone.
  But duty raps upon her doore for Verse.   5
  That makes her bleed a poem through her Searce.

When, Lord, man was the miror of thy Works
  In happy State, adorn'd with Glory's Wealth
What heedless thing was hee? The Serpent lurks
  Under an apple paring, and by Stealth   10
  Destroy'd his Glory. O poor keeper hee
  Was of himselfe; lost God, and lost his Glee.   [255]

Christ, as a Turtle Dove, puts out his Wing.
  Lay all on me, I will, saith hee, Convay
Away thy fault, and answer for thy sin.   15
  Thou'st be the Stowhouse of my Grace, and lay
  It and thyselfe out in my service pure
  And I will for thy sake the Storm Endure.

Jonas did type this thing, who ran away
    From God and shipt for Tarsus, fell asleep.   20
A storm lies on the ship; th[e] seamen: they
    Bestir their stumps, and at wits ends do weep.
    Wake Jonas, who saith, Heave me over deck.
    The Storm will Cease then, all lies on my neck.

They cast him overboard out of the Ship.   25
    The tempest terrible, lies thereby Still.
A Mighty Whale nam'd Neptunes Dog doth Skip
    At Such a Boon, Whose greedy gorge can't kill
    Neither Concoct this gudgeon, but its Chest
    Became the Prophets Coffin for the best.   30

He three dayes here lies trancifi'de and prayes.
    Prooves working Physick in the Fishes Crop
Maybe in th'Euxine, or the Issick Bay.
    She puking falls and he alive out drops.
    She vomits him alive out on the Land   35
    Whence he to Ninive receives command.

A sermon he unto the Gentiles preacht,
    Yet fortie dayes, and Ninus is destroy'd.
Space granted, this Repentance doth them teach.
    God pardons them, and thus they ruine 'void.   40
    Oh! Sweet Sweet Providence! rich Grace hath spic'te
    This Overture to be a type of Christ.

Jonas our Turtle Dove, I Christ intend
    Is in the ship for Tarsus undersaile.
A fiery Storm tempestiously doth Spend   45
    The Vessill, and its hands: all spirits faile.
    The Ship will sink or Wrack upon the rocks
    Unless the tempest cease the same to box.

None can it Charm but Jonas. Christ up posts,
    Is heaved overboard into the Sea.   50
The Dove must die; the storm gives up its Ghost   [256]

And Neptune's Dogg leapes at him as a Prey.
Whose stomach is his Grave where he doth Sleep,
Three Dayes sepulchred, Jonas in the Deep.

The Grave him swallow'd down as a rich Pill   55
Of Working Physick full of Virtue which
Doth purge Death's Constitution of its ill.
    And womble-Crops her stomach where it sticks.
    It heaves her stomach till her hasps off fly.
    And out hee comes Cast up, raisd up thereby.   60

In glorious Grace he to the Heathen goes,
    Envites them to Repentance, they accept.
Oh! Happy Message: squandering Curst foes.
    Grace in her glorious Charriot here rides deckt.
    Wrath's Fire is quencht, and Graces sun out shines.   65
    Death on her deathbed lies, Consumes and pines.

Here is my rich Atonement in thy Death,
    My Lord, nought is so sweet, though sweat it cost,
This turns from me Gods wrath: Thy sweet sweet breath
    Revives my heart; thy Rising up o're bosst   70
    My soule with Hope seeing acquittance in't.
    That all my Sins are killd, that did mee sinke.

I thanke thee, Lord, thy death hath deadned quite
    The Dreadfull Tempest; let thy Dovy wings
Ore shadow me, and all my Faults benight   75
    And with Celestiall Dews my soule besprindge.
    In Angells Quires I'le then my Michtams Sing:
    Upon my Jonah Elem Rechokim.

---

6 That *orig.* She ; poem *orig.* poem in dist[**]s[*]
22 do *ins.*
26 lies *ins.*
36 receives command *orig.* [***]e[*]ts with command
38 Ninus is *orig.* Ninus [***]ine
42 a *ins.*

60 raisd *orig.* raise
65 out *orig.* doth
66 deathbed *orig.* death

4.4M ⎱ MEDITATION 31. JOH. 15.13. GREATER LOVE
1699 ⎰ HATH NO MAN &C.

Its said Hispaniola doth enjoy
  A Tree of Gold whose Root is deemd t'have birth
At Centre of the Earth whose Spirits fly
  Ore all its body, blossoming on th'earth.
  Leaves * * * and Fruits grow on its twigs and limbs.   5
  That make a golden Smile on Spanish kings.   [257]

Yet this rich vegitable tree of Gold
  Is but a Toade Stoole bowre compar'd to thee
My blessed Lord, whose tent of Humane mould
  Shines like Gods Paradise, where springs the tree   10
  Of Pure, Pure Love that doth thy friends enfold
  In richer Robes than all those Leaves of gold.

Thy Love-Affection, rooted in the Soyle,
  Of Humane Nature, springing up all ore
With Sanctifying Grace, of brightest file   15
  Brings Loads of Love to Sinfull man all gore.
  Here is great Love, greaten'd by influences
  The which this Godhead to the same dispenses.

No spirits ever yet were founde within
  The golden Tree of Humane nature, bud   20
Or blossom such a Love, or Lovely thing
  As this thy nature doth So greate, so good.
  The Plant's set in a Soile Pure, faultless, stronge,
  Its fruite sores to the highst pitch, Good, Great Longe.

There is no Sin can touch this Lovely Love.   25
  It's Holy, with a perfect Holiness.
Its grown unto the highst Degree, above
  All stuntedness, or stately stintedness.
  The Soile is faultless, and doth give its strength.
  The Plant doth beare its fruite of largest length.   30

This Love in thee most pure, and perfect stands
  A Relative, and hath its object here
Which it befriends with all good things, and hands
  In holy wayes to heavenly Glory cleare.
  Oh! happy Such as with it are befriended: 35
  With perfect Love, to perfect bliss they're tended.

Make me thy Friend: Befriend me with thy Love.
  Here's cloaths more rich than silk or Cloth of gold.
I'le in the Circuite of thy Friendship moove
  So thy Warm Love enspire mine Organs would.   40
  My Garden will give Sweet, and Lovely Flowers
  If thou distill thereon thy Love in showres.   [258]

Lord, let thy Sunshine-Love, my Diall grace.
  Then what a Clock it is, it will display.
The glory of this Sunshine on its Face   45
  Will take the light and tell the time of Day.
  My * * * shall [**]eet this Shine as well
  With prais * * * tun'de on my bell.

---

20 bud *orig.* but
24 Greate *orig.* Greate and
42 distill *orig.* upon it distill ; thereon *orig.* therein
48 tun'de *orig.* tune

30.5M
1699
}
MEDITATION 32. JOH.[15.13.] GREATER LOVE HATH
NO MAN THAN THIS, THAT A MAN LAY DOWN HIS LIFE
FOR HIS FRIENDS.

Oh! that I could, my Lord, but chide away
　That Dulness and the Influences which
Thy All wise Providence doth brieze, display,
　Unedging of my Spiri[ts], them down pitch.
　Although thy quick'ning Love might make them spring   5
　With its War[m] Sun Shine * * * like birds they ring.

That Love of * * * that in thy Person dwells
　All Wonderfull in Birth, in Natures shine
In Union too, o're leaping Reason's shells,
　One made of two, of Humane, and Divine   10
　Of Infinite, and Finite, (take my Word)
　Compound, and Uncompound compose a Third.

That Love I see that in thy Person dwells,
　So Great and Good, nothing too good appeares
For it to give to Such on whom it fell.   15
　Although it shine on mee, I hang mine Eares,
　Although it smiles thy Providence doth scowle
　In Some things whence my Face * * * seems fowle.

Stupendous Love! Two objects * * * doth hug.
　Thy Life (that Wond'rous Life) of thine is One.   20
Thy people are the other, though they snug
　In Satans Arms, in Sin [and] Wrath are grown.
　This Object then must [**]er come * * *
　Unless thy Love * * * [**]me * * *

Love borrows Wisdome's Eyes and with them lookes   25
　O're Natures Cabbinett of Jewells bright
And then attemps th'Accounts down in Gods Books
　If Credit may be made, and they made right.
　But here she findes the Sums so greate, the Debt
　Exceed the Worth in Natures Cabinet.   [259] 30

Alass! what now? Shall Satans wiles out wit
  Wisdom itselfe? and take away Christs eye
His portion from him, and off tare and split
  The object of his Love and * * *
  Oh! Cursed Elfe * * * the foole   35
  Wilt dash thy brains o[**] * * * Wisdome's toole.

How doth she now my Lord * * * the Way
  Her object and thy intrest to set free?
She Comes to thee, and makes thy person pay
  Seing sufficient worth alone in thee,   40
  Hence to the Debt Book goes to end the striefe,
  Ore payes their debt in laying down * * * Life.

The Better object of Christs Love, Christs Love
  Surrenders up to ruin * * * redeem
The Other Object of it and remove   45
  That Wrath that else * * * ever on it been
  Which done it did resume the Life down laid.
  And both its Objects from the Curse free made.

O let thy lovely Streams of Love distill
  Upon myselfe and spoute their spirits pure   50
Into my Violl, and my Vessell fill
  With liveliness, from dulness mee secure.
  And I will answer all this Love of thine
  When with it thou hast made my * * * Divine.

What wilt thou, Lord, deny mee this, that would   55
  Not once deny to lay thy Choice life downe?
To make a Cabinet * * * more worth than gold
  To give to thine, and buy them Glories Crown,
  My Heart shall harbor better thoughts of thee
  If thou my dross dost but refine from mee.   60

Lord! make my Leaden Whittle, metall good,
  That in thy service it may Split an haire.
If thou wilt whet it on thy Holy Rub

T'will trim my Life of sin, and make mee fair.
And I will Sing a Song of Love to thee   65
In a Seraphick [tune] and full of glee.   [260]

---

3 doth *ins.*
15 on *orig.* as
25 with them *ins.*
42 debt *ins.*

MEDITATION 33. JOH. 15.13. GRETER LOVE HATH NO
1.8M   } MAN THAN THIS, THAT A MAN LAY DOWN HIS LIFE FOR
1699   } HIS FRIEND.

Walking, my Lord within thy Paradise
  I founde a Fruite whose Beauty smote mine Eye
And Tast, my Tooth that had no Core nor Vice
  An Hony Sweet, that's never rotting, ly
  Under a Tree, which view'd, I knew to bee   5
  The Tree of Life, whose Bulk's Theanthropie.

And looking up, I saw its boughs all bow
  With Clusters of this Fruit that it doth bring,
Nam'de Greatest LOVE, and well, For bulk, and brow,
  Thereof, of th'sap of Godhood-Manhood spring.   10
  What Love is here for kinde? What sort? How much?
  None ever, but the Tree of Life, bore such.

Who is the Object of this Love? And in
  Whose mouth doth fall the Apple of this tree?
Is Man? a Sinner? Such a Wormhol'de thing?   15
  Oh! matchless Love, Laid out on such as Hee!
  Should Gold Wed Dung, should Stars Wooe Lobster Cla[ws,]
  'Twould no wonder, like this Wonder, cause.

Is sinfull Man the Object of this Love?
  What then doth it for this its Object doe,   20
That doth require a purging far above

The whiteness, sope and Nitre can bestow,
(Else Justice will its Object take away.
Out of its bosome, and to hell't convay?)

Hence in it steps, to justice saith, I'll make   25
Thee Satisfaction, and my Object Shine.
I'l slay my Humane Nature for thy sake
Fild with the Worthiness of thy Divine.
Make pay therewith. The Fruite doth sacrifice
The tree that bore't. This for its object dies.   30

An Higher round upon this golden scale
Love cannot Climbe, than to lay down the Life
Of him that loves, for him belov'd to bale,
Thereby to satisfy, and end all strife.   [261]
Thou lay'st, my Lord, thy Life down for thy Friend   35
And greater Love than this none can out send.

Then make me, Lord, thy Friend: I humbly pray.
Though I thereby should be deare bought by thee
Not dearer yet than others, for the pay
Is but the same for others as for mee.
If I be in thy booke, my Life shall proove   40
My Love to thee, an Offering to thy Love.

Title hath no *ins.*
20 doe, *orig.* doe?
21 That *orig.* It
22 bestow, *orig.* bestow?
27 I'l slay my Humane Nature *orig.* This Nature Humane slayeth
29 Make *orig.* Makes
30 bore't *orig.* bore the
34 Thereby to *orig.* Thereby, and
36 can *ins.*

26.9M ⎤ 34. MEDITATION. REV. 1.5. WHO LOVED US AND WASHED
1699 ⎦ AWAY OUR SINS IN HIS BLOOD.

Suppose this Earthy globe a Cocoe Nut,
   Whose Shell most bright, and hard out challenge should
The richest Carbunckle in gold ring put.
  How rich would proove the kirnell, it should hold?
  But be it so, who then could breake this Shell,   5
  To pick the kirnell, walld within this Cell?

Should I, my Lord, call thee this nut, I should
  Debase thy Worth, and of thee basely stut.
Thou dost its worth as far excell as would
  Make it to thine worse than a worm eat nut.   10
  Were all the World a Sparkling pearle, 't would bee
  Worse than a dat of Dung if weighd with thee.

What Elemented bit was that, thine eyes
  Before the Elements were moulded, ey'd?
And it Encabbineting Jewellwise   15
  Up in thy person, hast nigh Deified?
  It lay as pearle in dust in this wide world,
  But thou it tookst, and in thy person firld.

To finde a Pearle in Oister shells, 's not strange:
  For in Such rugged bulwarks such abound.   20
But this rich Gem in Humane Natures grange,
  So bright could by none Eye but thine be found.
  It's mankinde flowr'd, searst, kneaded up in Love
  To Manna in Gods moulding trough above.

This bit of Humane Flesh Divinizd in   25
  The Person of the Son of God; the Cell
Of Soule, and Blood, where Love Divine doth swim
  Through veans, through Arteries, Heart, flesh, and fell,   [262]
  Doth with its Circkling Arms about entwinde
  A Portion of its kindred choice, Mankinde.   30

But these defild by Sin, Justice doth stave
  Off from the bliss Love them prepar'de, untill
She's satisfide, and sentence too she gave
  That thou should feel her vengeance and her will.
  Hence Love steps in, turns by the Conduit Cock.   35
  Her Veans full payment: on the Counter drop.

Now Justice satisfi'de, Loves Milke white hand
  Them takes and brings unto her Ewer of blood,
Doth make Free Grace her golden Wisp, and Sand
  With which she doth therein them Wash, scoure, rub   40
  And Wrince them cleane untill their Beauty shows
  More pure, and white, than Lilly, Swan, or Rose.

What love, my Lord, dost thou lay out on thine
  When to the Court of Justice cald they're judg'd.
Thou with thy Blood and Life dost pay their fine.   45
  Thy Life, for theirs, thy Blood for theirs must budge.
  Their sin, Guilt, Curse, upon thyselfe dost lay:
  Thy Grace, thy Justice, Life on them Convay.

Make such a Change, my Lord, with mee, I pray.
  I'le give thee then, my Heart, and Life to th'bargen.   50
Thy golden Scepter then my Soule shall sway
  Along my Path unto thy Palace garden.
  Wash off my filth, with thy rich blood, and I
  Will Stud thy praise with thankfull melody.

---

16 hast *orig.* so be'st
21 this rich Gem *orig.* t'finde this Gem
31 these *orig.* this
41 Wrince *orig.* Wince
45 pay *ins.*
53 filth, *orig.* filth, and

3:1M

1699/1700

} MEDITATION 35. JOH. 15.5. WITHOUT ME YEE
CAN DO NOTHING.

My Blessed Lord, that Golden Linck that joyns
  My soule, and thee, out blossoms on't this spruice
Peart Pronown: MY more spiritous than wines,
  Rooted in Rich Relation, Graces sluce.
    This little Voice feasts mee with fatter sweets   5
    Than all the stars that pave the Heavens streets.

It hands [***]e All, my heart, and hand to thee
  And up doth lodge them in thy persons Lodge
And as a Golden bridg ore it to mee
    Thee, and thine All to me, and never dodge.   [263]10
    In this small ship a mutuall Intrest sayles
    From Heaven and Earth, by th'holy spirits gales.

Thy Ware to me's so rich, should my Returns
  Be packt in sparkling Metaphors, out still'd
From Zion's garden flowers, by fire that burns   15
    Aright, of Saphire fuell and up filld
    And [**]nt in Jasper Vialls, all would bee
    As packs of guilded Non-Sense unto thee.

Suppose a Golden Palace Walled round
  With Walls made of transparent silver bright   20
With Towers of Diamonds and in't is found
    A Throne of sparkling Carbuncle like light
    Wherein sits Crownd one with the sunn. The same
    Would be but smoak compar'd to thy bright flame.

Thy Humane frame's a Curious Palace, raisd   25
  Of th'Creame of Natures top Perfection here,
Where Grace sits Sovereign that ere ore blazd
    The Splendent beams of precious stones most clear.
    Whose Mace, and scepter richer Matter shine,
    Than Berill, Amathyst or smaregdine.   30

Here is a Living Spring of power that tapt
　All-doing influences hence do flow.
What we have done undone us hath. (as't hapt)
　That we without thee now can nothing do
　We cannot do what do we should. (in Summ)   35
　Nor undo what undoes us, by us undone.

We have our Souls undone. Can't undo this.
　We have Undone the Law, this can't undo:
We have undone the World, when did amiss.
　We can't undoe the Curse that brings in Woe.   40
　Our Undo-Doings can't undo, it's true.
　Wee can't our Souls, and things undone, renew.

Without thee wee can nothing do, it's sure.
　Thou saidst the same. We finde thy saying true.
Thou canst do all things: all amiss canst cure.   45
　Undo our Undo-doing: make all new.
　Thou madst this World: dost it thy play-house keep
　Wherein the stars themselves do play Hide-and-Seek.

It is thy Green, where all thy Creatures play
　At Barly-Breaks and often lose their fleece.   50
But we poore wee our Soules a wager lay
　At Nine-Mens Morrice, and at Fox-and-Geese.   [264]
　Let me not play myselfe away, nor Grace,
　Nor lose my soule, My Lord, at prison base.

Reclaim thy Claim: finde me refinde; I'm thine.   55
　Without thee I can nothing do. Dispense
Thyselfe to me, and all things thine are mine,
　I'le not account of what thou countst offence.
　Give me thy Power * * * work, and thou shalt finde
　Thy Work attended with my hand, and minde.   60

---

10 me, and never *orig.* me run, and ne'er
15 fire *orig.* fires
23 one *ins.*
50 Barly-Breaks *orig.* Barly-Beaks
57 and *orig.* and I [****]

19.3M
1700
} 36. Col. 1.18. He is the Head of the Body.

An Head, my Lord, an honourable piece;
　Nature's high tower, and wealthy Jewelry;
A box of Brains, furld up in reasons fleece:
　Casement of senses: Reason's Chancery:
　Religions Chancell pia-mater'd ore　　　　　　　　　5
　With Damask Roses that sweet wisdom bore.

This is, my Lord, the rosie Emblem sweet,
　Blazing thyselfe out, on my mudd wall, fair.
And in thy Palace, where the rosy feet
　Of thy Deare spouse doth thee her head thus ware.　　10
　Her Head thou art: Head glory of her Knot.
　Thou art her Flower, and she thy flower pot.

The Metall Kingdoms had a Golden head,
　Yet had't no brains, or had its brains out dasht.
But Zions Kingdome fram'd hath better Sped　　　　　15
　Through which the Rayes of thy rich head are lasht.
　She wares thee Head, thou art her strong defence
　Head of Priority, and Excellence.

Hence art an head of Arguments so strong
　To argue all unto thyselfe, when bent　　　　　　　20
And quickly tongue ty, or pluck out the tongue
　Of all Contrary pleas or arguments.
　It makes them weake as water, for the tide
　Of Truth and Excellence rise on this Side.

Lord, let these barbed Arrows from thy bow　　　　　25
　Fly through mine Eyes, and Eares to strike my heart.
And force my Will, and Reason to thee so
　And stifle pleas made for the other part　　　　　　[265]
　That so my soule, rid of their Sophistry
　In rapid flames of Love to thee may fly.　　　　　　30

My Metaphors are but dull Tacklings tag'd

With ragged Non-Sense. Can such draw to thee
My stund affections all with Cinders clag'd,
  If thy bright beaming headship touch not mee?
  If that thy headship shines not in mine eyes.   35
  My heart will fuddled ly with wordly toyes.

Lord play thy Excellency on this pin
  To tongue ty other pleas my gadding heart
Is tooke withall. Chime my affections in
  To serve thy Sacred selfe with Sacred art.   40
  Oh! let thy Head stretch ore my heart its wing
  And then my Heart thy Headships praise shall sing.

---

10 doth *orig.* do
32 thee *orig.* thee?
39 Chime my affections *orig.* Chime all my 'ffections
42 Heart *orig.* Heat

14.5M
      } 37. Meditation. Col. 1.18. He is the Head, &c.
1700

It grieves mee, Lord, to thinke thy famous Name
  Should not be guilded ore with my bright Love.
Yet griev'd I am to thinke thy splendid fame
  Should be bedotcht by such poore stuff I moove.
  That thy Bright Pearle, impald in gold, My Theme,   5
  Should by my addle brains, finde a dull veane.

Thou art an Head, the richest, that e're wore
  A Crown of Glory, where the Kirnell lies.
Of deepest Wisdom, boxt in Brains, that sore
  In highest Notions, of the richest sise   10
  Compar'd whereto, man's Wisdom up doth rise
  Like Childrens catching speckled Butterflies.

Thou art the Head of Causes to thy Church:
  Its Cause of Reconciliation art,

Thou it Redeemdst, and hast gi'n hell the lurch.   15
  Thou sanctifiest it in Life, and Heart.
  Thou dost it Form, Inform, Reform, and Try
  Conform to thee, marre her Deformity.

A Glorious Heade of Choicest influence
  More rich than Rubies, golden rivlets lie   [266]20
Convaying Grace along these channells thence
  To heart, hand, foot, head, tongue, to eare, and eye.
  That man, as th'golden Tree, golde blossoms shoots.
  And glorifieth God with golden fruites

A Royall Head of Majesty to make   25
  Heade of thy foes th[y fo]otstoole stepping stone.
Thou giv'st forth Holy Laws, and up dost take
  The Ruling scepter over every one.
  The Golden Rule is ever in thy hand
  By which thine walk unto the golden strand.   30

Be thou my Head: and of thy Body make mee
  Thy Influences in my Cue distill.
Guild thou my Chamber with thy Grace, and take mee
  Under thy Rule, and rule mee by thy Will.
  Be thou my head, and act my tongue whereby   35
  Its tittle-tattle may thee glorify.

---

9 Of *orig.* In
26 thy *orig.* this
32 Cue *orig.* Cew
33 take *orig.* make

22.7M   } 38. MEDITATION. COL. 1.18. HE IS THE HEAD OF THE
1700   }   BODY, THE CHURCH, WHO IS THE BEGINNING.

If that my Power was answerable to
  My minde, my Lord, my little mite would rise
With something in its hand of Worth to 'stow
  And send to thee through the bright azure Skies.
  For next unto Infinity I finde   5
  Its Love unto thyselfe of boundless kinde.

Its Love, Desire, Esteem of thee all scorn
  Confining limits, whose Dimensions stand
Immeasurable, but my Power's down born,
  Its impotency; Cannot heave a Sand   10
  Over a Straw, that all the fruites my Will
  Can e're produce, can't t[**]e or one Sin kill.

This Wracks my heart, and low my person layes
  And rowles mee in the dust at thoughts hereon.
That thou, who dost deserve all glorious praise   15
  Should with an Empty Will, whose power is none
  Be pai'd, indeed; But yet. (O pardon mee)
  I want a power, not will to honour thee.   [267]

Thou Wisdom art, Wisdom's the heads Chiefe thing,
  Thou the Beginning art of Gods Creation.   20
And therefore art of Excellence the spring
  And the Beginning of all Holy station.
  First born from th'Dead: Sun like thy Excellence
  All Good things doth like sunbeames forth dispense.

All Love, and Praise, all service, Honour bright   25
  From all the Sons of men is but thy due.
Thou their beginning art: they and their might
  Should sing thy glory out and it forth show.
  But, oh my shame, I have no Power, nor skill
  To do the same, onely an Empty Will.   30

But, oh my Lord, thou the Beginning art,
  Begin to draw afresh thine Image out
In shining Colours, on my Life, and Heart.
  Begin anew thy foes in mee to route.
  Begin again to breize upon my Soule   35
  Breize after brieze untill I touch the goale.

Thou the Beginning art of Order, and
  Art Head of Principalities and Power
Archont of Kings, Archangell to the Band
  Of Angells, and Archangells in their flower.   40
  Thou art, Lord, Principall whence Beings run
  And all best things like Sun beames from the Sun.

Be ever, Lord beginning till I end,
  At carrying on thine Intrest in my soule.
For thy beginning will my marr'd minde mende   45
  And make it pray, Lord, take mee for thy tole.
  If mee as Wheate thy Tole-Dish doth once greet
  My tune's to thee Al-tashcheth Mictam sweet.

---

13 low *orig.* layes
41 whence *orig.* all
42 things *orig.* things hence
48 Al-tashcheth *orig.* [**]l-tasheth

[*].10M   ⎫   39. MEDITATION COL. 1.18. THE FIRST
1700   ⎭   BORN FROM THE DEAD.

Poor wither'd Crickling, My Lord, am I
  Whose shrunke up skin hidebounds my kirnell so   [268]
That Love its Vitall sparke's so squeezd thereby
  'T must breake the prisons Walls ere it can go
  Unto thyselfe. Hence let thy warm beams just   5
  Make it so grow that it may breake its husk.

Love like to hunger breaks through stone strong Walls.
  Nay brazen walls cannot imprison it
Up from its object, when its object calls
  In Beams attractive falling on it thick.   10
  My Chilly Love sick of the Ague lies.
  Lord touch it with thy Sunshine; make it rise.

Death shall not deaden it, while thy sun shines.
  The keyes of Hell, and Death are at thy side.
Thy Conquoring Pow're draws ore the grave thy lines.   15
  Whose darksom Dungeon thy dead body tri'de.
  Thou hast Deaths shady Region Conquoured,
  Rose, as the Sun, up First born from the Dead.

First Fruits of them that sleep to Sanctify
  The Harvest all, thou art; thou art, therefore   20
The First born from the Dead in Dignity
  In kinde, Cause, Order to dy, and rise no more.
  As those raisd up before must, whose Erection
  Rather Reduction was than Resurrection.

Thy Humane Nature in the Cock-Pit dread,   25
  Like as the morning birds when day peeps, strout
Stands Crowing ore the Grave, laid Death there dead.
  And ore its Carkass neckt, doth Crow about.
  Throws down the Prison doors, comes out, and lay
  Them ope that th'Prisoners may come away.   30

But Lord Strike down the iron Gate also
  Of spiritual Death. Unprison thus my soule:
Breath in the Realm of Life on it bestow,
  And in thy Heavenly Records me enrowle.
  And then my bird shall Crow thus roosted high.   35
  Death, where's thy sting? Grave, where's thy Victory?

The Golden Twist of Unity Divine
  Lord make the Ligaments to ty mee fast
Unto thyselfe, a Member W[i]th this twine

Binde me to thee, For this will ever last.   40
My Tunes shall rap thy prayses then good store
In Death upon the Resurrection Doore.   [269]

Date 10 *orig.* 9
Title 39 *orig.* 38
6 so *orig.* to ; may *ins.*
7 hunger *orig.* hunger will ; strong *ins.*
12 it *ins.*
18 Rose *orig.* And Rose
20 art *orig.* art still
23 before *ins.*
26 Like as the *orig.* And like the
32 Death *ins.*
34 thy Heavenly *orig.* thy Records
41 then good store *orig.* ever w[***]ere

[****]M ⎫   40. MEDITATION. COL 1.18. THAT IN ALL THINGS
1701   ⎬   HE MIGHT HAVE THE PREHEMINENCE.
         ⎭

Under thy Rod, my God, thy Smarting Rod:
   That hath off broke my James, that Primrose, Why?
Is't for my Sin? Or Triall? Dost thou nod
   At me, to teach mee? or mee sanctify?
   I needed have this hand, that broke off hath   5
   This Bud of Civill, and of Sacred Faith.

But doth my Sickness want such remedies,
   As Mummy draind out of the Body Spun
Out of my bowells first? Must th'Cure arise
   Out of the Coffin of a pious Son?   10
   Well: so be it. I'le kiss the Rod, and shun
   To quarrell at the stroake. Thy Will be done.

Yet let the Rose of Sharon Spring up cleare,
   Out of my James his ashes unto mee,
In radient Sweet and shining Beames to cheer   15

My sorrowfull Soule, and light my way to thee.
Let thy Preheminence which, Lord, indeed
Ore all things is, me help in time of need.

Thy Humane nature so divinely ti'de
  Unto thy Person all Divine's a Spring   20
So hath advanc'd, that in it doth reside
  Preheminence large over ev'ry thing.
  Thy Humane flesh with its Perfections shine
  Above all other Beauties in their prime.

The like ne're seen in Heaven, nor Earth so broad.   25
  Adorn'd with Graces all, grown ripe in glory.
Thy Person with all Excellency stowd
  Perfections shine is lodgd in ev'ry story.
  Here all Created, all Creating faire,
  And Increated Eminences are.   30

Here all Preheminence of Offices
  Priest, Prophet-King-Hood too, their glorys rise
Conferrd on thee, my Lord, and all their Keyes
  That open us thy shining Mysteries
  Which do enflame our hearts their heads to run   35
  Under the shining Wings of this bright Sun.   [270]

Lord lead my sight to thy Preheminence.
  Raise thou in mee right feare of thee thereby.
My Love to thee advance till it Commence
  In all Degrees of Love, a Graduate high,   40
  When thy Preheminence doth ply this pin.
  My Musick shall thy Praises sweetly bring.

---

8 draind out *orig.* draind of
15 and *ins.*
20 thy *orig.* the
24 Above *orig.* S

6.5M   41. MEDITATION. HEB. 5.8. HE LEARND BY THE
1701   THINGS WHICH HE SUFFERED.

That Wisdom bright whose vastness for extent
  Commensurates Dimension infinite
A Palace built with saphir-Battlement
  Bepinkt with Sun, Moon, Starrs, all gold-fire bright
  Plac'de man his Pupill here, and ev'ry thing,   5
  With loads of Learning, came to tutor him.

But he (alas) did at the threashould trip,
  Fell, Crackt the glass through which the sun should shine
That darkness gross his noble soule doth tip.
  Each twig is bow'd with loads of follies Rhime.   10
  That ev'ry thing in tutoring, is a toole
  To whip the scholler that did play the foole.

The Case thus stands: Hence matters up arose
  More sweet than Roses, and out-shine the sun:
That Living Wisdom put on dying Cloaths: 15
  In mortall roabs to Sorrows schoole house run.
  The Vessell full, can hold no more, doth goe
  To Schoole to learn, whose learning cannot grow.

Christ, where all Wisdom's Treasures hidden are,
  Is Schollar, Suffering's his Tutor-Master: 20
Obedience, is his Lesson, which (as fair
  As Light in th'Sun) flows from him, yea and faster.
  But how should he learn any learning more
  In whom all Learning's ever lodg'd before?

Surely it must be said, the Humane Hall,   25
  Though furnished with all Ripe Grace, yet was
Not all ore Window that no beame at all
  Of further light could have into it pass.
  He grew in Wisdom, Wisdom grew in him
  As in's, though's Godhead other wayes did't bring.   [271]30

Though Grace in Christ for ever perfect was
  And he e're perfectly was free from Sin
His progress yet in Knowledg needs must pass
  The Passes, humane modes, admit the thing.
  Hence learnd Obedience in his suff'ring-schoole.   35
  Experience taught him (though a Feeble toole).

O Condescention! Shall the Heavens do
  Low Conjues to the Earth? or Sun array
Itselfe with Clouds, and to a Glow worm go
  For Light to make all o're the World light day?   40
  That thou should learn in Sorrows schoole, in whom
  All learning is, and whence all learnings come?

Wonder, my soule, at this great Wonder bright,
  And in this frame, Lord, let my heart to thee
On Angells Wings fly, out of Earths Eyesight.   45
  Obedience learn in sorrows schoole of thee
  Till right Obedience me hath handed in
  Among thy Palace songs thy praise to sing.

---

5 man *orig.* man as
12 whip *orig.* whipt ; the foole *orig.* foole
17 no *ins.*
19 hidden *orig.* are
27 Not *orig.* Not o're
28 could *ins.*
36 (him] *orig.* though th'Mistress of a Foole ; though *ins.*
48 praise to *orig.* praises

31.6M   } 42. MEDITATION. HEB. 10.5. A BODY HAST THOU
1701   } PREPARED MEE. σῶμα δὲ κατηρτίσω μοι.

I fain would prize thee, Lord, but finde the price
  Of Earthy things to rise so high in mee.
That I no pretious matter in my choice
  Can finde within my heart to offer thee.

The price of worldly toyes is grown so deare,   5
They pick my purse; thy Coine is little there.

But oh! if thou one Sparke of heavenly fire
Wilt but drop on my hearth; its holy flame
Will burn my trash up, and refin'de desire
   Will rise to thee in th'Curlings of the Same.   10
   As Pillars of Perfuming incense rise,
   And surges bright of Glory, 'bove the skies.

Oh! that my soul was Walled round about
   With Orient Pearle fetcht out of holy Mine
And made a Castle, where thy Graces Stoute   15
   Keep garison against my foes and thine.   [272]
   Then they each peeping thought sent scout of sin
   Would quickly take, and gibbit up therein.

But, oh! the swarms of enemies to thee
   (Bold sawce boxes) make in these quarters spoile.   20
Make insurrection 'gainst the motions free
   Of thy good Spirit: Lord, come, scoure the Ile
   Of these, and quarter here each flourishing grace.
   The Whole will then be in a Wealthy Case.

Thou for this end, a Body hadst prepar'de: 25
   Where Sin ne'er Set a foot, nor shewd its head
But ev'ry grace was in it, and well far'de.
   Whose fruite, Lord, let into my heart be shed.
   Then grace shall grace my Soule, my Soule shall thee
   Begrace, and shall thy gracefull Palace bee.   30

Thy Body is a Building all like mine,
   In Matter, Form, in Essence, Properties.
Yet sin ne'er toucht it, Grace ne'er ceast in't'shine.
   It, though not Godded, next to th'Godhead lies.
   This honour have I, more than th'Angells bright.   35
   Thy Person, and my Nature do Unite.

Oh! Thanks, my Lord, accept this dusty thing:

If I had better, thou should better have.
I blush, because I can no better bring:
   The best I do possess, I for thee save.   40
   Wash in thy blood, my gift till white it bee:
   And made acceptable to God by thee.

In humble wise, I thee implore to make
   Me, what thou, and thy Father ever love.
Empt me of Sin: Fill mee with Grace: and take   45
   Up while I'me here, my heart to thee above.
   My soule shall sing Thanksgiving unto thee.
   If thou wilt tune it to thy praise in mee.

---

4 within *orig.* with
6 Coine *orig.* Gaine
11 Perfuming *orig.* Perfume
12 And *orig.* In
13 soul *orig.* heart
20 make in these quarters *orig.* these quarters all do

26.8M ⎱ MEDITATION. 43. ROM.9.5. GOD BLESSED
1701 ⎰ FOR EVER.

When, Lord, I seeke to shew thy praises, then
   Thy shining Majesty doth stund my minde.
Encramps my tongue, and tongue ties fast my Pen,
   That all my doings, do not what's designd.   [273]
   My speeches Organs are so trancifide   5
   My words stand startld, can't thy praises stride.

Nay Speeches Bloomery can't from the Ore
   Of Reasons mine, melt words for to define
Thy Deity, nor t'deck the reechs that sore
   From Loves rich Vales, sweeter than hony rhimes.   10
   Words though the finest twine of reason, are
   Too Course a web for Deity to ware.

Words Mentall are Syllabicated thoughts:
  Words Orall but thoughts Whiffld in the Winde:
Words Writ, are incky, Goose quill-slabbred draughts: 15
  Although the fairest blossoms of the minde.
  Then can such glasses cleare enough descry
  My Love to thee, or thy rich Deity?

Words are befould, Thoughts filthy fumes that smoake,
  From smutty Huts, like Will-a-Wisps that rise   20
From Quaugmires, run ore bogs where frogs do Croake,
  Lead all astray led by them by the eyes.
  My muddy Words so dark thy Deity,
  And cloude thy sun-shine, and its shining sky.

Yet spare mee, Lord, to use this hurden ware.   25
  I have no finer Stuff to use, and I
Will use it now my Creed but to declare
  And not thy Glorious Selfe to beautify.
  Thou art all-God: all Godhead then is thine
  Although the manhood thereunto doth joyne.   30

[handwritten margin note: But he tries it anyway]

Thou art all Godhead bright, although there bee
  Something beside the Godhead in thee bright:
Thou art all Infinite although in thee
  There is a nature pure, not infinite.
  Thou art Almighty, though thy Humane tent   35
  Of Humane frailty upon earth did sent.

He needs must be the Deity most High,
  To whom all properties essensiall to
The Godhead do belong Essentially
  And not to others: nor from Godhead go.   40
  And thou art thus, my Lord, to Godhead joynd.
  We finde thee thus in Holy Writ defin'de.   [274]

Thou art Eternall; Infinite thou art;
  Omnipotent, Omniscient; Erywhere
All Holy, Just, Good, Gracious, True, in heart,   45

Immortall, though with mortall nature here.
Religious worship hence belongs to thee
From men and angells: all, of each degree.

Be thou my God, and make mee thine Elect
  To kiss thy feet, and worship give to thee: 50
Accept of mee, and make mee thee accept.
  So I'st be Safe, and thou shalt served bee.
  I'le bring thee praise, buskt up in Songs perfum'de,
  When thou with grace my soule hast sweetly tun'de.

Date 8m *orig.* 7m
14 but *orig.* bee
19 filthy *orig.* gr[**]y
25 this *ins.*
27 it *orig.* it onely
29 not *ins.*
33 although *orig.* although there b
44 Omniscient, *orig.* Omniscient, Ubitary
46 here *orig.* w[***]y
48 angells: *orig.* angells from men and

28.10M   ⎫   MEDITATION. 44. JOH. 1.14. THE WORD WAS MADE
1701   ⎭   FLESH.

The Orator from Rhetorick gardens picks
  His Spangled Flowers of Sweet-breathd Eloquence
Wherewith his Oratory brisk he tricks
  Whose Spicy Charms Eare jewells do commence.
  Shall bits of Brains be candid thus for eares?   5
  My Theme claims Sugar Candid far more cleare.

Things styld Transcendent, do transcende the stile
  Of Reason, reason's stares neere reach so high.
But Jacobs golden Ladder rounds do foile
  All reasons Strides, wrought of THEANTHROPIE.   10
  Two Natures distance-standing, infinite,
  Are Onifide, in person, and unite.

In Essence two, in Properties each are
  Unlike, as unlike can be. One All-Might,
A Mite the other; One Immortall fair.   15
  One mortall, this all Glory, that all night,
  One Infinite, One finite, so for ever:
  Yet ONED are in Person, part'd never.

The Godhead personated in Gods Son
  Assum'd the Manhood to its Person known,   20
When that the Manhoods essence first begun
  That it did never Humane person own.
  Each natures Essence e're abides the same.
  In person joynd, one person each do claim.   [275]

Oh. Dignifide Humanity indeed: 25
  Divinely person'd: almost Deifide.
Nameing one Godhead person, in our Creed,
  The Word-made-Flesh. Here's Grace's 'maizing stride.
  The vilst design, that villany e're hatcht
  Hath tap't such Grace in God, that can't be matcht.   30

Our Nature Spoild: under all Curses groans
  Is purgd tooke, grac'd with grace, united to
A Godhead person, Godhead-person owns
  Its onely person. Angells Lord it's so.
  This Union ever lasts, if not relate   35
  Which Cov'nant claims Christs Manhood, separate.

You Holy Angell, Morning-Stars, bright-Sparks,
  Give place: and lower your top gallants; shew
Your top-saile Conjues to our slender barkes:
  The highest honour to our nature's due.   40
  It's neerer Godhead by the Godhead made
  Than yours in you that never from God stray'd.

Here is good anchor hold: and argument.
  To anchor here, Lord make my anchor stronge
And Cable, both of holy geer, out sent   45
  And in this anch'ring dropt, and let at length.

My bark shall Safely ride then though there fall
On't th'strongest tempests hell can raise of all.

Unite my Soule, Lord, to thyselfe, and stamp
  Thy holy print on my unholy heart.   50
I'st nimble be when thou destroyst my cramp
  And take thy paths when thou dost take my part.
  If thou wilt blow this Oaten straw of mine.
  The sweetest piped praises shall be thine.

---

12 Onifide *orig.* One
18 in *ins.*
20 Person *orig.* Person so
32 purgd *ins.* ; grac'd *orig.* washt, grac'd
34 Angells *orig.* Lord of Angells
45 geer, *orig.* geer, to hold fast, and

15.12M   ⎫ 45. MEDITATION. COL. 2.3. IN WHOM ARE HID
1701   ⎭   ALL THE TREASURES OF WISDOM.

My head, my Lord, that ivory Cabinet
  'S a nest of Brains dust-dry, ne're yet could Ware
The Velvet locks of Vertue for its deck
  Or golden Fleece of Wisdoms virdent hair.
  The scull without, not fring'd with Wisdom fleece,   5
  The pan within a goose pen full of geese.   [276]

There Reason, wick yarn-like ore twisted snarles
  Chandled with sensuall tallow out doth blaze
A smoaky flame upon its hurden harles
  That Wil-a-Wisps it into boggy wayes.   10
  Melt off this fat, my Reason make thy Candle,
  And light it with thy Wisdom's flames that spangle.

Thy Person's Wisdoms sparkling Treasury:
  Consisting of two natures: One of which
Runs parallell with blest infinity.   15

All treasures here of Wisdom ever pitch,
Wise Counsills all, of everlasting date.
And Wisdom them t'effect, here sits in state.

Th'other's a Locker of a Humane frame
  With richer than Corinthian Amber, tills,   20
And shelves of Emralds. Here to deck the same
  All Wisdom that's Created comes, and fills
  Created Wisdom all and all its Wealths
  Of Grace are treasur'de in these Tills and shelfes.

Like to a Sparkling Carbuncle up Caskt   25
  Within a Globe of Chrystall glass most cleare.
Fills't all with shine which through its sides are flasht,
  And makes all glorious shine: Is much more here.
  These treasures of thy Wisdom shine out bright
  In thee. My Candle With thy Flame, Lord, Light.   30

Or as the Sun within its Azure bowre
  That guilds its Chrystall Walls with golden rayes
And from its bowl like body, light out poures
  Exiling darkness, making glorious dayes.
  All Wisdom so, and Wisdoms Treasures all   35
  Are shining out in thee, their Arcinall.

Unlock thy Locker, make my faith Key here
  To back the Wards. Lord ope the Wicket gate
And from thine Emrald shelves, and Pinchase there
  A beame of every sort of Wisdom take   40
  And set it in the Socket of my Soule
  To make all day within, and night controle.

And from these tills, and drawers take a grain
  Of every sort of Sanctifying grace
Wherewith impregnate thou the former beame.   45
  Set in my Soule a lamp to light that place
  That so these beames let in, may generate
  Grace in my Soule, and so an Holy State.   [277]

If wisdom in the socket of my heart
   And Grace within its Cradle rockt do shine   50
My head shall ware a frindg of Wisdom's art.
    Thy grace shall guild this pilgrim life of mine.
    Thy Wisdom's Treasure thus Conferrd on mee
    Will have my glory all Conferrd on thee.

---

8 tallow *orig.* tallow ever
18 t'effect *orig.* to effect
23 Wealths *orig.* Welths
25 up *ins.*
28 Is *orig.* It's
30 thy *orig.* this
31 Azure *orig.* Chr
33 And *orig.* It
50 Grace within its Cradle rockt *orig.* in its Cradle Grace rockt there
51 frindg *orig.* fring

10.3M   ⎫   46. MEDITATION. COL. 2.9. THE FULNESS OF
1702   ⎭   THE GODHEAD DWELLETH IN HIM BODILY.

I drown, my Lord. What though the Streame I'm in
   Rosewater bee Or Ocean to its brinkes
Of Aqua Vitæ where the ship doth swim?
    The Surges drown the soul, oreflowd, that sinks.
    A Sea of Liquid gold with rocks of pearle   5
    May drownd as well as Neptune's Fishy Well.

Thy Fulness, Lord, my Filberd cannot hold.
   How should an acorn bowle the Sea lade dry?
A Red rose leafe the Suns bright bulk up fold?
    Or halfe an Ants egge Canopy the Sky?   10
    The world play in a sneale horn Hide, and seek
    May, ere my thimble can thy fulness meete.

All fulness is in thee my Lord, and Christ.
   The fulness of all Excellence is thine.
All's palac'de in thy person, and bespic'de   15

All Kinds, and Quantities of't in thee shine.
The Fulness of the Godhead in respect
Unto the Manhood's in thy person kept.

Hence all the Properties, that Godhead hath,
  And all their Godhead Operations brave,   20
Which are the Fulness Godhead forth display'th,
  Thy person for their Temple ever have.
All alwaye as transcendent Stones bright, set;
  Encabin'd are in thee their Cabbinet.

Oh! what a Lord and Lordship's here, my Lord?   25
  How doth thy Fulness, fill thy Hall with shine?
Some Rayes thereof my Cottage now afford
  And let these golden rayes its inside line.
Thy Fulness all, or none at all, Will goe
  Together, and in part will never flow.   [278]30

All, Lord, or None at all! this makes mee dread.
  All is so Good, and None at all so bad.
All, puts faith to't: but none at all strikes dead.
  I'le hope for all, lest none at all makes sad.
Hold up this hope. Lord, then this hope shall sing   35
  Thy praises sweetly, spite of feares Sad sting.

---

3 where *orig.* all where
5 A Sea *orig.* Will Drown
11 play *orig.* plays
14 all *ins.*
18 Manhood's *orig.* Manhood is

12.5M } 47. MEDITATION. JOH. 5.26. THE SON HATH LIFE
1702   }   IN HIMSELFE.

Noe mervaile if my mite amaized bee
　Musing upon Almighties Mighty ALL
In all its Fulness socketed in thee
　　As furniture, my Lord, to grace thy Hall.
　　Thy Work requires that so the Case should goe.　　　5
　　But oh! what Grace doth hence to Sinners flow?

I strike mine oare not in the golden Sea
　Of Godhead Fulness, thine essentially.
But in the Silver Ocean make my way
　　Of All Created Fulness, thine Most high.　　　10
　　Thy Humane Glass, God wondrously did build:
　　And Grace oreflowing, with All fulness Filld.

Thou dost all Fulness of all Life possess.
　Thy Life all varnisht is with virdent flowers
'Bove Sense and Reason in their brightest dress.　　　15
　　Lifes best top-gallant ever in thee towers.
　　The Life of Grace that Life of Life within
　　Thy knot in heavenly sparks is flourishing.

Besides thy proper Lifes tall fulness-Wealth,
　There Life in thee, like golden Spirits, stills　　　20
To ery member of thy Mystick Selfe,
　　Through secret Chases into th'vitall tills
　　Or like the Light embodi'd in the Sun
　　That to each living thing with life doth run.

A Well of Living Water: Tree of Life,　　　25
　From whom Life comes to evry thing alive:
Some Eate and Drink Eternall Life most rife
　　Some life have for a while by a reprive.
　　Who in this well do let their bucket down
　　Shall never in the lake of Lethe drown.　　　[279]30

Lord, bath mee in this Well of Life. This Dew

Of Vitall Fruite will make mee ever live.
My branch make green: my Rose ware vivid hew
  An Holy and a fragrant sent out give.
My kirnell ripe shall rattle out thy praise.   35
And Orient blush shall on my actions blaze.

---

16 Lifes *orig.* The
20 There *orig.* There's ; stills *orig.* stilld
24 living thing *orig.* thing alive

13.7M ⎱
1702   ⎰   48. MEDITATION. REV. 1.8. THE ALMIGHTY.

O! What a thing is Might right mannag'd? 'T will
  That Proverb brain, whose face doth ware this paint.
(Might ore goes Right) for might doth Right fulfill.
  Will Right revive when wrong makes Right to faint.
  Might hatches Right: Right hatches Might, they are   5
  Each Dam, and Chick, to each: a Lovely paire.

Then Might well mannag'd riseth mighty: yet
  Doth never rise up to Almightiness.
Almightiness nere's in a mortall bit.
  But, Lord, thou dost Almightiness possess.   10
  Might in its fulness: all mights Fulness bee
  Of ery sort and sise stow'd up in thee.

But what am I, poor Mite, all mightless thing!
  That cannot rive a rush, that I should e're
Adventure t'dress Almighty up, or bring   15
  Almightiness deckt in its mighty geere?
  Then Spare my stutting stamring, inky Quill,
  If it its bowells on thy Power distill.

My Mite (if I such solicisms might
  But use) would spend its mitie strength for thee   20
Of Mightless might, [o]r feeble stronge delight.

Its little ALL thy Sacrifice should bee.
For thee't would mock at all the Might and Power
That Earth, and Hell possess: and on thee shower.

A Fig for Foes, for Divells, Hell, and all   25
The powres of darkness, thou now on my side.
Their Might's a little mite, Powers powerless fall.
    My Mite Almighty will not let down slide.   [280]
    I will not trust unto this Might of mine:
    Nor in my Mite distrust, while I am thine.   30

Thy Love Almighty is, to Love mee deare,
    Thy Grace Almighty mee to save: thy Truth
Almighty to depend on. Justice cleare
    Almighty t'justify, and judge. Grace shewth.
    Thy Wisdom too's Almighty all to eye.   35
    And Holiness is such to sanctify.

If thy Almightiness, and all my Mite
    United be in sacred Marriage knot,
My Mite is thine: Mine thine Almighty Might.
    Then thine Almightiness my Mite hath got.   40
    My Quill makes thine Almightiness a string
    Of Pearls, to grace the tune, my Mite doth sing.

---

2 That *orig.* The
12 stow'd up *orig.* stored
21 [o]r *orig.* f
24 shower *orig.* p[**]
27 Might's *orig.* Mite's
30 Mite *orig.* Migh
39 Mine *orig.* thine
40 Then *orig.* Mine
41 makes *orig.* shall ; a *orig.* forth

8.9M
1702 } 49. Joh. 1.14. Full of Grace.

Gold in its Ore, must melted be, to bring
  It midwift from its mother womb: requires
To make it shine and a rich market thing,
  A fining Pot, and Test, and melting fire.
  So do I, Lord, before thy grace do shine   5
  In mee, require, thy fire may mee refine.

My Flame hath left its Coale, my fire's gone t'bed:
  Like Embers in their ashie lodgen gray.
Lord let the Influences of thy head
  Most graciously remoove this rug away.   10
  If with the Bellows of thy grace thou blow
  My ashes off, thy Coale will shine, and glow.

Thy Clay, and Mine, out of one pit are dug:
  Although with spades of vastest differing kinde.
Thine all bright Godhead; mine of mortall Wood,   15
  Thine shod with Glory, Mine with sin all rin'de.
  Thy Soule, and Mine made of one minerall
  And each made regent o're their Clayie Hall.

But oh! alas! mine's Wall is worm-hold, and
  My House and Household sogd with noisom sin   20
And no reliefe can have in Creature's hand
  While thine all Sparkling shines without, and in.   [281]
  Fild with all Grace, and Graces Fullness all
  Adorning of thy Household and thy Hall.

But woe is mee; uncleane, I am: my slips!   25
  Lord, let a Seraphim a live Coale take
Off of thine Altar, with it touch my lips.
  And purge away my sins for mercys sake.
  I thus do pray finding thy Cask within
  With Grace, and graces fulness fild to th'brim.   30

I empty, thou top full, of Grace! Lord, take
  A Gracious Cluster of thy glorious grace
And busk it in my bosom, Sweet to make
  It, and my life: and gracious, in thy face.
  If thou with gracious Sweetness sweeten mee   35
  My Life with Grace Sweetly perfum'de shall bee.

Can I a graceless member be of thee,
  While that thy head's a Spring of Grace? and Heart
All gracious is to give? Then influence mee
  With thy free Grace. Thou art my lovely marke.   40
  When thy rich Grace doth tune my song, sung high
  Thy Glory then shall rise its melody

---

6 may mee *orig.* mee t
10 this *orig.* the
15 mine *orig.* mine all
31 empty *orig.* emt

27.10M ⎫
         ⎬   50. Meditation. Joh. 1.14. Full of Truth.
1702   ⎭

The Artists Hand more gloriously bright,
  Than is the sun itselfe, in't's shining glory
Wrought with a stone axe, made of Pearle, as light
  As light itselfe, out of a Rock all flory
  Of Precious Pearle, a Box most lively made   5
  More rich than gold Brimfull of Truth enlaid.

Which Box should forth a race of boxes send
  Teemd from its Womb such as itselfe, to run
Down from the Worlds beginning to its end.
  But, o! this box of Pearle Fell, Broke: undone.   10
  Truth from it flew: It lost Smaragdine Glory:
  Was filld with Falshood: Boxes teemd of Sory.

The Artist puts his glorious hand again
   Out to the Worke: His Skill out flames more bright
Now than before. The worke he goes to gain,   15
   He did portray in flaming Rayes of light.   [282]
   A Box of Pearle shall from this Sory, pass
   More rich than that smaragdine Truth-Box was.

Which Box, four thousand yeares, o'r ere 'twas made,
   In golden scutchons lay in inke Divine   20
Of Promises; of a Prophetick shade,
   And in embellishments of Types that shine.
   Whose Beames in this Choice pearle-made-Box all meet
   And bedded in't their glorious Truth do keep.

But now, my Lord, thy Humane Nature, I   25
   Doe by the Rayes this Scutcheon sends out, finde
Is this smaragdine Box where Truth doth ly
   Of Types, and Promises, that thee out lin'de.
   Their Truth they finde in thee: this makes them shine.
   Their Shine on thee makes thee appeare Divine.   30

Thou givst thy Truth to them; thus true they bee.
   They bring their Witness out for thee. Hereby
Their Truth appeares emboxt indeed in thee:
   And thou the true Messiah shin'st thereby.
   Hence Thou, and They make One another true   35
   And They, and Thou each others Glory shew.

Hence thou art full of Truth, and full dost stand,
   Of Promises, of Prophesies, and Types.
But that's not all: All truth is in thy hand,
   Thy lips drop onely Truth: give Falshood gripes,   40
   Leade through the World to glory, that ne'er ends,
   By Truth's bright Hand all such as Grace befriends.

O! Box of Truth! tenent my Credence in
   The mortase of thy Truth: and Thou in Mee.
These Mortases, and Tenents make so trim,   45

That They and Thou, and I ne'er Severd bee.
Embox my Faith, Lord, in thy Truth a part
And I'st by Faith embox thee in my heart.

---

9 beginning *orig.* begining
19 o'r ere't *orig.* ere it
20 lay *orig.* layd
24 And *orig.* Em ; do *orig.* to
25 Lord *orig.* Glorious Lord
31 thus true *orig.* this makes
40 give *orig.* and

14.12 ⎱ 51. MEDITATION. EPH. 1.23. WHICH IS HIS BODY, THE
1702 ⎰   FULNESS OF HIM THAT FILLETH ALL IN ALL.

My Heart, my Lord, 's a naughty thing all o're:
   Yet if renew'd, the best in mee, 't would fain
Find Words to waft thy praises in, ashore,
   Suited unto the Excellence in thee.
   But easier 't is to hide the Sun up under   5
   Th'black of my naile, than words to weald this Wonder.   [283]

Had I Corinthian Brass: nay Amber here
   Nay Ophir Gold transparently refin'de.
Nay, th'heavenly Orbs all Quintessenced clear,
   To do the deed, 't would quite deceive my minde: 10
   Words all run wast, so these a nit may Weigh:
   The World in Scale, ere I thy wealth display.

Then what doe I, but as the Lady Bee
   Doth tune her Musick in her mudd wall Cell:
My Humming so, no musick makes to thee: 15
   Nor can my bagpipes play thy glory well.
   Amaizd I stand to see thee all Compleate:
   Compleated by a body, thou makst neate.

Thy Church, (what though its matter of it here
  Be brightest Saints, and Angells, all Compact   20
With Spirituall Glew, with grace out shining cleare
  And brimfull full of what the World ere lackt)
  Whom thou hast filld with all her fulness, shee
  Thy fulness is, and so she filleth thee.

Oh! wondrous strange. Angells and Men here are   25
  Incorporated in one body tite.
Two kinds are gain'd into one mortase, fair.
  Me tenent in thyselfe my Lord, my Light.
  These are thy body: thou their head, we see.
  Thou fillst them first, then they do fill up thee.   30

This gracious fulness thus runs to and fro.
  From thee to them: from them to thee again:
Not as the tides, that Ebbe, as well as flow.
  The Banks are ever Full, and so remain.
  What mystery's here. Thou canst not wanty bee.   35
  Yet wantest them, as sure as they want thee.

Necessity doth in the middle stand,
  Layes hands on both: constrains the body to
The head and head unto the body's band.
  The Head, and Body both together goe.   40
  The Head Compleats the body as its such:
  The Body doth Compleate the Head, as much.

Am I a bit, Lord, of thy Body? oh!
  Then I do claim thy Head to be mine own.   [284]
Thy Heads sweet Influence let to mee flow.   45
  That I may be thy fulness, full up grown.
  Then in thy Churches fullness thou shalt be
  Compleated in a Sense, and sung by mee.

---

5 't *orig.* it
11 so *orig.* and ; a *orig.* too. a ; Weigh *orig.* Way
21 out *orig.* o're
24 is *orig.* it

33 the tides *orig.* a tide ; Ebbe *orig.* Ebbs
41 the body *ins.*
42 as *orig.* and

11.2M   52. Meditation. Mat. 28.18. All Power in
1703   Heaven, and Earth is given mee.

What Power is this? What all Authoritie
  In Earth, and Heaven too? What Lord is here?
And given All to thee! Here's Majisty.
  All Worldly Power hence slinks away for feare.
  Then blush, my Soule that thou dost frozen ly: 5
  Under the beams of such bright Majesty.

What flying Flakes of Rapid flames of Love
  Scal'de from my heart by those bright beams that bed
Do in thyselfe, up mount to thee above
  Oretoping golden mountains with their head.   10
  But Why, my heart? O! why so drossy now;
  When such Authority doth to thee bow?

One Sprig of this Authority doth beare
  The Tree of Life, that spreads ore heaven quite
And sinners sprinkles with its sap t'make faire.   15
  And with its juyce doth quench Gods wrath out right.
  With God it maketh Reconciliation
  By offering, and Holy Intercession.

Within whose Shade my Sin-scorcht Soule doth bathe.
  In Gods bright sunshine, smiling heart-sweet beams.   20
Whose Rosie sents reviv'de my spirits have.
  Whose Spirits wash away my guilt, and stains.
  Amongst whose leaves my heart doth shroude its head
  And in whose buds my grounded hopes do bed.

O that I could once frown away my sloath: 25
  And dart my dulness through with glouts that stroy!

That mine Affections, (O! their sluggish growth)
  Might with seraphick Wings, Lord, swiftly fly,
  Unto thine Altar for an Holy Cure
  Produced by a Coale thence took most pure.   30

When this is gain'd, a Golden Trumpet I,
  All full of Grace shall be, wherein, in rayse
Of thy bright Priest-hood's sweet Authority
  My spirit trumpet shall, tun'd to thy praise
  Till when let this unskilfull ditty still   35
  Tunes in thine Eares, pipd through my sorry quill.   [285]

---

3 Majisty *orig.* Magisty
5 Soule *orig.* Sould
15 sap t'make *orig.* fr[** *]m
16 wrath *ins.*
27 That *orig.* And
34 My *orig.* The

13TH.4M   ⎤   53. MEDITATION. MAT. 28.18. ALL POWER IS GIVEN
1703   ⎦   ME IN HEAVEN, AND IN EARTH.

Were not my fancy Stagnate, and the Lake
  Of mine affections frozen ore with ice.
And Spirits Crampt or else Catochizate
  The Sweet brea[th'd] smells the briezes of the Spice
  My Theme doth vent, would raise such waves upon   5
  The Sea of Eloquence, they'd skip thereon.

Shall I be lumpish when such lightsom Showers
  Of livning influences still on mee?
Shall I be lowring, when Such lovely flowers
  Spring Smiling up, and Court mee too for thee?   10
  When Such heart liv'ning glances breake and fly
  Out through the sides of thy Authority?

Oh! that this, Thine Authority was made
  A Golden Anvill: and my Contemplation

A smiting Hammer: and my heart was laid   15
  Thereon, and hammerd up for emendation.
  And anvilld stoutly to a better frame
  To entertain thy rayes that round the same.

Thou hast the golden key, that doth unlock,
  The heart of God: Wisdoms bright Counsills Tower   20
All Power Prophetick This the boundless stock
  Of Gods Designs displayes in Gospell Showers.
  These gleames may liven our dead spirits then,
  File bright our rusty brains, and sharpen them.

Thou nothing but the Will of God declarst.   25
  And nothing less: For thine Authority
Should be abusd; if not improov'd, or spar'd.
  If't more or less than Gods good Will descry.
  This cannot be abusd: We therefore must
  The Lesson learn thou setst, and therein trust.   30

But here is still another gleame out breakes.
  All Royall Power in heaven, and earth do lodge
In thee, my Lord, this thou wilt not out leake
  Nor smoother up: it will not haft nor dodge.
  A right to mannage all things: therefore thou   35
  Wilt thine Secure, and make thy foes down bow.

Thou law deliverst: Thine Authority
  Cannot be idle; nor exceed the right.   [286]
Hence such as will not with thy rule Comply,
  Thou with thy iron scepter down wilt smite.   40
  This Power will raise the dead, and judge all too.
  His own will Crown with Life. To hell foes throw.

Lord let thy Doctrine melt my Soule anew:
  And let thy scepter drill my heart in mee:
And let thy spirits Cotters pierce it through   45
  Like golden rivits, Clencht, mee hold to thee.
  Then thou, and I shall ne'er be separate.
  Thy Praise shall be my Glory sung in state.

1 Stagnate *orig.* Sagnate
13 was *orig.* would
22 Designs desplayes *orig.* Designs do
25 God *ins.*
30 thou *orig.* hee
39 as *ins.*

22TH.6M ⎱ 54. MEDITATION. MATT. 28.18. ALL POWER IS GIVEN
1703 ⎰ MEE IN HEAVEN, AND IN EARTH.

Untun'de, my Lord. My Cankard brassy wire
  'S unfit to harp thee Musick. Angells pipes
Are squeaking things: Soon out of breath. Desires
  Exceed them; yet screwd highst up are but mites
  To meddle with the Musicking thy glory.   5
  What then's my jews trump meet to tune thy Story?

File off the rust: forgive my sin, and make
  My Heart thy Harp: and mine Affections brac'de
With gracious Grace thy Golden strings to shake
  With Quavers of thy glory well begrac'de.   10
  Though small's my mite, its dusty Wings e're will
  Sprindg out thy fame tun'de by thy spirits skill.

Three shining suns rise in the Chrystall skies
  Of Mankinde Orbs, and Orbs Angelicall.
Whose Rayes out Shine all pimping stars that rise   15
  Within these Spheres and Circuite through them all.
  These do evigorate all Action done
  By men and angells right, wherein they run.

The shine of these three Suns is all the same,
  Yet Sparkling differently according to   20
The Matter form'd therewith, and beares the Name
  Authority: and by the same doth goe
  Into a trine of Offices. Hence Springs
  Good warrant, for just Prophets, Priests and Kings.

These three are brightest suns, held in the skies   25
  Or Shining Orb of Man, or Angell kinde.
And all attain unto a Sovereign Sise
  Of shine, that hitherto ascend, we finde.   [287]
  The brightst brightness, and the mighti'st Might
  Is lodg'd in each one of these Balls of Light.   30

He that hath any one of these, doth weare
  A Supreme shine. But all these three suns came
To no man; but alone unto thy share,
  My Lord, they fall. Thou hast the sovereign name.
  And all the glorious Sunshine of these three   35
  Bright Suns, Shines bright and powerfull out in thee.

Here's threefold glory, Prophet's, Priest's and King's
  Trible Authority bestud thy Crown.
As Mediatour, all that Pow're within
  The Heaven, and Earth is thine. O bright Renown.   40
  To view those glories in thy Crown that vapor,
  Would make bright Angells eyes to run a-water.

O! plant mee in thy Priestly sunshine, I
  Shall then be reconcild to God. In mee
A beame of thy Propheticke sun imploy,   45
  'T will fill my Spirits Eye with light to see.
  Make in my heart thy Kingly sunshine flame.
  'T will burn my sin up, sanctify my frame.

My Gracious-Glorious Lord, shall I be thine?
  Wilt thou be mine? Then happy, happy mee!   50
I shall then cloath'd be with the sun, and Shine
  Crown'd with twelve Starrs, Moon underfoot too see.
  Lord, so be it. My rusty Wires then shall
  Bee fined gold, to tune thee praise withall.

---

1 Cankard *orig.* rusty
5 Musicking *orig.* Musiking
25 These *orig.* Though
27 a *ins.*

56. Meditation. Joh. 15.24. Had I not done
amongst them the works, that none other
man hath done, &c.

10.8m
1703

Should I with silver toole delve through the Hill
 Of Cordilera for rich thoughts, that I
My Lord, might weave with an angelick Skill
 A Damask Web of Velvet Verse thereby
To deck thy Works up, all my Web would run   5
To rags, and jags: so snicksnarld to the thrum.

Thine are so rich, Within. Without, Refin'd.
 No workes like thine. No Fruits so sweete that grow
On th'trees of righteousness, of Angell kinde,
 And saints, whose limbs reev'd with them bow down low.   10
 Should I search ore the Nutmeg Gardens shine
 Its fruits in flourish are but Skegs to thine.   [288]

The Clove, when in its White-green'd blossoms shoots,
 Some Call the pleasentst sent the World doth show.
None Eye e're Saw, nor nose e're Smelt such Fruits   15
 My Lord, as thine, Thou Tree of Life in'ts blow.
 Thou Rose of Sharon, Vallies Lilly true
 Thy Fruits most Sweet and Glorious ever grew.

Thou art a Tree of Perfect nature trim
 Whose golden lining is of perfect Grace   20
Perfum'de with Deity unto the brim,
 Whose fruits, of the perfection, grow, of Grace.
 Thy Buds, thy Blossoms, and thy fruits adorne
 Thyselfe, and Works, more shining than the morn.

Art, natures Ape, hath many brave things done   25
 As th'Pyramids, the Lake of Meris vast
The Pensile Orchards built in Babylon.
 Psammitich's Labyrinth. (arts Cramping task)
 Archimedes his Engins made for war.
 Romes Golden House. Titus his Theater.   30

The Clock at Strasburgh, Dresdens Table-sight.
   Regiamonts Fly of Steele about that flew.
Turrian's Wooden Sparrows in a flight.
   And th'Artificiall man Aquinas slew.
   Mark Scaliota's Lock, and Key and Chain   35
   Drawn by a Flea, in our Queen Betties reign.

Might but my pen in natures Inventory
   Its progress make, 't might make such things to jump
All which are but Inventions Vents or glory
   Wits Wantonings, and Fancies frollicks plump.   40
   Within whose maws lie buried Times, and Treasures
   Embalmed up in thick dawbd sinfull pleasures.

Nature doth better work than Art: yet thine
   Out vie both works of nature and of Art.
Natures Perfection and the perfect shine   45
   Of Grace attend thy deeds in ev'ry part.
   A Thought, a Word, and Worke of thine, will kill
   Sin, Satan, and the Curse: and Law fulfill.

Thou art the Tree of Life in Paradise,
   Whose lively branches are with Clusters hung   50
Of Lovely fruits, and Flowers more Sweet than spice
   Bende down to us: and doe out shine the sun,
   Delightfull unto God, doe man rejoyce
   The Pleasentst fruits in all Gods Paradise.

Lord, feed mine eyes then with thy Doings rare,   55
   And fat my heart with these ripe fruites thou bearst.
Adorn my Life well with thy works, make faire
   My Person with apparrell thou prepar'st.   [289]
   My Boughs shall loaded bee with fruits that spring
   Up from thy Works, while to thy praise, I sing.   60

---

2 rich *orig.* Wealthi'st
4 Verse *orig.* Velses
7 Thine *orig.* These ; Refin'd *orig.* so fine ; like *ins.*
14 show *orig.* know

20 golden lining *orig.* lining is
32 Regiamonts *orig.* Regsamonts
38 make *orig.* many
54 fruits *ins.*
57 well *orig.* will ; faire *orig.* fare

5.10M ⎫   58. Meditation. Matth. 2.15. Out of Egypt have I
1703 ⎭   called my Son.

When in Italian flourisht hand I would
  Lord, flourish up thy praise, my Quill's too dry,
My Inke too thick and naught (though liquid Gold).
    That will not write, this will not run; nay I
    My standish finde is empty, Paper loose,   5
    That drains all blotches from my inkie sluce.

What shall I then, Lord doe? Desist thy praise?
  Thou Canst amend it. Steep my stubborn Quill
In Zions Wine fat, mend my pen, and raise
    Thy right arms Vean, a drop of'ts blood distill   10
    Into mine inkhorn, make my paper tite
    That it may n't blot. In sacred Text I write.

Christen mine Eyeballs with thine Eye Salve then,
  Mine Eyes will Spy how Isra'ls journying
Into, and out of Egypt's bondage Den   15
    A Glass thy vissage was imbellisht in.
    Hunger Constrains. Jacob to Egypt highs.
    Herod Constrains and Christ to Egypt flies.

God Jacob calls. Jacobs son Joseph there
  Him brings and nourisht there, and God doth call   20
Jacobs son Joseph, Jesus brings there, where
    He nourisht him. This spills the Dragons gall
    And broke that aching tooth that at him snapt
    In Herods jaw bone and his Chops it flapt.

God Israel calls from Egypt: up he 'pears.   25
  God calls his Son from Egypt; up he highs.
The Wilderness tries Isr'el 40 years.
  Christ 40 days in Wilderness tri'de lies.
  The Cockatrice's egg in Jewry hatcht;
  He shuns, and Nazareth doth him in latch.   30

But Isra'ls coming out of Egypt thus,
  Is Such a Coppy that doth well Descry
Not onely Christ in person unto us.
  But Spirituall Christ, and Egypt spiritually.
  Egyptian Bondage whence goes Israel shows   35
  The Spirituall bondage whence Christs children goe.   [290]

The Bondage state to Sin and Satan stand,
  In Peckled Black, red hellish Colours laid,
By wicked Pharao, and his hellish hand
  On Egypts Bondage in the brickiln trade.   40
  God Israel Calls. Pharao and Egypt grin.
  God calls the Soule. Satan now greatens Sin.

God miracles doth work. Wonders out fly,
  Like flocks of birds with golden wings, and Claws.
For Israels Sake. Pharao and Egypt fry   45
  In fiery Wrath. Israel attends Gods Cause.
  So here, when once the soule doth Gods call heare
  Satan red mad doth rage. Wonders appeare.

Isra'l Complies: runs into fire by this,
  Which Pharao's Wrath, and Egypts rage procure,   50
Now Farewell Goshen; Farewell Rameses.
  Your Pleasures and Commotions we abjure.
  So here the Soule attends Gods Call. Farewell
  Worlds smiling sunshine; tole your passing bell.

Out Israel comes to succoth, and from thence   55
  To Etham. God his banner ore them bright
Erects. His Cloude and firy pillard fence

A Fence from foes, Lanthorn makes day of night.
Pharao, and's Peers, horse: hosts and Charet wheels
Rise and with flaming swords persue at heels.   60

So here, the Soul Call'd to Effect out goes
   To Succoth, to Gods tabernacles wings,
The firy flag, God, banner ore him throws
   To keep, and Conduct him in's journeyings.
   Though Hell is all in arms: persues him hard.   65
   The Cloud and Fiery Pillar doe him guard.

Isra'l thus bannerd Hiroths mouth attempt
   Whose teeth are Migdol, Baalzephon high.
And throate the red sea; Pharao's host them pen't
   Behinde up, they then terrifide out Cry.   70
   Moses his rod divides the red sea so
   They safely pass't but Pharao't ore doth flow.

So here, the Soule on goes into the jaws
   Of Worldly rage, with mountains him do round.
Hells armies Chase to tare him with their paws.   75
   The red sea of Gods wrath seems quite to drownd.
   He Cries, Christs Cross divides the sea whereby
   He passeth safe, and it his foes doth 'stroy.   [291]

Isra'l Sings praise, but yet finds weeping Cheere.
   Wilderness state is his and waters are   80
At Mara bitter. Yet God sheweth here
   A tree whose wood did sweetly them repare.
   So here the soul sings praise in Christ, yet shall
   The wilderness work griefe, but Christ makes all.

Isra'l to Elim comes. Sweet joyes here findes   85
   Twelves springs of Water Every tribe a Well.
And seventy Palm trees fruitfull to their minde
   A type that might things past, and future tell.
   Twelve Patriarchs the wells they sprung from so,
   And seventy Elders that from them did flow.   90

So here the soule in Christ at twelve wells drinks
    Of Living waters, twelve Apostles shew'd
Dates bore by seventy Palms set at their brincks.
    The seventy disciples, are this food.
    The Holy scriptures, and Christs Doctrine are   95
    Waters these Wells, and Dates these Palm trees bare.

Hence Israel goes the red sea back to see,
    To minde him of the mercy shewn him there,
And thence into the Wilderness goes hee
    Of Sin, where tried, and so to Sinai where   100
    By open Covenant God Israel takes
    His onely Church! and Select people makes.

Gives him his Laws and ordinances just.
    Erects his Worship, open fellowship
Holds with him in the same wherein he must   105
    In the desert through various Changes trip
    Some very sweet some of a bitter hande
    Untill they Come to keep in Canaans land.

So here indeed, the soul in Christ doth back
    From Elim pass unto the Red sea deare   110
Of Christ's rich blood the mercy of that track
    To take more in as he about to viere
    Thence through the Wilderness of sin, to rise
    In Covenant on Zion mount likewise.

And here enricht with Holy Oracles   115
    And fellowship in holy worship so
Through interchanging Course, like miracles,
    The Diaperd Encheckerd works must goe
    Of Providences, Honycombs and stings
    Till hee within Celestiall Canaan sings.   [292]120

What Wisdom's here? My Lord, What Grace? What bright
    Encheckerd Works, more rich than Rubies fair?
Doe thou my soule with this Rich trade delight
    And bring mee thus into thy promisd aire

Wherein my Virginalls shall play for joy   125
Thy Praise with Zions virgins Company.

Title Matth. 2.15 *orig.* Matth. 2.25 ; of *ins.*
19 Jacobs *orig.* Jose ; Joseph *orig.* him
20 and God doth] *orig.* God too
21 Jacobs *orig.* Jose
25 'pears *orig.* goes
27 orig. Isra'l [****] the Wilderness t[***] h[***] doth close.
28 Christ *orig.* And Christ
35 goes *orig.* int
36 bondage *ins.* ; whence Christs children goe *orig.* whence from Christs [****] goes
40 brickiln *orig.* brickiron
43 doth work *orig.* hath
46 attends *orig.* is
47 doth *orig.* attends
57 pillard fence *orig.* pillar for defence
58 of *ins.*
72 Pharao *orig.* Parao
73 jaws *orig.* burning jaws
74 him do *ins.*
76 Gods wrath *orig.* Christs blood
77 Cross *orig.* div
83 soul *orig.* souls
88 might *orig.* may
94 this *orig.* their
96 Wells *orig.* Walls
118 Diaperd *orig.* Diaperd of
126 virgins *orig.* virgind

6.12
1703 } 59. MEDITATION. 1 COR. 10.2. BAPTIZED IN THE CLOUD.

Wilt thou enoculate within mine Eye
    Thy Image bright, My Lord, that bright doth shine
Forth in the Cloudy-Firy Pillar high
    Thy Tabernacles Looking-Glass Divine?
    What glorious Rooms are then mine Eyeholes made.   5
    Thine Images on my windows Glass portrai'd?

Oh! Pillar Strange, made of a Cloude, and Fire.
  Whose Stoole is Israels Camp, it sits upon.
Whose skirts doe Canopy that Camp: Whose spire
  Doth kiss the Heavens, leading Israel on.   10
  Sure't is Christ's Charret drawn by Angells high.
  The Humane jacket, typ'te, of's Deity.

A Sun by night, to Dayify the dark.
  A shade by Day, Sunbeames to mollify.
The Churches Pilot out her way to mark: 15
  Her Quarter Master quarters to descry.
  It's Christs Watch tower over his Churches Host,
  With Angells kept. Tent of the Holy Ghost.

Christs Looking Glass that on his Camp gives shine.
  Whose backside's pitchy darkness to his foes   20
A Wall of Fire that 'bout his Israel twines
  To burn up all that offer to oppose:
  The Mediatory Province in a Map.
  The Feather in the Tabernacle's Cap.

Christ, in this Pillar, Godhead-Man'd doth rise   25
  The Churches King, to guid, Support, Defend.
Her Priest to Cleanse her: in the Cloud to baptize.
  And Reconcile with Incense that ascends.
  Her Prophet too that Lights her in her way
  By Night With Lanthorn Fire. With Cloud by day.   30

Then lead me, Lord, through all this Wilderness,
  By this Choice shining Pillar Cloud and Fire
By Day, and Night I shall not then digress.   [293]
  If thou wilt lead. I shall not lag nor tire
  But as to Cana'n I am journeying   35
  I shall thy praise under this Shadow sing.

---

6 my windows *orig.* mine
15 mark *orig.* pry
21 that 'bout *orig.* about

16.2M ⎱ 60[A]. Meditation. Joh. 6.51. I am the Living
1704 ⎰   Bread, that came down from Heaven.

Count me not liquorish if my Soule do pine
  And long for Angells bread of Heaven's wheate
Ground in thy Quorns, searcde in the Laws Lawn fine
  And bakt in Heavens backhouse for our meate
  I'st die of Famine. Lord, My stomach's weak.   5
  And if I live, Manna must be my meate.

I'm sick; my Sickness is mortality
  And Sin both Complicate (the worst of all).
No cure is found under the Chrystall sky
  Save Manna, that from heaven down doth fall.   10
  My Queasy stomach thus alone doth Crave.
  Nought but a bit of manna can mee Save.

This Bread came down from heaven in a Dew
  In which it bedded was, untill the sun
Remoov'd its Coverlid: and did it shew   15
  Disht dayly food, while fourty years do run.
  For Isra'ls Camp to feast upon their fill
  Thy Emblem, Lord, in prent by perfect skill.

Thou in thy word as in a bed of Dewes
  Like Manna on thy Camp dost fall and light   20
Hid Manna, till the Sun shine bright remooves
  The Rug, and doth display its beauty bright
  Like pearly Bdellium white and Cleare to set
  The Sight, and Appetite the Same to get.

This is a shining Glass, wherein thy face   25
  My Lord, as Bread of Life, is clearly seen.
The Bread of Life, and Life of lively Grace
  Of such as live upon't do flowrish Green.
  That makes their lives that on it live ascend
  In heav'nly rayes to heaven that have none end.   30

Refresh my sight, Lord, with thy Manna's eye.

Delight my tast with this sweet Honied Cake.
Enrich my stomach with this Cake bread high.
　And with this Angells bread me recreate.   [294]
　Lord, make my Soule thy Manna's Golden Pot   35
　Within thine Arke: and never more forgot.

Here's food for ery day, and th'seventh too:
　(Though't never fell upon the seventh day
But on the first, and ery weekday new)
　And now is on the Camp shour'd ery way.   40
　Yet where it is not rightly usd it turns
　To nauseous sent, and doth occasion worms.

It's first daye's Mess Disht up in Heavenly Dew.
　Lord feede mee all wayes with't; it will enable
Mee much to live up to thy praise anew.   45
　Angells delight, attending on this table.
　If on this Angell fare I'm fed, I shall
　Sing forth thy glory with bright Angells all.

---

11 doth *ins.*
21 bright *ins.*
23 Bdellium *orig.* D
25 thy *orig.* the
38 day *orig.* day)
44 feede *orig.* mee

30.5M ⎱ 60[B]. MEDITATION. 1 COR. 10.4. AND ALL DRUNK
1704   ⎰   THE SAME SPIRITUALL DRINKE.

Ye Angells bright, pluck from your Wings a Quill
　Make me a pen thereof that best will write
Lende me your fancy, and Angellick skill.
　To treate this Theme, more rich than Rubies bright
　My muddy Inke, and Cloudy fancy dark.   5
　Will dull its glory, lacking highest Art.

An Eye at Centre righter may describe
  The Worlds Circumferentiall glory vast
As in its nutshell bed it snugs fast tide,
  Than any angells pen can glory Cast   10
  Upon this Drink Drawn from the Rock, tapt by
  The Rod of God, in Horeb, typickly.

Sea water straind through Mineralls, Rock, and Sands
  Well Clarifi'de by Sun beams, Dulcifi'de,
Insipid, Sordid, Swill, Dish water stands.   15
  But here's a Rock of Aqua-Vitæ tride.
  When once God broacht it, out a River came
  To bath and bibble in, for Israels train.   [295]

Some Rocks have sweat. Some Pillars bled out tears.
  But here's a River in a Rock up tun'd   20
Not of sea Water nor of Swill. It's beere.
  No Nectar like it, yet it once Unbund
  A River down out runs through ages all.
  A Fountain opte, to wash off sin and Fall.

Christ is this Horebs Rock, the streames that slide   25
  A River is of Aqua Vitæ Deare
Yet Costs us nothing, gushing from his side.
  Celestiall Wine our sinsunk souls to cheare.
  This Rock and Water, Sacramentall Cup
  Are made, Lords Supper Wine for us to Sup.   30

This Rock's the Grape that Zions Vineyard bore
  Which Moses Rod did smiting pound, and press
Untill its blood, the brooke of Life, run ore.
  All Glorious Grace, and Gracious Righteousness.
  We in this brook must bath: and with faiths quill   35
  Suck Grace, and Life out of this Rock our fill.

Lord, oynt me with this Petro oyle. I'm sick.
  Make mee drinke Water of the Rock. I'm dry.
Me in this fountain wash. My filth is thick.
  I'm faint; give Aqua Vitæ or I dy.   40

If in this Stream thou cleanse, and Chearish mee
My Heart thy Hallelujahs Pipe shall bee.

---

20 in *orig.* from
22 it once Unbund *orig.* being [*** ***]und
29 Cup *orig.* Cupress

61. MEDITATION. JOH. 3.14. AS MOSES LIFT UP THE SERPENT IN THE WILDERNESS SO MUST THE SON OF MAN BE LIFT UP.

17.7M
1704

My Might's too mean, lend your Angelick might
  Ye mighty Angells brightly to define
A Piece of burnish't brass, formd Serpent like
  To Countermand all poison serpentine.
  No Remedie could cure the Serpents Bite   5
  But One: to wit The brazen serpent's sight.

Shall brass that bosoms poison in't, Contain
  A Counter poison, better than what beds
In Creatures bosoms? Nay. But th'vertue came
  Through that brass shapt, from God that healing sheds.   10
  Its Vertue rode in th'golden Coach of th'eyes
  Into the Soule, and Serpents Sting defies.   [296]

So that a Sight of th'brazen Serpent hung
  Up in the Banner standard of the Camp
Was made a Charet wherein rode and run   15
  A Healing vertue to the serpents Cramp.
  But that's not all. Christ in this snake shapt brass
  Raist on the standard, Crucified was.

As in this Serpent lay the onely Cure
  Unto the fiery Serpents burning bite:
Not by its Physick Vertue. (that is sure)   20
  But by a Beam Divine of Grace's might
  Whose Vertue onely is the plaster 'pli'de
  Unto the Wound, by Faith in Christs blood di'de.

A sight of th'Artificiall Serpent heales 25
 The venom wound the naturall serpent made.
A spirituall sight of Christ, from Christ down steals
 A Cure against the Hellish Serpents trade.
 Not that the springhead of the Cure was found
 In Christs humanity With sharp thorns Crownd. 30

This Brazen serpent is a Doctors shop.
 On ev'ry shelfe's a sovereign remedy.
The Serpents Flesh the sovereign salve is got
 Against the serpents bite, gaind by the eye.
 The Eye beames agents are that forth do bring 35
 The sovereign Counter poison, and let't in.

I by the fiery serpent bitt be here.
 Be thou my brazen serpent me to Cure.
My sight, Lord, make thy golden Charet cleare
 To bring thy remedy unto my sore. 40
 If this thou dost I shall be heald: My wound
 Shall sing thy praises: and thy glory sound.

---

2 brightly *orig.* to brightly
6 to wit *ins.*
9 th *ins.*
16 to *orig.* of
31 Brazen *orig.* Bras

18.9M
1704

62. MEDITATION. CAN. 1.12. WHILE THE KING SITTETH
AT HIS TABLE, MY SPICKNARD SENDETH FORTH THE
SMELL THERE[OF].

Oh! thou, my Lord, thou king of Saints, here mak'st
 A royall Banquet thine to entertain.
With rich, and royall fare, Celestiall Cates,
 And sittest at the Table rich of fame.
 Am I bid to this Feast? Sure Angells stare. 5
 Such Rugged looks, and Ragged robes I ware.

I'le surely come, Lord fit mee for this feast:
   Purge me with Palma Christi from my sin.
With Plastrum Gratiæ Dei, or at least
   Unguent Apostolorum healing bring.   [297]10
   Give mee thy sage, and savory: me dub
   With Golden Rod, and with Saint Johns Wort good.

Root up my Henbain, Fawnbain, Divells bit,
   My Dragons, Chokwort, Cross wort, Ragwort, vice,
And set my knot with Hony suckles; stick   15
   Rich Herb-a-Grace, and Grains of Paradise
   Angelica, yea Sharons Rose the best
   And Herba Trinitatis in my breast.

Then let thy sweet-spike Sweat its liquid Dew
   Into my Crystall Viall: and there swim.   20
And as thou at thy Table in Rich shew
   With royall Dainties, sweet discourse, as King
   Dost Welcome thine. My spicknard with its smell
   Shall vapour out perfumed Spirits Well.

Whether I at thy Table Guest do sit,   25
   And feed my tast: or Wait, and fat mine Eye
And Eare with Sights and Sounds, Heart Raptures fit:
   My Spicknard breaths its Sweet perfumes with joy
   My heart thy Viall with this Spicknard fill.
   Perfumed praise to thee then breath it will.   30

---

5 Am *orig.* I
16 Rich *orig.* With
22 sweet *orig.* and sweet
23 with *orig.* gives
24 perfumed *orig.* perfumes

4.12M ⎤   63. MEDITATION. CANT. 6.11. I WENT DOWN IN
1704 ⎦   TO THE GARDEN OF NUTS, TO SEE THE FRUITS &c.

Oh that I was the Bird of Paradise!
    Then in thy Nutmeg Garden, Lord, thy Bower
Celestiall Musick blossom should my voice
    Enchanted with thy gardens aire and flower.
    This Aromatick aire would so enspire   5
    My ravisht Soule to sing with angells Quire.

What is thy Church, my Lord, thy Garden which
    Doth gain the best of soils? Such spots indeed
Are Choicest Plots empalde with Palings rich.
    And set with slips, herbs best, and best of seed.   10
    As th'Hanging Gardens rare of Babylon
    And Palace Garden of King Solomon.

But that which doth excell all gardens here
    Was Edens Garden: Adams Palace bright,
The Tree of Life, and knowledge too were there.   15
    Sweet herbs and sweetest flowers all Sweet Delight
    A Paradise indeed of all Perfume
    That to the Nose, the Eyes and Eares doth tune.   [298]

But all these Artificiall Gardens bright
    Enameled with bravest knots of Pincks   20
And Flowers enspangld with black, red and White
    Compar'd with this are truely stincking sincks
    As Dunghills reech with stincking sents that dish
    Us out, So these, when balanced with this.

For Zions Paradise, Christs Garden Deare   25
    His Church, enwalld, with Heavenly Crystall fine
Hath evry Bed beset with Pearle all Cleare
    And Allies pald with Gold, and silver shrine.
    The Shining Angells are its Centinalls
    With flaming swords Chaunting out Madri'galls.   30

The sparkling Plants, Sweet spices, Herbs and Trees,
　The glorious shews of aromatick Flowers
The pleasing beauties soakt in Sweet breath lees
　Of Christs rich garden ever upward towers
　For Christs Sweet Showers of Grace makes on it fall.   35
　It therefore bears the bell away from all.

The Nut of evry kinde is found grow big,
　With food, and Physick, lodgd within a tower
A Wooden Wall with Husky Coverlid.
　Or shell flesht ore, or in an Arching bower   40
　Beech, Hazle, Wallnut, Cocho, Almond brave,
　Pistick or Chestnut in its prickly Cave.

These all as meate, and med'cine emblems choice
　Of spirituall Food, and Physike are which sport
Up in Christs Garden. Yet the Nutmeg's Spice   45
　A leathern Coate wares, and a Macie shirt,
　Doth far excell them all. Aromatize
　My Soule therewith, my Lord, in sprituall wise.

Oh! sweet Sweet Paradise, Whose spiced spring
　Will make the lips of him asleep to tune   50
Heart ravishing tunes, sweet Musick for our king
　In Aromatick aire of blesst perfume.
　Open thy garden doore: mee entrance give
　And in thy Nut tree garden make me live.

If, Lord, thou opst, and in thy garden bring   55
　Mee, then thy little Linet sweetly Will
Upon thy Nut tree sit and sweetly sing,
　Will Crack a Nut and eat the kirnell still.
　Thou wilt mine Eyes, my Nose, and Palate greet
　With Curious Flowers, sweet Odors, Viands sweet.   [299]60

Thy Gardens Odorif'rous aire mee make
　Suck in, and out t'aromatize my lungs,
That I thy garden, and its Spicie State

May breath upon with such ensweetned songs.
My Lungs and Breath ensweetend thus shall raise   65
The Glory of thy garden in its praise.

---

7 Garden *orig.* Garden?
10 herbs *orig.* and herbs
15 were *orig.* was
21 enspangld *orig.* enspang
23 stincking *orig.* sticking
28 pald *orig.* b
37 grow *orig.* to grow
38 With *orig.* Both
44 are which *orig.* which do
48 in *orig.* and
51 sweet *orig.* and sweet
56 Linet sweetly Will *orig.* bird'll sweetly sing

2.2M   64. MEDITATION. CAN. 6.11. TO SEE—IF THE VINE
1705   FLOWRISHT, AND THE POMEGRANATE BUD.

Oh! that my Chilly Fancy, fluttering soe,
   Was Elevated with a dram of Wine
The Grapes and Pomegranates do yield, that grow
   Upon thy Gardens Appletrees and Vines.
   It should have liquour with a flavour fraight   5
   To pensil out thy Vines and Pomgranates.

But I, as dry, as is a Chip, scarce get
   A peep hole through thy garden pales at these,
Thy garden plants. How should I then ere set
   The glory out of its brave Cherry trees?   10
   Then make my fancy, Lord, thy pen t'unfold
   Thy Vines and Pomegranates in liquid gold.

Whence come thy garden plants? So brave? So Choice?
   They Almugs ben't from Ophirs golden land:
But Vines and Pomegranates of Paradise.   15

Spicknard, Sweet Cane, and Cynamon plants here stand.
What heavenly aire is briezing in this Coast?
Here blows the Tradewinde of the Holy Ghost.

Thy Pomegranates that blushy freckles ware
    Under their pleasant jackets, spirituall frize,   20
And Vines, though Feeble, fine, and flowrishing are
    Not Sibmahs, but mount Zions here arise.
    Here best of Vines, and Pomegranates up hight
    Yea Sharons Rose, and Carmels Lillies White.

These trees are reev'd with Gilliads balm each one   25
    Myrrh trees, and Lign Aloes: Frankincense;
Here planted grow; here's Saffron Cynamon
    Spicknard and Calamus with Spice Ensenc'd.
    Oh! fairest garden: evry bed doth beare
    All brave blown flowers whose breath is heavenly aire.   30

Make me thy Vine and Pomegranate to be
    And in thy garden flowrish fruitfully
And in their branches bowre, there then to thee
    In sweetend breath shall come sweet melody.   [300]
    My Spirit then engrapd and pomegranat'de,   35
    Shall sweetly Sing thee o're thy garden gated.

---

1 fluttering soe *orig.* flappering low
3 and *orig.* or
5 It should *orig.* Ist have
6 orig. Thy Vine to paint out and thy Pomgranates.
9 ere *orig.* ever
14 They *orig.* Here ; ben't *orig.* are
28 Spice Ensenced *orig.* Spicde insence
29 beare *orig.* bare
35 pomegranat'de *orig.* pomegranated

4M.10.　⎤　65. MEDITATION. CAN 6.11. TO SEE THE FRUITS OF THE
1705　　⎦　　VALLY.

The Vines of Lebanon that briskly grew
  Roses of Sharon in their flowrish fair,
The Lillies of the Vallies Beauteous Shew
  And Carmels Glorious Flowery Robes most rare
  In all their lively looks bluft brisk, appeare　　　　　　5
  Dull Wanlookt things, Lord, to thy Gardens geere.

Engedi's Vineyard, that brave Camphire bower
  Though Cypress Banks and Beds of bravery
And Eshcol's Grapes that royall juyce out shower,
  And Wine of Hesbon in its flavor high　　　　　　　　10
  With Elevating Sparks, stand shrinking, blush
  To see the flowrish of thy Garden flush.

Mount Olivet with Olive Trees, full green,
  The flowrishing Almond in their smiling ray
And Sibma's vap'ring Wines that frolick seem　　　　　15
  Are all unmand as tipsy, slink away
  As blushing at their manners to behold
  Thy Nut tree Gardens buds and flowers unfold.

Whose Buds not Gracious but pure Grace do shine.
  Whose blossoms are not Sweet but sweetness brace　　20
Whose Grapes are not Vine berries, but rich Wine:
  Whose Olives Oyle springs be'n't but Oyle of Grace.
  When pound and presst, they Cordiall juyce bleed all
  And spirits Unction. Oh Sweet Hony fall.

These Buds are better than blown Roses fair:　　　　　25
  These Blossoms fairer bee than Carmels hew:
These Vines beare Grapes sweeter than Raisens are.
  These Nuts are better than ere Nutmegs grew.
  Olivets Olive's but a grease pots mate
  To thy Nut Gardens Vine and Pomegranate.　　　　　30

In thy Nut Garden make my heart a Bed,
  And set therein thy spicknard, Cypress, Vine
Rose, Olive, Almonds, Pares, Plumbs White, and Red,
  Pomegranats, Spices, Frankincense divine.
  If thou dost stud my heart with graces thus   35
  My heart shall beare thee fruits perfumed flush.   [301]

Make thou my soule, Lord, thy mount Olivet
  And plant it with thy Olive Trees fair Green.
Adornd with Holy blossoms, thence beset
  With Heavens Olives. Happy to be seen.   40
  Thy sacred Oyle will then make bright to shine
  My soul its face, and all the works of mine.

Set thou therein thy Pomegranate of State
  Thy Spice Trees, Cloves, and Mace, thy Cynamon.
Thy Lemons, Orenges, Nuts, Almonds, Dates.   45
  Thy Nutmeg trees and Vines of Lebanon
  With Lillies, Violets, Carnations rare,
  My heart thy spice box then shall breath Sweet aire.

My Vine shall then beare Raisens of the Sun,
  My Grapes will rain May shower of Sacred Wine.   50
The Smiling Dimples on my Fruits Cheeks hung
  Will as rich jewells adde unto their shine.
  Then plant my heart with thy rich fruit trees sweet
  And it shall beare thee Fruits stew'd in sweet reech.

---

2 Roses *orig.* The Roses
14 The *orig.* And
15 vap'ring *orig.* vaporing
21 are *ins.*
22 Olives *orig.* Olives are not
24 spirits *orig.* Unction of the spirits ; Unction. Oh *ins.*
26 fairer *orig.* fare ; hew *orig.* shew
31 make *orig.* give
34 Spices *orig.* Spicknard
38 fair *orig.* fare

19.6M
1705
} 66. MEDITATION. JOH. 15.13. GREATER LOVE HATH NO
MAN THAN THIS: THAT A MAN LAY DOWN HIS LIFE
FOR HIS FRIENDS.

O! what a thing is Love? who can define
  Or liniament it out? It's strange to tell
A Sparke of Spirit empearld pill like and fine
  In't shugard pargings, crusted, and doth dwell
  Within the heart, where thron'd, without Controle   5
  It ruleth all the Inmates of the Soule.

It makes a poother in its secret sell
  'Mongst the affections: oh! it swells; it's paind,
Like kirnells Soked untill it breaks its shell
  Unless its Object be obtain'd and gain'd.   10
  Like Caskd wines jumbled breake the Cask: this sparke
  Oft swells when crusht untill it breakes the Heart.

O! Strange strange Love! 'Stroy Life and'tselfe thereby;
  Hence lose its Object; lay down all't can moove.
For nothing! rather choose indeed to dy,   15
  And nothing be, than be without its love.
  Not t'be, than be without its fanci'de bliss!
  Is this Love's nature? What a thing is this?   [302]

Love thus ascending to its highest twig,
  May Sit and Cherp such ditties, sing and dy.   20
This highest Note is but a Black-Cap's jig
  Compar'd to thine my Lord, all Heavenly.
  A greater love than such man ne'er mentain'd
  A greater Love than such thou yet hast gain'd.

Thy Love laid down thy Life hath for thy sheep: 25
  Thy friends by grace: thy foes by Natures Crimes
And yet thy Life more precious is and sweet
  More worth than all the World ten thousand times.
  And yet thy Love did give bright Wisdoms shine
  In laying down thy precious life for thine.   30

This Love was ne'er adulterate: e're pure.
  Noe Whiffe of Fancy: But rich Wisdomes Beams,
No Huff of Hot affection men endure.
  But sweetend Chimings of Celestiall gleams
  Play'd and Display'd upon the golden Wyer   35
  That doth thy Human Cymball brave, attire.

Thy Love that laid thy life all down for thine
  Did not thereby destroy itselfe at all.
It was preserved in thyselfe Divine
  When it did make thy Humane selfe down fall   40
  And when thy body as the Sun up rose.
  It did itselfe like flaming beames, disclose.

Lord, let thy Love shine on my soule! Mee bath
  In this Celestiall Gleame of this pure Love.
O! gain my heart and thou my Love shalt have.   45
  Clime up thy golden Stares to thee above.
  And in thy upper Chamber sit and sing
  The glory of thy Love when Entred in.

---

4 and doth dwell *orig.* and p[***]ed well
8 swells *orig.* swells also
9 untill *orig.* till
40 thy *orig.* thyselfe ; selfe *ins.*

21.8   ⎫   67[A]. MEDITATION. MAL. 4.2. BUT UNTO YOU THAT
       ⎬   FEARE MY NAME, SHALL THE SUN OF RIGHTEOUS-
1705   ⎭   NESS ARISE.

My China Ware or Amber Casket bright,
  Filld with Ambrosian Spirits soak't and Bindg'd.
Made all a mass of Quicken'd metall right,
  Transparent silver Bowles with Flowers Enfringd
  Sent to the Temple by king Ptolemy   5
  Compar'd thereto are but vile Trumpery.

These spirits, drawn by heavens Chymistry

And Casked up, with Cask Conspire into
A Lump of sacred Fire that actively
  About thy sacred selfe entwine and grow   10
  So that this Cask bindgd with these spirits rise
  A fearer of Jehovah, holy wise.   [303]

In acting of the same with Holy skill
  And Sanctifying Sight as shining Eyes
Some soure, and muddy Humors soon do still   15
  When that the Glass is jumbled up arise
  Or in its China ware some Spot or Dimple.
  Or Amber Cask unhoopt hath Crack or Wrinkle.

The spirits and the Vial both are sick.
  The Lump Consisting of them both so trim   20
Is out of trim, sore wounded to the quick,
  Distemperd by ill Humors bred therein.
  Some poyson's in the golden Cup of wine.
  That treason works against the king Divine.

I fain would purge the poison out, and Cleare   25
  The liquor from the musty dregs therein.
The Bottle free from Crack, Dint, and bad geer,
  The China Ware from spot or Wrinkling
  And all the Quickend Lump I fain would Cure
  Of all ill Humors, Sickness, wound, or Sore.   30

But cannot do the same, yet this I finde,
  To them that feare thy Name Lord, there doth rise
The Sun of Righteousness, (this Cheers my minde)
  With healing in his Wings Physicianwise.
  This yields reliefe; some things in such as do   35
  Thee Fear are bad: in them diseases grow.

Mine argument let winde into thine heart,
  That hence I do assume seing it's sure
None that do feare thee, perfect bee, each part.
  I'm one of them or none of them I'm sure.   40
  If one of them, my bad Distempers shall

Not it disproove. I don't excell them all.

They want a Cure: and so do I: I'm not
    Pleasd with my mud: sin doth not tickle mee.
The Wrinkles Crest, or Dints my ware hath got.   45
    My sores and Sicknesses my Sorrows bee.
    I'l strive against them till I'st strive noe more
    While healing Wings abide, I'le not give o're.

The Objects of the Sun of Righteousness
    Doth with its healing wing rise Cleare upon.   50
Have need of healing. I do need no less.
    Our wants for kinde are equall hereupon.
    We both are of our Sickness sick. Hence shown
    We both are by the argument proovd one.   [304]

Hence this I pray. And pray no less than this.   55
    Grant, Lord, mine Eyes with acute sight not dim,
Thy shining Sun of Righteousness may kiss.
    And broodled bee under its Healing Wing.
    My Bird like to a Nighting gaile in th'spring
    With breast on sharpest thorn, thy praise shall sing.   60

---

2 Bindg'd *orig.* Bing'd
7 drawn by *orig.* L[***]d by
11 bindgd *orig.* bingd
12 A fearer *orig.* True fearers
17 Dimple *orig.* Wrinkle
18 Wrinkle *orig.* dimple
20 Lump *orig.* Lumb
23 poyson's in *orig.* poyson is
32 there *orig.* do
36 Thee Fear is *orig.* The Fear thee are
38 assume seing *orig.* assume by pious art
39 perfect *orig.* right perfect
45 Wrinkles *orig.* Rinkles
49 Object of the Sun *orig.* Objects that the So
50 rise Cleare upon *orig.* arise up Cleare
55 than *orig.* then
58 broodled *orig.* broodled up
59 gaile *orig.* Gaile

16.10M ⎱ 68[A]. MEDITATION. MAL. 4.2. THE SUN OF
1705 ⎰   RIGHTEOUSNESS. &C.

Methinks I spy Almighty holding in
    His hand the Crystall Sky and Sun in't bright:
As Candle and bright Lanthorn lightening,
    The World with this bright lanthorns flaming light
    Endungeoning all Darkness under ground   5
    Making all Sunshine Day Heavenward abound.

The Spirituall World, this world doth, Lord out vie.
    Its skie this Crystall Lanthorn doth orematch.
Its Sun, thou Art, that in'ts bright Canopy
    Out shines that Candle; Darkness doth dispatch   10
    Thy Crystall Globe of Glorious sunshine furld
    Light, Life and heate in't Sundayeth the World.

The World without the sun, 's as dungeon, darke.
    The Sun without its Light would Dungeon spring.
The Moon and Stars are but as Chilly Sparks   15
    Of Dying fire. The Sun Cheeres ery thing.
    But oh thy Light, Lightsom, delightsom falls
    Upon the Soul above all Cordialls.

All Light delights. Yet Dozde wood light is cold.
    Some light hath heate yet Darkness doth it bound   20
As Lamp and Glowworm light. The Stars do hold
    A twinkling lifeless Light. The sun is found
    A Ball of Light, of Life, Warmth to natures race.
    But thou'rt that Sun, that shines out, Saving Grace.

Doz'de wood-light is but glimmer, with no smoke.   25
    And Candle Light's a smoaky lifeless thing.
The light lodgd in the glowworms peticoate
    Is but a shew. Star light's nights twinkling.
    Moon light is nightish, Sun makes day: these all
    Without our Visive Organs lightless fall.   [305]30

But thou, my Lord no Dozed Wood shine art.

No smoky Candle Light rose from thy Wick.
Thy Light ne'er lin'de the glowworms velvet part.
Thy shine makes Stars, Moons, Sun Light darkness thick.
Thou art the Sun of Heavens bright light rose in   35
The Heavenly Orbs. And Heavens blesst glories Spring.

Were all the trees on earth fir'de Torches made,
    And all her Grass Wax Candles set on flame
This Light could not make day, this lightsom trade
    Would be a darksom smoke when sun shines plaine   40
    But thy Shine, Lord, darkens this Sun Shine bright
    And makes the seing Organ, and its Light.

Within the Horizontall Hemisphere
    Of this Blesst Sun, Lord, let mee Mansion have.
Make Day, thou shining Sun, unto mee Cleare.   45
    Thy sorry servant earnestly doth crave.
    Let not the Moon ere intervene or fix
    Between me and this sun to make Ecclipse.

O bright, bright Day. Lord let this sun shine flow.
    Drive hence my sin and Darkness greate profound   50
And up them Coffin in Earth, Shade below
    In darkness gross, on th'other Side the ground.
    Neer let the Soyle spew fogs to foile the Light
    Of this sweet Aire pregnant with sunbeams bright.

How shall my Soule (Such thoughts Enravish mee)   55
    Under the Canopy of this bright Day
Imparadisde, Lighten'd and Livend bee
    Bathd in this sun shine, 'mong bright Angells play
    And with them strive in sweetest tunes expresst
    Which can thy glorious praises Sing out best.   60

---

1 Methinks *orig.* Methings
4 this bright lanthorns *ins.*
9 that in'ts bright *orig.* in heavenly
22 sun is *orig.* sun light
24 shines out *orig.* shining

42 makes *orig.* makst
47 Moon *orig.* Sun

10.12M } 67[B]. Meditation. Mal. 4.2. With Healing
1705   }   in His Wings.

Doe Fables say, the Rising Sun doth Dance
  On Easter Day for joy, thou didst ascende.
O Sun of Righteousness; though't be a glance
  Of Falshoods spectacles on Rome's nose end?
And shall not I, furld in thy glorious beams,   5
Ev'n jump for joy, Enjoying such sweet gleams?   [306]

What doth the rising sun with its Curld Locks
  And golden wings soon make the Chilly world
Shook with an Ague Fit by night shade drops
  Revive, grow brisk, Suns Eyebright on it hurld?   10
  How should my Soule then sick of th'scurvy spring
  When thy sweet medicating rayes come in?

Alass! sweet Sun of Righteousness, Dost shine
  Upon such Dunghills, as I am? Methinks
My Soule sends out such putrid sents, and rhimes   15
  That with thy beams would Choke the aire with stincks.
  And Nasty vapors ery where, whereby
  Thy rayes should venom'd be that from thee fly.

The Fiery Darts of Satan stob my heart.
  His Punyards Thrusts are deep, and venom'd too.   20
His Arrows wound my thoughts, Words, Works, each part.
  They all ableeding ly by th'stobs, and rue.
  His Aire I breath in, poison doth my Lungs.
  Hence come Consumptions, Fevers, Head pains: Turns.

Yea, Lythargy, the Apoplectick stroke: 25
  The Catochee, soul Blindness, surdity,
Ill Tongue, Mouth Ulcers, Frog, the Quinsie Throate

The Palate Fallen, Wheezings, Pleurisy.
Heart Ach, the syncopee, bad stomach tricks
Gaul Tumors, Liver grown; spleen evills, Cricks.   30

The Kidney toucht, The Iliak, Colick Griefe
The Ricats, Dropsy, Gout, the scurvy, sore
The Miserere Mei. O Reliefe
 I want and would, and beg it at thy doore,
 O! Sun of Righteousness: Thy Beams bright, Hot   35
 Rafter a Doctors, and a Surgeons shop.

I ope my Case to thee, my Lord; mee in
 Thy glorious Bath, of sun shine, Bathe, and sweate.
So rout Ill Humors: And thy purges bring.
 Administer in Sunbeame Light, and Heate.   40
 Pounde some for Cordiall powders very small
 To Cure my Kidnies, Spleen, My Liver, Gaul.

And with the same refresh my Heart, and Lungs
 From Wasts, and Weakness. Free from Pleurisy,   [307]
Bad Stomach, Iliak Colick, Fever, turns,   45
 From Scurvy, Dropsy, Gout, and Leprosy.
 From Itch, Botch, scab. And purify my Blood
 From all Ill Humors: So make all things good.

Weave, Lord, these golden Locks into a web
 Of spirituall Taffity; make of the same   50
A sweet perfumed Rheum-Cap for my head
 To free from Lythargy, the Turn, and Pain,
 From Waking-sleep, sin-Falling Malady,
 From Whimsy, Melancholy Frenzy-dy.

Thy Curled Rayes, Lord, make mine Eare Picker   55
 To Cure my Deafeness: Light, Ophthalmicks pure
To heale my Eyes and make the sight the Quicker.
 That I may use sins spectacles no more
 O still some Beams, and with the spirits fresh
 My Palate Ulcerd Mouth, and Ill Tongue dress.   60

And ply my wounds with Pledgets dipt therein.
  And wash therewith my scabs and Boils so sore.
And all my stobs, and Arrow wounds come, bring
  And syrrindge with the same. It will them Cure.
  With tents made of these Beams well tent them all.   65
  They Fistula'es and Gangrenes Conquour shall.

Lord plaster mee herewith to bring soon down
  My swellings. Stick a Feather of thy Wing
Within my Cap to Cure my Aching Crown.
  And with these beams Heale mee of all my sin.   70
  When with these Wings thou dost mee medicine
  I'st weare the Cure, thou th'glory of this shine.

---

11 scurvy *orig.* survy
15 thy *ins.*
17 vapors *ins.*
30 evills *orig.* evills thick
32 scurvy, *orig.* scurvy, o're
41 some *ins.* ; very *orig.* some rayes
43 Heart *orig.* Heat
67 soon *orig.* all

28.2 M ⎫ 68[B]. MEDITATION. MAL. 4.2. YE SHALL GO FORTH
1706 ⎭ AND GROW AS CALVES OF THE STALL.

My megre Soule, when wilt thou fleshed bee,
  With Spirituall plumpness? Serpents flesh dost eat
Which maketh leane? The bones stick out in thee.
  Art thou Consumptive? And Concoctst not meat?
  Art not a Chick of th'Sun of Righteousness?   5
  Do not its healing Wings thy ailes redress?

Hast not Chang'd place with Mercury? And made
  Thy robes of Broadcloath of the Golden Fleece   [308]
Of Wooly Sun beams? (O! Warm shining trade!)
  Souls freshen sure in Cloaths of Such a piece.   10

And gloriously dance on these golden Cords.
Yet till a Cure is got, Griefe o're them Lords.

And if thou bruddled liest, (though Qualms arise)
  Under the healing wings of this bright sun
Of Righteousness, as Chicken Chearping wise   15
  Under its Dam, the Cure is surely Done.
  Some healing Beam a Certain med'cine brings
  To all Distemper'd souls under these wings.

This is the Heavenly Alkahest that brings
  Lean Souls t'ore thrive all Pharao's fattest Ware.   20
Grow like the Stalled Oxe, or Fattlings
  Plump, Fleshy, Fat, slick, brisk, and rightly fair.
  A Spirituall fat of Collops gracious greate
  Shall Cloath the Whole and make it grace-Compleat.

Though th'Wicker bird Cage is of rusty Wyer: 25
  This sunshine will imbellish it and bright.
Though th'bird in't of immortall breed, much tire
  These healing wings will make it fully ripe.
  My little Pipkin Soule of heavenly Clay
  Shall fatted to the brim with grace grow gay.   30

My Heade, O Sun, hide in thy healing Wing.
  Thy Warmth will to my megre soule flesh give.
My growth shall Beauty to thine Eyesight bring.
  Thy sight shall make mee plump and pleasant live.
  And all my Growth to thee shall bud with blooms   35
  Of Praises Whistling in Angelick Tunes.

Title 68 *orig.* 78
20 t'ore *orig.* ore
22 rightly *ins.*
23 gracious *ins.*
35 Growth *orig.* Growth shall

30.4M ⎫   69. Meditation. Cant. 2.1. The Lillie
1706 ⎭   of the Vallies.

Dull! Dull! my Lord, as if I eaten had
  A Peck of Melancholy, or my Soule
Was lockt up by a Poppy key, black, sad;
  Or had been fuddled with an Henbane bowle.
    Oh, Leaden temper! my Rich Thesis Would   5
    Try metall to the back, sharp, it t'unfold.   [309]

Alas! my Soule, Thy Sunburnt Skin looks dun:
  Thy Elementall jacket's snake like pi'de
I am Deform'd, and Uggly all become.
    Soule sicknesses do nest in mee: and Pride.   10
    I nauseous am: and mine iniquites
    Like Crawling Worms doe wormeaten my joys.

All black though plac'de in a White lilly Grove:
  Not sweet, though in a bed of Lillies rowle,
Though in Physicians Shop I dwell, a Drove   15
  Of Hellish Vermin range all ore my Soul.
    All spirituall Maladies play rex in mee.
    Though Christ should Lilly of my Vally bee.

But, Oh! the Wonder! Christ alone the Sun
  Of Righteousness, that he might do the Cure   20
The Lilly of the Vallies is become
  Whose Lillie properties do health restore.
    Its glory shews I'm filthy: yet must Spring
    Up innocent, and beautifull by him.

Its Vally state and Bowing Head declare   25
  I'm Haughty but must have a Humble minde.
Its Healing Virtue shew I'me sick: yet rare
  Rich Remedies I'st in this Lilly finde.
    Yea Christ the Lilly of the Vallies shall
    Be to mee Glory, Med'cine, Sweetness, all.   30

The Lillies Beautie, and its Fragrancy

Shews my ill-favourdness, and nauseous stinck:
And that I must be beautifull, fully,
  And breath a sweetness that the aire must drink.
This Beauty, Odour, Med'cin, Humble Case   35
This Vallys Lilly shall my Soul begrace.

Lord, make me th'Vally where this Lilly grows.
  Then I am thine, and thou art mine indeed.
Propriety is mutuall: Glorious shows
  And Odorif'rous breath shall in me breed   [310]40
  Which twisted in my Tunes, thy praise shall ring
On my shoshannims sweetest Well tun'de string.

---

4 with *orig.* in
12 Worms doe *orig.* vermin
15 Shop *ins.*
26 have a *ins.*
27 I'me *orig.* I
31 Beautie *orig.* Beauties
32 Shews *orig.* Shew
36 begrace *orig.* with grace
42 string *orig.* strings

25.6M
1706 } 70. MEDITATION. COL. 2.11.12. IN WHOM ALSO YE ARE
CIRCUMCISED WITH CIRCUMCISION MADE WITHOUT
HANDS, IN PUTTING OFF OF THE SIN OF THE FLESH
BY THE CIRCUMCISION OF CHRIST, BURIED WITH HIM
IN BAPTISM; &C.

I humbly Crave, this Riddle to unfold
  Seing, Lord, thou madst man Compleate at first,
How comes't to pass When Natures egge, that holds
  Her Chicken brake, the bird defilde out burst?
  A Callous doth the heart Disspiritualize   5
Till Gilgal's Razer doth it Circumcise.

Thy first Free Covenant, Calld not for this:
  Thy Covenant of Graces Quilting kinde,

Shall it require a Seale that Cutting is?
  That fleys the skin off, that the heart doth rinde?   10
  What is Rebellions Castle made the heart,
  Filld up with filth, to be skin'd off? O sharp.

Hath sin encrusted thus my heart? Sad! Sad!
  And latcht my Lips? And Eares made deafe, and ditcht?
O! Lord! pare off, I pray, what ere is bad: 15
  And Circumcise my Heart, mine Eares and Lips.
  This in thy Circimcisions heart doth bed.
  The same in baptism is bosomed.

What must Christs Circumcision pacify
  Gods Wrath? and's Blood of's Circumcision Sore,   20
Bring Righteousness, Purge Sin, and Mortify
  Proude Naughtiness? And wash with Grace mee o're?
  And my Uncircumcisedness all Slay?
  That I might walke in glorious Graces way?

The Infant male must lose its Foreskin first,   25
  Before Gods Spirit Workes as Pulse, therein
To Sanctify it from the sin in't nurst,
  And make't in Graces Covenant to spring.
  To shew that Christ must be cut off most Pure.
  His Covenantall blood must be mans Cure.   [311]30

And shall this sweet kinde Covenant of Grace
  Ware on't a Seale so keen and Cutting sharp
When it its brightst Edition doth embrace?
  No, no. Baptism is a better marke.
  It's therefore Circumcisions Rightfull Heir   35
  Bearing what Circumcision in't did beare.

Hence me implant in Christ, that I may have
  His Blood to wash away the filth in mee.
And finde his Wounds that are so deep, the grave
  Wherein my Sins ly dead and buri'de bee.   40
  From which let such sweet Exhalations rise
  As shall my Soule deck with an Holy guise.

Lord bed mee in thy Circumcisions Quilt.
   My wounds bathe with New Covenantall blood.
My ears with Grace Lord syringe, scoure off guilt.   45
   My Tongue With holy tasled Languague Dub.
   And then these parts, baptisde thine Organs keep,
   To tune thy Praise, run forth on golden feet.

Title off *orig.* off the body
3 When *orig.* th
6 Till *orig.* Untill
19 Christs *orig.* Christs Blood
22 wash *orig.* mee ; mee *orig.* Wash
28 make't *orig.* it make
36 what *orig.* in't all

20.8M ⎤   71. MEDITATION. 1 COR. 5.8. LET US KEEP THE
1706 ⎦   FEAST, NOT WITH OLD LEVEN.

Oh! What a Cookroom's here? all Deity
   Thick blancht all ore with Properties Divine
Varnisht with grace that shineth gloriously.
   Pollisht with glorious folds of brightest shine
   Enricht with Heavens Cookery the best   5
   The Turtle Dove, and Paschall Lamb's here dresst.

Oh! Dove most innocent. O Lamb, most White.
   A Spotless Male in prime. Whose blood's the Dier
That dies the Doore posts of the Soule most bright.
   Whose body all is rost at justice's fire   10
   And yet no bone is broken though the spit
   Whereon its rost runs, spearelike, thorow it.

This Choicest Cookery is made the Feast
   Where glories king doth entertain his Guests.
Whose Pastie past is Godhead: filld at least   15
   With Venison, of Paschall Lamb the best.

All spic'd and Plumbd with Grace, and disht up right
Upon Gods Table Plate Divinely bright.   [312]

This spirituall Fare in Ordinances, and
    The Wine bled from the Holy Grape, and Vine,   20
That's on the Table orderd by God's hand
    (The Supper of the Lord, the feast Divine),
    Gods Gospel Priests this to that Table beare,
    Where Saints are Guests: and Angells waiters are.

The Wedden garment of Christs Righteousness   25
    And Holy Cloaths of Sanctity most pure
Are their attire, their Festivall rich dress:
    Faith feeds upon the Paschall Lamb it's sure
    That on God's Porslain Dish is disht for them
    And drinks the Cup studded with graces Gem.   30

Let at this Table, Lord thy servant sit.
    And load my trencher with thy Paschall Lamb.
My Doore posts dy with the red blood of it
    The 'stroying angells weapon therewith sham
    And let my Faith on thy rost mutton feed   35
    And Drinke the Wine thy holy grape doth bleed.

Lord make my Faith feed on it heartily.
    Let holy Charity my heart Cement
Unto thy Saints: and for a Cordiall high
    Make mee partaker of thy sacrament.   40
    When with this Paschall bread and Wine I'm brisk
    I in Sweet Tunes thy sweetest praise will twist.

---

12 thorow *orig.* through
18 Plate *orig.* Gods Plate
21 That's *orig.* I
30 Gem *orig.* them

15.10 ⎱   72. MEDITATION. MAR. 16.19. SAT DOWN
1706 ⎰   ON THE RIGHT HAND OF GOD.

Enoculate into my mentall Eye
　The Visive Spirits of the Holy Ghost
My Lord, that I may see the Dignity
　Of thy bright Honour in thy heavenly Coast.
　Thou art deckt with as sunshine bright displaid   5
　That makes bright Angells in it, cast a Shade.

Enrich my Phansy with seraphick Life,
　Enquicknd nimbly to catch the Beams
Thy Honour flurs abroad: in joyous Strife
　To make sweet Musick on Such Happy Themes.   10
　That in such Raptures, and Transports of joy,
　Thy Honour brings I may my Phansy 'ploy.

At Gods Right Hand! Doth God mans parts enjoy?
　This with Infinity can never stande:
Yet so God sayes, His Son to Dignify   15
　Inmanhooded, said, Sit at my right hand.
　The manhood thus a brighter Honour bears
　By Deity than Deity ere wares.   [313]

The splendor of the matter of each story
　Of th'Heavenly Palace Hall all brightend cleare,   20
The Presence Chamber of the King of Glory
　Common with thee, to Saints and Angells there.
　They share with thee in this Celestiall shine.
　Although the[ir] share is lesser far than thine.

Yet they in all this glorious splendor bright   25
　So many suns like, shining on each other,
Encreasing each's glory, fall down right
　To kiss thy feet, whose shine thy glorie Covers.
　Their brightest Shine, in Glory's highest story,
　Is t'Stand before thee in thy bright-bright glory.   30

Thy Honour brightens theirs, as't on theirs falls.

Its Royall Honour thou inheritst, Cleare.
A Throne of Glory in bright glories Hall:
  At Gods right Hand, thou sits enthroned there:
  The Highest Throne in brightest glory thou   35
  Enjoyest. Saints, and Angells 'fore thee bow.

Come down, bright Angells, Now I claim my place.
  My nature hath more Honour due, than yours:
Mine is Enthron'de at Gods Right Hand, through Grace.
  This Grace for mine and not for yours, endures,   40
  Yours is not there, unless in part of mine,
  As *Species* in their *Genus* do combine.

Hence make my Life, Lord, keep thine Honour bright,
  And let thine Honour brighten mee by grace.
And make thy Grace in mee, thee honour right,   45
  And let not mee thy Honour ere deface.
  Grant me the Honour then to honour thee
  And on my Bells thine Honour chim'd shall bee.

---

3 see orig. *see aright*

9.12M ⎫   73. MEDITATION. 1.TIM. 3.16. RECEIVED INTO
1706   ⎬   GLORY.
       ⎭

Glory! oh Glory, Wonderfull, and more.
  How dost thou Croude with all thy Ranks most bright?
Thou never playdst Such Glorious Casts before
  Nor ever wor'st such flourishing delight.   [314]
  Thy heart doth leape for joy, to have the gain   5
  When thou Receivdst my Lord in Glories Flame.

Who can the Ranks of Glory ere relate,
  As they stand up in Honours Palace Hall?
They sparkle Flashing spangles, golden flakes
  Of burnisht shines with lowly Conjues all   10

To kisse thy hand, my Lord, and hande thee in
To tend thee and attend thee, her head spring.

Glory was never glorifide so much,
   She ne're receiv'de such glory heretofore.
As that that doth Embrace her, (it is such,)   15
   As She unto my Lord, doth ope her doore.
   When he receivd was into glory's Sphere
   Glory then found her glory brightest were.

When unto Angell's Glory opens doore,
   Or unto saints, all to be glorifi'de,   20
She well bestows herselfe, t'enrich her store:
   Yet blushes much to eye thy Glories tide.
   When She doth make herselfe thy Cloaths to bee,
   She's cloathd with brighter glory far by thee.

The greatest glory glory doth enjoy.   25
   Lies in her hanging upon thee Wherein
Glory that glorifies thee mightily,
   Is far more glorifi'de. Hence Glories spring,
   Now Graces Glory, Heavens Glory, and
   Gloryes of Saints, and Angells, guild thy hand.   30

A Glorious Palace, a Bright Crown of Glory
   A glorious train of Saints, and Angells Shine
And glorious exercise as sweetest posy.
   Do sacrifice themselves unto thy shrine.
   They give their all to thee, and so receive   35
   Therein from thee a much more brighter Wreath.

Let some, my Lord, of thy bright Glories beams,
   Flash quickening Flames of Glory in mine eye
T'enquicken my dull spirits, drunke with dreams
   Of Melancholy juyce that Stupify.   40
   A Coale from thy bright Altars Glory sure
   Kissing my lips, my Lethargy will Cure.

If Envy e're by sanctifying skill

Could gracious be, or be a Grace, I would
I could it on my Spirits Cold and Chill   45
    Well Exercise, that Love thus ever should   [315]
    Ly lockt by Melancholy's key up in my Heart.
    And hardly Smile when Glories beautyes dart.

Lord make thy beams my frost bit heart to warm.
    Ride on these Rayes into my bosom's till   50
And make thy Glory mine affections Charm.
    Thy rapid flames my Love enquicken will.
    Then I in Glories Tower thy Praise will sing
    On my Shoshanims tun'd on ev'ry string.

---

8 up *ins.*
17 receivd *orig.* receives
28 glorifi'de *orig.* glorified
46 thus *orig.* thus should ever
49 warm *orig.* Charm
51 affections *orig.* affections w
52 flames *orig.* flames will quicken
54 on *orig.* to

6.2M ⎫   74. MEDITATION. PHI. 3.21. HIS GLORIOUS
1707 ⎭   BODY. τῷ σώματι τῆς δόξης αυτοῦ.

I fain would have a rich, fine Phansy ripe
    That Curious pollishings elaborate
Should lay, Lord, on thy glorious Body bright
    The more my lumpish heart to animate.
    But searching ore the Workhouse of my minde,   5
    I but one there; and dull and meger finde.

Hence, Lord, my search hand thou from this dark Shop
    (It's foule, and wanteth sweeping) up unto
Thy Glorious Body whose bright beames let drop
    Upon my heart: and Chant it with the show.   10
    Because the shine that from thy body flows,

More glorious is than is the brightest Rose.

Sun shine is to this Glory but a smoke.
  Saints in their brightest shines are clouds therein.
Bright Angells are like motes i'th'Sun unto't.   15
  Its Beames gild heavens bright Hall, that's sparkling.
  Of all Created Glory, that doth shine
  Thy Bodies Glory is most bright and fine.

The Beauty of Humanity Compleate.
  Where ery organ is adepted right.   20
Wherein such spirits brisk, do act full neate
  Make Natures operations fully ripe.
  All Harmonizing in their actions done
  That ery twig's with glorious blossoms hung.

And still more sweet: thou'rt with more glory deckt.   25
  The Glory of ripe Grace of brightest kinde
Like lumps of living Fire, by nothing Checkt
  Thrumping the stars, as pinking things half blinde,
  This makes thy Bodies glory Choice and fine,
  A spirituall light in Corporall Lanthorn shine.   [316]30

Yea, still more Glory. Oh! thy Humane Frame
  Is th'brightst Temple of the Holy Ghost.
Whose Rayes run through the Whole in brightest flame
  Hence on thy body campeth Glories Hoast.
  What more can still be said? I add but this.   35
  That Glory bright thy Bodies Tilt-Clothe is.

Oh! Glorious Body! Pull my eye lids ope:
  Make my quick Eye, Lord, thy brisk Glory greet,
Whose rapid flames when they my heart revoke
  From other Beauties, make't for thee more sweet.   40
  If such blesst Sight shall twist my heart with thine.
  Thy Glory make the Web, thy Praise the Twine.

Title His *orig.* Thy

6 I *orig.* I see one
11 thy *orig.* my
16 that's *ins.*
25 thou'rt *orig.* and
28 Thrumping *orig.* Thruming
30 light *ins.*

1.4M ⎫ 75. MEDITATION. PHIL. 3.ULT. OUR VILE BODIE
1707 ⎭   τὸ σῶμα τῆς ταπεινώσεως ἡμῶν

Oh. strang, my Lord. Here's reason at a set.
  Run out of'ts Wits, construing Grace's style.
Nay shining Angells in an holy fret
    Confounded are, to see our Bodies Vile
    Made Cabinets of Sparkling Gems that far   5
    Out Shine the brightest shining heavenly Star.

Mudd made with Muscadine int'mortar Rich,
  Dirt wrought with Aqua-Vitæ for a Wall
Built all of Precious Stones laid in it, Which
    Is with leafe gold bespangled, 'maizes all   10
    Yet this Amaizment's scarce a minutes Sise
    Compar'd unto the matter 'fore our eyes.

Here is a Mudwall tent, whose Matters are
  Dead Elements, which mixt make dusty trade:
Which with Life Animall are wrought up faire   15
    A Living mudwall by Gods holy spade.
    Yet though a Wall alive all Spruice, and crouce,
    It's Base, and Vile, and baseness keeps its House.

Nature's Alembeck't is, It's true: that stills
  The Noblest spirits terrene fruits possess,   20
Yet, oh! the Relicks in the Caldron will
    Proove all things else, Guts, Garbage, Rotteness.
    And all its pipes but sincks of nasty ware
    That foule Earths face, and do defile the aire.

A varnisht pot of putrid excrements,   25
  And quickly turns to excrements itselfe,
By natures Law: but, oh! there therein tents
  A Sparke immortall and no mortall elfe.
  An Angell bright here in a Swine sty dwell!
  What Lodge of Wonders's this? What tongue can tell?   [317]30

But, oh! how doth this Wonder still encrease?
  The Soule Creeps in't. And by it's too defil'd
Are both made base, and vile, can have no peace
  Without, nor in: and's of its shine beguil'd.
  And though this Spirit in it dwells yet here   35
  Its glory will not dwell with such sad geere.

Both grac'd together, and disgrac'd. Sad Case
  What now becomes of Gods Electing Love?
This now doth raise the Miracle apace,
  Christ doth step in, and Graces Art improove.   40
  He kills the Leprosy that taints the Walls:
  And Sanctifies the house before it falls.

And nature here, though mean and base beside,
  With marks and stains of sin, and sin not dead
Though mortifi'de and dying, in't reside,   45
  With Graces precious Pearls its flourished.
  And in our bodies very vile and base
  Christ hath enthron'de all Sanctifying Grace.

That these dark Cells, and Mudwalld Tents defild,
  With nastiness should Cabinets be made   50
For th'Choicest Pearls in Glories ring enfoild
  Out shining all the shining starry trade.
  It's glorious Wonders, wrought by Graces hand
  Whereat bright Angells all amaized stand.

Oh! make my Body, Lord, Although it's vile,   55
  Thy Warehouse where Grace doth her treasures lay.
And Cleanse the house and ery Room from soile.
  Deck all my Rooms with thy rich Grace I pray.

If thy free Grace doth my low tent, perfume,
I'll sing thy Glorious praise in ery room.   60

---

7 Rich *orig.* which
14 dusty *orig.* dirty
19 Alembeck *orig.* Alimbick
35 this *orig.* the
42 before it *orig.* for
54 amaized *orig.* amaised
55 Although *orig.* although *orig.* though

27.5M
1707 } 76. MEDITATION. PHI.3.21. WHO SHALL CHANGE OUR
       VILE BODY, THAT IT MAY BE FASHIOND LIKE HIS
       GLORIUS BODY.

Will yee be neighbourly, ye Angells bright?
  Then lend mee your Admiring Facultie:
Wonders presented stand, above my might.
  That call from mee the highest Extasie,
  If you deny mee this: my pimping soule,   5
  These Wonders pins up in an Auger hole.

If my Rush Candle on its wick ware flame,
  Of Ignis lambens. Oh! bright garb indeed:
What then, when Flakes of flaming Glory train
  From thy bright glorious bulk to 'ray my weed.   10
  What my vile Body like thy Glorious, Formd?
  What Wonder here? My body thus adornd!   [318]

What shall mine hempen harle wove in thy Loome
  Into a web (an hurden web indeed)
Be made its Makers Tent Cloth? I presume.   15
  Within these Curtains Grace keeps Hall, and breeds:
  But shall my hurden hangings ever ware
  A bright bright glory like thy body faire?

Meethinks thy smile doth make thy Footstoole so
  Spread its green Carpet 'fore thy feet for joy.   20

And Bryers climb in t'bright Rose that flows
  Out in sweet reechs to meet thee in the sky:
  And makes the sportive starrs play Hide-and-Seek
  And on thy bodies Glory peeping keep.

And shall not I (whose form transformd shall bee   25
  To be shap'te like thy glorious body, Lord.
That Angells bright, as Gasterd, gaze at mee
  To see such Glory on my dresser board),
  Transported be hereat for very joy,
  Whose intrest lies herein, and gloriously?   30

What shall the frosty Rhime upon my locks,
  Congeale my brains with Chilly dews, whereby
My Phansie is benumbd: and put in Stocks,
  And thaws not into Steams of reeching joy?
  Oh! strange Ingratitude! Let not this Frame   35
  Abide, Lord, in mee, Fire mee with thy flame.

Lord, let thy glorious Body send such rayes
  Into my soule, as ravish shall my heart,
That Thoughts how thy bright Glory out shall blaze
  Upon my body, may such Rayes thee dart.   40
  My Tunes shall dance then on these Rayes and Caper
  Unto thy Praise. When Glory lights my Taper.

---

1 yee *orig.* bee
6 pins *orig.* pin
16 keeps *ins.*
18 A bright bright glory like *orig.* As bright a glory as ; faire *orig.* fare
21 climb in t'bright Rose that flows *ins.*
22 Out in sweet *orig.* And in flows
37 rayes *orig.* raises

5.8M ⎫ 77. MEDITATION. ZECH. 9.11. THE PIT WHEREIN
1707 ⎬ IS NO WATER.

A state, a state, Oh! Dungeon state indeed.
  In which mee headlong, long agoe sin pitcht:
As dark as Pitch; where Nastiness doth breed:
  And Filth defiles: and I am with it ditcht.
  A sinfull state: This Pit no Water's in't.   5
  A Bug bare state: as black as any inke.

I once sat singing on the summit high
  'Mong the Celestiall Choire in Musick sweet
On highest bough of Paradisall joy,
  Glory and Innocence did in mee meet.   10
  I as a Gold-Fincht Nighting Gale, tun'd ore
  Melodious songs 'fore Glorie's Palace Doore.   [319]

But on this bough I tuning Pearcht not long:
  Th'Infernall Foe shot out a Shaft from Hell
A Fiery Dart pilde with sins poison strong: 15
  That struck my heart, and so down I headlong fell.
  And from the Highest Pinicle of Light
  Into this Lowest pit more darke than night.

A Pit indeed of Sin: No water's here:
  Whose bottom's furthest off from Heaven bright.   20
And is next doore to Hell-Gate, to it neer:
  And here I dwell in sad and solemn plight
  My Gold-Fincht Angell-Feathers dapled in
  Hells scarlet Dy fat, blood red grown with sin.

I in this Pit all Destitute of Light   25
  Cram'd full of Horrid Darkness, here do Crawle
Up over head, and Eares, in Nauseous plight:
  And swinelike Wallow in this mire, and Gall:
  No Heavenly Dews nor Holy Waters drill:
  Nor sweet Aire Brieze, nor Comfort here distill.   30

Here for Companions, are Fears, Heart Achs, Grief

Frogs, Toads, Newts, Bats, Horrid Hob-Goblins, Ghosts:
Ill spirits haunt this Pit: and no reliefe:
Nor Coard can fetch me hence in Creatures Coasts.
I who once lodgd at Heavens Palace Gate   35
With full Fledgd Angells, now possess this fate.

But yet, my Lord, thy golden Chain of Grace
  Thou canst let down, and draw mee up into
Thy Holy Aire, and Glory's Happy Place.
  Out from these Hellish damps and pit so low   40
And if thy Grace shall do't, My Harp I'le raise,
Whose strings toucht by this Grace, Will twang thy praise.

---

13 bough *orig.* bow
25 I in *orig.* And
29 drill *orig.* drills
30 Nor *orig.* Nor brieze of sweet ; distill *orig.* distills
39 Glory's Happy Place *orig.* happy Glory's Rase

14.10M ⎫   78. MEDITATION. ZECH. 9.11. BY THE BLOOD OF THY
        ⎬   COVENANT I HAVE SENT FORTH THY PRISONERS
1707   ⎭   OUT OF THE PIT WHEREIN IS NO WATER.

Mine Eyes, that at the Beautious Sight of Fruite
  On th'Tree of Knowledge, drew black venom in
That did bemegerim my brains at root
  That they turnd round, and tippled me int'sin.
I thus then int'Barath'rick pit down fell   5
That's Waterless and next doore is to Hell:

No water's here: It is a Springless Well.
  Like Josephs Pit, all dry of Comforts spring:
Oh! Hopeless, Helpless Case: In such I fell.
  The Creatures bucket's dry, no help can bring: 10
Oh here's a spring; Indeed it's Lethe Lake,
Of Aqua-Infernalis: don't mistake.   [320]

This Pit indeed's sins Filthy Dungeon State,
  No water's in't, but filth, and mire, sins juyce.
Wherein I sinke ore Head, and Eares: Sad fate,   15
  And ever shall, if Grace hath here no Sluce.
  Its Well Coards whip Coards are: not Coards to draw
  (Like Pully Coards) out of this Dungeons maw.

Yet in the upper room of Paradise
  An Artist anvill'd out Reliefe sure, Good;   20
A Golden Coarde, and bucket of Grace Choice
  Let down top full of Covenantall blood.
  Which when it touches, oh! the happy Cry!
  The doores fly ope. Now's jayles Deliverie.

This is a spring of Liquour, heavenly, Cleare.   25
  Its streams oreflow these banks. Its boundless Grace
Whose spring head's Godhead, and its Channells where
  It runs, is Manhood veans that Christ keeps Chase
  For it, and when it makes a spring tide Flood
  This Pit is drown'd with Covenantall blood.   30

And now the Prisoners sent out, do come
  Padling in their Canooes apace with joyes
Along this blood red Sea, Where joyes do throng,
  And sayling in the Arke of Grace that flies
  Drove sweetly by Gales of the Holy Ghost   35
  Who sweetly briezes all along this Coast.

Here's Covenant blood, indeed: and't down the banks
  Of this dry Pit breakes: Also't is a key
T'unlock the shackles Sin hung on their shanks
  And wash the durt off: Send them cleane away.   40
  The Pris'ners freed, do on this Red Sea Swim
  In Zions Barke: and in their Cabbins Sing.

Lord let this Covenantall blood Send mee
  Poore Pris'ner, out of sins dry Dungeon pound:
And on this Red Sea saile mee safe to thee   45

In which none Israelite was ever drown'd.
My sayles shall tune thee praise along this coast
If waft with Gailes breath'd by the Holy Ghost.

---

3 bemegerim *orig.* bemegrim
5 then ins. ; int' *orig.* into th'
11 Oh *orig.* Yet
23 Cry *orig.* Sise
24 Deliverie *orig.* Deliveries
32 in *orig.* with
47 praise *orig.* praises

8.12M } 79. MEDITATION. CAN. 2.16. MY BELOVED IS MINE
1707   }   AND I AM HIS.

Had I Promethiu's filching Ferula
  Filld with its sacred theft the stoln Fire:
To animate my Fancy lodg'd in clay,
    Pandora's Box would peps the theft with ire.   [321]
    But if thy Love, My Lord, shall animate   5
    My Clay with holy fire, 't will flame in state.

Fables fain'd Wonders do relate so strange
  That do amuse when heard. But oh! thy Fame
Pend by the Holy Ghost, (and ne'er shall Change
    Nor vary from the truth) is wonders flame   10
    Glazde o're with Heavens Embelishments, and fan'd
    From evry Chaff, Dust, Weedy Seed, or Sand.

What wilt thou change thyselfe for me, and take
  In lew thereof my Sorry selfe; whereby,
I am no more mine own, but thine, probate,   15
    Thou not so thine, as not mine too, thereby?
    Dost purchase me to be thine own, thyselfe
    And dost exchange for mee, thyselfe, and wealth?

I'm Thine, Thou Mine! Mutuall propriety:
  Thou giv'st thyselfe. And for this gift takst mee   20
To be thine own. I give myselfe (poore toy)
  And take thee for myne own, and so to bee.
  Thou giv'st thyselfe yet dost thyselfe possess,
  I give and keep myselfe too neretheless.

Both gi'n away and yet retain'd aright.   25
  Oh! Strange! I have thee mine, who hast thyselfe,
Yet in possession Thou hast mee as tite,
  Who still enjoy myselfe. And thee my wealth.
  What strang appropriations hence arise?
  Thy Person mine, Mine thine, ever weddenwise?   30

Thine mine, mine Thine, a mutuall claim is made.
  Mine, thine, are Predicates unto us both.
But oh! the Odds in th'purchase price down laid:
  Thyselfe's thy Price, myselfe my mony go'th.
  Thy Purchase mony's infinitly high;   35
  Of Value for me: mine for thee, 's a toy.

Thou'rt Heire of Glory, dost Bright image stand
  Ev'n of the God of Glory. Ownest all.
Hast all Wealth, Wisdom, Glory, Might at hand
  And all what e're can to mans Glory fall,   40
  And yet thou giv'st thyselfe to purchase mee
  Ev'n of myselfe, to give myselfe to thee.   [322]

And what am I? a little bit of Clay.
  Not more, nor better thing, at all I give.
(Though give myselfe) to thee as Purchase pay.   45
  For thee, and for thy all, that I may live.
  What hard terms art thou held unto by me.
  Both in thy Sale, and Purchase, laid on thee?

But yet this thing doth not impov'rish thee
  Although thou payest down thy glorious selfe.   50
And my downlaying of myselfe I see

For thee, 's the way for mee to blessed wealth.
Thou freely givst what I buy Cheape of thee.
I freely give what thou buyst deare of mee.

The Purchasd Gift, and Given Purchase here   55
    (For they're both Gifts, and Purchases) by each
For each, make each to one anothers deare,
    And each delight t'heare one anothers speech.
Oh! Happy Purchase, and oh! Happy sale:
Making each others joye in joyous gales.   60

Let this dash out the snarling teeth that grin,
    Of that Damnd Heresy, calld SHERLOKISM,
That mocks, and scoffs the UNION (that blesst thing)
    To Christs Blesst Person, Happy Enkentrism
For if that's true, Christs Spouse spake false in this   65
Saying My Beloved's Mine, and I am his.

Hence, Oh! my Lord, make thou mee thine that so
    I may be bed wherein thy Love shall ly,
And be thou mine that thou mayst ever show
    Thyselfe the Bed my Love its lodge may Spy.   70
Then this shall be the burden of my Song:
My Well belov'de is mine: I'm his become.

---

2 filld with its *orig.* With 'ts [***] the
18 dost *orig.* do *orig.* be
31 is made *orig.* runs thus
32 are *orig.* is ; unto *orig.* to
37 Heire *orig.* Hair
39 at hand *orig.* and Power at hand
40 to *orig.* unto
42 to give *orig.* that to give
49 thing *orig.* bargain
57 make *orig.* that ; one *orig.* on
60 joye in *orig.* joyes
65 For if that's *orig.* For that is
66 Beloved's *orig.* Beloved is
70 its *orig.* may

80. MEDITATION. JOH. 6.53. EXCEPT YOU EATE THE
6.IM   FLESH OF THE SON OF MAN, &C: YE HAVE NO LIFE
1707/8   IN YOU.

This Curious pearle, One Syllable, calld LIFE,
  That all things struggle t'keep, and we so prize
I'd with the Edge of sharpend Sight (as knife)
  My understanding Sheath anatomize
  But finde Life far too fine, I cannot know't.   5
  My Sight too Dull; my knife's too blunt to do't.

And if you say, What then is Life? I say
  I cannot tell you what it is, yet know
That Various kinds of Life lodg in my clay.
  And ery kinde an Excellence doth show: [323]10
  And yet the lowest sort so secret lies
  I cannot finde it nor anatomize.

But here I finde, that all these kindes proove stares
  Whereon I do ascende to heaven to
My Lord, thyselfe, and so do mock earths snares   15
  Those Snick snarls, and thus my Soul steps goe
  From Vegetate to sensitive, thence trace
  To Rationall, and thence to th'Life of Grace.

What though I know not what it is? I know,
  It is too good to bee full known by any   20
Poor Perblinde man, that squints on things; although
  It's Life, it's quickening Life to very many.
  Yea t'all th'Elect. It is a Slip up bred
  Of Godlike life, in graces garden bed.

Grace is the Pearle, the Mother Pearle of Pearles   25
  In which this Pearle of Life is kirnell choice.
Christ dropt it in the Soule, which up it ferles
  A Lignum Vitæs Chip of Paradise.
  It's Heart and Soule of Saving Grace out spred
  And can't be had till Grace be brought to bed.   30

The Soule's the Womb. Christ is the spermodote
  And Saving Grace the seed cast thereinto,
This Life's the principall in Graces Coate.
  Making vitality in all things flow
  In Heavenly verdure brisking holily   35
  With sharp ey'de peartness of Vivacity.

Dead Looks, and Wanness, all things on them weare,
  If this Life Quickens not, Things Spirituall Dead
The Image too of God is grown thrid bare
  If this Choice Life ben't with Christ's body fed.   40
  All other lives dance on, in hellish wayes
  Eternally, unless this Life out blaze.

Thou art, my Lord, the Well Spring of this life.
  Oh! let this Life send Rivelets in my heart.
That I may by lifes Streames in Holy Strife   45
  Conquour that death, at whose dead Looks I startt.
  When of this Life my Soule with Child doth spring
  The Babe of Life swath'de up in Grace shall Sing.

---

4 understanding Sheath *orig.* understandings Sheath th
12 cannot *orig.* can't
14 heaven *orig.* heavens Throne and Palace,
17 trace *orig.* shall trace
22 It's *orig.* It is ; it's *ins.* ; very *ins.*
23 up bred *orig.* likewise
29 of Saving *orig.* of Saving of Saving
32 the seed *ins.*
37 weare *orig.* beare
38 If this Life Quickens not *orig.* Unless this Life them Quickens
39 is *orig.* is E**ld
48 Life *orig.* Grace ; Grace *orig.* Life

2.3M
1708
}

81. MEDITATION. JOH. 6.53. UNLESS YE EAT THE
FLESH OF THE SON OF MAN, AND DRINK HIS
BLOOD, YOU HAVE NO LIFE IN YOU.   [324]

I fain would praise thee, Lord, but often finde
    Some toy or trinket slipping in between,
My heart and thee, that whiffles hence my minde
    From this I know not how, and oft unseen.
    That such should interpose between my soule   5
    And thee, is matter for mee to Condole.

I finde thou art the spring of Life, and Life
    Is up Empon'd in thee, that's Life indeed,
Thou art Lifes Fountain and its Food. The strife
    Of Living things doth for Life sake proceed,   10
    But he that With the best of Lifes is spic'te
    Doth eate, and drinke the Flesh, and blood of Christ.

What feed on Humane Flesh and Blood? Strang mess!
    Nature exclaims. What Barbarousness is here?
And Lines Divine this Sort of Food repress.   15
    Christs Flesh and Blood how can they bee good Cheer?
    If shread to atoms, would too few be known,
    For ev'ry mouth to have a Single one.

This Sense of this blesst Phrase is nonsense thus.
    Some other Sense makes this a metaphor.   20
This feeding signifies, that Faith in us
    Feeds on this fare; Disht in this Pottinger.
    Faith feeds upon this Heavenly Manna rare.
    And drinkes this Blood. Sweet junkets: Angells Fare.

Christs works as Divine Cookery, knead in   25
    The Pasty Past, (his Flesh and Blood) most fine
Into Rich Fare, made with the rowling pin
    His Deity did use. (Obedience prime)
    Active, and Passive is the Food that all
    That have this Life feed on within thy Hall.   30

Here's Meate, and Drinke for souls to use: (Good Cheer,)
  Cookt up, and Brewd by Pure Divinity
The juyce tund up in Humane Casks that ne'er
  Were musty made by any sluttery.
  And tapt by Graces hand whose table hold   35
  This fare in dishes far more rich than Gold.   [325]

Thou, Lord, Envit'st me thus to eat thy Flesh,
  And drinke thy blood more spiritfull than wine.
And if I feed not here on this rich mess,
  I have no life in mee: no life Divine.   40
  The Spirituall Life, the Life of God, and Grace
  Eternall Life, obtain in me no place.

The Naturall Life the Life of Reason too
  Are but as painten Cloths to that I lack
The spirituall Life, and Life Eternall View.   45
  If none of mine, my Glorys face grows black.
  And how should I upon this food ere feed,
  If thou give unto me no vitall Seed?

Those Fruits (the Works) that gloriously do shine
  Upon thy Humane Nature Flesh and Blood   50
From thy Divine, are th'Purchase price, and th'Fine
  Set on our heads, and made our Spirituall Food.
  Faith that's the feeding on these pleasant flowers,
  Incorporates thy Flesh and Blood with ours.

Thy Flesh, and Blood and Office Fruites shall bee   55
  My souls Plumb Cake it eates, as naturally,
In Spirituallwise mixt with my soul, as wee
  Finde food doth with the body properly.
  So that my life shall be mentain'd and thrive
  Eternally when spiritually alive.   60

Oh! feed mee, Lord, on thy rich Florendine.
  Made of the Fruites which thy Divinity
As Principall did beare (more Sweet than wine)
  Upon thy Manhood, meritoriously.

If I be fed with this rich fare, I will   65
Say Grace to thee with songs of holy skill.

---

2 slipping in between *orig.* whiffling off my minde
10 for *ins.*
11 With *orig.* hath
13 Strang *orig.* Strng
19 nonsense *orig.* mere nonsense
30 within *orig.* in
37 Envit'st *orig.* Envitest
47 I *ins.*
53 these pleasant *orig.* this ple[**]sall
55 and *orig.* and its works
63 beare (more *orig.* beare, more

82. MEDITATION. JOH. 6.53. UNLESS YEE EATE THE
27.4M   }   FLESH OF THE SON OF MAN, AND DRINK HIS
1708   }   BLOOD, YE HAVE NO LIFE.

My tatter'd Fancy; and my Ragged Rymes
    Teeme leaden Metaphors: which yet might serve
To hum a little touching terrene shines.
    But spirituall Life doth better fare deserve.
    This thought on, sets my heart upon the Rack.   5
    I fain would have this Life but ha'n't its knack.   [326]

Reason stands for it, moving to persue't.
    But Flesh and Blood, are Elementall things:
That sink me down, dulling my spirits fruit.
    Life Animall a Spirituall Sparke ne'er springs.   10
    But if thy Altars Coale Enfire my heart,
    With this Blesst Life my soule will be thy sparke.

I'm Common matter: Lord thine Altar make mee
    Then Sanctify thine Altar with thy blood:
I'l offer on't my heart to thee. (Oh! take mee)   15
    And let thy fire Calcine mine Altars Wood.
    Then let thy Spirits breath, as Bellows, blow
    That this new kindled Life may flame and glow.

Some Life with spoon, or Trencher do mentain
  Or Suck its food through a small Quill, or Straw: 20
But make me, Lord, this Life thou givst, sustain
  With thy sweet Flesh, and Blood, by Gospell Law.
  Feed it on Zions Pasty Plate-Delights:
  I'de suck it from her Candlesticks sweet Pipes.

Need makes the Old wife trot: Necessity   25
  Saith, I must eate this Flesh, and drinke this blood.
If not, no Life's in mee that's worth a Fly,
  This mortall Life, while here eats mortall Foode.
  That Sends out influences to mentaine,
  A little while, and then holds back the Same.   30

But soule sweet Bread, is in Gods Backhouse, made
  On Heavens high Dresser Boarde and thro'ly bakd:
On Zions Gridiron; Sapt in'ts dripping trade,
  That all do live that on it do partake,
  It's Flesh, and Blood even of the Deity;   35
  None that do eat, and Drinke it, ever dy.

Have I a vitall Sparke even of this Fire?
  How Dull am I? Lord, let thy Spirit blow
Upon my Coale untill its heate is higher,
  And I be quickned by the same, and Glow.   40
  Here's Manna Angells food to fatten them.
  That I must eate or be a witherd stem.

Lord, make my Faith thy golden Quill where threw
  I vitall Spirits from thy blood may suck.
Make Faith my Grinders thy Choice Flesh to chew,   45
  My Witherd stock shall with frim Fruits be stuck.
  My Soule shall then in Lively Notes forth ring
  Upon her Virginalls, praise for this thing.   [327]

---

4 fare *orig.* fair
6 knack *orig.* nak
21 sustain *orig.* men
29 That *orig.* This ; to *orig.* that

36 None that do *orig.* It [**]ll do ; it, ever *orig.* that never
39 untill *orig.* up untill
43 threw *orig.* thro'

29.6M ⎫   83. MEDITATION. CAN. 5.1. I AM COME INTO MY
1708 ⎭   GARDEN. &C.

A Garden, yea a Paradise indeed,
  Of all Delightfull Beauteous flowers and sweet,
(A Cloud of rich perfume hence did proceed
  From sweet breathd plants,) first Adam was to keep.
  But sinning here he's from this Farm exilde: 5
  And th'Farm, Lord, thou camst to, 's a Garden stylde.

A Garden-Church, set with Choice Herbs and Flowers.
  Here Lign-Aloes. And th'Tree of Life.
Here trees of Frankincense and Myrrh up towers:
  Here's Sharons Rose and Lillie: Beauties strife.   10
  Here's Cassia, Cinnamon, Cloves, Nut Megs, Mace.
  Sweet Calamus: and all Heavens herbs of Grace.

Here's Order Choice, Beds, Allies all in print.
  Here bud sweet blushing Blossoms, sparkling brave
And Beautifull rich spangled Flowers bepinckt   15
  Which White, Red, Blushie, Cherry Cheekt smiles have.
  Making Celestiall aire their Civit Box
  Of Aromatick Vapors: Spirituall Drops.

This Garden, Lord, thy Church, this Paradise
  Thou com'st into, with thy Choice spirits Gales   20
Making all Plants of Grace gust out like spice
  Their sweet perfumed breath that us assailes.
  And sacrifice their spirits sweet upon
  Their Beauties Altar to thee, Holy One.

This Garden too's the soule, of thy Redeem'd: 25
  When thou thy spirits plants therein hast set

In their Conversion, now most Choicely 'steemd,
  Embeautified with Graces bracelet.
  If that my Soule thy Paradise once bee:
  Thou wilt emparadise it e're with thee.   30

Make mee thy Garden; Lord, thy Grace my plant:
  Make mee thy Vinyard, and my plants thy Vine:
Then come into thy Garden: view each ranck.
  And make my Grape bleed in thy Cup rich wine.
  When thou comest in, My Garden flowers will smile   35
  And blossom Aromatick Praise the while.   [328]

---

5 here *ins.*
16 Blushie *orig.* Bushie
22 us *orig.* th
27 now most Choicely 'steemd *orig.* now of Choice esteemd

17.8M ⎫ 84. MEDITATION. CAN. 5.1. I HAVE GATHERD
1708   ⎬   MY MYRRH WITH MY SPICE.

Hast made mee, Lord, one of thy Garden Beds?
  And myrrhiz'd mee with bitter Exercise?
Stubd up the Brush, toore up the Turfy head?
  And Combd it with thy Harrow teeth likewise?
  Hast set therein thy Myrrhy Trees, that so   5
  Sweet spice might in this Garden bed forth flow?

This Bitter myrrh will keep Corruption out,
  Will kill the worms that Worm hole do my heart:
Will breath sweet breath of rich perfumes about,
  That sweetest sents though bitter tast impart.   10
  Such med'cine, Lord, I lack my sin to calm:
  To kill Corruption and my soule Embalm.

But doth thy Myrrh tree Flowrish in my Soule?
  Doth it bleed Myrrh, and Myrrhy blossoms beare?
Do thy Convictions bring mee to Condole   15

My sinfulness with griefe, Hearts bitter fare?
And pickle up my soule in teares whereby
My sins are mortif'de repentingly?

Is this the state, Lord, of my Garden Bed?
  And com'st thou in thy Garden, Lord, anew?   20
And gatherst thou thy Myrrh that's therein bred.
  With thy sweet spices? Oh! this matter shew.
  Thy bitter Myrrh that then my sins doth quell,
  Will mee revive with its sweet gracious smell.

How graciously then dost thou deale with mee,   25
  Wrapping this bitter myrrh in Odours Sweet?
Though'ts bitter rellish yet sweet sented wee
  Do finde it: when our Senses do it greet.
  Its bitter kills the Vermin in my Hive:
  The Sweetness makes my inward man revive.   30

This myrrh in killing putrid vermin Sins,
  Will keep my soule from putrifying here.
Will ease the Conscience of its dreadfull stings:
  And sweeten all with its perfumed Cheere.   [329]
  Thou art delighted in this Myrrh For Why?   35
  Thou dost it gather with thy spice, oh! Joy.

Then Spice my Soule, Lord, with Sweet myrrh that drop[s]
  Off of my Myrrh tree in thy garden Bed.
Thou gatherdst't with thy spice, this garden Crops,
  Thy Garden bore thee: Oh! Choice Crop it bred.   40
  Apply this Myrrh on me, and on mee keep't.
  My Soules Cure lies indeed in Bitter-sweet.

If with thy Myrrh, thou cur'st my mallody
  Which hitherto hinders my songs of Praise
And with its spicy gales that from it fly,   45
  Thou dost perfume my spirits, songs to raise
  My spirits stufft with Sweetest joy will bring
  Thy Glory tun'de on my perfumed string.

6 forth flow *orig.* might glow
8 worms that *ins.*
11 my sin to calm *orig.* to kill my sin *orig.* my
19 Garden *orig.* soul?
28 Do *orig.* It
30 my *ins.*
37 Sweet myrrh that drops *orig.* thy Sweet myrrh thus got
39 My *orig.* Her
47 My *orig.* Her ; sweetest *orig.* sweets:

26. ⎫
10M ⎬   85. MEDITATION. CAN. 5.1. I HAVE EATEN MY
1708 ⎭   HONY COME WITH MY HONY. I HAVE DRUNK MY
                WINE WITH MY MILK.

Oh! Angells, stand agasttard at my song;
  The Aire scar[c]e e're sedans such news as this.
The Soule Christs spouse his garden Bed's become
  Where Christ doth walk in Aromatick bliss.
  Sin slaying Grace he gets as Myrrh, and spice: 5
  Grace Nutritive's his Wine, Milk, Hony Choice.

Repentance, Patience, and Humility.
  And Graces Such that mortify our Sin
Thou gatherst up as garden fruits with joy,
  Thy bitter Myrrh and sweet spice note this thing.   10
  The Exercising of these graces Choice.
  Perfume thy Ambient aire with Holy spice.

Faith, Hope, and Love with Heavenizing Joy.
  These graces Nutritive to souls arise
As Honey in its Comb, deliciously   15
  Unto thy Palate in their Exercise
  Thou in the Garden eats as Hony Good.
  And drinkst as wine and milk, sweet Sillibub.

Hast set these slips, Lord, of the Holy Ghost.
  In me thy gardens bed? Do they grow there   [330]20
And bear thee spirituall fruits the which thou dost

Delight thy Palate with, as Choicest Cheere?
Oh! Do these graces that thou sets in mee
Thy Hony, Wine, and Milk Cook up for thee?

Who could believe it, if thou hadst not said   25
    I'm come into my Garden, in its shine
Have got my myrrh with spice up. (Oh! Sweet trade)
    My Hony ate and drunk with milk my Wine?
    Hast Eate and drunk my Holy Fair and Good?
    Hony in'ts Comb, and Winemilk Sillibub?   30

What thing is this? How sweet? How Good? How brave?
    Oh! Leape my Soule for joy: art thou become
A spice bed in Christ's Garden where * * * Wave
    Of spiced aire brieze all his Walks along:
    Oh! dress thy Garden, Lord; it fatten well   35
    That I its bed may with such Fruits excell.

Be thou my Gardener, Lord, make my soule
    Thy Gardens Knot. Thy Grace my plants set there.
And make my fruits, thy Myrrh and Spice out rowle,
    My Hope, Faith, Charity, thy Chiefe good cheere.   40
    Then Hony Wine, and Milk Well spic'de by mee
    Shall disht with Praise, thy entertainment bee.

---

2 e're *orig.* ever
12 aire *orig.* are
21 the which *orig.* whose
30 Comb *orig.* Come
33 where * * * Wave *orig.* whereon Waves

21.12M   ⎱   86. MEDITATION. CAN. 5.1. EAT OH! FRIENDS
1708   ⎰   DRINK, YEA DRINK ABUNDANTLY OH! BELOVED.

Sometimes, my Lord, while that my soule enwarms
   Heroicks to thy Viall, I did finde,
My heart enchanted with thy Ambient Charms,
   That like an Angell, agitate my minde,
   Soaring't as on seraphick wings on high.   5
   But now, like lead, I Cold, and Heavy lie.

Lord, touch it with thine Altars quick, live Coale,
   And then my spirits, (oh! how brisk? How Quick?)
Will sweetest melody upon thee rowle.
   Their Tunes shall with thy praises frisk and skip.   10
   When on thy sillibubb I sup and bib.
   Thy wine and milk will make my Notes run glib.

But is it thus? Do graces blossoms grow
   As Myrrh? And Spice? Hony? And Hony Comb?
Yea Wine, and Milk, which as they overflow?   [331]15
   For thee, thou eatst, and drinkst, and sayst come come.
   Furnish my Table with the same; I'l cry
   Eat here my Friends, drink, drinke abundantly?

Wilt thou me spice with spice that spiceth thee?
   Shall I eat of the Hony Comb thou eatst?   20
Shall I drinke of the Cup thou drinkst of? See!
   Drink of thy Wine and Milk! eat of thy meats?
   What Love? What Honour? Shall I have such Share
   And hearty welcome of thy Trencher fare?

Oh! that the Quintessence, Lord, of mee here   25
   In the pure spirits then of Zions Wine
Extracted were all into Praise most cleare
   I'd rise to thee Up Praise, I'd all be thine.
   Could I refine myselfe thus melt to praise
   All should be thine on this account, and blaze.   30

Then make mee, Lord, one of thy garden beds.

The Herb of Trinity set in my Heart.
Herb True Love, Herb of Grace with Rosie sheds.
  Which springing up may beauties sweet impart.
  Then I shall yield thee Hony, Milk and Wine: 35
  And spice too, sweet to thee, and t'sweeten thine.

Mee gracious make, then Graces fruits I'st beare.
  Which thou, Lord, callst thy Myrrh, thy spice and Milk
Thy Wine thy Hony too, of which a share
  To mee to wonderment, impart thou wilt.   40
  Eate at thy Table, and drinke too shall I?
  Then o're this Feast, I will say *Grace* for joy.

---

9 sweetest *orig.* sweet
12 will make *ins.*
26 the *orig.* pure
27 all *ins.*
28 I'd rise *orig.* I rise would ; Praise *orig.* Praises
29 I *orig.* I but
34 springing *orig.* spring

17.2M   ⎫   87. MEDITATION. JOH. 10.10. I AM COME
1709   ⎭   THAT THEY MIGHT HAVE LIFE.

Life! Life! What's That? It is a Taske too hard
  For my Goose Quill with 'Bellisht Definitions
To set it out: It would thereby be marrd:
  My inke would black it, though a gold Edition.   [332]
  It's Natures Principall, that makes all brisk,   5
  Peart, Flowerish, Glorious where it consists.

It's such a Thing that makes all things in which
  It doth embower, and while they're with it frought
To be full Worthy, Beautifull and Rich
  While in them. But when Gone, they're good for naught.   10
  Where ere it is, it's th'chiefest excellence:
  And where it is not, is no Worth, nor Sense.

It's such a thing, that all things else attende.
  Earths Golden Fleece, and Flourish, Fruits, and Flower
Of ery sort, their sweet Consent do sende,   15
  To Honour, and mentain it in its Tower.
  Heaven smiles on't and in'ts Crystall Candlestick
  Stand sun, Moon, stars blazing to Lighten it.

It from the Worlds Birth runs unto its End
  Along Lifes Channells of each sort of things   20
And all their peart Ey'de beauty doth them send.
  What of all worldly Glory is the spring.
  Whose brightest Flower of all this Beauty bright
  Is Humane Life. Oh a most beautious sight.

This Life adepts mans Person to be made   25
  All Glorious with shining Grace indeed,
And in this glory in Gods Holy trade
  Of Grace unto his Glory to proceed.
  But oh! sin fould this Glory: Man hath lost it:
  Death by a sinfull Morsell killd and crost it.   30

But oh! what Grace, my Blessed Lord, hast thou?
  What vallue set'st thou on mans life, now vile?
Prize it thou dost 'bove all the world, that Now
  To save't from Death, thou leapest ore the stile
  Dy'dst in our stead, that wee might still have Life   35
  Appeasing Justice, Ending thereby strife.

But oh! how precious is this Life of Man,
  Seing thou cam'st from heaven for this end
That we might live, Do Satan what he can,   [333]
  Myselfe to thee, my Lord, I therefore give.   40
  Give me, Lord, Life and Grace to boot; then I
  Will give My Life and Selfe to thee with Joy.

---

2 with *orig.* and
11 orig. Where ere it is Its such a thing that all things else attend
15 do *ins.*
24 Oh a *orig.* Oh [**] is

32 thou *ins.*
63 Justice, *orig.* Justice, and

12.4M ⎤   89. MEDITATION. JOH. 10.10. I AM COME THAT THEY
1709 ⎦   MIGHT HAVE LIFE.

What Birth of Wonders from thy Fingers ends
  Dropt, when the World, Lord, dropt out of the Womb
Of its Non-Entity for to attende
  Thy Will its Cradle. And its Midwife strong.
  Non-Entity in Travell fill did bare   5
  The World, big belli'd with all Wonders rare.

The Infant born, in'ts Cradle dorment lay.
  As Dead, yet Capable of Ery Form.
A jumbled Lump of all things ery Way
  Not any Single birth of it's yet born,   10
  But when this Lump enjoy'd a Vitall Heate
  All Kinds of things did from its belly leape.

Life Vegetative now hatcht in the Egge,
  Flourishing some things nobler than the rest.
Life sensitive gives some of these its Head,   15
  Inspiring them with honour next the best.
  And some of which Life Rationall Enfires,
  Cloathd with a Spiritualizing Life, aspires.

This Life thy Fingers freely dropt into
  The Humane shaped Elements and made   20
The same Excell the Rest and nobler goe
  Enspirited with all Heavenizing trade.
  But man by sin hath lost all life, and marr'd
  Himselfe eternally. Death's his reward.

But, thou my Lord, before its Execution   25
  Didst step from heaven down Death to deterr
And that we might have life: making solution

Unto the Creditor, dost Grace Conferr,
Oh! what a thing is life then. Choice? how Good,
In that thou camst to buy it with thy blood?   [334]30

Life Naturall indeed is in the Bill
Thou with thy Father drewst up, it to buy.
Life Spirituall much more; which ever Will
As Heaven doth, Earth, all Naturall Life out Vie.
Life Naturall is Common, makes alive   35
Things Vegetative, and things sensitive.

The Spirituall Life is never founde but where
Life Naturall indeed doth make its nest,
Which builds as well in Bruits and Wicked geers.
As in Gods Children, and in holy breasts: 40
But Spirituall Life falls onely to Gods sons
And Out in Holy Conversation runs.

It doth Saints souls, and Conversation gild
With Godlike Glory of a Gracious shine,
Brightens its superstructure where it builds   45
A Lofty Tower of Holy Life Divine.
The Richest Jewell in the Cabinet
Of Nature made, this Spirituall Life is set.

The Spirituall Life is nighst Gods Life in kinde.
In Godlike Properties it doth Consist.   50
Hence't glorifies the Soule and Life with it lin'de.
Lord, in my Soul and Life this life entwist.
Thou cam'st that I might live thus. Then grant me
This Life. And I shall Glory beare for thee.

---

11 enjoy'd *orig.* injoy'd
22 all *ins.*
26 Didst step *orig.* step[e]st *orig.* Did step
34 doth *ins.*
43 gild *orig.* guild
49 in *ins.*
50 In *orig.* It

14.6M ⎤   90. Meditation. Joh. 10.28. I give unto them
1709 ⎦   Eternall Life.

Eternall Life! What Life is this, I pray?
  Eternity snicksnarls my Brains thought on:
It's the Arithimaticians Wrack each way.
  It hath begining, yet it end hath none.
  He that hath been ten thousand years therein,   5
  'S as far from'ts end, as when they did begin.

Eternity indeed is Adjunct to
  The Life of Man: Of all men, Good, and Bad.
As to Deaths Darksom Entery they goe
  They e're shall live: and joyous be, or Sad.   [395]10
  Eternall life, then is dicotomizd
  Into a Life of Joy or miseries.

This last is Calld Everlasting Punishment
  Or Everlasting sad Distruction.
Or second Death. Not Life. It's Life all shent   15
  Of Good, and filld with Deaths Edition.
  This though the Worm's alive, is Living Death,
  A thousand times worse than to have no breath.

Eternall Life then's in a right sense this.
  That All things blissfull do to it belong.   20
Life Naturall, and Spirituall Life's in bliss
  Eternizde in Eternall Joyes that throng.
  Though all by Nature Death indeed doth fine.
  Yet, Lord, thou giv'st Eternall Life to thine.

Oh! what a Lord is mine? How rich? that he   25
  Gives his, Eternall Life: that doth Contain
All Heaven and its Glory, Bliss, and Glee
  Within it, Hee is Rightfull Lord of th'same.
  For none can give that which he never had:
  Wheather the gift he gives be good, or bad.   30

And though he give this Gift so rich to his

His Wealth and Glory's not thereby Diminisht.
He hath the spring of Life, and Life of bliss
  When they their Pilgrimage have fully finisht.
  Out of His spring of life and Bliss that flowth,   35
  Confer Eternall Life on them he doth.

Life Naturall (although Essentiall to
  All Living things) and spirituall Life indeed,
Peculiar to Rationalls also
  Containd are in Christs Gift as in a seed,   40
  Are both Adjuncted with Eternity
  In that he gives them them Eternally.

Ripe Grace in all its Orient Blossoms bright,
  Ripe Glory in its flower of brightest shine:
Ripe Joy upon the highest branch full ripe   45
  Adorn this Life Eternall made most fine,
  All blanched o're in Orient Glory all
  Do send their shining Rayes on them to fall.   [336]

Oh! Boundless sea, and Bottomless, of Love,
  Confer'd on Saints: Oh! richest gift e're gi'n!   50
Worth more than thousands Worlds: all Heaven above,
  Whole Heavens of Love; and God to boot therein.
  God, Bliss, Joy, Glory, Eternall Life enjoy'de
  Oh! Happiness: Saints Happy shall abide.

Hence, Lord, I kiss thy Feet, and humbly Cry   55
  Give mee this Gift, Eternall Life I pray.
'T will gild my Harp O're very gloriously,
  And spiritualize my strings thy tunes to play.
  Life Naturall's the Base. The Spirituall is
  The Meane: the Tenour is Eternall Bliss.   60

Lord, make my Person, subject of thy Gift
  Eternall Life its Adjunct gi'n by thee.
My Person then, thy Well-Tun'de Harp shall lift
  Thy Praises up in Tunes sung forth by mee.

Then on my Spirituall Wiars harmoniously   65
Thy sweetest Tunes shall ring Eternall Joy.

---

2 my *orig.* in
19 then's *orig.* then
39 to *ins.*

2.8m ⎫   91. MEDITATION. MATTH. 24.27. SO ALSO SHALL
1709 ⎭   THE COMING OF THE SON OF MAN BE.

What once again, my Lord, allowst thou mee,
    Ev'n Mee, poore Dusty thing thus to enjoy,
With Thee, ev'n thee, 'fore whom, 't's said, *Bow the Knee*
    Ye Angells bright, Communion Graceously?
        Thou art so glorious, thy very Feet   5
        It's glory to the Angells bright to greet.

And shall I on thy Table Fare, Lord, feed,
    That is Cookt up by much more Whiter hands
Than ever Angells usd? Thy flesh indeed
    Is meate, and Blood is Drink and on it stands.   10
        The Waiters are bright Angells all in Shine
        Of their White, Holy, Sapphick Robes Divine.

The thoughts hereof entring upon my Heart
    Nigh sink, and drown my fainty soule ev'n in
The Ocean Sea of Flaming Joy best part.   15
    As she attempts *Magnificat* to sing   [337]
        And plunging down and up herein, oft Cries,
        As she pops up her head, *Raptures of Joyes.*

And now, my Lord, me with thy foode sustain:
    Mee in good liking make, yea Fat, and fine,   20
To wait on thee, when thou shalt come again:
    For Come thou wilt, and kindely visit thine.
        Thou lov'dst our Nature that its Blossoms hang

In thy Description. Hence the son of Man.

Thou art Continually a Coming, it's true,   25
  In Providences Some, that scowle and lower,
That Thunder sharp, and fiery lightening spew
  Yet Roses some, and Merygolds out shower.
  Thou comst in Ordinances too: and dost
  The golden gifts give of the Holy Ghost.   30

But still besides this, there's another which
  Our text Embellisheth in glory bright.
Part of thy Exaltation's Glory rich
  When thou comst with all Angells train of Light.
  Then by thy present Comings furnish mee   35
  That I when thou shalt come, may wait on thee.

Hence loade my Trencher with thy Flesh Divine:
  It's Angells foode. My soule doth almost sink:
And press thy Grape into my Cup: Rich Wine
  Lord make thy Blood indeed, my dayly drinke   40
  When with thy Fare my Vessell's fild to th'brim,
  Thy Praise, on my shoshannims, Lord, shall Ring.

---

3 Bow *orig.* bow
10 is *orig.* as
15 Flaming *orig.* Flaing
26 Providences *orig.* Providence
34 all *ins.*
41 fild *orig.* fill

27.9M ⎫ 92. MEDITATION. MATTH. 24.27. SO ALSO SHALL
1709 ⎭   THE COMING OF THE SON OF MAN BE.

It grieves mee, Lord, my Fancy's rusty: rub
  And brighten't on an Angells Rubston sharp.
Furbush it with thy spirits File: and Dub
  It with a live Coale of thine Altars Spark:

Yea, with thy holly Oyle make thou it slick   5
Till like a Flash of Lightning, it grow Quick.   [338]

My Heart may ake to finde so bright a Theme
    Which brighten might even Angells wits, to bee,
By my thick, Rusty Fancy, and dull Veane,
    Barbd of its brightsom sparkling shine by mee,   10
    Quicken my Fancy Lord; and mend my Pen:
To Flowerish up the same, as brightest Gem.

What is thy Humane Coach thy soule rides in,
    Bathing in Bright, Heart ravishing glory all
In Gods Celestiall splendent Palace trim,   15
    Full of th'Effulgient Glory of that hall?
    And wilt thou from this glorious Palace come
Again to us on Earth, where sinners throng?

Meethinks I see, when thou appearest thus
    The Clouds to rend and skies their Crystall Doore   20
Open like thunder for thy pass to us
    And thy Bright Body deckt with shine all Ore
    Flash through the same like rapid Lightening Waver
That gilds the Clouds, and makes the Heavens Quaver.

Proud sinners now that ore Gods Children crow,   25
    Would if they could creep into Augur holes,
Thy Lightening Flashing in their faces so,
    Melts down their Courage, terrifies their Souls.
    Thy Rapid Lightning Flashes pierce like darts
Of Red hot fiery arrows through their hearts.   30

Now Glory to the Righteous is the song.
    Their dusty Frame drops off its drossiness
Puts on bright robes, doth jump for joy, doth run
    To meet thee in the Clouds in lightning Dress.
    Whose nimble Flashes dancing on each thing   35
While Angells trumpet-musick makes them sing.

Make Sanctifying Grace, my tapestry,

My person make thy Lookinglass Lord, clear
And in my Looking Glass cast thou thine Eye.
Thy Image view that standeth shining there.   40
Then as thou com'st like Light'ning I shall rise
In Glories Dress to meet thee in the skies.

---

9 Fancy, *orig.* Fancy, and Dull Fancy
20 *orig.* Thy Glorious body Deckt with shine all o'er
22 And thy Bright *orig.* Thy glorious
35 each *orig.* ech
38 My *orig.* And make my

22.11 ⎫ 93. Meditation. Joh. 14.2. In my Fathers house
1709 ⎭   are many Mansions.   [339]

Could but a Glance of that bright City fair,
    Whose walls are sparkling Pretious stones, whose Gates
Bright pollisht splendent Pearls, Whose Porters are
    Swash Flaming Angells, and Whose streets rich Plates
    Of pure transparent Gold mine Eyes enjoy,   5
    My Ravisht heart on Raptures Wings would fly.

My Lumpish soule, enfir'd with such bright flame
    And Quick'ning influences of this sight
Darting themselves through out my drossy frame
    Would jump for joy, and sing with greate delight   10
    To thee, my Lord, who deckst thy Royall Hall,
    With glorious Mansions for thy Saints even all.

Thy Lower House, this World well garnished
    With richest Furniture of Ev'ry kinde
Of Creatures of each Colours varnished   15
    Most glorious, a Silver Box of Winde.
    The Crystall skies pinkt with Sun, Moon, and Stars
    Are made its Battlements on azure spars.

But on these Battlements above, thou'st placdst

Thy Upper House, that Royall Palace town,   20
In which these Mansions are, that made thou hast
   For Saints and Angells Dwellings of renown.
   Should we Suppose these mansions, Chambers neate
   Like ours, 't would sordid be, not fit this seate.

But if these Mansions, built so very bright   25
   Beyond the worlds Bright Battlements, yet should
Be of materialls Celestiall right
   Streets of such Houses, of transparent gold
   For Saints and Angells to possess in Glory's
   Would they unfit thy Upper House as Stories.   30

Though we can't ken these Mansions, now, yet this
   Our Faith doth dwell upon while on this Shore
That there are Mansions, in Celestiall Bliss
   For Saints and Angells t'dwell in ever more.
   Then cheer up, Soule, and take the Kings path brave   35
   Unto these Mansions promises do pave.

Bright Jasper Hall Walld with translucid Gold,
   Floors pav'd with Pearls to these are durty sells,
Then what bright lives ought all men here uphold
   That hope within these mansions ere to dwell?   [340]40
   Adorne my Soule, Lord, with thy Graces here
   Till by their shine I'm fitted to dwell there.

Let as I bring thy Glory home, in mee
   Grace shine, and me thy paths tread pav'de with jems,
Unto thy house, wherein these Mansions bee,   45
   And let mee dwell within their Curtain Hems.
   Thy Praise shall then my Virginalls inspire
   To play a Michtam on her golden wyer.

---

24 sordid be *orig.* be sordid and
25 very *ins.*
32 while on *orig.* within
38 Pearls *orig.* Peals
44 Grace *orig.* Thy Grace

19.1M ⎫ 94. MEDITATION. JOH. 14.2. IN MY FATHERS
1709/10 ⎭   HOUSE ARE MANY MANSIONS.

Celestiall Mansions! Wonder, oh my Soul!
  Angells Pavillions surely: and no Halls
For Mudwalld Matter, wherein Vermins rowle:
  Wormeaten'd ore with sin, like wormhold Walls.
  Shall Earthen Pitchers set be on the shelfe   5
  Of such blesst Mansions Heavenly Plate of Wealth?

May I presume to screw a Single thought
  Well splic'de with saving Faith, into my Heart,
That my poore Potshread all o're good for nought
  May ever in these Lodgens have a part.   10
  The influences of the same would fly
  With rapid flashes through my heart of joy.

Oh! that thy spirit would my Soule Inlay
  With such rich lining, Graces Web, that would
While in my Loom, me in these Tents convay   15
  And that thy Sovereign Love might ever hold
  Me in the paths that to these Mansions bring,
  That I might ever dwell with thee therein.

Oh! that my Meditations all were frindg'd
  With Sanctifying Gifts: and all my wayes   20
Borderd were with Obedience rightly hindg'd
  Lord on thy word thy Honour bright to raise.
  Oh! that my Paths were pav'de with Holiness
  And that thy Glory were their shining dress.

Array me, Lord, with such rich robes all ore   25
  As for their Matter, and their modes usd are
Within these Mansions. Dye them all therefore
  Deep in thy blood: to make them gracious Ware.   [341]
  If with thy * * * [***]de thou dress me here
  My present tunes shall [s]ing thy praise when there. 30

5 Pitchers *ins.*
10 Lodgens have a part *orig.* Rest a part
11 same *orig.* same that fly
15 these *orig.* these Lodgens gay
19 frindg'd *orig.* fring'd
21 hindg'd *orig.* hing'd

14.3M ⎫ 95. MEDITATION. JOH. 14.2. I GO TO PREPARE A PLACE
1710   ⎭   FOR YOU.

What shall a Mote up to a Monarch rise?
  An Emmet match an Emperor in might?
If Princes make their personall Exercise
  Betriming mouse holes, painting with delight!
  Or hanging Hornets nest with rich attire,   5
  All that pretende to Wisdome would admire.

The Highest Office and Highst Officer
  Expende on lowest intrest in the world
The greatest Cost and wealthi'st treasure far
  'T would shew mans wisdom's up in folly furld.   10
  That Humane Wisdom's hatcht within the nest
  Of addle brains which wisdom ne'er possest.

But blush, poor Soule, at th'thought of such a thought
  Touching my Lord, the King of Kings most bright
As acting thus, for us all over nought,   15
  Worse than poor Ants, or Spider catchers mite
  Who goes away t'prepare's a place most cleare
  Whose shine o're shines the shining sunshine here.

Ye Heavens wonder, shall your maker come
  To Crumbs of Clay, bing'd all and drencht in Sin   20
To stop the gap with Graces boughs, defray
  The Cost the Law transgresst, doth on us bring?
  Thy head layst down under the axe on th'block,
  That for our sins did off the same there lop.

But that's not all. Thou now didst sweep Deaths Cave   25
  Clean with thy hand: and leavest not a dust
Of Flesh, or Bone that there the Elect dropt have.
  But bringst out all, new buildst the Fabrick just
  (Having the scrowle of Gods Displeasure clear'd)
  Bringst back the Soule, puts't in its tent new rear'd.   30

But that's not all: Now from Deaths realm, erect,
  Thou gloriously gost to thy Fathers Hall:
And pleadst their Case, preparst them place well dect
  All with thy Merits hung. Blesst Mansions all
  Dost ope the Doore lockt fast 'gainst sins that so   35
  These Holy Rooms admit them may thereto.   [342]

But that's not all. Leaving these dolefull roomes,
  Thou com'st and takst them by the hands, Most High,
Dost them translate out from their Death bed toombs,
  To th'rooms prepar'd filld with Eternall joy   40
  Them Crownst and thronst there, there their lips be shall
  Pearld with Eternall Praises; that's but all.

Lord let me bee one of these Crumbs of thine.
  And though I'm dust adorn me with thy graces
That though all flect with sin, thy Grace may shine   45
  As thou Conductst me to thy furnisht places.
  Make mee thy Golden trumpet Sounded bee.
  By thy Good Spirits melody to thee.

---

5 Hornets *orig.* Hornests
25 didst *orig.* did
27 that there *ins.* ; dropt *orig.* dropt there have
34 thy *ins.*
41 there their *orig.* and there their
42 that's *orig.* and that's
46 thy *orig.* these
47 Golden trumpet *ins.*

9.5M   }   96. MEDITATION. CANT. 1.2. LET HIM KISS ME WITH
1710   }   THE KISSE OF HIS MOUTH.

What placed in the Sun: and yet my ware,
   A Cloud upon my head? an Hoodwinke blinde?
In middst of Love thou layst on mee, despare?
   And not a blincke of Sunshine in my minde?
   Shall Christ bestow his lovely Love on his,   5
   And mask his face? allowing not a kiss?

Shall ardent love to Christ enfire the Heart?
   Shall hearty love in Christ embrace the Soule?
And shall the sprituall Eye be wholy dark.
   In th'heart of love, as not belov'd, Condole?   10
   In th'midst of Loves bright Sun, and yet not see
   A Beame of Love allow'd to lighten thee?

Lord! read the Riddle: Shall a gracious heart
   The object of thy love be Sick of Love?
And beg a kiss, under the piercing smart.   15
   Of want thereof? Lord pitty from above.
   What wear the Sun, without a ray of light?
   In midst of sunshine, meet a pitchy night?

Thy foes, whose Souls Sins bowling alley's grown
   With Cankering Envy rusty made, stand out   20
Without all sense of thy sweet Love ere shown
   Is no great wonder; thou lov'st not this rout.
   But wonder't is, that such that grudge their hearts
   Hold love too little for thee, should thus smart.

Nay, nay, stand Sir: here's wisdom very cleare: 25
   None Sensibly can have thy love decline:
That never had a drop thereof: nor ere
   Did tast thereof; this is the right of thine.
   Such as enjoy thy Love, may lack the sense
   May have thy love and not loves evidence.   [343]30

Maybe thy measures are above thy might.

Desires Crave more than thou canst hold by far:
If thou shouldst have but what thou would, if right,
   Thy pipkin soon would run ore, breake, or jar.
   Wisdom allows enough; none wast is known.   35
   Because thou hast not all, say not, thou'st none.

Christ loves to lay thy Love under Constraint.
   He therefore lets not's Love her Candle light,
Too see her Lovely arms that never faint
   Circle thyself about, with greate Delight.   40
   The prayers of Love ascend in gracious fume
   To him as Musick, and as heart perfume.

But listen, soule, here seest thou not a Cheate.
   Earth is not heaven: Faith not Vision. No.
To see the Love of Christ on thee Compleate   45
   Would make heavens Rivers of joy, earth overflow.
   This is the Vale of tears, not mount of joyes.
   Some Crystal drops while here may well suffice.

But, oh my Lord! let mee lodge in thy Love.
   Although thy Love play bow-peep with me here.   50
Though I be dark: want spectacles to prove
   Thou lovest mee: I shall at last see Clear.
   And though not now, I then shall sing thy praise.
   In that thy love did tende me all my dayes.

---

4 blincke *orig.* blinke
10 th' *orig.* the
20 made *orig.* grown
24 too *orig.* to
31 thy *ins.*
32 canst *orig.* cast
34 ore *ins.*
41 fume *orig.* tune

3.7M   97. MEDITATION. CAN. 1.2. LET HIM KISS ME WITH
1710   THE KISSES OF HIS MOUTH.

My onely Lord, when with no muddy sight,
  Mine Eyes behold that ardent Flame of Love,
Thy Spouse, when that her day light seemed night
  In passionate affection seemd to move.
    When thou to her didst onely Cease to show   5
    Thy sweet love token: makes me cry out, Oh.

Although in trying, I through grace can finde
  My heart holds such Conclusions in't, that I
Account this World, Silver, and Gold refinde
  Pearles, Pretious Stones, Riches, and Friends a toy.   10
    Methinks I could part with them all for thee
    Yet know not what I should if tri'de should bee.

I dare not say, such ardent flames would rise
  Of true Loves passion, in its Blinks or Blisses,
As in thy Holy Spouse's heart that cries   15
  Oh! let him kiss mee with his orall kisses.
    Should she but Stop such acts of love and grace
    Making dark Clouds mask up his brightsom face.   [344]

If such strong Flame of Love, be made the mark
  And Cata Pantos of true Love, then who   20
Can prove his marriage knot to Christ in's heart
  That doth not finde such ardent flames oreflow?
    When thy bright sun-shine Face doth weare a Cloude
    Methinks my Soule in sorrows thicket shroudes.

Yet pardon, Lord, give me this word again: 25
  I feare to wrong myselfe, or Gracious thee.
This I can Say, and can this Say mentain,
  If thou withdrawst, my heart soon sinks in mee.
    Though oftentimes my Spirits dulled grow,
    If so I am, I am not always Soe: 30

When thou dost shine, a sunshine day I have:

When I am cloudy then I finde not thee:
When thou dost cloud thy face, thy Face I crave.
  The shining of thy face enlivens mee.
  I live and dy as smiles and Frowns take place: 35
  The Life, and Death of Joy Lodge in thy face.

But yet methinks, my pipkin is too small.
  It holds too little of Loves liquour in't.
All that it holds for thee seems none at all.
  Thou art so dear, it is too cheape a Drink.   40
  If I had more thou shouldst have more of mee
  If Better, better too. I all give thee.

If thou, my Lord, didst not accept a mite
  More than a mountain, if the mite doth hold
More than a mountain of the heart Love right   45
  I should be blankt, my heart would grow so cold.
  A Quarter of a Farthen, halfe a mite
  Of Love thou likest well; its heart delight.

Then let thy Loveliness, Lord touch my heart:
  And let my heart imbrace thy loveliness: 50
That my small mite of Love might on thee dart,
  And thy great selfe might my poor love possess.
  My little mite of Love shall musick sweet
  Tune forth on thee, its harp, that heaven shall greet.

---

2 that *orig.* thy
6 makes *orig.* she makes ; out *ins.*
12 if tri'de should bee *orig.* should I tride bee
14 Blinks *orig.* Binks
29 grow *orig.* bee
52 might *orig.* mite
53 mite *orig.* might

29.8M   }   98. MEDITATION. CAN. 1.2. THY LOVE IS
1710   BETTER THAN WINE.

A Vine, my Lord, a noble Vine indeed
  Whose juyce makes brisk my heart to sing thy Wine.
I have read of the Vine of Sibmahs breed,
   And Wine of Hesbon, yea and Sodoms Vine.
    All which raise Clouds up when their Liquour's High   5
    In any one, but thine doth Clarify.

The Choicest Vine, the royallst grape that rose,
  Or ere in Cana'ns vinyard did take Root,
Did Emblemize thyselfe the True Vine; those
   Are not like thee for Nature, nor for fruite.   [345]10
    Thy noble royall nature Ever blesst
    Produceth spiced juyce by far the best.

The Vine deckt in her blosoms frindge the Aire
  With sweet perfume. O! smell of Lebanon!
Her Grapes when pounded and prest hard (hard fare)   15
   Bleed out both blood and spirits leaving none
    Which too much tooke, the brain doth too much tole,
    Though't smacks the Palate, merry makes the Soule.

But, oh! my Lord, thou Zions Vine most deare,
  Didst send the Wealthi'st juyce and spirits up to   20
Thy Grape which prest in Zions Wine fat Geere
   Did yield the Wealthi'st wine that ere did flow.
    It's Loves Rich liquour spice't with Grace even thine,
    And thus thy love is better far than wine.

This Wine thy Love bleeds from thy grape, how sweet?   25
  To spiritualize the life in every part.
How full of spirits? And of a spirituall reeck,
   To th'blood and spirits of the gracious heart?
    How warming to the Chilly person grown?
    And Cordiall to spirituall feeble one?   30

How sweet? how warm? how Cordiall is thy Love

That bleeds thy grapes sweet Juyce into the soule?
How brings it Grace, and Heaven from above.
  And drops them in the Heart its Wassell bowle?
  Wine th'Nectar of all juyces with its sapor   35
  Compared to thy love is but a Vaper.

It's not like other wine which took too much
  Whose spirits vapor, and do wise men foole.
But this the more is tooke, the Better such
  Servants and service best, best grace the schoole.   40
  Lord tun this Wine in me and make my savour
  Be ever richly filled with its flavour.

Lord make mee Cask, and thy rich Love its Wine.
  Impregnate with its spirits Lord my heart.
And make its heat my heart and blood refine.   45
  And Sweetness sweeten me in ery part.
  Give me to drinke the juyce of this true Vine.
  Then I will Sing thy Love better than Wine.

---

5 raise Clouds up *orig.* bring vapours
13 blosoms *orig.* blosomes ; frindge *orig.* fring
22 Wealthi'st *orig.* Welthi'st
35 sapor *orig.* Vapor,
36 Vaper *orig.* saper
38 do *orig.* make ; foole *orig.* fools
43 mee *orig.* my

24.10M } 99. MEDITATION. ISA. 24.23. HE SHALL WALK BEFORE
1710   }   HIS ANCIENT GLORIOUSLY.

Glory! what art? O! Sparkling spark all bright,
  Thy shining Robes all gallantry do ware   [346]
Dazling the Eye of such as have the sight
  Of any one deckt with thy sparklings rare.
  Guilding the Ambient aire with golden shine   5
  In which its subjects stande in glory fine.

This pale facde Moon that silver snowball like
  That Walkes in'ts silver Glory, paints the skies
This tester of the Bed, where day and night
    Each Creature Coverd ore with glory lies,   10
    She with her silver Rayes envarnish doth
    In silver paint, the skies as out she go'th.

But, oh! the Sun, that golden Ball of Glory
  That Walkes in his Celestiall Galleries.
If flaming Broad cloth, wove, in th'Highest story,   15
    Of Glories Rayes, and aires fine twine webwise
    Doth make her golden Beams, her tapestry
    Which gilds the heavens ore, hung out on high.

But all this glory pleasent to behold,
  Is but a drop of inck compar'd with thine,   20
My Deare-Dear Lord, whose sparkling glory would
    Enravish all that see but halfe its shine.
    The bodies eyes wante strength to beare a sight
    From sinking when a beam of't on't doth Light.

Thy elementall Frame, that China Dish,   25
  Varnisht with nature's rich perfection o're,
The top of beauty, humane nature's bliss,
    Most naturally deckt with all beauties glore,
    A Crystall Glass, Transparent Silver bowle.
    Or Golden Tabernacle of the soule.   30

Eyes ne'er beheld Humanity so brave,
  So Beautifull a piece of manhood-frame.
Filld all with graces glory, whose bright Wave
    Is dasht all ore, with orientall flame.
    A Golden Viol full of gracious Grace   35
    Whose flashing shine outshines the Angells face.

Hence ery thought that in thy heart was hatcht.
  And ery word that from thy lips did fall
And ery act thy person ere dispatcht,
    Came glorifide with graces glory all   40

That eyes enlighten'd with thy glory said
We saw his glory as God's Son's, displaid.   [347]

When thou the Curtain backtst a little t'shew
  A little flash of thy greate glory bright
Thy Countenance did shine like lightning: true,   45
  Thy Raiment was as white as Snow, or light.
  Angells adore and Saints admire thy brightness
  And hunger to bee filled with thy likeness.

Lord, make me with thy likeness like to thee.
  Upon my soule thy shining Image place.   50
And let thy glorious grace shine bright in mee.
  Enlay my thoughts, my words, and Works with Grace.
  If thou wilt dub mee with bright gracious geere.
  I'le sing thee songs of Grace in Glories spheare.

---

2 do *orig.* doth
4 with *orig.* up wth
7 that *orig.* walking
8 That *ins.* ; Walkes *orig.* Walking
14 That *ins.* ; Walkes *orig.* Walking
20 inck *orig.* ink
23 eyes *ins.* ; wante *orig.* wants
24 of't on't doth *orig.* on't doth it
29 Glass *orig.* Mass
36 Whose *orig.* A
37 in *orig.* ere in

18.12M ⎫
      ⎬   100. MEDITATION. ISAI. 24.23. THE LORD OF HOSTS
1710 ⎭   SHALL REIGN IN MOUNT ZION, AND IN JERUSALEM
          AND BEFORE HIS ANCIENTS GLORIOUSLY.

Glory, What art thou? tell us: Dost thou know?
  It's native to our nature to desire
To weare thy shine. Our sparkling Eyes bestow
  Their kisses on the Cheeks thou dost attire.
  Our Fancies fed therewith grow lively briske.   5
  Acts always lodgd in happy glances frisk.

Then Glory as a Metaphor, I'l'tende
  And lay it all on thee; my Lord to bring
My Heart in Flames of love, its rayes out send
  Whose Curled tops shall ever to thee cling.   10
  But all the glory sun beams on them beare
  Is but a smoaky vapour to thy Weare.

To see thee king it in mount Zion bright
  And in Jerusalem, wherein the shine
Of thy Right scepter pinkt with starrs of Light   15
  Thy Gospell Law, and Miracles Divine,
  Enravish may my soule untill it flies
  To thee upon the Wings of Extasies.

To see thee thron'de in Spirituall Zion Bright,
  Where Sanctifying Grace doth gild the Throne   20
Raisd in the heart. In which thou sitst as Light
  And swayst the Realm of thoughts, now gracious grown
  Where sins arreignd are sentenced and slain
  Will hearts with rapid raptures entertain,

To see thee reign in Heavenly Zion, Oh!   25
  Wherein the Throne of Glory all beset   [348]
With sparkling Angells round about it throw
  Bright flashes of their glory as they step
  Thee to attend, exceeds all sight each way
  And make might to my soule, all Heavenly day.   30

The suns bright Glory's but a smoky thing
  Though it oft 'chants mans fancy with its flashes,
All other glories, that from Creatures spring
  Are less than that; but both are sorry swashes,
  But thine is purely bright, and spotless cleare   35
  That will inravish in the Heavenly Sphere.

Then set thy Throne, Lord, in my Souls bright Hall:
  And in thy throne let Grace enthroned bee
And let thy Grace gild ore thy Palace Wall
  And let thy scepter sway and rule in mee.   40

While in my heart thou'rt thron'd my Quill shall greet
Thyselfe with Zions Songs in musick sweet.

---

4 the *orig.* thy
11 beare *orig.* weare
18 To *orig.* With
23 sentenced *orig.* sentencd
26 Wherein the *orig.* Whereon
38 let *orig.* of ; enthroned bee *orig.* plac'd in my heart
40 and rule in mee *orig.* in ery part

101. MEDITATION. ISAI. 24.23. THEN SHALL THE MOON
BE CONFOUNDED, AND THE SUN ASHAMED WHEN
THE LORD OF HOST SHALL RAIN IN MOUNT
ZION—GLORIOUSLY.

15.2M ⎫
1711 ⎭

Glory, thou shine of shining things made fine
  To fill the Fancy peeping through the Eyes
At thee that wantons with thy glittering shine
  That onely dances on the Outside guise
  Yet art the brightest blossom fine things bring   5
  To please our Fancies with and make them sing.

But spare me, Lord, if I while thou dost use
  This Metaphor to make thyselfe appeare
In taking Colours, fancy it to Choose
  To blandish mine affections with, and Cheare   10
  Them with thy glory, ever shining best.
  Thus brought to thee so takingly up dresst.

May I but Eye thy Excellencys guise
  From which thy glory flows, all Sparkling bright
Th'Property of all thy Properties   15
  Being both inside, and their Outside Light,
  The flowing flakes of brightest glories flame
  Would my affections set on fire amain.

Thy Holy Essence, and its Properties
  Divine and Human all this Glory ware.   20

Thou art Bright Sun Glorie its Beams our Eyes
  Are gilded with which from its body are.
  Magnetick vertue raising Exhalation
  Out of the humble soule unto thy station.   [349]

My blissfull Lord, thou and thy properties   25
  And all thy Adjuncts that upon thee thrung
Enbedded alltogether up arise
  And moulded up into a Splenderous Sun
  And in thy Kingly Glory out do shine
  In Zions mount, out shineing Glories line.   30

Created Glory dangling on all things
  Of brightest sweet breathd flowres and Fields and glaze
The spurred starry Tribes whose Sparkling wings
  Flur glory down in shining Beames and Rayes
  Do blush and are asham'de of all their grace   35
  Beholding that bright Glory of thy Face.

The silver Candlesticks of th'heaven bright,
  Bearing the Blazing torches round about,
The Moon and Sun, the Worlds bright Candle-light
  These Candles flames thy Glory blows all out.   40
  These Candle flames lighting the World as tapers,
  Set in thy sunshine seem like smokie vapors.

The Glory bright of Glorified Saints
  And brightest Glory sparkling out with grace
Comparde with thine my Lord is but as Paint   45
  But glances on them of thy glorious Face.
  Its weak reflection of thy glories shine,
  Painting their Walls not to compare with thine.

But, Lord, art thou deckt up in glory thus?
  And dost thou in this Glory come and Wo[o]e   50
To bring our hearts to thee compelling us
  With such bright arguments of Glories hew?
  Oh! Adamantine Hearts if we withstand
  Such taking Charming pleas in Glories hand.

Thy splendid glory lapt in Graces mandle   55
    Confer on mee Lord, with thy gracious hand.
Let not my feet upon such glory trample
    But make me for thee and thy Glory stand.
    If that thy Gracious Glory win my Heart
    Thy Glory's Grace I'le on Shoshannims harp.   60

---

11 ever shining *orig.* shining ever
13 Excellencys guise *orig.* Excellency so
18 set on fire *orig.* all enfire
20 Human *orig.* Humall
21 its *orig.* the
22 are *orig.* rare
26 all *ins.*
32 flowres *orig.* flowers
37 th' *ins.*
44 out with *ins.*
46 on *orig.* of
49 up in *orig.* there
59 Glory *orig.* Glory doth

10.4M ⎫ 102. MEDITATION. MAT. 26.26. WHILE THEY WERE
1711   ⎭   EATING, HE TOOK BREAD AND BLESSED &C:

What Grace is here? Looke ery way and see
    How Grace's splendor like the bright sun, shines
Out on my head, and I encentred bee
    Within the Center of its radien lines,
    Thou glories King send out thy Kingly Glory   5
    In shining Institutions laid before mee.   [350]

The Basis of thy gracious functions stands
    Ensocketted in thy Essentiall Grace.
As its foundation, Rock (not loose loose sands)
    Bearing the splendor of this shining face   10
    Th'New Covenant, Whose Articles Divine
    Do far Surmount lines wrote in Gold for Shine.

And as the King of Zion thou putst out
  Thy Institutions, Zions statutes, th'Laws
Of thy New Covenant, which all throughout   15
  Thy bright Prophetick trumpet sounds, its Cause
  To this New Covenant, thou sets thy hand
  And Royall seale eternally to stand.

A Counterpane indented right with this
  Thou givst indeed a Deed of Gift to all   20
That Give to thee their Hearts, a Deed for bliss.
  Which with their hands and seales they sign too shall.
  One seale th[e]y at the Articling embrace:
  The other oft must be renew'd, through grace.

Unto the Articles of this Contract   25
  Our Lord did institute even at the Grave
Of the last Passover, when off its packt.
  This seale for our attendence oft to have.
  This seal; made of New Cov'nat wax, red di'de.
  In Cov'nat blood, by faith's to be appli'de.   30

Oh! this Broad Seale, of Grace's Covenat
  Bears, Lord, thy Flesh set in its rim aright.
All Crucifide and blood, (Grace hath no want)
  As shed for us, and on us us to White.
  Let's not neglect this gracious law nor breake   35
  But on this Flesh and blood both drinke and Eate.

Seing thou, Lord, thy Cov'nant writst in blood
  My blood red sins to blot out quite from me
Bathe thou my soule in this sweet gracious flood.
  Give mee thy Grace that I may live to thee.   40
  My heart, thy harp make, and thy Grace my string.
  Thy Glory then shall be my song I'l sing.

---

6 shining *orig.* shing
10 Bearing *orig.* Baring
14 Institutions, *orig.* Institutions, these
20 Deed *orig.* Deed to all

21 thee *orig.* these
22 too *orig.* it
23 th[e]y *orig.* ev'n
25 of *ins.* ; Contract *orig.* Compact
33 hath *orig.* its
37 Cov'nant *orig.* Cov'nat
40 mee *orig.* my
41 string *orig.* sing

12.6M   }   103. MEDITATION. MAT. 26.26. AS THEY WERE EATING
1711   }   HE TOOKE BREAD &C.

The Deity did call a Parliament
  Of all the Properties Divine to sit
About mankinde. Justice her Law out went.
    All Vote mans life to stand or fall by it,
    But Grace gave band securing Gods Elect.   5
    Justice, if Wisdom tended Grace, accepts.   [351]

Man out doth come, and soon this Law disgrac't.
  Justice offended, Grace to worke doth Fall
And in the way of Purest wisdom, trac'd
    New Covenants man and to return him calls.   10
    Erects New Cov'nant Worship suited to
    His present state to save him from all Woe.

And in this Course Glory to offer bright
  Through Graces Hand unto Almighty God
Her Credits Good: Justice therein delights.   15
    Rests in her Bill yet Grace prepares a Rod
    That if her subjects her sweet rules neglect,
    She with her golden rod may them Correct.

New Covenant worship Wisdom first proclaims
  Deckt up in Type[s] and Ceremonies gay.   20
Rich Metaphors the first Edition gains.
    A Divine key unlocks these trunks to lay
    All spirituall treasures in them open Cleare.

The Ark and Mannah, in'ts Christ and Good Cheere.

This first Edition did the Cov'nant tend   25
  With Typick Seales and Rites and Ceremonie
That till the Typick Dispensations end
  Should ratify it as Gods Testimony.
  'Mong which the Passover (whose Kirnell's Christ)
  Tooke place with all its Rites, graciously splic't.   30

But when the Pay day came their kirnells Pickt.
  The shell is cast out hence. Cloudes flew away,
Now Types good night; with Ceremonies strict,
  The Glorious sun is risen, it's broad day.
  Now Passover Farewell, and leave thy Place.   35
  Lords Supper seales the Covenant of Grace.

But though the Passover is passt away.
  And Ceremonies that belong'd to it,
Yet doth its kirnell and their Kirnell stay
  Attending on the seale succeeding it.   40
  The Ceremony parting leaves behinde
  Its spirit to attend this Seale designd.

As it passt off, it passt its place o're to
  The Supper of the Lord (Choice Feast) to Seale
The Covenant of Grace thus, even So   45
  The Ceremoniall Cleaness did reveale
  A Spirituall Cleaness qualifying all
  That have a Right to tend this Festivall.   [352]

All must grant Ceremonies must have Sense.
  Or Ceremonies are but Senseless things.   50
Had God no reason when, for to dispense
  His Grace, he ope'd all Ceremoniall Springs?
  The reason why God deckt his Sacred shine
  With senseless Ceremonies, here Divine.

A Typick Ceremony well attends   55
  A Typick Ordinance, these harmonize

A spirituall Ordinance the Type suspendes
  And Onely owneth Spirituall Qualities
  To have a right thereto. And this the Will
  Thy dying Ceremony made, stands Still.   60

Morall, and Ceremiall cleaness, which
  The Pascall Lamb requir'd Foreshow the Guests
Must at the Supper Seale with Spoiles be rich
  Of sin and be with Saving Grace up dresst.
  God Chose no Ceremonies for their sake   65
  But for Signification did them take.

Give me true Grace that I may grace thy Feast.
  My Gracious Lord, and so sit at thy Table.
Thy Spirituall Dainties this Rich Dress at least
  Will have the Guests have. Nothing less is able   70
  To prove their right to't; this therefore bestow.
  Then as I eate, my lips with Grace shall flow.

---

9 way *ins.* ; trac'd *orig.* traced
16 Rests *orig.* Yet
30 splic't *orig.* spic't
45 thus *orig.* this
51 Had *orig.* Did
62 requir'd *orig.* required
67 Feast *orig.* Table
72 this *orig.* Give this

30.7M   }   104. MEDITATION. MATTH. 26.26.27. HE TOOKE
1711   }   BREAD.—AND HE ALSO TOOKE THE CUP:

What? Bread, and Wine, My Lord! Art thou thus made?
  And made thus unto thine in th'sacrament?
These are both Coridall: and both displai'd.
  Food for the Living. Spirituall Nourishment.
  Thou hence art food, and Physick rightly 'pli'de   5
  To Living Souls. Such none for dead provide.

Stir up thy Appetite, my Soule, afresh,
   Here's Bread, and Wine as Signs, to signify
The richest Dainties Cookery can Dress
   Thy Table with, filld with felicity.   10
   Purge out and Vomit by Repentance all
   Ill Humours which thy Spirituall Tast forestall.

Bread, Yea substantiall Bread dresst daintily
   Gods White bread made of th'kidnie of Wheate
Ground in his Mill to finest Flowre, we spy,   15
   Searc'de through his Strict right Bolter, all compleate   [353]
   Moulded up by Gods hand and baked tite
   In Justices hot oven, Gods Cake bread white.

It is Gods Temple bread; the fine Flower Cake.
   The pure shew Bread on th'golden Table set,   20
Before the Mercy-Seate in golden Plate,
   Thy Palate for this Zions Simnill whet.
   If in this oyled Wafer thou dost eate
   Celestiall Mannah, Oh! the Happy meate.

But that's not all. Here's wine too of brave state.   25
   The Blood, the pure red blood of Zions Grape
Grounde in the Mill of Righteousness to 'bate
   Gods firy wrath and presst into the shape
   Of Royall Wine in Zion's Sacred bowles
   That Purges Cleanse and Chearish doth poore Soules.   30

This Bread, and Wine hold forth the selfesame thing
   As they from their first Wheat and Vine made flow
Successively into their Beings, bring
   The manner of Christs Manhood and forth show
   It was derived from th'head Humanity   35
   Through Generations all Successively.

And as this Bread and Wine receive their forms
   Not fram'd by natures acting, but by Art.
So Christs Humanity was not ere born
   By natures Vertue, which she did impart.   40

But by Almighty power which acted so
Transendently, did nature overdoe.

These two are of all food most Choice indeed
  Do Emblemise Christ's Elementall frame
Most Excellent and fine, of refinde seed   45
  With sparkling Grace deckt, and their Works in flame
  As grafted in and flowing from his Nature
  And here is food of which his are partaker.

Bread must be broke and Eate, Wine pourd out too
  And drunke and so they feed and do delight.   50
Christ broken was upon Gods wheele (it's true)
  And so is Spirituall bread that feeds aright
  And his Choice blood shead for our sins is made
  Drinke for our Souls: a Spirituall Drinke displaid.

Food though it's ne're so rich, doth not beget   55
  Nor make its Eaters; but their Lives mentain.
This Bread and Wine begets not Souls; but's set
  'Fore spirituall life to feed upon the same.
  This Feast is no Regenerating fare.
  But food for those Regenerate that are.   60

Spit out thy Fur, my Tongue; renew thy tast
  Oh! whet thine Appetite, and cleanly brush   [354]
Thy Cloaths, and trim thy Soule. Here food thou hast
  Of Royall Dainties, that requires thee thus
  That thou adorned be in spirituall state.   65
  This Bread ne're moulds, nor wine entoxicate.

They both are Food, and Physick, purge out sin
  From right Receivers. Filth, and Faults away:
They both are Cordialls rich, do Comfort bring.
  Make sanctifying Grace thrive ery day,   70
  Making the spirituall man hate Spirituall Sloath
  And to abound in things of Holy growth.

Lord, feed me with th'Bread of thy sacrament:

And make me drinke thy sacramentall Wine:
That I may Grow by Graces nourishment   75
    Washt in thy Vinall liquour till I shine.
And 'rai'd in sparkling Grace unto thy Glory,
    That so my Life may be a gracious Story.

---

12 thy *orig.* thy Tast do qu[**]te
20 th' *orig.* the
38 acting *orig.* actings
42 did *orig.* and
45 fine, *orig.* fine, and ; refinde *orig.* refined
71 hate *orig.* to hate
76 Washt *orig.* And wash't ; thy *ins.*

23.10M ⎫   105. MEDITATION. MATT. 26.26. JESUS TOOKE BREAD
1711   ⎬   AND BLESSED IT, AND BRAKE IT.
       ⎭

✓ Smelting again

If I was all well melted down, refinde
    In graces Furnace and ran in the mould
Of bright bright Glory, that with Glory shinde
    More bright than glory doth, my Lord I would
Crown thee therewith thou shouldst have all, except   5
    The dross I in refining did eject.

Hast thou unto thy Godhead nature tooke   *Inca*
    My nature and unto that nature joyn'de
Making a Union thereby, whose root
    Too deep's for reasons delving toole to finde,   10
Which is held out thus, by thy Taking Bread,
    In this sweet Feast in which our Souls are fed?

This Union, that it is, wee clearely See
    But se not How, or What it is; although
We stande and gaze on't, at't amazed bee.   15
    But Why it is Grace graciously doth show,
These natures thus United have (as't shown)
    Each done by each, what neither could alone.

The Reason of it Grace declares, whose hand
  This Union made, it's made (and thinke hereon)   20
That so our Nature Cansell might the Bande.
    She'd forfeited, and Justice sude upon.   [355]
    For natures Purse could not the Fine defray.
    Hence She had Gold from Godheads Mint to pay.

This Mystery more rich than massy gold   25
  Our Lord lapt up in a Choice napkin fine
Of Heavenly trade an Ordinance that hold
    The same out doth to us all sweet, Divine,
    That this might live, he in his Dying night,
    Portraide it on his supper last, as light.   30

To shew that he our nature took, he then
  Took breade, and wine best Elementall trade,
Designed as the sign thereof. Which when
    He had his blessing over it display'de.
    To shew his Consecration, then it brake.   35
    To signify his sufferings for our sake.

Hence in this Bread, and Wine thou dost present
  Thyselfe, my Lord, Celestiall Food indeed,
Rich spirituall fare, soul-Food, Faiths nourishment.
    And such as doth all saving Graces feed.   40
    For which an Heaven full of thanks, all free,
    Is not too much my Lord to render thee.

Yet my poore Pipe can hardly stut a tune
  Above an hungry thanks unto thy name
For all this grace, My Lord, My heart perfume   45
    With greater measures, till thy Grace out flame
    And leade mee on in Graces path along
    To Glory, then I'l sing a brighter Song.

---

1 well *ins.* ; down *orig.* well down
2 in *orig.* into
3 with *orig.* my
12 in *orig.* at
42 Is *orig.* In ; Lord *orig.* Lod

17.12M   106. MEDITATION. MATTH. 26.26.27. — TAKE EATE
1711   DRINKE YEE.

I fain would Prize, and Praise thee, Lord, but finde
  My Prizing Faculty imprison'd lyes
That its Appreciation is confinde
  Within its prison walls and small doth rise.
  Its Prizing Act it would mount up so high   5
  That might ore mount its possibility.

I fain would praise thee, but want words to do't:
  And searching o're the realm of thoughts finde none
Significant enough and therefore vote
  For a new set of Words and thoughts hereon   10
  And leap beyond the line such words to gain
  In other Realms, to praise thee: but in vain.   [356]

Me pitty, parden mee and Lord accept
  My Penny Prize, and penny worth of Praise.
Words and their sense within thy bounds are kept   15
  And richer Fruits my Vintage cannot raise.
  I can no better bring, do what I can:
  Accept thereof and make me better man.

With Consecrated Bread and Wine indeed
  Of Zions Floore, and Wine press me sustain.   20
Those fruits thy Boddy, and thy blood doth breed
  Thy Pay and Purchase for mee mee to gain.
  Lord make thy Vitall Principall in mee
  In Gospellwise to eate and drink on thee.

These acts of mine that from thy Vitall spark   25
  In mee bring to thyself, my Lord, my Deare,
As formative in touching thee their marke
  Of this thy sacrament, my spirituall Cheere,
  Life first doth act and Faith that's lifes First-born
  Receiving gives the sacramentall form.   30

Hence it's as needfull as the forme unto
  This Choice formatum. Hypocrites begon.

Elfes Vizzarded, and Lambskinde Woolves hence goe.
  Your Counterfeted Coine is worse than none.
  Your gilding though it may the schoole beguile   35
  The Court will Cast and all your gilt off file.

Morality is here no market ware.
  Although it in the Outward Court is free.
A state of sin this Banquet cannot beare.
  Old, and New Cov'nant Guests here don't agree.   40
  The Wedden Robe is Welcome, but the back
  This supper cloaths not with, that doth it lack.

Food is for living Limbs, not Wooden legs:
  Life's necessary, unto nourishment.
Dead limbs must be cut off: the Addle Eggs   45
  Rot by the heat the dam upon them spent.
  A state of sin that take this bread and Wine
  From the signatum tareth off the signe.

A Principle of life, to eate implies,
  And of such life that sutes the Foods desire.   50
Food naturall doth naturall Life supply.
  And spirituall food doth spirituall life require.
  The Dead don't eate. Though Folly childish dotes
  In th'Child that gives his Hobbyhorses oates.   [357]

To Eat's an Act of life that life out sent   55
  Employing Food. Life's property alive
Yet acts uniting with foods nourishment
  Which spreads o're nature quite to make it thrive.
  Life Naturall and sprirituall Life renewd
  Precedes their Acts, their Acts precede their food.   60

Then form mee Lord, a former here to bee
  Of this thy sacrament receiving here
And let me in this Bread and Wine take thee:
  And entertain me with thy spirituall Cheer.
  Which well Concocted will make joy up start,   65
  To make thy praises leape up from my heart.

6 ore *ins.*
7 thee *ins.*
11 leap *orig.* leaping
12 Realms *orig.* Relms
13 Lord *orig.* me
15 Words *orig.* Th
36 all *ins.*
38 is free *orig.* may bee
58 o're *orig.* over ; quite *ins.*
60 their Acts, their Acts *orig.* the Acts, the Acts ; their food *orig.* the food
66 To *orig.* And ; praises leape *orig.* praise to leap

13.2M ⎫ 107. MEDITATION. LU. 22.19. THIS DO IN
1712   ⎭   REMEMBRANCE OF MEE.

Oh! what a Lord is mine? There's none like him.
 Born heir of th'Vastest Realms, and not Confinde,
Within, nor o're the Canopy or rim
 Of th'starry Region, and as vastly kinde.
 But's bright'st Dominion gloriously lies   5
 In th'Realm of Angells above the starry skies.

When man had sin'd he saw that nothing could
 In all's Dominnion Satisfaction make
To milke white Justice, but himselfe, who should
 Then drinke Deaths health, he did the matter take   10
 Upon himselfe by Compact, new and good
 On such Conditions that requir'd his blood.

Yet entred he in Cov'nant with God.
 The Father for to do the thing himselfe
Which to perform he took a Humane Clod   15
 In union to his Godhead, it enwealth,
 That he might in it fully pay the score
 Of's fallen friends and them from death restore.

And having in our nature well sufficde
 The hungry law, with active Righteousness   20

His life did pay our debt. Death him surprizde.
  His blood he made the Law's sufficing mess.
  With Active and with Passive duties hee
  Balanc't th'accounts, and set the Captives free.

But drawing nigh upon Death's Coasts indeed   25
  He made his Will bequeathing legacies   [358]
To all his Children, a Choice Holy seed.
  As they did up in Covenant new arise
  He his last Night them feasts and at that meale
  His supper institutes his Cov'nant seale.   30

Four Causes do each thing produc'd attend:
  The End, Efficient, Matter and the Form.
These last th'Efficient passt through to the End,
  And so obtains the same, the babe is born.
  So in this supper causes foure attend   35
  Th'Efficient, Matter, Form, and now the End.

The Primall End whereof is Obsignation
  Unto the Covenant of Grace most sweet.
Another is a right Commemoration
  Of Christs Rich Death upon our hearts to keep   40
  And to declare his own till he again
  Shall come; this Ordinance doth at these aim.

And secondary Ends were in Christ's Eye
  In instituting of this sacrament
As Union, and Communion sanctity   45
  Held with himselfe by these usd Elements
  In Union and Comunion which are fit,
  Of Saints Compacted in Church Fellowship.

But lest this Covenat of Grace should ere
  Be held by doubting Saints all Violate   50
By their infirmities as Adams were
  By one transgression and be so vacate
  Its seale is food and's often to be usd,
  To seale new pardons freshening faith, misusd.

Then make me, Lord, at thy sweet Supper spy   55
  Thy graces all well flourishing in mee.
And seale me pardons off and ratify
  Thy Covenant with mee; thus gracious bee.
  My Faculties all deckt with grace shall Chime
  Thy praise, with Angells and my grace shall shine.   60

---

5 bright'st *orig.* brightest
16 Godhead *orig.* Godhead and
17 fully *orig.* totally ; pay *ins.*
39 a right *ins.*
41 own *ins.* ; he again *orig.* he shall come
42 Shall *orig.* Again Shall
49 Covenat *orig.* Covent
54 faith *orig.* their faith

8.4M ⎫   108. MEDITATION. MATT. 26.26,27. JESUS TOOK
1712 ⎭   BREAD—AND HE TOOK THE CUP:

What Royall Feast Magnificent is this,
  I am invited to, where all the fare
Is spic'd with Adjuncts, (ornamantall bliss)
  Which are its robes it ever more doth ware?   [359]
  These Robes of Adjuncts shining round about   5
  Christs golden sheers did cut exactly out.

The Bread and Wine true Doctrine teach for faith
  (True Consequence from Truth will never ly).
Their Adjuncts teach Christs humane nature hath
  A Certain place and not Ubiquity,   10
  Hence this Condemns Ubiquitarians
  And whom deny Christs Manhood too it damns.

It Consubstantiation too Confounds.
  Bread still is bread, Wine still is wine; it's sure.
It Transubstantiation deadly wounds.   15
  Your touch, Tast, sight say true. The Pope's a whore.

Can Bread and Wine by words be Carnifi'de?
And manifestly bread and Wine abide?

What monsterous thing doth Transubstantiation
  And Consubstantiation also make   20
Christs Body, having a Ubique-station
  When thousands sacraments men Celebrate
  Upon a day, if th'Bread and wine should e're
  Be Con-, or Trans-Substantiated there?

If in Christs Doctrine taught us in this Feast,   25
  There lies No ly. (And Christ can never ly)
The Christian Faith cannot abide at least
  To dash out reasons brains, or blinde its eye,
  Faith never blindeth reasons Eye but cleares
  Its sight to see things quite above its sphere.   30

These Adjuncts shew this feast is 'ray'd in ware
  Of Holiness enlin'de with honours shine.
It's Sabbath Entertainment, Spirituall fare.
  It's Churches banquet, Spirituall Bread and Wine.
  It is the signet of the Kings right hande.   35
  Seale to the Covenant of Grace, Gods bande.

The Sign, bread made of th'kidnies of Wheate,
  That grew in Zions field: And th'juyce we sup
Presst from the grape of Zions Vine sweet, great
  Doth make the signall Wine within the Cup.   40
  These signalls Bread and Wine are food that bear
  Christ in them Crucified, as spirituall fare.

Here is a feast indeed! in ev'ry Dish
  A Whole Redeemer, Cookt up bravely, Good,
Is served up in holy sauce that is,   45
  A mess of Delicates made of his blood,
  Adornd with graces sippits, rich Sweet-Meats,
  Comfect and Comforts sweeten whom them eats.

Lord, Make thou me at this rich feast thy Guest.
  And let my food a whole redeemer bee. [360]50
Let Grace Carve him for mee in ev'ry mess:
  And rowle her Cuttings in this sawce for mee.
  If thou me fatten with this Faire While here.
  Hereafter shall thy praise be my good Cheere

---

7 true *ins.* ; teach *orig.* true
15 deadly wounds *orig.* t[*****] gives
19 monsterous thing *orig.* monster then [***]
20 also *orig.* too
29 blindeth *orig.* blindes

3.6M }   109. Meditation. Mat. 26.26:27: And gave it to his
1712 }   Disciples.

A Feast is said to be for Laughter made.
  Belshazzars Feast was made for Luxury.
Ahashueru's feast for pomp's displayde.
  George Nevill's Feast at Yorks, for gluttony.
  But thou my Lord a spirituall Feast hast dresst   5
  Whereat the Angells gaze: and Saints are Guests.

Suppose a Feast in such a Room is kept
  That's deckt in flaming Guildings everywhere,
And richest Fare in China Chargers deckt
  And set on golden Tables. Waiters there   10
  In flaming robes waite pouring Royall wine
  In Jasper Cups out. Oh! what glories shine?

But all this Glorious Feast seems but a Cloud,
  My Lord, unto the Feast thou makst for thine.
Although the matters thou hast thine allowd,   15
  Plain as a pikestaffe bee, as Bread and Wine.
  This feast doth fall below thine, Lord, as far
  As the bright Sun excells a painted Star.

Thine is a Feast, the Funerall feast to prize
  The Death, Oh! my Redeemer, of the Son   20
Of God Almighty King of Heaven and'ts joys,
  Where Spirituall food disht on thy Table comes.
  All Heavenly Bread and Spirituall Wine rich rare.
  Almighty gives, here's Mannah, Angells Fare.

This Feast indeed yields gracious Laughing ripe   25
  Wherein its Authour laugheth Hell to Scorn:
Lifts up the soule that drowns in tears, a wipe
  To give th'old Serpent; now his head piece's torn.
  Thou art, my Lord, the Authour, and beside
  The Good Cheer of this Feast, as Crucifide.   30

The Palace where thou this dost Celebrate
  Is New Jerusalem with Precious Stones
Walld in: all pavde with Gold: and Every Gate.
  A precious pearle: An Angell keeps each one.
  And at the Table head, more rich than gold,   35
  Dost sit thyselfe, and thy rich fare unfold.   [361]

Thy Table's set with fare, that doth Excell
  The richest Bread, and Wine that ever were.
Squeezd out of Corn or Vines: and Cookt up well.
  It's Mannah, Angells food. Yea, Heavens Good Cheer.   40
  Thou art the Authour, and the Feast itselfe.
  Thy Table Feast hence doth excell all wealth.

Thou sittest at the table head in Glory,
  With thy brave guests With grace adornd and drest.
No Table e're was set like thine, in story,   45
  Or with such guests as thine was ever blesst.
  That linings have embroider'd as with gold.
  And upper robes all glorious to behold.

They're Gods Elect, and thy Selected Ones,
  Whose Inward man doth ware rich robes of Grace.   50
Tongues tipt with Zion Languague. Precious stones.
  Their Robes are quilted ore with graces lace.

Their Lives are Checker work of th'Holy Ghost.
Their 'ffections journy unto Heavens Coast.

The subjects, that at first sat at this feast   55
    With Christ himselfe, faithfull Disciples were
Whose gracious frames 'fore this time so increast
    Into Apostleship that brought them here.
    Who when Christ comes in Glory, saith, they shall
    Sit with him on twelve thrones in's Judgment hall.   60

These sample out the subjects and the Guests.
    That Welcome are unto this Table bright,
As Qualifi'de Disciples up well drest
    In sprituall apparell whitend white
    Else spots they're in this feast; they cannot thrive   65
    For none can eate, or ere he be alive.

Thou satst in flaming Grace at table head
    Thy flaming Grace falling upon the rest
That with thee sat, did make their graces shed
    Their Odours out most sweet which they possesst.   70
    Judas that graceless wretch packt hence before.
    That onely gracious ones enjoyd this store.

Lord Deck my soule with thy bright Grace I pray:
    That I may at thy Table Welcome bee.
Thy hand Let take my heart its Captive prey   75
    In Chains of Grace that it ne're flip from thee:
    When that thy Grace hath set my heart in trim
    My Heart shall end thy supper with an Hymn.

---

6 Whereat *orig.* Where
20 The *orig.* Thy
21 God *orig.* the
24 here's *ins.*
45 e're *orig.* er'y
50 ware *ins.*
65 spots they're *orig.* spots are
67 in *orig.* at th'Table in
75 Thy hand Let *orig.* Let grace too ke**

5.8M ⎫   110. MEDITATION. MATT. 26.30. WHEN THEY HAD SUNG
1712 ⎭   AN HYMN.

The Angells sung a Carole at thy Birth:
  My Lord, and thou thyselfe didst sweetly sing
An Epinicioum at thy Death, on Earth.
  And order'st thine, in memory of this thing
  Thy Holy supper, closing it at last   5
  Up with an Hymn, and Choakst the foe thou hast.

This Feast thou madst in memory of thy death.
  Which is disht up most graciously: and towers
Of reeching vapours from thy Grave (Sweet breath)
  Aromatize the skies. That sweetest showers   10
  Richly perfumed by the Holy Ghost,
  Are rained thence upon the Churches Coast.

Thy Grave beares flowers to dress thy Church withall.
  In which thou dost thy Table dress for thine.
With Gospell Carpet, Chargers, Festivall   15
  And spirituall Venison, White Bread and Wine
  Being the Fruits thy Grave brings forth and hands
  Upon thy Table where thou waiting standst.

Dainties most rich, all Spiced o're with Grace,
  That grow out of thy Grave do deck thy Table   20
To entertain thy Guests, thou callst, and place
  Allowst, with welcome. (And This is no Fable)
  And with these Guests I am invited to't
  And this rich banquet makes me thus a Poet.

Thy Cross planted within thy Coffin beares.   25
  Sweet Blossoms and rich Fruits, Whose steams do rise
Out of thy sepulcher and purge the aire
  Of all Sins damps and fogs that Choake the skies.
  This Fume perfumes saints hearts as it out peeps
  Ascending up to bury thee in th'reechs.   30

Joy stands on tiptoes all the While thy Guests
  Sit at thy Table, ready forth to Sing
Its Hallilujuhs in sweet musicks dress
  Waiting for Organs to imploy herein.
  Here matter is allowd to all, rich, high,   35
  My Lord, to tune thee Hymns melodiously.

Oh! make my heart thy Pipe: the Holy Ghost.
  The Breath that fills the Same and Spiritually.
Then play on mee thy pipe that is almost
  Worn out with piping tunes of Vanity.   40
  Winde musick is the best if thou delight
  To play the same thyselfe, upon my pipe.   [363]

Hence make me, Lord, thy Golden Trumpet Choice
  And trumpet thou thyselfe upon the same
Thy heart enravishing Hymns with sweetest Voice.   45
  When thou thy Trumpet soundst, thy tunes will flame.
  My heart shall then sing forth thy praises sweet
  When sounded thus with thy sepulcher reech.

Make too my Soul thy Cittern, and its wyers
  Make my affections: and rub off their rust   50
With thy bright Grace. And screw my strings up higher
  And tune the same, to tune thy praise most Just.
  I'le close thy Supper then with Hymns, most sweet
  Burr'ing thy Grave in thy sepulcher's reech.

---

2 sweetly *orig.* sing
3 at *orig.* ore
22 And This *orig.* This ; is *ins.*
23 to't *orig.* to to
26 Sweet *ins.* ; rich *ins.*
29 This Fume perfumes *orig.* These Fumes perfume ; it *orig.* they ; peeps *orig.* peep
44 thou *ins.*
51 up *orig.* much

7.10M
1712
} 111. MEDITATION. 1 COR. 10.16. THE CUP OF BLESSING
WHICH WEE BLESS, IS IT NOT THE COMUNION OF
THE BODY OF CHRIST? &C.

Oh! Gracious Grace! whither soarst thou? How high?
　Even from thy root to thy top branch dost tower?
Thou springst from th'essence of blesst Deity
　And grow'st to th'top of Heavens all blissfull flower.
　Thou art not blackt but brightend by the sin   5
　Of Gods Elect, whom thou from filth dost bring.

Thou Graces Egg layst in their very hearts,
　Hatchest and brudl'st in this nest Divine
Its Chickin, that its fledge. And still imparts
　It influences, through their lives that shine.   10
　Them takest by the hand, and handst them o're
　The Worlds wild waves to the Celestiall shoare.

And as thou leadst them 'long the way to glory
　Thou hast the Wells of Aqua Vitæ cleare.
For them to take good drachms of (Oh! blesst story)   15
　And Inns to entertain them with good Cheere.
　That so they may not faint, but upward grow
　Unto their ripeness, and to glory Soe.

They take a drachm of Heavenly spirits in,
　From every Duty. Here is blessed Ware.   20
Thou hast them draughts of spirituall Liquour gi'n
　And ev'ry Sabbath tenders us good fare,
　But oh! the Supper of our Lord! What joy?
　This Feast doth fat the Soul most graceously.   [364]

Theandrick Blood, and Body With Compleate   25
　Full Satisfaction and rich Purchase made
Disht on this golden Table, Spirituall meate
　Stands. And Gods saints are Welcom'd with this trade
　The Satisfaction, and the Purchase which
　Thy Blood and Body made, how Good? how rich?   30

Oh! blesst effects flow from this table then.
  The feeding on this fare and spiritually
Must needs produce a spirituall Crop for them;
  That rightly do this table fare enjoy
  Whatever other Ordinances doe!   35
  This addeth seale, and sealing wax thereto.

This is a Common that consists of all
  That Christ ere had to give. And oh! how much!
Of Grace and Glory here? These ripe fruits fall
  Into saints baskets: they up gather such.   40
  All fruits that other ordinances which
  Are Edifying, Do this Feast enrich.

But still besides these there are properly
  Its own effects which it doth beare and hath.
It's Spirituall Food that nourisheth spiritualy   45
  The new born babe to thrive in using Faith.
  The Soule it quiets: Conscience doth not sting.
  It seales fresh pardon to the soul of sin.

It maketh Charity's sweet sweet rosy breath
  Streach o're the Whole society of saints.   50
It huggeth them, that nothing of the Earth
  Or its infection its affections taints.
  Grace now grows strong, Faith sturdy. Joy, and Peace
  And other Vertues in the Soule encrease.

Gods Love shines brighter now upon the heart,   55
  In that he seals Christ Dying with a Feast;
Wherein he smiles doth on the soul impart:
  With all Christs Righteousness: Joy now's increast.
  The soul grows valient and resists the foe.
  The spirituall Vigour vigorous doth grow.   60

Lord, on thy Commons let my Spirits feed
  So nourish thou thy new Born babe in mee:
At thy Communion Table up mee breed.
  Communicate thy Blood and Body free.

Thy Table yielding sprituall Bread and Wine   65
Will make my soul grow brisk, thy praise to Chime.   [365]

---

6 thou *ins*.
8 brudl'st in this *orig*. brudlest up in
12 to *orig*. unto
15 good *orig*. their good
40 saints *orig*. their
42 Do *orig*. too
48 fresh *orig*. a
49 sweet sweet *orig*. sweet ; rosy *orig*. rosy wings
58 Christs *orig*. Christs Satisfaction
66 make *ins*.

15.12 }   112. MEDITATION. 2 COR. 5.14. IF ONE DIED FOR
1712 }   ALL THEN ARE ALL DEAD.

Oh! Good, Good, Good, my Lord. What more Love yet.
  Thou dy for mee! What am I dead in thee?
What did Deaths arrow shot at me, thee hit?
  Didst slip between that flying shaft and mee?
  Didst make thyselfe Deaths marke shot at for mee?   5
  So that her shaft shall fly no far than thee?

Did'st dy for mee indeed, and in thy Death
  Take in thy Dying thus my death the Cause?
And lay I dying in thy Dying breath,
  According to Graces Redemption Laws?   10
  If one did dy for all, it needs must bee
  That all did dy in one, and from death free.

Infinities fierce firy arrow red
  Shot from the splendid Bow of Justice bright
Did smite thee down, for thine Thou art their head.   15
  They di'de in thee. Their death did on thee light.
  They di'de their Death in thee, thy Death is theirs.
  Hence thine is mine, thy death my trespass clears.

How sweet is this: my Death lies buried
   Within thy Grave, my Lord, deep underground,   20
It is unskin'd, as Carrion rotten, Dead.
    For Grace's hand gave Death its deadly wound.
    Death's no such terrour in the saints blesst Coast.
    It's but a harmless shade: No walking Ghost.

The Painter lies: the Bellfrey Pillars weare   25
   A false Effigies now of Death, alas!
With empty Eyeholes, Butter teeth, bones bare
    And spraggling arms, having an Hour Glass
    In one grim paw; th'other a spade doth hold
    To shew deaths frightfull region under mould.   30

Whereas its sting is gone: its life is lost.
   Though unto Christless ones it is most Grim
It's but a Shade to Saints whose path it Crosst.
    Or shell or Washen face, in which she sings
    Their Bodies in her lap a Lollaboy   35
    And sends their souls to sing their Masters joy.

Lord let me finde sin, Curse and Death that doe
   Belong to me ly slain too in thy Grave.   [366]
And let thy law my clearing hence bestow
    And from these things let me acquittance have.   40
    The Law suffic'de: and I discharg'd Hence sing
    Thy praise I will over Deaths Death and Sin.

---

5 shot at *orig.* for mee
10 to *orig.* unto
12 That *orig.* Then
23 in the *orig.* unto
24 harmless *orig.* shade
25 weare *orig.* wares
28 spraggling *orig.* spaggling
38 Belong *orig.* Belong in [***] ; too *ins.*
42 Death *orig.* Deaths

12.2M   ⎫   113. MEDITATION. REV. 22.16. I AM THE ROOT &c.
1713   ⎬   OFFSPRING OF DAVID.

Help, oh! my Lord, anoint mine Eyes to see
  How thou art Wonderfull thyselfe all ore.
A Common Wealth of Wonders: Rich Vine tree
  Whose boughs are reevd with miracles good store.
  Let thy sweet Clew lead me thy servant right   5
  Through out this Labyrinth of Wonders bright.

Here I attemp thy rich delightfull Vine,
  Whose bowing boughs buncht with sweet clusters ripe
Amongst the which I take as Cordiall wine
  This Bunch doth bleed into my Cup delight.   10
  It Cramps my thoughts. What Root, and Offspring too
  Of David: Oh! how can this thing be true?

What top and bottom, Root and Branch unto
  The selfesame tree, how can this bee? ah-fiddle!
It cannot be; this thing may surely goe   15
  As harder far to read than Sampsons Riddle.
  A Father and a Son to th'selfesame man!
  This wond'rous is indeed; read it who can.

The Root the tree, the Tree the branch doth beare.
  The tree doth run between the branch, and Root.   20
The root and branch are too distinct a pair
  To be the same: Cause and Effect they sute.
  How then is Christ the Root, and Offspring bright
  Of David, shew, come, read this riddle right.

Lend me thy key, holy Eliakim,   25
  T'unlock the doore untill thy glory shine.
And by thy Clew me thorow lead, and bring
  Cleare through this Labyrinth by this rich twine
  Posamniticks Labyrinth now doth appeare
  An Easy thing unto the passage here.   30

But this doth seem the key unto the Lock.
  Thy Deity, my Lord, is Davids root,
It sprang from it: it's rooted on this rock,
    Thy Humane nature is its Offspring-sute.   [367]
    Thy Deity gave David Being, though   35
    Thy Humane Being did from David flow.

Hence thou both Lord, and Son of David art,
  Him Being gav'st, and Being tookst of him:
This doth unbolt the Doore, and light impart
    To shew the nature of this wond'rous thing.   40
    Hence two best natures do appeare to stand
    United in thy Person hand in hand.

My blessed Lord, thou art like none indeed:
  Godhead, and Manhood harmonize in thee.
Hence thou alone wee mediator read,   45
    'Tween God, and Man, and setst Gods Children free
    From all Gods wrath, and wholy them restore
    Into that Favour, which they lost before.

Hence give thou me true Faith in thee to have:
  Make me thy branch, be thou my root thyselfe,   50
And let thy Grace root in my heart, I Crave.
    And let thy purchase be my proper Wealth:
    And when this sweet hath in my heart full sway
    My sweetest musick shall thy praise display.

---

4 boughs *orig.* bows
9 take *orig.* take this one most fine
14 ah-fiddle *orig.* it
17 Father *orig.* Fath
18 it *orig.* it read
38 gav'st *orig.* giv'st
42 thy *orig.* his
44 Manhood *orig.* Manhead
47 them *orig.* dost
48 that *orig.* this

9.6M ⎱   114. MEDITATION. REV. 22.16. THE BRIGHT
1713 ⎰   AND MORNING STAR.

A Star, Bright Morning Star, the Shining Sun
  Of Righteousness, in Heaven Lord thou art.
Thou pilotst us by night, which being run
  Away, thou bidst all darkness to depart.
    The Morning Star peeps up an usher gay   5
    'Fore th'Sun of Righteousness to grace the day.

All men benighted are by fall, and Sin:
  Thou Graces pole Star art to pilote's from it:
The night of sorrow and Desertion spring,
  Thou morning starr dost rise, and not a Comet.   10
    This night expired now, is dead and gone:
    The Day spring of sweet Comfort cometh on.

The Morning Star doth rise, Dews gracious fall:
  And spirituall Herbs, and sweet Celestiall flowers
Sprinkled therewith most fragrantly do call   15
  The Day star up with golden Curls, and Towers
    Put back the Curtains of the azure skies
    And gilde the aire while that the sun doth rise.   [368]

The night of Persecution up arose.
  Not Even, but the morning Star thereto   20
Soon riseth: vant ill looks: the last Cock Crows
  The Morning Star up: out the sun doth go.
    Farewell darke night, Welcome bright gracious day.
    As Joy Divine comes on, Griefe goes away.

This world's a night-shade, or a pitchy night.   25
  All Canop'i'de with storms and Cloudes all darke.
Sending out thunders, Lightnings and with might,
  But thou our Pole Star art, which we must marke,
    While th'morning Star hands dawning light along.
    Let Grace sing now, Birds Singing time is come.   30

Whilst thou, my Pole-star shinst my Lord, on mee,
  Let my poore pinnace saile thereby aright.

Through this darke night until its harbor bee
 The Daystars bay, the spring of dayly light,
 The Usher bidding of the night good night   35
 And Day, Good morrow lightend with delight.

If I by thee, my Pole Star, steere aright
 Through this dark night of foule hard weather here
My Vessell safely to the harbour bright
 Of thee, my Morning Star, ere shining clear.   40
 I then shall soon Eternall day possess
 Where ever shines the Sun of Righteousness.

Grant me, my Lord, by thee, my star to steere.
 Through this darke vale of tears untill I meet,
Thee here my morning star out shining cleare,   45
 Shewing my night is past, and day doth peep.
 When thou my sun of Righteousness makst day.
 My Harp shall thy Eternall praise then play.

Thou Jacobs star, in's Horizon didst rise.
 And fixt in Heaven, Heavens steeridge star.   .   50
To steer poor sinners out from Enemies
 Coasts unto Graces Realm, (Best state by far).
 Thou sentst a star in th'East to lead Wise men
 Thence to thyselfe, when born in Bethlehem.

The golden locks of this bright star, I pray,   55
 Make leade us from sins quarters to the Coast
Of Graces tillage: darkness from to th'Bay
 Of Consolation, and the Holy Ghost
 And from this Vale of tears to Glory bright
 Where our tunde breath shall ne're be Choakt by th'night.   60

---

3 pilotst *orig.* pil[*]te
6 Righteousness *orig.* Righteous ; pilote's *orig.* pilate's
16 Towers *orig.* Showers
31 shinst *orig.* shineth
36 lightend *orig.* lighted
52 unto *orig.* to
57 tillage: *orig.* tillage: from affection ; from *ins.*
60 by th'night *orig.* by night

4.7M
1713 } 115. MEDITATION. CANT. 5.10. MY BELOVED.

What art thou mine? am I espousd to thee?
　What honour's this? it is more bright Renown
I ought to glory more in this sweet glee
　　Than if I'de wore greate Alexanders Crown.
　　Oh! make my Heart loaded with Love ascend,   5
　　Up to thyselfe, its bridegroom, bright, and Friend.

Her whole delight, and her Belov'de thou art
　Oh! Lovely thou: Oh! grudg my soule, I say,
Thou straitend standst, lockt up to Earths fine parts
　　Course matter truly, yellow earth, Hard Clay.   10
　　Why should these Clayey faces be the keyes
　　T'lock, and unlock thy love up as they please?

Lord, make thy Holy Word, the golden Key
　My soule to lock and make its bolt to trig
Before the same, and Oyle the same to play   15
　　As thou dost move them off and On to jig.
　　The ripest Fruits that my affections beare
　　I offer, thee. Oh! my Beloved faire.

Thou standst the brightest object in bright glory
　More shining than the shining sun to 'lure.   20
Unto thyselfe the purest Love, the stories
　　Within my Soule can hold refinde most pure
　　In flaming bundles pollishd all with Grace
　　Most sparklingly about thyselfe t'imbrace.

The most refined Love in Graces mint   25
　In rapid flames is best bestowd on thee
The brightest: metall with Divinest print
　　Thy tribute is, and ever more shall bee.
　　The Loving Spouse and thou her Loved sweet
　　Make Lovely Joy when she and thee do meet: 30

Thou art so lovely, pitty 't is indeed
  That any drop of love the Heart can hold
Should be held back from thee, or should proceed
  To drop on other Objects young, or old.
  Best things go best together: best agree: 35
  But best are badly usd, by bad that bee.

Thou all o're Lovely art. Most lovely Thou:
  Thy spouse, the best of Loving Ones: Her Love,
The Best of Love: and this shee doth avow
  Thyselfe. And thus she doth thyself approve.   40
  That object robs thee of thy due that wares
  Thy spouses Love. With thee none in it shares.   [370]

Lord fill my heart with Grace refining Love.
  Be thou my onely Well-Belov'd, I pray.
And make my Heart with all its Love right move   45
  Unto thyselfe, and all her Love display.
  My Love is then right well bestowd, alone
  When it obtains thyselfe her Lovely One.

My Best love then shall on Shoshannim play.
  Like David her sweet Musick, and thy praise   50
Inspire her songs that Glory ever may
  In sweetest tunes thy Excellency Glaze.
  And thou shalt be the burden of her song
  Loaded with Praise that to thyselfe belong.

---

12 unlock *orig.* unlock up ; please *orig.* plase
15 to *orig.* with ; same *orig.* same with
30 she and *orig.* thee
34 on *orig.* on any
37 o're *orig.* o're lovely
40 doth *ins.*

21.9M
1713
} MEDITATION 116. CAN. 5.10. MY BELOVED
is WHITE, AND RUDDY, THE CHIEFEST
AMONG TEN THOUSAND.

When thou, my Lord, mee mad'st, thou madst my heart
  A seate for love, and love enthronedst there.
Thou also madst an object by thy Art
    For Love to be laid out upon most Cleare.
    The ruling stamp of this Choice object shows   5
    God's Beauty, beautifuller than the rose.

I sent mine Eye Loves Pursevant to seek
  This Object out, the which too naturall
I found it mixt with White and Red most sweet.
    On which love naturall doth sweetly fall   10
    But if it's spirituall, then Orient Grace
    Imbellisheth the object in this Case.

Such Beautie rose in Sharon's Rose and keeps
  Its pleasing blushes of pure White, and Red
Where spirituall blossoms give their Spirituall Reech   15
    And in thy spirituall Countenence do bed.
    Thou art this Rose Whose rosy Cheeks are found
    In purest White and Red of Grace abound.

Thou art arrayed in Gods Whitest Lawn
  And with the purest ruddy looks sweet Rose,   20
White Righteousness, And sufferings too out drawn.
    Thy purest blood thy blessed veans did lose
    Was Lasht, Gasht slain paying our debts in which
    Thy beauty rose unto the highest pitch.

Hence purest White and red in spirituall sense   25
  Make up thy Beauty to the spirituall Eye.
Thus thou art object to love spirituall. Hence
    The Pur'st Spirituall Love doth to thee high.   [371]
  * * * * * *

  * * * * * *
          30

Thou art the loveli'st object over spread
  With brightest beauty Object ever wore
Of purest flushes of pure white and red,
  That ever did or could the Love allure,
  Lord make my Love and thee its Object meet   35
  And me in folds of such Love raptures keep.

Oh! thou most beautifull of Objects gay
  Dart out thy Heavenly beams into my breast.
And make thy Beauty Lord, thy Golden key
  For to unlock and open right my Chest   40
  Loves Cabinet and take the best thyselfe
  Of all my Love therein; it's all thy Wealth.

When I bring forth the best of Love to thee
  And poure its purest streams all reeching Warm
The best of Love, and Beautiest object bee   45
  Then met together, Love by Beauties Charm
  Embrace thyselfe in her pure milkewhite Hands.
  Thy Holy beauty lays my love in bands.

Thy beauty then shall weare the best of mee.
  My Love shall then the best of Beauties have.   50
My Love's my best; thy Beauty's best in thee.
  For thy Best Beauty my best love I save.
  While my best love doth thy best beauty greet
  My purest Love shall sing thy Beauty sweet.

---

5 object *orig.* object rose
12 the *orig.* th'
15 give *orig.* giving ; their *ins.*
20 sweet *orig.* seet
21 too *ins.*
22 thy *orig.* doe thy
25 red in *orig.* rudy
28 The Pur'st *orig.* Purest
47 milkewhite *orig.* milke
48 beauty *ins.*
53 doth *orig.* on

117. MEDITATION. CANT. 5.10. THE CHIEFEST
AMONG TEN THOUSAND. מִדְּבָבוֹת דָּגוּל VER

17.11M   ILLAROUS E MYRIADE: JEROM. ELECTUS E

1713   MILLEBUS. ELECTUS EX INSIGNIS PR[E] DECEM.
MAR. STANDARD BEARER ABOVE TEN THOUSAND.
OR THE CHOICE ONE OF TEN THOUSAND.

A King thou art, my Lord, yea King of Kings
  All Kings shall truckle and fall 'fore thee down.
Thou hast a Kingdom too Whose greate bell rings
  A Passing peale to Worldly Kings and Crowns.
  Thou art the King of Saints and Angells bright   5
  Thou art the King of Glory, and all Light.   [372]

Thy Kingdom is with walls encircled
  Stronger than Walls of Brass or solid Gold.
It's walld about with fire: stones Cemented
  With all the Promises Gods booke doth hold.   10
  And all its buildings laid upon the Rock
  Eternall: that Hell gates can't make them shock.

Thou hast a Throne, Crown, Scepter, Mace all Rich
  Richer than golden Crowns, pearld all about.
Thou hast a Body of just Laws: all Which   15
  Transcend all Lawes that ever Kings put out.
  Thou also hast both Foes and Enemies
  That up against thee and thy Realm arise.

Thou hast a Standard and a Banner greate.
  Thy Gospell and all Gospell Grace, its flag: 20
Thy standards Colours blancht with Grace compleat
  Enrich thy Banner doth (that is no rag).
  Thou hast a Drum thou beatest up apace
  For Volunteers, that thou enlists with Grace.

Thy souldiers that unto thy standard high   25
  Deckt in thy Colours up thou trainst aright
To hande their Weapons well and dextrously
  And rightly use Shield, Arrow, Sworde and Pike.

And leadst them out against thy foes, the King
Abaddon, Divells, Wicked Ones and Sin.   30

Their glittering swords and spears Edgd sharp with Grace
  Wherewith they are well arm'd do surely bring
Thy Adversaries under and apace
  Their hearts do pierce that foes do rise to Ring.
  And from the fight to th'Throne triumphantly   35
  Them leadest while Drums beat and Colours fly.

All these thy men under thy flag that fight
  In ranke and file, and Graces Exercise
In all the way go 'till they Come aright
  Unto thy Palace back triumphing wise.   40
  Their Colours on their golden streamers flying
  Do with thy glorious selfe there enter, joying.   [373]

Under thy Banner Lord, enlist thou mee,
  Make me to ware thy Colours, *Saving Grace.*
Them flourish in my Life, and make thou mee   45
  To beare thy standerd and thy Banner trace
  And so me to thy Palace Glory bring
  Where I thy standards Glory ere may sing.

Title illarous *orig.* illatus
3 greate bell rings *orig.* bells do ring
12 that *orig.* and
28 use *ins.*
33 Thy *orig.* His
34 to *ins.* ; Ring *orig.* th [**]ing
36 leadest *orig.* leads ; beat *orig.* do beat
40 back *orig.* in

14.1M   ⎤   118. MEDITATION. CAN 5.11. HIS HEAD IS MOST
1713   ⎦   FINE GOLD.

Oh! Hidebound Heart. Harder than mountain Rocks.
  Cannot one beam of this bright golden Head
Have enterance, that's trim'd with black Curld Locks
  In all its vigrous green up flowerished
  My Child affections thus to touch and thaw.   5
  And to thy golden head their spirits draw?

The stateliest Head that ever body Bore
  Not gilt but finest gold, of Heavens Gold.
The golden Head that Neb'chadnezzer wore
  Was but a durt ball to't of tainted mould.   10
  It's true indeed, I call't not Deity,
  But a Bright Emblem of bright Majesty.

This Golden head holds Sovereignity
  And Sovereignity being relative
Constrains a golden body Worthily   15
  Both politick, and properly native.
  The Best of Humane Bodies Golden should
  And politicke, ere weare this head of Gold.

These Bodies fitted to this Golden Head
  Must needs be golden. Oh the best of all,   20
Because it is their sovereign: and doth bed
  And board the best things in its golden Hall
  Faith, Hope and Charity and graces still
  Out from this Head, and every member fill.

The Brains that in this golden brain Pan dwell   25
  Must needs be golden, Golden Wisdom breed.
Its Eyes weare Golden Apples. Th'Senses Cell
  Is all fine Gold, all Golden trade indeed,
  If Wisdoms Palace is the finest Gold,
  Then Golden laws, and statutes hence behold.   [374]30

Hence Golden influences out are sent

To Every member of this Golden Head,
The Body Naturall, Whose acts intent
  Upon their Golden Rule are Golden bread
  And hence a golden life my Lord did lead,   35
  From top to toe, most gloriously displayd.

Also the Body Politick, the Realm
  Having its members every one possess
These golden influences from their Helm
  Do make all golden motions ever fresh.   40
  Hence th'golden Laws with Golden influences
  A golden race produce and in all tenses.

Thy Golden Head a golden Kingdom hath
  To which it Golden Statutes out doth give
And golden influences it display'th,   45
  That make the subjects golden lives to live,
  And by these golden Laws thy walke to hold
  Thy glorious City to, whose streets pure gold.

Oh! glorious Lord, make mee make thy Gold Head
  To bee my Sovereign, and make thou mee   50
A member of thy Golden body led
  By its blesst Golden Lines that lead to thee
  That as my Life thy lines do parallell.
  My Harp shall play: thy Golden head Excell.

---

5 thus to touch and thaw *orig.* till they thee [*]s[**]ile touch
10 to't *orig.* to this Gold
16 politick *orig.* [***]live, and also
18 And *orig.* And bodies
23 and *orig.* and all
25 Pan *ins.*
27 Th' *orig.* the
30 Then *orig.* Hence ; and *ins.*
47 thy *orig.* my
49 make *ins.* ; Gold *orig.* Golden
50 bee *orig.* make
52 that *orig.* to

119. Meditation. Can. 5.12. His Eyes are as the
9.3M   Eyes of Doves by Rivers of Waters washed
1714   with milk, and fitly set.

My Lord! my Love! what loveliness doth ly,
    In this pert percing fiery Eye of thine?
Thy Dovelike Eyes orevarnish gloriously
    Thy Face till it, the heavens over shine.
    No Eye did ever any face bedight   5
    As thine with Charming Beauty and Delight.

No Eyeholes did at any time enjoy,
    An apple of an Eye like this of thine
Nor ever held an Apple of an Eye
    Like that thine hold. Apple and Eyehole fine   [375]10
    Oh! How these Apples and these Eyeholes fit,
    Its Eye Omniscient in its fulness sits!

Never were Eyeballs so full trust with might
    With such rich, sharp, quick visive spirits tite
Nor gave such glances of such beauty bright   15
    As thine, my Lord, nor wore so smart a Sight.
    All bright, All Right, all Holy, Wise, and Cleare
    Or ere discover did such beauty here.

Look here, my Soule, thy Saviours Eye most brisk
    Doth glaze and make't most Charming beauty weare   20
That Ever Heaven held, or ever kisst.
    All Saints, and Angells at it Gastard Stare.
    This Eye with all the beauties in his face
    Doth hold thy heart and Love in a blesst Chase.

Lord let these Charming Glancing Eyes of thine   25
    Glance on my Souls bright Eye its amorous beams
To fetch as upon golden Ladders fine
    My Heart and Love to thee in Hottest Steams.
    Which bosom'd in thy brightest beauty cleare
    Shall tune the glances of thy Eyes Sweet Deare.   30

5 Eye *ins.*
12 in *orig.* on
14 such *ins.*
15 beauty *orig.* beaty
19 Eye *orig.* Eye ins head
24 heart *orig.* heat

4.4M   ⎱   120. Meditation. Can. 5.13. His Cheeks are as
1714   ⎰   a Bed of Spices, as Sweet Flowers &c.

My Deare-Deare Lord! What shall my Speech be dry?
  And shall I court thee onely with dull tunes?
When I behold thy Cheekes like brave beds ly
    Of Spices and Sweet flowers, reechs of Perfumes?
    Sweet beauty reeching in thy Countenance.   5
    Oh! amorous Charms: that bring't up in a Trance!

Oh! brightest Beauty, Lord, that paints thy Cheeks
  Yea Sweetest Beauty that Face ere did ware,
Mans Clayey Face ne're breathd such ayery Reechs
    Nor e're such Charming sweetness gave so fair.   10
    If otherwise true Wisdoms voice would bee,
    That greater Love belong'd to these than thee,

If so, Love to thyselfe might slacke its pin
  And Love to Worldly Gayes might screw up higher
Its rusty pin, till, that her Carnall string   15
    Did raise Earths tunes above the Heavenly Quire.   [376]
    Shall Vertue thus descend, and have Disgrace?
    Shall brightest beauty have the lowest place?

Shall dirty Earth out shine the Heavens bright?
  Our Garden bed out shine thy Paradise?   20
Shall Earthy Dunghills yield more sweet Delight?
    Be sweeter than thy Cheeks like beds of Spice?
    Are all things natur'de thus and named wrong?
    Hath God that made them all made all thus run?

Where is the thought that's in Such dy pot di'de?   25
  Where is the mouth that mutters Such a thing?
Where is the Tongue that dare such Speech let slide?
  As Cramps the Aire that doth such ditties ding
  Upon the Eare that wound and poison doe
  The Auditory Temple where they goe?   30

Such things as these indeed are Hells black Smoke
  That pother from its Chimny tunnells vile
To smut thy perfect beauty, Damps thence broke
  Out of the serpents smokehole, to defile,
  And Choake our Spirituall smell and so to Crush   35
  Thy sweet perfum out of these briezes thus.

But Oh! my Lord, I do abhorr such notes
  That do besmut thy Beautious Cheeks like spice:
Like Pillars of perfume; thy Cheeks rich Coats,
  Of purest sweetness deckes in's th'beauty Choice.   40
  My bliss I finde lap't in my Love that keeps
  Its station on thy sweet, and Beautious Cheeks,

Lord lodge my Eyes upon thy Cheekes that are
  Cloathd ore with orient beauty like as't were
A Spice bed shining with sweet flowers all fair   45
  Enravishing the very Skies so Cleare
  With their pure spirits breathing thence perfumes
  Orecoming notes that fill my Harpe with tunes.

---

2 thee *ins.*
11 would *orig.* be
22 sweeter *orig.* sweter
23 natur'de thus *orig.* thus natur'de
28 doth *orig.* so
33 thence *orig.* thence out broke
35 so to *ins.*
38 like *orig.* of
40 th' *ins.*
42 sweet, and Beautious Cheeks. *orig.* Beautious Cheeks, and th[*] reecks

28.9M ⎤   121. Meditation. Cant. 5.13. His Lips are
1714 ⎦   like Lillies, dropping sweet smelling Myrrh.

Peart Pidgeon Eyes, sweet Rosie Cheeke of thine
  My Lord, and Lilly Lips, What Charms bed here?
To Spiritualize my dull affections mine
    Untill they up their heads in Love flames reare.
    The flaming beames sent from thy beautious face   5
    Transcend all other beauties and their grace.   [377]

Thy Pidgen Eyes dart piercing, beames of Love.
  Thy Cherry Cheeks sende Charms out to Loves Coast.
Thy Lilly Lips drop myrrh down from above
    To medicine our Spirituall ailes, greate host.   10
    These spirituall maladies that do invest
    The Spirituall man are by thy myrrh redresst.

Art thou the Myrrh tree Lord? thy mouth the Sorce,
  Thy Lilly Lips the bancks the rivers to
Wherein this Myrrhie Juyce as water-Course   15
    Doth glide along? And like Choice waters flow?
    Lord make thy lilly Lips to ope the Sluce
    And drop thy Doctrine in my Soule, its juyce.

These golden Streames of Gospell Doctrine glide
  Out from thy Lilly Lips aright, my Lord,   20
Oh! spirituall myrrh! And raise a Holy Tide
    Of flowing Grace, and graces Sea afford.
    This is the Heavenly shoure of Myrrh that flows
    Out of this Cloude of Grace thy lips disclose.

That Grace that in thy lips is powered out   25
  So that these lillie Lips of thine ere bee
The graceous Floodgate whence thy graces spout,
    My Lord, distill these drops of Myrrh on mee,
    If that thy lilly Lips drop on my heart
    Thy passing myrrh, 't will med'cine ev'ry part.   30

If that these lilly Lips of thine drop out

These Myrrhie drops into mine hearts dim Eye
And are to mee rich Graces golden Spout
  That poure out sanctifying Grace, Oh! joy,
  This myrrh will medicine my heart that falls   35
  Out of thy Lilly Lips, on graces Hall.

When these thy Lips poure out this myrrh on mee:
  I shall be medicinde with myrrhed Wine
And purifide with Oyle of Myrrh shall bee
  And well perfumde with Odours rich divine.   40
  And then my life shall be a Sacrifice
  Perfum'de with this Sweet incense up arise.

---

2 Charms *orig.* Charming Love
7 of Love *orig.* t'charm
11 maladies *orig.* medicines
12 man *orig.* man that by
14 bancks the *orig.* banks the
21 Oh *orig.* Of
23 Heavenly *orig.* Heavenly Myrrh
27 graceous *orig.* gracious
32 These *orig.* This
36 on *orig.* for

122. MEDITATION. CANT. 5.14. THY HANDS ARE
AS GOLD RINGS נלילי ORBS SET ממלאים FILLD
WITH BERILL.

30.11M
1714

My Deare! Deare Lord! while mine Affections act,
  Upon thyselfe, no better words I have
To set them out than this Word Deare, that lack:
  Doth length and breadth to shew them. Hence I crave   [378]
  Thy Pardon 'Cause such feeble terms I use   5
  Whose selvedge, Hem, and Web weare sorry shews.

I also crave thy pardon still because
  My Muses Hermetage is grown so old
Her spirits shiver doe, her Phancy's Laws

Are much transgresst. She's far too Crampt with cold.   10
Old age indeed hath finde her, that she's grown
Num'd, and her Musicks Daughters sing Ahone.

But is the shine, thus of thy Precious hands
  Whose fingers each are girdled rich all round
With Rims of Gold, all Decorated stand.   15
  Puncht with green Berill which therein abound,
  Do by their vivid glances make alive
  My frozen Phancy, that it doth revive.

Thy Hands wherein's thy mighty power displaide,
  Hold out afore us, thy brave Operation   20
Of Mediatory Acts, most golden trade
  Of Spirituall Luster, in thy Holy station.
  May my Chil'd spirits into raptures put
  Of right delight of an Extatick Cut.

But yet methinks the glory of thy hands   25
  As handling thy mediatoriall Acts
Metaphorized here too faintly stands
  Englisht [gold rings] for th'Hebrew terms exact.
  For in our text the Hebrew predicates
  Thy hands as Golden Orbes of Berill mates.   30

But now, my Lord, are thy brave hands, so bright
  The golden Orbs Celestiall filld up cleare
With this brave Oyle-green Berill all delight
  With all rich Grace of graces Charter Deare?
  Are all th'Celestiall Orbs of Graces right   35
  The spirits predicate of thy hands tite?

In that thy hands this golden Orb is made
  This Orbe is emblem of the sphere of Grace:
And doth Contain thy mediatory Trade.
  Redemption of thy blesst Elected race.   40
  And Application too, to them, do stand.
  With grace laid on, thee on the same to hand.

What are thy hands the golden Orbs of Grace?
  Then they must be the spirits nest also
Wherein the spirit doth an holy race   45
  Hatch, and doth rain sweet shoures for grace apace   [379]
  And hands that hand thy spouse up tenderly
  To thy Bride Chamber of Eternall joy.

Lord! let these golden Orbs thy hands that have
  All Graces Operations in them cleare   50
Bestow thy Holy Berill green and brave
  Upon my Soule, and rain sweet Dews down there.
  Upon my Heart and make the Application
  Of thy rich Grace, and mee its Habitation.

And let this golden Sphere of Grace shoure down   55
  Celestiall showers of Grace on mee I pray,
And let thy golden hands me lead and Crown
  With glory's Diadem in Graces way.
  Then as I Crownd in Glories Orb do stand
  I'le Sing the golden glory of thy Hand.   60

---

5 Pardon *orig.* Pardon for
12 *orig.* BeNum'd, and her Daughters Musick all doe sing ahone
18 that *orig.* till
26 As *orig.* As they
30 of *orig.* full of Green
37 Orb *orig.* Orb of Grace
38 Orbe is *orig.* Orbe's
45 doth ins.

3.2M   123[A]. MEDITATION. CANT. 5.14. HIS BELLY: [I,E,
1715   BOWELLS] IS AS BRIGHT IVORY OVERLAID WITH
                  SAPHIRES

The Costli'st Gem kept in Christs Ivory Box
  O're laid with Saphires such none else ere had,
Christs Key of grace this Cabinet unlocks
  And offers thee. Why then art thou so sad?

Such bright Affection in's bright bowells boiles 5
Up to thyself, may, glaze thy Cheeks with smiles.

That Precious Gem yea preciousest of all
Embedded in Christs bowells as they shine
Ore Covered with asure saphirs, Call
   To welcome it with brightsome looks of thine. 10
   Oh Happy thou! waring the brightest thing
   That Christs bright bowells alwaye weare within.

Then why shouldst thou, my soule, be dumpish, sad?
Frown hence away thy melancholy Face.
Oh! Chide thyselfe out of this Frame so bad. 15
   Seing Christs precious bowells thee Embrace
   One flash of this bright Gem that these bowells bring
   Unto thyselfe, may make thy heart to singe.

Thy Ivory Chest with Saph'rine Varnish fine
Ope Lord, give me thy Bowells Gem all deare. 20
My lumpish Lookes shall then yield smiles and shine.
   Thy brightsomness shall make my looks shine clear.
   If that love in thy Ivory Chist is mine
   My Countenance thy bowells Love shall Chime. [380]

---

3 this Cabinet *orig.* most graceously
5 in's *orig.* his
9 saphirs *orig.* saphers
10 it *orig.* them
12 alwaye weare *orig.* alwayes wears
20 Gem *orig.* Gem and then
23 in *ins.*
24 thy *orig.* shall thy

[**]4M   MEDITATION 123[B]. CANT. 5.15. HIS LEGS ARE AS
1715   PILLARS OF MARBLE SET (FOUNDED) ON SOCKETS [אֲדָנֵי
           BASES] OF FINE GOLD.

My search, my Lord, now having passed o're
  The province of my soule, to finde some geere
That for thyselfe is fit to Set before
  And Wellcome thee withall, But no good Cheare
  I in my Cogitations Orb can finde: 5
  Whose limits are too little for my minde.

My barren Heart is such an hungry Soile
  No Fruits it yields meet for thyselfe, my King,
Either for food or Raiment but defile
  What they come nigh. Parden then what I bring.   10
  Fain I would brighten bright thy glory, but
  Do feare my Muse will thy bright glory smoot.

Thy spirits Pensill hath thy Glory told
  And I do stut, commenting on the same,
While some bright flashes of thy glory, Would   15
  If touch my Windows, guild my glasses flame.
  This Pensill Rapts thee up in Glorys fold
  From thy gold head quite to thy Feet of gold.

Thy legs like Marble Pillars streight Strong, bright,
  Do beare and Carry all thy Bodie too,   20
That founded are upon thy Feet upright
  As golden Socks or Sockets, Tressles true
  Do fitly hold out that strong might of thine
  That bears up, and mentains thy Realm and'ts Shine.

They shew thy mighty strength, that doth mentain   25
  Thy Kingdom's Upright, Stately Welthy, and
Majesticke Righteous, Glorious right and Gain,
  All Conquoring and Ever more shall stand,
  And though thy Marble legs with feet of gold
  Treade on the dirty ground, most pure they hold.   30

Thy Marble Pillar-Legs on golden Feet
  Beare up and Carry on thy Realm in State
Among thy golden Candlesticks most sweet.
  Thou Walkst thereon and breakst all that thee hate.
  These are thy Pounderall wherewith thy foe   35
  Whether Sins, or Divells dasht to pieces goe.

O! let these marble legs and golden feet
  That do up hold, and Carry on aright
Thy blessed kingdom as it is most meet
  And make its shining glory shine most bright   [381]40
  And make my heart unlock its box of Wealth
  And thence its Love, thy treasure, send thyselfe.

Oh! that this stately, Wealthy Glorious Might
  Of thine, my Lord, inchant my heart might so
That all my heart and hearty Love most right   45
  Leap thence and lodge might in thy heart and go
  And on thy golden head sit singing sweet
  The Glory of thy Legs and golden feet.

---

12 Do *orig.* But
15 of *ins.*
16 glasses *orig.* glassey
23 hold *ins.*
25 mighty *ins.*
27 right and *ins.*
29 Marble legs *orig.* Marblegs ; feet *orig.* feed
35 wherewith *orig.* wherewithy Foes ; foe *orig.* foes
38 on *ins.*
40 its shining glory shine *orig.* it shine
41 box *orig.* box and
47 sit singing *orig.* might sing most

6.6M ⎫ 125. MEDITATION. CANT. 5.15. HIS COUNTENANCE IS
1715 ⎭ LIKE LEBANON, EXCELLENT AS THE CEDARS.

Lead me, my Lord upon mount Lebanon,
  And shew me there an Aspect bright of thee.
Open the Valving Doors, when thereupon
  I mean the Casements of thy Faith in mee
  And give my Souls Cleare Eye of thee a sight   5
  As thou shinst its bright looking Glasses bright.

If I may read thee in its name thou art
  The Hill, it metaphors, of Frankincense,
Hence all atonement for our Sins thy heart
  Hath made with God: thou pardon dost dispense.   10
  So thou dost whiten us, who were all O're
  All fould with filth and Sin, all rowld in goare.

What Costly stones, red Marble, Porphory
  And Cedars Choice in Lebanon abound
What Almugs and what Vines deliciously   15
  That Smell, are in this Lebanon then found?
  All Grace and gracious Saints are hereupon
  Compared to the smell of Lebanon.

When thou hast cleard my Faiths round appled Eye
  My Souls peirt Eye and Lebanon display   20
Her Glory and her Excellency high
  In Sweet perfumes and gaudie bright array
  And all grow tall, Strong, fragrant up from thee
  And of these Cedars tall I sprung one bee.

Then I shall see these precious square wrought stons   25
  Are to thy Zion brought, foundations laid,
And all these Cedars Choice, of Lebanon
  Are built thereon and spirituall Temples made.
  And still thy spirits Breathings make them grow
  And forth they flowrish, and their smell doth flow.   30

Lord let me stand founded on thee by grace
  And grow a Cedar tall and Upright here.   [382]
And sweeten me with this sweet aire apace.
  Make me a grape of Leb'nons Vine up peare.
  Let me then See Thy Glory, Lebanon   35
  And yield the smell of those sweet vines thereon.

My Circumcised Eare, and Souls piert Eye,
  Having their Spirituall Casements opening
And thou displaying thy bright majesty
  Thy shine and smell of Lebanon Crowd in   40
  At these gold-Casements of mine Ears and Eyes.
  They'l fill my Soul with Joyous Extasies.

Lord, make thine Aspect then as Lebanon.
  Allow me such brave sights and sents so sweet
Oh! Ravishing Sweet pour'd out my Soule upon.   45
  Fill all its empty Corners and there keep
  That so my breath may sing thy praise divine
  All smelling of thy Lebanons rich wine.

---

6 shinst *ins.*
18 Compared *orig.* Compar'd are
24 I sprung one bee *orig.* tall to spring in mee
29 Breathings *orig.* Beathings [**] them
46 empty *orig.* emty

9.8M	126. MEDITATION. CANT. 5.16.	חכן PALATE
1715	HIS MOUTH IS MOST SWEET	OR WINDPIPE, LATINE GUTHER

My Lord, my Love, my sov'reign, and supreme,
  Thy Word's my Rule, thy Law's my Lifes sweet line.
All Law subordinate not to this Beame,
  No right contains: but is of Sodoms shrine.
  Thy mouth's most sweet, the Windepipe of thy Lungs   5
  Conveighs all sweetness from thy Heart that throngs.

The spring of Life, and all lifes sweetness Choice
  Hatcht in thy Heart. (Oh! how sweet is this Chest?)
Comes bubbling up this path of Breath and Voice?
  This Highway is the thro'fare of thy Breast: 10
  Wherein its Vitall Breath runs in, and out
  Well loaded with sweet languague all about.

The golden Current of sweet Grace sprung in
  Thy Heart, Deare Lord comes Wafting on thy Tast
Sweetning thy Palate passing by its ring,   15
  And rowling in our borders thus begrac'te.
  Come tast and see How sweet his Current is.
  Oh! sweet breath passage, sweetend sweet as bliss.

The golden mine of sanctifying Grace
  That in thy heart is glorious indeed   20
In Golden streames come flowering out apace
  Through thy rich golden pipe, and so in speed,
  As golden liquour, running thence all ore
  Into thy Spouse's heart from Graces store.   [393]

That golden Crucible of Grace all sweet,   25
  Is thy sweet Heart, The golden pipe of Fame
Is thy sweet Windpipe, where thy spirits reech
  Comes breizing sweet perfumes out from the same.
  This is the golden gutter of thy Lungs
  And through thy mouth, by th'Palate sweetly runs.   30

Thy Palate hence not sweet but sweetness is
  It being made the thoroughfaire or way
Of all that sweetness of thy heart, and bliss
  That from thy heart to us thou dost Conveigh.
  How sweet then must thy Holy mouth neede bee   35
  Through which thy sweetning heart breath comes from thee?

Lord, make my Palates Constitution right
  Like to thy Palates Constitution fine:
That what comes from thy heart in heart delight
  Sweet to thy Palate may thus sweeten mine.   40

Then what disrellish to thy Palate shall
Shall to my Palate bee disrellisht all.

Then what shall to thy tast be sweet indeed
  Shall be most sweet unto my tast likewise.
What bitter to thy Palate doth proceed   45
  Shall to my Palate bitter up arise.
    Thy Hearts sweet Steame that doth thy Palate greet
    Will make my Tast with thy heart sweetness sweet.

Those Hony falls that in thy heart rise high
  Of Grace, and through the pipes of thy pure Lungs   50
Are brought into thy mouths bright Canopy
    And on my Garden herbs are shower'd in throngs
    Will sweeten all my flowers and herbs therein
    And make my Winde Pipe thy sweet praises sing.

---

6 from *orig.* in
17 his *orig.* this
30 th' *orig.* the
42 bee disrellisht *orig.* too disrellish
46 bitter *orig.* bitter bee
49 rise *orig.* arise

127. MEDITATION. CANT. 5.16. —HE IS ALTOGATHER
LOVELY נלן מחמדים ALL OF HIM, OR OF HIS EJUS
VEL IPSIUS TOTUM IS DESIRABLE.

4.IOM
1715

My Lord, when thou didst form mankinde the hand
  Of thine Omnipotency then did hold
The Vessell rightly well Engravd, and cleansd
  From dust right stild Omnisciencies Mould
    Wherein mankinde was run and shapt most bright   5
    With Properties, that fix on Objects right.   [384]

Hence I have power to Love and to desire.
  These brave Affections Choose such Objects which
Desireable and Lovely are t'infire

These bright affections that upon them pitch.   10
Such objects found by these affections sweet,
Desire draws in, and Love goes out to meet.

Of all things in the Orbs of Entity
Such as are best deckt up with such attire
Do these affections onely satisfy,   15
Which ever to the best of things aspire:
Though these may in some few things here up thrive
They're in thee, Lord, super-superlative.

Some things there bee within this Orb full fine,
And be desirable yet nothing here   20
Do all desirable, and Lovely shine
But all of thee, and thine most Lovely clear
For Excellency in thee's the Foundation
That to Desire and Love yieldes firmest station.

Thou altogether Lovely art, all Bright   25
Thy Loveliness attracts all Love to thee:
Yea all of Thee and Thine is Fair and White
Together or apart in highst degree.
Thy Person, Natures Properties all thine
Thy Offices, and Acts most lovely shine.   30

Rich Personated Deity most bright,
Milk white Humanity by God begot
Deckt with transplendent Graces shining Light
And sparkling Operations without spot.
All Gods Elect, Angells and saints All thine.   35
Thy Word and Ordinances most Divine.

A Spirituall ministry of Gracious Ware:
A path of Holiness: Blesst Conduct in't.
A way of Right pav'de ore beyond Compare
To thy Celestiall blissfull Palace mint   40
Where thou dost intertain thy saints in joy
Oh. Loveliness. Desirable and high.

All thee, and all of thee and thine arise
   Thus Lovely and Desireable appere
The Object of All Love, and purest joyes   45
   Exactly minted in Loves mold most cleare.   [385]
   Be thou the Object then that I attire
   With my best Love, and loveliest desire.

Then thou desirable and Lovely Rose
   Each part alone, or altogether art.   50
Oh! make thy Takingness that thus oreflows
   Take to thyselfe my love and all my heart.
   Then my Desire and Love shall sing this story
   That all of thee is lovely, in thy Glory.

---

1 mankinde *ins.*
2 Omnipotency *orig.* Omnipotence
7 power to *orig.* properties
9 are t'infire *orig.* mostly are to infire
21 shine *orig.* ware
22 most Lovely clear *orig.* [**] Lovely Cleare shine
25 Bright *orig.* White
27 Thine is *orig.* Thine's ; and *orig.* or
30 most *orig.* a most
41 Where thou dost *orig.* Wherein thou
49 Rose *orig.* [*]a[**]est Rose

12.12M ⎤   128. MEDITATION. CANT. 6.1. WHITHER IS THY
1715   ⎦   BELOVED GONE, OH! THOU FAIREST AMONG
                 WOMEN? &c.

My Dear-Deare Lord, my Heart is Lodgd in thee:
   Thy Person lodgd in bright Divinity
And waring Cloaths made of the best web bee
   Wove in the golden Loom of Hum'nity.
   All lin'de and overlaid with Wealthi'st lace   5
   The finest silke of sanctifying Grace.

Hence ev'ry minim of thy Humane Frame.
   Deckt up with Nature's brave perfections right,

And Decorated with rich Grace, Whose Flame
  In sparkling shines do ravish with delight   10
  So that thy Nature, and its Acts all shine
  And never miss the Right an Haire breadth fine.

Thy soule Divine array'de in Splendent Grace,
  The spirituall Temple, pinckt with precious Stones:
Like sparks of Glory glaze thy Spirits Face   15
  And glorious make thy Will with graces tones.
  Not one black tittle ere is in it found
  To dim the shine that in it doth abound.

Thy soule's a Spirituall Treasury, in Which
  Are Precious stones and spirituall Jewells laid,   20
The spirits spicery the gold mine rich
  Of Precious Grace. And Graces sugar Trade,
  The Warehouse of all Humane thoughts well Wrought
  In which there never came an Evill thought.

Thy Eares and Nose ware Graces Jewells bright.   25
  Thy sight walks out in Graces Paradise:
Thy smell is Courted with perfum'de delight.
  Thy Garden Flowers breath sweeter breath than spice,
  But if the serpent on these objects spit
  Sighs from thy soul, blow hence the venom quick.   30

Thy Feet o're burnished with glorious Grace
  Make all right steps, and not one step awry,
Leave Every footstep guilt with grace, a trace
  And golden track unto Celestiall Joy.
  Thy Tongue's tipt with sweet Heavenly Rhetorick   35
  Ne're spake amise. Grace from thy lips doth skip.   [386]

Thy Hands, milk white, were never yet beguild
  In Graces Almond milke washt ware no spot.
Thy fingers never toucht what sin defilde.
  Grace at thy fingers ends doth ever drop.   40
  Thy Head's a golden Pot of Manna fine
  A silver Tower of Gospell Weapons Prime.

Oh! what a glorious Lord have I? See here.
  When in the Gospell Glass his Beams dart on
The Brides [****]ve bridemaids looking on him cleare   45
  And make them ask her, Whither is he gone?
  Oh! Whither's thy Beloved bright declin'de
  Declare, thou fairest of All Womankinde.

Our heart is ravisht with his glory bright.
  Oh! Whither whither is he turnd aside?   50
Wee now indeed do greatly wish we might
  Him seeke with thee. His Spouse and blessed Bride!
  That happiness lodg'd in his Glorious face
  Will thence when seen slide int'our Hearts with Grace.

Lord, let thy Glorious Excellencies flame   55
  Fall through thy Gospells Looking Glass with might,
Upon my frozen heart, and thaw the same
  And it inflame with flaming Love most Light
  That in this flame my heart may ride to thee,
  And sing thy Glories Praise in Glories glee.   60

---

5 with *orig.* are with the
17 *orig.* And not a tittle black is in it found
20 Are *orig.* All ; laid *orig.* Cl[***]
31 burnished *orig.* burnisht *orig.* bur'd
32 *orig.* Do gild each foot
33 Leave *orig.* And leave
43 I? *ins.*
45 [****]ve *ins.*
50 whither *ins.*
59 may *ins.*
60 sing *orig.* sing the praise

25.1M   } 129. MEDITATION. CAN. 6.2. MY BELOVED IS
1715/6   }   GON INTO HIS GARDEN.

My Glorious Lord, what shall thy spouse, descry
    That flaming Glorious Beauty, Rich Divine,
Before mine Eyes? And shall my heart out cry
    Where's thy Beloved gone hence with his shine?
    That I may seeke him or shall she me sham,   5
    When saying; to his garden which I am?

This Garden which he's gone to can it bee
    Thyselfe thou fairest of all Women kinde?
Can he go from, and yet abide with thee?
    It must be so, if th'Garden's his Church designd.   10
    It rather shews where his he entertains
    Than th'sense that saith, and that unsaith the same.

Garden delights when he therein descends
    He makes his entertainments sweet for all.
These dainty Dishes disht up for Choice Friends   15
    Who enter there attendents to his Call.
    Eyesight Delights and blushy Rosey Flowers
    Clouds aromatick lodge in our Warm Towers.   [387]

Heart Ravishments: Delightfull joyes unto
    The highst inchantings of Nose, Eares and Eyes   20
With spirituall tunes, Perfumes and Beauties show
    Enriched all with all Celestiall joyes,
    The sweet sweet Gales of the spirits sweet Air
    With which Clouds aromatick can't compare.

Lord! let thy Holy spirit take my hand   25
    And opening thy Graces garden doore
Lead mee into the same that I well fan'd
    May by thy Holy Spirit bee all ore
    And make my Lungs thy golden Bagpipes right
    Filld with this precious Aire, thy praises pipe.   30

4 Beloved *orig.* Belov'd
5 him *ins.*
13 he therein *orig.* therein he
17 Rosey *orig.* Roses
23 the *orig.* the Sweet
25 my *orig.* mee by
26 And *orig.* My Hand, and ; Graces *ins.*

20.3M ⎫   130. MEDITATION. CANT. 6.2. MY BELOVED IS GONE
1716 ⎭   DOWN INTO HIS GARDEN, TO THE BEDS OF SPICES.

My sweet-sweet Lord who is it, that e're can
   Define thyselfe, or Mine affections strong
Unto thyselfe with inke? Who is the man
   That ever did, or can these riches sum?
     Thy sweetness no description can define   5
     Nor Pen and Inke can my hearts Love out line.

The Breathings of thy Spice beds Gardens Spot,
   And of thy Sweet spot o'flowers stowd in the Aire
This sweet breath breatht out from thy Garden knot
   Perfume the skies and all their riches fair.   10
     Thy Gardens Bed thy Civet Box gives vent,
     To th'Gales of Spiced Vapors, Sweetest sent.

Thy Bed of spices in thy Garden Spots,
   Perfumes most sweetly as they are inspir'd.
With thy rich spirits breath: thy flower Pots   15
   Breathe out such sweetness, that's by saint's desir'd
     Ascending up in gracious exercise
     Making these b[e]ds of spices thy sweet Joyes.

Thou dost delight to visit these, and make
   These spicy beds thy blissfull Couches bright   20
And Visits them even from thy Palace Gate
   And walkst their alies with most sweet delight.
     This sweetness that perfumes bright Glory clear
     Perfumes thy joyes, perfumed joyes are here.

And all the sweetness of these Beds of Spice   25
   Doth Spiritually perfume these beds of saints
That they breath in and out perfume, whose price
   Excells all precious jewells, never faints.
   Set me a Lilly in thy Bed of Spice,
   With sweeten'd breath, my Lord ere to rejoyce.   [388]30

If thou allowst me setting in this Bed,
   Of Spices set in spirituall ranks therein
With Gusts of spirituall Odors over sored,
   (Oh! Sweet perfum! oh blessed blissfull thing)
   I shall suck in and out as sweetend fare,   35
   As ever did perfume the Clear cleare Aire.

Lord, make my sweetned Lungs out sweet Breath send
   'T will make thy spice Beds still more sweet to bee.
This Aire all sweetned will its sweetness lend,
   And make my heart thereby more sweet for thee.   40
   I shall breath sweetness in and out to thee
   And in my spicy Lodgen will lodge thee.

The gales of Graces breath shall rise most sweet
   To thee, my Lord, me sweet with Graces spice.
A mutuall sweetness then shall be the reek.   45
   Thy Garden aire that [c]arrys there, my voice
   Then shall my tongue thy sweetend praises sing
   In tunes perfumed, thus on ery string.

---

11 Bed *orig.* Bed and
29 a Lilly *orig.* my Lord, a Lilly
30 my Lord ere *orig.* ever
47 sweetend *ins.*

15.4M   131. Meditation. Cant. 6.2. To the Beds of Spice to
1716   feed in the Garden, and to gather Lillies.

Dull, Dull, my Lord, my fancy dull I finde.
  Hast thou allowd no Grindlestone at all,
Unto thy Zion Fancies dull to grinde
  And make sharp edged when that thou dost call
  Thy servants up to carry on thy worke   5
  That from the same they may not ever shurk?

Will not the Vine of Lebanon yield Wine,
  To quicken up my Spirits? or have I
Not tasted of thy Wine, for to refine
  My Fancy at thy feast and't vivify?   10
  How should my heart vent bitter groans, to finde
  Such Spirituall deadness deadening my minde?

Dost thou come down into thy garden brave
  To feed and gather Lillies, fragrant, bright?
Shall I no Bed of Spice, or Spices have   15
  Rise up to entertain thee with Delight?
  Nor shall thy spicy Garden green, and Vine
  Hence entertain thee with her Lilly-Shine?

If thou feedst on my spice, my spice must flow,
  Then thou wilt feed my soull on spice Divine: 20
Com'st thou to get thy Lillies? get me so.
  Then I shall be well fed, and made all fine.
  Thine Ordinances then brieze spicy gailes
  Filling of thy, and my Delights the sails.   [389]

The Clouds of Grace in thy New Covenant skie   25
  By thy descent tapt soile down on this plot,
Their Sweet Spice-Showers of Precious grace, whereby
  Sweet showers of Grace upon thy Garden drop:
  And graces golden Pestill too doth pound
  Her Herbs, and spices, that sweet smells abound.   30

Here thus is Entertainment Sweet on this.
  Thou feedst thyselfe and also feedest us.
Upon the Spiced dainties in this Dish.
    Oh pleasant food! both feed together thus;
    Well Spicde Delights do entertain thee here.   35
    And thou thine entertain'st with thy good Cheare.

And yet moreover thou in thy spice beds dost
  Thy Elect Lillies gather and up pick
Out of the throng of stinking Weeds: and stowst
    Their natures with thy holy graces thick.   40
    That they of Lillies are made lillies fresh
    Which thou dost gather glories Hall to dress.

If thou, my Lord, thy spice bed make my Heart
  My Heart shall welcome thee with spiced joy.
If I'm thy lilly made by Graces Art   45
    I shall adorn thy Palace fragrantly.
    And when thou mee thy Spi[c]e bed interst in
    I'le thee on my Shoshannim Spic'de Songs sing.

---

2 allowd *orig.* allowd Zions
3 dull *orig.* sharp
6 they *ins.*
7 Wine, *orig.* Wine?
8 To *orig.* That
26 soile *orig.* down
32 also *ins.*
37 moreover *orig.* more
38 gather *orig.* gatherst ; pick *orig.* pickst
41 made *orig.* pure
48 orig. Spic'de tunes to thee shall my Shoshannim

9TH.7M
1716

132. MEDITATION. CAN. 6.3. — HE FEEDS AMONG THE
LILLIES.

Pardon my Lord, I humbly beg the same
  Of thy most blessed Gracious selfe thy hand.
For if I nothing touch thy glorious name
  Shewing its praise I shall unworthy stand.
  And if I 'tempt to celebrate thy fame   5
  It is too bright: my jagging pen will't stain.

The words my pen doth teem are far too Faint
  And not significant enough to shew
Thy Famous fame or mine affection paint
  Unto thy famous selfe in vivid hew.   10
  My jarring Pen makes but a ragged line
  Unfit to be enricht with glories thine.

But thus I force myselfe to speake of thee.
  If I had better thou shouldst better have.
It grieves me I no better have for thee.   15
  Finding thou art the Lilly growing brave
  Even of the Vally rich where lillies grow
  Of Graces Bright making a gracious show.   [390]

Those Lillies White all glorious shining bright
  'Mongst which thou feeding art sweet breathing flower   20
That Entertain thy sight and smell most right
  With sweetest Splender of rich Grace in power.
  I hope I am one of these Lillies pure
  Whose breath and Beauty do thy joy procure.

Lord make my Heart the Vally, and plant there   25
  Thyselfe the Lillie there to grow. No scorns
Shall me amuse, if I'me thy Lilly clear,
  Allthough I be thy Lilly midst of thorns.
  If I thy Lilly Fair and Sweet be thine
  My heart shall be thy Harbor. Thou art mine.   30

If I thy Vally, thou its Lilly bee.
  My Heart shall be thy Chrystall looking Glass
Shewing thy Lillies Face most cleare in mee
  In shape and beauty that doth brightly flash.
  My Looking Glass shall weare thy Lillies face   35
  As 'tis thy Looking Glass of Every Grace.

My Heart shall then yield thee the Object right
  Of both thy spirituall sight and smell most clear
Standing inrounded in in sweet delight.
  Thou growing Lilly in't dost feed too there   40
  Thus in the Vally and growst, very cleare
  And fill my vally with perfumed fare.

Make mee thy Lilly, Lord and be thou mine.
  Be thou the Lilly, me its vally right.
Thou th'lillie then shalt make my Vallys shine   45
  Thou feeding mongst the lillies, with delight,
  I then shall weare thy lillies Whitness fair.
  My Lungues like bellows shall puff out sweet air.

My Vally then shall filld be with sweet air.
  My songs shall blow out sweetend breath therein   50
That shall perfume the very aire that wears
  The aromatick breaths breathd out most thin.
  If thou my Lilly, I its Vally bee.
  My Breath shall lilly tunes sweet sing to thee.

---

9 fame *orig.* faint
25 the *orig.* thy
27 I'me *orig.* if thou makest me
32 Heart *orig.* Hart
34 orig. in shape and beauty that gives sparkling flash
35 face *orig.* Face
36 of Every *orig.* holding out
39 inrounded *orig.* rounded
40 in't *orig.* there ; feed *orig.* feed indeed
41 growst. *orig.* growst. oh! blesst seed.

11.9M   }   133. MEDITATION. CANT. 6.2. I AM MY
1716   }   BELOVEDS AND MY BELOVED IS MINE.

Ye Daughters of Jerusalem I pray
  Delude you not yourselves, think not
To steale from me my souls belov'd away.
  I my Beloveds am, and he my lot.
  He and his All yea all of him, is mine   5
  His Person, offices, his Grace and shine.

The Bridsgroom's all the Brids; his all is hers.
  He's not partable nor by parts give out;
Who hath him hath him all, all bright no blurs.   [391]
  He's what's hers. Or she's all him without.   10
  He faithfull to his spouse will ever bee.
  He'l not bag such that to him spoused flee.

Ye Daughters of Jerusalem ne'er please
  Your fancies with such thoughts as tell you do
That you may rob me of my Loved, and ceize   15
  Him for your own, oh never deale you so.
  The Bridsgroom, and his bride are Relates sure
  That never separation can endure.

Christ will not play the knave to shab me thus
  Though knaveishness of such sort youths oft Use.   20
And youthish Damsells to do so don't blush
  Yet shamefull't is and grossly to abuse.
  Your Virgin beauty will not taking bee
  Him by his Eyes t'inchant his love from mee.

Whom Christ espouseth is his spouse indeed.   25
  His spouse or bride no single Person nay.
She is a[n] agrigate so doth proceed
  Ad on it fore and can't be stole away
  And if yee thus be members made of mee
  He'l be your Bridsgroom, you his spouse shall be.   30

Thus you in me enjoynd shall be made bright
  And thus united his Choice spouse be made.
You'st be his Bride the Bridesgrooms great delight
  And thus we both shall bee most bright displaid.

Oh! Daughter then ye of Jerusalem   35
  Rest not in your Degenerate case at all
With all your soul endevour allwayes then
  To be espousd in heart to Christ, so shall
  Then my beloved in his glory bright
  Discoverd * * * shall be your hearts delight.   40

Then my Beloved your beloved shall bee
  And both make him one Spouse enrichd with grace
And when dresst up in glory and bright glee
  Shall sing together 'fore his blessed face
  Our Wedden Songs with Angell melody   45
  In ravishing notes throughout Eternity.   [392]

---

4 he my *orig.* he is mine
5 him, *orig.* him, that shines
7 Brids *orig.* Brids yet ; is *ins.*
16 oh never *ins.*
17 bride *ins.*
28 Ad *orig.* In[****]se Ad
30 Bridsgroom *orig.* Bridg
33 great *ins.*
34 bee *ins.* ; bright *orig.* Happy
36 case *ins.*

26.[*]M ⎫   134. MEDITATION. CANT. 6.4. THOU ART BEAUTIFUL
1716   ⎭   AS TIRZAH O MY LOVE COMELY AS JERUSALEM.

Thou fairest of the Fairest kind alive
  Thy Beauty doth ascend above Compare.
Thy shining face super superlative
  Like to Jerusalem most comely fair.
  Thy brightness, and thy Comeliness shines like   5

Most Happy Brides the bravest Beauty bright.

That eye that never did want sight to see,
   Nor t'see into the Nature of what's seen
Inravisht with thy Beautys glorious glee.
   Hath seen't and sets upon it highst Esteem.   10
   Though by Comparison it's not to lower
   Its excellence but raise our 'steem on't more.

Oh bright bright Beauty all of glorious Grace
   How doth its beams dance on thy Cheeks all cleare?
Setting both beauty and terrour on thy face   15
   Pleasant in Christs Eye and terrour to's foes all here
   A pleasing shine to Christ and yet send darts
   Of Terrour terrifying Wicked hearts.

Hence thou enjoyst a rich sunshining Grace
   Which most bright beams of beauty ever play   20
Most gloriously th'alurements of thy face
   Making the same Christ flower knot th[**] oft [*]ay
   That in this beautious rich thou reeching stand
   That Christ doth Come and taketh by the hand.

And to himselfe presents thee pleasantly   25
   A glorious bride without all spot or blame.
His Eyes and hearts delight eternally.
   Oh Bride most beautifull of blisfull fame
   The Hearts delight, Christ wears thee in his heart.
   His Eyes delight that ne're doth from thee part.   30

Thy Beauty is made of Heavenly Paint all Grace
   Of Sanctity Holy Within and Out
A Bride most bright for the King of Glorys face
   Whose beauty laid in Heavenly Colurs about
   That ravish doth the Eyes of Angells which   35
   Can't but gaze on't and all amaizd at it pitch.

And lest perchance any wrinckle on it light
   Or any freckle on thy beautious face

The silk and satin Robe, than milk more white
  Of Christ's own Righteousness o're all hath place.   40
  Hence all thy Beauty fits thee for Christ's Bed
  And he will Cover thee, with's White and Red.   [393]

---

10 highst *ins.*
21 th' *ins.*
22 th[**] oft [*]ay *orig.* of Delight
24 and *orig.* to
33 Bride *orig.* Bide
37 wrinckle *orig.* winckle
41 all *ins.*
42 will *orig.* will ever

14.11 }   135. MEDITATION. CAN. 6.4. TERRIBLE AS AN
1716   }   ARMY WITH BANNERS.

Thou far the fairest of all female dress
  Whose spirituall beauty doth arise with shine,
Of the Beams of the blesst son of Righteousness,
  Glazing thy face with glory all Divine.
  All sparkling Glory like as Moses's Face   5
  Shining was dreadfull so is thine with grace.

Thy Intellects a saphrin socket bears.
  Christ's flaming Torch of Grace that sanctifies
Thy Will Christs Cabinet of Rich Grace Wares
  Top full of Grace of Every sort and sise.   10
  Thy Body's like a golden Lanthorn trim
  Through which the lamps of Grace shine from within.

Thine Eye balls rowle like fiery balled sparkes
  That graces beams like fiery arrows fling
Whose fiery bullets, Graces flaming Darts   15
  Most terrible to such as rowle in sin.
  Thy Mouths Christs Morter piece lets granade fly
  Of th'holy Ghost all wicked Ones to 'stroy.

Nay Still th'more Artiliry is there.
   Thy Brazeel Bow's thy mouth, thy Tong's the string   20
That shoots his Arrows pild, both in and through
    The sinners soules that make deep wounds therein.
    Yet more, thy mouth doth use his furbusht sword.
    By thy bright tongue in truth his dreadfull word.

Christs golden Canon Balls that dash asunder   25
    Whereby thou Satans garrisons dost bomb.
Thy hands cast out like lightening sharp and Thunder
    And herewith thou dost Satans Souldiers Thum[p].
    Thy Mouth, thy Tongue, thy Eyes and Face are steeld
    With terrour when thou meets the foe in th'field.   30

And thou art armed in thy Coate of Male
    Made all of Graces golden Wyer bright
By th'best of artists ere in Heavens pale
    The holy Ghost that made it strong and tite.
    No Arrow that the foe lets flie can dint   35
    Or pierce it through or break thereof a lin[k].   [394]

Thou'rt rightly trained by thy Captain, who
    Hath rightly learnt thee words of his command.
Thou well * * * and Fiter fears no foe
    And makst good use of th'Weapons in thy hand.   40
    Thy Helmet Hope, thy Belt Christ's Truth, thy shie[ld]
    Of Faith all right, thy Fortitude have steeld.

Thy Excellency gracious hath thee made
    Full Terrible, in fight while thou art Eying
Thy bright bright Captain whose rich skill displaid   45
    Leading thee home with songs and Colours flying,
    And thus thou terrible in gracious manners
    Appearest like an Armed troop in Banners.

---

18 wicked *orig.* wiked
19 th' *orig.* theres *orig.* the
20 Thy *orig.* Chris
37 Captain, *orig.* Captain, and
39 well *orig.* well dost
46 thee *orig.* thee out of th'field

6.3M   136. Meditation. Cant. 6.5. Turn away thine
1717   Eyes from mee. For they have Overcome mee.

Oh! what a word is this thy Lips Let fall.
  Here in these drops of Honey dews whereby
Thou dost bedew mine Olive Copses all
    Within the garden of my Soul and joy?
    It's such a word so wondrous and so high   5
    Hadst not thou said that sure't was blasphemy.

How should it be, that thou should charge thy spouse
  To turn away her glanc[i]ng Eyes from thee?
Whose Charming glances are quick Flaming to ro[use]
    The dull affections in th'flaming Glee.   10
    And these glances which most delightfull bee
    That thou should say they overcome have mee.

What do these Eyes then raise thy Joys so much:
  And do they so dilate thy Spirits pure
To such a breadth though thou dost joy in such,   15
    Thy Spirits run so from thy heart, it's sure.
    What [do] these [Ey]es then rob thy heart of all
    Its Vitall spirits that it fainting falls?

O wondrous * * * that doth sorely Cramp
  Our Wondring Faculty and make it Strain   20
Untill it feeble grows and groweth faint:
    If such Eyes sparkling dart us with their flame!
    Art thou my Lord who art too strong for all
    Orecome hereby when they upon thee fall?

But yet this thy serprize seems Rationall   25
  In some respect seing thy glorious selfe
Stand glor[i]ously portrayed Ever shall
    Within thy Spouses Eyes in th'richest Wealth
    That Graces gold mine hath in it that it seems
    Thou must these Eyes esteem, or thy honor 'steems: [395]30

[***]ing thy Spouse that doth consist of all
  Gods blesst Elect regenerate within
[T]he tract of time from first to last send shall
  From her bright Eyes her gracious beams and fling
  I wonder't would be topping very high   35
  If that such Eyes should not advance thy joy.

Then let the Beams of my souls eyes ev'n meet
  The brightsome Beams of thy blesst Eye my Lord,
And in their meeting let them sweetly greet
  And back return laded as each affords.   40
  Mine then return'd well loaded with thines flame
  Shall tune my * * * to sing thy glory's fame.

My Soul then quickend by thy beames brought in
  By my souls Eyebeams and glaz'd be thereby
With glorious Grace that will mee make more Sing   45
  Thy praise, my Lord, then shalt thou have more joy.
  My Soul strung with thy grace as golden Wier,
  Will by its musick Raise thy joy the Higher.

---

1 thy Lips *orig.* my Lord
8 Eyes *orig.* face
9 Flaming *orig.* Flaming Glee
10 The *orig.* That will the ; affections *orig.* affections up t[******]se
11 glances *orig.* glances should thee see [*****] Eyes be
12 have *ins.*
25 this *orig.* this they
29 hath *orig.* hath so ; in it *ins.*
32 regenerate *orig.* regenerated
35 be *ins.*
44 and glaz'd *orig.* glazed shall
45 that *orig.* that make

15.7M   }   137. Meditation. Cant. 6.5. Thy hair is like a
1717   }   flock of Goats that graze on mount Gilliad.

How precious are thy thoughts my Lord, to mee?
   O that my thoughts on mee were Crystalliz'd
Within the same, like Gems all sparkling bee
   Like Gilliads flock of Goats by his so prizde,
   A precious remedy for th' Souls Distempers.   5
   A spirituall Cure on which my soule adventures.

How doth this praise thy Spouse whose Hair doth shine
   Here like a flock of Goats that Gilliad [g]raze
And by their keepers set and Order'd fine,
   And Stately go in their slick Glory rayes,   10
   These hairs assembled like a flock in fold
   On Gilliads top, there feeding on to hold.

Thy Gilliads top Thy Testimonies place,
   In Zions mount thy testimonies there
Thy Spirituall pasture whose frim grass is Grace.   15
   The Spouses Hairs, thy flock, feed on this Cheere.
   With Grace thou feedst and fatst thy flock and down
   Dost make them ly, and in these folds them Crown.   [396]

In the High places of the City where
   Wisdome lifts up her Voice and food in't gives   20
Unto the Flock upon her head and there
   Administers them grace that they may live,
   These Spirituall Hairs do ware a Spirituall grace
   Feeding in Graces pastures thrive apace.

Are these thy spouses Curled hairs trimd fine   25
   Adorning her all in rich Graces shine
Like Gilliads Flocks that Graze her sweet herbs prime?
   Make me then one of them an hair of thine
   Fed in thy fold. Assemblies pure and fair
   With spirituall Crisping pins adorn my hair.   30

If thou dost make mee thus one of the Hairs
  Even of thy spouse and in thy 'semblies fit
Me with thy Spirits Crisping pins prepare
  Me as a Curled lock thy glory t'hit,
    I'st honour then thy Spouse and thee also   35
    As I like one of Gilliads flock do grow.

---

2 mee *orig.* thee
3 like Gems all *orig.* Gems all bee
4 flock *orig.* flock [***] would they sh[****]ing
8 that *orig.* that graze doth [****] graze *orig.* on gilliad doth graze
9 And *orig.* And tended ; set *ins.*
10 go *orig.* going ; slick *orig.* slick chose
20 her *orig.* her head
31 mee *orig.* my
33 prepare *orig.* pure *orig.* prepare

<table>
<tr><td rowspan="3">25.9
1717</td><td>138. MEDITATION. CAN. 6.6. THY TEETH ARE LIKE A</td></tr>
<tr><td>FLOCK OF SHEEP THAT COME UP FROM WASHING</td></tr>
<tr><td>WHEREOF EVERY ONE BEARS TWINS.</td></tr>
</table>

My blessed blessing Lord I fain would try
  To heave thy Glory 'bove the Heavens above,
But finde my lisping tongue can never prie
  It up an inch above this dirt nor move
    Thy brightsom glory o're this dirty slough   5
    We paddle in below and Wallow now.

But though I can but stut and blur what I
  Do go about and so indeed much marre
Do thy bright shine. I fain would slick up high
  Although I foul it by my pen's harsh jar.   10
    Pardon my faults: they're all against my Will.
    I would do Well but have too little skill.

What Golden words drop from thy gracious lips.
  Adorning of thy speech with Holy paint,
Making thy spouses teeth like lambs that skip,   15
  Or flock of sheep that come from Washing quaint.

Each bearing twins a pleasant sight to spy
Whose little lambs have leaping play and joy.   [397]

* * * [**]ne whose Teeth
  * * * a flock of pure Washt Sheep most white: 20
* * * borne babe and Church that hath reliefe
  Whose name is in the book of life wrote right
  The Newborn Soule and the society
  Of such espoused to my Lord most High.

[W]hat are these Teeth? pray shew, Some do suppose   25
  They are the spouses Military armes:
The Arguments that do destroy her Foes,
  And do defend the Gospell truths from harms,
  But Teeth in Sheep are not their Wepon though
  The Lions teeth and Cur dogs teeth are so.   30

[Bu]t others * * * they note Christ's ministers:
  That dress the Spouses food. Yet such from Cooks.
* * * these are 'ployd like teeth 'bout meat as its dresser
  Yet still this seems a lesson not in books.
  Methinks Christs Ministers may rather beare   35
  The name of Cooks, than Teeth, that eat the fare,

Hence methinks that they righter judge, that hold
  These Teeth import true Faith in Christ alone
And Meditation on the Gospell, should
  Be signifide thereby to everyone.   40
  Teeth are for the eating of the Food made good
  And Meditation Chawing is the Cud.

The proper use of Teeth gives the first stroke
  Unto the Meat and food we feed upon
And fits it for the stomach there to soake   45
  In its Concoction for nutrition.

And Meditation when't is Concocted there
  Takes its rich liquour having nurishment,
And distributes the same Choice Spirituall Cheer

Through all the new man by its instrument,   50
And hence the means of Grace do as I thinke
Give nurishment hereby, as meate and drinke.

This Faith, and Meditation a pair appeare
As two like to the two brave rows of Teeth
The Upper and the neather, well set cleare   55
Exactly meet to chew the food, beliefe
Doth eate by biting; meditation
By Chewing spiritually the Cud thereon.

* * * two those two exactly answer right
* * * Grindeing them and operation.   [398]60
Those in a naturall sense in spirituall * * *
These two, and so they pare each in their Station
The fore and hinder teeth, that bite and Grinde.
So spiritually these bite and Chew in minde.

They paire each other too, in whiteness cleare   65
As those like Olivant, these sparkling show
With glorious shine in a most brightsome geare
Of spirituall whitness that exceeds pure snow
Christ's milkwhite Righteousness and splendent Grace
Faith doth and Meditation ever trace.   70

---

number 138 *orig.* 128
15 lambs *orig.* lams
37 that *ins.*
38 and *conj.*
42 chawing *orig.* chaing
45 to *orig.* doth
51 do as *orig.* thus
58 the Cud *ins.*
59 right *orig.* aright
66 sparkling *orig.* sparkling whiteness
67 brightsome *orig.* bright
70 ever *orig.* ever shine

MEDITATION 139. CANT. 6.[7.] LIKE A PIECE OF A
POMEG[RA]NATE ARE THY TEMPLES WITHIN THY LOCKS.

My Deare, Deare Lord, oh that my Heart was made
   Thy Golden Vissell filld with Graces Wine.
Received from thy Fulness and displai'de
   Even by thy spouse in her sweet Wine Cup fine
   Unto thy blessed Selfe to drinke at Will.   5
   Of her sweet Wine unto thy very fill.

Thy Love * * * in thy Spouses Countenance.
   Is so deli[ghted] with her Temples State,
The Seate of Modesty that in't doth glance;
   Her Temples like a piece of Pomegranate   10
   That with Arteriall blood blossom with blushes,
   That in her Temples yield do spirituall flushes.

The Temples where's the purest blood indeed
   Impregnate with the working Spirits ripe.
That Warm and work the Brains they proceed,   15
   Even from the Heart through th'Arteriall pipe
   Hence modest Looks and head that contemplate
   The Temples proper exercise and State.

The Temples like a piece of Pomegranate
   Import thy spirituall Beauty and spirits high   20
In purest heart blood through th'Arteriall Gate
   Into the Head. Hence these thy Visage dy
   Pomegranat-like with Ruby blushey stains
   And sharpen do thine Eyes with spirituall strains.

And through thy Temples Silver Wickets go   25
   Int'Contemplations Temple brave and here
In Spirituall Contemplations labour do
   On Christs rich Grace, and Glory everywhere.
   And how to manage well in Graces wayes
   Sin to destroy. Gods Ordinances raise.   [399]30

Number 139 *orig.* 129
2 with *orig.* with thy
13 where *orig.* were
15 Brains *orig.* Brains as
16 th' *orig.* the
20 Beauty *orig.* Beauty that up fly
24 do *ins.*
26 Temple *orig.* Temple wheres brave

14.9M ⎫   [MEDITATION] 140. CANT. 6.7. AS A PIECE OF A
1717   ⎬   POMEGRANATE ARE THY TEMPLES WITHIN THY LOCKS.
       ⎭

My all Deare Lord, I fain would thee adore
    But finde my Pen, and Inke too faint to doe't.
And all the Praise with which my heart runs ore
    Unto thyself is but a poor dull note,
        That thou in thy great love thy blesst Delight   5
        Should set upon thy Spouse and to such hight.

Them which thou here thus dost Court saying even thus,
    Like to a piece of a Choice Pomegranate
Thy Temples shine and glaze thy Cheeks that blush,
    With their Arteriall heart blood, modest state.   10
        Whose Vitall heate and Spirits in those pipes
        Make peart thy Countenance in gracious plites.

Th'Arteriall pipes that from thy heart do run
    Conveigh unto thy Temples the best Cheare
Of Hearty spirits that to thy Temples come,   15
    And dy them like a pomegranate looks cleare.
        And make thy Cheeks to ware a Scarlet Maske
        Of Modest blushes, on thy Cheeks well dasht.

Thy Countenance hence is the Looking Glass
    Into thy heart wherein in cleare cleare Shapes   20
Appear doth Choice Humility that doth pass
    Most Currant coin in Graces Markets, Mates.

These pomegranated Temples exercise
A Contemplation of a Spirituall Guise.

A spirituall Beauty on the spouse hence flames   25
  That's Emblemized by the Pomegranate
Unto us on the temples by its grains
  Wearing a Scarlet dy upon their shape
  All holding out a spirituall Beauty fresh
  And Chiefly to Christ's Eye in loveliness.   30

My Lord my Temples pomegranate make thus
  That I may ware this Holy Modesty
Upon my Face maskt with thy Graces blush.
  That never goes without Humility.
  Thy lovely object then all grac'd shall bee   35
  And Humbly sing forth graces notes to thee.   [131]

---

3 the *orig.* my
9 that *orig.* with
14 Cheare *orig.* Cheere
15 that *ins.*
21 that *orig.* that was
22 Markets *orig.* courts
31 make *orig.* thou
35 grac'd *orig.* grace

2.1M
1717/8   }   MEDITATION 141. CANT. 6.8.9. THERE ARE
THREESCORE QUEENS, AND FOURSCORE CONCUBINES,
AND VIRGINS WITHOUT NUMBER.

My Only Dear, Dear Lord I search to finde
  My golden Arck of Thoughts, thoughts fit and store.
And search each Till and Drawer of my minde
  For thoughts full fit to Deck thy kindness o're.
  But find my storehouse Empty of such thoughts   5
  And so my words are Empty, ragged, naught.

Thoughts though the fairest Blossoms of my minde,
  Are things too loose and light t'strew at the gate
Of thy bright Palace. My words hence are winde
  Moulded in print up thee to decorate.   10
  Hence th'glory of thy Love Whose Sunshine here
  I shall but darken with my dusty geere.

Hence I do humbly stand, and humbly pray,
  Thee to accept my homely Style although
It's too too hurden a bearing blancket, nay   15
  For to lap up thy Love in, it to show.
  When spruiced up therein, it seems like thatch
  Upon a golden Palace (Dirty slatch.)

Thy Love dropt on thy spouse's Loveliness
  Out measures all Dimention ne'er so wide.   20
Nay Angills pen can't pencill out its dress
  Nor can its length or breadth ere out describe:
  They never can thy gloryous Love out lay
  Whose brightness doth out shine the brightest day.

All Virgins in their Virginall Attire: 25
  Ladies of Honour eighty in array
And threescore Queens robde shining out like fire
  Can never match thy spouses Beauty gay.
  Though these for Number and for Glory rise
  In sparkling glory yet not to her Sise.   30

Thy boundless Love thy spouses boundless prove
  Doth take up all and in't did ever latch.
Oh Boundless Loveliness, and boundless Love
  You neither either ever over match.
  Yet know this thing, thy Boundless Love hath made   35
  This Loveliness thus boundless where it's laid.

Oh! let thy boundless Love my Lord, a Kiss
  Bestow on me and joyn me to thy Dove
That is but one, Whose members have such Bliss

And in its blissfull beams I'st ever move,   40
My portion then shall far excell the share
These Queens and Concubines and Virgins weare.   [132]

If one bright beam of this thy boundless Love
  Do light on me, enlightend I shall bee
To Cooe thy praise as joyned to thy Dove   45
  And double back thy Love with songs to thee.
    Thy Love I'le thus requite with Songs I'le sing
    Unto thy lovely selfe, under loves Wing.

---

8 the *orig.* thy
9 are *orig.* are but
12 geere *orig.* geer
14 accept *orig.* except
15 a *ins.*
18 Dirty *orig.* a Dirty
31 prove *orig.* Beauty
32 ever *orig.* ever laye
34 match *orig.* dodge *orig.* Charge
45 joyned *orig.* joynd

4.3M   ⎫   142. MEDITATION. CAN. 6.9. MY DOVE IS ONE THE
       ⎬   ONELY ONE OF HER MOTHER THE CHOICE ONE OF
1718   ⎭   HER THAT BARE HER. &C.

What shall I say, my Deare Deare Lord? most Deare
  Of thee! My choisest words when spoke are then
Articulated Breath, soon disappeare.
  If wrote are but the Drivle of my pen,
    Beblackt with my inke, soon torn worn out unless   5
    Thy Holy spirit be their inward Dress.

What, what a say is this? Thy spouse doth rise.
  Thy Dove all Undefiled doth excell
Allthough but one the onely in thine Eyes
  All Queens and Concubines that beare the bell.   10
    Her excellence all excellency far
    Transcends as doth the sun a pinking star.

She is the Onely one her mother bore.
   Jerusalem * * * above esteems
Her for her Darling, her choice one therefore   15
   Thou holdst her for the best that ere was seen.
   The sweetest Flower in all thy Paradise
   And she that bore her Made her hers most Choice.

That power of thine that made the Heavens bow,
   And blush with shining glory ever cleare   20
Hath taken her within his glorious brow
   And made her Madam of his Love most Deare,
   Hath Circled her within his glorious arms
   Of Love most rich, her shielding from all harms.

She is thy Dove, thy Undefiled, she shines   25
   In thy rich Righteousness all Lovely, White
The onely Choice one of her Mother, thine
   Most beautifull beloved, thy Delight.
   The Daughters saw and blessed her, the Queens
   And Concubines her praisd and her esteem.   30

Thy Love that fills the Heavens brimfull throughout
   Coms tumbling on her with transcendent bliss
Even as it were in golden pipes that spout
   In streams from heaven, Oh! what love like this?
   This comes upon her, hugs her in its Arms   35
   And warms her spirits. Oh! Celestiall Charms.   [133]

Make me a member of this spouse of thine
   I humbly beg deck thus, as Tenis Ball
I shall struck hard on th'ground back bounce with shine
   Of Praise up to the Chamber floor, thy Hall,   40
   Possesses. And at that bright Doore I'l sing
   Thy sweetest praise untill thou'st take me in.

---

2 words *orig.* words spoken then are
3 Articulated *orig.* Are but articulated
5 my *ins.* ; torn *orig.* torn and
11 Her excellence *orig.* Whose excellence doth
20 glory *orig.* glory cleare
23 within his *orig.* with thy

13.5M
1718 } 143. MEDITATION. CAN. 6.10. WHO IS SHE THAT LOOKS FORTH AS THE MORNING. FARE AS THE MOON CLEARE AS THE SUN. TERRIBLE AS AN ARMY WITH BANNERS.

Wonders amazed! am I espousd to thee?
  My Glorious Lord? what shall my bit of Clay
Be made more bright than brightest Angells bee.
  Looke forth like as the Morning every way?
  And shall my lump of Dirts ware such attire?   5
  Rise up in heavenly Ornaments thus, higher?

But still the Wonders stand, shall I looke like
  The glorious morning that doth gild the skie
With golden beams that make all day grow light
  And View the World ore with its golden Eye?   10
  And shall I rise like fair as the fair Moon,
  And bright as is the Sun, that lights Each room?

When we behold a piece of China Clay
  Formd up into a China Dish compleat.
All spiced ore as with gold sparks display   15
  Their beauty all under a glass robe neate.
  We gaze thereat and wonder rise up will
  Wondring to see the Chinees art and skill.

How then should we and Angells but admire
  Thy skill and Vessell thou hast made bright thus   20
Out for to look like to the Morning tire
  That shineth out in all bright Heavenly plush,
  Whose golden beams all Varnish ore the skies
  And gild our Canopy in golden wise?

Wonders are nonplust to behold thy spouse   25
  Look forth like to the morning whose sweet rayes
Gild ore our skies as with transparent boughs
  Like Orient gold of a Celestiall blaze.
  Fair as the Moon, bright as the sun most cleare
  Gilding with spirituall gold graces bright Sphere.   30

O Blessed! Virgin Spouse shall thy Sharp lookes
  Gild o're the Objects of thy shining Eyes
Like fairest Moon, and Brightest Sun do th'Fruits
    Even as they make the morning shining rise?   [134]
    The fairest moon in'ts socket's Candle light   35
    Unto the Night and th'sun's days Candle bright.

Thy spouses Robes all made of spirituall silk
  Of th'Web wove in the Heavens bright Loom indeed,
By the Holy spirits hand more whit than milk
    And fitted to attire thy soule that needs.   40
    As th'morning bright's made of the suns bright rayes
    So th'spirits Web thy souls rich Loom o're layes.

Oh! spouse adorned like the morning Cleare
  Chasing the night out from its Hemesphere.
And like the fair face of the Moon: whose Cheere,   45
    Is very brave and like the bright sun peares,
    Thus gloriously fitted in brightest story
    Of Grace espousd to be th'king of glory.

And thus deckt up methinks my Eare attends
  Kings, Queens and Ladies Query. Who is this?   50
Enravisht at her sight, how she out sends
    Her looks like to the morning filld with Bliss,
    Fair as the Moon, Clear as the Sun in'ts Costs
    And terrible as a bannerd host?

And all in Graces Colours thus bedight   55
  That do transend with glorys shine, the sun
And Moon for fairness and for glorious light
    As doth the sun a gloworms shine out run.
    No wonder then and if the Bridesgroom say
    Thou art all fair my Love, Yea Every way.   60

May I a member be, my Lord, once made
  Here of thy spouse in truest sence, though it bee
The meanest of all, a Toe, or Finger 'rayde
  I'st have enough of bliss, espousd to thee.

Then I in brightest glory ere't belong   65
Will Honour thee singing that Wedden Song.

---

20 Thy *orig.* This
27 our *orig.* our Batlements ; transparent *orig.* transparent layers
33 th' *orig.* the
34 shining *orig.* shining as they rise
39 By *orig.* All by
40 soule *orig.* soule and feed
46 peare *orig.* Chee
48 th' *orig.* th'unto the
52 to *ins.* ; as *orig.* as is
54 as *orig.* as is
56 do *orig.* to
63 of all *orig.* member
66 singing *orig.* sing

14.7M ⎫   144. MEDITATION. CANT. 6.11. I WENT DOWN INTO
1718   ⎬   THE GARDEN OF NUTS TO SE THE FRUITS OF THE
       ⎭   VALLY, TO SE WHETHER THE VINE, FLOWERISHED
                AND THE POMEGRANATE BUDDED.

Eternall Majesty, my blessed Lord,
    Art thou into thy Nutty Garden come?
To se the Vallys fruits on thy accord:
    Whether thy Vines do flowrish and thick hunge
    To se whether thy Pomegranates do bud?   5
    And that thy nuttree gardens fruit is good?

Am I a grafted Branch in th'true true Vine?
    Or planted Pomegranat thy Garden in
And do I flowerish as a note of Wine?
    And do my pomegranates now bud and spring?   [135]10
    Oh let my blossoms and my Buds turn fruite
    Lest fruitless I suffer thy prooning Hook.

And with thy spirituall Physick purge thou mee:
    My very Essence that much fruite't may beare.
Most joyous and delightfull unto thee.   15

Yea spirituall Grapes and Pomegranates most fare.
If in thy Nut Tree Garden I am found
Barren, thy prooning knife will Cut and Wound.

If in thy nuttery, I should be found
   To beare no Nutmegs, Almonds, but a nut   20
All Wormeate, or in barrenness abound
   I well may feare thy prooning hook will Cut
   And Cut me off as is the fruitless Vine:
   That evermore doth fruitfulness decline.

But when thou in thy garden dost descend   25
   And findst my branch clusterd with spirituall Grapes;
And my trees limbs with fruits downward to bend.
   Each bow's full reev'd with spirituall Pomegranates.
   My Vines and blossom and the Grapes thereon
   Will smell indeed like smell of Lebanon.   30

Shall this poore barren mould of mine e're bee
   Planted with spirituall Vines and pomegranates?
Whose Bud and Blossome flowrish shall to thee?
   And with perfumed joys thee graciate?
   Then spirituall joyes flying on spicy Wings   35
   Shall entertain thee in thy Visitings.

And if thou makest mee to be thy mold
   Though Clayey mould I bee, and run in mee
Thy spirits Gold, thy Trumpet all of gold,
   Though I be Clay I'st thy Gold-Trumpet bee,   40
   Then in Angelick melody I will
   Trumpet thy Glory and with gracious Skill.

---

2 thou *orig.* thou come
20 Almonds *orig.* Almonds filberts
25 thou *orig.* thou dost ; dost *orig.* down
30 like *orig.* like Lebanon
38 and *orig.* and therein
39 spirits *orig.* spirits mettle

19.9M } 145. Meditation. Can. 6.12. Or ere I was aware
1718   }   my soule had made mee like the Chariots of
       }   Aminadab.

Alas! my Lord, how should my Lumpish Heart,
    Ascend the golden Ladder of thy praise
With packs of sweetest Tunes prest like a Carte
    Loaded with cold hard iron, sorrows layes?
    Seing thy people tread down under feet,   5
    Thy will reveald, as dirt within the street.   [136]

I do constrain my Dumpishness away
    And to give place unto a spirituall Verse
Tun'd on thy glorious joys and to Conveigh
    My notes upon the same, and my heart seirce   10
    From all such dross till sweet tund prais pierce thro'
    Those Clouds of Damps to come thy throne unto.

What shall mine Ears, thy Rhetorick displaid
    Be lind with Melancholy Dark and sad?
Whilest thus thou singst, My soule I wist not, made   15
    Me like the Chariots of Aminadab?
    Whirld up in heart transporting Raptures bright
    And spiced incoms Wonderfull Delights.

Oh! what a speech is this, thy lips do vent.
    My soul as I walk in my Nut tree Vaile   20
I wist not how its flourishing Vines out sent
    Such reechs about me now within'ts pales,
    That me enravished and me they did
    Make like the Chariots of Aminadib.

Thy Gardens Graces breizing on thee bring   25
    Thee Welcome when thou Visitst it all bright
Transport thy soul as it on Angells Wings
    Flyes to thy Paradise of all delight
    Or ere I wist thou saist. And I it see
    To be a word too wonderfull for mee.   30

My Gracious Lord, take thou my heart and plant
  Each sanctifying Garden Grace therein.
Make it thy nut tree Vaile [***] have no want
  And tune its graces to thy songs, My King,
    When thou unto thy praise my heart shalt tune   35
    My heart shall tune thy praise in sweetest fume.

---

4 cold hard iron, sorrows *orig.* iron, prest down sorrows
6 within *orig.* is in
11 till *orig.* and
16 Aminadab *orig.* Aminadib
18 incoms *orig.* incoms of
23 did *orig.* bad
24 Make *orig.* Made ; Aminadib *orig.* Aminadab
28 thy *orig.* my
33 Vaile *orig.* Vally ; to *conj.* ; have *ins.*

11.11M ⎱ 146. MEDITATION. CANT. 6.13. RETURN, OH
1718   ⎰   SHULAMITE, RETURN RETURN.

My Deare Deare Lord I know not what to say:
  Speech is too Course a web for me to cloath
My Love to thee in, or it to array
  Or make a mantle; wouldst thou not such loath?
    Thy Love to mee's too great, for mee to shape   5
    A Vesture for the same at any rate.   [137]

When as thy Love doth Touch my Heart down tost
  It tremblingly runs, seeking thee its all
And as a Child, when it its nurse hath lost
  Runs seeking her, and after her doth Call.   10
    So when thou hidst from me, I seek and sigh.
    Thou saist return return Oh Shulamite.

Rent out on Use thy Love thy Love I pray.
  My Love to thee shall be thy Rent and I
Thee Use on Use, Intrest on intrest pay.   15
    There's none Extortion in such Usury.

I'le pay thee Use on Use for't and therefore
  Thou shalt become the greatest Usurer.
But yet the principall I'le neer restore.
  The same is thine and mine. We shall not Jar.   20
  And so this blessed Usury shall be
  Most profitable both to thee and mee.

And shouldst thou hide thy shining face most fair
  Away from me. And in a sinking wise
My trembling beating heart brought nigh t'dispare   25
  Should cry to thee and in a trembling guise,
  Lord quicken it; drop in its Eares delight
  Saying Return, Return my Shulamite.

---

3 in, *orig.* in. ; Such stuff I loath, th[***] ; or it *ins.*
11 hidst *orig.* didst
13 Love thy Love *orig.* Love my Lord
14 Rent *orig.* Rent I pay
16 such *orig.* this

1. OF IM   }   147. Meditation. Cant. 6.13. That wee may
1719   look upon thee.

Had I Angelick skill and on their wheele
  Could spin the purest puld white silk into
The finest twine and then the same should Reele
  And weave't a satten Web therein also
  Or finest Taffity with shines lik'of gold   5
  And Deckt with pretious stones, brightst to behold.

And all inwrought with needle work most rich,
  Even of the Holy Ghost to lap up in.
My Heart full freight with love refinde, the Which
  Upon thy Glorious selfe I ever bring   10
  And for thy sake thy all fair spouse should wear't
  Some glances of the same I to her beare

That Cloath her may who in her mourning Weeds

As sorrowing she searches thee about
That saith: Oh Shulamite Our eye much bleeds.   15
Turn turn that it may look on thee right out.
That we may looke upon thee, and behold
Thy ravishing beauty that thy sweet face unfolds.   [138]

That sparkling Airiness thy Cheeks do lodge
Laid on them by the Holy Ghost in Grace   20
Do send such sparkling flashes without Dodge
Those Charms that took our Eyes * * * a pace
A sight thereof: and ever more would bed
Upon these Cheeks of all their sight the head.

The brightest beauty Pensill ever drew   25
Laid in the Richest Colours gold could gain,
The shiningst glory the suns face ere knew,
The sparklingst shine nature did ere attain
Are but black spot and smoot on brightest faces
Unto thy beauty enlaid all with graces.   30

The bodies Eyes are blind; no sight therein
Is Cleare enough to take a sight of this.
It's the internall Eye sight takes this thing;
This glorious sight the sin-blind Eye doth miss.
Th'Internall Eye with Christ's Eye salve annointed   35
Is on this beauteous face alone well pointed.

Hence 'noint mine Eyes my Lord with thine Eye salve
That they may view thy spouses Beauty pure.
Whose sight passt on thyselfe do thence Resolve
To lodge and with the Shulamite Endure   40
That grace that from this fulness make her shine
Brightst in mine Eyes to sing her praise a[nd] thine.

---

1 Angelick skill *orig.* Angeliskill ; wheele *orig.* Wheele,
4 weave't *orig.* weave it
11 should *orig.* doth
12 I to her beare *orig.* thus do her give t
13 *orig.* That thus her courts Cloathd in her Sighing Weeds.

14 she *orig.* she [***] her search for thee about
15 That saith *orig.* Turns turn
22 that took *ins.*
39 lodge *orig.* lodge on

3.3M ⎫
    ⎬   148. MEDITATION. CAN. 7.1. HOW BEAUTIFUL ARE
1719 ⎭   THY FEET WITH SHOOES, OH PRINCES DAUGHTER?
            THE JOYNTS OF THY THIGHS ARE AS JEWELLS &C.

My Blessed Lord, should I arrive unto
    That rich propriety that makes mee thine,
If otherwise though thou thereto say'th noe.
    I am in a bad case indeed and pine.
    If I be thine thou then wilt set thine Eye   5
    Upon my feet; their beauty thou will spy.

In my returning unto thee wilt say
    How beautious are thy feet with shooes, behold.   [139]
Then thou indeed wilt praises give my way.
    My feet do take, my thigh joynts like rich gold   10
    Adornd with Jewels gloriously do shine,
    The work of an Artificers hand most fine.

As I return to thee my errours fro
    Thou wilt mee see and say of Mee behold:
Thy feet all beautious with shooes up grow.   15
    Thy walke's more shines than paths all pavde with gold;
    Thy beauteous shooes all laid all ore so trim
    And jew'ld thigh joynts grace the way Walkt in.

My walk to thee then in the Way of Faith
    And of Repentance where each step is filld   20
With prints of Grace, of which our Lord Christ saith
    How beautious are thy feet with shooes that guild
    Do every step with wealthy grace inlaid
    Thy Huckle joynts with jewells glorious trade.

Shall traitor Beckets tripping slippers bee   25

Dawbed all ore with Gold lace, studded too
With precious stones? that evry step that he
　　Did take that sun like sparks thence flew?
　　And shall Christs bride with brightest grace begracd
　　With blacksome shew have her bright path defacd?　　　　30

Her spirituall shooes ore lai'd with spirituall Lace
　　Studed with spirituall pearls and precious stones,
Fitted to stick in glory's Crown where Grace
　　Shines in't as brightest Carbuncles ever shown
　　Which makes her path she walks in ware a shine　　　　35
　　As she walks to Christ, glazd with rayes divine.

Her bright affections and Choice thought, her feet
　　Shod all with grace, Choice shooes indeed the best
In Graces market had, good Cheape most meet
　　For th'princes Daughters * * * and all her Vests　　　　40
　　Are answerable thereunto. That bee
　　All beauteous for delight in heavenly Glee.

These shooes do make her walke to Christ appear
　　More glorious by far than is Romes street
Stild Via Auri, or triple Crowns costly Geare　　　　[140]45
　　Or Balams toes that Emperours Passing greet.
　　How glorious with shooes blest Madam sweet.
　　Thy thigh joynts buncht with Pearls so beautious keep.

My Lord, may my Souls feet but wear such shows
　　And my thigh joynts be lashed, such jewells ware,　　　　50
I then shall statly go and bravely Close
　　Even with thyselfe and keep the way most fair.
　　But evry step will lined be with grace
　　And fill the Aire with songs while thee I chase.

6 beauty *ins.*
7 unto thee *orig.* thou
9 thou *ins.*
17 shooes *orig.* feets
18 grace *orig.* all grace

21 our Lord *ins.*
23 Do *orig.* Hath
26 Dawbed *orig.* Dawbd ; studded *orig.* and studded
28 Did *orig.* Doth ; that *orig.* where ; thence *orig.* out
30 With blacksome shew *orig.* What With this black shine
34 in't as *orig.* in its
36 she *orig.* she doth walk ; with *orig.* with these
41 bee *orig.* Chose
49 may *orig.* my ; shows *orig.* shoes
50 such jewells ware *orig.* with such jewells *orig.* with such pearles

5.5M
1719
}

149. MEDITATION. CAN. 7.2. THY NAVILL IS A ROUND
GOBLET אנ BASON EXO: 26. THY BELLY IS A HEAP
OF WHEATE SET ABOUT WITH LILLIES.

My blessed-Glorious Lord, thy spouse I spie
  Most Glorious in thine Eye, that ther is none
That may compare with her under the skie,
  Nay Heaven itselfe can't shew such other One.
  Her wandring t'seek thee when that thou withdrew   5
  Didst from her, caused her heart ach sobs renew.

Then thy sweet calls thus said, Return Return
  Oh! Shulamite, return and do not feare:
And as this gladsom sound forbad to mourn.
  Did touch her heart as it did touch her Eare.   10
  That vitall faith turnd from her wandring state
  Shee findes her soule enricht with Graces plate.

Her steps returning, her Lord beholds her shooes
  Ore laid with beauty far outshining Gold.
Her huckle joynts like precious pearls he viewes   15
  Like precious stones that golden rings enfold,
  Which he beholding doth to her thus crie,
  Oh Beautious daughter and for very joye.

Thy spirituall Navill like the Altars Bowle
  Filld full of spirituall Liquour to refresh   20
The spirits babes conceived in thy soule,

The Altars Bason that its blood to dress
The Altar sprinkled with it and t'atone
Herself and hers and ease her of her Grone.   [141]

Her Belly where her spirituall Offspring's bred   25
   Is like an heap of Wheate most Choice and fine
With fragrant Lillies richly selvidged
   Making the whole most beautifully shine.
   Her spirituall strength these arteries and nerves keep
   Holding up, and upholding of all most sweet.   30

Here's spirits of the spirits Chymistrie
   And Bisket of the spirits Backhouse best
Emblems of sanctifying Grace most high
   Water and Bread of spirituall life up dresst.
   Here's Meat and Drinke to nourish grace in sum   35
   And feed the spouses infants in her womb.

Hereby is shewn her spirituall growth in Grace,
   Whereby she able rises to bring forth
Her spirituall offspring of a spirituall race
   Her saints, and sanctifying Grace their growth.   40
   Her spirituall Navill buttoning all her store
   Of Liquour rich, the spirits Wine fat pure.

Of spirituall rich distilled sanctity
   Its sweetest dews to moisten all her fruite.
Here's food to feed her infant saints whereby   45
   They up are Cherisht well in branch and root;
   Races of saints do from her belly flow
   That to supply her spousehood up do grow.

Hence spirituall Babes hang sucking of her breasts
   And draw thence th'spirituall milk of these milk bowles   50
And of this Wheat eate plumb bread too the best.
   That nurish do and fatten holy souls.
   My Bisket sap her Basons liquour in
   And feed me with, I'le then thy praises sing.

3 That *orig.* That there is
6 renew *orig.* up grew
13 Lord *orig.* deare Lord
17 doth to her thus crie *orig.* he unto her cries
18 Oh *orig.* Out doth. Oh ; joye *orig.* joyes
24 Herself *orig.* Thyself ; hers *orig.* thine ; ease her *orig.* ease thee ; of her *orig.* of thy
30 Holding up, and upholding of *orig.* Upholding, and holding
42 spirits *orig.* spirits liquour
48 do *orig.* that
50 th *ins.*
51 plumb *orig.* plum ; eate *orig.* eath

6.7M } 150. MEDITATION. CANT. 7.3. THY TWO BREASTS ARE
1719 }   LIKE TWO YOUNG ROES THAT ARE TWINS.

My Blessed Lord, how doth thy Beautious spouse
   In stately stature rise in Comliness?
With her two breasts like two little Roes that browse
   Among the lillies in their shining dress
   Like stately milke pailes ever full and flow   5
   With sprituall milke to make her babes to grow.   [142]

Celestiall Nectar Wealthier far than Wine,
   Wrought in the spirits brew house and up tund
Within these Vessells which are trust up fine
   Likend to two pritty neate twin Roes that run'd   10
   Most pleasently by their dams sides like Cades,
   And suckle with their milk Christs spirituall Babes.

Lord put these nibbles then my mouth into
   And suckle me therewith I humbly pray.
Then with this milke thy spirituall Babe I'st grow.   15
   And these two milke pails shall themselves display
   Like to these pritty twins in pairs round neate
   And shall sing forth thy praise over this meate.

Title young *ins.*
4 shining *orig.* frisk

7 Nectar *orig.* Nectar more Wealthy
10 two *ins.* ; twin *orig.* two
11 by *orig.* and by ; sides like *orig.* side brave
12 suckle *orig.* suckle doe

151. MEDITATION. CANT. 7.4. THY NECK IS LIKE A
31.8M ⎱ TOWER OF IVORY: THINE EYES ARE LIKE
1719 ⎰ THE FISHPOOLS OF HESHBON, AT THE GATE OF
BATH RABBIM: THY NOSE IS LIKE THE TOWER OF
LEBANON THAT LOOKETH TOWARDS DAMASCUS.

My Glorious Lord, how doth the Worlds bright Glory
  Grow great? yet, loe, thy spouse doth ware a shine
That far ore shines the Worlds bright shining story
  More than the sun a glow worms glitter prime.
    Thy Neck is like a Tower of Ivory   5
    White, pure and bright, streight upright, neatly High.

Noting thy Pretious Faith which Pillar like
  Bears up the golden Head: and joyns it to
Herselfe, thy Body mystick, thy delight:
    And is the very pipe through which do flow   10
    All Vitall spirits from the head t'revive
    And make the Bodies members all to thrive.

This Neck Compleats thy spouse, her stately steps,
  As a Celestiall Majesty Upright
Not [ry] nor Rugged Whight smooth, hath no frets.   15
    Thyselfe her Head fix on her neck all White.
    It never breaks but make[s] the spouse a neate
    And statly person, Body and head compleate.

All spirituall Vitall Influences soaking through
  They through it drench all its passports, or wayes   20
Though never so secret to each member so
    And make them grow most gay.   [143]
    This office performs and uniting hold
    The Head and Body, feet more bright than gold.

Her Eyes, the fayer glory, the Looking Glass   25
   Wherein her minde sees all things shining peep.
They are like Heshbons fish pooles sparkling as
   The Lymphick Rayments scally Robes there keep
   Her cleare clear knowledge in her spirituall Eye
   As Viewing things Divine is held thereby.   30

These Fish pools then of Heshbon of rare Art
   And at Bath Rabbims gate erected cleare
Bright shining do unto us thus impart
   As they stand at the Rabbins Hall door neer.
   That bright bright Light that doth thy spouse attend   35
   That doth all Hellish darkness quite dispend.

It is the Holy Ghosts bright Lanthorn in Her hand
   That lights her feet to take the path of Grace.
And make the night time daylight, No stop nor stand.
   Hence she hath as she doth to glory trace   40
   The sun of Righteousness'es beams make day
   Within, through these and out; hence she sees th'right way.

Her Nose, the Faces Ornamentall Dress
   Like Lebanon's brave tower, that hath its Eye
Upon Damascus which Enemies possess.   45
   And smells the actions of Christs Enemy.
   The senses and the Neck, Eyes, Nose speake beauty bright
   Being Compleat and Watchfull Weights.

And hence these Metaphors we spirituallized
   Speake out the spouses spirituall Beauty cleare: 50
And morallizd do speake out Enemies
   And hence declare the spouses Lovely deare
   To be the best and Enemies hath though they
   Assaulting her shall perish in th'assay.

Make me a member of thy Beautious Bride,   55
   I then shall wear thy lovely spouses shine
And shall envest her with my Love beside
   Which with thy graces shall adorn her fine.

I'st then be deckt up in thy Glorious vests
And sing the Bridall Melodies out best. 60

---

2 great? *orig.* great,
15 hath *orig.* and hath
18 Body *orig.* of Body
26 shining *orig.* shing
28 Rayments *orig.* garments
45 Damascus *orig.* Damaskus
49 we *ins.*
52 spouses *orig.* spouses [*********]ssos
53 hath *orig.* too [******]ess
55 thy *orig.* this
56 I *orig.* I'st
57 with *ins.*

27.10M
1719
} 152. MEDITATION. CAN. 7.5. THY HEAD
UPON THEE IS [LIKE] CARMEL AND
THE HAIR OF THY HEAD [LIKE] PURPLE. [144]
THE KING IS HELD IN THE GALLERIES.

My Deare Deare Lord! my Soul is damp Untun'd.
  My strings are fallen and their screw pins slipt,
When I should play thy praise with grace perfumd
  My strings made fit with graces wax most slick.
  My notes that tune thy praise should pleasently 5
  Will onely make an harish sympheny.

Thou gildest ore with sparkling Metaphors
  The Object thy Eternall Love fell on
Which makes her glory shine 'bove brightest stars
  Carbuncling of the skies Pavillion 10
  That pave that Crystal Roofe, the Earth's Canopy
  With golden streaks, borderd with Pomell high.

The inward Tacles and the outward Traces
  Shine with the Varnish of the Holy Ghost
Are th'Habit and the Exercise of Graces 15
  Sent out with glorifying a part an host.

Yea every part from top to toe do shine
Or Rather from the toe to th'top Divine.

Thus waring of the sparkling shine most bright.
  Of sanctifying Grace in evry part   20
She is an Object of thy blesst delight
  That with her beauty doth attack thy heart.
  Hence in her Galleries doth * * * thy Eye
  Detains thyselfe surprised with such joy.

Then make me, Lord a member of thy spouse   25
  Thus Varnisht with thy spirit, purest Gold,
A Toe, a Foot, Navill, or Nose, Eye brows,
  An Arm, an Hand, a lock of hair, or fold.
  All sparkling with thy Grace in brightest layes
  And golden Tunes I'le ever sing thy praise.   30

---

1 damp *orig.* dampish
2 slipt *orig.* slipp
6 onely make *orig.* make onely
9 shine *orig.* outshine
29 layes *orig.* praise

12M   }   153. MEDITATION. CANT. 7.[6.] HOW FAIR?
1719   }   AND HOW PLEASANT ART THOU O LOVE FOR DELIGHT:

My Glorious Lord thy work upon my hand
  A work so greate and doth so Ample grow
Too larg to be by my Souls limits spand.
  Lord let me to thy Angell Palace goe   [145]
  To borrow thence Angelick Organs bright   5
  To play thy praises with these pipes aright.

You Holy Angells lend yee mee your skill
  Your Organs set and fill them up well stuft
With Christs rich praises whose lips do distill
  Upon his spouse such ravishing dews it gusts   10

With silver Metaphors and Tropes bedight.
How fair, how pleasant art, Love, for delight?

Which Rhetorick of thine my Lord descry
  Such influences from thy spouses face
That do upon thee run and raise thy Joy   15
  Above my narrow Fancy to uncase
  But yet demands my praise so high, so much
  The which my narrow pipe can ne'er tune such.

Hence I come to your doors bright starrs on high
  And beg you to imply your pipes herein.   20
Winde musick makes the sweetest Melody.
  I'le with my little pipe thy praises sing.
  Accept I pray and what for this I borrow.
  I'le pay thee more when rise on heavens morrow.

---

3 Too larg to be by my Souls limits *orig.* Too large within my narrow limits
9 whose lips do distill *orig.* tunde [**** ***] bravest
10 it gusts *orig.* [***] tast
11 bedight *orig.* are bedight
13 descry *orig.* display

10.5M ⎫
         ⎬ [154] MEDITATION. HEB. 11.6. WITHOUT FAITH ITS
1720   ⎭   IMPOSSIBLE TO PLEASE GOD.

Faith! Faith! my Lord! there is none other Grace.
  Like suitable thyself to grace most High.
Of all thy glorious Graces, oh! the place,
  That Faith obtains 'mongst them to magnify
  Thyselfe, it is the Golden Twist thou hast   5
  To tie my soule to thee my Lord most Fast.

That Golden Lace thy Ephod fast to ty
  Unto thy Glorious Breast plate deckt with stones
Rather the golden Button Curiously
  Together on thy shouldier bone alone   10

On golden Girdle that the Breast plate ties
Upon thy breast, my Lord, my High Priest wise.   [146]

* * * * * *
* * * * * *
* * * * * *   15
* * * * * *

Within whose folds those Oracles Divine
The Urim and the Thummim doe outshine.

Which utter Oracles of shining Light,
   That shine among the Glittering precious stones,   20
Oucht in their rows upon the Breastplate right
   Dancing among their sparkling glances known
   Upon the High Priest in his rich Robes drest.
   Stars in his glorious breast plate on his breast.

Faith doth ore shine all other Grace set in   25
   The soule, that Cabbinet of Grace up fild,
As far as doth the shining sun in'ts r[im]
   Walking within its golden path ore gild
   The little pinking stars playing boe peep.
   As walking in their azure room they keep.   30

And though their glorys brave, its borrow shine
   And when each doth its glorious glory lay
Upon the heap of eachs glory fine
   That lump this made's but nighty, makes no day,
   But when the sun with its Curld locks out Crowds   35
   They blush as shamd and hide but in the Clouds.

Even such is Faith amongst these Graces all,
   It is a grace that doth them grace indeed.
It layes a shine upon their Glory all
   That further glory hence on them proceed.   40
   They in its Glory do more glorious grow.
   It strengthens and doth nourish them also.

Faith is the Curious Girdle that ties to
   The King of Glory, glorifide with Grace

The bundled beams of th'sun, Gods son that flow 45
  In graces sunshine on the soul apace
  Making their graces all invest them bright
  In brightest Robes by Faith, more light than Light.

It is Golden Bosses of Gods Booke that do
  Clasp it and soule and yea God and seals up fast. 50
The Golden Belt that doth unite also
  Christ and the soule together: buckled clasp
  Christ and the soule the so[**] of Grace and brings
  All grace with't to the soul Gods praise to sing. [147]

Title Without *orig.* He that Without
2 thyselfe *orig.* to this
5 Twist *orig.* Twist that [**]de
6 To *orig.* To thy
8 Unto *orig.* Thy ; stones *orig.* rich stones
9 Button *orig.* Button buttoning
10 Together *orig.* Curiously together
11 Breast plate *orig.* Breast ties
18 doe *orig.* oracles
23 in *orig.* Within
25 in *orig.* within
27 r[im] *orig.* race
32 glorious *ins.*
38 them *ins.*
50 orig. Clasp it and the [**]ght soul and God up fast

155. MEDITATION. 2 COR. 13.5. EXAMINE

THE 18.   YOURSELVES WHETHER YOU BE IN THE FAITH:
OF 7M 1720   KNOW YOU NOT YOURSELVES THAT CHRIST IS
             IN YOU EXCEPT YOU BE REPROBATS?

My blessed Lord, I fain would thee advance
  But finde my Pen is workt to th'very stumps.
My tongue my speeches tabber stick can't dance
  Unto thy prais as I would have it jump.
  My Drumb stick thin of Dogtree Wood is made 5
  And is unfit to beat thy praises Crade.

Thou bidst me try if I be in the Faith,
  For Christ's in me if I bee'nt Reprobate.
Thou me dost Check if ignorance displai'th
    Itself in me. And I know not my state.   10
    A Reprobate my Lord, let not this come
    On mee to be the burden of the song.

Grant me thy spectacles that I may see
  To glorify aright thy glorious selfe.
And see this saving Faith grafted in mee.   15
    Then thou wilt me inrich with Gospell Wealth.
    This Faith most Usefull is I ever finde
    To glorify thyself, of all Grace-kinde.

It Usefull is for every Duty here
  Thou calst us to and to the same fit make.   20
Its subject doth, for * * * Prayer most deare
    And for the Lord's rich supper to partake.
    It Oyles indeed the very Wheels of Grace
    And makes them bravely run aright apace.

It is the Grace of Grace begracing all.   25
  Usefull for Grace, for sacraments and Prayer.
Religion is without it an empty Call
    And Zeale without it is a fruitless Care.
    Preaching without it's as a Magpies Chatter
    And as a little tittle tattles Clatter.   30

Prayer without Faith is but as prittle pratle.
  Fasts and Thanksgiving are but barren things
And sacraments without it's but as rattles
    But where this faith is all things gracious spring.
    What ere it fills it Midas like is't's told.   35
    It Certainly turns into gospell Gold.

The Heart that it doth make its Feather Bed
  It purifies, makes graces Lodgen Roome.
It makes th'Tongue tipt with it silver; the Couch orespreds
  With Gospell Pillows, sheets and sweet Perfumes   40

And sweetest tunes sings in the spirit Halls
Sweet musick on the spirits Virginalls. [148]

Lord give me saving Faith and then my Heart
 Thou'lt make thy gospell golden mine of Grace.
Studded with precious stones in every part 45
 Of thy sweet spirit guilding ery place.
 If thou wilt give me this, my heart shall sing
 On'ts Virginall, thy holy praise, within.

---

20 same *orig.* same prepares [**]
27 is *ins.*
28 And Zeale *orig.* Prayer
34 things *orig.* doth ; spring *orig.* sing
35 fills *orig.* filld
36 It *orig.* Doth ; turns into gospell Gold *orig.* [****] doth into go
38 makes *orig.* and
39 silver *orig.* silver well is spredd *orig.* silver well is set
40 With *orig.* and deckt with
44 make thy *ins.* ; Grace *orig.* richest Grace

THE 12.9M ⎫ MEDITATION 156. CANT. 5.1. EATE OH FRIENDES
1720 ⎭ AND DRINK YEA DRINK ABUNDANTLY OH BELOVED.

Callst thou me Friend? What Rhetorick is this?
 It is a Piece of heavenly Blandishments.
Can I befriend thee, Lord? Grace dost thou miss,
 Miss name me by such lushous Complements.
 The Poles may kiss and Paralells meet I trow 5
 And sun the Full moon buss, e're I do so.

'T would be too much for speeches Minted stamp.
 Sure it would set sweet Grace nigh on the Wrack
To assert I could befriend thee and her Cramp.
 Methinkes this tune nigh makes thy Harp strings crack. 10
 Yet Graces note claims kindred nigh this knell
 Saying Eate Oh Friends, Yea drinke Beloved Well.

Friend, and Belov'd calld to and welcom'd thus
  At thy Rich Garden feast with spiced joy.
If any else had let such Dainties rush   15
  It would be counted sauced blasphemy.
  But seing Graces Clouds such rain impart,
  Her Hony fall for joy makes leape my heart.

A Friend, yea the best friend that heaven hath
  Thou art to me; how do thy sweet lips drop   20
Thy Gospell Hony Dews her sky display'th
  Oh sweetness such never to be forgot.
  All Trees of spices planted in this plot
  Rich hung with Hony dews that on them dropt.

Thou drinkst thy Gardens syllabub in trine   25
  Honide with the drops thy Hony Comb distills.
Thou drinkst a Cup to me of'ts spiced wine
  And bidst mee pledg thee and I pledg will:
  My heart top full of these sweet dainties comes
  Runs over with thy praise in sweetest songs.   [149]30

---

4 name me by such *orig.* nameing by thy
6 e're *orig.* than e're
8 Sure *orig.* It Sure ; sweet Grace *orig.* sweet sweet Grace
13 Belov'd *orig.* Beloved ; to *orig.* unto
15 let such *ins.* ; rush *orig.* fall
25 thy *orig.* trine thy
30 over *orig.* ere

5.12M
      } 157[A]. Meditation. Cant. 2.[4.] He brought
1720   me into his Banqueting house
          and h[is] Bann[er] over me was Love.

How Blesst am I having such blesst a Lord
  If I improve my Happiness aright?
He loves me so that he doth me afford,
  A Banquet such that none can make the like.

It's not a single meate but certainly   5
It life sustains unto Eternity.

The sweetest dainties that were ever disht:
  On any table in best Cookery
In Heaven's made. It's Mannah: Angells feast
  Ye Holy Angells with your melody   10
  That in the Golden pot kept in memento
  Was a black shadow unto this and ment so.

Ground in Gods mill in Heaven, hence finest floure
  And made the [***] pasty paste that ere we made
And filld with Paschall [Mutton] that nere doth soure   15
  Bakt in the Backhouse of Free Grace displaid,
  Serv'd up in Gospell Chargers, pure and bright
  By shining Angells all arraied milk white.

When this Grist in Free Graces mill ground * * *
  Bolted most fine [in] Gospell Tiffany   20
And made in shew Bread Cakes * * * shew stand
  Ore the golden Altar shew bread gloriously
  Yet that of Manna's wheat's but grudgens bakt
  But oh this Banquet's all Shugar Cake.

This Meat and drink the best ten thousand fold   25
  The Paschall [mutten] th'fattest of the flock
And cookt by Grace, in Chargers fine of Gold
  This [is] the Banquets fare, [Ch]rist on the rock.

It's Wisdoms rost meat on free graces spit.
  All Saints * * * their bread in dripping shall   30
And on this table's fare s[weet] eate each bit
  And never let the least crumb from them fall.
  T[he] Liquour that his table holds is fine,
  Is richer spirits far than Cana['s] wine.   [150]

5.12M
1720

157[B]. Meditation. Can. [2.]4. He brought me into the Banqueting house, and his Banner over me was Love.

How Blest am I having so blesst a Lord
  If I improve in blessedness a right
He loves me so that he doth mee afford
    * * * Banquet such that none can make the like.
    It's not a single meate but certainly   5
    * * * life mentains and that eternally.

* * * sweetest dainties that were ever disht
    * * * any Table by Best Cookery
[I]n Heaven's made. It's Mannah true, a feast
  Ye holy Angells with your praises joy   10
  That in the golden Pot kept in the Arke
  Was but black smoke to this of Graces Art.

Ground in Gods mill in heaven, Hence finest flouer
  Made into Pasty Paste, by Holy Ghost
Filld with the Paschall Mutton, spice on it shouers   15
  Bakt in the Backhouse of Free Graces Craft
  Serv'd up in Gospell Chargers pure and bright
  By shining Angells, waiting all in white.

This Grist of Mannah ground in Gods sweet mill
  When bolted in Christ's pure fine Tiffiny   20
And dresd in various Dishes by's [***]ksy skill
  In glorious shine at the Epiphany
  That of the Mannahs wheat's mere grudgens bakt
  But this Christs Banquet's all of sugar Cake.

This Meate and Drink is best ten thousand fold   25
  Of th'Paschall Mutten the fattest of the Flock
Cookt up by Grace in Chargers all of Gold:
  This Banquits Fare, it is Christ himself th'Rock
  Is Wisdoms rost meat rost on graces spit
  Whose Dripping, Saints their bisket in't do dip.   30

The sweetest dainties cookt most curiously
  Is truly man * * * spiced Mess.
And tis the Holy Ghost sweet [***]iously
  This is the Banquets fair Christ * * *
    The liquour at this table's Juyce of the Vine   35
    Far richer spirit than the Cana wine.   [152]

This Drinke here drunk is Zions rose red wine.
  It is the Blood of the best Grape that grew
In Gods sweet Vineyard on that noblest Vine
    The true true Vine; and from this press grape drew.   40
    What wine is this? it's bled out of Christs side
    Tapt by the speare. Doth always best abide.

Oh! what a banquet's here? Saints are the Guests,
  Angells the servitors pra[****] on th'Best.
The Holy Ghost's spice seasons every * * *   45
    And by the King of Glory ever blesst
    All things hereof super superlative.
    All graces in the Guests hereby much live.

Hence banquet me my Lord here 'mongst thy gues[ts]
  And load my Trencher with this choicest Fare,   50
And let my golden Beker too at least
    Be blesst with the blest Wine beyond compare
    And then my Viall shall thy praises ring
    All Heaven ore sweet praise on ery string.

---

2 in *orig.* aright in
14 by Holy Ghost *orig.* that wee will saver
22 at *orig.* will stand at
23 the *ins.*
32 spiced *orig.* spiced trade

14.3M
1721
}

MEDITATION 158. ON JOH. 1.14. WE BEHELD HIS
GLORY AS THE GLORY OF THE ONELY BEGOTT SON,
FULL OF GRACE AND TRUTH.

My Deare Deare Lord what shall I render thee?
  Words spoken are but breesing boxed Winde.
If written onely inked paper bee.
  Unless truth mantle, they bely the minde.
  Is this sylabicated jumble whist   5
  Out of my pen, for thee fit mov'd by my fist?

My deare dear Lord, thou king of Gloriousness,
  Who can sufficiently thyself admire?
The Heavens themselves cannot the same express.
  It then their Covering ascends still Higher.   10
  Nor can the Heavens e're thy glory hold.
  Its brightness doth exceed all pearls, and Gold.

I fain would give thee all my Love and all
  Its Cabbinet wherein it keeps its Case.
My heart with it, yea, and myselfe too shall   15
  Go with it to thyself in holy chase
  Is all too foule and small a thing for thee.
  Yet I no better finde to furnish mee.   [153]

If thus my Love dresst with the Quintessence
  Of its choice Faith * * * dear affections   20
Extract by their spirits Chymistry, expence
  Being for this thing their rich and right Ejections
  'T would be onely sweate of thy drops of Grace
  Upon my heart, thus trickling down my face.

These spirits of Love with th'Quintesses pure   25
  Of all affection never could the Eye
Ever behold thy Glory, nor endure
  To look upon it without dazling joy.
  Thy beaming Glory falling on its sight
  Would make its Vision darke as dark as night: 30

Thy Glory Lord all other glory blinds.
  The glory of thy Nature pure Divine.
The glory that thy Human Nature joyns.
  Out shines all mortalls glory that doth shine.
  Thy Persons glory makes all others smutt   35
  And seem to it but like to Chimny sut.

The Glory of thy Human birth, by right
  Did make an Host of glorious Angells sing.
And all their spirituall instruments and pipes
  Melodiously tune praises to our King.   40
  Thus when God brought his First born Son to light
  He said ye Angells Worship him aright.

Thy glory shone through ery step thou tookst
  And did attend each word dropt from thy tongue.
Thy Doctrine did shine out thy life like shoots   45
  And glorious miracles went with't along.
  With these thy life did shine indeed most clear
  And made the actions of thy life bright here.

The glory of thy powerfull words did make
  The fiends of hell to tremble and to fly.   50
And made their stoughtest blades their hearts to quake.
  And turn away their feet, and out to cry.
  The wind and sea amaizd stand still. Divills shrinke.
  The sun within the skies hereby's made blinke.

The Grave is gilded where thy body lay   55
  Even with thy glory. That sting of death puld out.   [154]
The Earth adancing fell when thy bright day
  Of its uprising shining all about
  Angells put on their glorious robes to tend
  Thy tryumph over death and as thy friends.   60

And still to make our Happiness compleate
  Thou art top full of Grace and truth Wherby
The Object art of Intellects the seate
  In us and of our Wills, therein to 'ploy

Themselves in truth and Goodness at their Will   65
These Faculties with happiness, to th'fill.

Then thou upon the Wings of Glories Beams
    Ridst through the realm of th'Enemies, the skies:
Unto thy throne of Glorys brightest streams
    And hosts of sparkling Angells glorious wise.   70
    And whilst thy Captives thou dost Captive bring
    The Heavens do thy Triumphant glory sing.

Such glory ne'er seen under the Canopy
    The Copes of Heaven these golden letters favour.
This th'truth, we saw his Glory gloriously   75
    As th'glory of the onely Son of th'Father.
    Lord ope mine eyes to se thy glory bright
    And tune thy praise in beams of glorious light.

---

2 spoken *ins.* ; boxed *orig.* agitated
16 thyself in holy chase *orig.* thee. yet all gifts [****] face
21 Extract *orig.* Extracted ; their *orig.* thy
23 drops *orig.* one drop
43 Thy *orig.* His
45 Thy *orig.* His ; thy *orig.* his ; life *orig.* life alonge
46 miracles *orig.* miracles rayes that [**** *****]t *orig.* miracles [****]ge allonge
48 the *orig.* thy
51 stoughtest *orig.* stout
65 Goodness *orig.* Goodness that will
73 seen *orig.* were seen
75 gloriously *orig.* ly gloriously

[**]8M   ⎫   MEDITATION 159. REV. 2.17. HE THAT OVERCOMES WILL I
1722   ⎬   GIVE TO EAT OF THE HIDDEN MANNAH.
            ⎭

Pardon my Lord; this is my great request.
    For that thy Table of such spirituall Cheere
Hath been by me so long a time undresst
    My tenderness to that Offender were

A cause of this long intermission, 5
Yet it at length producde Confession.

And now dear Lord, I do return thee praise
For such forbearance and such Victory
Over the powers of darkness, that did raise
The storm to blow the Candle out thereby 10
But Faith that gains the Conquest over hell
Hath here tryumphd. And born away the bell.

Thou saist thou'lt feed with hidden Mannah them
That in the spiritual Combate overcom.
Give mee I pray this Conquouring Faith and then 15
I'le sing a Tryumph: it shall be my song. [155]
I honour will my Captain, sing his praise
Who leads me on and in triumphing wayes.

He in the War knows well us to Command.
The word is very ready in his lip. 20
He leads us on whenever hits us stand.
Lets not us fall, although we've many a slipp.
He gives us Heart a grace: come on brave boys;
I'le give you Angells Dainties, heavenly joyes.

He'l feast us now with farest feast ere made. 25
George Nevills feast although prodigeous't were
With dainties, things all fat and Ce[**]ish trade
Was but like th'indian broths of Garbagd deer
With which the Netop entertains his guests
When almost starved, yea Welcome Sir; it's our Mess. 30

Ahashuerus his banquet long and linde
And larded too with fatness and the Choicest Wines
Was but a little milk wash in it lin'd
To be compar'd to this that is all divine.
It is a feast so sweet, so taking flavour, 35
That make the very Angells mouths to water.

The Table, Benches, Chairs and Cushens and
    Their Table cloaths and Napkins all of Grace.
The drinking Cups and Trenchers all at hand,
Gold hath no market for this feasting place.   40
    The Guests are saints, the Waiters Angells are,
    The Entertainment Mannah, Angells fare.

The Drinking Glass is of sapharine full of Grace.
    The Pasty past is of the Wheat of Heaven.
The Holy Ghost managed the Cooke's choice place.   45
    The Venison it's filld with free from Leaven
    Was taken in Gods parke and dresst, but where
    By Whom it matter not, it's Choicest cheare.

Minced pies most choise spic'd with the richest Spice
    Enriched with the Wealthi'st wine indeed   50
And plumbd with raisins those of Paradise.
    Our Mannah thus prepar'd let's now proceed.
    Lord make me then to overcome I 'treat.
    Then thou will give mee hid'n mannah t'eate.   [156]

---

27 Ce[**]ish *orig.* Ce[**]ish ate deare
28 like *orig.* to this like
32 too *ins.*
34 is *ins.*
40 for this feasting place *orig.* but have no place
47 dresst *orig.* dresst I tell not here
51 plumbd *orig.* plumbed ; those *ins.*

WESTFIELD   }   MEDITATION 160. CANT. 2.1. I AM THE LILLY
22.10M 1722 }   OF THE VALLIES.

My Lord my Love I want word fit for thee
    And if't were otherwise, affections want
To animate the word that they might bee
    A mantle to send praise to praises camp

But want I word and spirits for the same.   5
If I omit thy praise I sure have blame.

Lord make my heart in mee an humble thing.
  The humble heart's thy Habitation bright,
It's fatted then by thee and thou therein
  Enrich it wilt with thy Celestiall Light.   10
  Thyselfe, dear Lord, shall be its gloryous shine
  Wherewith it shall adorned be and fine.

I being thus become thy Vallie low.
  O plant thyselfe my lilly flower there.
Sure then my lilly in it up will grow   15
  In beauty. And its fragrancy will fleer.
  My heart thy spirituall valie all divine,
  Thyselfe the lilly of the Vally thine.

I am thy Vally where thy lilly grows,
  Thou my White and Red blesst lilly fresh,   20
Thy Active and thy Passive 'bedience do
  Hold out Active and Passive Right'ousness
  Pure White and Red making a lovely grace
  Present thee to our Love to hug and 'brace.

The Medicenall Virtue of the lilly speake   25
  That thou my Lilly are Physician who
Healst all Diseased souls both small and greate
  None dy of any spirituall sores that to thee goe.
  The Vally lilly then doth Emblemize
  Thy fitness for thy Mediatoriall guise.   30

Shall Heaven itselfe with all its glorious flowers
  Stick them as feathers in thy Cap my king
And in this glory bow to plant in power
  Them as a lilly flower my Vall in;
  Which is not onely deepe but durty too,   35
  What wonder's this? What praise and thanks hence due?

But oh! alas my pin box is too small
  To hold praise meet for such praiseworthiness.
Ye Angells and Archangells in Gods hall
  Mee your shoshannim tend then to adress   40
  My Lord with praises bright in highest tunes
  And though they are stuttings they are sweet perfumes.

If thou the Lilly of my Vally bee
  My Vally shall then glorious be and shine
Although it be a barren soile for thee: 45
  The Lilly of my Vally is divine.
  I'le borrow heavenly praise for thee my king
  To sacrifice to thee on my Harps sweet string.   [157]

---

2 affections *orig.* I want a
6 I sure *orig.* and hav
12 fine *orig.* shin
16 fleer *orig.* spring
19 am *ins.*
20 fresh *orig.* shew
30 for *orig.* to appear for

WESTFIELD   ⎫   161[A]. MEDITATION ON CANT. 2.3. [AS THE]
12M 3 DAY ⎬   APPLE [TREE] AMONG THE TREES OF THE
1722   ⎭   WOOD SO IS MY BELOVED AMONG THE SONS.

My double Deare Lord, and doubl't ore and ore
  Ten thousand times it would indeed still rise
A bulke too smale to knock at thy blesst doore
  Of Loveliness, ten thousand times to thy Sise.
  It would be a gift ten thousand times too low   5
  Though't is the best I have on thee t'bestow.

My Love alas is but a shrimpy thing,
  A sorry Crickling, a blasted bud,
A little drachm, too light a gift to bring.
  It's but a grain weight and scarce ever good,   10

And shall I then presume thee to obtain
  If I should rob thee of so small a grain?

Thou art as Apple tree 'mong sons each man
  As was the Apple tree amonge the trees
That many are, (the Worlds geese are white swans   15
  In its account), but thou excellst all these
  Ten thousand times, bearing on every limb
  All golden apples; ripest grace that springs.

Not like the tree that once in Eden grew
  Amongst whose fruits the serpent old soon lops   20
And in his very teeth the poison threw
  Into our Mother Eves her sorry Chops.
  Nor like the serpents Egge the squerill held
  Secur'd its intrails from th'serpant fell.

Lord shake their bows, and let these apples fall   25
  Into my Wicker basket and it fill.
Then I shall have rich spirituall food for all
  Occasions as they offer me or still
  And I shall feed * * * grace my fare
  As they drop from thy Apple tree most rare.   30

As thou servst up in thy Charger bright
  A messe of these rich apples, sweet imbrace
I tasting them and * * * them with delight
  And over them will surely sing thee grace.

Thou tree of Life that ever more dost stand   35
  Within the Paradise of God and hast
The Promise to him gi'n whose happy hand
  Doth overcome, shall of it eate and tast.
  Lord feed mee with this promisd food of Life
  And I will sing thy praise in songs most rife.   40

---

9 too light a gift to bring *orig.* nay not a sixty [**]t[*]ing
11 orig. And shall I then presume this, Ist then have blaim
13 'mong *orig.* amongst

21 the poison *orig.* the Apple
24 its intrails *orig.* itself ; th' *orig.* th'snake that it [*****]st
31 As *orig.* And as ; thy *orig.* thy choice
33 with *orig.* pleasant
35 ever *orig.* ever standing host
38 it *orig.* it eate its surely

WESTFIELD ⎫ 162[A]. MEDITATION CANT. 2.3. I SAT UNDER HIS
31.12M 1723 ⎭   SHADOW WITH GREATE DELIGHT.

A shadow, Lord, not such as types do show
  Nor such as Titerus his broad Beech flings
In which on's oat pipe his muse sung so
  A forrest song. (Such are dark black sorry things)
  But Lord, * * * thyselfe madst it for delight.   5
  It is a milke white golden shadow bright.

It doth rejoyce the Saints when sorrowise
  And ting its string that they make ragged sounde.
Yea, that they are nigh burnt apieces, joyes
  Can't dance upon them, joyous come.   10
  It doth revive the soule When sorrows heate
  Doth feeble, set it in a fainty sweet.

This shade will make me Cheery bee
  When sorrows searching sun shine seekes mee
When thy blest Spirits brezzes * * *   15
  And my soul basks under thy shade as glee.
  Hence Lord thy shadow will my soul refresh
  To sing thy praise here in this shady dress.

2 Beech *orig.* Beech down
3 muse *orig.* muse sing so
5 orig. But such a shadow ne'er the like was known ; thyselfe madst *orig.* thyselfe hast made
10 joyous come *orig.* Sorrows so abound.
12 orig. Doth make feeble, brings in't a fainty sweet
16 orig. Basking my soul under thy Apple tree
17–18 orig. When thy sweet spirit in this shad [****]l / Breath on mee it my Soule refresh me will

WESTFIELD } MEDITATION 161[B]. CANT. 2.3. AS THE APPLE
22.3M 1723 } TREE AMONG THE TREES OF THE WOOD, SO IS MY
                BELOVED AMONG THE SONS.

My double Deare Lord, yea doubld ore and ore
  Ten thousand times, it would indeed still rise
Too little for to knock at thy blesst doore
  Of Loveliness ten thousand times * * * sise.
    'T would be a gift ten thousand times too small   5
    For my poore love to honour thee wit[hall].

My Love alas is a small shriv'led thing
  A little Crickling and [a] blast[ed] bud,
Scarce a grain in weight that can't unto thee bring
  Scarce lump the s[***]es nor give them up or hub   10
    And shall I then presume therewith to greet
    Th[e] * * * jewells that adorn thy feet?   [159]

Thou as the Apple tree, in wood dost rise
  Even such among the sons and them Excellst.
The world * * * are * * * in many's eyes   15
  But thou these White-white * * * then tellst,
    'T would this gold Martyre * * * relats in's streams.
    I trust indeed it's but * * * golden dreams.

Not like the tree that once in Eden grew
  Out of whose bows th'old serpent drops   20
Into our Mother Eve's lap the apple threw
  The which she quickly mumbld in her Chops.
    That tree of Life gods Paradise [wi]thin
    That healing fruite brings forth to heale 'gainst sin.

It's better far then was the snakes eges found   25
  By the poore squerrell and did arm itself
Therewith held in its teeth when th'snake did round
  Assault it who held them unto this Elfe.
    She tenderd the Eggs held in its mouth strange fate,
    And so repelld away the Rattle snake.   30

Oh! Shake the tree and make these apples fall
  Into my Wicker Basket; oh how free
Art thou my Apple tree, surpassing all
  Then spirituall Food and Physick curing mee.
  Then I shall have rich spirituall Balms, once had   35
  The Balm of Gilliad to make me glad.

Lord serve up in thy Saphire Charger bright
  A service of these golden Apples brave
Whose sight and sent will fill me with delight
  As they come tumbling on in a rowling Wave,   40
  My food will Food and Med'cine to mee bee
  Which Grace itselfe cooks up aright for mee.

Thou tree of Life yea life erelasting stand
  Within the Paradise of God; thou hast
Thus promisd them that hath that happy hand   45
  As to overcome shall Eating of it tast.
  Lord feed me with this promisd bread of Life,
  And I will Sing thy Grace with gracious strife.

---

21 the orig. *and under*

<table>
<tr><td>WESTFIELD</td><td rowspan="3">}</td><td>MEDITATION 162[B]. CANT. 2.3. I SAT UNDER</td></tr>
<tr><td>31,12M</td><td>HIS SHADOW WITH GREATE DELIGHT</td></tr>
<tr><td>1723</td><td>AND HIS FRUIT W[AS] SWEET TO MY TA[STE.]</td></tr>
</table>

A shadow, Lord, not such as any here
  Nor such as Titerus his broad Beech made   [160]
In which he with his Oate straw pipe there
  A Forrest march; such is dark blackish trade.
  But 'tis a milke white shadow sparkling bright   5
  That doth excell all excellent delight.

It doth delight the saints in glorious wise
  As shadow of a rock in weary land.

It doth revive them when the Clouds arise
 And maske the brows of heaven's shining hand.   10
 Grace gilds this shade with brightsom shines Godward
 And manward doth bring each a best reward.

A shadow not a scowling cloud that rose
 Big belld with hard Cracks of frightfull thunder
And rapid frightfull firy flashes throws   15
 A * * * with horrid rending thunder
 Making the hinds to calve and Lebanon
 To skip like * * * a Frighted Unicorn.

A shade indeed * * * * did hap
 [As] Cluster of bright Angells m[***] up   20
Made a Brave feather to adorn the Cap
 Upon the tabernakes * * *
 By Day and Night the Camp as on they stand
 Through the Wilderness to the promisd land.

Lord let this shadow as a Canopy   25
 Catch all perfumes that from the Earth arise
* * * suck them * * * in to fill * * *
 My drinking cup, when squezd I shall this prize.
 Then when my Crystall Cup grows full to the brim
 Thy praise sweet to my tast my harp shall sing. 30

---

3 there *orig.* there plaid
9 the *ins.* ; rise *orig.* arise
10 heaven *orig.* heaven bright
12 each a blest *orig.* these a Cordiall reward

MEDITATION 163. CANT. 2.3. HIS FRUIT WAS SWEET TO MY TAST.

Sweet Lord, all sweet from top to bottom all
 From Heart to hide, sweet, mostly sweet.
Sweet Manhood and sweet Godhead and ere shall.
 Thou art the best of sweeting. And so keep.

Thou art made up of best of Sweetness brast.   5
Thy Fruit is ever sweet unto my tast.

Thou art my sweetest one, my Onely sweet
    From kirnell to the rinde, all sweet to mee.
Thy bitterness is sweet: no choaking reech,
    Nor damping steams arise to damp from thee   10
    The sacred spices Stacte, Galbanum
    Are unto thee smell like to feted gum.   [161]

Thou unto mee art onely sweet all sweet
    Sweet in the Virgin wombe and horses Manger.
Sweet in thy swath band and childhood meeke   15
    Yea sweet to all to neighbour and to stranger.
    Sweet in thy Life and Conversation, friends
    Thy sweetness drop't * * * thine fingers End.

My Lord, my Love, my Lilly, my Rose and Crown
    My brightest Glory, and my Hony sweet   20
My Happiness, my Riches, my Renown.
    My shade for Comfort, in thee good things meet.
    Not one thing in thee that admits of spot,
    All Heavens scutchen, a bright Love knot:

Heavens Carnation with most sweet perfume,   25
    Pinkes, Roses, Violets that perfume the Aire
Inchant the Eyes and fansy in their bloome
    Entoxicate the Fancy with their Ware
    That fuddled turne and reele and tumble down
    From holly sweet to Earthly damps like a Clowns.   30

It gathers not the Lillys nor doth't Picke
    This double sweet rose Zions Rose tree breede
Nor climbs this Apple tree, nor doth it sit
    At all in'ts shade, nor on its Apple feed.
    It's lost within the fog and goes astray   35
    Like to a fuddled person out of way.

But Oh! my Lord, how sweet art thou to mee

In all thy Mediatoriall actions sweet
Most sweet in thy Redemtion all way free
  Thy Righteousness, thy holiness, most meeke.   40
  In Reconciliation made for mee
  With God offended in the highst degree.

A Cabbinet of Holiness, Civit box
  Of Heavenly Aromatick, still much more,
A Treasury of spicery, rich knots,   45
  Of Choicest Merigolds, a house of store
  Of never failing dainties to my tast
  Delighting holy Palates, such thou hast.

A sugar Mill, an Hony Hall most rich
  Of all Celestial viands, as Golden box   50
Top full of saving Grace, a Mint house which
  Is full of Angells, and a cloud that drops
  Down better fare than ever Artist could,
  More pleasant than the finest liquid Gold.   [162]

Then glut me Lord, ev'n on this dainty fare,   55
  Here is not surfeit took upon this dish:
All is too little to suffice, this fare
  Can surfeit none that eatest; none eate amiss,
  Unless they eat too little: So disgrace
  The preparation of the banquit place.   60

While I sat longing in this shadow here
  To tast the fruite this Apple tree all ripe
How sweet these sweetings bee. Oh! sweet good Cheere
  How am I filld with sweet most sweet delight.
  The fruite, while I was in its shady place   65
  Was and to mee is now sweet to my tast.

---

9 sweet *orig.* sweetness not stincking reech
18 thy *orig.* their
22 things *orig.* things ever
24 and a bright *orig.* carnation
27 and *orig.* the ; in their *orig.* when they
28 Fancy *orig.* Fancy make it fuddled ware

30 a *ins.*
31 doth *orig.* doth't
32 breede *orig.* breeds
46 house *orig.* store house
48 Palate's *orig.* Palate's very high
49 most rich *orig.* A Sumptuary rich
51 which *orig.* rich
63 Oh! sweet *orig.* Oh! sweet sweet

MONTH 6TH ⎫ MEDITATION 164. CANT. 2.4. HE BROUGHT MEE
ANNO 1723 ⎬ INTO HIS BANQUETING HOUSE (HOUSE OF WINE)
            ⎭ AND HIS BANNER OVER ME WAS LOVE.

Words are Dear Lord, notes insignificant
 But Curled aire when spoke sedan'd from the Lip
Into the Eare, soon vanish, though don't Cant,
 Yea run on tiptoes, and hence often trip,
 Sometimes do poother out like th'Chimny smoake,   5
 Hence often smut the matter, and nigh Choake.

Hence my Dear Lord, the mantle I would make
 Thee, I do feare will run all Counter buffe
To my design and streakt be like a snake,
 That's new crept out of'ts garment, a slunk slough.   10
 Or have a smoaky smell, and Choaky, lodge
 Within its Nap. And so it proove a bodge.

But, oh Dear Lord, though my pen pukes no gold
 To lace these robes with, I would dress thee in
And it's a shame that Tinsyl ribbon should   15
 Be all the triming that I * * * to bring
 Yet seeing, Lord, my shop board hath no better,
 I do presume thou'lt take it of thy debtor.

Thou hast me brought into thy house of Wine
 The saphire Caske of thy rich precepts * * *   20
And thy Carbunkled Firkins tappt most fine
 And choicest Nectar * * * as well   [163]

When thou hast * * * me * * * drinke * * *
Thy sweetest praise my Muse shall melodiously out sing.

9 a *orig.* to a
16 own to *orig.* should borrow
21 most fine *orig.* divine
22 *orig.* Streams of Nectar in sweet Promises
24 Thy *orig.* My

Month 8 } 165. Meditation. Cant. 2.5. I am sick of Love.
1725 }

Heart sick my Lord heart sick of Love to thee
   * * * pain'd in Love oh see
Its parchment's ready t'crack, it runs so free.
   It so affects true love * * *
     As token sends to * * * it bears my Lords pledge   5
     But seeing it's so small and hence not fledge,

It hates confinement, can't confine its Love
   It sends to thee, disdains an Hidebound gift.
But ever doth esteem great Love to move
   Unto thyself my Lord from all else rifts   10
     All hatcht in heaven of an heavenly Egge
     The Holy Ghost layd there in'ts feather bed.

If it be hatcht in Heaven, and thence brought
   * * * in the bill of th'brightest Angel there
My heart would feare it was but stolen, ore and caught   15
   Thence and me given, unfit for thee most deare.
     The Holy spirits Egg hatcht in this nest
     Would onely bee a gift, of Gifts the best.

I do bewaile my heart hath little of this
   Thee to assail therewith, but oh the smell   20
Of such a gift, that thou art pleast with, yes.

Hence hope there's something in't will please thee well.
Hence Lord accept of this, reject the rest.
I grudg my heart if it send not thee th'best.

Had I but better thou shouldst better have.   25
    I naught withold from thee through nigerdliness
But better than my best I cannot save
    From any one, but bring my best to thee.
    If thou acceptst my sick Loves gift I bring
    Thy it accepting makes my sick Love sing.   [164]30

---

7 *orig.* My heart is sick it hold such promisde Love in't bound
8 *orig.* It hates confinement and all hide bound bounds
10 Lord *orig.* Lord thy Lovely breas
14 * * * *orig.* Down
18 Would *orig.* Would be an onely gift ; bee a *ins.*
19 heart *orig.* heart so little hath of
30 Thy *orig.* Thy accepting

GLOSSARY

The following definitions are determined using a variety of sources, primarily the *Oxford English Dictionary* and the *English Dialect Dictionary*. Other crucial sources are James Strong, *Exhaustive Concordance of the Bible* (Madison, N.J., 1890); *The Interpreter's Dictionary of the Bible*, ed. G. A. Buttrick et al. 4 vols. (New York: Abingdon Press, 1962); *Dictionary of the Bible*, by John L. McKenzie, S.J. (New York: Collier, 1965); *Leicestershire Words, Phrases, and Proverbs*, ed. Sebastien Evans (London: Trubner and Co., 1881); and *A Latin Dictionary*, by Charlton T. Lewis and Charles Short (Oxford: Clarendon Press, 1879). Also helpful for quickly surveying the instances of a word in Taylor's poetry are Gene Russell's *A Concordance to the Poems of Edward Taylor* (Washington, D.C.: Microcard Editions, 1973), which is a concordance to Donald Stanford's *The Poems of Edward Taylor*, and Raymond A. Craig's *A Concordance to the Minor Poetry of Edward Taylor*, which is a concordance to *MP*.

This glossary, however, is not exhaustive. I have not included all of Taylor's biblical and topical references; nor have I listed all the forms of an entry word in Taylor's poetry; and words commonly found in standard dictionaries are not included. When Taylor uses a word in more than one sense, but only one of those needs to be defined here, I give a location of that special occurrence in parentheses. (See, for example, "bells" below.)

Abaddon: "angel of the bottomless pit" in Rev. 9:11; in Hebrew meaning "destruction" or "perdition."
acquittance: usually a legal term referring to the removal of debt or obligation.
agastard: aghast, terrified, amazed.
Ahashueru's feast: the seven-day feast given by Ahashueru, the king of Persia, to display the greatness of his kingdom (Esther 1).
ahone: a sigh of lament.
alkahest: in alchemy, the "universal solvent."
almugs: a tree; brought from Ophir. Variant of algum, said to be either acacia, cedar, cypress, or sandalwood (1 Kings 10:11–12).

Altaschat: Al-taschith, literally "Thou must not destroy." Used in titles of Psalms 57, 58, 59, and 75; probably the opening words of a popular song.

amercement: the imposition of an arbitrary penalty.

amoring: loving, in the context of courtship.

amuse: to cause to "muse" or stare; to confound, bewilder.

Anakims: "sons of Anak," a pre-Israelite tribe of Canaan referred to as "giants" (Deut. 2:10–11); conquered by the Israelites.

angelica: an aromatic herb of the parsley family used in medicine, cooking, and in a confection called "candied angelica."

angel: an old English coin, the "Angel-Noble," depicting the archangel Michael standing on and piercing the dragon.

anti-type: that which the Old Testament "type" foreshadows, usually Christ and New Testament events involving Christ.

aqua vitæ: "water of life," a strong distilled alcohol; in alchemy, ardent or flammable spirits.

Arrians: those who denied that Christ was "consubstantial," or of the same essence with God. Arius was of fourth-century Alexandria.

aurum vitæ: "gold of life"; a preparation containing or resembling gold.

Baalzephon: village in northeastern Egypt that was a station of the Exodus (Exod. 14:2, 9).

baracadoes: plural of "barricado": a hastily formed barrier of earth- and stone-filled barrels and other materials such as wagons, timber, and furniture.

Barath'rick: adjective from "Barathrum," the pit of hell; a deep pit in Athens into which criminals were thrown to die.

barleybreaks: a game of chase-and-catch played by three couples; one couple has to catch the others from within a middle region called "hell."

Bath Rabbim: one of the gates of Heshbon; fish pools were nearby (Canticles 7:4).

bdellium: variously defined as a gum or resin and as a precious stone or pearl; used to describe the whiteness of manna in Numbers 11:7.

beam: the wooden cylinder in a loom on which the warp is wound before weaving.

bells: bubbles; pocks or blisters (*GD* 1390).

Belshazzar's feast: the feast at which the drunken Chaldean king Belshazzar derided the God of Israel (Daniel 5).

bemegrim: to inflict with a "megrim," a painful headache often accompanied by vertigo.

bepinckt: adorned; decorated with cut or punched perforations to display a contrasting lining.

besprindge: bespreng: to sprinkle over with moisture or powder; besprinkle.

bib: to drink.

bibble: to drink with the bill, as a dabbling duck.

bindgd: past of "binge," to make a wooden barrel watertight by soaking.

bituminate: covered or cemented with bitumen, a kind of mineral pitch; asphalt.

black-cap: chickadee.

blin: to cease, leave off, desist.

bodge: a botched piece of work.

bloomery: a smelter in which metal is first melted from ore.

bolt: to sift flour by passing it through a seive or bolting cloth.

boss: a raised ornament in metal or wood on a book's cover.

bowl: to roll, to convey on wheels, as in a carriage.

Bozrah: a fortified city in Edom; symbol of Edom's strength. The Hebrew word denotes an enclosure or sheepfold (Isaiah 63:1).

brast: possibly, braised (*PM* 2.163.5).

Brazeel bow: a bow made of Brazil-wood, known for its hardness and its use in making red, orange, or peach-colored dyes.

bruddled: treated as a broodling, a young bird or nestling.

bub: pustule.

bucking tub: a tub used to bleach ("buck") cloth or yarn by steeping or boiling in a lye of wood ashes.

buff: a hit or buffet. "Buff" and "counterbuff" were fencing terms.

buskt: busked, dressed, attired.

buss: kiss.

butter teeth: buck teeth.

cade: a young animal, often wild, raised by hand.

calamus: sweet calamus, either an aromatic Eastern plant or European sweet flag.

cant: to lurch as in the pitching of a ship; to tilt suddenly.

cassia: the aromatic bark of an Eastern tree used to prepare fragrant oils.

cast: in law, to defeat or condemn (*PM* 1.38.34, 2.106.36).

cata pantos: or "kata pantos": the first of Aristotle's three laws of method adapted by the logician Peter Ramus (1515–1572); according to this law, the major premise of a syllogism allows no restrictions or exceptions.

catholicon: a universal medical remedy, often in the form of a syrup.

catochee: catochus, an older term for catalepsy, a disease characterized by a seizure or trance.

cawle: caul, an enveloping membrane; the amnion.

Chalybdine: made of strong steel, like that of Chalybes, an ancient nation of Asia Minor famous for its work in iron.

chase: a hunting ground, unenclosed parklike land. In printing, the quadrangular frame holding the type in place.

chat: a small branch or twig used for kindling.

cheape: a bargain.

chuffe: swollen or puffed out; stern, morose.

cield: past of "ciel" or "ceil": to line interior walls or roof with wood or plaster to conceal beams or rafters.

cittern: cithern, a sixteenth-century guitarlike instrument.

clagd: clotted or bedaubed with a sticky or miry substance.

clew: a ball of thread, such as that used to find one's way through a maze.

closestoole: close-stool; a chamber pot enclosed in a chair or stool.

collop: a thick fold of fatty flesh on a body.

comfect: confect; a sweetmeat made of fruits and seeds preserved in sugar.

concoct: to digest; to put up with, "stomach."

conjue: congee; a bow of salutation.

consent: agreement; in music, concent, harmony.

consonant: agreeable, harmonious.

cony cut: a rabbit "run."

Cordilera: cordillera; a mountain chain, generally the parallel chains of the Andes.

Corinthian: of Corinth, a city of ancient Greece celebrated for the arts of adornment.

Coursey Park: course-a-park; a country game in which a girl calls a boy to chase her.

covenant: the first or old covenant is the Covenant of Works, whereby humankind owes God obedience; by the new covenant, or Covenant of Grace, humankind owes God faith.

crade: crate.

cribb: crib; a wickerwork basket, pannier; generally, a framework.

crickling: a crinkling, crinchling, a small, wrinkled apple.

crosswort: one of a variety of plants having leaves in the shape of a cross.

crotchets: whimsical fancies; peculiar notions opposed to common opinion.

crouce: crouse; lively in spirit, bold, daring.

cue: a container to hold a small amount; denoted by the letter "q" (for "quadrans"). Sometimes equated with half a farthing.

cupping glass: a glass vessel with an open mouth applied to the skin in cupping; a method of drawing blood.

dant: daunt.

Darchont: Greek *archon:* ruler, magistrate.

dead head: *caput mortuum;* the residuum after distillation or sublimation; worthless residue.

delph: delf, quarry.

distraint: "to distrain" is to force someone to fulfill an obligation by the seizure of a chattel or thing.

divells bit: a common meadow herb with blue flowers; so called because its root is truncate, as if bitten or broken off.

dorst: dorsed; a "dorse" is the back of a book; "to dorse" is to place on the back.

dozde: of wood; having lost its tenacity of fiber, as by dry rot.

dragons: popular name of dragonwort.

drugstery: drugs, collectively.

dub: to dress, adorn, array; to stick or attach, as with ornaments.

dunce: to make a dunce of; to dull.

Edom: an Old Testament land that extended from south of the Dead Sea to the Gulf of Aqaba encountered by the Israelites in their passage from Egypt to Canaan. The Hebrew word refers to its reddish soil.

Eliakim: royal chamberlain to King Hezekiah of Judah; Isaiah prophesied Eliakim would succeed Hezekiah.

Elim: a camp of the Israelites in their passage from Egypt to Canaan with twelve springs and seventy palm trees.

emmet: an ant.

empon'd: "ponded up," stored as in the form of a pond.

Engedi: an oasis of Judah (Canticles 1:14).

enkentrism: an ingrafting; from ἐγκευτρίζω, meaning "to prick in, ingraft"; used in Paul's analogy of grafting wild olive branches onto the cultivated stock; hence, union with Christ (Romans 11:17–24.)

enrin'de: placed within a rind or outer crust.

enucleate: to remove the kernel or nucleus from; remove from disguise, lay open, explain.

epha: a Hebrew dry measure, variously said to have contained from four and a half to nine gallons.

ephod: a garment worn over the upper body of the high priest. Its rich shoulder straps were ornamented with two onyx stones in which were engraved the names of the twelve tribes of Israel (Exodus 28:6–14; 39:2–22); its breast plate was adorned with twelve different stones, each symbolizing one of the tribes.

epinicioum: epinicion; an ode sung in honor of the victor of the Greek games; a song of triumph.

Eschol: a valley near Hebron that produced the gigantic cluster of grapes carried back by the Israeli spies (Numbers 13:23–24). The Hebrew word denotes a cluster of grapes (or of other fruit).

Etham: the Israelites' first stop after leaving Succoth (Exodus 13:20).

Euxine: the Black Sea, called in Latin "Pontus Euxinus," or the "hospitable" sea.

fardell: bundle, parcel, burden of sorrow.

fat: wine cask, vat (*PM* 2.58.9, 2.77.24).

fayer: fair.

Feast of Booths: a seven-day feast that commemorated the Israelites' wandering in the wilderness (Leviticus 23:33–43; Numbers 29:12–32).

ferula: the giant fennel; a cane, rod or flat piece of wood (ferule) used for punishment.

fet: fetched.

feted: fetid.

filberd: filbert, the nut of the cultivated hazel; the shell of this nut.

fillitt: to fillet, to bind using a strip of material; or the fillet itself.

finde: past participle of "to fine"; to finish off, bring to an end (*PM* 2.122.11).

fistulate: in the form of a fistula; a long, sinuous pipelike ulcer with a narrow orifice.

fleer: to make a wry face, grin, grimace, laugh mockingly; also a variant of "flare."

flesh flie: a blow-fly.

Florendine: Florentine; a meat pie or tart baked in a dish covered with a paste.

flory: showy, fleury.

flout: an object of flouting or mockery.

flur: to flurr, scatter, throw about.

foild: foiled; to be placed in foil, as a gem, for contrast.

foist: fustiness, as the smell from a wine cask.

formatum: past participle of the Latin *formare*; a thing formed.

forme: from printing, the body of type held in place by the chase or frame.

fox and geese: a board game of pursuit and evasion played with pegs, pebbles, or corn kernels.

freehold: an estate held for a tenure of life, or the tenure itself.

freestone: a fine-grained sandstone or limestone that can be cut or sawn easily.

fret: to rub, chafe.

frim: luxuriant in growth, full-fleshed, vigorous.

frize: frieze; a coarse woollen cloth with a nap usually on one side only; the nap or down of a plant.

frob: variant of "throb."

frog: a disease of the tongue or throat, common in children; the thrush.

fulld: past of "to full"; to tread or beat cloth to cleanse and thicken it.

fur: variant of "far" or "farther."

galbanum: a sweet spice of Exodus 30:34 used in holy incense; a resinous gum from a species of giant fennel.

garland: garlanded; crowned or ornamented with a garland.

Garzia Horti: a play on Garcia de Orta (whose Latin name was "Garcia ab Horto"), author of a well-known herbal (see Davis, *A Reading* 211 n.8).

gastard: aghast, frightened, amazed.

George Nevill's feast: a remarkably elaborate feast that marked George Neville's becoming Archbishop of York in 1470.

Gilgal: Joshua's base where the twelve commemorative stones were set up and where Israelites were circumcised (Joshua 4:19–20, 5:7); the end of the Israelites' journey from Moab to Canaan. The Hebrew word denotes a circle.

Gilliad: Gilead; a hilly, fertile territory east of the Jordan famous for good pasture land and the movements of flocks (Numbers 32:1, Canticles 4:1).

Giliads balm: a gold-colored resin used to heal wounds.

gird: to tighten.

glaver: to deceive with flattery.

glew: variant of glow.

glore: glory, related to glow and glare.

glout: to frown, sulk.

Goshen: the place of good pastures in Egypt where Joseph settled the Israelites; called the land of Rameses (Genesis 47:11).

grain: the kermes dye that produces a scarlet color. To dye in grain is also to dye in any fast color, to dye thoroughly.

grindlestone: grindstone.

grudgens: gurgeons; coarse meal, the coarse refuse from flour.

gudgeon: a small European freshwater fish used for bait.

gum'd: gummed; stiffened or coated with gum.

hanck: to hank; fasten by a hank or loop; entangle.

harish: harelike; mad, foolish.

harle: fibre of flax or hemp; a tangle or knot; confusion.

haump: dialect variant of "hamp"; a kind of smock-frock; commonly in the phrase "hardin hamp."

henbain: henbane; a European plant with an unpleasant smell and narcotic or poisonous properties.

herba trinitatis: herb trinity, old name for the pansy *viola tricolor.*

herb-a-grace: old name for the herb rue; more generally, an herb of some strength or properties.

Hesbon: Heshbon, a city of Moab and capital for the Amorite King Sihon (Numbers 21:25f; Canticles 7:4).

hin: a Hebrew liquid measure of about a gallon.

Hiroth: Pi-hahiroth, a town the Israelites camped near early in the Exodus (Exodus 14:2; Numbers 33:8).

hopple: to fasten an animals' legs together to keep it from straying.

Horeb: Mount Sinai, the scene of several events of the Exodus, including the smiting of the rock (Exodus 17:6).

hurden: harden; a coarse fabric made from hurds or hards, the coarser parts of flax or hemp.

hyssop: a marjoram of the mint family whose wiry stem and bunches of flowers and stems made it useful for sprinkling water or blood in Hebrew rituals (Exodus 12:20, 9:19).

ignis lambens: a lambent or "licking" flame, one that plays lightly on a surface without burning it.

iliak: ileus, a painful intestinal obstruction in the ileum, frequently fatal; known also as "iliac passion."

imply: to enfold, involve.

Issick Bay: the Gulf of Issus, now Gulf of Iskenderun, Turkey's port city in the extreme northeast of the Mediterranean Sea.

jet: to strut, swagger, assume a pompous gait; to caper.

Jews' trump: a trump, Jews' harp.

jing: a card game, also called "jinks" or "jink game"; related to the card game "spoil five."

Jonath Elem Rechokim: opening words of a popular song used in the heading of Psalm 56; it translates as "Dove on far-off Terebinths."

junket: one of a variety of sweet dishes consisting of sweetened curds under a layer of scalded cream; called "curds and cream."

keck: to make a sound as if to vomit; to retch.

ken: to descry, catch sight of.

kid: a faggot or bundle of twigs, brushwood, gorse; as kid-wood.

kit: a small fiddle.

kit-cat: the game of tip-cat, in which the tip-cat (a short piece of wood tapered at both ends) springs up when struck with a stick and then is knocked a distance.

knop: a knob, a boss, a rounded protuberance.

knot: a flowerbed of intricate design; a laid-out garden plot.

lade: to take up water from a river or vessel with a ladle or scoop; to bale.

Lake of Meris: the Lake of Moeris, an artificial lake in Egypt some fifty miles wide, designed as a reservoir to hold water from the Nile floods.

lawn: a fine sieve used for sifting flour or straining liquids (*PM* 2.60[A].3); also a kind of fine linen.

layes: short lyric or narrative poems intended to be sung; strains or tunes (*PM* 2.3.36, 2.26.35).

let: to hinder; or a hindrance.

lign-aloes: the wood of aloes, an aromatic wood (Numbers 24:6).

linsy-wolsy: woven from a mixture of wool and flax; an inferior, coarse material.

lymphic: lymphatic; frenzied, visionary.

macie: like a mace, the spiked metal club.

mammocks: scraps, shreds, broken or torn pieces.

mammulary: the olfactory nerves, referred to in the seventeenth century as "mammulares processus"; but also "mamillary," of or relating to the mamilla, the nipple of the female breast.

mandle: variant of mantle.

Mara: Marah, source of bitter water the Israelites found in the wilderness of Shur (Exodus 15:23). The Hebrew word means "bitter."

maukin: malkin; a ragged puppet or effigy.

michtam: used in the headings of Psalms 16 and 56–60; of uncertain etymology, possibly indicating a psalm of expiation.

Migdol: a place on the route of the Exodus near Pi-hahiroth and Baal-zephon. The Hebrew word denotes a tower (Exodus 14:2).

miserere mei: "have mercy on me"; a name for the iliac or iliac passion.

morrise: merels or nine-men's morris, a board game played by two players each with an equal number of pebbles or pegs; somewhat similar to checkers.

mould: the earth, soil, or dust of which humankind is made, as well as the world itself.

mullipuff: a fuzz-ball; also a term of contempt.

mummy: a medicinal preparation of the substance of embalmed bodies.

muscadalls: the muscatel or muscadine grape, known for its flavor or odor of musk.

muth labben: cue words appearing in the headnote of Psalm 9, variously translated as "To die for the son," "Upon Maiden," and "To the son."

neckt: necked; killed by striking or pulling the neck, as fowls or rabbits.

netop: from an Algonquin word meaning "friend"; often used generically for "Indian."

nine holes: a game in which balls are rolled into an arrangement of nine holes, each having a different scoring value; also a similarly structured board game.

Ninus: another name for Nineveh.

noddy: a card game resembling cribbage.

non-suite: to subject to a non-suit, to cause a judge to stop a suit when in his opinion the plaintiff fails to establish a defensible case or to present sufficient evidence.

obsignation: the act of sealing or formally ratifying.

oculated: having eyes, and thus being sharp-sighted; having eyelike spots or holes; also "inoculated," having an "eye" or bud engrafted.

officine: officina, a pharmaceutical office or workshop in a monastery.

olivant: probably "oliphant"; ivory.

one-and-thirty: a card game similar to black-jack, in which each player receives three cards, the third face-up.

onica: onycha, the aromatic mussel used in the mixture to be burned on the altar of incense (Exodus 30:34).

Ophir: a place on the southwestern coast of Arabia on the Red Sea (Psalm 45:9); noted for its highly esteemed gold.

ophthalmic: a medicine or remedy for a disease of the eye.

oucht: ouched; held in place by an ouch, a brocade, reticulated setting for a gem (Exodus 39:13).

paintice: variant of "pentice"; a sheltering structure with a sloping roof attached to a main building; penthouse.

palate fallen: term for a "relaxed uvula," a painful condition.

pald: paled; enclosed with pales, fenced.

palma christi: "palm or hand of Christ," the castor-oil plant.

panchin: pancheon; a large, shallow earthenware bowl, wider at the top than at the bottom, used in separating cream from milk.

parg'd: past tense of "to parge"; to put on a coating of plaster, especially inside a chimney. The parget was made of cow dung and lime.

parging: plastering, as in the lining of a chimney.

peckled: speckled.

peg: one of the sharp points on the rowel of a spur.

pensile: suspended from above; pendent.

peps: to pepse; to throw at, pelt.

pericarde: pericardium; the membranous sac enclosing the heart.

Petro oyle: oleum petroli; a purgative.

phlebotomizd: past tense of "phlebotomize"; to let blood by opening a vein.

pia-mater: "thin or tender mother," a name for a thin membrane enveloping the brain and spinal cord.

pick: to pitch.

pickpack: pick-a-back, piggy-back.

pild: piled; of a javelin or arrow, having a pile or pointed metal head.

pillard: a plunderer, robber; also "pillared," supported by pillars.

pimping: small, paltry; sickly.

pinck: a small, sweet-smelling garden flower. Also, as a verb, to ornament, as by perforations; to peep, twinkle.

pincky eyes: winking of half-closed eyes.

pingle: a small enclosure or croft.

pipkin: a glazed vessel, usually small and of brown earthenware.

plastrum gratiæ dei: a medicinal plaster made of wax, turpentine, and aromatic gum resins from one of two plants: the hedge hyssup and the lesser centaury, both of which were called *gratia dei*.

pledget: a small compress of absorbent material to apply to a wound.

plite: plait, in the sense of a fold, wrinkle, or crease in a natural structure such as an ear, lip, or brow.

pomell: pommel, a spherical ornament, knob.

poother: pother, a disturbance, confusion, squabble; also smoke or steam, as in "a pother of smoke."

Posamnitick's Labyrinth: a renowned ancient Egyptian labyrinth.

post and pare: post and pair; a card game in which each player receives three cards and then bids on them.

pots: sheep-folds or cattle stalls (from Psalms 68:13).

pottinger: a pot, mug, or cup; a porringer.

pound: an enclosure maintained by authority for the detention of stray or trespassing cattle (*GD* 809).

pounderall: an intensified form of "pounder," an instrument for pounding.

pranck: to prance, to be forward or pert.

pritch: a prick or spur.

propence: propense, inclined, disposed.

purdue: perdue; to lie perdue is to lie in ambush.

purse: the scrotum of an animal.

pursevant: variant of "pursuivant"; a nobleman's attendant or messenger.

put: or "putt," a card game involving the taking of tricks.

quaile: to fail, become faint or feeble.

quilting: soft, gentle, as a quilt.

quinsie throate: quinsy, an inflammation of the throat; tonsillitis.

quintess: quintessence; the substance of heavenly bodies latent in all things; the goal of alchemical distillation.

'quittance: acquittance (see above).

quorn: quern; a simple apparatus for grinding corn between circular stones; also a small hand mill for grinding peppercorns and other spices.

radien: having the nature of a ray or of a radius line.

ragnell: probably related to "rag," meaning a low, worthless person, and "raggil," a rascal, scoundrel, worthless vagabond of some mischief.

ragwort: a common plant of unpleasant taste.

refelld: past tense of "refell"; to refute, repel.

Rameses: the Egyptian city of royal residence from which the Exodus began (Genesis 47:11).

reev'd: past of reeve, to twine, twist; to thrust or pass through an opening, as a rope.

riggalld: past tense of "riggell"; to cut a groove in, to notch.

rinde: to rind, to strip away the rind or bark; also, as an adjective, to have a rind or bark.

rive: to pull down or tear out; split.

rots: a disease (normally of sheep) characterized by pocks or eruptive pustules.

rowell: to spur (as a horse) with a rowel; the star-shaped wheel of a spur.

rubstone: a stone used for sharpening or smoothing.

ruff-and-trumpt: a common card game, associated with whist.

Sabellians: followers of Sabellius, a third-century African who denied the Christian Trinity.

Saint Johns Wort: St. Johns-wort, common English name for plants of the genus *hypericum*.

Saint 'Tony Cross: the cross of St. Anthony, or "Tau Cross," in which the transverse bar lies on top of the upright, as in the letter T.

sampler: a model or pattern; a child's exercise in embroidery usually containing the alphabet, a motto, and decorative devices.

Sanctuary: the *sanctum sanctorum* of the Mosaic tabernacle.

saphrin: sapphrine, consisting of sapphire.

sawcebox: saucebox; a mouth; an impudent, saucy person; a pert child.

scar-fire: scare-fire; a sudden conflagration.

screw pin: an adjusting screw, finger screw.

searce: a sieve, sifter, or strainer.

secundine: the placenta or after-birth.

selvedge: the edging of a woven material that prevents raveling out of the weft.

severall: enclosed as opposed to common pasture land; privately owned land over which a person has a particular right (*GD* 805).

shab: to sneak off; to get rid of, smuggle away.

shackeroon: probably variant of "shackerell"; vagabond.

shalm: an oboe.

sheed: dialect pronunciation of "shed."

shekel: a coin. God commanded Moses to require "half a shekel" as a ransom for each adult male's soul (Exodus 30:12–14).

Sherlockism: William Sherlock (1641–1707) attacked various aspects of Puritan spirituality, especially the doctrine that one can know the mercy of God only through Christ.

shew: to sue (*GD* 471).

shew bread: "bread of the presence" (Exodus 25:30; Leviticus 24:5–9); the offering of bread placed in the sanctuary.

Shiloam: a pool in Jerusalem in which Christ told a man born blind to wash, after which he was sighted (John 9:7).

Shittim wood: the acacia wood used to make the Ark of the Covenant (Exodus 25:10).

shiver: fragment, chip, splinter.

shooclout: a clout or rag for cleaning or shining shoes.

shoshannim: another enigmatic musical term used in Psalm headings. The Hebrew word means "lily" and is given as part of the title of a well-known song. Taylor seems to refer to his *PM* as "shoshannims" and to convert them metaphorically thereby into stringed instruments.

Shulamite: Solomon's betrothed in Canticles 6:13.

Sibmah: a city west of the Jordan famous for its vineyards; given to the tribe of Reuben (Isaiah 16:8).

signatum: that which is signified; past participle of the Latin *signare*, to sign or signify.

sillibub: sillabub, a drink of milk curdled by wine or cider, sometimes sweetened.

simnill: simnel cake, a rich cake of flour, spice, plums, and currants, traditionally eaten during Lent.

sippit: sippet, a small piece of bread, toasted or fried, served with meat, gravy, or soup.

skeg: a name applied to various types of wild plum, some noted for a very harsh taste.

slatch: noun from the verb "to slatch"; to dabble in mire.

slickt up: polished, shined by rubbing or filing.

slough: soft, miry, or muddy ground; a skin that is shed.

slunk: adjective from the past participle of "to slink."

sluttery: impurity, filth; sluttishness.

snick snarl: an entanglement of thread or yarn.

Socinians: a sect co-founded by Faustus Socinus, a sixteenth-century Italian theologian who denied the inherent divinity of Christ.

sogd: past of "to sog," to soak, saturate.

sory: a mineral ore that yields vitriol; or a kind of vitriol.

spagyrist: alchemist.

spermodote: literally "seed giver."

spraggling: straggling, sprawling.

spicknard: spikenard, or nard; a costly fragrant ointment prepared from an Indian herb (Canticles 1:12, 4:13–14).

spiles: piles; pointed stakes or posts driven into a riverbed or marshy ground to support a pier or building.

spiracle: inspired substance, breath of life (cf. "spiraculum vitæ" of Genesis 2:7).

sprindge: variant of springe and sprenge; to sprinkle, scatter, disperse.

spruice: variant of spruce; brisk, lively; trim, dapper.

sprunt: to struggle convulsively.

squibd: past tense of "squib"; to throw forth a remark after the fashion of a squib, a type of firework that shoots out sparks.

squitchen: diminutive of "squitch," a dialect form of "switch"; a twig or small stick used for punishment; a ferule.

stacte: one of the four aromatic ingredients of the holy incense (Exodus 30:34). The Hebrew root meaning suggests the droplets of gum from a variety of shrubs or trees.

stob: to stab, pierce, prick.

stoole: the base of a plant whose shoots or branches have been fastened down and partly covered with earth so that they may take root while still attached to the parent stock and thereby propagate the plant (*GD* 1488).

stowhouse: storehouse.

stranging: being surprised or wondering.

strout: variant of strut.

sub forma pauperis: "in forma pauperis"; the legal designation as a pauper that exempts one from paying the costs of a legal action.

sublune: beneath the sphere of the moon; worldly.

Succoth: the first stop of the Israelites in their flight from Egypt. The Hebrew word denotes "tents" or "booths."

surdity: deafness.

swash: a style of capital letter with flourished strokes; ostentatious, swaggering.

sweetspike: French lavender, noted for its essential oil.

syncopee: syncope, heart failure.

tantarrow: to announce or welcome with a flourish of trumpets.

tent: attentive (*PM* 2.2.4); also, a probe (*PM* 1.47.2).

tester: a canopy held over a bed, pulpit, or podium by posts or suspended from a ceiling.

theanthropy: the doctrine that in Christ divine and human natures are unified.

thresher: thrasher; a type of shark (fox-shark) with a very long upper tail division with which it was said to lash an enemy.

thrum: the ends of the warp threads left unwoven and attached to the loom when the web is cut off.

Thummim: see "Urim and Thummim."

tipple: tumble, topple.

tole-dish: toll-dish, a container used to measure the toll of grain due to the miller of a mill.

topping: very high or superior in position, distinguished.

trig: to move quickly or briskly; trip (related to "trigger").

tumberill: tumbrel; a cart whose body tips over for dumping; a dung-cart.

tund: tunned; stored in or put into a tun or large cask (usually for wine, beer, or ale); also tuned (*PM* 2.145.9).

turn: a brain disease (usually of sheep and cattle) characterized by dizziness.

type: a person, ceremony, or event of the Old Testament that foreshadows and is fulfilled by Christ and certain events of the New Testament.

Ubiquitarians: those Lutherans who maintained that Christ's body was everywhere present at all times.

unguent apostolorum: the Apostles' ointment or salve; a purifying ointment composed of twelve ingredients.

unlute: to un-loot, remove the loot from; or to unlute, remove the lute (clay or cement used to seal vessels or pipes) from.

Urim and Thummim: the oracular devices on the ephod's Breastplate of Judgment through which the priest could consult Yahweh (Exodus 28:30).

vend: to vent; of animals, to cast out, expel, or discharge.

venom: venomous (*GD* 1020; *PM* 2.61.26).

wamble: to feel nausea.

wards: the ridges projecting from the inside plate of a lock (*PM* 1.42.15); also the incisions in the bit of a key corresponding to these ridges (*GD* 1713).

wash: hogwash; kitchen swill as food for swine.

wassell: wassail; from the Old English *wes hal* ("Be in good health"); the salutation uttered in drinking to someone's health or the liquor in the bowl.

waybred: waybread, plantain; of various herbal and culinary uses.

weight: wight; living being, creature (*PM* 2.151.48).

welt: to roll

welted: adorned or trimmed with welts (ornamental and structural strips, fillets, or edging), as in garments.

whelm'd down: turned upside down so as to cover something.

whiffle: to blow in puffs or slight gusts; also a trifle.

whimsy: dizziness, giddiness.

whittle: a knife; a term that denotes either large or small knives.

wine fat: wine vat; the vat in which grapes are pressed in making wine.

wisp: a bundle of straw or other material used for wiping or scouring.

womble-crop: to be affected with nausea.

wooling: woolgathering; indulging in purposeless thinking, being in an absent-minded state.

writh: enveloped or swathed by winding or folding; wrenched, twisted.

yawn: variant of awn, the spiny end of the grain-sheath of barley, oats, and other grasses.

TEXTUAL NOTES

Gods Determinations

title page As closely as type will allow, I have reproduced the title as it appears in PW; Taylor has carefully centered it in the top half of the title page, the four margins of which he has ruled. Below the title, in a hand other than Taylor's, is the following:

> This a MS. of the Rev. Edward Taylor
> of Westfield, who died There A. D. 1728. or 1729
> Aetat. circa 88. velsupra.
>> Attest Ezra Stiles
>> His Grandson.
>> 1786.

Below this, in yet a different hand, appears the following:

> Henry W Taylor
>> his Great Grandson.
>> *1868*

Penciled in beside Stiles's name is "DD" and beside Henry Taylor's name "LLD."

title, verso This page is blank except for "Eliza Taylor," written twice, in a hand other than Taylor's, in the top, left corner.

39 A stain at the top of the manuscript has partially obscured Taylor's insertion "man."

153 After 152 Taylor began to copy the next stanza. He wrote and then canceled:

> Mer:
> All this I'le do, and do it o're and o're
> Before my

208 This line has been cut away at the bottom of the page.

208f At the top of ms. 6, Taylor has written the title:

A Dialogue between $\left\{\begin{array}{l}\text{Mercy and}\\ \text{Justice}\end{array}\right.$

617 The speaker indication preceding 617 was originally "Sat."

791 An "o," raised above the line, appears just before "leave."

799–924 Throughout "Christs Reply," the left margin is indented three spaces.

869 Taylor has indented this line approximately three spaces farther than 868 and has indicated with a zigzag mark that it should be brought back in line with 868.

949–1012 After the first six four-line stanzas of "An Extasy of Joy," Taylor pairs them as eight-line stanzas, concluding with a four-line stanza.

1178 The bottom of "minde" is cut away. The period is conjectural.

1222 This line has been cut away. The tops of several letters are visible.

1400 Below this line Taylor wrote "Saint," indented as if to begin the next stanza.

1446 The end of this line is cut away at the bottom of the page; however, the "i" of "is," the dot above the "i" of "in," and the "t" are visible.

1491 Most of 1491 and all of 1492 are cut away.

1535 Taylor originally indented at the beginning of this line and wrote the speaker indication "Soul."

1572 The "i" of "in" is almost blotted out by ink. Under the ultraviolet light, the "i" is legible.

1580 At the bottom of ms. 36, indented from the left margin, Taylor has written the next speaker indication: "Saint."

1770 At the bottom of ms. 40, a line has been cut away; the tops of a few letters are visible. At the very top of ms. 41, higher on the page than Taylor usually begins to write, he has written the missing line 1770.

1843–66 In PW, Ranks Two and Three are designated by numerals.

1847–48 Taylor has indented these lines and made zigzag marks which indicate that they should be brought back to the left margin.

1864 At the bottom of ms. 42, line 1864 has been cut away. Taylor has written the line at the top of the next page.

2039–72 With each successive stanza on ms. 47, Taylor has slightly deepened the indentation of the third, fifth, and sixth lines.

2102f On the bottom half of ms. 48, in a much later hand, Taylor has written the title and the first sixteen lines of "My Valediction to all the world preparatory to Death."

Preparatory Meditations

1 Across the top of this page and above Taylor's title is written the following in a hand other than Taylor's: "Sacramental Meditations for 35 y. from 1682 to 1725." An original end date of "1717" has been crossed out and corrected with "1725." In the space above this first Meditation, Taylor has written: "Preparatory Meditations before my Approach to the Lords Supper. Chiefly upon the Doctrin preached upon the Day of administration." In yet another hand, beginning to the right of "1. Meditation" and continuing down the right margin, appears the following:

By Rev. Edward Taylor A. M.
   Attest Ezra Stiles
      his Grandson
         1786.

7.9 Having omitted line 10, Taylor wrote it in the right margin at the end of line 9.

16.13 A blot over the "s" in "Conseald" obscures an original reading; Taylor inserted the "e."

26.4 Taylor simply omitted this line in copying into PW.

36.34 Taylor's illegible insertion obscures two words in this line.

39.7 The first letter of "Coop" is a hybrid, combining the internal structure of Taylor's "C" with the right-leaning loop of his "k."

40.31 The first letter has flaked away with the page edge.

41.5 An ink smear makes illegible the first letter of "[m]ark." Stanford reads "dark," apparently taking a "t" that shows through from the other side of the page as the loop of a "d." Since the ink smear does not reach higher than the top of the "a," the loop of a "d" would be visible; therefore, "mark" seems most likely.

45.23 & 34 The last letters of these lines flaked away with the page edge.

45.35 The last two letters of "Glory" flaked away at the page edge; the "y" is written beneath the line.

46.36 A hole in the page takes letters from "g[***]ious."

46.53 The last letter flaked away with the page edge.

47.8 A hole in the page runs the length of a word written, and probably canceled, between "Bodys" and "Soile."

48.date The day of the month flaked away with the page edge.

SECOND SERIES

Title page PW contains no title page for the Second Series.

1–2.36 The first sheet of the second series is bound out of place in the rice-paper binding. This sheet (ms. 167 and 168) contains *PM2.1* and the first six stanzas of *PM2.2*. The first series resumes with ms. 169.

1.date Much of the date is flaked away with the page edge.

1.title After "to" the page edge is flaked away.

6.50 In altering the first letter or two of "send," Taylor left it unclear; it is not clearly "s," resembling equally his "f" and "t."

8.35 A blot obscures the last letter of "it[s]."

11.22 Taylor originally wrote "makest"; then, to improve the line's meter, he placed the apostrophe directly above, but neglected to cancel, the "e."

17.25 Taylor clearly canceled the first "m" in his original "phlegmbotomizd"; the "g," however, is not clearly canceled.

19.18 In "frindge," the "g" is written directly over the "d." I leave both letters, Taylor's typical spelling of the word.

21.23 Above line 23, Taylor wrote and then canceled "These Feasts all."

21.58 The last letters flaked away with the page edge.

21.61–82 The following twenty-two lines are canceled:

> But now I from the New Moon Feast do pass
> And pass the Pass o're o're unto Gods Seales.
> And come to Whitsuntide, and turn its glass
> To Search for pearles amongst its sands and meals.
> For Israel had not fifty dayes been out   65
> Of Egypt, ere at Sinai Law did spout
>
> So Christ our Passover had not passt ore
> Full fifty dayes before in fiery wise
> The Law of Spirit and of Life much more
> Went out from Zion: Gospell Law did rise.   70
>
> The Harvest of the former yeare is in'd.
> Injoy'd, and Consecrated Thanks for't pay'd.
> All holding out the Right in things we Sind
> Away restored is, and they all made
> Fit for our use, and that we thankfully   75
> Ourselves unto the using them should ply
>
> Then make me to this Penticost repare
> Make mee thy Guest, Lord, at this feast, and live
> Up to thy Gospell Law. and let my Fare

Be of the two Wave Loaves this Feast doth give.   80
If th'Prophets Seed time spring my harvest I
Will, as I reape't, Sing thee my harvest joy

Within these lines, Taylor made the following three revisions: line 66
spout *orig.* shout; line 73 out *orig.* out hereby; line 82 reape't, *orig.* reape't,
make

22.date Taylor omitted the date.

23.4 This line was originally written at the top of the following page (ms.
245); in a later hand, Taylor copied it at the bottom of ms. 244 because it
had been partially trimmed away at the top of ms. 245.

23.72–73 In both lines, "gift" occurs, but Taylor altered them, inserting an
illegible letter (or two) in 72 before the "i" and in 73 inserting a letter,
possibly "e," after the "i" and altering the "f." Since his intent is unclear,
I leave "gift" in both places.

24.18 This line is written in the margin at the end of line 17 in two half-
lines, each of which loses one or more letters from trimming.

24.28 Taylor wrote the "re" of "here" below the line apparently after trimming it away.

24.30 The last letter is trimmed away.

26.36 The last letter flaked away at the page edge.

27.49 & 51 The first letters are trimmed away.

29.34 A stain obscures the "b" of "[b]ecause."

30.21 A blot obscures the last letter of "th[e]."

31.43–2.32.66 This entire sheet (ms. 259–60) is brittle; pieces have fallen
away leaving holes, and show-through and blotting present additional
problems. The microfilm, made before PW was placed in rice paper, pre-
serves a number of readings.

31.47 This line runs through the darkest area of a stain. Stanford reads:
"My Hammer then shall greet this Shine as well."

32.37 Between "Lord" and "the," the stain obscures the line; Stanford reads
"spy out."

33.17 The last letters flaked away at the page edge.

39.39 In revising, Taylor partially obscured "W[i]th"; no "i" is visible.

40.date The day and month are trimmed away.

48.21 Taylor's revision obscures the word following "might"; the "r" is clear.

53.3–4 Taylor miscopied these two lines but corrected them with a mar-
ginal note keyed for insertion after "Crampt" in line 3. What I take to be
"brea[th'd]" is trimmed at the page edge.

67[B].26 Following line 25, Taylor copied and canceled a version of line 27:
"Ill Tongue, Mouth ulcers, the Frog, Angina Throate."

72.24 A stain obscures "the[ir]."

77.16 Taylor's caret indicates that "so" is to be inserted from above; he made no cancellations to improve meter.

77.21 A stain obscures an original reading following "Hell-Gate."

79.56 Taylor inserted "too" after "Purchases," writing it both above the line (with a caret below) and in the right margin; he tried to smear away "too" in the margin. I omit the word.

84.37 An ink blot obscures the final letter.

85.10 The "s" of "sweet" is written directly over "and."

85.33 In revising "whereon," Taylor did not form a clear word.

92.27 Taylor indented the line but indicated with a zigzag mark that it should be brought back to the left margin.

93.35–36 Taylor originally omitted these lines; later, with a duller quill and darker ink, he crowded them in.

94.29 Faded ink and show-through make part of this line illegible.

99.16 In the right margin, Taylor wrote "aires" and keyed it for insertion in the line after "and."

101.50 A blot obscures one letter in "Wo[o]e."

102.23 In altering "ev'n," Taylor neglected to form an "e" for "they."

103.20 A blot obscures the last letter of "Type[s]."

107.38 Of the "a" in "Covenant," Taylor formed only the vertical stroke.

115.49–54 In a later, shakier hand (while revising PW generally), Taylor revised the last four lines of this poem, apparently mistaking them for an incomplete stanza. He might have seen them so because the customary space between stanzas is lacking between this poem's last two stanzas and because such a space does separate the final four lines from the first two lines of their stanza. I take this as Taylor's error and retain the original version of the lines in question. The single change Taylor makes in line 49 is to substitute "raise" for "play," creating what appears to him as the final couplet of the preceding stanza. The following is the sestet (as indented in PW) Taylor produced by revising the final four lines:

> Inspire her songs that Glory may orcome
>> In sweet tunes and may thy Excellency Glaze.
>> And thou shalt be the burden of her song
>> Loaded with Praise that to thyselfe out blaze.
>> When thou heart inspirth my heart shall run
>> Thy praise in sweetest tunes most sweetly sung

116.6 In revising an initial letter or two, Taylor imperfectly formed the "od" of "God."

116.7 Taylor wrote "Pursevanto" apparently intending "Pursevant to."

116.29–30 The lines are not trimmed away; they're simply missing from PW.

118.31 & 33 Taylor indented these, but his zigzag marks bring them back to the margin.

122.28 The square brackets are Taylor's.

123[A].title The square brackets are Taylor's.

123[B].title The square brackets are Taylor's.

128.29–30 Taylor initially omitted these lines, crowding them in later.

130.18 A blot obscures the middle of "b[e]ds."

131.44 Taylor originally wrote "spiced" but revised to "spic'de"; since this seems a metrical error, I retain the original.

131.47 A blot obscures a letter in "Spi[c]e."

132.34 After omitting and then crowding this line in, Taylor wrote its revision down along the right edge of the page.

132.42 Taylor mistakenly inserted this line between lines 48 and 49.

133.28 Before "Ad," "In [****]se" has been canceled. The ink is faded here, but "Ad on it fore" is fairly clear; its sense is not clear.

135.39 Taylor's alterations make part of this line illegible.

135.41–42 Taylor wrote a version of these lines following line 36, indented as if they completed that preceding stanza: "Thy Helmet Hope, thy Belt of Truth, Thy shield / Of Faith all * * * will never yield."

136.6 After "said," Taylor inserted the raised "t" standard in his abbreviation "y^t"; the "y," however, is missing.

136.9 The final word flaked away with the page edge.

136.17 A long, dark cancellation on the opposite side of this page obscures a few letters in the first half of this line.

136.19 Taylor canceled "[***]den" and placed a caret beneath it; he then neglected to supply the new word.

136.42 A stain obscures here a word of four or five letters.

137.title Taylor drew a line across the page after this title.

138.19–21 Ms. 398 is badly flaked at the top and outer edges.

138.31 A stain obscures a word of five or six letters following "others."

139.date Taylor omitted a date for this Meditation.

139.title Taylor left a space for the Bible reference but did not fill it in.

139.8 Following "so," a word is blotted out; Taylor wrote in the right margin "deli[ghted]," which is partly flaked away at the page edge.

139.30f The final stanza of this Meditation is at the top of the verso ms. 400 (the final page in PW). It is too faint to read, except for an occasional word. Following the line across the page at the end of that stanza, Taylor wrote: " * * * other Meditations see back before the beginning."

140 After "Prologue," which is well centered on the entire ms. 129, and which precedes all the Meditations, the verso is blank. At the top of ms. 131, above the heading for *PM* 2.40, in a hand clearly older than the 1717 hand of 2.140, Taylor wrote: "Se the following meditations * * * that should have been in the End of the book." He then drew a line to separate that note from 2.40.

143.6f Between the first two stanzas are these two lines, which have been canceled: "Oh see [*]ow floo forth like th'morning very faire / As shines the Moon and bright bright sun faire."

145.11 I do not expand the abbreviation "thro'" here because of the visual rhyme Taylor achieves with "unto" in line 12.

147.22 A lengthy, illegible cancellation follows "our"; Taylor crowded in "a pace" beneath it. He provided no other word or phrase to fill out the line.

147.42 After "praise," an "a" is legible among other illegible marks.

151.15 The difficult letters most closely resemble "ry." The entire line is puzzling.

152.23 The word following "doth" is illegible because of cancellations, show-through, and blotting ink.

154.13–16 Taylor omitted these lines when transcribing. Since the preceding stanza is based on Exodus 28:28, and the last two lines of this stanza are based on Exodus 28:30, the missing lines are likely based on Exodus 28:29.

157[A].34f Ms. 151 is blank.

157[B].4–9 Faded ink and a stain make several initial letters illegible.

158.45 Written above the canceled "alonge" is "his bookes"; this phrase is not canceled, but Taylor, in darker ink and at the end of the line, wrote "like shoots."

158.46–47 Taylor's multiple cancellations make these lines difficult. In faint, gray ink, resembling show-through, he made his revisions in the space to the right of the lines.

161[A].29 An ink smear covers the word following "feed"; a bold "h" stands to the right of the smear and before "grace."

161[B].10 The last word is clearly "hub."

162[A] This Meditation contains many cancellations and revisions, including several entire lines canceled. It is clearly an earlier version of 162[B]. Stanford omitted it as a "rough draft."

162[A].6f Below line 6 is a canceled line, which is partially legible: "Making t[***] s[***]t and I [***]ll take delight."

162[A].16f Below line 16 and above the canceled original lines 17 and 18 is an uncanceled line, a caret indicating that it should replace the original line 17: "Il shadow that will me cheery greet."

163.date Taylor left the space but did not supply the date.

163.11–12 These lines contain many cancellations and illegible words not canceled. Uncanceled at the beginning of an otherwise canceled line following line 11 is "And Onica."

164.16 Taylor's insertion after "I" is not clear; Stanford reads "own."

164.22 A line cancels the original "Streams of" but then continues just below the rest of the line. At the bottom of the page, Taylor wrote the revised line, a portion of which is too faint to read.

165.1–6 This first stanza contains many cancellations and illegible revisions.

165.14 Taylor's revision of the original "Down" is illegible.

165.18 In revising this line, Taylor canceled the original "be" but neglected to cancel "an."

EMENDATIONS

The emended reading of this edition is given to the left of the square bracket; the manuscript reading is indicated to the right. To the right of the bracket, the tilde (~) represents a word that was unchanged; the caret (∧) represents the absence of the punctuation reported to the left of the bracket.

20 It's] Its
58 Life,] ~∧
58 Fortify.] ~∧
61 hence;] ~∧
79 where.] ~∧
90 lap;] ~∧
105 'rain'd] rain'd
122 is] as
123 Face.] ~∧
136 a way] away
136 be found] befound
137 show.] ~∧
140 Violence.] ~∧
145 below,] ~∧
146 unto the] unto
150 cry,] ~∧
153 spare,] ~∧
186 Stands.] ~∧
188 hands.] ~∧
201 bee.] ~∧
203 it's] its
210 yet's] yets
214 hee.] ~∧
221 feare,] ~.
223 Will.] ~∧
224 head,] ~∧
242 rake.] ~∧

249 Let's] Lets
279 Whos'ever] Whosever
383 finde.] ~∧
389 in.] ~∧
399 it's] its
411 down.] ~∧
412 frown.] ~∧
413 wamble,] ~∧
425 Small,] ~∧
442 other] othe
459 Their] There
472 before.] ~∧
476 Whom] whom
479 fist,] ~∧
483 fell;] ~∧
501 You] you
503 You'st] You st
507 that's] thats
510 Wee?] ~.
541 Will.] ~∧
551 Fight,] ~∧
554 lie.] ~∧
557 field.] ~∧
560 Engins] Engims
581 smut,] ~∧
594 Coate,] ~∧
608 It's] Its
609 It's] Its
611 may.] ~∧

614 much as] much
631 Sin.] ~_∧
647 mee.] ~_∧
649 anatomize;] ~_∧
684 it's] its
685 there,] ~.
698 Embrace.] ~_∧
699 aright;] ~_∧
705 Weigh,] ~_∧
722 purg'd] purgd
723 itselfe,] ~.
758 pipe.] ~_∧
763 Her] her
765 Sin,] ~.
803 too] to
829 Head,] ~_∧
836 is,] ~_∧
843 t'hunt] t'hunts
875 God's] God
892 It's] Its
916 Silver-like] Silver like
948 ring.] ~_∧
951 pipe?] ~.
954 ring?] ~.
966 Emmet] Emmets
1002 Sound.] ~_∧
1014 Angells] Angell
1025 what's] whats
1027 saw,] ~_∧
1027 Smelt] smest
1027 tasted,] ~_∧
1028 It's] Its
1032 Figitive?] ~.
1051 Slavery.] ~_∧
1055 Greate.] ~_∧
1056 is] ~ is
1061 Side.] ~_∧
1064 what's] whats
1065 trust.] ~_∧
1069 Yet] yet
1079 It's] Its
1091 it's] its
1102 there,] ~.
1114 wonder's] wonders
1120 Darke] ~,

1121 it's] its
1136 ev'ry] e'vry
1139 Brain:] ~,:
1159 it's] its
1165 impart:] ~_∧
1173 we rue,] ~, ~
1176 a Case] Case
1192 Charge!] ~.!
1203 It's] Its
1203 word.] ~_∧
1207 It's] Its
1213 doe.] ~_∧
1217 would,] ~_∧
1229 wee,] ~.
1231 pray'reless] pra'yreless
1259 ours,] ~.
1269 angry] argry
1284 'tis] tis
1290 wilt.] ~_∧
1313 It's] Its
1319 do?] ~,?
1338 Stacks,] ~.
1341 I'le] Ile
1355 It's] Its
1355 so,] ~.
1366 They] The
1381 behold;] ~_∧
1386 bow,] ~_∧
1405 wish,] ~.
1415 bee.] ~_∧
1417 thought,] ~.
1434 i'th'] i th'
1439 s'e're] se're
1446 Wilfull,] ~_∧
1462 own.] ~_∧
1503 Genuine.] ~_∧
1504 It's] Its
1513 Patience,] ~_∧
1520 It's] Its
1544 more,] ~_∧
1545 can't] cant
1556 He'l] Hel
1563 fall,] ~_∧
1578 minde.] ~_∧
1586 It's] Its

1587 those] thoses
1588 thoughts] thought
1596 Same,] ~.
1601 foe?] ~ₐ
1626 rowle] ~,
1646 Hard-thoughted] Hard thoughted
1646 black-thoughted] black thoughted
1647 Renew] Rewew
1650 frailty,] ~ₐ
1650 a new] anew
1657 Contend.] ~ₐ
1671 excludes,] ~ₐ
1688 it's] its
1691 it's] its
1695 Calls,] ~ₐ
1714 away.] ~ₐ
1715 grave.] ~ₐ
1716 It's] Its
1751 Glasses] Grasses
1767 ejects,] ~ₐ
1769 There's] Theres
1771 it's] its
1772 Cast.] ~ₐ
1783 time,] ~ₐ
1786 Face.] ~ₐ
1796 It's] Its
1799 one,] ~ₐ
1800 upon.] ~ₐ
1810 harms.] ~ₐ
1812 In Spite] ~ Spit
1825 it's] its
1840 thee,] ~.
1860 Sincks] Sinck
1863 it's] its
1867 fall,] ~ₐ
1914 thereof;] ~ₐ
1914 pay.] ~ₐ
1929 It's] Its
1940 Christ's] Christ
1952 Porters] Porter
1975 Passions] Passion
1982 it's] its
1982 know.] ~ₐ
1994 splic'te.] ~ₐ
2006 that's] thats

2016 Contents.] ~ₐ
2043 Instruments] ~.
2059 it's] its
2064 Voice.] ~ₐ
2083 Christ's] Christ

PREPARATORY MEDITATIONS

FIRST SERIES

2.7 'bide.] ~ₐ
2.20 therein.] ~ₐ
3.35 Caves;] ~.
Exp.17 I'le] Ile
Exp.22 Deity.] ~ₐ
Exp.28 bring.] ~ₐ
Ret.6 thee.] ~ₐ
Ret.7 with] whith
Ret.33 glorify,] ~ₐ
Ret. 35 thee.] ~ₐ
Ret.38 Out of] Outed
Ret.42 thee.] ~ₐ
4.10 shines;] ~ₐ
4.33 wrackt,] ~ₐ
4.34 Wound.] ~ₐ
4.40 Cure.] ~ₐ
Ref.5 Guest] Guess
Ref.6 dry.] ~ₐ
Ref.14 Ravishment] Ravishm[nt]
Ref.24 Unlockt] Unlock
Ref.25 Pearle-like] Pearle like
Ref.28 Fall.] ~ₐ
5.11 bereave.] ~ₐ
Ano.title Meditation] Mediation
Ano.3 I'me] Ime
7.2 filld,] ~ₐ
7.16 foild.] ~ₐ
7.17 Gold.] ~ₐ
8.27 take;] ~ₐ
8.29 It's] Its
8.30 It's] Its
9.4 Pish,] ~.
9.22 It's] Its
10.6 Sun.] ~ₐ
10.19 brew'd,] ~.
10.32 praise.] ~ₐ

10.34 raise.] ~ₐ

11.24 Guests] Guess

11.27 here;] ~.

12.1 Doores:] ~ₐ

12.6 It's] Its

12.8 pure.] ~ₐ

12.14 Blaze.] ~ₐ

12.16 thousand] thosand

12.38 reare.] ~ₐ

12.48 bee.] ~ₐ

13.15 benights.] ~ₐ

13.16 It's] Its

14.11 answerable,] ~.

15.58 ever.] ~ₐ

17.5 Magnificent.] ~ₐ

17.34 disdaind.] ~ₐ

17.41 Record.] ~ₐ

17.42 Lords.] ~ₐ

18.5 it's] its

18.8 Slime.] ~ₐ

19.1 ground.] ~ₐ

19.6 Hell.] ~ₐ

19.9 milke-white] mike white

19.24 it's] its

19.29 mall.] ~ₐ

19.36 where's] wheres

20.26 melodies.] ~ₐ

20.32 below?] ~ₐ

22.4 by't.] ~ₐ

22.7 glorifi'de:] ~,:

23.8 'Twould] T'would

23.11 'Twould] T'would

23.26 Worms] Worm

24.24 i'th'] ith'

23.43 it's] its

25.9 undone.] ~ₐ

25.31 Choicest] Coicest

26.2 holds] hold

26.8 Same.] ~ₐ

26.11 It's] Its

27.3 That's] Thats

27.4 inclinde.] ~ₐ

27.18 thyselfe.] ~ₐ

27.38 Angells,] ~.

27.42 us.] ~ₐ

27.48 mee.] ~ₐ

28.4 minde.] ~ₐ

28.17 it's] its

28.21 My] By

28.27 Well;] ~.

28.30 Grace.] ~ₐ

29.4 Divine,] ~.

29.16 its] it's

29.41 Stock.] ~ₐ

29.42 Crop.] ~ₐ

30.1 ever] every

30.11 It's] Its

30.12 hold.] ~ₐ

31.4 Nose,] ~.

32.18 displac'te.] ~ₐ

32.26 Golden] Goldens

32.34 Supply.] ~ₐ

32.42 chime.] ~ₐ

33.38 live.] ~ₐ

33.42 grow.] ~ₐ

34.2 pass.] ~ₐ

34.10 Enfoild,] ~ₐ

34.14 reliefe.] ~ₐ

34.18 brakest:] ~.

34.22 Piety.] ~ₐ

34.23 Death's] Death

34.30 grace.] ~ₐ

34.31 Washt] Whasht

34.38 indeed.] ~ₐ

34.42 sting?] ~ₐ

35.4 on't,] ~.

35.6 overstockt] overstock

35.6 overstockt,] ~.

35.6 fed.] ~ₐ

35.23 Men,] ~ₐ

35.30 thing;] ~.

35.43 sight:] ~.

36.14 Confine.] ~ₐ

36.15 disdain.] ~ₐ

36.16 thine.] ~ₐ

36.30 of't,] ~.

36.31 feele.] ~ₐ

36.34 hand.] ~ₐ

36.42 can't] cant

36.70 stock.] ~ₐ

37.28 Fruites of] Fruites
37.28 Life:] ~.
37.28 it's] its
38.25 tri'de] ~ˌ
38.28 Case;] ~.
38.31 nay.] ~ˌ
38.32 came.] ~ˌ
38.35 Case,] ~ˌ
38.40 it's] its
39.17 poyson] poyson'
39.22 it's] its
39.22 plaint] paint
39.28 therefore.] ~ˌ
39.36 praise.] ~ˌ
39.40 'gainst] gainst
39.40 fulfill.] ~ˌ
39.45 Pleas] Plea's
39.45 mine;] ~.
40.title Propitiation] Propi/tiation
40.17 herein.] ~ˌ
40.21 Hell.] ~ˌ
40.23 Post-and-Pare] Post,-and-Pare
40.23 Post-and-Pare,] ~ˌ
40.26 out,] ~.
40.27 Faith's] Faiths
40.34 afresh,] ~.
40.35 now,] ~ˌ
40.36 not] rot
40.40 spirit's] spirits
40.48 Grace.] ~ˌ
40.61 sun] sun,
40.64 streams.] ~ˌ
41.3 Spiracles] Spirit'les
41.19 tallons,] ~ˌ
41.25 in't] ~.
41.38 silent] silence
41.40 style.] ~ˌ
42.title me] we
42.2 appitite,] ~.
42.6 nest.] ~ˌ
42.36 fall?] ~:?
43.7 Corrupt,] ~ˌ
43.15 Love;] ~.
43.41 then] when
44.1 Righteousness.] ~ˌ

44.4 pay.] ~ˌ
44.14 nay.] ~ˌ
44.19 it's] its
44.31 Righteousness,] ~.
44.34 part.] ~ˌ
44.35 I'st] Ist
44.41 I'le] Ile
44.41 come.] ~ˌ
45.6 leasure.] ~ˌ
45.14 Gamesters;] ~ˌ
45.20 Grace.] ~ˌ
45.25 yet,] ~.
45.27 brightest] brighest
45.34 's] s
45.36 story.] ~ˌ
45.40 pin.] ~ˌ
45.42 ring.] ~ˌ
46.19 Wit,] ~.
46.26 it's] its
46.48 it's] its
46.54 best.] ~ˌ
48.9 ore;] ~.
48.12 Love;] ~.
48.32 Smiles] Smile
48.34 all,] ~.
48.41 make] makes
49.1 great.] ~ˌ
49.4 box.] ~ˌ
49.16 stand.] ~ˌ
49.22 are,] ~.
49.27 'T] T
49.28 glass,] ~.
49.28 hop.] ~ˌ

SECOND SERIES
1.22 nat,] ~.
2.27 above.] ~ˌ
2.28 Copses;] ~.
2.29 Father's] Father
2.37 Brother.] ~ˌ
3.4 Crown.] ~ˌ
3.10 shrine,] ~ˌ
3.11 makes] make
3.19 'peare] peare
3.23 high] hugh

4.9 pinck;] ~‸

4.17 round,] ~.

5.5 Oar.] ~‸

5.8 because] ~.

5.14 Christ's] Christ

5.42 Mines.] ~‸

6.16 alone;] ~.

6.21 Grief;] ~‸

6.26 two.] ~‸

7.2 skin.] ~‸

7.10 thou;] ~.

7.12 Bits;] ~.

7.14 Divell,] ~.

7.17 run.] ~‸

7.28 messe.] ~‸

7.39 thine.] ~‸

7.40 therein.] ~‸

7.42 glorify.] ~‸

8.13 Doves] Dove

8.15 Guncrack,] ~.

8.19 son,] ~‸

8.37 Send.] ~‸

9.14 thee.] ~‸

9.15 persecuted;] ~.

9.26 Wilderness?] ~‸

9.30 Serpents,] ~.

9.34 shame.] ~‸

9.42 so,] ~.

9.42 it's] its

9.58 dross,] ~.

9.60 outwarp.] ~‸

10.title Jesus,] ~.

10.28 Cooke.] ~‸

10.51 cleane.] ~‸

10.54 praise,] ~.

10.54 part.] ~‸

11.1 thick,] ~.

11.2 butt] but

11.22 mak'st] mak'est

11.26 May] may

11.36 o'th'] oth

11.38 Oh,] ~.

11.53 sunshine;] ~‸

11.54 poure.] ~‸

12.24 that's] thats

13.23 smite.] ~‸

13.25 shown?] ~.

13.27 Throne] Thone

13.29 strong.] ~‸

13.37 springs,] ~.

13.44 thy] ~,

14.5 Shell.] ~‸

14.6 wallow,] ~.

15.2 Jasper,] ~.

15.9 Grace's] Grace'es

15.18 Soure;] ~.

15.20 not;] ~.

15.24 sweet,] ~.

16.6 declare.] ~‸

16.14 Soule:] ~,:

16.22 Crown,] ~‸

16.38 beare?] ~.

17.18 told.] ~‸

17.19 Christ] ~,

17.22 fine.] ~‸

17.24 Wood.] ~‸

17.25 type;] ~‸

17.26 Fire;] ~.

17.28 Peace,] ~‸

17.32 thine.] ~‸

17.32 pray.] ~‸

17.33 retrograde.] ~‸

17.36 do.] ~‸

17.42 myselfe.] ~‸

17.46 kind.] ~‸

17.48 gift;] ~.

17.48 mee.] ~‸

17.50 too] to

17.51 Child,] ~.

18.8 Alley;] ~‸

18.9 led.] ~‸

18.10 there.] ~‸

18.44 thee?] ~.

18.46 bone.] ~?

18.49 Amen,] ~.

18.51 shrine.] ~‸

19.3 Excellency] Excelleny

19.20 Thine] thine

19.23 Lavender] ~.

19.26 Guests] Guess

20.9 again.] ~∧
20.24 Oyle,] ~.
20.26 influences;] ~.
20.41 in't,] ~.
20.42 Seate,] ~.
20.54 Play-House,] ~.
20.59 herein] ~.
21.9 Month] Mon'th
21.12 out.] ~∧
21.23 Feasts,] ~.
21.37 own.] ~∧
21.41 Earthward,] ~∧
21.61–82 [See Textual Note]
22.1 month] mon'th
22.2 Full] ~.
22.6 Grave,] ~.
22.6 Crown.] ~∧
22.18 hearbs,] ~.
22.23 I'le] Ile
22.33 I'le] Ile
22.37 apace.] ~∧
22.43 I'le] Ile
22.48 Deliverance.] ~∧
22.50 farewell;] ~∧
22.50 shew,] ~.
22.70 give.] ~∧
23.4 Delight.] ~∧
23.10 beg.] ~∧
23.21 day,] ~.
23.24 sweet.] ~∧
23.33 dy.] ~∧
23.34 declines.] ~∧
23.35 away.] ~∧
23.52 thereby;] ~.
23.64 Fly,] ~.
23.66 mee?] ~.
23.75 that's] thats
24.28 here?] ~∧
24.32 thine] ~.
24.34 mine.] ~∧
24.42 Sin,] ~.
24.45 tuch.] ~∧
24.46 my] ~,
25.4 fire,] ~.
25.5 Pericarde.] ~∧

25.13 are.] ~∧
25.15 Wear,] ~∧
25.33 accurst.] ~∧
25.44 nullitie.] ~∧
25.47 makes] make
25.47 frim.] ~∧
25.49 I'le] Ile
25.52 stills.] ~∧
25.54 I'le] Ile
26.1 Undone,] ~.
26.21 assign'd.] ~∧
26.22 feate,] ~.
26.34 clear.] ~∧
27.18 Uncleane,] ~.
27.20 Cure.] ~∧
27.27 the] The
27.34 it] it'
27.38 Shiloam,] ~.
27.54 th'] th
27.66 besprinkled,] ~.
28.10 Vengeance,] ~.
28.10 straw.] ~∧
28.11 benighted,] ~∧
28.25 I've] Ive
28.35 City;] ~.
29.4 Cart.] ~∧
29.7 are.] ~∧
29.9 tare.] ~∧
29.12 abound.] ~∧
29.13 Ark,] ~.
29.15 boats,] ~.
29.24 give.] ~∧
29.33 Sinke] ~.
29.34 without.] ~∧
29.38 Lamb,] ~∧
29.38 Crib.] ~∧
29.48 higher.] ~∧
30.12 himselfe;] ~.
30.15 sin.] ~∧
30.21 ship;] ~.
30.23 deck.] ~∧
30.29 gudgeon,] ~.
30.30 best.] ~∧
30.33 Bay.] ~∧
30.39 teach.] ~∧

30.40 them,] ~.

30.40 'void] void

30.40 'void.] ~ₐ

30.46 hands:] ~.

30.46 faile.] ~ₐ

30.49 posts,] ~'

30.50 Sea.] ~ₐ

30.51 die;] ~.

30.58 sticks.] ~ₐ

30.61 goes,] ~ₐ

30.65 quencht,] ~.

30.70 heart;] ~ₐ

30.74 Tempest;] ~.

31.4 th'earth.] ~ₐ

31.22 good.] ~ₐ

31.26 It's] Its

31.37 Love.] ~ₐ

31.39 I'le] Ile

31.45 its] it's

31.48 bell.] ~ₐ

32.6 birds] bird

32.18 fowle.] ~ₐ

32.19 hug.] ~ₐ

32.28 made,] ~.

32.30 Cabinet.] ~ₐ

32.41 striefe,] ~ₐ

32.42 Life.] ~ₐ

32.48 made.] ~ₐ

32.52 liveliness,] ~ₐ

32.54 Divine.] ~ₐ

32.62 haire.] ~ₐ

33.9 LOVE,] ~.

33.13 is] iss

33.28 Divine.] ~ₐ

33.30 bore't.] ~ₐ

33.34 satisfy,] ~.

34.8 stut.] ~ₐ

34.19 shells,] ~.

34.23 It's] Its

34.28 Heart,] ~ₐ

34.30 Mankinde.] ~ₐ

34.32 untill] ~.

34.34 will.] ~ₐ

34.36 drop.] ~ₐ

34.38 blood,] ~ₐ

34.40 Wash,] ~ₐ

34.45 fine.] ~ₐ

34.54 melody.] ~ₐ

35.26 here,] ~.

35.38 Law,] ~.

35.41 undo,] ~.

35.41 it's] its

35.43 it's] its

35.43 sure.] ~ₐ

35.46 Undo-doing:] ~ₐ

35.54 base.] ~ₐ

35.55 thine.] ~ₐ

35.56 Dispense] ~.

36.23 water,] ~.

36.30 fly.] ~ₐ

37.15 lurch.] ~ₐ

38.9 Immeasurable,] ~.

38.31 oh] ô

38.40 flower.] ~ₐ

39.7 breaks] breake

39.12 Sunshine;] ~.

39.17 Conquoured,] ~ₐ

39.20 art;] ~,

39.20 art,] ~.

39.26 Like] like

39.36 Victory?] ~.

39.40 last.] ~ₐ

40.11 Rod,] ~.

40.22 thing.] ~ₐ

40.24 other] others

40.33 thee,] ~.

40.40 Love,] ~.

41.7 trip,] ~ₐ

41.9 tip.] ~ₐ

41.16 run.] ~ₐ

41.18 learn,] ~.

41.22 faster.] ~ₐ

41.36 taught] teaght

41.36 him] (him

41.36 (though] ₐthough

42.title prepared] pre/pared

42.6 purse;] ~.

42.9 up,] ~.

42.16 thine.] ~ₐ

42.23 these,] ~.

42.23 grace.] ~ˌ

42.24 Case.] ~ˌ

42.25 end,] ~.

42.27 it,] ~.

42.43 I] ~.

43.4 doings,] ~.

43.4 what's] whats

43.4 designd.] ~ˌ

43.10 rhimes.] ~ˌ

43.25 ware.] ~ˌ

43.46 here.] ~ˌ

43.48 degree.] ~ˌ

44.10 THEANTHROPIE.] ~ˌ

44.11 infinite,] ~.

44.13 two,] ~.

44.14 All-Might,] ~ˌ

44.16 night,] ~ˌ

44.17 finite,] ~.

44.18 Person,] ~.

44.28 stride.] ~ˌ

44.34 it's] its

44.38 gallants;] ~.

44.41 It's] Its

44.52 part.] ~ˌ

44.54 thine.] ~ˌ

45.title 2.3.] 2ˌ3.

45.4 hair.] ~ˌ

45.5 fleece,] ~ˌ

45.10 wayes.] ~ˌ

45.12 spangle.] ~ˌ

45.15 infinity.] ~ˌ

45.18 state.] ~ˌ

45.24 shelfes.] ~ˌ

45.28 here.] ~ˌ

45.30 Light.] ~ˌ

45.34 dayes.] ~ˌ

45.39 shelves] slelves

45.45 beame.] ~ˌ

45.48 Soule,] ~.

45.51 art.] ~ˌ

45.52 mine.] ~ˌ

46.title 2.9.] 3.9.

46.title The] The the

46.6 Neptune's] Neptune

47.6 Sinners] Sinnes

47.15 dress.] ~ˌ

47.28 reprive.] ~ˌ

47.32 live.] ~ˌ

47.36 blaze.] ~ˌ

48.3 goes] goe's

48.11 its] it's

48.15 up,] ~ˌ

48.26 side.] ~ˌ

48.36 sanctify.] ~ˌ

48.39 Might.] ~ˌ

49.15 Wood,] ~ˌ

49.22 Sparkling] Sparklingl

49.25 mee;] ~.

50.10 Broke:] ~.

50.22 embellishments] embellisments

50.28 Promises,] ~.

50.31 them;] ~.

50.40 gripes,] ~ˌ

51.8 transparently] trasparently

51.9 Nay,] ~ˌ

51.9 th'heavenly] 'th'heavenly

51.11 wast,] ~.

51.34 Full,] ~.

51.37 stand,] ~ˌ

51.44 own.] ~ˌ

52.2 Earth,] ~.

52.6 Majesty.] ~ˌ

53.36 Secure,] ~.

53.41 dead,] ~.

53.41 too.] ~ˌ

53.46 thee.] ~ˌ

54.7 off] of

54.7 sin,] ~.

54.10 begrac'de.] ~ˌ

54.14 Orbs,] ~.

54.21 therewith,] ~.

54.22 goe] ~.

54.23 Offices.] ~ˌ

54.39 Mediatour,] ~.

56.10 low.] ~ˌ

56.14 show.] ~ˌ

56.22 Grace.] ~ˌ

56.40 Wantonings,] ~.

56.46 part.] ~ˌ

56.56 bearst.] ~ˌ

56.60 sing.] ~ ̬

58.2 Quill's] Quills

58.3 Gold).] ~) ̬

58.4 run;] ~.

58.16 in.] ~ ̬

58.17 highs.] ~ ̬

58.24 flapt.] ~ ̬

58.25 'pears.] ~ ̬

58.26 Egypt;] ~ ̬

58.26 highs.] ~ ̬

58.27 The] the

58.27 years.] ~ ̬

58.28 lies.] ~ ̬

58.34 spiritually.] ~ ̬

58.36 goe.] ~ ̬

58.40 trade.] ~ ̬

58.54 sunshine;] ~.

58.64 in's] ins

58.64 journeyings.] ~ ̬

58.69 sea;] ~.;

58.70 Cry.] ~ ̬

58.74 rage,] ~ ̬

58.74 round.] ~ ̬

58.75 paws.] ~ ̬

58.76 drownd.] ~ ̬

58.78 'stroy] stroy

58.79 praise,] ~.

58.79 Cheere.] ~ ̬

58.84 work] works

58.84 griefe,] ~.

58.93 brincks.] ~ ̬

58.111 Christ's] Christ

58.114 likewise.] ~ ̬

58.118 Encheckerd] Encleckerd

58.120 sings.] ~ ̬

58.126 Company.] ~ ̬

59.7 Strange,] ~.

59.17 It's] Its

59.21 'bout] bout

59.36 sing.] ~ ̬

60[A].5 I'st] Ist

60[A].7 sick;] ~.

60[A].8 all).] ~) ̬

60[A].18 skill.] ~ ̬

60[A].26 seen.] ~ ̬

60[A].32 Cake.] ~ ̬

60[A].36 forgot.] ~ ̬

60[A].44 with't;] ~.

60[A].46 table.] ~ ̬

60[A].48 all.] ~ ̬

60[B].19 Pillars] Pillar

60[B].21 It's] Its

60[B].21 beere.] ~ ̬

60[B].22 it,] ~.

60[B].40 faint;] ~.

60[B].40 dy.] ~ ̬

61.2 define] ~.

61.4 serpentine.] ~ ̬

61.9 bosoms?] ~,

61.9 th'] th

61.21 (that] th(at

61.31 shop.] ~ ̬

62.10 bring.] ~ ̬

62.12 Saint] Saints

62.14 Chokwort,] ~ ̬

62.15 suckles;] ~ ̬

62.28 Spicknard] Spickward

62.29 fill.] ~ ̬

63.4 flower.] ~ ̬

63.14 bright,] ~ ̬

63.18 tune.] ~ ̬

63.24 this.] ~ ̬

63.30 Madri'galls] Macri'dalls

63.35 fall.] ~ ̬

63.41 Hazle, Wallnut] ~ Wall, nut

63.41 brave,] ~ ̬

63.48 wise.] ~ ̬

63.52 perfume.] ~ ̬

63.57 sing,] ~ ̬

63.58 still.] ~ ̬

63.66 praise.] ~ ̬

64.14 ben't] be'nt

64.15 Paradise.] ~ ̬

64.27 grow;] ~.

64.27 here's] heres

64.30 aire.] ~ ̬

64.34 melody.] ~ ̬

64.36 gated.] ~ ̬

65.22 Grace.] ~ ̬

65.33 Olive,] ~ ̬

65.33 Almonds,] ~ₐ

65.45 Almonds,] ~ₐ

65.47 Lillies,] ~ₐ

65.47 Violets,] ~ₐ

65.48 aire.] ~ₐ

65.50 Wine.] ~ₐ

65.54 reech.] ~ₐ

66.title Life] Live

66.2 It's] Its

66.5 heart,] ~.

66.5 where] whre

66.6 Soule.] ~ₐ

66.8 'Mongst] Mongst

66.8 affections:] ~,:

66.8 swells;] ~ₐ

66.8 it's] its

66.10 gain'd.] ~ₐ

66.13 Love!] ~,!

66.13 'Stroy] Stroy

66.13 Life] Live

66.13 thereby;] ~ₐ

66.14 Object;] ~.

66.20 ditties,] ~.

66.42 beames,] ~.

66.45 have.] ~ₐ

66.48 in.] ~ₐ

67[A].title name,] ~.

67[A].3 right,] ~ₐ

67[A].18 Wrinkle.] ~ₐ

67[A].19 sick.] ~ₐ

67[A].21 quick,] ~ₐ

67[A].24 Divine.] ~ₐ

67[A].35 reliefe;] ~ₐ

67[A].36 are] is

67[A].38 it's] its

67[A].41 Distempers] Distembers

67[A].42 all.] ~ₐ

67[A].45 got.] ~ₐ

67[A].48 I'le] Ile

67[A].51 less.] ~ₐ

67[A].52 hereupon.] ~ₐ

67[A].60 sing.] ~ₐ

68[A].8 orematch.] ~ₐ

68[A].13 darke.] ~ₐ

68[A].14 spring.] ~ₐ

68[A].19 cold.] ~ₐ

68[A].28 twinkling.] ~ₐ

68[A].31 art.] ~ₐ

68[A].34 Stars,] ~ₐ

68[A].36 Spring.] ~ₐ

68[A].42 Light.] ~ₐ

68[A].49 flow.] ~ₐ

68[A].54 bright.] ~ₐ

68[A].60 best.] ~ₐ

67[B].9 drops] ~.

67[B].10 brisk,] ~.

67[B].20 deep,] ~.

67[B].21 thoughts] thougts

67[B].21 part.] ~ₐ

67[B].22 rue.] ~ₐ

67[B].29 syncopee,] ~.

67[B].30 evills,] ~ₐ

67[B].30 Cricks.] ~ₐ

67[B].37 thee,] ~.

67[B].39 bring.] ~ₐ

67[B].44 Pleurisy,] ~ₐ

67[B].45 Colick,] ~ₐ

67[B].45 Fever,] ~ₐ

67[B].45 turns,] ~:,

67[B].47 Botch,] ~ₐ

67[B].48 good.] ~ₐ

67[B].53 Malady,] ~ₐ

67[B].59 Beams,] ~.

67[B].64 Cure.] ~ₐ

67[B].70 sin.] ~ₐ

68[B].18 Distemper'd] Distemer'd

68[B].31 Wing.] ~ₐ

68[B].32 give.] ~ₐ

69.title 2.1.] 2.2.

69.2 Melancholy,] ~.

69.12 joys.] ~ₐ

69.23 Its] It's

69.28 finde.] ~ₐ

69.33 beautifull,] ~.

69.34 drink.] ~ₐ

70.17 bed.] ~ₐ

70.35 It's] Its

70.44 blood.] ~ₐ

71.6 dresst.] ~ₐ

71.13 Choicest] Coicest

71.21 That's] Thats
71.26 pure] ~.
71.27 attire,] ~.
71.28 it's] its
71.34 'stroying] stroying
72.4 Coast.] ~ˬ
72.16 hand.] ~ˬ
72.28 Covers.] ~ˬ
72.30 glory.] ~ˬ
72.39 Right] ~.
72.47 honour] hornour
73.21 herselfe,] ~.
73.35 thee,] ~.
73.49 warm.] ~ˬ
73.52 will.] ~ˬ
73.54 string.] ~ˬ
74.8 It's] Its
74.14 therein.] ~ˬ
74.15 i'th'] ith'
74.16 sparkling.] ~ˬ
74.40 sweet.] ~ˬ
74.42 Web,] ~.
74.42 Twine.] ~ˬ
75.2 Wits,] ~.
75.18 It's] Its
75.18 Vile,] ~.
75.19 It's] Its
75.33 vile,] ~.
75.53 It's] Its
75.55 it's] its
75.57 soile.] ~ˬ
75.58 pray.] ~ˬ
77.8 Choire] Coire
77.10 meet.] ~ˬ
77.16 heart,] ~.
77.21 Hell-Gate,] ~.
78.title Covenant] Coven
78.2 Knowledge] Knowled
78.6 That's] Thats
78.10 bucket's] buckets
78.11 it's] its
78.14 in't,] ~.
78.20 Good;] ~ˬ
78.29 tide] ti'de
78.40 away.] ~ˬ

78.46 drown'd.] ~ˬ
79.2 Filld] filld
79.16 too,] ~.
79.25 aright.] ~ˬ
79.29 arise?] ~,?
79.31 made.] ~ˬ
79.38 all.] ~ˬ
79.39 Wealth,] ~ˬ
79.39 Wisdom,] ~ˬ
79.48 Purchase,] ~.
79.53 thee.] ~ˬ
79.59 Purchase,] ~.
79.65 that's] thats
79.71 Song:] ~ˬ
80.8 is,] ~.
80.12 anatomize.] ~ˬ
80.17 sensitive,] ~ˬ
80.21 things;] ~.
80.22 it's] its
80.26 choice.] ~ˬ
80.27 Soule,] ~.
80.29 It's] Its
80.30 bed.] ~,
80.36 Vivacity.] ~ˬ
80.40 Christ's] Christ
80.43 life.] ~ˬ
81.4 unseen.] ~ˬ
81.8 that's] thats
81.19 thus.] ~ˬ
81.24 Fare.] ~ˬ
81.32 Divinity] Divinty
81.36 Gold.] ~ˬ
81.40 Divine.] ~ˬ
81.42 place.] ~ˬ
81.52 Food.] ~ˬ
81.53 that's] thats
81.54 ours.] ~ˬ
81.66 skill.] ~ˬ
82.title Meditation] Medition
82.title drink] drinks
82.4 deserve.] ~ˬ
82.5 Rack.] ~ˬ
82.6 knack.] ~ˬ
82.16 Wood.] ~ˬ
82.17 Bellows,] ~)

82.26 blood.] ~ₐ
82.27 that's] thats
82.31 Backhouse,] ~.
82.35 It's] Its
82.36 Drinke] ~,
82.40 same,] ~.
82.43 threw] thre'w
83.6 stylde.] ~ₐ
83.28 bracelet.] ~ₐ
83.35 in,] ~.
84.7 out,] ~ₐ
84.28 finde] ~:
84.31 vermin] ver in
84.39 gatherdst't] gatherdstt
84.40 bore] bores
84.48 string.] ~ₐ
85.title Hony.] ~ₐ
85.title drunk] druk
85.4 Christ] Chrst
85.10 thing.] ~ₐ
85.18 sweet] sweed
85.30 in'ts] ints
85.33 Christ's] Christ
86.16 come.] ~ₐ
86.17 same;] ~ₐ
86.28 I'd] Id
86.31 beds.] ~ₐ
86.40 wonderment] wondement
87.2 'Bellisht] Bellisht
87.4 Edition.] ~ₐ
87.5 It's] Its
87.6 consists.] ~ₐ
87.7 It's] Its
87.11 it's] its
87.13 It's] Its
87.13 attende.] ~ₐ
87.16 Tower.] ~ₐ
87.24 sight.] ~ₐ
87.40 give.] ~ₐ
87.41 boot;] ~ₐ
87.42 Joy.] ~ₐ
89.10 it's] its
89.13 hatcht] ha'tcht
89.35 Common,] ~ₐ
89.44 shine,] ~ₐ

89.48 made,] ~.
89.49 kinde.] ~ₐ
89.50 Consist.] ~ₐ
89.51 lin'de.] ~ₐ
89.53 thus.] ~ₐ
90.3 It's] Its
90.4 It] If
90.5 therein,] ~.
90.15 It's] Its
90.16 Edition.] ~ₐ
90.17 Worm's] Worms
90.20 belong.] ~ₐ
90.28 th'same] th same
90.43 bright,] ~ₐ
90.52 therein.] ~ₐ
90.53 Glory,] ~ₐ
90.58 play.] ~ₐ
90.62 thee.] ~ₐ
90.65 Spirituall] Spiritu ll
91.6 It's] Its
91.10 meate,] ~.
91.25 it's] its
91.27 lightening] lighteing
91.28 shower.] ~ₐ
91.33 Exaltation's] Exaltations
91.38 It's] Its
91.42 Ring.] ~ₐ
92.6 Quick.] ~ₐ
92.28 Courage,] ~.
92.42 skies.] ~ₐ
93.8 Quick'ning] Quick'ming
93.8 influences] infuences
93.19 thou'st] thoust
93.28 transparent] tranparent
93.30 Stories.] ~ₐ
93.31 now,] ~.
93.34 more.] ~ₐ
93.36 pave.] ~ₐ
93.40 mansions] mansion
94.10 part.] ~ₐ
94.30 there.] ~ₐ
95.2 might?] ~ₐ
95.10 'T] T
95.22 bring?] ~.
95.30 Soule,] ~ₐ

95.30 puts't] putst
95.31 that's] thats
95.33 Case,] ~∧
95.37 that's] thats
95.37 all.] ~∧
95.40 th'] th
95.42 Praises;] ~∧
95.44 I'm] Im
95.48 thee.] ~∧
96.22 wonder;] ~.
96.23 their] there
96.28 thereof;] ~.
96.34 ore,] ~∧
96.35 enough;] ~∧
96.44 No.] ~∧
97.title mouth.] ~∧
97.10 toy.] ~∧
97.20 Love,] ~.
97.21 in's] ins
97.44 mountain,] ~∧
97.47 Farthen,] ~∧
97.48 well;] ~.
97.54 greet.] ~∧
98.2 juyce] juyces
98.2 Wine.] ~∧
98.3 Vine of] Vine
98.6 one,] ~.
98.6 Clarify.] ~∧
98.9 Vine;] ~∧
98.10 fruite.] ~∧
98.22 flow.] ~∧
98.23 It's] Its
98.37 It's] Its
98.47 Vine.] ~∧
99.title before] be/fore
99.4 with] wth
99.8 in'ts] ints
99.18 high.] ~∧
99.21 sparkling] sprkling
99.22 see] sees
99.22 shine.] ~∧
100.2 It's] Its
100.5 Fancies] Fances
100.5 briske.] ~∧
100.7 I'l] Il

100.32 'chants] chants
100.34 swashes,] ~∧
100.40 mee.] ~∧
100.42 sweet.] ~,
101.6 Fancies] Fances
101.6 sing.] ~∧
101.12 dresst.] ~∧
101.16 Light,] ~∧
101.17 brightest] brighest
101.18 amain.] ~∧
101.20 ware.] ~∧
101.24 station.] ~∧
101.30 mount] mout
101.39 Sun,] ~∧
101.40 out.] ~∧
101.52 hew?] ~∧
101.54 pleas] plea's
101.54 hand.] ~∧
102.6 Institutions] Insticutions
102.16 sounds,] ~.
102.34 White.] ~∧
103.3 went.] ~∧
103.5 Elect.] ~∧
103.7 disgrac't.] ~∧
103.21 gains.] ~∧
103.33 night;] ~.
103.34 it's] its
103.36 Grace.] ~∧
103.40 it.] ~∧
103.53 deckt] deck
103.60 Still.] ~∧
103.64 dresst.] ~∧
103.71 to't;] ~.
103.71 bestow.] ~∧
103.72 flow.] ~∧
104.4 Nourishment.] ~∧
104.6 provide.] ~∧
104.9 Dress] ~.
104.10 with,] ~.
104.12 forestall.] ~∧
104.40 Vertue,] ~.
104.44 Christ's] Christ
104.46 their] theirs
104.49 Eate,] ~∧
104.50 delight.] ~∧

104.51 it's] its
104.55 it's] its
104.56 mentain.] ~_^
104.58 spirituall] spiritull
104.76 Washt] wash't
104.78 Story.] ~_^
105.4 glory] gloly
105.11 thus,] ~.
105.12 Souls] Soals
105.20 made,] ~..
105.20 it's] its
105.39 fare,] ~_^
105.42 too] to
106.4 rise.] ~_^
106.6 possibility.] ~_^
106.14 Praise.] ~_^
106.16 raise.] ~_^
106.20 sustain.] ~_^
106.29 that's] thats
106.31 it's] its
106.32 begon.] ~_^
106.33 goe.] ~_^
106.52 require.] ~_^
106.54 oates.] ~_^
106.66 make] makes
107.title remembrance] remem/brance
107.18 restore.] ~_^
107.21 surprizde.] ~_^
107.24 free.] ~_^
107.25 Coasts] Costs
107.27 seed.] ~_^
107.32 Form.] ~_^
107.36 Form,] ~.
107.38 sweet.] ~_^
107.42 come;] ~.
107.43 Christ's] Christ
107.54 misusd.] ~_^
107.58 mee;] ~.
107.58 bee.] ~_^
107.60 praise] paise
108.3 ornamantall] ~.
108.8 ly).] ~)_^
108.13 Confounds.] ~_^
108.14 wine;] ~_^
108.14 it's] its

108.15 wounds.] ~_^
108.16 whore.] ~_^
108.30 sphere.] ~_^
108.31 'ray'd] ray'd
108.33 It's] Its
108.34 Wine.] ~_^
108.36 Grace,] ~_^
108.40 Cup] Cap
108.47 sippits,] ~.
108.50 bee.] ~_^
109.8 That's] Thats
109.9 Chargers] Charges
109.16 bee,] ~.
109.28 Serpent;] ~.
109.28 torn.] ~_^
109.40 It's] Its
109.44 drest.] ~_^
109.49 They're] They'r
109.51 stones.] ~_^
109.53 Ghost.] ~_^
109.54 Coast.] ~,
109.65 feast;] ~.
110.6 hast.] ~_^
110.13 Grave] Graves
110.40 Vanity.] ~_^
110.42 pipe.] ~_^
110.45 Voice.] ~_^
110.46 flame.] ~_^
110.52 same,] ~.
110.52 Just.] ~_^
110.53 I'le] Ile
110.54 reech.] ~_^
111.1 high?] ~_^
111.7 hearts,] ~_^
111.9 imparts] impartst
111.17 faint,] ~.
111.30 Good?] ~,?
111.31 then.] ~_^
111.36 thereto.] ~_^
111.40 such.] ~_^
111.42 enrich.] ~_^
111.45 It's] Its
111.46 Faith.] ~_^
111.47 sting.] ~_^
111.51 them,] ~.

111.58 increast.] ~ₐ

111.59 resists] resist

111.63 breed.] ~ₐ

111.64 free.] ~ₐ

112.7 Did'st] Di'dst

112.12 That] Thet

112.12 free.] ~ₐ

112.16 light.] ~ₐ

112.17 theirs.] ~ₐ

112.18 clears.] ~ₐ

112.21 unskin'd,] ~.

112.22 wound.] ~ₐ

112.23 Death's] Deaths

112.24 It's] Its

112.29 paw;] ~.

112.31 lost.] ~ₐ

112.33 It's] Its

112.34 sings] sing

112.38 too] to

113.10 delight.] ~ₐ

113.14 tree,] ~ₐ

113.15 be;] ~.

113.31 Lock.] ~ₐ

113.33 it's] its

114.29 th'] th

114.30 come.] ~ₐ

114.49 in's] ins

114.52 far).] ~)ₐ

114.53 th'] th

114.60 night.] ~ₐ

115.1 thee?] ~ₐ

115.4 I'de] Ide

115.12 please?] ~ₐ

115.31 lovely,] ~ₐ

115.33 should] shoud

115.43 Love.] ~ₐ

115.46 display.] ~ₐ

115.48 thyselfe] thyselfer

116.6 God's] God

116.7 Pursevant] Pursevan

116.7 to] ~.

116.8 too] to

116.11 it's] its

116.21 drawn.] ~ₐ

116.37 Objects] Objejects

116.42 therein;] ~.

116.42 it's] its

116.47 Hands.] ~ₐ

116.48 bands.]~ₐ

116.51 best;] ~.

116.51 Beauty's] Beautys

116.52 save.] ~ₐ

116.54 sweet.] ~ₐ

117.2 down.] ~ₐ

117.4 Crowns.] ~ₐ

117.6 Light.] ~ₐ

117.8 Gold.] ~ₐ

117.9 It's] Its

117.22 rag).] ~)ₐ

117.28 Shield,] ~ₐ

117.36 and] ~ and

117.40 wise.] ~ₐ

117.42 joying.] ~ₐ

117.44 *Grace*.] ~ₐ

118.2 this] thiss

118.2 bright] brigh

118.3 that's] thats

118.10 mould.] ~ₐ

118.18 Gold.] ~ₐ

118.24 fill.] ~ₐ

118.30 statutes] statute

118.30 behold.] ~,

118.36 toe,] ~.

118.42 tenses.] ~ₐ

118.44 Statutes] Statues

119.1 Lord!] ~,!

119.1 Love!] ~,!

119.4 shine.] ~ₐ

119.22 Stare.] ~ₐ

119.24 Chase.] ~ₐ

120.5 Countenance.] ~ₐ

120.10 fair.] ~ₐ

120.16 Quire.] ~ₐ

120.25 that's] thats

120.29 doe] ~?

120.30 The] They

120.40 in's] ins

120.40 th'] th

120.48 tunes.] ~ₐ

121.3 dull] ~.

121.7 of] on
121.10 host.] ~ₐ
121.12 redresst.] ~ₐ
121.30 't] t
121.34 Grace,] ~ₐ
121.42 arise.] ~ₐ
122.3 Deare] Dears
122.5 'Cause] Cause
122.10 too] to
122.22 station.] ~ₐ
122.23 Chil'd] Child
122.60 Hand.] ~ₐ
123[A].title Bowells]] ~)]
123[A].5 boiles] boile
123[A].6 smiles.] ~ₐ
123[A].8 Christs] ~,
123[A].10 thine.] ~ₐ
123[A].11 thou!] ~,!
123[A].13 sad?] ~,?
123[A].14 Face.] ~ₐ
123[A].15 bad.] ~ₐ
123[A].18 singe.] ~ₐ
123[A].20 deare.] ~ₐ
123[A].21 shine.] ~ₐ
123[A].22 clear.] ~ₐ
123[A].24 Chime.] ~ₐ
123[B].Date 1715] 1714
123[B].10 bring.] ~ₐ
123[B].12 smoot.] ~ₐ
123[B].18 gold.] ~,
123[B].24 and'ts] and't
123[B].33 sweet.] ~ₐ
123[B].34 hate.] ~ₐ
123[B].36 goe.] ~ₐ
123[B].44 heart] heard
123[B].48 feet.] ~ₐ
125.10 dispense.] ~ₐ
125.12 goare.] ~ₐ
125.30 flow.] ~,
125.33 apace.] ~ₐ
125.34 peare.] ~ₐ
125.36 thereon.] ~ₐ
125.42 Extasies.] ~ₐ
125.43 Lebanon.] ~ₐ
125.45 upon.] ~ₐ

126.2 line.] ~ₐ
126.4 shrine.] ~ₐ
126.14 Wafting] Wasting
126.16 thus] this
126.18 passage,] ~.
126.34 Conveigh.] ~ₐ
126.54 sing.] ~ₐ
127.7 power] prower
127.7 desire.] ~ₐ
127.18 super-superlative.] ~ₐ
127.25 art,] ~.
127.28 degree.] ~ₐ
127.36 Divine.] ~ₐ
127.38 Conduct] ~.
127.40 Palace] ~.
127.41 intertain] intertainst
127.54 Glory.] ~ₐ
128.1 Lord,] ~.
128.3 web] webe
128.14 Temple,] ~.
128.16 tones.] ~ₐ
128.19 soule's] soules
128.20 laid,] ~ₐ
128.23 thoughts] thougts
128.24 thought] thoughtt
128.25 bright.] ~ₐ
128.27 delight.] ~ₐ
128.30 quick.] ~ₐ
128.32 awry,] ~ₐ
128.33 Leave] leave
128.33 grace,] ~.
128.36 skip.] ~ₐ
128.38 spot.] ~ₐ
128.42 Prime.] ~ₐ
128.48 Womankinde.] ~ₐ
128.52 Bride] Brde
128.54 int'] in't
128.54 Grace.] ~ₐ
129.1 Lord,] ~.
129.6 saying;] ~';
129.8 kinde?] ~ₐ
129.10 Garden's] Garden
129.18 Towers.] ~ₐ
129.30 pipe.] ~ₐ
130.1 sweet-sweet] sweet-speet

130.8 spot o'flowers] spotoflowers
130.12 sent.] ~.,
130.16 Breathe] Breaths
130.18 these] thise
130.20 Couches] Coaches
130.22 delight.] ~ₐ
130.28 jewells,] ~ₐ
130.38 bee.] ~ₐ
130.40 thee.] ~ₐ
130.41 sweetness] sweeness
130.44 Lord,] ~:.
131.1 finde.] ~ₐ
131.4 call] ~.
131.33 Dish.] ~ₐ
131.44 spiced] spic'de
131.44 joy.] ~ₐ
131.48 sing.] ~ₐ
132.6 stain.] ~ₐ
132.13 thee.] ~ₐ
132.14 have.] ~ₐ
132.18 show.] ~ₐ
132.20 'Mongst] Mongst
132.22 power.] ~ₐ
132.30 mine.] ~ₐ
132.36 'tis] ti's
132.36 Grace.] ~ₐ
132.39 delight.] ~ₐ
132.41 growst,] ~.
132.44 Lilly,] ~ₐ
132.44 right.] ~ₐ
132.47 fair.] ~ₐ
132.48 air.] ~ₐ
132.49 air.] ~ₐ
132.53 bee.] ~ₐ
133.3 away.] ~ₐ
133.4 lot.] ~ₐ
133.7 Bridsgroom's] Bridsgrooms
133.7 Brids;] ~ₐ
133.7 hers.] ~ₐ
133.8 He's] Hes
133.9 all,] ~ₐ
133.10 what's] whats
133.10 without.] ~ₐ
133.24 mee.] ~ₐ
133.25 indeed.] ~ₐ

133.30 be.] ~ₐ
133.33 You'st] Youst
133.34 displaid.] ~ₐ
133.38 espousd] esousd
133.42 Spouse] Spou ~
133.44 'fore] fore
133.46 throughout] thoughout
133.46 Eternity.] ~ₐ
134.11 it's] its
134.12 'steem] steem
134.24 hand.] ~ₐ
134.26 blame.] ~ₐ
134.27 eternally.] ~ₐ
134.29 delight,] ~ₐ
134.29 heart.] ~ₐ
134.36 on't] ont
134.37 perchance] perchanch
134.40 Christ's] Christ
134.41 Christ's] Christ
134.42 with's] withs
134.42 Red.] ~ₐ
135.7 bears.] ~ₐ
135.8 Christ's] Christ
135.12 within.] ~ₐ
135.13 balled] bulled
135.13 sparkes] sparke
135.17 fly] ~.
135.18 'stroy] stroy
135.20 Bow's] Bows
135.20 Tong's] Tongs
135.22 therein.] ~ₐ
135.24 word.] ~ₐ
135.28 Thum[p].] ~ₐ
135.29 Mouth,] ~ₐ
135.30 field.] ~ₐ
135.33 artists] artist
135.34 tite.] ~ₐ
135.35 lets] let
135.35 flie] flies
135.36 lin[k].] ~ₐ
135.38 command.] ~ₐ
135.41 Christ's] Christ
135.42 right,] ~.
135.46 flying,] ~ₐ
136.5 It's] Its

136.6 thou] though
136.10 th'] th
136.16 it's] its
136.16 sure.] ~∧
136.23 art] aret
136.30 'steems] steems
136.36 joy.] ~∧
136.46 shalt] sho'nt
136.46 joy.] ~∧
136.48 Higher.] ~∧
137.6 adventures.] ~∧
137.18 ly,] ~.
137.22 live,] ~∧
137.24 apace.] ~∧
137.27 prime?] ~∧
138.3 prie] ~.
138.4 move] ~.
138.10 pen's] pen
138.11 Will.] ~∧
138.12 too] to
138.31 Christ's] Christ
138.33 'ployd] ployd
138.33 its] it
138.48 Takes] Take's
138.50 its] it
138.52 Give] Gives
138.64 minde.] ~∧
138.69 Christ's] Christ
139.title Pomeg[ra]nate] Pomeg[ra]/nate
139.22 Head.] ~∧
139.24 strains.] ~∧
140.Number 140] 129
140.12 plites.] ~∧
140.18 blushes,] ~.
140.26 That's] Thats
140.30 Christ's] Christs
140.34 Humility.] ~∧
140.36 thee.] ~∧
141.Number 141] 130
141.6 Empty,] ~∧
141.7 minde,] ~.
141.12 geere.] ~∧
141.15 It's] Its
141.36 it's] its
141.40 I'st] Ist

141.42 Queens] Queen
141.44 me,] ~∧
141.47 I'le] Ile
141.48 Wing.] ~∧
142.Number 142] 131
142.title Meditation] Medtation
142.2 My] my
142.4 pen,] ~∧
142.7 this?] ~∧
142.7 Thy] thy
142.7 rise.] ~∧
142.10 Queens] Queen
142.11 far] fur
142.12 Transcends] Transcend
142.13 bore.] ~∧
142.15 Darling,] ~.
142.18 her] hers
142.22 Deare,] ~∧
142.24 harms.] ~∧
142.30 Concubines] Concubine
142.41 I'l] Il'
143.Number 143] 134
143.title Fare] Fore
143.23 beams] beam
143.29 Moon,] ~∧
143.39 By] by
143.46 peares] peare
143.48 th'] th
143.59 Bridesgroom] Bridesgroon
143.64 I'st] Ist
144.Number 144] 135
144.title flowerished] flower/ished
144.10 pomegranates] pomegranate
144.16 Yea] Ye
144.18 Barren,] ~∧
144.28 bow's] bows
144.39 Gold,] ~∧
144.40 I'st] Ist
145.Number 145] 136
145.11 thro'] tho'
145.14 Be lind] Belind
145.22 me] we
145.29 ere] eare
145.32 therein.] ~∧
145.36 sweetest] sweest

146.Number 146] 137

146.2 too] to

146.3 in,] ~.

146.4 mantle;] ~.

146.4 loath?] ~ₐ

146.15 Use,] ~ₐ

146.26 guise,] ~ₐ

146.27 it;] ~.

147.Number 147] 138

147.5 shines] shins

147.12 glances] glance

147.21 such] shuch

147.26 gain,] ~ₐ

147.27 knew,] ~ₐ

147.28 ere] ear

147.31 blind;] ~ₐ

147.31 sight] sights

147.32 this.] ~ₐ

147.33 It's] Its

147.33 thing;] ~ₐ

147.34 sin-blind] sinₐblind

147.35 Christ's] Christ

148.Number 148] 139

148.3 say'th] say,'th

148.6 feet;] ~ₐ

148.8 behold.] ~ₐ

148.11 shine,] ~ₐ

148.14 behold:] ~ₐ

148.16 walke's] walkes

148.16 gold;] ~ₐ

148.23 step] stept

148.37 thought,] ~ₐ

148.38 grace,] ~ₐ

148.47 sweet.] ~ₐ

148.50 lashed,] ~ₐ

148.50 ware,] ~ₐ

149.Number 149] 140

149.2 Eye,] ~.

149.6 caused] cause

149.13 returning,] ~ₐ

149.14 Gold.] ~ₐ

149.21 soule,] ~ₐ

149.34 Bread] Bead

149.42 rich,] ~ₐ

150.Number 150] 141

150.1 Lord,] ~.

150.3 breasts] breast

151.Number 151] 142

151.3 bright] brigh

151.4 prime] prine

151.9 Herselfe,] ~ₐ

151.18 compleate.] ~ₐ

151.24 Body,] ~.

151.30 thereby.] ~ₐ

151.36 darkness] darknest

151.37 Lanthorn] Lathorn

151.39 daylight,] ~ₐ

151.39 stand.] ~ₐ

151.42 out;] ~ₐ

151.46 Enemy.] ~ₐ

151.47 Neck,] ~ₐ

151.58 her] here

151.59 I'st] Ist

151.60 Bridall] Bidall

152.Number 152] 143

152.1 Soul] Souls

152.4 slick.] ~ₐ

152.11 Crystal] Crysal

152.11 Roofe,] ~ₐ

152.18 to] ~'

152.18 th'] th

152.19 sparkling] sprkling

152.27 Nose,] ~ₐ

152.27 brows,] ~ₐ

152.28 Arm,] ~ₐ

152.28 Hand,] ~ₐ

153.Number 153] 144

153.22 sing.] ~ₐ

153.24 morrow.] ~ₐ

[154].Number [154]] ₐ

[154].8 deckt] deck

[154].10 Together] together

[154].23 Priest] Priests

[154].25 shine] shines

[154].26 soule,] ~ₐ

[154].26 fild,] ~ₐ

[154].34 day,] ~ₐ

[154].38 indeed.] ~ₐ

[154].40 proceed.] ~ₐ

[154].41 grow.] ~ₐ

[154].45 th'] th
[154].54 sing.] ~ˌ
155.number 155] 146
155.2 workt] work
155.2 th'] th
155.18 thyself] thysell
155.20 make.] ~ˌ
155.22 Lord's] Lord
155.29 it's] its
155.33 it's] its
155.35 is't's] is'ts
155.35 told.] ~ˌ
155.38 purifies,] ~ˌ
155.39 Tongue] Thongue
155.39 silver;] ~ˌ
155.40 With] with
155.45 stones] stone
155.47 this,] ~ˌ
156.number 156] 147
156.3 thee,] ~.
156.3 miss,] ~ˌ
156.6 buss,] ~.
156.7 'T] T'
156.7 Minted] Minttd
156.10 Methinkes] Methinke
156.10 makes] make
156.18 makes] make
156.20 me;] ~ˌ
156.27 of'ts] of't
157[A].Number 157[A]] 148
157[A].5 It's] Its
157[A].9 Heaven's] Heavens
157[A].9 It's] Its
157[A].12 so.] ~ˌ
157[A].15 soure] soures
157[A].19 Graces] Grace
157[A].23 wheat's] wheats
157[A].24 Banquet's] Banquets's
157[A].29 It's] Its
157[A].29 spit.] ~ˌ
157[A].33 fine,] ~ˌ
157[B].Number 157[B]] 14[8]
157[B].title house,] ~.
157[B].4 like.] ~ˌ
157[B].5 It's] Its

157[B].9 Heaven's] Heavens
157[B].9 made.] ~ˌ
157[B].9 It's] Its
157[B].13 heaven,] ~ˌ
157[B].18 Angells] Angell
157[B].20 Christ's] Christ
157[B].30 Dripping,] ~ˌ
157[B].37 wine.] ~ˌ
157[B].40 drew.] ~ˌ
157[B].41 it's] its
157[B].42 abide.] ~ˌ
157[B].43 banquet's] banquets
157[B].44 Best.] ~ˌ
157[B].47 things] thing
157[B].47 superlative.] ~ˌ
157[B].49 'mongst] mongst
158.Number 158] 149
158.3 bee.] ~ˌ
158.4 mantle,] ~ˌ
158.6 fist?] ~ˌ
158.7 Gloriousness,] ~,?
158.8 admire?] ~.
158.9 express.] ~ˌ
158.14 Case.] ~ˌ
158.15 too] to
158.23 'T] T'
158.24 face.] ~?
158.26 all] ~ 't
158.42 aright.] ~ˌ
158.43 through] though
158.44 tongue.] ~ˌ
158.46 along.] ~ˌ
158.53 Divills] Divill
158.64 'ploy] ~.
158.66 happiness,] ~.
158.68 Enemies,] ~.
158.70 Angells] Angell
158.74 favour.] ~ˌ
158.75 th'] th
159.Number 159] 150
159.title 2.17.] 3.10.
159.1 Lord;] ~.
159.5 intermission,] ~ˌ
159.14 overcom.] ~ˌ
159.18 wayes.] ~ˌ

159.22 not] ~.

159.23 grace:] ~‸

159.23 boys;] ~‸

159.25 made.] ~‸

159.27 dainties,] ~‸

159.29 entertains] entertain

159.30 Sir;] ~.

159.30 it's] its

159.31 linde] lind'e

159.34 divine.] ~‸

159.37 Benches,] ~‸

159.41 Waiters] Waters

159.41 are,] ~‸

159.42 Mannah,] ~‸

159.43 Grace.] ~‸

159.44 Heaven.] ~‸

159.45 Cooke's] Cooke

159.45 place.] ~‸

159.46 it's] its

159.48 it's] its

159.51 Paradise.] ~‸

160.Number 160] 151

160.5 same.] ~‸

160.6 omit] omnt

160.7 thing.] ~‸

160.8 heart's] hearts

160.9 It's] Its

160.13 low.] ~‸

160.14 there.] ~‸

160.17 divine,] ~‸

160.19 grows,] ~‸

160.20 blesst] bless

160.21 'bedience] bedien

160.24 'brace.] ~‸

160.30 guise.] ~‸

160.33 in] ~.

160.34 Vall in] Vallin

160.37 too] to

160.38 praiseworthiness.] ~‸

160.39 Angells] Angell

160.48 string.] ~‸

161[A].Number 161[A]] 152

161[A].5 times] time

161[A].7 thing,] ~‸

161[A].8 Crickling,] ~‸

161[A].8 bud,] ~‸

161[A].10 It's] Its

161[A].12 grain?] ~.

161[A].15 swans] ~)

161[A].16 account),] ~.)

162[A].Number 162[A]] 153

162[A].5 delight.] ~‸

162[A].6 bright.] ~‸

162[A].8 sounde.] ~‸

162[A].10 them,] ~.

162[A].10 come.] ~‸

162[A].12 sweet.] ~‸

162[A].16 And] and

162[A].16 glee.] ~‸

162[A].18 dress.] ~‸

161[B].Number 161[B]] 152

161[B].2 times,] ~.

161[B].5 'T] T'

161[B].14 Excellst.] ~‸

161[B].17 'T] T'

161[B].17 streams.] ~‸

161[B].18 it's] its

161[B].25 It's] Its

161[B].30 snake.] ~‸

161[B].32 Basket;] ~‸

161[B].44 God;] ~‸

162[B].Number 162[B]] 153

162[B].title shadow with] shadowith

162[B].4 march;] ~‸

162[B].5 'tis] tis

162[B].10 heaven's] heaven

162[B].24 Through] Though

162[B].28 cup,] ~.

163.Number 163] 154

163.7 sweet] sweet sweet

163.9 reech,] ~.

163.23 spot,] ~‸

163.32 rose] roses

163.35 It's] Its

163.43 Holiness,] ~‸

163.52 Is] is

163.52 Angells] Angell

163.58 eatest;] ~‸

163.59 little:] ~‸

163.62 fruite] fruite to taste the fruit

163.63 sweetings] sweeting

163.64 sweet] seet

163.66 tast.] ~∧

164.Number 164] 155th

164.4 trip,] ~∧

164.5 smoake,] ~∧

164.8 buffe] ~.

164.10 That's] Thats

164.10 garment,] ~.

164.15 it's] its

165.Number 165] 156

165.3 parchment's] parchments

165.6 it's] its

165.8 thee,] ~.

165.11 hatcht] hatch

165.12 bed.] ~∧

165.18 best.] ~∧

165.22 well.] ~∧

165.23 rest.] ~∧

165.24 best.] ~∧

165.25 have.] ~∧

165.30 sing.] ~∧

VARIANTS

Following is a list of variants between this edition, *Edward Taylor's* Gods Determinations *and* Preparatory Meditations: *A Critical Edition* (*ET*) and *The Poems of Edward Taylor* (*Poems*), edited by Donald Stanford (New Haven: Yale University Press, 1960). The *unemended* manuscript reading (as reported in *ET*) appears to the left of the central bracket; to the right of that bracket is the corresponding reading as it appears in *Poems*. The tilde (~) to the right of the central bracket represents a word repeated from the reading to the left of the bracket without change. The caret (^) to the right of the bracket emphasizes that a point of punctuation that occurs in the present edition does not occur in *Poems*.

In many cases, a reading that *Poems* reports as the manuscript reading agrees with an *emended* reading in *ET*. For example, at *GD* 1446, the *Poems* reading "Willful," agrees with the emended reading in *ET*, where the list of emendations reports that no comma follows "Willful" in the manuscript. All such variants are included here.

Variants involving conjectural readings also occur. At *PM* 2.136.33, for example, *Poems* reports a conjectural (*conj.*) "tract" while *ET* reports that "tract" is legible in the manuscript. In some cases, a reading that *Poems* reports as conjectural is partially legible; *ET* reports the legible portions. For example, at *PM* 2.135.41, the word "shield," which Stanford gives as conjectural, is partially legible and so reported in *ET* as "shie[ld]." The variants between *ET* and *Poems* in the evidence of Taylor's manuscript revision (given at the end of each poem herein) are not reported.

GODS DETERMINATIONS

title &c] and
16 down] ~,
37 Man,] ~^
37 indeed] ~,
39 man] then
58 Fortify] ~.
68 Findes,] ~^
78 trace:] ~.
87 himselfe] himself
102 Sin.] ~,

108 nought] ~,
111 Breast.] ~^
115 Array'de] Array'd
122 as] is
137 show] ~.
140 Violence] ~.
150 buckling,] ~^
155 it o're,] ~^ ~^
159 beare] ~,
163 fall;] ~:
179 What] ~,

185 shall] ~,
186 Stands] ~.
188 hands] ~.
201 bee] ~.
221 feare.] ~,
223 Will] ~.
227 abusde] abus'de
235 lessoning] lessening
242 rake] ~.
243 ar'] are
254 He'st] Ile'st
293 mee,] ~.
311 Soule,] ~ˌ
318 lai'n] lain
327 come,] ~ˌ
338 waft] wast
340 goe.] ~,
354 raisd] rais'd
356 opprest.] ~,
372 guessts] guests
383 finde] ~.
389 in] ~.
402 Eternall] Eternal
408 reare.] ~ˌ
411 down] ~.
412 frown] ~.
414 thereat,] ~ˌ
414 throw.] ~,
425 Small] ~.
428 To all] ~ ~,
428 inclinde:] ~ˌ
441 rancks,] ~ˌ
466 away.] ~,
472 before] ~.
473 red-hot-firy] ~-~ˌ~
474 ingage,] ~ˌ
476 whom] Whom
479 fist] ~.
487 feeble hearted] ~-~
494 aide] aid
501 foe.] ~,
513 Presumption] ~,
541 Will] ~.
542 Still.] ~,
554 lie] ~.

557 field] ~.
578 were.] ~,
594 Coate] ~,
595 Eyes,] ~ˌ
602 fall.] ~,
609 Its] It's
611 may] ~.
622 be;] ~,
626 Cry.] ~,
630 Knife.] ~ˌ
631 Sin] ~.
666 Pick-pack] Pickpack
673 yourself] yourselfe
685 finde] ~,
688 adde] add
698 Embrace] ~.
699 aright] ~.
715 Place] place
723 itselfe.] ~,
728 amuzde] amus'de
758 pipe] ~.
763 Conscience.] ~,
765 Sin.] ~,
769 Well] ~,
782 Pardons] ~,
787 mee;] ~,
788 makes,] ~ˌ
794 Stray] ~.
797 first,] ~.
817 fur] far
829 Head] ~.
836 is] ~.
840 I'le] I'l
840 Severely] severly
850 Repentance] Repentence
854 may;] ~:
860 Soul] ~,
885 Spare.] ~,
898 Faith] faith
902 fur] far
922 Mock:] ~.
926 Rear!?] ~!ˌ
927 Mite!] ~:
935 Fly,] ~ˌ
948 ring] ~.

963 Gulph,] ~∧
970 thee] ~,
993 Fall:] ~∧
997 Soule,] ~∧
997 thus,] ~∧
1002 Sound] ~.
1041 Stirdy] sturdy
1042 Grace,] ~∧
1051 Slavery] ~.
1055 Greate] ~.
1056 is is] is
1059 impart,] ~∧
1064 whats] what's
1065 trust] ~.
1121 true:] ~,
1125 Demand] Command
1131 part;] ~:
1136 e'vry] ev'ry
1173 we, rue] ~, ~.
1178 Good] ~,
1192 oh] ~,
1203 word] ~.
1209 do] Do
1213 doe] ~.
1215 what] What,
1224 yourselves,] ~∧
1231 pra'yreless] pray'reless
1237 not] ~,
1245 mercy] Mercy
1261 Crackt] Crack't
1267 brinck.] ~∧
1290 wilt] ~.
1313 Cawle wrought] ~--~
1315 Lodge, which] Lid∧ ~,
1316 rowles] shuts
1319 do,?] ~∧?
1349 Strange.] ~:
1360 Grace:] ~.
1388 Crookt] Crook't
1395 Sins] ~,
1415 bee] ~.
1417 thought.] ~,
1429 fraught] ~,
1431 Methinkes] Methinks
1445 flint;] ~,

1446 Wilfull] ~
1449 quite.] ~,
1453 well.] Well,
1462 they'l] thy'l
1462 own] ~.
1480 aright:] ~.
1488 root:] ~.
1494 deem'st] deemst
1500 appears,] ~.
1503 Genuine] ~.
1507 Soule] ~,
1513 Humility.] ~,
1515 sure.] ~,
1528 just] Just
1533 He'de] He'd
1551 What] ~!
1553 better,] ~∧
1556 Cut] cut
1563 fall] ~.
1564 you had] ~, ~
1572 in] on
1575 Tho] The
1578 lose,] ~∧
1578 minde] ~.
1586 Its] It's
1588 Vip'rous]Viprous
1596 spoile] spoil
1596 Same.] ~,
1614 Untill] Until
1622 Sin.] ~,
1624 much,] ~∧
1634 Splended] splendid
1637 obtain.] ~,
1647 Rewew] Renew
1650 frailty] ~,
1657 Contend] ~.
1667 blinding,] ~∧
1686 forg'in] forgi'n
1688 its] it's
1690 begun,] ~.
1691 its] it's
1691 done] ~,
1695 Calls] ~.
1700 doubts.] ~:
1714 away] ~.

1715 grave] ~.
1716 Its] It's
1721 Serve] ~,
1744 These] Those
1755 Taffity] ~,
1757 are.] ~:
1760 rise] ~,
1767 ejects] ~.
1769 Theres] There's
1769 New] new
1769 finde] find
1772 Cast] ~.
1786 Sublune] Sublime
1786 Face] ~.
1796 Worldliness;] ~:
1799 one] ~.
1800 upon] ~.
1810 harms] ~.
1811 fly.] ~,
1821 Providence] ~,
1825 firled] foiled
1829 Snarle] snarld
1851 presume,] ~∧
1861 But,] ~∧
1863 its] it's
1868 motes.] ~,
1886 ALL.] ~∧
1914 thereof] ~.
1914 pay] ~.
1925 Yea] ~,
1927 inlai'de] inlaide
1930 Ordinance,] ~∧
1963 Itself] Itselfe
1979 purdue.] ~,
1982 know] ~.
1994 splic'te] ~.
2010 Angels] Angells
2016 Contents] ~.
2030 Heaven] heaven
2043 Instruments.] ~∧
2049 otherwise,] ~∧
2055 Winde-Instruments] ~∧~
2063 theft] heft
2064 Voice] ~.
2068 Angells] Angels

2079 Enfirde] Enfir'de
2085 soon,] ~∧

PREPARATORY MEDITATIONS

FIRST SERIES

1.7 Oh.] ~,
2.1 Call.] ~:
2.2 art] ~,
2.5 Low,] ~;
2.17 Lord] ~,
2.22 herein] therein
2.23 Box] box
"The Experience":
20 farther] further
23 first,] first∧
"The Return":
5 me] mee
46 Charity.] ~,
50 assume:] ~.
4.3 Box] ~,
4.4 pick,] pick∧
4.11 unlocks] Unlocks
4.33 shes] she's
4.38 Vertues] Virtues
4.42 Rose.] ~,
4.49 need,] need∧
"Another Meditation":
8 dim,] ~;
7.17 poured] pourd
9.4 Pish.] ~,
10.28 Lord,] ~.
10.31 jar] Jar
11.18 joy.] ~!
11.25 Fast, &] Fasting
12.22 about.] ~:
12.25 Curtains;] ~,
13.8 wherein] Wherein
13.20 Shine,] ~∧
13.20 distille] distill
13.24 stought] Stoughd
14.11 answerable.] ~,
14.12 Glory] glory
14.14 Man:] ~∧
14.34 Desires,] ~∧

16.13 Conseald] Conceald

17.title Meditations] Meditation

17.21 twist] ~,

17.38 mee] Mee

17.40 live,] ~∧

18.34 Cures;] ~,

19.4 buride] buri'de

19.33 beside:] ~,

20.4 Angell like] Angell-like

23.32 is;] ~,

23.38 Coy] Clay

24.6 would] Would

24.32 Divine,] ~∧

25.26 it,] ~.

25.34 Complement:] ~.

25.36 Cabbinet;] ~,

26.2 hold] holds

27.5 cannot] ~,

27.20 Fulness:] ~;

27.35 Flow're] ~,

27.38 Angells.] ~∧

29.5 limbs,] ~∧

29.7 Tree.] ~∧

29.10 writh] Writh

29.12 stock] ~,

29.14 all.] ~∧

29.16 fall.] ~,

29.35 thing.] ~,

29.37 burnisht] burnish't

30.3 stateli'st] statelist

30.26 Palace.] ~,

30.27 Flesh,] ~∧

30.32 gild] guild

30.41 sign.] ~∧

30.46 anew.] ~,

31.1 Begrac'de] Begracde

32.1 Lord, 's] Lord's

32.6 Harp] ~,

33.13 amazde] amaz'de

33.24 killd] kill'd

33.35 Ark,] ~;

33.40 Liveing] Living

34.4 Worth.] ~,

34.10 Wilt] Will

34.11 dropd] drop'd

34.17 Pluckt'st] Plucktst

34.41 Oh!] ~∧

34.42 Triumph!] ~∧

34.42 sting] ~?

35.11 Powers,] ~∧

35.11 Lord,] ~∧

35.12 'ffections] 'Fections

35.22 selfe] self

35.25 Troops,] ~∧

35.43 sight.] ~,

35.43 dart:] ~.

36.9 unrivetted] onrivetted

36.10 saith,] ~∧

36.27 unsay] Unsay

36.47 Their] These

36.52 gain.] ~;

36.67 all:] ~.

37.9 Ragnell] ~.

37.10 yet;] ~,

37.11 Cap] ~,

37.24 Rose,] ~∧

37.27 apples:] ~;

37.28 Life.] ~:

39.14 oh!] ~,

39.25 give.] ~:

39.41 fields,] ~∧

39.45 mine.] ~∧

40.15 talk.] ~∧

40.17 stall's] stale's

40.23 Post,-] ~∧-

40.23 Pare] ~,

40.50 Propiciation] Propitiation

40.56 tub:] ~∧

41.14 Just.] ~∧

41.18 'Quittance] Quittance

41.33 appeare;] ~,

41.47 do] so

42.1 Apples,] ~∧

42.16 enlivend] enliven'd

42.32 fine.] ~∧

42.36 blesst] bless't

43.5 thee;] ~,

43.7 Corrupt] ~,

43.15 Love.] ~:

44.29 thee,] ~∧

44.31 Righteousness.] ~ˏ
45.2 Swomp] Swamp,
45.25 yet.] ~:
45.33 ware] Ware,
45.38 Verse.] ~:
46.2 'ray'd] ray'd
46.5 Elements.] ~ˏ
46.10 thus;] ~.
46.15 morn,] ~ˏ
46.16 Nay] ~,
46.17 such:] ~.
46.19 Wit.] ~,
46.38 excell;] ~ˏ
46.54 best] best [conj.]
47.2 joy.] ~:
47.4 die.] ~ˏ
47.8 Bodys Soile] Body: soile
47.13 hell,] ~:
47.24 housd] hous'd
47.25 Seraphims.] ~,
47.26 Carbuncle] carbuncle
48.3 craul] crawl
48.9 ore.] ~,
48.37 waftings] Castings [conj.]
48.41 mee,] ~ˏ
49.2 vitiate,] ~.
49.3 eate.] ~ˏ
49.14 heart.] ~:
49.18 heart,] ~.
49.20 And's] And
SECOND SERIES
1.title to] to come
1.8 Th'] The
1.31 fault.] ~:
2.2 with] With
2.3 wrack] Wrack
2.13 these] those
2.14 melt] make
2.39 other.] ~:
3.10 Emblemizd] Emblemiz'd
3.16 Sin.] ~,
3.26 elfe] else
4.1 doe;] ~:
4.10 Nay] ~,
4.28 Soule;] ~,

4.33 grow] grows
4.34 Figure] Figures
4.35 them] ~,
5.2 One,] ~ˏ
5.7 Antitype.] ~ˏ
5.8 because.] ~ˏ
5.9 cought] caught
5.15 Cought] Caught
5.16 Knife.] Knife:
5.21 Oh.] ~ˏ
5.23 this,] ~ˏ
5.33 sweet;] ~,
5.37 Mutten] Mutton
6.3 blood:] ~ˏ
6.13 saith,] ~ˏ
6.16 alone.] ~,
6.19 shews,] ~ˏ
6.22 wor'st] wer'st
6.27 came'st,] ~ˏ
6.28 wooe] Wooe
6.29 gain.] ~,
6.37 Love,] ~ˏ
6.40 with] in't
6.43 trash.] ~:
6.45 Love] love
6.47 prize,] ~ˏ
6.47 thee:] ~, [PW thee.]
6.47 finde] sende
6.50 [s]end] send
6.51 shall] shalt
7.4 vertue.] ~ˏ
7.9 pickt] pick't
7.12 Bits.] ~,
7.26 bubbles] babbles
7.30 joy] Joy
7.37 bewaile,] ~ˏ
7.41 on] in
8.2 Vane,] ~ˏ
8.2 Bears] Wears
8.3 do.] doˏ
8.5 very] Very
8.13 Dove] Doves
8.15 Guncrack.] ~:
8.16 day.)] ~).
8.20 One)] ~),

8.22 Commends.] ~,

8.24 rich] ~,

8.25 Love.] ~,

8.33 Deare)] ~,) [conj.]

9.27 bring'st] bringst

9.44 well] Well

9.53 glory-darte] ~ˌ~

10.13 Promis'd] Promisd

10.17 fair.] ~,

10.21 Ware.] ~,

10.26 offshook] off took

10.34 Trumpits] Trumpets

10.34 hirld] hurld

10.40 fall.] ~ˌ

10.45 fling.] ~ˌ

10.49 Beam,] ~ˌ

11.13 spouse;] ~,

11.22 mak'st] makest [PW make'st]

11.38 One.] One,

11.45 shows] show:

11.51 Foes,] ~.

12.17 thee,] ~ˌ

13.3 should;] ~,

13.13 stok] stock

13.19 him] he's

13.32 the] thy

13.36 amaz'd] amazed [PW amaze'd]

13.44 in thy,] ~ ~ˌ

13.45 Cup,] ~ˌ

14.10 stripes.] ~,

14.33 Story)] ~).

15.6 Sapphires] Sapphire's

15.9 Grace'es] Grace's

15.10 Gods] God's

15.10 Hall] ~.

15.16 Kirnelld] Kirnells

15.16 Chink] ~:

15.25 Crown.] ~ˌ

15.30 they'le] they'l

15.37 pray] ~,

15.39 thyselfe.] ~,

16.16 in] on

16.19 beares] Grows

16.23 tauny] tawny

16.37 I,] ~ˌ

16.43 Pride,] ~ˌ

16.44 laid.] ~ˌ

17.1 One.] ~:

17.17 mould] would

17.19 bailes,] ~.

17.26 Fire.] ~:

17.32 thine,] ~ˌ

17.35 mee,] ~.

17.40 Tinder.] ~,

17.45 bulke] ~,

17.48 gift.] ~,

17.49 sacrifice.] ~,

17.50 mee.] ~,

17.51 Child.] ~,

17.51 prize.] ~,

18.8 Alley] ~.

18.10 pingle:] ~.

18.11 Coursy] Coursey

18.13 Attonement] Atonement

18.21 Godhead] ~,

18.24 mens] men's

18.33 'tire.] ~ˌ

18.41 Claw] ~,

18.49 climb,] ~ˌ

18.62 High.] ~ˌ

19.3 Excelleny,] ~ˌ

19.4 [*]ich] reech [conj.]

19.13 delight,] ~ˌ

19.15 bright,] ~ˌ

19.19 Circuite-Table] ~ˌ~

19.22 An[d]] And

19.23 Lavender.] ~ˌ

20.6 hell.] ~:

20.24 Oyle.] ~ˌ

20.27 wall] Wall

20.33 within:] ~ˌ

20.41 Stowd] stand

20.41 in't.] ~,

20.42 Seate.] ~,

20.46 Holies.] ~,

20.50 thee.] ~,

20.54 House.] ~,

20.55 mee.] ~,

20.58 its] thy

20.59 me:] ~.

20.59 herein.] ~ˌ

21.2 makst] makest

21.5 clearly] ~,

21.9 Mon'th] Month

21.23 Feasts.] ~,

21.25 aide.] ~ˌ

21.25 refine.] ~ˌ

21.28 fly,] ~.

21.44 day.] ~ˌ

21.52 Ecclipsd] Ecclipsed

21.55 Earth,] ~ˌ

21.56 me] ~,

21.62 Seales.] ~,

21.70 Zion:] ~.

22.2 Full.] ~ˌ [PW ~,]

22.6 Grave.] ~ˌ

22.10 when] When

22.10 Free'd] Freed

22.17 updresst.] ~,

22.18 hearbs.] ~,

22.22 fall.] ~,

22.23 I le] I'le

22.24 Corner all] ~ ~,

22.33 I le] I'le

22.34 good.] ~,

22.35 hand.] ~,

22.40 Food,] ~ˌ

22.40 with] With

22.43 I le] I'le

22.51 Whitsuntide,] ~;

22.52 anew] ~.

22.53 fifti'th] fift'th

22.55 our] oure

22.61 inn'd] ~,

22.63 typifying] typefying

22.67 this] the

22.68 Feast:] ~,

23.1 Lord] ~,

23.3 Eare.] ~;

23.14 makst] makest

23.21 Curtain.] ~,

23.37 t'] to

23.41 incense] Incense

23.41 Prayer.] ~ˌ

23.54 'Ray] Ray

23.64 Fly.] ~,

23.71 thyself] thyselfe

23.77 Wyers] ~,

23.78 ALTASCHAT] ALTASCHAT

24.18 tol[d]] told

24.23 mee,] ~ˌ

24.28 here] ~?

24.30 war[e]] ware

24.32 thine.] ~ˌ

24.56 Lease] Leafe

24.57 live:] ~.

25.3 are] o're

25.8 heart.] ~,

25.15 Wear] Weare

25.26 Christ.] ~,

25.27 wine] Wine

25.31 first.] ~ˌ

25.32 Wherefore] ~,

25.39 What] ~!

25.46 Containd] Contained

25.47 Feeble] feeble

26.1 vile,] ~ˌ

26.2 Defil'd] Defild

26.12 Church-fellowship] ~ˌ~

26.14 Holiness.] ~:

26.19 heifers] heifer's

26.20 Water] ~,

26.22 feate.] ~ˌ

26.30 whiter than,] ~, ~ˌ

27.2 alone:] ~,

27.3 Gold;] ~:

27.11 Runs: my] Running

27.12 Coverd] Covered

27.14 botchd] botch't

27.17 too] ~,

27.17 cry.] ~,

27.18 Uncleane, Uncleane.] Unclean, Unclean,

27.19 mee!] ~.

27.23 nay:] ~,

27.25 cought] caught

27.27 Natures.] ~,

27.32 twine] ~,

27.33 diptd] dipted

27.34 times.] ~ˌ

27.35 appli'de] applide
27.36 purifi'de] purifide
27.43 Sacrifice] Sacrifices
27.46 bring.] ~,
27.49 [A]nd] And
27.51 [T]his] Thy [conj.]
27.56 sanctifie] sanctify
27.65 praise.] ~,
28.1 build.] ~∧
28.2 ev'ry] every
28.5 Bell;] ~:
28.6 Shell.] ~!
28.8 Law.] ~,
28.9 Wealth.] ~,
28.10 Vengeance.] ~,
28.18 Refuge-Citie's] ~∧~'s
28.20 way:] ~.
28.21 City:] ~,
28.26 Selfe-Murderer] ~∧~
28.31 me] ~,
28.31 Aire.] ~,
28.33 Refuge,] ~∧
28.35 City.] ~,
28.35 me] mee
29.2 wormholes] Wormholes
29.13 Ark.] ~:
29.15 boats.] ~,
29.17 thou] ~,
29.18 Waves,] ~∧
29.18 toss!] ~∧
29.22 Propitiatory.] ~∧
29.25 flood;] ~:
29.27 spouts,] ~∧
29.33 Sinke.] ~∧
29.34 Hell] ~,
29.35 thyselfe,] ~∧
29.38 Lamb] ~,
30.1 Sin!] ~∧
30.3 Th[**]] Thus
30.11 his] her
30.21 Seamen:] ~∧
30.22 ends] end
30.23 Wake] ~,
30.23 saith,] ~∧
30.29 gudgeon.] ~,

30.40 them.] ~,
30.41 Providence!] ~,
30.63 Message:] ~∧
30.70 heart.] ~:
30.72 killd] kill'd
30.73 Lord,] ~.
30.77 Sing:] ~,
31.1 Hispaniola] H * * *
31.4 body,] ~∧
31.4 th'] the
31.10 where] Where
31.18 The which] To ~
31.18 this] thy
31.20 bud] ~,
31.22 greate,] ~∧
31.24 Greate Longe] ~, and ~
31.39 I le] I'le
31.45 this] the
32.4 pitch.] ~,
32.6 War[m]] Warm
32.6 ring] sing
32.9 shells,] ~∧
32.10 two, of] twoness
32.17 Providence] * * *
32.18 things] Things
32.18 Face] * * *
32.19 Stupendous] * * *
32.19 Two objects] One Object
32.19 doth hug] * * *
32.21 are] * * *
32.21 other,] ~∧
32.23 must [**]er come] much * * *
32.24 * * * [**]me * * *] from * * *
32.25 borrows] borrows [conj.]
32.26 Natures] Nature's
32.28 made.] ~∧
32.30 Natures] Nature's
32.32 itselfe?] ~∧
32.35 Elfe] Elf
32.35 foole] fool
32.36 Wilt dash thy brains o[**]]* * *
    dost thy beams of
32.37 Lord] ~,
32.38 intrest] merit
32.40 thee,] ~.

32.42 debt] debts [conj.]

32.42 * * *] her

32.43 of Christs] of thy

32.46 been] ~,

32.54 my * * *] me all

32.59 harbor] harbor [conj.]

32.59 thoughts of thee] than * * *

32.61 Whittle] Whistle [conj.]

*33.*title Greter] Greater

33.2 founde] finde

33.2 smote] smites

33.3 Tast,] Taste∧

33.6 Life,] ~∧

33.13 iss] is

33.23 away.] ~∧

33.37 Friend:] ~,

33.37 pray.] ~∧

*34.*title Loved] loved

34.1 Nut,] ~∧

34.3 put.] ~∧

34.4 kirnell,] ~∧

34.12 dat] dot

34.16 hast] be'st

34.19 shells.]~∧

34.21 grange,] ~∧

34.23 mankinde] mankind

34.32 untill.] ~∧

34.35 Cock.] ~:

34.47 Curse,] ~∧

35.3 Pronown:] ~∧

35.14 still'd] stilld

35.16 fuell and] Battlements [conj.]

35.17 [**]nt] sent [conj.]

35.17 all] it

35.18 As packs] A pack

35.19 Suppose a] Such * * *

35.26 here.] ~∧

35.31 that] which

35.33 as't] sad [conj.]

35.37 undone.] ~,

35.38 Law.] ~,

35.41 Doings] Doing

35.45 cure.] ~,

35.50 Breaks] Breake

35.52 Fox-and-Geese] ~∧~∧~

35.56 do.] ~,

35.56 Dispense.] ~,

35.59 Power [***] work]
Power to work

36.8 fair.] ~,

36.32 thee] thee [PW the]

37.11 whereto,] ~∧

38.5 Infinity] ~,

38.12 produce,] ~∧

38.12 t[**]e] * * *

38.17 pai'd] paid

38.17 yet.] ~,

38.29 Power,] ~∧

38.31 ô] O

38.33 Heart.] ~∧

38.41 Principall] ~:

38.41 whence] whose [conj.]

38.42 things] ~,

38.45 marr'd] marrd

38.46 pray,] ~∧

39.6 so] to

39.7 hunger] hunger'll

39.8 walls] Walls

39.12 Sunshine.] ~,

39.15 Pow're] Powre

39.15 lines.] ~,

39.17 Deaths] Death's

39.22 more.] ~,

39.27 dead.] ~,

39.28 about.] ~,

39.32 spiritual] spirituall

39.32 soule:] ~.

39.35 high.] ~∧

39.39 W[i]th] with

40.1 Rod:] ~,

40.8 the] that

40.11 Rod.] ~,

40.24 Above] So 'bove

40.33 thee.] ~,

40.40 Love.] ~,

40.40 high,] ~.

40.41 pin.] ~,

41.17 full,] ~∧

41.27 Window] ~,

41.43 bright,] ~∧

42.2 mee.] ~ˍ

42.6 Coine] Gaine

42.10 Same.] ~,

42.11 Perfuming] Perfumeing

42.20 spoile.] ~,

42.23 these.] ~ˍ

42.25 end.] ~,

42.25 prepar'de:] preparde,

42.43 wise,] ~ˍ

42.43 I.] ~ˍ

43.2 minde.] ~,

43.3 tongue,] ~ˍ

43.4 doings.] ~,

43.5 speeches] speeche's

43.14 Winde:] ~.

43.15 draughts:] ~,

43.32 bright:] ~.

43.42 defin'de] definde

43.44 Omniscient;] ~,

43.44 Erywhere] ~,

44.13 two.] ~,

44.32 purgd] purg'd,

44.34 Angells] ~,

44.37 bright-sparks] ~ˍ~

44.44 Lord] ~,

44.44 anchor] Anchor

45.2 dust-dry] dust, dry [PW dust. dry]

45.7 Reason] Reason's

45.11 Candle,] ~ˍ

45.16 pitch,] ~.

45.17 date.] ~,

45.20 Amber,] ~ˍ

45.20 tills,] ~ˍ

45.26 cleare.] ~ˍ

45.27 flasht,] ~ˍ

45.28 Is] so

45.48 Soule.] ~,

46.2 bee] ~,

46.33 All,] ~ˍ

47.6 Sinnes] Sinners

47.16 top-gallant] ~ˍ~

47.20 There] There's

47.25 Life,] ~ˍ

47.35 praise.] ~ˍ

48.3 fulfill.] ~ˍ

48.22 should] showld

48.42 Pearls,] ~ˍ

48.42 tune,] ~ˍ

49.16 Glory,] ~;

49.22 Sparklingl] Sparkling

49.25 uncleane,] Unclean ˍ

49.38 head's] hand's

50.2 in't's] in'ts

50.3 axe,] ~ˍ

50.20 lay] lay'd

50.21 Promises;] ~,

50.24 do] to

50.31 them.] ~,

50.40 Truth:] ~, [PW ~.]

51.8 refin'de] refinde

51.31 fro.] ~ˍ

51.33 tides,] ~ˍ

51.43 oh] Oh

51.45 flow.] ~,

52.2 Earth.] ~ˍ

52.19 sin-scorcht] ~ˍ~

52.19 bathe,] ~ˍ

52.22 guilt,] ~ˍ

52.33 Priest-hood's] Priesthoods

53.2 ice.] ~ˍ

53.3 Crampt] ~,

53.31 breakes.] ~,

53.34 haft] hast

53.37 law] Law

54.title in] In

54.22 Authority:] ~, [PW ~.]

54.29 brightst] brightest

54.39 Mediatour.] ~ˍ

54.45 imploy,] ~.

56.1 toole] tooles

56.4 Verse] Verse [PW Velse]

56.7 rich,] ~:

56.9 kinde,] ~ˍ

56.27 Babylon.] ~,

56.31 Table-sight.] ~ˍ

56.41 lie] lies

56.54 Pleasentst] pleasentst

56.55 Lord,] ~ˍ

56.60 praise,] ~ˍ

58.title Matth.] Math.

58.5 loose,] ~∧
58.7 Lord] ~,
58.29 hatcht;] ~∧
58.35 goes] gates
58.39 Pharao,] ~∧
58.41 Calls.] Calls . . .
58.50 procure,] ~.
58.57 Erects.] ~∧
58.58 foes,] ~.
58.59 horse:] ~,
58.65 arms:] ~, [PW ~.]
58.69 sea.,] ~,
58.69 pen't] pent
58.73 here,] ~∧
58.92 shew'd] shewd
58.93 brincks] brinks
58.102 Church!] ~:
58.102 people] peoples
58.118 Encleckerd] Encheckerd
58.121 What Grace] what ~
59.21 that bout] about
59.25 Christ,] ~∧
59.31 Wilderness,] ~∧
60.2 Heaven's] Heavens
60[A].5 Famine.] ~,
60[A].7 sick.] ~;
60[A].23 white] White
60[A].44 with't.] ~:
60[B].3 skill.] ~∧
60[B].5 dark.] ~,
60[B].27 Costs] costs
61.1 Might's] Mights
61.2 Angells] ~,
61.3 burnish't] burnisht
61.6 wit] ~, [conj.]
61.7 that] the
61.7 in't,] ~∧
61.9 Nay.] ~,
61.9 th] its
61.10 shapt,]~∧
61.13 th'] the
61.20 bite:] ~,
61.21 Vertue.] ~,
62.5 stare.] ~,
62.14 Chokwort] Chokewort,

62.22 discourse,] ~∧
62.28 Spickward] Spicknard
63.15 there.] ~∧
63.28 pald] Opald
63.30 Macri'dalls] Madrigalls [PW Macridalls]
63.32 Flowers] ~,
63.37 found] ~ to
63.48 in] and [PW orig: in]
63.62 lungs,] ~.
64.5 should] shouldst
64.17 briezing] breezing
64.20 jackets,] ~∧
64.23 hight] ~,
64.26 Frankincense;] ~,
64.29 Oh!] ~∧
64.35 pomegranat'de,] ~∧
65.5 bluft] blusht [PW blust]
65.7 bower] ~,
65.8 Tho] The
65.11 Sparks,] ~∧
65.13 Trees,] ~∧
65.14 Almond] Almonds
65.15 vap'ring] vaporing
65.18 tree] trees
65.22 be'n't] ~,
65.24 Oh] ~!
65.40 Olives.] ~,
65.44 Cloves,] ~∧
65.47 rare,] ~.
66.8 affections,:] ~:
66.8 swells] ~,
66.10 obtain'd] obtained
66.11 Cask:] Caske,
66.12 crusht] ~:
66.13 Love,!] ~!
66.15 nothing!] ~∧
66.42 beames.] ~∧
67[A].title name.] ~,
67[A].2 soak't] soakt
67[A].3 right] ~,
67[A].17 Dimple.] ~,
67[A].35 reliefe] ~.
67[A].36 Thee] The
67[A].47 noe] no

67[A].*50* upon.] ~ˏ

67[A].*57* kiss.] ~ˏ

68[A].*10* Candle;] ~,

68[A].*24* out,] ~ˏ

68[A].*34* Sun Light] sunlight

68[A].*51* Earth,] Earths

68[A].*57* Lighten'd] Lightend

68[A].*58* shine,] ~ˏ

67[B].*5* furld] furled

67[B].*9* drops.] ~,

67[B].*13* Alass] Alas

67[B].*35* Righteousness:] ~ˏ

67[B].*37* thee.] ~,

67[B].*41* Pounde] Pound

67[B].*45* Iliak] ~,

67[B].*45* Fever] ~,

67[B].*45* turns:,] ~,

67[B].*46* Leprosy.] ~ˏ

67[B].*62* sore.] ~,

68[B].*10* piece.] ~ˏ

68[B].*34* live.] ~,

69.*2* Melancholy.] ~:

69.*3* sad;] ~:

69.*12* wormeaten] worm eat on

69.*17* mee.] ~,

69.*27* I'me] I'm

69.*32* nauseous] Nauseous

69.*40* Odorif'rous] Oderif'rous

69.*42* shoshannims] Shoshannim's

70.title sin] sins

70.title baptism;] ~:

70.*1* Crave,] ~ˏ

70.*35* Its] It's

70.*35* Circumcisions] Circumcision's

71.*12* runs,] ~ˏ

71.*17* Plumbd] Plumb'd

71.*17* Grace,] ~ˏ

71.*22* (The] ˏ~

71.*22* Divine),] ~ˏˏ

71.*23* beare,] ~ˏ

71.*24* Guests:] ~ˏ

71.*26* Cloaths] Cloathes

71.*27* attire] atire

71.*31* Lord] ~,

71.*31* sit.] ~,

72.*12* Thy] To

72.*12* brings] kings

72.*14* stande:] ~.

72.*16* Inmanhooded] In manhood

72.*24* the[ir]] their [conj.]

72.*28* thy glorie] this ~

72.*34* Hand,] ~ˏ

72.*34* there:] ~.

72.*39* Right. Hand] Right-Hand

72.*45* right,] ~.

72.*48* chim'd] chimed

73.*1* Glory,] ~!

73.*3* Casts] Cast,

73.*14* receiv'de] receiv'd

73.*21* herselfe.] ~,

73.*21* enrich] enriche

73.*28* glorifi'de] glorifide

73.*28* spring,] ~.

73.*33* posy.] ~,

73.*43* e're] ere

73.*50* till] chill

74.*4* lumpish heart] ~-~

74.*28* blinde,] ~.

75.*1* Oh.] ~!

75.*19* Alembeck] Alembick

75.*33* vile.] ~,

75.*53* hand] ~,

76.title fashiond] fashioned

76.title Glorius] Glorious

76.*4* Extasie,] ~.

76.*17* hurden hangings] ~-~

76.*36* mee,] ~.

77.*3* Pitch;] ~,

77.*11* I] I,

77.*16* heart.] ~,

77.*16* and so] and

77.*20* bright.] ~,

77.*21* Hell-Gate] ~ˏ~

77.*22* plight] night, [*conj.*]

77.*23* Angell-Feathers] ~ˏ~

77.*31* Heart Achs] ~-~

78.*2* of] ~,

78.*11* Oh] ~,

78.*11* spring;] ~:

78.*24* jayles] jayle's

78.29 ti'de]tide
78.44 Pris'ner] Prisner
78.44 pound:] ~.
79.16 too.] ~ₐ
79.18 dost] be'st
79.23 thyselfe] ~,
79.28 myselfe.] ~,
79.29 arise,?] ~?
79.32 thine,] ~ₐ
79.40 fall,] ~.
79.44 thing,] ~ₐ
79.48 Purchase.] ~,
79.62 SHERLOKISM] SHERLOSISM
80.title etc:] ~.
80.3 sharpend] sharpen'd
80.4 Sheath] sheath'th
80.14 heaven to] ~ ~ ~,
80.22 many.] ~,
80.28 Chip] chip
80.33 Coate.] ~,
80.34 flow] ~,
80.43 Well Spring] ~-~
80.46 startt] start
81.8 indeed,] ~.
81.10 proceed,] ~.
81.22 fare;] ~,
81.23 rare.] ~ₐ
81.25 works] ~,
82.6 ha'n't] han't
82.8 things:] ~.
82.16 Wood] ~,
82.31 house.] ~,
82.33 Gridiron;] ~,
82.38 Lord,] ~ₐ
82.39 Coale] ~, [PW ~.]
82.39 heate] heart
82.45 Grinders] ~,
83.title Garden.] ~,
83.5 exilde:] ~,
83.9 towers:] ~.
83.15 rich] ~,
83.16 Cheekt] Cheek't
83.20 com'st] comst
83.27 Conversion,] ~ₐ
83.27 'steemd,] ~ₐ

83.32 Vinyard] Vineyard
83.33 ranck.] ~:
84.4 Combd] Combt
84.11 calm:] ~,
84.21 bred.] ~ₐ
84.27 Tho"ts] Tho'ts
84.28 finde:] ~ₐ
84.39 Crops,] ~ₐ
85.title Hony] ~.
85.1 agasttard] agastard
85.4 Chrst] Christ
85.5 Myrrh,] ~ₐ
85.5 spice:] ~.
85.7 Humility.] ~ₐ
85.11 Choice.] ~,
85.33 * * *] each
85.41 Hony] ~,
86.2 finde,] ~ₐ
86.11 bib.] ~,
86.25 Oh!] ~ₐ
86.28 Praise,] ~.
86.33 Love,] ~.
86.33 sheds.] ~,
86.42 Grace] GRACE
87.8 frought] fraught
87.21 Ey'de] Eyde
87.22 spring.] ~,
87.24 Oh] ~!
87.32 set'st] sets't
87.34 stile] ~,
89.7 lay.] ~,
89.11 enjoy'd] einjoy'd
89.22 with all] with ₐ [all cancelled?]
89.34 doth,] ~ₐ
89.35 alive] to live
89.39 geers.] ~ₐ
89.40 breasts:] ~.
89.43 souls,] ~ₐ
89.53 thus] ~.
90.2 Brains] ~,
90.5 therein.] ~,
90.8 Man:] ~.
90.8 men,] ~ₐ
90.10 live:] ~ₐ
90.11 dicotomizd] dicotamizd

90.30 the] that
90.34 finisht.] ~,
90.44 shine:] ~,
90.45 Joy] joy
90.46 Adorn] Are in
90.47 Orient] orient
90.49 Bottomless,] ~ˍ
90.50 Saints:] ~.
90.52 therein] ~:
90.53 Glory] ~,
90.53 Eternall] Eternal
90.54 Happiness:] ~!
90.59 Base.] ~:
90.62 Eternall] Eternal
91.2 thing] ~,
91.5 very] Very
91.10 meate.] ~,
91.10 is] is [PW as]
91.21 thee,] ~ˍ
91.21 shalt] hast
91.25 Coming] Comming
91.27 sharp,] ~ˍ
91.28 Merygolds] Mary golds
91.31 still] ~,
91.41 Vessell's] Vessels
91.41 fild] fill
92.title Matth] Math
92.4 Spark:] ~.
92.9 Fancy,] ~ˍ
92.9 Veane,] ~ˍ
92.10 mee,] ~.
92.16 th'Effulgient] it's Fulgient
92.19 thus] ~,
92.20 rend] ~,
92.25 crow,] ~ˍ
92.28 Courage.] ~,
92.41 Light'ning] ~,
93.2 sparkling] ~,
93.37 Gold] gold
93.38 sells,] ~.
93.42 shine] ~,
94.3 rowle:] ~,
94.9 Potshread] ~,
94.29 If with thy * * * [***]de thou dress
me here]

If with thy precious robes will't dress
me here [Entire line conj.]
95.5 attire,] ~ˍ
95.9 wealthi'st] wealthiest
95.12 possest] possesst
95.22 bring.] ~? [PW ~ˍ]
95.23 block,] ~ˍ
95.24 lop.] ~:
95.25 Deaths] Death's
95.27 have.] ~,
95.28 just] ~,
95.37 all] ~.
95.37 roomes,] ~ˍ
95.43 let] Let
95.46 thy] these
95.47 mee] ~,
95.47 trumpet] ~,
96.4 blincke] blinke
96.9 dark.] ~,
96.10 love] Love
96.15 kiss,] ~ˍ
96.15 smart.] ~,
96.25 cleare:] ~.
96.34 ore] ~,
96.35 enough] ~:
96.35 none wast] none t'wast
96.41 fume] tune
97.title mouth,] ~.
97.3 light] Light
97.6 Oh.] ~!
97.9 Gold] ~,
97.20 Love.] ~,
97.21 ins] in's
97.29 dulled] ~,
97.37 methinks,] ~ˍ
97.49 heart:] ~.
98.2 juyces] juyce
98.4 Vine.] ~,
98.6 one.] ~:
98.8 vinyard] Vinyard
98.13 blosoms] blosom
98.15 prest] presst
98.22 Wealthi'st] Welthi'st
98.22 flow] ~.
98.27 reeck] reech

98.37 much] ~,
98.44 spirits] ~,
98.44 Lord] ~,
99.4 wth] with
99.7 pale facde] ~-fac'de
99.9 This] The
99.14 Galleries.] ~ˬ
99.15 cloth,] ~ˬ
99.23 wante] want
99.41 glory] ~,
99.53 geere.] ~,
100.title Zion,] ~ˬ
100.6 lodgd] lodged
100.8 thee;] ~,
100.8 Lord] ~!
100.21 heart.] ~ˬ
100.23 arreignd] arraignd
100.32 flashes,] ~.
100.34 that;] ~:
100.42 sweet,] ~.
101.13 Excellencys] Excellency's
101.21 its] the
101.26 thrung] throng
101.27 alltogether] altogether
101.30 mout] mount [orig: mont]
101.38 about,] ~ˬ
101.39 Candle-light] Candle's light
101.54 plea's] pleas
101.55 mandle] mantle
102.6 Insticutions] Institutions
102.20 givst] giv'st
102.29 seal;] ~ˬ
102.29 Cov'nat] Cov'nant
102.30 Cov'nat] Cov'nant
102.30 faith's] faith
102.31 Covenat] Covenant
102.39 flood.] ~,
102.40 mee] me
102.41 harp] ~,
103.4 mans] man's
103.9 trac'd] traced
103.15 Good:] ~.
103.24 in'ts] in't,
103.30 splic't] spic't
103.32 away,] ~.

103.35 Farewell] farewell
104.3 displai'd.] ~ˬ
104.9 Dress.] ~ˬ
104.18 Cake bread] ~-~
104.40 Vertue.] ~ˬ
104.58 spiritull] spirituall
104.61 tast] Tast
104.65 state.] ~:
104.76 shine.] ~,
104.77 'rai'd] ˬrai'd
105.11 thus.] ~ˬ
105.16 show,] ~.
105.29 night,] ~ˬ
106.8 o're] ore
106.32 formatum.] formation [PW
    formatum(?)]
106.32 begon] beg on
106.37 ware.] ~,
106.40 Old,] ~ˬ
106.47 take] takes
106.66 To] That
107.13 God.] ~,
107.18 friends] ~,
107.34 same,] ~ˬ
107.36 Form.] ~,
107.42 this] This
107.44 sacrament] ~,
107.49 Covenat] Covenant
107.57 pardons] pardon
107.57 off] up [conj.]
108.3 ornamantall.] ornamentallˬ
108.10 Ubiquity,] ~.
108.17 Carnifi'de] Carnifide
108.28 eye,] ~.
108.35 hande.] ~,
108.37 bread] ~,
108.37 wheate,] ~ˬ
108.40 Cap] Cup
108.41 These] Those
108.41 signalls] Signals
108.47 sippits.] ~:
108.47 Meats,] ~.
108.48 Comfect] Comfort
109.6 gaze:] ~.
109.16 Wine.] ~,

109.23 Wine] ~,

109.37 fare,] ~‸

109.46 blesst.] ~,

109.47 gold.] ~,

109.50 Grace.] ~,

109.51 Languague.] ~,

109.61 Guests.] ~‸

109.63 Qualifi'de] Qualifide

109.65 spots] spot

109.65 they're] there's

109.74 bee.] ~,

109.76 flip] slip

109.76 thee:] ~.

110.1 Birth:] ~,

110.3 Earth.] ~‸

110.7 death.] ~‸

110.13 Graves] Grave

110.22 welcome.] ~,

110.25 beares.] ~‸

110.31 While] while

110.37 Ghost.] ~‸

110.52 same.] ~‸

111.33 them;] ~‸

111.55 heart,] ~:

111.56 Feast;] ~‸

111.62 mee:] ~.

111.65 Bread] ~,

112.2 What] ~,

112.3 me,] ~‸

112.12 Thet] That

112.15 thine] ~.

112.21 rotten,] ~‸

112.23 in] on [orig: in]

112.23 the] th'

112.33 Crosst.] ~,

112.41 discharg'd] ~,

112.42 Death] ~,

113.title &c] and

113.2 ore.] ~,

113.7 Vine,] ~‸

113.8 clusters] ~,

113.14 ah] oh

113.18 indeed;] ~:

113.27 lead,] ~‸

113.32 root,] ~:

113.33 rock,] ~.

113.40 wond'rous] wondrous

113.43 indeed:] ~.

113.51 Crave.] ~‸

114.25 night.] ~,

114.26 Canop'i'de] Canopi'de

114.28 marke,] ~.

114.29 along.] ~:

114.31 mee,] ~‸

114.32 aright.] ~,

114.35 night] ~,

114.41 Eternall] Eternal

114.42 Where ever] Wherever

114.50 fixt] fix't

114.53 th] th'

114.57 from] ~,

114.58 Consolation,] ~‸

115.4 Ide] I'd

115.5 ascend,] ~‸

115.21 Love,] ~.

115.31 lovely] ~,

115.34 Objects] ~,

115.37 art.] ~,

115.39 shee] she

115.44 Belov'd,] ~‸

115.47 bestowd] bestow'd

115.51 songs] ~,

115.53 the] that

116.6 God] God's

116.7 Eye] ~,

116.7 Loves] love's

116.7 Pursevan to.] Pursevant, to‸

116.12 the] th'

116.15 Reech] ~,

116.16 in] on

116.28 Pur'st] Purest

116.33 red,] ~‸

116.34 allure,] ~.

116.37 beautifull] beautiful

116.51 best.] ~,

116.51 Beautys] Beauty's

116.52 Beauty] ~,

117.title ver] vir

117.title illarous] illustrus

117.title pr[e]] supra

117.title thousand.] ~_∧_

117.2 'fore] _∧_fore

117.3 greate] great

117.15 Laws:] ~,

117.29 leadst] lead'st

117.43 mee,] ~.

117.44 *Saving Grace*] SAVING GRACE

118.2 thiss] this [PW thus]

118.20 all,] ~!

118.23 and] and all

118.28 indeed,] ~.

118.29 Wisdoms] Wisdom's

118.30 laws,] ~_∧_

118.30 behold,] ~.

118.32 Head,] ~_∧_

118.42 tenses] senses [conj.]

118.53 parallell.] ~,

119.1 Lord,!] ~,_∧_

119.1 my] (~

119.1 Love,!] ~,)

119.4 it,] ~_∧_

119.4 heavens] Heavens

119.4 shine] ~.

119.10 hold] held

119.12 in] on

120.12 thee,] ~;

120.16 tunes] Tunes

120.25 thats] that's

120.29 Eare] Ear

120.29 doe] ~?

120.34 defile,] ~_∧_

120.38 besmut] besmoot

120.38 spice:] ~.

120.40 decke ins th] decke't in's [PW decke(?) decketh(?)]

120.41 lap't] lapt

120.42 sweet,] ~_∧_

120.42 Cheeks,] ~.

120.45 fair] ~,

121.3 dull.] ~_∧_

121.4 Untill] Until

121.6 beauties] ~,

121.14 bancks] ~,

121.14 to] too

121.15 this] thy

121.19 Streames] Streams

121.24 lips] Lips

121.27 spout,] ~.

121.31 lilly] Lilly

121.34 joy,] ~.

121.37 mee:] ~,

121.39 Oyle] oyle

122.3 Dears] Deare

122.3 lack:] ~_∧_

122.4 shew] show

122.10 She's far to] She sits so [sits (conj.) orig: is]

122.13 shine,] ~_∧_

122.15 stand.] ~,

122.28 Englisht] Englishd

122.35 Celestiall] Celestial

122.39 Trade.] ~,

122.41 stand.] ~_∧_

122.47 up] ~,

123[A].title [i.e. Bowells)]] (i.e. Bowells)

123[A].*11* thou,!] ~!

123[A].*12* alwaye] always

123[A].*13* dumpish,] ~_∧_

123[A].*17* that these] these

123[A].*21* smiles] ~ [PW smils]

123[A].*23* Chist] chest

123[B].*9* Raiment] ~,

123[B].*10* then] ~,

123[B].*18* gold,] ~.

123[B].*26* stately] ~,

123[B].*28* Conquoring] Conquering

123[B].*35* thy] the

125.29 make] makes

125.35 Glory,] ~_∧_

126.3 Beame,] ~_∧_

126.7 lifes] life's

126.16 this] thus

126.38 fine:] ~.

126.42 bee] be

127.4 Mould] ~,

127.7 prower] power [conj. orig: proper]

127.9 Desireable] Desirable

127.20 desirable] ~.

127.20 yet] Yet
127.26 thee:] ~.
127.34 spot.] ~,
127.38 Conduct.] ~ₐ
127.40 Palace.] ~ₐ
127.41 Where] Wherein
127.41 dost intertainst] intertainst
127.44 appere] appeare
127.46 Loves] Love's
127.54 lovely] Lovely
128.1 Dear] Deare
128.4 golden] golde
128.4 Hum'nity] Humanity
128.13 array'de] arrayde
128.14 Temple.] ~ₐ
128.28 spice,] ~:
128.30 soul,] ~ₐ
128.32 steps,] ~ₐ
128.32 step] strey
128.34 Celestiall] Celestial
128.37 beguild] beguil'd
128.43 here.] ~ₐ
128.46 ask] ~,
128.46 her] Where
128.50 whither] Whither
128.52 thee.] ~,
129.2 flaming] ~,
129.6 saying';] ~ₐ;
129.10 his Church] his
129.14 all.] ~,
129.15 Friends] friends
129.20 highst] highest
129.20 Nose,] ~ₐ
129.23 spirits] sweet spirits
130.8 spotoflowers] sweet flowers [PW spot(?)flowers]
130.8 the] th'
130.18 thise] these
130.30 sweeten'd] sweetend
130.31 Bed,] ~ₐ
130.33 sored] fared
130.44 Lord:,] ~;
130.48 on] in
131.26 soile] 'still [PW *still* changed to *drill*(?)]

131.27 spice-showers] ~ₐ~
131.32 us.] ~,
132.19 Those] These
132.35 face] Face
132.36 ti's] tis
132.41 growst.] ~ₐ
132.45 lillie] Lillie
132.46 delight,] ~.
132.47 *lillies*] *Lillies*
*133.*title beloveds] beloved
133.3 belov'd] beloved
133.7 Brids] ~,
133.9 all all] ~, ~ [PW ~. ~]
133.10 whats] what's
133.15 Loved] Lord
133.15 ceize] seize
133.16 deale] ~ [conj.]
133.16 you] not
133.19 thus] ~,
133.20 knaveishness] knavishness
133.20 Use.] ~:
133.25 espouseth] espousseth
133.27 a[n]] an
133.28 Ad on it fore] And in it sure
133.29 yee] you
133.30 Bridsgroom] Bridegroom
133.32 united] ~,
133.33 You'st] You'll
133.33 Bride] ~,
133.33 Bridesgrooms] Bridegrooms
133.33 great] Great
133.34 bee] be
133.34 bright] True [orig: Happy]
133.40 Discoverd * * *] ~ be
133.42 grace] Grace
133.45 Wedden] Weddin
133.45 Angell] Angells
133.45 melody] mild * * *
133.46 thoughout] throughout
*134.*title O] Oh
134.1 kind] kinde
134.5 brightness,] ~
134.5 shines] shinst
134.8 t'] to
134.9 Beautys] Beauty's

134.12 on't] on't [PW ont]

134.14 cleare?] ~ˌ

134.17 send] sendst

134.20 ever] ere can [conj.]

134.21 face] ~,

134.22 th[**] oft [*]ay] thereof gay

134.24 taketh] take thee

134.28 blisfull] blissfull

134.34 Colurs] Colours

134.39 Robe] Robes

134.40 Of] Oh

134.42 thee,] ~ˌ

134.42 withs] with's

135.2 shine,] ~ˌ

135.3 the] th'

135.5 Moses's] Moses

135.13 bulled] balled

135.15 Graces] graces

135.17 granade] granades

135.17 fly.] ~ˌ

135.19 th'] the

135.20 Thy] A

135.20 Bows] Bow's

135.20 Tongs] Tong's [PW Tongs(?) Tonge(?)]

135.24 truth] ~,

135.25 asunder] ~,

135.28 Satans] Satan's

135.28 Thum[p]] Thump

135.36 a lin[k]] a link [conj.]

135.39 Thou well * * * and Fiter fears no foe] Them well doth like and Fiter than the foe [entire line conj.]

135.41 shie[ld]] shield [conj.]

135.42 right.] ~,

135.42 steeld] ~ [conj.]

136.4 and] oh [conj.]

136.6 tho'] thou

136.6 that] it

136.7 should] shouldst

136.7 be,] ~ˌ

136.8 glanc[i]ng] glancing

136.8 Eyes] face

136.9 Flaming to ro[use]] Flames to rouse [conj.]

136.10 in th] rich

136.13 much:] ~ˌ

136.17 What [do] these [Ey]es] * * *

136.17 rob] robs

136.21 faint:] ~ˌ

136.22 dart] start [conj.]

136.23 aret] are

136.27 glor[i]ously] graciously

136.27 Ever] ~ [conj.]

136.28 in th'] with

136.29 gold] Gold

136.29 hath] ~,

136.29 in it] so

136.30 or] ere

136.30 honor] heart [conj.]

136.30 steems:] 'steems.

136.31 [***]ing] Seeing

136.33 [T]he] The [conj.]

136.33 tract] ~ [conj.]

136.37 eyes] eye

136.42 * * *] harp [conj.]

136.42 glory's] glories

136.46 praise,] ~ˌ

137.Date 15.] 14. [orig: *14 (24?)*]

137.1 mee?] ~!

137.2 Crystalliz'd] Crystallizd

137.3 all] that

137.4 flock] Flock

137.8 [g]raze] graze

137.9 fine,] ~ˌ

137.34 hit,] ~.

138.3 prie.] ~ˌ

138.6 paddle] puddle

138.9 shine.] ~:

138.13 lips.] ~,

138.16 Or] Oh

138.19 * * * [**]ne whose Teeth] * * * * * *

138.20 most] more

138.21 reliefe] relief

138.22 life] Life

138.23 the] that

138.24 Of such] I such

138.25 [W]hat are] What ~ [conj.]

138.25 shew] show

138.27 Foes,] ~:

138.31 [Bu]t] And [conj.]
138.32 from] seem
138.36 Teeth,] ~ₐ
138.37 that they] they the
138.45 soake] sooke
138.51 the] that
138.51 do] doth
138.52 hereby,] ~ₐ
138.53 Faith,] ~ₐ
138.53 appeare] appears
138.57 Doth] Both
138.62 pare] ~,
138.63 Grinde.] ~,
139.2 Vissell] Vessel
139.2 Wine.] ~ₐ
139.3 displai'de] displaide
139.4 Cup] cup
139.8 deli[ghted]] delighted
139.9 glance;] ~,
139.16 th'] the
139.22 Head] ~.
139.23 Pomegranat-like] ~ₐ~
139.23 blushey] blushes
139.26 here] there
139.29 Graces] Grace's
139.30 Gods] God's
140.2 Pen,] ~ₐ
140.2 doe't] do't
140.3 the] my
140.7 which thou] thou

[At this point this list ceases to report most variants in punctuation.]

140.11 those] these
140.24 Contemplation] contemplation
140.35 grac'd] grace
141.2 Thoughts] Thought
141.5 storehouse] foreheade
141.6 Empty] simply
141.6 naught] nought
141.19 spouse's] spouses
141.40 Ist] I'st
141.42 These] Those
142.10 beare] bear
142.11 fur] far

142.14 * * * above] ever above
142.41 Il'] I'l
143.2 what] What!
143.22 plush,] ~?
143.54 as] as is
144.1 Eternall] Eternal
145.9 Tun'd] Tund
145.12 Damps] Dumps
145.22 'ts] its
145.25 breizing] briezing
146.9 its] his
147.10 Upon] Up on
147.22 Eyes] Eye
147.23 and] which
147.28 ear] ere
147.30 enlaid all] all enlaid
147.34 sight] light
147.41 that] shed [conj.]
147.42 a[nd]] and
148.title Princes] Prince's
148.title daughter?] ~:
148.3 say,'th] say'th
148.4 case] use
148.16 walkes] walkst
148.23 Do] Hath
148.26 Dawbed] Dawbt
148.27 evry] every
148.28 Did] Didst
148.28 flew] out flew
148.29 begracd] be graced
148.31 lai'd] laid
148.42 beauteous] beautious
148.46 Balams toes that Emperours kissing greet] Besems toes of Emperours Passing great
148.49 shows] Shooes
148.50 such jewells ware] such jewells weare [conj.]
148.53 evry] every
149.20 Liquour] Liquor
149.37 shewn] shown
149.51 eate] eat
149.53 sap]sop
150.15 milke] milk
151.27 Heshbons] Heshbon's
151.32 Rabbims] Rabbim's

151.*39* make] makes
152.title [like]] like
152.title [like]] like
152.title Galleries] galleries
152.*5* pleasently] pleasantly
152.*6* sympheny] symphony
152.*11* Crysal] Crystal
152.*12* borderd] border'd
152.*17* top] leg
152.*19* sprkling] sparkling
152.*20* evry] every
152.*23* Galleries] galleries
152.*23* doth * * *]thou'rt held [conj.]
152.*26* purest] a part of
152.*27* Navill] a ~
152.*27* or Nose Eye] Nose or
152.*29* layes] Rayes
152.*30* I'le] I'l
152.*30* sing thy] singing
153.title Fair?] ~ₐ
153.title [O love]] O love
153.title delight:] ~?
153.*10* it gusts] to gust
153.*15* thee] me [conj.]
153.*18* ne'er] neer
154.*5* Twist] twist [conj.]
154.*11* On] Or
154.*17* folds] fold
154.*17* those] these
154.*21* Oucht] Oucht [conj.]
154.*27* rim] run
154.*30* azure] Azure
154.*36* but] out
154.*57* so[**]] seal [conj.]
155.*9* displai'th] displaith
155.*21* * * * Prayer] every prayer [conj.]
155.*29* it s] it's
155.*46* guilding] gilding
156.*12* Friends] Friend
156.*13* Belov'd] Beloved
156.*18* make] makes
156.*28* pledg] pledge
157[A].title his] the
157[A].title Bann[er]] banner
157[A].*2* aright?] a right,ₐ
157[A].*5* It s] It's

157[A].*9* It s] It's
157[A].*10* Ye] The
157[A].*10* with your melody] * * *
157[A].*11* pot] poet
157[A].*11* in memento] * * * to
157[A].*12* and ment so] * * *
157[A].*13* Gods] God's
157[A].*13* hence finest] finest
157[A].*14* the [***]] into a
157[A].*14* that ere we made] * * *
157[A].*15* [Mutton]] Mutton
157[A].*15* doth soures] soures
157[A].*16* Bakt] Backt
157[A].*18* arraied] arrayd
157[A].*20* Tiffany] Tiffiny
157[A].*21* Cakes] Wafers
157[A].*22* Ore the] * * *
157[A].*23* wheat s] wheat's
157[A].*24* Banquets 's] Banquet is
157[A].*25* the] is
156[A].*28* [is]] is
157[A].*28* fare, [Ch]rist] * * *
157[A].*30* their bread in] * * *
157[A].*31* on] of
157[A].*31* s[weet]] Saints
157[A].*33* T[he]] The
157[A].*34* wine] Wine
157[B].*10* Ye] The
157[B].*13* Hence finest] finest
157[B].*13* flouer] floure
157[B].*14* by Holy Ghost] the Holy * * *
157[B].*15* shouers] showers
157[B].*21* [***]ksy] Cook's
157[B].*26* Mutten] Mutton
157[B].*28* it is] it's
157[B].*28* th'] the
157[B].*29* on graces spit] in graces sops
     [*sops* conj.]
157[B].*30* dip] sop
157[B].*31* curiously] graciously [conj.]
157[B].*33* [***]iously] * * *
157[B].*34* fair] * * *
157[B].*35* Juyce] juyce
157[B].*37* rose red wine] water red
157[B].*38* best Grape that grew] Grape
     that * * *

157[B].*39* Vine] * * *

157[B].*40* and from] from

157[B].*40* drew] * * *

157[B].*41* its] it's

157[B].*41* Christs] Christ's

157[B].*43* the] its

157[B].*44* pra[****]] * * * all

157[B].*45* Ghost's] Ghosts

157[B].*46* ever] it is

157[B].*48* live] make

157[B].*49* gues[ts]] Feast [conj.]

157[B].*50* this] his

157[B].*52* the] thy

157[B].*53* Viall] Violl

157[B].*53* thy praises ring] this * * *
   wing

158.title begott] begot

158.*6* mov'd] meed [conj.]

158.*6* fist] ~?

158.*16* thyself] thee, that

158.*20* * * *] and

158.*20* affections] affection

158.*21* their] thy

158.*21* expence] Expence [conj.]

158.*22* their rich and right Ejections]
   this rich Ejection

158.*24* face?] ~.

158.*34* mortalls] mortall

158.*43* though] through

158.*46* went with't] were * * *

158.*47* these thy life did shine indeed
   most] * * * this life full

158.*47* clear] cleare

158.*60* friends] freinds

158.*65* their] thy

158.*76* the] th'

159.*18* triumphing wayes] my song him
   grace [conj.]

159.*21* whenever hits] when weary bids
   [conj.]

159.*24* Angells] ~,

159.*25* farest feast ere] such a feast as
   [conj.]

159.*27* Ce[**]ish] * * *

159.*28* Garbagd] Garbag'd

159.*30* starved] starv'd [conj.]

159.*32* Wines] Wine

159.*33* in] * * *

159.*34* that is] that's

159.*41* Waters] Waiters

159.*43* sapharine] sapharin

159.*51* plumbd] plumbt

159.*52* let's] lets

160.title Vallies] Vallie

160.*1* word] words

160.*4* mantle] mantle [conj.]

160.*6* omnt] omit

160.*10* wilt] will

160.*25* Medicenall] Medicinall

160.*45* Although] Allthough

161[A].*1* Deare] Dear

161[A].*3* bulke] bubbe

161[A].*3* smale] small

161[A].*6* t'] to

161[A].*13* each] of

161[A].*16* excellst] excellest

161[A].*24* its intrails from th'serpant]
   itselfe from th'venom that on it
   [*venom that on it* conj.]

161[A].*25* bows] bower

161[A].*28* offer me or] essences do
   [conj.]

161[A].*29* * * *] on their rich [conj.]

161[A].*31* As] And as

161[A].*33* and * * * them with] do in
   their reech [*do* conj.]

162[A] [Note: This Meditation is
   omitted from all previous editions.]

161[B].title Beloved] beloved

161[B].*4* times * * *] times its [conj.]

161[B].*6* poore] poor

161[B].*6* wit[hall]] withall [conj.]

161[B].*7* shriv'led] shrivled

161[B].*10* the s[***]es nor give them up
   or hub] * * * nor give * * *

161[B].*15* * * * are * * *] * * *

161[B].*15* many's] envy's [conj.]

161[B].*16* White-white * * *] White * * *

161[B].*16* then] thou

161[B].*18* I trust] * * *

161[B].22 mumbld] mumbled

161[B].23 gods] god's

161[B].24 forth] froth

161[B].29 tenderd] tendered

161[B].40 on in a rowling] * * *

161[B].47 feed] send

161[B].47 bread] branch

162[B].title shadowith] shadow with

162[B].1 any] types show [conj.]

162[B].3 Oate] Oat

162[B].3 pipe] pipe't

162[B].10 heaven] heaven's bright

162[B].12 each] * * *

162[B].12 best] blest

162[B].14 frightfull] frightful

162[B].15 frightfull] frightful

162[B].18 Frighted] frighted

162[B].20 Cluster] cluster

162[B].24 Though] Through

162[B].27 suck them * * *] * * *

162[B].28 this] it

163.7 sweet sweet] sweet

163.11 spices] ~.

163.11 Stacte, Galbanum] Muske * * * * * * them

163.12 smell] sweet

163.12 feted] faded [conj.]

163.15 childhood meeke] thy Childhood meete

163.18 drop't * * * thine] dropest from thy

163.27 fansy] fancy

163.30 a Clowns] Clowns

163.31 doth't] doth

163.32 roses] rose in

163.36 of] of's

163.49 Hall] Hive [conj.]

163.50 as Golden] golden

164.4 tiptoes] tiptoe

164.10 Thats] That's

164.12 Nap] Clasp

164.12 bodge] blodge

164.13 pukes] pikes

164.16 triming] trimming

164.16 * * *] own

164.21 most fine] divine

164.23 hast] hath

165.1 thee] ~!

165.3 t'] to

165.3 runs] was

165.5 token sends to * * * it bears] taken * * * * sends

165.26 naught] nought

Edward Taylor's Gods Determinations *and* Preparatory Meditations
was designed and composed by Christine Brooks
in 10/14 Janson Text;
printed on 50# New Age Totally Chlorine-Free stock
by Thomson-Shore, Inc. of Dexter, Michigan;
and published by
THE KENT STATE UNIVERSITY PRESS
Kent, Ohio 44242